Theories of Informetrics and Scholarly Communication

Theories of Informetrics and Scholarly Communication

Edited by
Cassidy R. Sugimoto

A Festschrift in honor of Blaise Cronin

DE GRUYTER

ISBN 978-3-11-057860-7
e-ISBN (PDF) 978-3-11-030846-4
e-ISBN (EPUB) 978-3-11-038823-7

Library of Congress Cataloging-in-Publication Data
A CIP catalog record for this book has been applied for at the Library of Congress.

Bibliographic information published by the Deutsche Nationalbibliothek
The Deutsche Nationalbibliothek lists this publication in the Deutsche Nationalbibliografie;
detailed bibliographic data are available on the Internet at http://dnb.dnb.de.

© 2016 Walter de Gruyter GmbH, Berlin/Boston
This volume is text- and page-identical with the hardback published in 2016.
Cover image: © Rafael Cronin
Typesetting: PTP-Berlin, Protago-TEX-Production GmbH, Berlin
Printing and binding: CPI books GmbH, Leck

♾ Printed on acid-free paper
Printed in Germany

www.degruyter.com

Foreword

I would not want to miss the opportunity to acknowledge my old comrade-in-arms, Blaise Cronin, on the occasion of this Festschrift. There are very few theoreticians that I have known and admired amongst the community of citationists. Blaise is one of them. However, I believe that this volume contains contributions from most if not all of those living scholars who deserve similar recognition.

I consider my own work more a contribution by a pragmatist, constantly juggling the exigencies of meeting payrolls and weekly deadlines. Well, those mundane concerns were over when ISI was sold to Thomson Reuters over twenty years ago. I am amazed that colleagues would still be seeking commentary from me.

My 1979 book, "Citation Indexing: Its theory and application in science, technology, and humanities", was published before we heard of the Internet. In the early days we lived with the constraints of the printed versions of the *Science Citation Index* and the *Social Sciences Citation Index*. Later on we added the *Arts and Humanities Citation Index*. Keeping up with rapidly changing technology we moved into the eras of the CD-Rom and online. From there we moved into the age of the Internet. By then bibliometrics became more than just the obsession of a few citation analysts like myself and the growing informetrics community. During all these decades of change Blaise Cronin was there and played a key role as constant critic and gatekeeper.

While many publishers and scientists are preoccupied with journal impact factors we must always remind them that the SCI was invented as a solution to the problem of information retrieval. And as early as 1965 it was already providing alerting services (selective dissemination of information) even before SDI became a dirty word. And in spite of their suspicions and doubts about citation analysis, administrators and editors know that high citation counts are justifiably associated with work of Nobel class.

Given the ubiquitous use of these metrics in higher education and science policy, it is only fitting that a body of work be collected addressing the state of theories in the field.

Eugene Garfield
Founder & Chairman Emeritus
Institute for Scientific Information
(now Thomson Reuters Scientific)
President & Founding Editor
The Scientist

Prologue

This Festschrift is compiled for Blaise Cronin upon the occasion of his retirement. Unlike some Festschrifts, you will not find in these pages honorific essays or deeply intimate recollections of the man. This is not an opportunity for his coevals to wax eloquent on his legacy. Such a Festschrift would not befit an individual of such professionalism and scholarship. Rather, the objective is to demonstrate Cronin's deep contextualization in the areas of informetrics and scholarly communication and to explore the ways in which he shaped a theoretical foundation for the field through his work, both critical and empirical (thus demonstrating Hjorland's notion of critical informetrics).

We honor the man by honoring his scholarship—what White terms the "author as person". However, we would be remiss were we to forget the "somatics of science" (Ekbia)—that this, to ignore the physicality of scientific practice. Cronin's position as Dean of the School of Library and Information Science at Indiana University allowed him the opportunity to bring together and mentor some of the most active scholars in informetrics and scholarly communication. He collaborated with a number of faculty members and students and his presence indelibly altered the scholarship of these individuals. He hired, inspired, and provoked and, in doing so, created a vibrant center of scientometric activity in Middle America. Two of his hires (Ekbia and Börner) are featured as contributors, and the editor of this volume was in the last cohort of hires for the School.

In the Festschrift Cronin edited on the occasion of Eugene Garfield's 75th birthday, he commented: "It is all too clear that a second volume could have been mustered without much additional effort or any loss of quality. All those whom we approached were heartily supportive of the idea and keen to show their affection and respect for the man and his multifarious accomplishments." Much the same could be said for the present Festschrift—there was no shortage of potential contributors and only I am blame if highly relevant authors were overlooked. I offer my apologies to these individuals here.

To those who were able to contribute, I offer my thanks. The authors represent some of the foremost scholars in scientometrics—among the contributors to this volume are nine awardees of the coveted Derek de Solla Price award (including, of course, the honoree of this volume). I am grateful that these authors offered their time and expertise. I would also like to express gratitude to my students, Nora

Wolfgang Glänzel and András Schubert
From Matthew to Hirsch: A Success-Breeds-Success Story —— 165

David Bawden and Lyn Robinson
Information's Magic Numbers: The Numerology of Information Science —— 180

Part IV: Authorship theories

Howard D. White
Authors as Persons and Authors as Bundles of Words —— 199

Nadine Desrochers, Adèle Paul-Hus, and Vincent Larivière
The Angle Sum Theory: Exploring the Literature on Acknowledgments in Scholarly Communication —— 225

Hamid R. Ekbia
The Flesh of Science: Somatics and Semiotics —— 248

Part V: Knowledge organization theories

Wolfgang G. Stock
Informetric Analyses of Knowledge Organization Systems (KOSs) —— 261

Loet Leydesdorff
Information, Meaning, and Intellectual Organization in Networks of Inter-Human Communication —— 280

Michael Ginda, Andrea Scharnhorst, and Katy Börner
Modeling the Structure and Dynamics of Science Using Books —— 304

Part VI: Altmetric theories

Michael Thelwall
Webometrics and Altmetrics: Home Birth vs. Hospital Birth —— 337

Contents

Foreword —— V

Prologue —— VI

Cassidy R. Sugimoto
Introduction —— 1

Part I: Critical informetrics

Blaise Cronin
The Incessant Chattering of Texts —— 13

Birger Hjørland
Informetrics Needs a Foundation in the Theory of Science —— 20

Part II: Citation theories

Henry Small
Referencing as Cooperation or Competition —— 49

Paul Wouters
Semiotics and Citations —— 72

Christine L. Borgman
Data Citation as a Bibliometric Oxymoron —— 93

Part III: Statistical theories

Jonathan Furner
Type-Token Theory and Bibliometrics —— 119

Ronald Rousseau and Sandra Rousseau
From a Success Index to a Success Multiplier —— 148

Wood, Andrew Tsou, Maureen Fitz-Gerald, and Bradford Demarest, who assisted in the production of the Festschrift.

Finally, I am deeply indebted to Blaise Cronin, without whom, none of this would have been possible.

Cassidy R. Sugimoto
Associate Professor
School of Informatics and Computing
Indiana University Bloomington

Lutz Bornmann
Scientific Revolution in Scientometrics: The Broadening of Impact from Citation to Societal —— 347

Henk F. Moed
Altmetrics as Traces of the Computerization of the Research Process —— 360

Stefanie Haustein, Timothy D. Bowman, and Rodrigo Costas
Interpreting 'Altmetrics': Viewing Acts on Social Media through the Lens of Citation and Social Theories —— 372

Biographical information for the editor and contributors —— 407

Index —— 414

Cassidy R. Sugimoto
Introduction

It has been suggested that crafting a theory of citation is a "Sisyphean undertaking" (Cronin & Sugimoto, 2015, p. 25) and one that might be best avoided (Cronin, this volume). Yet, while there may be no single unifying theory, there are a multitude of theories that are employed in informetrics and the study of scholarly communication. The chapters in this Festschrift—compiled on the occasion of Blaise Cronin's retirement—describe, extend, and propose several theories of informetrics and scholarly communication.

One might question the coupling of informetrics and scholarly communication in the title of the Festschrift: it could be argued that informetrics is a domain, while scholarly communication is merely an object of study. However, Cronin's oeuvre is an ideal justification for the pairing of these terms. As noted by a number of contributors to this volume (e.g., Glinda, Scharnhorst, Börner; White; Leydesdorff), Cronin's work bridges the gap between informetrics and scholarly communication. Cronin cites a number of prominent sociologists to theorize about scholarly communication, while his "image-makers" (those who frequently cite him) reinforce his relevance for statistical studies of informetrics (White). Cronin is therefore emblematic of the triangulation of theories and methods that bridge informetrics and scholarly communication.

One difficulty in identifying theories of informetrics and scholarly communication is the diversity of terminology around theories. In this volume, contributors discuss models (Glinda, Scharnhorst, & Börner; Leydesdorff), taxonomies (Bornmann), typologies (Desrochers), frameworks (Haustein, Bowman, & Costas; White), indices (Rousseau & Rousseau), hypotheses (Thelwall), and principles (Borgman), in addition to theories (Hjørland; Small; Furner). Several authors use the terms synonymously. For the purpose of this compilation, a theory will be defined as *a set of statements, systems, or principles used to describe or explain phenomena*, thereby providing an umbrella term under which all of these terms fall.

Informetrics has been defined as a quantitative domain (Stock) and one whose theories are often methodological (Thelwall). The numerical and methodological emphases of informetrics has been used to argue that this is an atheoretical domain. However, as Bawden cautions, "the actual number is less important that the theoretical perspective to which it points." There are a number of methodologically-oriented informetric theories with deep theoretical underpinnings. Hjørland, for example, describes the several similarity measures employed by informetricians and calls for a greater scrutiny of the theoretical assumptions of these measures.

Many theories have been imported from other disciplines to describe patterns and phenomena within informetrics and scholarly communication. These theories are conceptualized in other domains, but tested and empirically validated within informetrics. Sociologist of science Robert K. Merton's body of work is a ready example of this. With the exception of Blaise Cronin, Merton is referenced in more chapters in this volume than any other author and his theories are used as the foundation for empirical studies. Wolgang and Glänzel, for example, provide a statistical model for operationalizing Merton's "Matthew principle".

Informetric studies often draw from physics and other more quantitatively-oriented fields: a third of the contributors to this Festschrift cite physicist Mark Newman and a quarter cite physicist Albert-Lázsló Barabási. Other disciplines are also present: theories are drawn from evolutionary biology (Small), linguistics (Furner), psychology (Bawden), and communication (Leydesdorff), to name but a few. The appropriation of theories from other fields may speak to the inherently interdisciplinary nature of the domain or possibly reflect the status of informetrics as a meta-science (Hjørland). One thing is clear: there is an abundance of available theories of informetrics and scholarly communication.

1 Overview

The chapters in this Festschrift are organized into six sections, though these are not exclusive categories. For example, the perspectives are nearly all critical, in that they are reflexive about informetrics and consider biases and multidimensionality in the scholarly communication system (critical informetrics). This multidimensionality requires theories that address all research objects: data, documents, references, and scholars as individual human agents (citation theories and author theories). Observed regularities in research events form the basis of statistical theories of informetrics (statistical theories). However, informetric units are rarely independent and theories of informetrics must take into account the relational and organizational aspects of knowledge (knowledge organization theories). The Festschrift ends by looking towards the future and examining the role of theory in contemporary metrics, particularly those derived from social media and other web-based sources (altmetric theories).

1.1 Critical informetrics

Cronin adopts the role of *advocatus diaboli* in his contribution to this volume. This is not an unusual position for Cronin—his work and professional life are characteristically provocative. In one of his earliest works, *The Citation Process* (1984), Cronin challenged a major theoretical premise of the field, by questioning the validity of citations as proxies for quality. In the present contribution, Cronin criticizes the search for a unifying theory of citation, but does not leave the reader without a set of objectives for moving forward.

These objectives could easily fall within what Hjørland calls "critical informetrics"—a theoretical position proposed as an alternative to a positivist model of bibliometrics. Hjørland argues that numerous arbitrary constructs are used in informetric studies that produce a kind of hermeneutic circle in interpreting the results of studies drawn from biased data and proposes the adoption of an iterative and reflexive process to guide informetric studies.

Cronin and Sugimoto's edited compilation, "Scholarly Metrics Under the Microscope: From Citation Analysis to Academic Auditing" (2015) can be seen as a foundational text for critical informetrics. Collected in the volume are decades of criticisms of informetrics—examining issues of validity, bias in data sources, ethics of indicators, and the systemic effects of informetric analyses on the scholarly communication system. In chronicling these criticisms, Cronin and Sugimoto do not attempt to displace informetric research, but to improve the rigor of the methods and the ethical use of the results. A similar sentiment echoes throughout the chapters of the present volume (e.g., Hjørland; Borgman; Leydesdorff; Bornmann). The ubiquity of metrics in the evaluation of scholars and scholarship, the rampant proliferation of novel metrics, and the increasing use of metrics by amateur bibliometricians further fuels the need for a critical discourse of informetrics.

1.2 Citation theories

The debate between normative and social constructivist views is prominent in informetric and scholarly communication research and in the pages of this Festschrift (e.g., Cronin; Hjørland; Small; Bornmann; Haustein, Bowman, & Costas). Small provides an overview of these perspectives on science and finds them both lacking. He offers, as an alternative, theories of cooperation and competition drawn from evolutionary biology. These evolutionary theories provide an explanation of the strategies used by scholars in selecting references—evoking notions of generosity and reciprocity. Referencing is seen as a signaling behavior—communicating a message to the group or community.

Citations as signs, or semiotic devices, is a constant thread in theories of citation. Wouters and Furner, respectively, build upon Cronin's use of Peirce's "sign triad" for a more holistic understanding of the scholarly communication system (Cronin, 2000). Wouters argues for adoption of "material semiotics" in informetric research—in which the reference, citation, and the "citation as part of the citation index" are seen as ontologically different, but related objects—and urges the informetric community to accept multiple realities. Wouters agrees with Cronin's assertion that a need for a unifying theory of citation is nonsensical and instead argues for "a number of partly contradictory, and partly overlapping *set* of citation theories, each emerging in a particular set of knowledge practices."

The need for multiple theories of citation is reinforced by Borgman, who notes the inadequacies of citation theories for data citation. The increasing heterogeneity of the scholarly communication system has challenged the degree to which novel forms of scholarship can be understood under the existing frameworks. Data, for example, are not equivalent to publication—argues Borgman—and the fundamental differences must be fully understood before adopting citation theories for application to data.

1.3 Statistical theories

Citations are the coin of the realm for academic writing—those who corner more of the citation market are seen of as having higher value than those whose work fails to receive citations (Cronin, 2005). Success—in scientometric terms—is largely a function of heightened output and impact. The theory of success is explored in mathematical terms by Glänzel and Schubert and, separately, by Rousseau and Rousseau. Glänzel and Schubert build upon Merton's "Matthew principle", which describes a positive feedback loop in the reward structure of science, whereby those who are successful have more ease at achieving additional success. In short, "success breeds success" (Glänzel & Schubert).

Rousseau and Rousseau examine input-output indicators of success, treating the citation system as analogous to an economic one, in which authors seek to game the system for personal reward. As noted, "input-output indicators reinforce the current culture of assessing academic success in terms of publications and citations, rather than stimulating original research as valuable in its own right". This research combines both references and citations in the operationalization of success.

Seeking statistical regularities in human behavior—argues Furner—is a relatively recent phenomenon. Yet, as numerical regularities are observed, the product gains theoretical significance (Bawden). Bawden describes a few such regularities and the degree to which these can be used to "capture the structures and patterns of the information world". Common distributions were observed by Zipf, Lotka, and Bradford—a familiar trio to anyone in informetrics. Furner explores these and other power-law distributions in the context of type-token theory, continuing the long-standing bibliometric tradition of wedding linguistics and statistical studies for application to science studies.

1.4 Author theories

Cronin dedicated numerous publications to studying the notion of authorship and subauthorship in scientific publishing (e.g., Cronin, 2005). Among other contributions, Cronin is credited with coining the term "hyperauthorship"—to denote massive numbers of authors on the byline of a scientific article (Cronin, 2001). At the time of coining, the scientific community balked at 500 authors on an article. Numbers of co-authors have since increased by orders of magnitude: a recent paper from the Large Hadron Collider at CERN set the record with more than 5000 authors and the trend towards increased collaboration rates are consistent across all disciplines. These trends demonstrate a heightened need for theories of authorship—particularly those which apply a critical lens to understanding the components of contributorship and the place of the author in the scientific system.

White proposes a theory for understanding authors as "persons" and as "bundles of words". In this theory of authorship, White draws upon empirical studies of bibliometrics which demonstrate that authors behave in particular ways as citers—that is, they cite themselves and those they know disproportionately and create unique patterns of citing. As "bundles of words", authors exhibit a distinct discourse and cite in topically relevant ways. White thus elegantly weaves author theories, citation theories, and linguistic theories for a greater understanding of the function of authorship in scholarly communication.

The manifestation of a field in the person of a scientist (Bourdieu's *homo academicus*) is explored in Desrochers, Paul-Hus, and Larivière's contribution in this volume. Expanding upon Cronin's theory of the "reward triangle" of science, the contributors examine the vector of subauthorship in the form of acknowledgements—a line of inquiry highly promoted by Cronin. They emphasize the relational nature of science—that is, the intersection of citing, acknowledging, and authorship—as fundamental in the reward system of science.

The theories of White and Desrocher and colleagues emphasize the multidimensionality of an author as a writer, citer, and contributor. However, Ekbia argues that we should also examine the degree to which the embodiment of an "author as person" transforms science. Ekbia proposes "somatics of science": a theory which assumes that bodily relationships—"from physical proximity to friendship and romantic attachment"—affect the practice of science. This theory builds upon Cronin's rich micro-level analyses (e.g., Sugimoto & Cronin, 2012), in which he has demonstrated the importance of place and personal relationships in mediating scholarly communication behavior.

1.5 Knowledge organization theories

The importance of knowledge organization systems for informetrics should not be underestimated. One could argue that the maturation of scientometrics into a vibrant field was entirely dependent upon the construction of the Web of Science and subsequent citation indices. These systems have a powerful influence upon science studies. However, Hjørland's argument about search engines could apply generally for knowledge organization systems: they are cultural-political agents "making priorities in relation to what content should be relatively findable and what should remain relatively invisible."

They are also relational databases—which establish connections among various objects and actors in the scholarly communication system. While there have been many criticisms of these systems (see Cronin & Sugimoto [2015] for a review), few have developed frameworks for evaluating the quality of knowledge organization systems within the context of informetrics. In proposing such a framework, Stock's chapter is simultaneously forward looking and deeply embedded in the systems orientation of informetrics.

Knowledge organization can be embodied in a database, but can also be constructed by examining the relationship among various information objects. Relational aspects of scholarly communication—for example, citation relations among authors and documents—have formed the theoretical backbone for citation analyses and science mapping projects (Leydesdorff). However, Leydesdorff argues that "meaning nor knowledge is purely relational" and argues for theories that understand units positionally, rather than relationally. Building upon Shannon and Weaver's communication theory, Leydesdorff provides a layered theory of informetrics moving from the relational to positional and finally to the development of perspectives and translations. Leydesdorff uses Cronin as a case study to examine redundancy among authored, citing, and cited sources. This is demonstrated graphically through the use of networks, an increasingly common approach in informetric studies.

The influence of network science on informetrics is particularly evident in models of science. The landscape of models of science is examined in Glinda,

Scharnhorst, and Börner's chapter: the authors identify relevant items and create semantic networks of topical clusters using World Cat data of library catalog records, subject headings, and classification codes. In this way, the chapter serves both to provide an overview of models of science and to demonstrate the common use of knowledge organization systems and mapping exercises to provide depictions of a domain (the "mirror metaphor" as discussed by Hjørland).

1.6 Altmetric theories

One might question the prominent place in a Festschrift of what might seem a relatively new area of study. However, nearly two decades before the term "altmetrics" was coined, Cronin predicted a transformation of the scholarly communication system in which "networked hypertext systems will promote popular authorship, radiated reading and global gossip", where "[m]ultimedia assemblages will replace monotexts, delivered on-demand and in real-time" (Cronin, 1992, p. 23). Cronin's prescience put him first on the scene during the birth of webometrics (Thelwall) and arguably preempted the altmetric movement: Cronin has sought, throughout his career, to make manifest invisible traces of scholarly activity (Haustein, Bowman, & Costas).

The pressure to track and analyze altmetric data has been spurred in large part by the growing emphasis placed on the community by funding agencies in demonstrating societal impact of research (Moed). This pressure has challenged traditional understandings of the term *impact* in informetric research (Bornmann). Bornmann argues that the broadening of impact from citation to societal represents a scientific revolution in the scientometrics. He presents altmetrics as a potential source of data for measuring societal impact, but cautions that these may not capture the wider sphere of public engagement activities. He suggests that the taxonomic change in impact will lead to similar modifications of concepts such as output or productivity. Moed, however, argues that altmetrics do not track research *outputs*, but rather research *process*. Moed describes altmetrics as "traces of the computerization of the research process" noting the importance of knowledge organization systems (Stock) in framing the conversation around traditional bibliometrics.

Webometrics can, in many ways, be seen as the precursor to or umbrella term for altmetrics. Thelwall contextualizes webometrics as a subfield of information science "concerned with quantitative analyses of web data for various purposes." His depiction of the domain is largely a methodological one: he presents a theoretical framework for link analysis and theoretical hypotheses regarding commercial search engines, both of which focus on appropriate approaches to data collection and the interpretation of the results (reinforcing the embeddedness of critical informetrics [Hjørland] in contemporary research). Thelwall introduces altmetrics and ends by leaving these metrics "in the hands of the next generation of information scientists".

This challenge is accepted by Haustein, Bowman, and Costas who evaluate the application of citation and social theories to altmetrics—which they refer to as a "group of metrics based (largely) on social media events relating to scholarly communication." The authors provide a novel framework focused on the notion of engagement, which focuses more on the mechanisms underlying acts of altmetrics rather than the derivation of indicators from the counts of these acts. The authors provide numerous examples of the application of their framework—highlighting the nimbleness of this framework for the contemporary scholarly communication system.

2 Continuing the conversation

Cronin suggests that we understand citations as conversations between texts. A deliberate conversation with Cronin can be seen within these chapters: 43 unique works of Cronin's were cited, demonstrating the wide diversity and utility of his oeuvre. The contributors were also in conversations with one another—demonstrated by the high degree of references to other contributors within the volume. However, chitter chatter among the contributors does not imply that everyone is in concert—in fact, many disagreements can be seen in the text particularly in debating the existence of a singular reality and the degree to which informetrics can be seen as representations of reality. What emerges from the Festschrift is a web of dialogue around theories of informetrics and scholarly communication.

This Festschrift is not meant to end the conversation, but rather to start it. As many contributors note, the dynamicity and increasing heterogeneity of the scholarly communication system challenges contemporary theories. Furthermore, if informetrics is, as Bornmann argues, in a time of revolution, there may be a need for the construction of new theories that can adapt to the transformation of key concepts in the domain. In charting the path ahead, informetricians would do well to heed Cronin's advice to "pay more attention to what is actually being said, by whom, to whom, in what ways, and when". Only with deep engagement with the content and connectivity of conversations can we continue to develop robust and useful theories of informetrics and scholarly communication.

Cited References

Cronin, B. (1984). *The citation process: The role and significance of citations in scientific communication.* London: Taylor Graham.

Cronin, B. (1992). Contoured convenience. *Aslib Information, 20*(1), 23.

Cronin, B. (2000). Semiotics and evaluative bibliometrics. *Journal of Documentation, 56*(4), 440–453.

Cronin, B. (2001). Hyperauthorship: A postmodern perversion or evidence of a structural shift in scholarly communication practices? *Journal of the American Society for Information Science and Technology, 52*(7), 558–569.

Cronin, B. (2005). *The hand of science: Academic writing and its rewards.* Landham, MD: The Scarecrow Press.

Cronin, B., & Sugimoto, C.R. (Eds.) (2015). *Scholarly metrics under the microscope: From citation analysis to academic auditing.* Medford, NJ: Information Today, Inc./ASIST, pp. 976.

Sugimoto, C.R., & Cronin, B. (2012). Bio-bibliometric profiling: An examinination of multifaceted approaches to scholarship. *Journal of the American Society for Information Science & Technology, 63*(3), 450–468.

Part I: **Critical informetrics**

Blaise Cronin
The Incessant Chattering of Texts

> "All the really good ideas I've ever had came to me while I was milking a cow. You don't get panicky about some '-ism' or other while you have Bossy by the business end."
>
> Grant Wood (painter of "American Gothic")[1]

Citation attracts metaphors as flame attracts moths. You will find citations described variously, though by no means exhaustively, as scholarly bricks (Price, 1963), as signposts left behind (Smith, 1981), as applause (Nelson, 1997), as gifts (Hagstrom, 1982), as forms of reward or income (Ravetz, 1971), as tools of persuasion (Gilbert, 1977), as pellets of peer recognition (Merton, 2000), as paratextual baubles (Cronin, 2014), or, verging on the poetic, as frozen footprints on the landscape of scholarly achievement (Cronin, 1981). Such is the chameleon nature of citation.

Citations are both instrumental (they direct the reader to related and potentially relevant work) and symbolic (they commodify kudos) in nature, at once straightforward and ramified: "constitutionally complex," as Leydesdorff (1998, p. 6) put it. It may help, therefore, to think of citation as a cluster-concept[2]. Common sense, a sometimes undervalued asset, tells us that the institutionalized practice of sprinkling a paper with references is to no small extent rule-based and normatively governed, even if it is also inherently subjective, motivationally messy and susceptible to abuse. These factors, taken together, make the (questionable) quest for a theory of citation[3] about as likely to succeed as the search for the Loch Ness Monster—and I speak as a sometime Nessie-spotter!

Metaphors are handy devices for helping us better understand concepts or practices that are arcane, specialized, or resistant to easy grasp, but they do have their limits and a downside is that they may encourage reductionist thinking. (It was Samuel Taylor Coleridge, I think, who famously said: "No simile runs on all four legs.") None of the metaphors I just mentioned quite does justice to the complexity of a practice—for some one hardly deserving of an afterthought—that has

---

[1] Quoted in: Evans, R. T. (2010, October 15). Departmental Gothic: Grant Wood at the U. of Iowa. *Chronicle of Higher Education*, B10–11.
[2] See: http://itisonlyatheory.blogspot.com/2010/01/cluster-concepts.html
[3] You won't, for what it is worth, find an entry for theory of citation or theory of referencing in: Bothamley, J. (2004). *Dictionary of Theories: More than 5000 Theories, Laws and Hypotheses Described*. New York: Barnes & Noble.

become a sine qua non of academic writing, a literary convention and accounting mechanism rolled into one, without which it would be impossible to imagine contemporary science, certainly not its formal communication processes and (increasingly) its formalized evaluation mechanisms.

When it comes to metaphors I confess to having a personal favorite: Barbara Czarniawska-Joerges's idea of citation as conversation between texts—albeit, I might add, a particular kind of slow, asynchronous conversation. As she so aptly put it some years ago, long before Twitter and tweets, Facebook and 'likes' became part of the socio-scholarly communications mix, the patterning of references reveals "a trace of conversations between texts" (Czarniawska-Joerges, 1998, p. 63). By embedding a bibliographic reference to an earlier work in his paper an author establishes a connection between the citing and cited works. Now imagine the universe of papers on any given topic and all of the inter-citations and associated co-citation networks—the "transtextual relationships," to use Genette's term (1997, p. 1)—contained therein. A simple, one-off exchange has scaled up to become a multi-person, snowballing conversation—the 'incessant chattering' of my title—albeit one that for much of the time remains dimly perceived. Just as we occasionally talk sotto voce in the physical world, so it is in the penumbral world of citation, with the sustained susurration of texts. And in this vein we might think of self-citation as analogous to intrapersonal conversation, with each invoking of one's prior work a way of showing how the pith and substance of one's thesis, theory, or standpoint evolved over time. These different kinds of conversations really only become apprehensible when we conduct a bibliometric analysis and visualize the networked threads. Then we can see who talks to whom, which voices and conversations seem to matter most. Of course, if no one pays any attention to what is being said, a deathly silence ensues.

It is not uncommon for writers on the subject of citation behavior to speak of two camps or worldviews, the normative and the relativistic. This is an admittedly somewhat simplistic characterization of what is in reality a highly nuanced debate, but it does at least capture the interpretative polarization that exists, and, indeed, has existed for decades in the literature: for a chronology of the persistent skepticism, intellectual indignation, and irruptions of ideological fervor, I recommend our edited volume, *Beyond Bibliometrics*, and, for good measure, a contemporaneous companion compilation, *Scholarly Metrics Under the Microscope*, both of which examine academe's growing fascination with (one is tempted to say fetishization of) metrics (Cronin & Sugimoto, 2014, 2015). In one corner we have Merton (2000), arguing elegantly that authors' citing behaviors are neither inherently random nor whimsical in nature. In the main authors adhere to a more or less codified, tacitly understood, and collectively enforceable set of norms, knowledge of which may be acquired in a number of ways: osmotically; through apprenticing; in graduate seminars; via mentoring programs, etc. In the other corner, there are the doughty MacRoberts, who have long argued that citation behavior is prone to errors and biases of different kinds; they, in fact, maintain that citation is systemically biased and, as a consequence, citation analysis (and by extension the paraphernalia of evaluative bibliometrics) is an illegitimate tool for use in research performance assessment exercises (MacRoberts & MacRoberts, 1989): garbage in, garbage out, as it were. One has only to dip into the extensive literature on citation practices and motivations to see that generality (there is observable consistency in the way authors cite, the intensity with which they cite, where in the text they cite, the ostensible functions their citations perform) and particularity (an author's decision to cite A rather than B remains a private choice influenced by factors such as the author's awareness of all candidate citations, their accessibility, and their perceived relevance) co-exist when it comes to the dispensing of citations. 'Twere ever thus and likely always will be.

Human nature being what it is, normative drift inevitably occurs, to a greater or lesser extent: authors mis-cite, over-cite, under-cite, or cite preferentially (Liang, Zhong, & Rousseau, 2014). We may, through laziness or plain ignorance, fail to cite an important source, or we may choose for reasons of collegiality or self-interest to cite the work of a friend or colleague rather than the equally (perhaps more) relevant work of another scholar. Or we may seem to indulge rather too much in self-citation, though self-citation is no bad thing in itself; as already noted, it serves an important purpose, akin in some regards to redundancy in everyday speech, by allowing us to display the trajectory of our thinking and connect the reader to our oeuvre. I doubt that such venalities and inadvertent errors rise in most people's estimation to the level of crimes and misdemeanors, but for some they are evidence aplenty of the inherently random nature of citation behavior. And yet, are we really supposed to believe that Thomson Reuters' Web of Science and Elsevier's Scopus are in essence "nothing more than gigantic houses of cards resting on citational quick sands" (Cronin & Sugimoto, 2015, p. 934)? Is it the case that these huge databases are the byproducts of "a hundred million acts of whimsy" (Cronin, 2005, p. 1505)?

Fifty years ago, Eugene Garfield presciently envisaged intelligent software that would automatically 'dress' scholarly articles with all the necessary citations (Garfield, 1965) thereby relieving authors of the irksome responsibility. But even with prodigious advances in artificial intelligence in the interim, the solution that Garfield proposed remains elusive, and for good reason: the selection of citations by an author is a residually (and necessarily) subjective act, impossible to predict or second guess with certitude. Authors are human, citational perfection ultimately unattainable. The governing norms that Merton invoked are thus perhaps best viewed as aspirational in nature—stretch goals, in business jargon. This, of course, holds for other spheres of daily life; the aspirational and actual frequently diverge, which helps explain the success of *Weightwatchers*.

But back to chitter chatter. Think for a moment of a typical exchange between two persons and how it unfurls. Conversation, as philosophers and socio-linguists have shown, consists of a number of different kinds of speech acts (assertives, directives, commissives, etc.) and is governed by certain norms or implicit rules (e.g., turn-taking, avoidance of face-threatening acts). Here, by way of illustration, is what Grice (1989, p. 33) has to say: "Make your contribution such as it is required, at the stage at which it occurs, by the accepted purpose or direction of the talk exchange in which you are engaged." But as we all know, rational co-operative action is often as much observed in the breach as the observance: as with citation, so with conversation. Prescription (how we should behave) is not description (how we actually behave). One knows that one shouldn't interrupt or talk over one's interlocutor, but the excitement of the moment, the need to correct a factually incorrect statement, or some other factor may cause one to overstep the bounds of etiquette.

Conversation can be viewed as a set "collective social practices" (Hyland, 2000, p. 1), one that sometimes breaks down. In that regard it is not greatly different from citation behavior, another set of collective social practices that sometimes breaks down, or at least falls short of the Platonic ideal when authors are less than scrupulous in their referencing of prior work, or, somewhat rarer, attempt to game the system. Conversation (or discourse) analysis is an approach to studying naturally occurring, primarily verbal, interactions between individuals. To the best of my knowledge the considerable body of research that has been carried out in this area has not yet resulted in the creation of a universally accepted theory of conversation. That being so, I fail to see why we would expect the last sixty or so years of research in citation analysis to have produced a grand, unifying theory of citation behavior. To be sure, there is no shortage of metaphors to help us get to grips with the nature, purpose and practice of citation, and while these may well be illuminating and insightful, it has to be said that a congeries of metaphors does not a theory make.

Permit me now to adopt the role of *advocatus diaboli*. Although I once authored a paper with the title "The need for a theory of citing" (Cronin, 1981) I am not altogether convinced that constant self-flagellation and fretting about the absence of an all-embracing theory are the most productive uses of our time—more likely another case, I fancy, of what the literary scholar/critical theorist Stanley Fish (1985, p. 112) called "theory hope." Even if someone were to come up with a humdinger of a theory, I fail to see how the well-documented problems (validity, reliability, etc.) associated with citation analysis, evaluative bibliometrics, and the new wave of alternative metrics can be glossed over or made to disappear

(Cronin, 2013). Theory or no theory, the ineradicable messiness (of meaning and motivation) cannot simply be wished away: it is constitutive of citation behavior. Perhaps, as Wouters (1999) has suggested, we need to give up on the Holy Grail and approach the matter of theory construction from an oblique angle. In so doing we would not be alone; other academic tribes face similar challenges, have to deal with similar frustrations. In the spirit of ludic irreverence, therefore, let me quote a few lines from Thomas Erickson's (2000) ditty "Theory Theory," which was written specifically with the human-computer interaction (HCI) research community in mind. It seems to me that Erickson's message has potential relevance well beyond the borders of HCI.

> The world is messy, fuzzy, sticky.
> Theoretically 'tis all quite tricky.
> Theories keep it at a distance,
> Cov'ring up the awkward instance
> ...
> So let not theory serve as blinders,
> welcome disruptions as reminders!

I concluded my aforementioned 1981 article with a low-key motherhood and apple pie statement: "If authors can be educated as to the informational role of citations and encouraged to be restrained and selective in their referencing habits, then it should be possible to arrive at greater consistency in referencing practice generally" (Cronin, 1981, p. 22). Some 35 years on and the need for critical self-reflexivity is no less pressing, especially in light of the importance attached to citation data in so many personnel evaluation and program assessment exercises. The metricization of the academy is now in full swing and all hands are needed on deck to ensure that best practices are followed, as far as humanly possible. Thus, and to be more concrete, I would like to see the scientometrics community, loosely defined and scattered though it is, channel more of its collective energies into activities such as the following: (a) encouraging informed discussion within academe on the instrumental role and symbolic significance of citations (and other putative performance indicators) in scholarly communication; (b) promoting better understanding of the strengths and limitations of citation analysis and related techniques among different stakeholder groups; (c) developing, testing and refining new scientometric methods and tools sets; (d) critically examining the validity and ethicality of evaluative bibliometrics in research assessment exercises; and (e) exploring the use and significance of alternative metrics in the scholarly communication process. The Leiden Manifesto[4] is a commendable step in the right direction.

---

4 http://www.leidenmanifesto.org

Although I, unlike Grant Wood (author of this essay's epigraph), have very limited experience of milking cows, I can nonetheless sympathize, up to a point at any rate, with the artist's jadedness when it comes to "-isms". Perhaps pragmatism (an unsophisticated "-ism" in many people's eyes, I don't doubt) is the best way forward. Instead of trying to weight contributions, quantify outputs, measure quality, and calibrate downstream scholarly impact—in the process falling prey to what Collini (2012, p. 108) calls the "fallacy of accountability"—we should instead pay more attention to what is actually being said, by whom, to whom, in what ways, and when. In other words, we should listen attentively to the chattering of texts and develop better ways of capturing what is being said in the docuverse and demonstrating how conversations spark, splutter, and spiral off in multiple directions across time and disciplinary lines. Historiographical analysis of this kind, coupled with textual engagement—i.e., actually *reading* what an author has written—can probably teach us more about the process of scholarly communication, while also providing important insights into the issues and themes that matter most to those at what Mr. Wood folksily termed "the business end." In my view, that is where we should be directing our energies: perhaps the search for an overarching theory can—and here I risk incurring the wrath of the long-suffering editor of this volume or, worse, excommunication from the fold—be left for another day.

Cited References

Collini, S. (2012). *What are universities for?* London: Penguin.
Cronin, B. (1981). The need for a theory of citing. *Journal of Documentation*, 37(1), 16–24.
Cronin, B. (2005). A hundred million acts of whimsy? *Current Science*, 89(9), 1505–1509.
Cronin, B. (2013). Editorial. The evolving indicator space (iSpace). *Journal of the American Society for Information Science and Technology*, 64(8), 1523–1525.
Cronin, B. (2014). The penumbral world of the paratext. In: D. Apollon & N. Desrochers (Eds.). *Examining paratextual theory and its applications in digital culture.* Hershey, PA: IGI Global, 1–6.
Cronin, B. & Sugimoto, C. R. (Eds.). (2014). *Beyond bibliometrics: Harnessing multidimensional indicators of scholarly impact*. Cambridge, MA: MIT Press.
Cronin, B. & Sugimoto, C. R. (Eds.). (2015). *Scholarly metrics under the microscope: From citation analysis to academic auditing.* Medford, NJ: ITI/ASIS&T.
Czarniawska-Joerges, B. (1998). *Narrative approach to organization studies.* London: Sage.
Erickson, T. (2000). Theory theory: A designer's view. Available online at: http://www.visi.com/~snowfall/theorytheory.html
Fish, S. (1985). Consequences. In: W. J. T. Mitchell (Ed.). *Against theory: Literary studies and the new pragmatism*. Chicago, IL: University of Chicago Press, 106–131.
Garfield, E. (1965). Can citation indexing be automated? In: M. E. Stevens, V. E. Giuliano & L. B.

Heilprin (Eds.). *Statistical association methods for mechanized documentation, Symposium Proceedings, 1964.* Washington, DC: National Bureau of Standards, 189–192.

Genette, G. (1997). *Palimpsests: literature in the second degree.* Lincoln, NB: University of Nebraska Press.

Gilbert, G. N. (1977). Referencing as persuasion. *Social Studies of Science,* 7, 113–122.

Grice, H. P. (1989). *Studies in the way of words.* Harvard, MA: Harvard University Press.

Hagstrom, W. O. (1982). Gift giving as an organizing principle in science In: B. Barnes & D. Edge (Eds.). *Science in context: Readings in the sociology of science.* Cambridge, MA: MIT Press, 21–34.

Leydesdorff, L. (1998). Theories of citation? *Scientometrics,* 43(1), 5–25.

Liang, L., Zhong, Z., & Rousseau, R. (2014). Scientists' referencing (mis)behavior revealed by the dissemination network of referencing errors. *Scientometrics,* 101(3), 1973–1986.

MacRoberts, M. H. & MacRoberts, B. R. (1989). Problems of citation analysis: A critical review. *Journal of the American Society for Information Science,* 40(5), 342–349.

Merton, R. K. (2000). On the Garfield input to the sociology of science: A retrospective collage. In: B. Cronin & H. Barsky Atkins (Eds.). *The web of knowledge: A festschrift in honor of Eugene Garfield.* Medford, NJ: ITI/ASIS, 435–448.

Nelson, C. (1997). Superstars. *Academe,* 87(1), 38–54.

Price, D. J. de Solla (1963). *Little science, big science.* New York: Columbia University Press.

Ravetz, J. R. (1971). *Scientific knowledge and its social problems.* Oxford: Clarendon Press.

Smith, L. C. (1981). Citation analysis. *Library Trends,* 30(1), 83–106.

Wouters, P. (1999). Beyond the Holy Grail: From citation theory to indicator theories. *Scientometrics,* 44(3), 561–580.

Birger Hjørland
Informetrics Needs a Foundation in the Theory of Science

1 Introduction

The terms "bibliometrics", "informetrics" and "scientometrics" are—unless otherwise specified—considered synonymous in this chapter. They refer to quantitative studies of documents, collections of documents, and derived patterns (e.g., maps based on co-citations or bibliographic coupling, or evaluative techniques such as journal impact factor (JIF), or the h-index). They also cover webometrics and statistical patterns such as Bradford's law, Lotka's law, and Zipf's law.

Traditionally, many informetrics studies have been made by using scientific and scholarly databases (e.g., the *Science Citation Index*) and those studies thereby represent studies of scholarly literatures (thus this subset of informetrics may be termed "scientometrics"). By implication, scientometrics is a "science of science", a "metascience" or a field of "science studies" as also put forward by Bates (1999, p. 1044). The family of metasciences includes fields such as the history of science, the philosophy of science, and the sociology of science, mentioning only the most important,[1] where the term "science" is not limited to natural science but covers all fields of scholarship. The main points in this paper are: (1) information science with informetrics belongs to the meta-sciences, (2) these meta-sciences are mutually interdependent, (3) all meta-fields are also dependent on subject knowledge, and (4) "post-Kuhnian" views of knowledge are based on social, historical, and pragmatic perspectives (rather than on individualistic and foundational perspectives).

We shall start by having a brief introduction to the most important meta-sciences: *history of science* typically studies lines of development (*diachronic analysis*) in science and the life and works of great scientists often based on scientific literature as well as unpublished sources focusing on science as a whole, a single discipline, or a specific period or aspect. The principles of such historical studies are developed in the field called historiography and the principles of the history of science are developed in the subfield called historiography of science.

---

[1] Here, I am using science studies in a broader way than, for example, Collin (2011) who does not consider philosophy of science as a part of science studies.

Philosophy of science is typically based on *rationalist principles* putting forward normative criteria for scientific work and scientific methodology and is not usually based on empirical or historical studies.[2] The *logical positivists* suggested one family of norms in the first part of the 20th century: there is a universal and a priori scientific method; theories must be translatable into observational terms; the doctrines of behaviorism, operationalism, and methodological individualism; and the reduction of research objects into "variables". Such norms can still be found in textbooks of empirical methodologies in the social sciences, although logical positivism today is generally considered an unsuccessful project based on unfruitful premises. *Philosopher Karl Popper* developed another set of norms based on the principle of falsificationism whereby good research should: (1) provide scientific statements, hypotheses, and theories which are precise in having an inherent possibility to be proven false, (2) should not be based on empirical generalisations, but should put forward theories which are bold and courageous, and (3) should submit scientific theories to rigorous tests. The implications of theories should be logically deduced and empirically tested; the best scientific knowledge is able to resist careful scrutiny from the scientific community. *Philosophical positions and traditions such as hermeneutics, pragmatism, critical studies, and qualitative methodologies* developed another set of norms which tend to emphasise the historical nature of thinking; the active role of the researcher; the study of conceptions, theories, and the dialectics between subject and object; and emphasize that an object is always an object for a subject and a subject is always historically, socially, and culturally situated.

Sociology of science typically studies *empirical studies* on scientific activities, both internally in science and in their relations to broader society (power, economy, and policies). The field of scientometrics is often considered by sociologists of science as a part of their field (just as we in information science consider it part of our field). The field is closely related to "cultural studies of science". Among the important concepts in the sociology of science are "Mode 2" research and "triple helix" which emphasise the growing influence of industrial and commercial interests in the scientific system. Other important questions involve gender issues, the role of social class and ethnicity, the career system, and issues that motivate scientists to do things in the way they are done (versus how they could have be done).

Information science with informetrics typically studies information systems and information services; "memory institutions" such as research libraries, bib-

---

[2] Although Kuhn's philosophy of science, for example, represents a historicist philosophy of science.

liographic databases, knowledge organisation systems (see Stock, this volume); as well as the users, non-users, and potential users of such information systems and services. This field studies the whole system of actors, institutions, and services connecting information producers and users (cf., Søndergaard, Andersen, & Hjørland, 2003). Information science is largely an empirical field, but is also a normative field (studying, promoting, and providing standards for many aspects of scientific communication). While relatively distinct from the other meta-sciences given its purpose to contribute to optimal scientific communication and utilisation of recorded knowledge, information science often represents *a design or construction perspective* and a relation to the practice of librarianship, documentation, and information services that makes it relatively unique.

When it is claimed that informetrics belongs to the meta-sciences, it may be argued that this field is much broader than the scientific domain and today includes, among other things, webometrics and thus link-structures from all sectors of broader society as well as ordinary peoples' relation to information. Although this is correct, two things should be recognized: (1) Within the narrower field of science, it is important to consider the relation between scientometrics and the domain of science in order to understand and explain bibliometric patterns; and (2) In the broader field of other sectors of society and of everyday information use, the same principles may also provide a fruitful basis for understanding information science and informetrics. It is wrong and harmful to ignore the field of meta-sciences because it is considered too narrow (which is an argument frequently encountered in schools of library and information science because of the emphasis often placed on public libraries and information services for broader society). We shall return to the importance of the philosophy of science for non-scientific domains later.

Meta-sciences are mutually interdependent and all of them are also—first and foremost—dependent on subject knowledge of the fields of knowledge they are studying. In order to understand and evaluate research on say, the history of psychology, one must do so based on knowledge about the field of psychology, what counts as psychological knowledge, and what is a success or a blind alley in psychology. The same is the case when we have to interpret or evaluate a bibliometric map of psychology—in order to even draw it, first we need to identify which documents are psychological on which to draw the map (this is discussed in detail later in this chapter). In both cases, we have an example of a hermeneutic circle: in order to study a domain, you must delimit it, and in order to delimit it, you must have knowledge about it. In other words: A lack of subject knowledge on the part of meta-scientists may provide problematic interpretations of the empirical patterns observed.

Examples of interaction between the meta-sciences are Garfield's (2004) bibliometric contribution to historiography and Griffith's (1979) bibliometrically based criticism of some assumptions in the philosophy of science. On the other hand, Kuhn's (1962) theory of paradigms inspired bibliometric researchers to try to identify paradigms empirically (cf. Chen, 2003). This chapter will briefly introduce the relation between philosophy of science and other meta-sciences, but will mainly focus on the relation between the theory of science and informetrics.

2 Philosophy of science after logical positivism

Often stated, Thomas Kuhn's (1962) book *The Structure of Scientific Revolutions* brought an end to logical positivism. Although this is disputed,[3] the opposition between "positivism" and "post-Kuhnian philosophy" provides the foundation for this chapter; but what is (logical) positivism and what—if anything—has really changed in the ground swell of Kuhn?

Defining "positivism" is not easy.[4] There are many different positions in both classical and logical positivism, just as there are different interpretations of these positions (see, for example, Reisch, 2005 for a recent re-interpretation). A common view is that the term "positivism" includes three main characteristics:
1. the use of quantitative methodologies,
2. the use of scientific methods (as opposed to hermeneutic methods in the social sciences and humanities), and
3. the belief in realism and objectivity.

Given that Kuhn opposed positivism, an easy conclusion is that the understanding of positivism expressed in the first and second points must be wrong. Kuhn was a physicist by training and physics is based on measurements—hence a quantitative discipline. Of course, Kuhn did not end physics or its quantitative methodology and therefore it does not make sense to understand positivism in the first and second sense. Kuhn's revolution in the philosophy of science must have another

---

[3] The Danish philosopher Stig Andur Pedersen (1995) demonstrated that even if Kuhn's theory represents a clash with positivist ideas it is in many ways a natural continuation of the work of the logical positivists in the 1940s and 1950s . Friedman (2003), Moges (2010) and Reisch (1991) made related observations. Tsou (2015), however, maintains that the logical positivism of Rudolf Carnap and Kuhn's work represent two distinctive traditions of doing philosophy of science.

[4] "Questions such as 'Is thesis T a positivist (empiricist, idealist, realist etc.) thesis?' are notoriously difficult." (Bird, 2004, p. 338).

meaning (if the first view was correct, informetrics per definition would be positivist, which I will argue it cannot be).

The third view (that positivism is a realist position) is more complicated, but is generally considered wrong in the philosophy of science. For logical positivism, speaking about any reality behind observations or causing observations is metaphysical and metaphysics is considered illegitimate. "What exists in reality" is considered a metaphysical question and opposed to the positivist spirit. It is rather well-established in the philosophy of science that empiricism/positivism and realism are different positions. It can even be argued that positivism is less realistic compared to more interpretative positions because it is better to have explicit subjectivity than to have subjectivity disguised as objectivity. Such an argument will be put forward below.

What then is positivism? Perhaps we can best describe it as the belief in "the Leibnizian ideal":

> The Leibnizian ideal holds that all disputes about matters of fact can be impartially resolved by invoking appropriate rules of evidence. At least since Bacon, most philosophers have believed there to be an algorithm or set of algorithms which would permit any impartial observer to judge the degree to which a certain body of data rendered different explanations of those data true or false, probable or improbable [...] But whether optimists or pessimists, rationalists or empiricist, most logicians and philosophers of science from the 1930s through the 1950s believed, at least in principle, in the Leibnizian ideal.
>
> (Laudan, 1984, p. 5–6)

Although Kuhn was not the first to question this ideal,[5] *The Structure of Scientific Revolutions* nonetheless had the greatest impact on the fall of the Leibnizian ideal. What Kuhn brought to the forefront in the philosophy of science was the understanding that scientists are trained and socialized in paradigm-centered scientific communities and much of what they do and think is based on the experiences from their daily work with experiments. According to Mallery, Hurwitz, and Duffy (1992), the notion of a paradigm-centered scientific community is analogous to Gadamer's notion of a linguistically encoded social tradition. Therefore, we could say that Kuhn's philosophy is closer to hermeneutics than to positivism. Kuhn thus contributed in changing philosophy of science from an individualist to a social epistemology (cf. Wray, 2011). Not only do explicit theories govern scientists' activities, but also do tacit knowledge.

---

5 Names like Dewey (1929), Feyerabend (1975), Hanson (1958) and Toulmin (1953) deserve to be mentioned in this context.

Logical positivism must therefore be understood in contrast to socially and historically oriented philosophies of science. Logical positivism was an attempt to combine two former traditions—rationalism and empiricism:

> logical positivism arose as the joint product of two intellectual traditions [rationalism and empiricism] that conflicted deeply with one another: In attempting to unite these traditions, its adherents created an extremely influential approach to philosophy but one that embodied serious intellectual tensions from its dual ancestry.
>
> (Smith, 1986, p. 64)

In order to understand philosophy of science after logical positivism, it is therefore important to understand the inherent limitations of empiricism and rationalism (in this paper only empiricism is analyzed).

As a doctrine in epistemology, empiricism holds that all knowledge ultimately is based on experience; but empiricism should not be confused with the need for science to be empirical, is it rather about certain ideals governing empirical studies. Widely recognised today, sciences are empirical in a broad understanding of the term. In psychology, empiricism is in particular associated with behaviorism, the "objective" study of stimuli and responses in organisms. The limitations of behaviorism were strongly exposed by the linguist and cognitive scientist Noam Chomsky (who explicitly subscribed to rationalism), who wrote:

> A typical example of 'stimulus control' for [the behaviorist] Skinner would be the response to a piece of music with the utterance Mozart or to a painting with the response Dutch. These responses are asserted to be 'under the control of extremely subtle properties' of the physical object or event (108). Suppose instead of saying Dutch we had said Clashes with the wallpaper, I thought you liked abstract work, Never saw it before, Tilted, Hanging too low, Beautiful, Hideous, Remember our camping trip last summer?, or whatever else might come into our minds when looking at a picture (in Skinnerian translation, whatever other responses exist in sufficient strength). Skinner could only say that each of these responses is under the control of some other stimulus property of the physical object.
>
> (Chomsky, 1959, p. 31)

The behaviorism of Skinner is a version of logical positivism attempting to predict and control human behavior in terms of "stimuli" and "responses". It may understand itself as "objective science" but, as Chomsky's criticism demonstrates, in the case where a human being is looking at a painting and provides some response, we are unable to tell what in the painting elicited the specific response: the stimulus is not objectively given for the researcher. Because there is no objective way to identify the stimulus, there is of course a great possibility that the behaviorist/positivist psychologist uses his/her own subjective perception of the picture as the basis for studying other peoples' stimulus-response relations. If the psychologist is unaware of how the picture may be understood by different cultures and subcultures, his/her own cultural understanding may influence his/her perception of the psychology of the observer.

An example from history may also illustrate the same point. When history was established as a scholarly discipline in the United States, "universalism" was assumed, i.e., that,

> Truth was one, the same for all people. It was, in principle, accessible to all and addressed to all. Particular commitments —national, regional, ethnic, religious, ideological—were seen as enemies of objective truth [...] The close connection which historians saw between detachment and objectivity made them sympathetic to Mannheim's celebration of the vantage point of free-floating and socially detached observers, whose liberation from particularist loyalties allowed them to approach closer to objectivity.
>
> (Novick, 1988, p. 469)

However, this universalism was later challenged:

> The entry of large numbers of Jews into the upper reaches of the [historical] profession in the 1950s and early 1960s was widely seen as the fulfillment of universalist norms. It was otherwise with the arrival of blacks and women from the late sixties and onward. For their rise to prominence within the profession coincided with a new, assertive, particularist consciousness which both directly and indirectly challenged universalist norms. They defined themselves not as "historians who happened to be Negroes," with a consensually acceptable integrationist standpoint, but as *black* historians, committed to one or another form of cultural nationalism ...
>
> (Novick, 1988, p. 470; emphasis in original)

In short: Positivism is associated with the idea that researchers' subjectivity does not matter or may be eliminated while post-Kuhnian philosophy acknowledges the influence of subjectivity. The idea that male, middle-class, white historians may be able to describe history in neutral ways has been challenged just as has the idea about behavioral psychologists being able to describe stimulus-response patterns objectively. Somewhat paradoxically this makes positivism a less objective and less realist science compared to hermeneutics and related traditions: positivism turns out to be a form of subjective idealism in which the researcher's cultural background and theoretical understanding is neglected and therefore cannot be taken into account.[6]

---

[6] An anonymous reviewer commented: "positivism turns out to be a form of subjective idealism—only if you're characterizing positivism from an anti-positivist position, surely? There's no 'paradox' there." Answer: Yes, there is a real paradox in positivism. You cannot get rid of this criticism just by ignoring it. The implication of what the reviewer says is that any position is a

Kuhn introduced the concept of "paradigms", which has been heavily discussed. In this chapter a paradigm is understood as a system of assumptions, concepts, values, and practices that constitute a way of viewing reality. Paradigms influence the way scientists see things and describe them. Perception is not a neutral process of collecting data on which theories are afterwards developed, but perception itself is theory-laden. Scientists in different paradigms see the world differently and describe it differently. Concepts in one paradigm are not the same in another paradigm thus making paradigms incommensurable. This is in sharp conflict with the Leibnizian ideal because it changes the nature of scientists from objective calculators to socially conditioned subjects. It also means that scientific knowledge is not seen as a commonly agreed body of knowledge, but as different theories full of disagreements (although Kuhn himself saw science as governed by one paradigm at a time, the general post-Kuhnian tendency is to understand science as consisting of competing paradigms at any point in time). Kuhn added the historicist understanding that knowledge develops in historically constituted paradigms and this historical or evolutionary dimension (in addition to the social dimension) is important in order to understand the development of science. Finally, Kuhn also added the axiological dimension: Scientists may be governed by different goals and values.

The following quote by Michael Kleineberg expresses a view that has gained a stronghold today:

> In the process of knowing, the known and the knower seem to be inextricably interwoven. Knowledge as it appears in the consciousness of human beings is always knowledge about something for someone. The now widely accepted epistemic pluralism maintains that the validity of knowledge claims depends on the epistemic framework of the knower and cannot be judged from a neutral "view from nowhere". The knower as an agent of epistemic activity is always already embodied as a material organism and embedded in a social and cultural environment at a certain point in time and space. In other words, the prerequisites to create, represent, organize, and communicate knowledge or information are limited by preconditions which are investigated by theories of knowledge and constitute the epistemological dimension.
>
> (Kleineberg, 2014, p. 80)

This quote may sound relativistic (and Kuhn is often accused of being relativist).[7] Of course, any paradigm is not as fruitful as any other, although the difficulty is

---

fruitful as any other and that disagreeing arguments can just be ignored. To say that any theoretical position is true from its own point of view represent a problematic relativism.

[7] An anonymous reviewer of this chapter wrote: "In this very interesting chapter, the author argues that, as meta-scientists, designers and evaluators of informetric studies should heed certain claims of "post-Kuhnian" philosophy of science—e.g., that the goal of science/meta-science is

again that an evaluation of paradigms cannot be accomplished from a neutral "view from nowhere". However, as Kleineberg (2014) writes: "If the claim 'nothing is valid for all contexts' was true, then it would contradict itself since this statement appears as a universal claim as well" (p. 85).

We conclude this section with a quote from historian Christopher Lloyd:

> "Perhaps the greatest advance in understanding the nature of explanation made in the post-positivist and post-Kuhnian era is the general realization that methodologies, theories, and explanations are related to each other via extra-logical, historically variable constellations variously described as 'background knowledge', 'traditions', 'paradigms', 'research programmes', 'fields', or 'domains'. We can call all of these 'framework concepts.'
>
> (Lloyd, 1993, p. 32)

3 Intermezzo: social constructivism is not an alternative to positivism

Before we consider the implications of the Kuhnian revolution in the philosophy of science, it is necessary to consider social constructivism because this position is strongly influential today:

> Originally proposed by sociologists of science, constructivism or social constructivism is a view about the nature of scientific knowledge held by many philosophers of science. Constructivists maintain that scientific knowledge is made by scientists and not determined by the world. This makes constructivists antirealists. [...] Constructivism is more aptly compared with Berkeley's idealism.
>
> (Downes, 1998, vol. 2, p. 624)

Sociologists of science, such as Bloor (1991), a main figure in the so-called "Strong Programme", conduct empirical studies of (natural) scientists and some of them claim from such findings to demonstrate how scientists construct scientific knowledge (rather than discover the truth). Bloor based the sociology of science on the following principles (here quoted from Finn Collin):

---

not to discover objective (i.e., mind- or context-independent) truths about the world; that, in any case, there is no way (e.g., a neutral "view from nowhere") for scientists to discover objective truths about the world; that, in any case, there are no objective truths about the world; that, in any case, there is no objective reality—and should recognize the historically-, culturally-, and institutionally-specific nature of their findings." Answer: I did not made these claims, these are something that the reviewer read into the chapter. The pragmatic view of truth and objectivity is complicated, but most pragmatists do think that it is possible to give a pragmatic account of objectivity that avoids bad relativism and conventionalism; see Bernstein (2010, 106–124).

1. It [the sociology of science] would be causal, that is, concerned with the conditions which bring about belief or states of knowledge. Naturally there will be other types of causes apart from social ones which will cooperate in bringing about belief.
2. It would be impartial with respect to truth and falsity, rationality or irrationality, success or failure. Both sides of these dichotomies require examination.
3. It would be symmetrical in this style of explanation. The same types of cause would explain, say, true and false beliefs.
4. It would be reflexive. In principle its patterns of explanation would have to be applicable to sociology itself. Like the requirement of symmetry this is a response to the need to seek for general explanations. It is an obvious requirement of principle because otherwise sociology would be a standing refutation of its own theories.

These conditions are meant to express a commitment to what Bloor sees as an uncontroversial, mainstream conception of science; thereby, he intends to safeguard the scientific credentials of the programme.

(Collin, 2011, p. 37)

Collin continues pointing out how the above characteristics looks like a commitment, not to scientific rigor as such, but to the idealized conception of science constructed and propagated by logical positivism. Other philosophers (e.g., Kjørup, 2008) have also shown how Bloor's ideas are related to those of logical positivism. My own thoughts related to the problem of subject knowledge (or lack thereof) in much of meta-science come to the same conclusion: How is it possible for sociologists to study the activities of scientists without proper knowledge about the subject matter of those activities? (Recall Skinner's interpretation of peoples' reaction to a painting.) How can sociologists decide which acts are important and which are trivial? How is it decided which acts turn out to be fruitful and which are futile? In order to make these decisions, one needs detailed knowledge about the arguments for and against a given theory strengthened or falsified by those acts. To claim that a neutral and objective description of scientific activities is possible without proper subject knowledge is a mistake related to positivist doctrines. As formerly described, such positivist "objectivity" has often been demonstrated as imposing upon the researcher his/her own subjective biases into descriptions and claims.

Social constructivism seems to be based on a paradox: its own research is "true" in claiming the impossibility of objective research. Additionally, it seems to underestimate how difficult it is to produce knowledge and theories that are consistent (i.e., how much resistance reality makes in the construction of theories). While they are right that there is an element of contingency in science this does not mean that scientists can produce any truth they like. We shall return to this issue in relation to bibliometric maps.

Thomas Kuhn has often been used to support relativists and social constructivists, but Kuhn's philosophy does not imply a strong kind of constructivism (see Wray, 2011) and Kuhn (2000, p. 110) famously rejected the Strong Programme as "deconstruction gone mad". It is important, in the words of Brian Cantwell Smith, "to steer a path between the Scylla of naive realism and the Charybdis of pure constructivism" (Smith, 1996, p. 3). It is ironic that social constructivism –which tends to regard positivism as its enemy par excellence—itself seems to be based on the same problematic assumptions about the neutrality of the researcher. Therefore, (strong) social constructivism is not an alternative to positivism.

4 Post-Kuhnian perspectives on the meta-sciences

The issue of "positivism" versus "paradigm theory" is important in all specific sciences (like physics, biology, psychology, and history) as well as in the meta-sciences described above. In the field of history, Novick (1988) is a valuable example of how the American historical profession has dealt with the idea and ideal of objectivity from its foundation in the 1880s until the book was written. Its particular value is that it describes concretely how the ideal of objectivity was elaborated, challenged, modified, and defended over the last century. The study is based on, among other sources, the archives of the *American Historical Review*, and is thus a demonstration of how different philosophical norms have influenced decisions for the acceptance of papers for publication in a leading journal (philosophical norms are thus not "merely" philosophical). My analysis of how "post-Kuhnian" perspectives have changed the meta-sciences does not have the same differentiated and balanced treatment as Novick, but is here presented in a purely schematic and tentative form.

A scientific document is a report by a scientist observing the world and a scientometric study is a report by a scientist observing the reports of other scientists. In both cases, the ways the reports are made reflect norms in the theory of science (even if these norms are implicit or unconscious). The argument is wider, however: Even if the documents are not scholarly papers, they are influenced by philosophical views or ideologies (e.g., by different kinds of -isms in art). All documents are influenced by some views and interests, and all studies of documents are also influenced by some kinds of subjectivity, which are partly culturally and socially shaped. There are thus two levels at play: (1) the traditions and epistemologies underlying document production and (2) the traditions and epistemologies underlying informetrics, information science, and the study of scholarly communi-

Tab. 1: Paradigm shifts in the meta-sciences.

	Philosophy of science	History of science	Sociology of science	Information science with scientometrics
More traditional/ positivist views	Principles about logics and empirical data. "the Leibnizian ideal": Neutral researchers decide objectively whether or not a given set of data confirms or disconfirms a theory. Emphasis on verification of facts and verified facts.	Science is seen from an internal perspective "Whiggish" historiography: focusing on the successful chain of theories and experiments that led to present-day science, while ignoring failed theories and dead ends.	"the Leibnizian ideal" sociologized: Scientific controversies will stop, when things are "properly" studied. Scientific theories are not understood in relation to social issues.	The scientific authority and consensus is taken as a point of departure. (Or alternatively: the users' individual preferences are taken as a point of departure.) Information systems and services are predominantly understood as technological issues.
More hermeneutic/ constructivist/ post-Kuhnian views	Emphasis on theories and values and on the theoretical assumptions, which influence observational reports.	History of science includes an externalist perspective and more attention given to disagreements and views different from mainstream.	More emphasis placed on controversies and considering science and scientific theories in relation to broader social and cultural conditions and economics.	Information services, information systems, search engines, bibliometric maps, etc. cannot be neutral in relation to scientific theories and paradigms. These are not purely technical, but involve issues of subject knowledge, values, and epistemology.

cation. This paper claims that the important theories of level 1 are identical with the important theories of level 2 in that both levels may reflect a positivist or alternatively a post-Kuhnian philosophy. How post-Kuhnian perspectives have affected the meta-sciences is outlined in Table 1.

5 Post-Kuhnian perspectives on informetrics

Belver C. Griffith (1979) criticised how history and philosophy of science neglected bibliometric findings (including Solla Price, 1965, and his own research). Griffith claims that the empirical studies of science (bibliometrics) have challenged many claims in history and philosophy of science including Kuhn's rejection of "crucial experiments" in physics: "To have taken this image [provided by bibliometrics] seriously would have wiped out many 'hard won distinctions' that philosophers had wrested from their own scholarship" (p. 384). Griffith also praised two books in information science (Brittain, 1970; Meadows, 1974) writing: "The books are, however, philosophically blind—but perhaps nothing really was lost." In other words, in contrast to this article, Griffith did not expect philosophy of science to be important for information science.

That philosophy is indeed important for science can be expressed with a quote by Albert Einstein:

> The reciprocal relationship of epistemology and science is of noteworthy kind. They are dependent upon each other. Epistemology without contact with science becomes an empty scheme. Science without epistemology is—insofar as it is thinkable at all—primitive and muddled.
>
> (Einstein, 1949, p. 683–684)[8]

My aim is thus twofold: (1) To argue the importance of philosophy of science (against Griffith, 1979, among others, probably including the silent majority of researchers), and (2) to outline what I see as the most important philosophical perspective for informetrics.

---

[8] Einstein's relation to positivism is expressed in this quote: "I am not a Positivist. Positivism states that what cannot be observed does not exist. This conception is scientifically indefensible, for it is impossible to make valid affirmations of what people 'can' or 'cannot' observe. One would have to say 'only what we observe exists', which is obviously false" (Einstein, 2005, p. 238). This quote is of course too simplistic to say something about positivism as well as Einstein's philosophy of science—or to indicate that Einstein would support my interpretation of post-Kuhnian philosophy (see Howard, 1993 for a deeper discussion). It is cited only to indicate that positivism is not necessarily the scientists' philosophy and that it is justified to challenge it.

5.1 The mirror metaphor

Griffith's article, entitled *Bibliometrics: How faulty a mirror of knowledge?* did not, however, address the problem of its title (but was, as mentioned above, a criticism that philosophy of science neglected what he considered relevant bibliometric findings). Here, however, the problem will be directly considered: How faulty a mirror of science is a bibliometric map? (Moreover, how can we examine this?) My first comment concerns the mirror metaphor,[9] according to which scientific knowledge shall be understood as representing a mirror of nature and bibliometric maps as representing mirrors of science.

John Dewey (1929, p. 215) criticized what he labelled "the spectator theory of knowledge" (i.e., the view that the knower is only passively related to the thing known) as did the pragmatic tradition to which he belonged (see also Rorty, 1979). The pragmatic alternative to the mirror metaphor considers knowledge (and knowledge representations such as bibliometric maps) as *tools* and therefore they do not evaluate them according to how faulty (or how precise) a mirror they provide, but according to how well they fulfil their functions as tools for given tasks (implying that different tasks may require different perspectives). An example: Boyack and Klavans (2010) asked "Which citation approach represents the research front most accurately?" Asking the question this way reveals a view of knowledge corresponding to the mirror metaphor. One of the problems in asking which approach is best is that an answer to that question presupposes that there is a neutral platform from which different approaches may be compared, that we have a key on which to evaluate different approaches. But we do not have such a key; we only have different, more or less equivalent approaches, each of which may claim to be the best. The alternative is to ask: Which bibliometric approach provides the best tool for a given task? Based on this pragmatic view, I consider co-citation analysis and bibliometric coupling as two different approaches that should not be evaluated on providing the most accurate picture, but as different tools suited for different kinds of tasks (see Hjørland, 2013). To understand bibliographical coupling is to understand the degree of overlap in different authors' citation identity, while to understand co-citation patterns is to understand the reception history and scholarly impact of documents. My suggestions may of course be questioned and further examined, but the point here is to follow John Dewey and question the mirror view of knowledge and its use in informetrics today.

---

[9] The mirror metaphor is also known as "the picture theory of knowledge", "the mimetic nature of information", and "the spectator theory of knowledge".

5.2 Selection of sources: a hermeneutical circle

A strong argument about the non-neutrality of bibliometric maps concerns the selection of the journals (or other sources) on which a given map is constructed. In a former paper I wrote:

> Imagine that we are going to create a map of LIS. As Åström (2002) showed, former maps, such as that of White and McCain (1998), seem to have a bias towards information science. In order to provide a better alternative, Åström also included more library-oriented journals in his study. However, there is no objective criterion for judging which documents best represent LIS, and *any selected set of journals can always be shown to have a bias in some direction or another.*
>
> (Hjørland, 2013, p. 1322; emphasis in original)

Bibliometric researchers are mostly explicit about which journals they used in their studies, and thus about their selection. This means that their research is objective in the sense that other researchers may replicate it. However, the claim put forward here is that bibliometricans do not usually make explicit arguments for how the journals were selected in relation to their conception of the field. It is as if the researchers' view of the domain in question is considered 'obvious' or of no consequence, or that this would provide a kind of subjectivity that is antithetical to the positivist ideals of the authors. White and McCain (1998, p. 329), for example, wrote about co-citation maps: "The maps transcend the viewpoint—and the individual biases—of any one observer." The authors also argued that their choice of journals reflects "mainstream information science" and "journals with strong IS [information science] orientations, as indicated by title and scope statements". However, from my point of view their conception of information science seems to be biased towards "library automation". If I had to make the choice of journals, other journals should have been added (or replaced the library automation journals), because in my conception information science is less technology-oriented and more socially-oriented. My point is that we all have our different views of what the core information science journals are and our perspectives influence our study of the field. Therefore a bibliometric map is a subjective representation, not an objective one. Any researcher may have a specific interest (e.g., in facet analysis) and the journals/information sources with the best coverage of that focus could be determined. If not included in the bibliometric investigation, this could be considered a "bias" in the study. This is not an insignificant complaint because such maps are extremely vulnerable to such choices.

A study by Schneider (2010) may also confirm this view:

> The highly specialized character of *Scientometrics* compared to the other journals in this set, i.e., a larger share of publications and the large number of unique authors that only publish

> in the journal, obviously exacerbates the influence of this journal to the arbitrary construct named IS. This raises some important questions on how fields ought to be delimited if at all and how publications should be selected for mapping purposes. It is first of all a sampling problem rather than a normalization problem. It is not a question of right or wrong. It is the simple fact stemming from the phenomena of skewed distributions. Very few mapping studies address this issue.
>
> (Schneider, 2010, p. 257)

Schneider says that the domain under study, information science, is an "arbitrary construct" and that it has important consequences whether a given journal is or is not considered a part of the domain. I see this as a very strong support of my claim that informetrics researchers have to base their studies on an explicate view of what the field is, and what it should be.

We have a kind of hermeneutic circle: How can we identify a field by a set of journals, a set of departments, a set of scholars, etc., unless we already know the field? And how can we know the field unless we know its journals, its research institutions, and its leading scholars? The answer is not that it is hopeless, but that it requires an iterative process whereby the views of the informetrics researchers must be developed, considering the perspective of other meta-sciences, and used to inform their opinion of which views of the field their map is meant to be a tool to support.

A basic principle of critical theory has been formulated in this way:

> In retrospect the most important contribution of critical theory to philosophy in the late twentieth century would seem to be their criticism of positivism and their demand that social theory be reflective; that is, that theorists try to be as aware as possible of their own position, the origin of their beliefs and attitudes, and the possible consequences their theorizing might have on what they are studying.
>
> (Geuss, 1998, p. 728)

Using this principle of critical theory in bibliometrics may be termed "critical informetrics" and here we shall have a look at how former bibliometric investigations have been re-examined from such a critical perspective. Spear (2007) criticized former bibliometric studies of the so-called cognitive revolution in psychology. Among his findings are that subfields may develop independently to overall paradigm shifts in a discipline and that scholarly fields may have self-interest in appearing successful. Therefore, "flagship publications" may not be a good place to look for criticism of main stream assumptions (see also Toomela, 2014, about common assumptions in mainstream research). Spear provided convincing arguments and new empirical results questioning former studies. Spear also emphasised the important ethical issues in simplistic bibliometric conclusions:

We can argue about indicators, data sources, and forms of analysis, but in the end what we likely learn is that there are many ways to tell a complex story. The problem, of course, is that the outcome of this story has real and important implications for the distribution of organizational resources. If indeed every dean, every granting agency, and every department head "knows" that there has been a cognitive revolution or that a cognitive neuroscience revolution is afoot, then where does that leave the claims of those who do not identify themselves with cognitive psychology or, worse yet, those who identify with behavioral analysis? There is much at stake in how the history of psychology is told.

(Spear, 2007, p. 377)

This may be generalized: there is much at stake in how the history and bibliometric patterns of any domain are represented.

5.3 Is the pragmatic/critical view trivial?

Are informetrics researchers well aware of the importance of the pragmatic/critical philosophy outlined in this article? Is it a triviality? In my opinion, it is not. Although there have been some critical voices, mainstream research in this field is still reflecting the positivist model. For example, Henry Small has claimed that co-citation studies—in opposition to manually constructed bibliographies—does not involve subjective decisions:

> Either an existing bibliography is used, or subject experts are called upon to comb the literature and select relevant items. The bibliography then becomes the data base for subsequent analyses of the specialty, including its growth and structural characteristics. To the extent that this approach is based upon subjective decisions of relevance by the individual(s) compiling the bibliography, the analysis is open to criticism for possible bias and lack of reproducibility. The principal difficulty with this approach is that it is almost impossible to establish precise criteria as to what should or should not be included within the boundaries of the subject. The method employed here, on the other hand, uses a clustering algorithm to establish these boundaries; *it involves no subjective decisions on what is to be included or excluded from the specialty literature.*

(Small, 1977, p. 140, italics added)

Precisely the same argument was put forward 37 years later by Andersen, Bazerman and Schneider (2014, p. 317), who wrote: "Scientometric maps provide a kind of description of the cognitive or social structure of a research area independent of subjective judgments and relevance criteria"[10] and I have already discussed how Boyack and Klavans (2010) asked "Which citation approach represents the

---

10 Subsequently Bazerman wrote in an email: "Birger, Good point. [...] Nonetheless, the sentence does not say that the description provided is definitive or an ultimate or fully objective reality–

research front most accurately" as an example that I find represent mainstream informetrics research. Furthermore, informetric research often uses similarity measures about which Ellis, Furner-Hines and Willett wrote:

> Even in the field of numerical taxonomy, where the use of similarity coefficients has been even more widespread than in information retrieval, Jackson, Somers and Harvey (1989) were moved to conclude that 'the choice of a similarity coefficient is largely subjective and often based on tradition or on a posteriori criteria such as the 'interpretability' of the results", and went on to quote Gordon (1987): 'Human ingenuity is quite capable of providing a post hoc justification of dubious classifications.'
>
> (Ellis et al. 1993, 144)

They conclude:

> We agree with Kruskal (1964) 'that each scientific area that has use for different measures of proximity should after appropriate argument and trial, settle down on those measures most useful for its needs.' For most applications in information retrieval, the historical attachment to the simple, linear, association coefficients provided by the Dice and cosine formulae is in no need of revision.
>
> (Ellis et al., 1993, 145)

What I miss in this paper—and in the whole of mainstream research in information retrieval and bibliometrics—is the consideration that any two things may be considered similar in many different ways. There is no such thing as measuring similarity objectively. There should always be an argument about the perspective from which two things (e.g., documents) are considered similar. This is a well-known problem in biological taxonomy in which different species may have developed similar bones and other criteria of similarity in order to adjust to the same environmental possibilities.

There have, of course, been researchers who have pointed out bias, uncertainty, theoretical divergences, and subjectivity in informetrics research (for a compilation, see Cronin & Sugimoto, 2015). What I believe has seldom—if ever—been claimed explicitly is *the principal unavoidability of such bias and subjectivity* and, by consequence, the necessity of acknowledgement of the researcher's standpoint.

---

only that it provides a description that is independent of interpretive judgments. But of course scientometric methods themselves include criteria and procedural judgments. While it is hard to reconstruct my state of mind while revising the text, I likely was thinking that it referred to the kinds of narrative interpretation that historians or participants might give and I did not stop to consider the assumptions embedded within scientometrics. [...] Chuck"

One argument that my claim is trivial was put forward in an informal communication with a bibliometric scholar:

> It is well known that the results of bibliometric investigations often are expressed as probabilities—usually a confidence interval at 95 percent is accepted. In other words is it accepted that there may be up to five percent probability that the result is due to random outcome. This is more or less accepted standard in the social sciences. In this is also given a clear expression that the result is not necessarily "the objective truth".
>
> (Informal communication, January 12, 2015)

This argument does not catch my point, however. One thing is whether there is a statically uncertainty in results, another thing is whether there is a *systematic* bias due to the researcher's subjectivity. The belief that a certain result is within a certain confidence interval is still based on positivist assumptions. As an anonymous reviewer of this chapter wrote:

> The general argument that the results of informetric studies should not be treated as objective truths is by no means new.[11] I think there is scope for making reference to a wider selection of previous work, published in the information science literature, in which similar conclusions are drawn.

The reviewer subsequently, on demand, referred to Edge (1979), Hicks (1987), MacRoberts and MacRoberts (1989) and Sullivan, White, and Barboni, (1977).

My first answer is that it is correct that there have been critical voices about bibliometric studies, and I consider the four examples mentioned by the reviewer as being outside mainstream informetrics research. Of these four papers two (Edge, 1979 and Sullivan, White, & Barboni, 1977) are more in line with my post-Kuhnian position while the other two seem to be more in line with the positivist position.

Hicks (1987) compared co-citation analysis with a manually generated bibliography in the specialty of "spin glass" and found that co-citation analysis is a "premature" method for science policy decisions, but that further work may improve its reliability and robustness. She describes the subjectivity involved in co-citation analysis but overall her paper seems to suggest—in contradiction to the present chapter—that such subjectivity may be removed when the method becomes mature. She further wrote that "The identification of 'specialties' is fraught with theoretical and empirical difficulties, which remain unresolved" (p. 304), which we have already discussed.

---

[11] See footnote 7 about the pragmatic view of realism and objectivity and the reviewer's misinterpretation of my statements.

MacRoberts and MacRoberts (1989) discussed seven kinds of problems in citation analysis (i.e., formal influences not cited; biased citing; information influences not cited; self-citing; different types of citation; variations in citation rate placed to type of publication, nationality, time period, and the size and type of specialty; and technical limitations of citation indices and bibliographies). They concluded:

> Consequently, whether or not, and in what ways, citations can be used as data remains unclear and will continue so until all aspects of citation analysis—the theories and assumptions that inform it, as well as the data upon which it is based—are subjected to careful scrutiny. Until this is done, any results obtained by using citations as data will, at best, have to be considered tentative.
>
> (MacRoberts and MacRoberts, 1989, p. 347)

This study also tries to identify kinds of errors in order to eliminate them rather than reflecting the view that the bibliometric analyst should argue about his or her view of the represented domain (although this view may be implicit in the paper).

Sullivan, White, and Barboni (1977) examined Henry Small's claim that co-citation analysis "involves no subjective decisions on what is to be included or excluded from the specialty literature" and concluded:

> The potential biases of which Small speaks [in constructing manual bibliographies] are real, and we find it necessary in our work to be as aware as possible of them. But there are biases involved in co-citation analysis, as well.
>
> (Sullivan, White, & Barboni, 1977, p. 236)

In other words, this paper confirms the thesis about the subjectivity in informetrics. About the data used for examining the co-citation structure, the authors admit (p. 225): "We do not claim that this intellectual history is necessarily the true picture". The difference between this view and my own is that I would assume that any intellectual history reflects a specific perspective, and therefore suggests that some work is made illuminating different possible perspectives and how different methodological choices supports one or another perspective.

Edge (1979) is the paper that comes closest to my own view. He discusses quantitative methods in historical and sociological studies of modern astronomy and writes:

> ... my overall approach is critical. I am not convinced by the stronger claims of the proponents of these quantitative methods. I want to argue that those who adopt these methods (and, in particular, citation analysis) make implicit assumptions about the nature of science: and, moreover, that what they gloss over as unproblematic are precisely the points which many of us find to be crucially at issue.
>
> (Edge, 1979, p. 102)

One of the important conclusions in his paper is:

> These [bibliometric] data certainly make our case more convincing! However, it is important to stress the *derivative* quality of these figures, which have (in my mind) the status of *secondary validation* only. Essentially, our picture is derived from our 'soft' data.
>
> (Edge, 1979, p. 126)

Edge is not rejecting quantitative studies, but finds that they should be used critically and based on qualitative knowledge. He is not—as I am—referring to philosophy of science, Thomas Kuhn, critical theory or pragmatism, but his paper is explicitly "critical". Perhaps an explicit engagement with critical philosophy could have made his analyses even deeper by helping to uncover conflicting perspectives and interests in the qualitative and quantitative analysis of the domain.

The examples given in this section demonstrates, in my opinion, that the philosophical position defended in this paper is not trivial.

5.4 The historicist revolution and its implications for informetrics and information science

We saw that Kuhn introduced a historicist approach in the philosophy of science. The historical perspective has changed biological taxonomy (under the name "cladism") and may also have the potential of making a scientific revolution in information science and informetrics:

> Citation analysis can be compared to the paradigm shift in biological taxonomy over recent decades. The classical approach to biological classification (exemplified by the Linnaean taxonomy) is based on classifying organisms on the basis of shared properties (e.g., number of stamens), that is to classify according to similarity of certain properties. Cladism represents a paradigm shift in biology in which organisms are classified solely on the basis of a common ancestor (by Ereshefsky, 2000, called 'the historical approach'). This new approach has made fundamental changes in the classification of plants and animals and this revolution is not yet complete. In the same way as cladism represents a revolution in biological taxonomy, citation analysis may be considered a revolution in KO [knowledge organization] and information retrieval. Both are based on a historical rather than a structural approach to classification. The implication for KO is that the domains and scholarly traditions to which documents belong are considered their most important criteria of classification (rather than, for example, their statistical word patterns). Scholarly theories determine what is to be considered related and different theories imply different criteria of relatedness.
>
> (Hjørland, 2013, p. 1321)

Traditional information science and information retrieval tend to consider documents as isolated phenomena and to compare their individual characteristics.[12] Informetrics is the most obvious perspective to consider documents as part of a tradition and therefore to apply a historicist perspective (although this is not always the case). At this point, it shall just be stated that a more consequent historicist philosophy may have the potential to transform the field in a fruitful direction.

5.5 Non-scholarly domains

We have now considered informetrics in the perspective of the philosophy of science. Are these perspectives also relevant to broader perspectives than just scholarly domains? To make such a generalisation means to move from the theory of science to the theory of knowledge and cognition. My answer is yes: Any domain (e.g., sport, religion, education, law, eHealth or e-commerce) may be perceived differently, there is never just one, neutral and objective, way to describe a field. It is important to consider from which perspective and for which purpose documents are described and the relevance of information is evaluated. Google, for example, is not a neutral search engine (even if we consider only so-called "organic search" as opposed to advertisements). One could say that in principle any search engine is always a cultural-political agent making priorities in relation to what content should be relatively findable and what should remain relatively invisible.

Kuhn's theory has not just been influential in the philosophy of science, but also, for example, in psychology. "Theory theory" (Weiskopf, 2011) is a psychological theory that understands children's thinking as corresponding to scientists' way of thinking: Children have "theories" which may change like paradigm shifts. Therefore, principles from the philosophy of science may have potential as a general foundation for informetrics.

---

[12] An anonymous reviewer commented: "I would disagree, given the emphasis even in 'traditional' information retrieval on measures like tf.idf that take into account the collection-wide frequencies of terms as well as within-document frequencies, on thesauri built on term co-occurrence data, etc. Today's web search algorithms, of course, are heavily link-based, and in no sense treat documents as independent." Answer: Yes, traditional IR often considers documents as parts of collections or as being interlinked. Still, however, they do not consider the single document as part of a genre and a tradition and none of the approaches mentioned by the reviewer can be considered historicist. In biology related methods are known as numeric taxonomic approaches, but they are considered different from cladistics (historical) methods.

5.6 A paradox

This chapter is termed *Informetrics needs a foundation in the theory of science*. However, the theory of science distinguishes between two kinds of epistemology: (1) Foundationalism (a secure foundation of certainty exists) and (2) Anti-foundationalism (no fundamental belief or principle provides the basis or foundation for inquiry and knowledge); justification of knowledge claims is understood here as a function of a relationship between beliefs, none of which are privileged as maintained by foundationalist theories of justification. The paradox is that the philosophical foundation I suggest for informetrics is anti-foundationalism. This is, however, only a contradiction in the word used in the title: there is no contradiction in subscribing to anti-foundationalism.

6 Conclusion

The main point raised in the present paper is that insights from the theory of science are important for informetrics. A bibliometric study or measure cannot be judged from a neutral "view from nowhere", but is always—consciously or unconsciously—engaged in the theoretical issues in the field studied. The two most important implications of a post-Kuhnian view of informetrics are:
1. Bibliometric researchers need to consider domain-knowledge and its theoretical foundation: they have to stand in relation to different views on the domain being investigated; and,
2. The objects of bibliometric studies—the documents—must be understood in relation to the broader contexts in which they are produced, used, and cited. Concepts like "research tradition", "paradigms", "genres", "activity systems", and the like are framework concepts necessary for deeper interpretation and analysis of bibliometric patterns.

Where is Blaise Cronin situated in relation to this view of information science? The following quote illuminates this question:

> The texts we write and the texts we cite bear the marks of the epistemic cultures, sociocognitive networks and physical places to which we belong at the different stages of our professional lives.
>
> (Cronin, 2005, p. 1)

This understanding of "epistemic cultures" and their importance for informetrics and information science reflects the basic idea of the present chapter: The fruitfulness of a social and epistemological basis for the field.

Acknowledgment

Thanks to Cassidy Sugimoto and an anonymous reviewer for fruitful suggestions that improved the article.

Cited References

Åström, F. (2002). Visualizing library and information science concept spaces through keyword and citation based maps and clusters. In H. Bruce, R. Fidel, P. Ingwersen & P. Vakkari (Eds.), *Emerging frameworks and methods: Proceedings of the fourth international conference on conceptions of library and information science (CoLIS4)* (pp. 185–197). Greenwood Village: Libraries Unlimited.
Andersen, J.; Bazerman, C. & Schneider, J. (2014). Beyond single genres: Pattern mapping in global communication. In: Eva-Maria Jakobs and Daniel Perrin (Eds.), *Handbook of Writing and Text Production* (pp. 305–322). Berlin: Walter de Gruyter GmbH.
Bates, M. J. (1999). The invisible substrate of information science. *Journal of the American Society for Information Science, 50*(12), 1043–1050.
Bernstein, R. J. (2010). *The pragmatic turn*. Cambridge, UK: Polity.
Bird, A. (2004). Kuhn, naturalism, and the positivist legacy. *Studies in History and Philosophy of Science, 35*(2), 337–356.
Bloor, D. (1991). *Knowledge and social imagery*. London: Routledge & Kegan Paul, 2nd edition, Chicago: University of Chicago Press.
Boyack, K. W., & Klavans, R. (2010). Co-citation analysis, bibliographic coupling, and direct citation: Which citation approach represents the research front most accurately? *Journal of the American Society for Information Science and Technology, 61*(12), 2389–2404.
Brittain, M. J. (1970). *Information and its users: A review with special reference to the social sciences*. Bath, UK: Bath University Press.
Chen, C. M. (2003). Visualizing scientific paradigms: An introduction. *Journal of the American Society for Information Science and Technology, 54*(5), 392–393.
Chomsky, N. (1959). Review of B. F. Skinner's Verbal Behavior. *Language, 35*(1), 26–58.
Collin, F. (2011). *Science studies as naturalized philosophy*. Dordrecht: Springer.
Cronin, B. (2005). Warm bodies, cold facts: The embodiment and emplacement of knowledge claims. In P. Ingwersen & B. Larsen (Eds.), *Proceedings of the 10th International Conference on Scientometrics and Informetrics* (pp. 1–12). Stockholm: Karolinska University Press.
Cronin, B. & Sugimoto, C. R. (Eds.) (2015). *Scholarly metrics under the microscope: From citation analysis to academic auditing*. Medford, NJ: Information Today, Inc./ASIST, pp. 976.

Dewey, J. (1929). *The quest for certainty: A study of the relation of knowledge and action*. New York: Putnam.

Downes, S. M. (1998). Constructivism. In E. Craig (Ed.), *Routledge Encyclopedia of Philosophy* (Version 1.0). London: Routledge.

Edge, D. (1979). Quantitative measures of communication in science: A critical review. *History of Science*, 17(2), 102–134.

Einstein, A. (1949). Remarks concerning the essays brought together in this co-operative volume. In P. A. Schlipp (Ed.), *Albert Einstein, philosopher-scientist* (pp. 663–688). New York: Tudor Publishers.

Einstein, A. (2005). *The quotable Einstein* (edited by A. Calaprice). Princeton, NJ: Princeton University Press.

Ellis, D., Furner-Hines, J., & Willett, P. (1993). Measuring the degree of similarity between objects in text retrieval systems. ¤Perspective in Information Management¤, 3, 128–149.

Ereshefsky, M. (2000). *The poverty of the Linnaean hierarchy: A philosophical study of biological taxonomy*. Cambridge: Cambridge University Press.

Feyerabend, P. (1975). *Against method*. London: New Left Books.

Friedman, M. (2003). Kuhn and logical empiricism. In T. Nickles (ed.), *Thomas Kuhn* (pp. 19–44). Cambridge: Cambridge University Press.

Garfield, E. (2004). Historiographic mapping of knowledge domains literature. *Journal of Information Science, 30*(2), 119–145.

Geuss, R. (1998). Critical theory. In *Routledge Encyclopedia of Philosophy*, Vol. 2, 722–728. London: Routledge.

Gordon, A. D. (1987). A review of hierarchical classification. *Journal of the Royal Statistical Society*, Series A (General) 150(2), 119–137.

Griffith, B. C. (1979). Science literature: How faulty a mirror of science? *ASLIB Proceedings, 31*(8), 381–391.

Hanson, N. R. (1958). *Patterns of discovery*. Cambridge: Cambridge University Press.

Hicks, D. (1987). Limitations of co-citation analysis as a tool for science policy. *Social Studies of Science*, 17(2), 295–316.

Hjørland, B. (2013). Citation analysis: A social and dynamic approach to knowledge organization. *Information Processing & Management, 49*(6), 1313–1325.

Howard, D. (1993). Was Einstein really a realist? *Perspectives on Science, 1*(2), 204–251. Retrieved from https://www3.nd.edu/~dhoward1/Was%20Einstein%20Really%20a%20Realist.pdf

Jackson, D. A., Somers, K. M. & Harvey, H. H. (1989). Similarity coefficients: measures of co-occurrence and association or simply measures of occurrence? *The American Naturalist* 133(3): 436–453.

Kjørup, S. (2008). *Menneskevidenskaberne* [The human sciences]. 2nd Ed. Vol. 1–2. Frederiksberg: Roskilde Universitetsforlag.

Kleineberg, M. (2014). Integrative levels of knowing: An organizing principle for the epistemological dimension. *Advances in Knowledge Organization, 14*, 80–87.

Kruskal, J. B. (1964). Multidimensional scaling by optimizing goodness-of-fit to a non-metric hypothesis. *Psychometrika, 29*(1), 1–27.

Kuhn, T. S. (1962). *The structure of scientific revolutions*. Chicago: University of Chicago Press.

Kuhn, T. S. (2000). *The Road Since Structure: Philosophical Essays, 1970–1993*, with an Autobiographical Interview. J. Conant & J. Haugeland (Eds.). Chicago: University of Chicago Press.

Lloyd, C. (1993). *The Structures of History*. Oxford, UK: Blackwell.
MacRoberts, M. H. & MacRoberts, B. R. (1989). Problems of citation analysis: A critical review. *Journal of the American Society for Information Science*, 40(5), 342–349.
Mallery, J. C., Hurwitz, R., & Duffy, G. (1992). Hermeneutics. In S. C. Shapiro (Ed.), *Encyclopedia of Artificial Intelligence* (2nd ed., Vol. 1–2, pp. 596–611). New York: John Wiley & Sons.
Meadows, A. J. (1974). *Communication in science*. London: Butterworths.
Moges, A. (2010). Thomas Kuhn: Assassin of logical positivism or its double agent? The Heretic in Philosophy of Science. Retrieved from http://www.galilean-library.org/site/index.php/page/index.html/_/essays/philosophyofscience/thomas-kuhn-assassin-of-logical-positivism-or-r96
Novick, P. (1988). *That noble dream: The "objectivity question" and the American historical profession*. Cambridge: Cambridge University Press.
Pedersen, S. A. (1995). Kuhns videnskabsfilosofi, dens udvikling og betydning. [Kuhn's philosophy of science: its development and impact]. In: *Videnskabens revolutioner*. Ny udgave (pp. 7–44). København: Forlaget Fremad.
Price, D. J. de S. (1965). Network of scientific papers. *Science*, 149(3683), 510–515.
Reisch, G. A. (1991). Did Kuhn kill logical empiricism? *Philosophy of Science*, 58(2), 264 – 277.
Reisch, G. A. (2005). *How the cold war transformed philosophy of science: To the icy scopes of logic*. New York: Cambridge University Press.
Rorty, R. (1979). *Philosophy and the mirror of nature*. Princeton, NJ: Princeton University Press.
Schneider, J. W. (2010). Critical issues in science mapping: Delimiting fields by journals and the influence of their publication activity. *Eleventh International Conference on Science and Technology Indicators* (pp. 255–257). Leiden, the Netherlands. http://cwts.nl/pdf/BookofAbstracts2010_version_15072010.pdf#page=255
Small, H. G. (1977). A co-citation model of a scientific specialty: A longitudinal study of collagen research. *Social Studies of Science*, 7(2), 139–166.
Smith, B. C. (1996). *On the origin of objects*. Cambridge, MA: The MIT Press.
Smith, L. D. (1986). *Behaviorism and logical positivism. A reassessment of the alliance*. Stanford University Press, Stanford, CA.
Søndergaard, T. F.; Andersen, J. & Hjørland, Birger (2003). Documents and the communication of scientific and scholarly information. Revising and updating the UNISIST model. *Journal of Documentation*. 59(3), 278–320.
Spear, J. H. (2007). Prominent schools or other active specialties? A fresh look at some trends in psychology. *Review of General Psychology*, 11(4), 363–380. Retrieved from http://www.jmu.edu/socanth/sociology/wm_library/Spear_gpr-11-4-363.pdf
Sullivan, D.; White, D. H. & Barboni, E. J. (1977). Co-citation analyses of science: An evaluation. *Social Studies of Science*, 7(2), 223–240.
Toomela, A. (2014). Mainstream psychology. In T. Teo (Ed.), *Encyclopedia of critical psychology* Vol. 1–4 (Vol. 3, pp. 1117–1125). New York: Springer.
Toulmin, S. (1953). *An introduction to the philosophy of science*. London: Hutchinson.
Tsou, J. Y. (2015). Reconsidering the Carnap-Kuhn connection. In W. J. Devlin & A. Bokulich (Eds.). Kuhn's structure of scientific revolutions – 50 years on (pp. 51–69). Cham: Springer.
Weiskopf, D. A. (2011). The theory-theory of concepts. *The Internet Encyclopedia of Philosophy*. Retrieved from http://www.iep.utm.edu/th-th-co/

White, H. D., & McCain, K. W. (1998). Visualizing a discipline: An author co-citation analysis of information science, 1972–1995. *Journal of the American Society for Information Science, 49*(4), 327–355.

Wray, K. B. (2011). *Kuhn's evolutionary social epistemology*. New York: Cambridge University Press.

Part II: **Citation theories**

Henry Small
Referencing as Cooperation or Competition

1 The Citation Process Revisited

Blaise Cronin's book *The Citation Process* (1984) gave the information science and bibliometrics communities their first major statement on citation theory. It framed the theoretical discussion around the two principal approaches to science studies at the time, the Mertonian normative view and the post-modernist social constructivist view. The book saw the conflict in sharp terms: between those who espouse a positivist, normative, and aggregationist view of citation, and those who see it as subtle, individualistic, and a product of research-in-practice, where norms carry little or no weight.

Rereading *The Citation Process* after a hiatus of 30 years recalled feelings of both excitement and depression. I was energized by these tentative theoretical steps, but disheartened by his suggestion that we should follow the lead of the social constructivist. As someone trained in science and the history of science, the constructivist view did not ring true. Perhaps I was stuck in my story-book version of science. In any event, the bibliometrics community ignored the new sociology and remained largely empirical and atheoretical.

In a later paper, Cronin (1998) revisited the problem of citation theory in a way more congenial to me, proposing a middle ground between the normative and constructivist approaches, and then later even seemed to return to a more normative position in the context of semiotic theory (2000).

This long interlude of three decades saw many shifts in the positions of major players in the contending camps, among these, the split between the bibliometricians and constructivists with the formation of ISSI in 1993 and the burgeoning of the 4S society. My purpose in revisiting this debate is to better understand the fundamental issues it raised regarding the nature of science, the shortcomings of both constructivist and normative theories, and to suggest some possible ways forward based on recent theories in evolutionary biology which give a rationale for cooperative behavior.

2 Social Construction and Its Problems

One of the fundamental tenants of social construction is that science does not have direct access to the "reality" of the external world. Rather, that access is so thoroughly mediated by devices, presuppositions, and social constraints that our knowledge is not about the external world at all. Furthermore, what knowledge we do have is relative to the framework and circumstance in which it is created, and no one framework is more valid or closer to reality than any other. In Latour and Woolgar's (1979) view, scientists in the lab are engaged in processes of inscriptions that lead to the creation of a "mythology." Inscription devices in the lab act as black boxes allowing social interactions to dictate their output: "There thus occurs a transformation of the simple end product of inscription into the terms of the mythology which informs participants' activities" (Latour & Woolgar, 1979, p. 63).

From the "strong program" of the Edinburgh school, we have the view that scientific knowledge is no different from any other belief system, including those of primitive cultures, and the notion that "belief systems cannot be objectively ranked in terms of their proximity to reality or their rationality" (Barnes, 1974, p. 154). Knorr-Cetina, in *The Manufacture of Knowledge* asks (1981, p. 2), asks: "Why should our interest-geared, instrumentally-generated world order mirror some inherent structure in nature?" She claims that the lab is an artificial and constructed environment, and this social environment and its instruments manufacture what we call science, which bears no necessary relationship to the world.

According to Latour and Woolgar, the ultimate aim of the lab is the production of papers. In writing papers the task is to persuade fellow scientists and the outside world that the mythology they have created in the lab is valid. It is impossible for facts and theories to be convincing on their own because, as myth, they can only be made convincing by rhetorical means.

Knorr-Cetina sees the scientific paper as yet a further construction with its own unique arguments and end products which bear little or no resemblance to what went on in the lab. In fact: "Compared with the work observed in the laboratory, the written paper is ... a first complete perversion" (Knorr-Cetina, 1981, p. 132). One reason for this is that the paper does not reveal the more or less irrational and haphazard path that went on in the lab. The paper constructs a different "logic" and sequence of events for the benefit of various audiences. Knorr-Cetina's view is echoed by the rhetorician Ken Hyland who states: "Texts ... can never be regarded as accurate representations of what the world is like ... Reality is constructed through processes that are essentially social and involve crafting texts in ways which will be persuasive to readers" (2009, p. 12).

The message is that we need to analyze the various rhetorical devices that scientists use to convince (i.e., mislead) readers into thinking that the writer is describing the physical world. As Swales puts it: "The art of the matter, as far as the creation of facts is concerned, lies in deceiving the reader into thinking that there is no rhetoric ... that the facts are indeed speaking for themselves" (1990, p. 112).

To show how "facts" are created in the lab, Latour introduces the idea that there is a gradation in the so-called "facticity" of knowledge-claims. This is embedded in statements scientists make about these claims and is marked by the use of "modalities" which, to varying degrees, cast doubt on or boost the credibility of given assertions. Modalities are expressed by words or phrases such as "premature," "suggested," "reported," "first described," "assumed," "confirmed," etc. The goal of the lab is to move statements from low to high facticity by rhetorical persuasion such that all modalities disappear from the language. "Facticity" does not mean that some fact about the real world has been established, only that actors view it as such.

Latour introduces a theory of citation in *Science in Action*. In the citation context, the text surrounding the reference, modality words and phrases are deployed either to strengthen those who support the author or weaken the opposition. References are massed as opposing armies on a battlefield. In citation warfare all distortions of the meaning of the prior text is fair game: "... do whatever you need to the former literature to render it as helpful as possible ..." (1987, p. 37) and "... all deformations are fair" (1987, p. 40). Referencing becomes part of the process of persuasion in which one mythical version of the world is promoted over another.

Constructivist theory is now under attack from within, in part, because it has been hijacked by reactionary groups that invent their own versions of science (Latour 2004; Collins, 2014). Nevertheless, it is useful to review some of the objections that have a bearing on a theory of citation.

One problem is that fraud or error in science would be indistinguishable from any other type of science. If facts are socially constructed, then error and fraud are as well. Failure to replicate or corroborate an author's result would carry no weight because these activities are not anchored in the real world. Replication or reproducibility is, however, the basis for the detection of fraud or error in science and is fundamental to the normative operation of science (Zuckerman, 1977; Hull, 1988, p. 435).

For constructivists there is no way of evaluating or comparing the relative merits of one group's scientific views over another group's because neither is based on reality. Each group can provide persuasive arguments for the validity of its beliefs. Kuhn (1962), however, rejected this extreme relativism and conjectured that there could be progress through scientific revolutions. Because of the increasing growth and specialization of science through a revolution "... both the list of problems solved by science and the precision of individual problem-solutions will grow and grow" (p. 169).

Constructivists rely on rhetorical persuasion (Gilbert, 1977) to convert nonbelievers to believers presumably because the evidence is not sufficiently compelling on its own. Rhetorical devices include hedging and purging personal motives (Swales, 1990, p. 112). However, if rhetorical persuasion is all that it takes to win converts, it is unlikely that Einstein's theory of relativity or Heisenberg's matrix mechanics would have gained many converts. Persuasion can also come about by presenting a coherent framework of theory and observations. In some cases, a new finding is compelling enough to bring about the emergence of a new research area (Small, Boyack, & Klavans, 2014). This is because rhetoric is weak compared to the perception of a new ordering of facts and theory (Cole, 1992, p. 47).

It could also be argued that the rigid form of the modern scientific paper (Swales, 1990, p. 134) militates against persuasive presentation. The conventional IMRD format (introduction, methods, results, discussion) forces papers to present their findings in a uniform manner which may facilitate their browsing, comparison, and registration in databases, but does not facilitate discursive argument (Zuckerman, 1977, p. 125). Unlike the earliest scientific reports published in journals such as the *Philosophical Transactions of the Royal Society*, the modern scientific paper is not designed to be a first-hand account of an author's observations in the lab and does not allow the "virtual witnessing" that Robert Boyle practiced (Shapin & Schaffer, 1985, p. 55).

Regarding Latour's views on referencing as a strengthening of allies and a weakening of enemies, there is little evidence that such a nuanced deploying of individual references has much effect on a paper's impact. Much more depends on the actual findings reported in the paper, on the data or theory it presents. Watson and Crick's 1953 paper on the structure of DNA had only six references, Darwin's *Origin of Species* relatively few, while Einstein's 1905 paper on special relativity contained no references at all. A careful deploying of modalized references is not enough to make a trivial paper convincing.

3 The Realist Alternative

The idealist position espoused by the constructivists can be contrasted with the realist position that we are observers of a world which we have access to through our senses (Leplin, 1984). We extend the power of our senses by inventing instruments and analytical methods that magnify or probe our environment. The instruments are not the black boxes of the constructivists because they obey the same physical laws as the thing being observed. To understand the world, we make systematic observations, and invent hypotheses and theories to explain our observations. When our observations and theories agree, we claim to have discovered something about the world, but discoveries are always tentative and subject to revision by more accurate observations or different theories that have better agreement with the observations. We can think of this tentativeness of knowledge as a norm which resulted from the numerous theories in history which turned out to be false.

Despite this rosy picture, the signals from nature are not always clear. They can be noisy, contaminated, ambiguous, and affected by our prejudices, preconceptions, biases, and expectations. When an experiment is successful, it is not always apparent that it is until it can be replicated or corroborated by other experiments or with theory. Scientists can disagree about the meaning and interpretation of these signals. The realist response is to call for more research, and scientists are always thinking about their next experiment.

Most scientists committed to a theory are aware of the possibility that new evidence might prove them wrong. But the amount of effort required to develop and test a theory requires a level of commitment that makes it difficult to keep an open mind to alternative theories (Mitroff, 1974). However, what scientists work toward is a plausible basis for further research, and this may involve abandoning one hypothesis in favor a more plausible one. Latour's levels of facticity are also relevant in a realist approach as a means of sorting the plausible from the implausible. Thus, an important question is what makes some theories more plausible than others?

The colloquialism "the facts speak for themselves" expresses the common sense notion that the plausibility of hypotheses depends on their degree of fit with the existing body of facts and theories, like the fitting together of pieces of a puzzle. For example, quantum mechanics fits with the ionization potentials of simple atoms. The double helix model of DNA fits with the concept of genetic replication. Human-caused global warming is consistent with an increase in the burning of fossil fuels and more carbon dioxide in the atmosphere.

Each of these examples of consistent theory and observation can be expanded into networks comprised of many elements that fit together in a larger puzzle. For example, the quantum mechanical theory of the atom is also consistent with the electromagnetic spectrum of the atom and the quantum nature of light. Anthropogenic global warming is consistent not only with rising carbon dioxide levels in the atmosphere, but also with the decrease in energy being re-radiated back into space, and the wavelength of the main component of re-radiated energy is consistent with the energy spectrum of carbon dioxide. A similar point was made by

Gingras and Schweber in their critique of a social constructivist account of quarks (1986, p. 379). In theory choice, scientists consider a network of multiple facts and predictions, not single facts in isolation.

The general approach to fitting facts and theories together is called consilience and derives from the work of the 19th century philosopher and historian William Whewell (1847) recently made popular by E. O. Wilson (1998). Whewell wrote: "The consilience of induction takes place when an induction, obtained from one class of facts, coincides with an induction obtained from another different class" (1847, p. 469). A related network approach called "explanatory coherence" has been proposed by Paul Thagard (1992; 2007). In this approach various types of coherence relations are treated as constraints and the network having the highest constraint satisfaction is considered the most likely to be true, or at least, the best one given the currently available facts and theories. Explanatory coherence provides an approximate guide to theory choice and a way of understanding the history of science.

In writing scientific papers, authors are also engaged in fitting together the pieces of a large puzzle that represents the problem space of their research area. Some of this fitting together (but not all) is evident in the references authors cite which associate facts, theories, or methods with prior papers. In fact, Thagard applies his explanatory coherence to the process by which scientists arrive at a consensus which, he notes, requires communication among researchers (2000, p. 223).

Referencing is a passive form of communication between the cited and citing authors so we can use this to illustrate consilience. Citation contexts, that is, the portions of text where the papers are referenced, can reveal how authors see the prior literature. For example, a citation might represent the linking of a cause and effect, where the effect is an observation and the cause is a deduction from theory (Hanson, 1972).

To illustrate how a scientific paper builds a network of coherent facts and theories through its references, we use a paper that was part of a co-citation cluster from 2007 on the water pollution by estrogens (Small & Klavans, 2011). Focusing on a single randomly selected citing paper (Thorpe, Benstead, Hutchinson, & Tyler, 2007) from this cluster, all the contexts were extracted in which references were made (see Table 1).

The 23 contexts are arranged sequentially by the section of the paper. Content words have been removed, leaving the non-technical or general words. This allows us to see more clearly the function of the reference in the authors' presentation. The cited references within each context are denoted by integers in square brackets. Some contexts reference multiple items, so-called redundant references, and some items are cited repeatedly throughout the paper, the op. cit. references.

Tab. 1: Reference structure of a scientific paper: citation contexts stripped of content words.

Introduction
1. It is now well-established that ... may impair ... with potential detrimental consequences [5, 7, 8, 9, 13, 14]
2. ... implicated as causative [3] ... were not previously subject to routine monitoring due to ...
3. In this regard ... has been widely employed ... that induce ... response [23]
4. ... that is produced ... in response to ... [29, 17, 27]
5. ... but exposure to ... has been shown to result in ... [23, 29]
6. There is some evidence that ... production ... as a consequence of ... [6, 11, 21, 31, 4, 22, 10] but the implications of ... are less clear.
7. Even less is known on the consequences of ... although an association between ... has been reported [11] ...
8. ... provide the majority ... [30] and therefore ... could potentially impact on ...
9. ... but is of considerable ... relevance and was therefore used in ... to expand on the earlier work of [11] who investigated for association between ...

Materials and Methods
10. ... basic design ... same ... replicate treatment in experiment ... [26 self]
11. ... samples were assayed ... using [28]

Results and discussion
12. ... is consistent with reports from earlier investigations using ... [24 self, 19] and indicates that ... significantly exceeds ...
13. This supports the results of an earlier investigation reporting ... [20]
14. ... it has been hypothesized that ... is thought to result in ... [6, 21]
15. Indeed, a number of investigators have reported ... effects ... which are hypothesised to result from ... [11, 1, 12, 22, 10]
16. The effect ... [25 self] shows ...
17. This compares with previous observations where ... were linked with ... effects ... but not in ... [11, 1, 12, 22,10]
18. It has previously been demonstrated that ... are associated with ... results in ... leading to ... [4].
19. The observed ... here is consistent with a previous investigation [2] ...
20. This may reflect alterations ... due to ... and supports the earlier work of [2] who showed ... through ... examination of ...

Conclusions
21. The collective results from these investigations support an earlier investigation [11] in demonstrating that ... signals ... adverse ... impact ...
22. The poor ability ... however could lead to ... that have adverse health effects during ... as can occur ... and should be considered further [16, 18]
23. This further supports the work of [11, 15] in demonstrating that ... could potentially be used to signal for adverse ... health effects.

For example, the first context in the Introduction refers to "well established" facts that potentially lead to detrimental consequences. In other words, the established facts form a coherent picture and together with theory predict certain undesirable effects. In the ninth context earlier work was expanded on because an association was found. Associations suggest possible causes. The contexts in the introductory section emphasize causation using words such as "causative", "induce", "in response to", "result in", etc. Words like "may", "could", and "potentially" act as hypothetical connections that require further investigation.

Contexts in the Results and Discussion section focus mainly on documenting the consistency of the paper's results with empirical findings and hypotheses of earlier papers. Words such as "consistent", "supports", and "compares" build a web of relationships between the authors' current results and the previous literature. These relationships differ from the cause-effect relationships of the Introduction in that they are mainly about similarities and parallels between results by different investigators.

Instead of focusing on all contexts from a single paper, we can also look across all contexts at a particular cited reference. In the selected paper, reference #11 had the highest op. cit. rate, suggesting that it was of particular importance to the authors. There were a total of 16 contexts for reference #11 across the 868 contexts from all papers in the sample. We then selected the most characteristic of these contexts by computing the cosine vector similarity of each of the 16 contexts against a composite of all 16. The context with the highest cosine vector (0.61) was the seventh context in Table 1, and is thus the most representative of the 16:

> Even less is known on the consequences of disruptions in VTG dynamics in females and although an association between VTG induction and reduced egg production has been reported [11], the effects on egg production were only observed at concentrations that were toxic to males.

(Thorpe et al., 2007, p. 177)

Thus, this most typical context reports an association, or consilience, between three observations: VTG induction, egg production, and toxicity to males. These examples show that references serve to link observations with theory and effects with varying degrees of certainty.

4 The Problem of Norms in Science

What is missing in the previous discussion of the coherence model of plausibility is what establishes the acceptable forms of coherence between the pieces of the puzzle. A few of these noted already are the degree of fit between theory and experiment, the accuracy of theoretical predictions, and the qualitative agreement of a model and the evidence. Thagard mentions explanation, deduction, and association (2000, p. 17). But where do these criteria come from?

One answer is that these are technical or epistemic norms analogous to the norms that govern the social conduct of scientists proposed by Robert Merton, such as, universalism, communality, disinterestedness, skepticism, and originality. Merton considered social norms necessary for the "extension of certified knowledge" (1973 p. 270). Among the technical methods that allowed the creation of certified knowledge were empirical confirmation and logical consistency. The social norms supported the goal of certified knowledge.

Merton, however, does not spell out the "technical methods" that should govern scientific practice, or where they came from. These are discussed in greater detail in a long article by Zuckerman (1977). She called them "cognitive norms and methodological canons" (1977, p. 87), and related them to the philosophical concept of demarcation, that is, the rules that define what it is to be scientific.

The problem with both technical and social norms is that they appear to come out of nowhere, although Merton's early writings (1938) suggest a possible link to the Puritan values held by many members of the Royal Society in the 17th century. Zuckerman hints at the possible dynamic nature of norms when she discusses how the norm of disinterestedness, which encourages unrestrained pure research, comes into conflict with the social hazards of certain scientific findings (1977, p. 122). This suggests that under some circumstances restraints on pure research may be necessary. Thus, a dynamic and evolutionary theory of social and cognitive norms seems to be called for.

Mulkay rejects the idea that norms affect or control behavior. He sees moral precepts as embodied in Mertonian norms as flexible vocabularies that are invoked rhetorically to rationalize scientists' interests (Mulkay, 1991, p. 69). Yet, just paying lip service to norms does not seem adequate to explain why so many scientists adhere to formal conventions and rules in their work, and how these conventions and rules arose and become sustained.

Technical norms could be collectively considered part of the "scientific method" (Gower, 1997) for a given historical period. Francis Bacon provided many examples of technical prescriptions for science including the method of induction, the gathering of systematic observations, and the conducting of experiments. Philosophers of science have proposed criteria on which to judge the adequacy of theories called criteria for theory choice. Kuhn provided a short list of what he considered key criteria or "values": the accuracy of theoretical predictions, the consistency of the theory with other accepted knowledge, the ability of the theory to expand its scope to predict other phenomena, the need for a theory to be simple or parsimonious, and fruitful in generating new problems and solutions (1977, p. 322). Rather than seeing these as givens, however, it should be possible to trace their origins in history.

Technical norms clearly change over time and are subject to selection and extinction: what is acceptable or required in today's science is not what was acceptable or required in earlier historical periods. But norms probably change in a reactive rather than a proactive manner. As Hull puts it, "The nature of science is constantly under negotiation, and the currency of these negotiations is success" (1988, p. 297). The availability of a successful or highly visible social or technical practice might first become fashionable then later on required. That "accounts" should "save appearances" is one of the oldest technical norms perhaps having its origin in ancient Egyptian and Mesopotamian creation myths (Frankfort & Frankfort, 1949, p. 11).

Examples of technical norms that have gone extinct are the requirement that theories be consistent with the writings of the ancients, or with the teaching of the Church. A norm that emerged in the scientific revolution was that predictive theories should be mathematical in form. This norm was spurred by the success of Newton in predicting the motions of celestial bodies (and perhaps earlier according to Crombie [1959]). Likewise, Lavoisier's theory of combustion resulted in adoption of quantitative criteria in the explanation of chemical change (Kuhn, 1977, p. 336).

A technical norm of more recent origin is the notion of symmetry which was introduced in particle physics and relativity theory. Medicine has introduced its own norms such as double-blind clinical trials and evidence based medicine. Besides being induced by scientific discoveries or successes, it is likely that norms migrate from one branch of science to another. An example is the diffusion of statistical methods to various disciplines. Practical innovations can also be exemplars for new epistemic norms. For example, as new and more accurate scientific instruments are introduced, the standards of measurement increase and higher precision becomes required.

A potential difficulty in theory selection arises when a new discovery stimulates the adoption of a new norm which is then used to rationalize the discovery (Kuhn, 1977). It is not clear how often this situation arises, but it may account for the delays in acceptance of some theories, such as relativity or string theory where radical new ways to understand the world are proposed which are not easily testable. However, if the theory has multiple confirmatory paths, some of which rely on traditional criteria, this circularity is less problematic.

Mulkay argues that scientists often justify their behavior using a wide range of rules—some of which are contradictory—and their behavior can contradict their own stated rules (1980; 1991). He also notes, referencing Kuhn (1977), that when technical norms are applied to theory selection, different scientists can arrive at different choices. It is not difficult to envision situations where norms come into conflict, for example, when an author attempts to publish a paper that violates technical norms. Merton (1963) recognized that conflicting norms create ambivalence towards them, for example when originality conflicts with humility. The complex and contradictory nature of norms does not, however, invalidate their importance.

The social norms discussed by Merton under broad categories probably also evolved from exemplars of good practice or as reactions to new social realities. For example, the norm of universalism may be related to the rise of distinctive styles of national science in Europe (Ben-David, 1984), and the need to assert that scientific findings are valid across national boundaries. The invention of the scientific journal in the 1600s may have crystallized the norm of communality as well as numerous publishing conventions as the medium evolved.

Norms also carry different weights and are associated with varying degrees of sanctions, and the importance of a norm and the sanction that accompanies its violation would likely change over time. For example, the norm of openness is probably more important today than it was the in 17th century when many scientists kept their discoveries secret for fear of not receiving proper credit.

The norm of honesty, which falls under Merton's category of disinterestedness, however, carries a more severe sanction. Fraud, if proved, can jeopardize the scientist's career. Without adherence to the norm of honesty the scientific community would probably cease to function. Scientists could no longer trust one another and would lose the support of the larger society (Zuckerman, 1977). The norm of honesty in reporting scientific results may derive, in part, from the impracticality of eye witnessing experiments (Shapin & Schaffer, 1985) and was a necessity if scientists were to work independently.

5 Norms and the Scientific Paper

Central to the integrity of science is the connection between what is done in the lab and the final written scientific paper. Knorr-Cetina has shown that the relationship between what happens in the lab and the final report for publication is complex (1981, p. 94). Results are selected, not reported as they actually happened, and the argument may be reframed for various audiences. However, through these transformations the author must take care not to misrepresent his or her results. In some labs this norm is enforced by requiring the maintenance of lab notebooks and diaries which can be reviewed in cases of suspected misconduct (Gaulton,

2004). What is missing from Knorr-Cetina's account is the powerful effect exerted on the authors by both social and technical norms. The social norm of honesty is the most important, but many other norms and conventions govern the form and content of the paper, its style, sections, and references. Failure to follow generally accepted technical norms and conventions may jeopardize publication.

We could speculate about what the scientific "paper" would look like if we stripped away the norms and editorial conventions. Loss of a standardized format or organization would make science appear more "literary" or perhaps autobiographical. The personalization of the paper would probably result in fewer collaborators and co-authors. The paper would likely not start with a review of the state of knowledge with references to prior literature. The most dramatic effect would be loss of trust. Authors would have no need to tell the truth, and would not be held accountable. Readers would no longer have confidence that the author actually observed what was observed or did what was said was done.

In 1988, Merton explicitly discussed referencing as a normative constraint in science as part of the "composite cognitive and moral framework" (p. 622) which had historically evolved. He pointed to its main function as a "moral obligation to acknowledge one's sources" and explained its origin as a response to the social problem of plagiary in the 17th century. In 1965, Kaplan noted that there were few if any normative guides for citation practices in the available style handbooks. Nowadays we find many such guides and prescriptive texts (e.g., see Kamat & Schatz, 2014).

So how do we know that a norm of citation is operating and has an effect on behavior? Referee reports and letters to the editor are filled with complaints that author X has failed to cite author Y (Retraction Watch, 2014; Hagstrom, 1974). One kind of evidence is psychological discomfort: an author's real or imagined embarrassment on failing to cite an obvious precursor (Wilson & O'Gorman, 2003). Perhaps worse than the guilt the author may feel is concern that the omission will be found out by colleagues. And there is always the nagging feeling that somewhere in the literature another author has made the same point and the feeling of relief when a literature search fails to find anything of relevance. Sanctions can be psychological as well as social.

As Merton suggests, the social norm of referencing perhaps began with scholars wanting to lay claim to their ideas and avoid priority disputes. At first, the only option was to keep their ideas secret, deposit sealed notes or anagrams, and refrain from publication as Newton and others did. With the advent of the scientific journal, scientists were able to disseminate and date their ideas. Thus, the journal acted as a registry of their contributions. The author could then point to this registry if a question of priority arose and this function gradually evolved into the formal bibliographic reference. Thus, we would expect that the early referencing would be skewed toward self-citations, and that self-citations would be more complete in terms of specifying the cited item than citations to others, and there is some evidence that this is the case (Small, 2010).

The reference format has evolved over time as shown by studies of journals such as the *Philosophical Transactions of the Royal Society of London* which began publication in 1665 (Allen, Qin & Lancaster, 1994). Early references were usually embedded in the text, and often consisted only of an author name (italicized or bolded), and, occasionally, a source. Later, references became more complete, giving pages, years, etc., and moved from embedded text to side notes, footnotes, and finally endnotes.

Normative expectations probably evolved along with these changes in printing and format. In addition to allowing the ownership of ideas and discouraging plagiarism, referencing became a tool to carve out a niche for your idea by demonstrating that it was different from those of other authors (Gilbert, 1977)—effectively an extension of knowledge claiming.

Another evolutionary thread developed around summarizing the current state of knowledge on a topic, what we would call a review of the literature. The tradition of reviewing prior opinions on a topic goes back to the writings of Aristotle (Small, 2010), and many examples of such proto-reviews can be found in the *Philosophical Transactions*. The review, while not a novel knowledge claim, can be a new synthesis and useful to others.

In referencing others either for differentiation or for review, we can speculate that the norm of generosity of referencing came into being. What was originally a defensive practice could also be used in a generous way to credit other authors for their ideas. From this point the practice evolved from being customary, to one that is expected and eventually required. Readers would then expect certain authors to be credited if a topic was reviewed or a related knowledge claim was made. Authors who failed to reference would be suspected of intellectual theft or, at best, ignorance, and referencing others became a norm of scholarly practice.

In contrast to this normative account, in the constructivist approach, references are only made for persuasive reasons motivated by self-interest. In this world authors would be less likely to cite prior work closely related to their own claim since it might jeopardize their own priority. Authors would be more likely to distort or misrepresent prior work to support their own point of view (Nicolaisen, 2007). Authors would be less likely to cite items that serve only to provide the reader with background information, and they would be more likely to self-cite. In addition, as White has argued (2004), constructivist authors would tend to cite leading figures in order to convince readers, but this was not empirically supported.

In constructivist citation contexts we would expect to frequently encounter modality terms that weaken or cast doubt on the cited work. However, studies of citation contexts have found the rate of negative citations to be relatively low, about 6 % over seven separate studies (Small, 1982). In addition, in a random sample of 265 citation contexts containing the word "not", it was found that in about 85 % of cases the citing authors were supporting a negative finding of an earlier author, and were not themselves directly negating a cited work, in effect a negation by indirection.

As we have seen, Latour's theory calls for a no-holds-barred approach to referencing. However, in a norm-governed publication world, misquoting or distorting a prior author's work would not be regarded with equanimity. These instances could be classified as "constructivist" (Small, 2004) and are relatively rare. Most references are normative in the sense of adhering to some literal message in the cited text. This is supported by the word similarity of citing and cited texts (Peters, Braam & van Raan, 1995).

This does not mean that a range of interpretations of the cited work is not possible. In fact, capsulizing, summarizing, and pigeonholing a prior text is part of the compacting of knowledge, the process of creating symbols for ideas (Small, 1978), and a step toward Merton's obliteration by incorporation (1968, p. 35). There is, in addition, a gray area between distortion and legitimate interpretation. This provides some room for reconciliation between normative and constructivist positions (Luukkonen, 1997) because differences of interpretation and debate are expected in cases where the signals from nature are ambiguous, or there is ambiguity in the cited text. Cozzens shows that interpretations of specific papers can differ within a field of science (1982). Cole (1992) also sees the lack of consensus at the research front as an area of potential agreement between realists and constructivists. Riviera (2013) uses normative theory to describe the phenomenon of high citation rate and constructivist theory to explain low rates. However, interpretations can also converge—as seen in the emergence of regularized language in citation contexts of highly cited papers indicating the formation of a consensus (Small, 1978). In such cases, the significance of the paper for a majority of citing authors is shared.

In the previous discussion we have shifted the focus from the citing side to the cited side and the formation of consensus. Here a reconciliation of normative and constructivist theories is less likely. For example, Mulkay (1980) argues that scientists do not apply technical norms in a consistent way, and the meaning of rules varies depending on the situation and who is applying them. In this view it is difficult to see how a consensus could emerge, and yet, citation studies have shown that consensus formation can be rapid and dramatic (Cole, 1982, p. 48).

A citing theory deals with individual decisions on what to cite and cited theory with aggregate citation phenomena and the perspective of a community. Since the sum of all the citing acts results in what we see on the cited side, it might appear that a theory of citing is all we need. The resulting distributions of citations are typical of cumulative advantage processes, or, to use current nomenclature, preferential attachment networks, where the number of future cites depends on the number already accumulated (Newman, 2010). To get such distributions there must be some kind of coordination of action among citing authors, an awareness of the references of other authors or a shared reaction to the cited work. Seeing that an author has referenced a particular paper may motivate other authors to read and cite the paper, but there also needs to be recognition of the paper's value or relevance (White, 2011). Of course, many social and intellectual factors could contribute to citation inequality. Following Thagard's (2007) theory, value may derive from better alignment of theory and observation or, following sociological theory, a higher degree of utility (Cole, 1982, p. 47; Hull, 1988, p. 301).

6 Generosity in Referencing

We tend to think of science as a competitive activity with scientists striving for priority, recognition, and funding (Hagstrom, 1974). But scientists also act generously and cooperatively by sharing work and collaborating. The Mertonian norms, of course, embody generosity in the norm of "communalism." In constructivism, by contrast, scientists are driven by self-interest. Mertonian referencing is generous in giving credit to others, but could such behavior also be motivated by self-interest? In biology, Richard Dawkins (2006) is known for his rejection of altruistic behavior, favoring selfish behavior at the level of the gene. However, others have argued that altruistic behavior—benefiting others at a personal cost—is reasonable both biologically and psychologically (Sober & Wilson, 1998). Evolutionary biologists and philosophers have long struggled with how cooperative behavior could have existed at all in the face of fierce evolutionary competition. Yet both cooperation and competition seem ubiquitous in human and animal societies. E. O. Wilson recently described the inherent conflict between wanting to behave competitively and cooperatively which has been hardwired in our genes by evolutionary forces (2014, p. 24).

The decision to cite or not to cite a finding similar to our own is a difficult one for authors who want to claim as much credit as possible. In some instances authors may not go out of their way to find others who have expressed similar ideas. When we reference others, we are giving up credit to others that could have, hypothetically at least, come to us (Small, 2004; Hull, 1988, p. 319). This is especially true when the cited work is intellectually close to our own. At first glance, this seems to be an act of generosity, a sacrificing of a portion of our originality to others. On the other hand, we are motivated to cite others whose work is similar to ours in order to demonstrate that our contribution is distinctive, and to avoid negative sanctions for failing to cite related work. Thus, whether referencing is a selfish or generous act is ambiguous. Sober and Wilson point out the hypothesis of generosity is difficult to prove because, regardless of the apparent selfless act, we can always think of some way the actor could have benefited.

Nicolaisen (2007) makes a related point inspired by a theory from evolutionary biology called the "handicap principle" or "costly signaling" (Zahavi, 1975). In nature, animals engage in behaviors such as ostentatious displays, bluffs, and mock threats which serve to enhance the fitness of the performer and protect the herd from predators. Hence, costly signaling is behavior that risks our own well-being for the apparent benefit of others and might be interpreted as generous or altruistic. Nicolaisen sees referencing as costly signaling because the author is taking a risk and going out on a limb which could easily be cut off if a diligent reader discovers that the reference is irrelevant or fallacious. Here he sees a connection to Latour's theory of citation which is based on self-interested manipulation of the prior literature. Hence, referencing is a handicap and a gamble in the interest of gaining advantage. Thus, although referencing may appear to benefit others, it is actually done out of self-interest, to advance our own interests. The handicap principle does not accord well with normative theory because the behavior is based on trickery and deception.

The handicap principle is one of a number of theories now current in evolutionary biology which may serve to stimulate further theorizing on citations and other issues in science studies. Two of the most relevant theories are "reciprocal altruism" and "strong reciprocity". "Reciprocal altruism" is the tendency to help those who are likely to return a favor (Arrow, 2007). But this form of altruism still has a selfish motivation. Reciprocal altruism would work for referencing only if the cited author is likely or capable of returning the citation. If the cited author is incapable of reciprocating, as is often the case, this mechanism fails.

In another approach called "strong reciprocity" (Fehr, Fischbacker, & Gachter, 2002) cooperators are rewarded and non-cooperators are punished but at a cost to those who punish (the strong reciprocators). Under certain conditions this model has been shown to lead to sustained cooperation in social groups. Unlike reciprocal altruism or costly signaling, strong reciprocity is consistent with the existence of norms which define what it means to cooperate, but it requires that someone is willing to sanction the norm violators.

One version of this model begins with a population of three types of agents: cooperators who obey the norms but do not punish, selfish agents who violate the norms, and strong reciprocators who obey the norms and punish violators (Bowles & Gintis, 2003). In referencing, we can imagine that the selfish agents do not cite others, the cooperators cite others, and the strong reciprocators cite others and "punish" the non-referencing violators. Of course interactions of these agents would run over years, not generations, as in evolutionary models.

Cozzens (1989) has studied the degree to which scientists involved in a priority dispute over the discovery of the opiate receptor behaved generously in their referencing. She looked at each of the main co-discoverers and how they credited the other co-discoverers. Over time there was a tendency for some co-discoverers to be more generous in their referencing, and less inclined to claim the credit exclusively for themselves. Also, the trend over time is toward a more standardized and less specific or qualified citation of the competitor's work as evidenced in citation contexts. The initial divergence of views at the time of discovery is followed by a convergence over the next few years as distinctions and qualifications are dropped, suggesting greater generosity over time. In addition, one co-discoverer played the role of enforcer by complaining to the others about the excessive priority claiming of one of the co-discoverers.

Another well known "multiple" is the discovery of oxygen involving Lavoisier, Priestley, and Scheele. Lavoisier had received information from the others that he was able to put to good use in making his discovery. However, initially he claimed credit for himself and failed to acknowledge the contributions of the others. Priestley, however, played the role of strong reciprocator and wrote a letter to Lavoisier complaining about his failure to credit others. Subsequently Lavoisier did acknowledge his fellow co-discoverers but not without pointing out how their discoveries differed from his (Small, 2010).

Einstein's special relativity paper, although not a multiple discovery, is also an example of delayed generosity. His celebrated 1905 paper contains no references to other papers. Notable for its absence was the work of Michelson and Morley on the constancy of the speed of light relative to the ether. However, two years later Einstein wrote a longer article on relativity which contained a number of references among them the Michelson-Morley paper (Small, 2010). Many years later, Einstein claimed that he had been unaware of the earlier work and would have cited it had he known about it (Holton, 1973, p. 282). It is not known if pressure was brought to bear on Einstein to acknowledge others.

A possible hypothesis is that over time there is an increase in generosity of referencing which is marked by a spreading of credit to multiple individuals, a lessening of the tendency toward the differentiation of the contributions, and an increasing standardization of language in the citation contexts. This can occur in the evolution of a single author's work, in the work of independent co-discoverers, or within an invisible college. There is some evidence of strong reciprocators acting to enforce normative compliance.

Other evolutionary models of cooperation use "multilevel" strategies, advocated by Sober and Wilson (1998), where selection occurs at the level of both the individual and the group. When the focus changes from individual to the group level success, it turns out that groups with many altruists are favored over groups with more selfish individuals (Arrow, 2007). Taking this perspective requires that we can think of science in functional terms at the group level. Because scientists comprise a relatively distinct social group, it is possible that behaviors could have evolved that enhanced group success. Historically we know that scientists often had to defend their views from attack by various outside authorities, whether political, economic, religious, or scientific. At the same time, scientists depended on these authorities for their support. Under these external threats it is not unexpected to find that cooperative behaviors and norms evolved that increased the fitness and success of the community. Such cooperative mechanisms could have included norms of behavior, the punishing of deviant behavior, and the mechanisms for recognition. These mutual support mechanisms would be magnified by the sub-structure of invisible colleges where individuals come face to face. Evolution at the sub-group level might also give rise to other specialized technical norms.

The next step might be to apply game theory to the process of writing papers and making references. For example, Chatterjee and Chowdhury (2012) have applied game theory to citation networks. Another possibility is to model the writing process as a game between an author and an imagined reader or critic. Each move in the writing process could be scored as cooperative or competitive in a balancing act to maximize the paper's strengths and minimize its weaknesses. For example, not citing a precursor or citing an irrelevant paper would be scored as selfish, while citing a review or rival would be seen as generous and enhance the score. Obviously the paper's fitness is not just a matter of what references are cited, but what connections are made to experiment and theory, that is, the paper's explanatory coherence, which is as we have seen partially revealed in its citation contexts.

7 Conclusions

Social construction leads to an anti-realist position on scientific knowledge and a community of scientists bent on self-interests. In this view, facts and theories have no basis in reality, and the only means of convincing others of the "truth" of a knowledge claim is rhetorical persuasion—even if that involves deception or fabrication. In constructivism it would be impossible to detect fraud or error in science or make a rational choice between theories. Deception, fabrication, and distortion would become institutionalized norms of behavior.

The realist view, on the other hand, affirms that "eternal and immutable regularities" exist in nature (Hull, 1988, p. 476). Because science relies on the arbiter of our senses, it does not require rhetorical persuasion or deception. The principle of consilience, favoring theories that have multiple empirical confirmations, offers an approximate guide to theory selection and how science evolves. Citation contexts in papers are shown to be a rich source of connections between theory and observations, and can be used for the construction of consilience networks.

Both technical and social norms are pervasive in science and are critical in regulating behavior. But their origin and evolution are little understood. Technical norms govern what counts as a consilience and the general procedures we call the "scientific method". Changes in technical norms are perhaps spurred on by major scientific successes or technical innovations that employ novel methods. If a new method becomes popular and incorporated into general practice, it will eventually be seen as a rule. Social norms may have evolved from general cultural values, but also from new social realities such as the rise of national styles of science and the need to insure the integrity of independent researchers.

The invention of the scientific journal gave rise to numerous norms and conventions, perhaps the most important of which was the communalism of scientific knowledge. Numerous other norms pertain to the acceptable style and structure of scientific papers. The norm of referencing may have originated as a means to claim priority, to show how your work differs from others, and to review what is known on a topic. Once specific concepts became associated with prior works, normative expectations were raised that these works would be cited when these concepts were used.

Competition and cooperation are pervasive in science as they are in all human endeavor, but cooperation is difficult to account for in an evolutionary view stressing individual survival. Strong reciprocity, where cooperators are rewarded and non-cooperators punished, is one viable mechanism for the emergence of cooperation. Here norms play a critical role in defining what it means to cooperate. An alternative explanation is multi-level selection, where individual selfishness is counteracted by society level norms. Here norms act as group level adaptations to maximize the fitness and success of the group. It seems obvious that science is a mix of selfish and altruistic individuals, but, perhaps, each individual is also a mix of these tendencies.

Referencing appears to fit the model of strong reciprocity where generous citation is rewarded and non-citers are sanctioned. Historical examples of co-discoveries offer a preliminary confirmation. Referencing may trend toward a sharing of credit and symbolic consensus in cases of multiple discovery or priority disputes.

The tools of game theory and computer simulation now being used by evolutionary biologists and economists to study cooperation and competition may offer a promising new avenue for research into citation practice and social norms in science. While referencing decisions are undoubtedly situationally complex, we can expect that both competitive and cooperative motives are at work.

Acknowledgment

Citation context data for the publication year 2007 was generously provided by Elsevier under an agreement with SciTech Strategies, Inc. I would like to thank Mike Patek for programming support, and David Pendlebury and an anonymous reviewer for helpful suggestions.

Cited References

Allen, B., Qin, J., & Lancaster, F. W. (1994). Persuasive communities: a longitudinal analysis of references in the Philosophical Transactions of the Royal Society, 1665–1990. *Social Studies of Science, 24,* 279–310.

Arrow, H. (2007). The sharp end of altruism. *Science, 318* (Oct. 26), 581–582.

Barnes, B. (1974). *Scientific knowledge and sociological theory.* London: Routledge & Kegan Paul.

Ben-David, J. (1984). *The scientist's role in society: a comparative study.* Chicago: University of Chicago Press.

Bowles, S. & Gintis, H. (2003). Evolution of strong reciprocity: cooperation in heterogeneous populations. *Theoretical Population Biology, 65*(1), 17–28.

Chatterjee, K. & Chowdhury, A. (2012). Formation of citation networks by rational players and the diffusion of ideas. *Review of Network Economics, 11*(3), article number 6.

Cole, S. (1992). *Making science: between nature and society.* Cambridge, Mass.: Harvard University Press.

Collins, H. (2014). *Are we all scientific experts now?* Cambridge, England: Polity Press.

Cozzens, S. E. (1982). Split citation identity: a case study from economics. *Journal of the American Society for Information Science, 33*(4), 233–236.

Cozzens, S. E. (1989). *Social control and multiple discovery in science: the opiate receptor case.* Albany, New York: State University of New York Press.

Crombie, A. C. (1959). The significance of medieval discussions of scientific method for the scientific revolution. In M. Clagett (Ed.), *Critical problems in the history of science.* (pp. 79–101). Madison, Wisconsin: University of Wisconsin Press.

Cronin, B. (1984). *The citation process: the role and significance of citation in scientific communication*. London: Taylor Graham.

Cronin, B. (1998). Metatheorizing citation. *Scientometrics. 43*(1), 45–55.

Cronin, B. (2000). Semiotics and evaluative bibliometrics. *Journal of Documentation, 56*(4), 440–453.

Dawkins, R. (2006). *The selfish gene. 30th anniversary edition.* . Oxford: Oxford University Press.

Einstein, A. (1905). Zur Elektrodynamik bewegter Körper. Annalen der Physik, 17, 891–921. Reprinted in *The Collected Papers of Albert Einstein*, volume 2. Translated by Anna Beck, consultant Peter Havas, pp. 140–171. Princeton: Princeton University Press.

Fehr, E., Fischbacker, U., & Gachter, S. (2002). Strong reciprocity, human cooperation, and the enforcement of social norms. *Human Nature and Interdisciplinary Biosocial Perspectives, 13*(1), 1–25.

Frankfort, H. & Frankfort, H. A. (1949). Myth and reality. In H. Frankfort, H. A. Frankfort, J. A. Wilson, & T. Jacobsen (Eds.), *Before philosophy: the intellectual adventure of ancient man.* (pp. 11–36). Baltimore, Maryland: Penguin Books.

Gaulton, G. N. (2004). *Ethical conduct in biomedical research: a handbook for biomedical graduate studies students and research fellows*, 3rd edition. Biomedical graduate studies program, the University of Pennsylvania. Retrieved July 9, 2014, from https://www.med.upenn.edu/bgs/docs/BIOETHICSHANDBOOK4-04.pdf

Gilbert, G. N. (1977). Referencing as persuasion. *Social Studies of Science, 7*(1), 113–122.

Gingras, Y. & Schweber, S. S. (1986). Constraints on construction. Social Studies of Science, 16(2), 372–383.

Gower, B. (1997). *Scientific method: an historical and philosophical introduction*. London: Routledge.

Hagstrom, W. O. (1974). Competition in science. *American Sociological Review, 39*(1), 1–18.

Hanson, N. R. (1972). *Patterns of discovery: an inquiry into the conceptual foundations of science*. Cambridge: Cambridge University Press.

Holton, G. (1973). *Thematic origins of scientific thought: Kepler to Einstein*. Cambridge, Mass.: Harvard University Press.

Hull, D. (1988). *Science as a process*. Chicago: University of Chicago Press.

Hyland, K. (2009). *Academic discourse: English in a global context*. London: Continuum.

Kamat, P. & Schatz, G. C. (2014). Cite with sight. *Journal of Physical Chemistry Letters, 5*(7), 1241–1242.

Kaplan, N. (1965). The norms of citation behavior: prolegomena to the footnote. *American Documentation, 10*(3), 179–184.

Knorr-Cetina, K. D. (1981). *The manufacture of knowledge: an essay on the constructivist and contextual nature of science*. Oxford, England: Pergamon Press.

Kuhn, T. S. (1962). *The structure of scientific revolutions*. Chicago: University of Chicago Press.

Kuhn, T. S. (1977). Objectivity, value judgment and theory choice. In *The Essential Tension*. Chicago: University of Chicago Press.

Latour, B. & Woolgar, S. (1979). *Laboratory life: the social construction of scientific facts*. Beverly Hills: Sage Publications.

Latour, B. (1987). *Science in action: how to follow scientists and engineers through society*. Cambridge, Mass.: Harvard University Press.

Latour, B. (2004). Why has critique run out of steam? From matters of fact to matters of concern. *Critical Inquiry, 39*, 225–248.

Leplin, J. (1984). Introduction. In J. Leplin (Ed.), *Scientific realism.* (pp. 1–7). Berkeley, California: University of California Press.

Luukkonen, T. (1997). Why has Latour's theory of citations been ignored by the bibliometric community? discussion of sociological interpretations of citation analysis. *Scientometrics, 38*(1), 27–37.

Merton, R. K. (1938). *Science, technology and society in seventeenth century England.* Bruges, Belgium: Saint Catherine Press.

Merton, R. K. (1942). Science and technology in a democratic order. *Journal of Legal and Political Sociology, 1,* 115–126. Reprinted in: *The sociology of science: theoretical and empirical investigations.* Chicago: University of Chicago Press, 1973, 267–278.

Merton, R. K. (1963). Resistance to the systematic study of multiple discoveries in science. *European Journal of Sociology, 4,* 250–282.

Merton, R. K. (1968). *Social theory and social structure.* New York: Free Press.

Merton, R. K. (1988). The Matthew effect in science. 2. cumulative advantage and the symbolism of intellectual property. *ISIS, 79,* 606–623.

Mitroff, I. I. (1974). *The subjective side of science.* Amsterdam: Elsevier.

Mulkay, M. (1980). Interpretation and the use of rules: the case of the norms of science. In T. Gieryn (Ed.), Science and social structure: a festschrift for Robert K. Merton. *Transactions of the New York Academy of Sciences.* Series 2, 39, 111–125.

Mulkay, M. (1991). *Sociology of science: a sociological pilgrimage.* Bloomington, Indiana: Indiana University Press.

Newman, M. E. J. (2010). *Networks: an introduction.* Oxford, England: Oxford University Press.

Nicolaisen, J. (2007). Citation analysis. *Annual Review of Information Science and Technology, 41,* 609–641.

Peters, H. P. F., Braam, R. R. & van Raan, A. F. J. (1995). Cognitive resemblance and citation relations in chemical engineering publications. *Journal of the American Society for Information Science, 46*(1), 9–21.

Retraction Watch: Lack of citation prompts correction in Nature journal. April 10, 2014. Retrieved July 9, 2014, from http://retractionwatch.com/2014/04/10/lack-of-citation-prompts-correction-in-nature-journal/#more-19753

Riviera, E. (2013). Scientific communities as autopoietic systems: the reproductive function of citations. *Journal of the American Society for Information Science and Technology, 64*(7), 1442–1453.

Shapin, S. & Schaffer, S. (1985). *Leviathan and the air-pump: Hobbes, Boyle and the experimental life.* Princeton, New Jersey: Princeton University Press.

Small, H. (1978). Cited documents as concept symbols. *Social Studies of Science, 8,* 327–340.

Small, H. (1982). Citation context analysis. In B. Dervin & M. J. Voigt, (Eds.), *Progress in Communication Sciences,* 3 (pp. 287–310). Norwood, N. J.: Ablex Publishing Corp.

Small, H. (2004). On the shoulders of Robert Merton: towards a normative theory of citation. *Scientometrics, 60*(1), 71–79.

Small, H. (2010). Referencing through history: how the analysis of landmark scholarly texts can inform citation theory. *Research Evaluation, 19*(3), 185–193.

Small, H. & Klavans, R. (2011). Identifying scientific breakthroughs by combining co-citation analysis and citation context. *Proceedings of the 13th International Conference of the International Society for Scientometrics and Informetrics,* Durban, South Africa.

Small, H., Boyack, K. W. & Klavans, R. (2014). Identifying emerging topics in science and technology. *Research Policy, 43,* 1450–1467.

Sober, E. & Wilson, D. S. (1998). *Unto others: the evolution and psychology of unselfish behavior*. Cambridge, Mass.: Harvard University Press.

Swales, J. M. (1990). *Genre analysis: English in academic and research settings*. Cambridge, England: Cambridge University Press.

Thagard, P. (1992). *Conceptual revolutions*. Princeton, New Jersey: Princeton University Press.

Thagard, P. (2000). *Coherence in thought and action*. Cambridge, Mass.: MIT Press.

Thagard, P. (2007). Coherence, truth and the development of scientific knowledge. *Philosophy of Science*, *74*, 26–47.

Thorpe, K.L, Benstead, R., Hutchinson, T. H., & Tyler, C. R. (2007). Associations between altered vitellogenin concentrations and adverse health effects in fathead minnow (Pimephales promelas). *Aquatic Toxicology*, *85*, 176–183.

Watson, J. D. & Crick, F. H. C. (1953). A structure for deoxyribose nucleic acid. *Nature*, *171*, 737–738.

Whewell, W. (1847). *Philosophy of the inductive sciences, founded upon their history*. Vol. I. London: John W. Parker.

White, H. (2004). Reward, persuasion and the Sokal hoax. *Scientometrics*, *60*(1), 93–120.

White, H. (2011). Relevance theory and citations. *Journal of Pragmatics*, *43*, 3345–3361.

Wilson, D. S. & O'Gorman, R. (2003). Emotions and actions associated with norm-breaking events. *Human Nature: An Interdisciplinary Biosocial Perspective*, *14*(3), 277–304.

Wilson, E. O. (1998). *Consilience: the unity of knowledge*. New York: Alfred A. Knopf.

Wilson, E. O. (2014). *The meaning of human existence*. New York: Liveright Publishing Corp.

Zahavi, A. (1975). Mate selection: selection for a handicap. *Journal of Theoretical Biology*, *53*(1), 205–214.

Zuckerman, H. (1977). Deviant behavior and social control in science. In E. Sagarin (Ed.), *Deviance and social change*. (pp. 87–138). Beverley Hills, California: Sage Publications.

Paul Wouters
Semiotics and Citations

In his essay "Semiotics and Evaluative Bibliometrics", Blaise Cronin discusses the implications of a tight link between research funding and citation analysis. He calls attention to a marketplace for a new species of sign—the citation (Cronin, 2000)—and suggests that semiotics offers the bibliometric community a suite of supra-disciplinary tools to "develop greater sensitivity to the variable symbolic significance of the signs they routinely manipulate and treat as quasi-objective indicators of quality, impact and esteem" (p. 450). This chapter aims to honor and further develop this perspective. I explore to what extent a semiotic approach may enable us to better understand the "constitutive effects" of performance indicators (Dahler-Larsen, 2013) and how this perspective can further contribute to a more inclusive attitude to the problem of citation theory (Nicolaisen, 2007).

Before recapitulating the key elements of Cronin's (2000) argument, we need to clarify what we mean by semiotics. It is usually presented as the science of signs (Eco, 1976), but can perhaps better be summarized as the systematic scholarly analysis of sign systems. Eco's (1976) definition of a sign is straightforward: "Everything that, on the grounds of a previously established social convention, can be taken as something standing for something else" (cf. Walker, 2014, p. 317). Semiotics has developed two different mainstream approaches, one developed by the father of structuralist linguistics, Ferdinand de Saussure (Day, 2005) (who used the term 'semiology'), and the other by the inventor of pragmatist philosophy, Charles Sanders Peirce (James, 1898). Saussure's thinking is firmly within the domain of the symbolic and focuses on structural motifs and differential inter-textual positions. Its analysis is confined to relations among signifiers and signifieds, and since signifieds are conceptual in nature, they too are part of the linguistic system. They are meanings, not actual objects of reference (Keane, 2003, p. 412). Peirce is interested in the link between signs and real world objects, based on his pragmatist philosophy. Consequently, both define the concept of "sign" rather differently. For de Saussure, the radical separation of the word and the world is fundamental (Irvine, 1989). Peirce, on the contrary, places as central the linkages between sign vehicles and real world objects. Given Cronin's interest in contributing to citation theory and making the link between citations and research behavior, it is not surprising that he adopted Peirce's approach.

For Cronin (2000), the usefulness of semiotics is evident: "What, after all, are references and citations if not signaling devices?" (Cronin, 2000, p. 440). However, this obvious fact is "all too easily overlooked", by which Cronin meant that he had overlooked it himself in his previous work on the citation process (Cronin,

1984). Many authors, inside of bibliometrics as well as outside of the field, still use the terms "reference" and "citation" interchangeably and see the difference between the two signs as trivial. With his essay, Cronin clarified this nontrivial distinction and drew the attention of the bibliometric community to the potential of semiotics to explain the differential roles of the reference, acknowledgement, in-text citation, and citation as measurement instruments, freed from the original citing context. In summary, the essay sought to demonstrate "how semiotics can contribute to the ongoing debate on the role and significance of citations in the primary communication system" (Cronin, 2000, p. 440).

Cronin was not the first to call attention to these important differences in bibliometric signs. Derek de Solla Price (1970) first made the distinction between the words *reference* and *citation*. Narin (1976, p. 3) an others (e.g., Nicolaisen & Frandsen, 2008; Egghe & Rousseau, 1990) followed suit. Egghe and Rousseau (1990) summarized the distinction as follows:

> If one wishes to be precise, one should distinguish between the notions 'reference' and 'citation'. If paper R contains a bibliographic note using and describing paper C, then R contains a reference to C and C has a citation from R (Price, 1970). Stated otherwise, a reference is the acknowledgement that one document gives to another, while a citation is the acknowledgement that one document receives from another. So, 'reference' is a backward-looking concept while 'citation' is a forward-looking one. Although most authors are not so precise in their usage of both terms, we agree with Price (1970) that using the words 'citation' and 'reference' interchangeably is a deplorable waste of a good technical term.
> (Egghe & Rousseau, 1990, p. 204)

It would be silly to claim that bibliometricians would not be aware of the differences in characteristics of the distribution of references versus citations. After all, the study of characteristics of these distributions belongs to the core of the field. Nevertheless, most scientometricians have tended to use the term 'citation' and 'reference' interchangeably. Not only is this in accordance with the meaning of the English word 'citation', it also facilitates the explanation of the number of citations as a measure of scholarly quality or impact. After all, it seems obvious that a work to which many researchers have referred is of more importance than a work that is hardly cited.

Wouters (1998) was the first to make the difference between the two signs the central point of departure for the development of citation theory. Building on this, Wouters (1999) concluded that a theory of referencing behavior should be seen as fundamentally distinct from a theory of evaluative bibliometrics. This was based on the statement that there is a fundamental distinction between *reference* and *citation*. By analyzing references and citations as different signs, they were essentially positioned as different objects. Their relation is one of descent: the *citation* emerges in an act of "semiosis" (the creation of a novel sign) from the *reference*. This has an important implication: it is no longer the scientist who creates the citation. Its source lies in the citation index and the producer of that index is the creator of the sign *citation*.

Of course, this does not mean that the citation is created out of nothing, although it must be said that Wouters (1999) did not pay enough attention to this implication of his proposal. The raw materials of the citation signs are still the references and the link patterns among the references form constraints on the possible citation patterns. These constraints are relatively flexible. Herein is the expertise of the evaluative bibliometrician. Evaluative bibliometrics consists of the fine-tuned creation of different citation indicators from the pool of links between references and documents as well as from the links among references. Field-normalized citation indicators are an example of such fine-tuning. Some indicators are even combinations of citations and references, for example source-normalized indicators (Waltman & Eck, 2012) or other improved journal indicators (Nicolaisen & Frandsen, 2008). The need for technical expertise in evaluative bibliometrics to create and measure these indicators, whether this expertise is built into bibliometric algorithms or delivered by scientometricians, is itself an indication that the relationship between *reference* and *citation* is anything but self-evident or given.

Cronin (2000) developed this semiotic approach in much more detail than Wouters (1999), extending his earlier analysis of the citation process (Cronin, 1984). Moreover, Cronin (2000, p. 441) already expected forms of altmetrics:

> The web is giving rise to new modes of communication, representation, recommendation and invocation. The ways in which, and reasons why, individual researchers and scholars are mentioned, or linked to on the web, are multifaceted. It is conceivable that novel forms of signalling will evolve, which could also be used as indicators of cognitive or social influence within specific disciplines or communities of professional practice.

His essay emphasizes the polysemy of signs: "Multiple interpretations of references and their extra-textual import are possible" (Cronin, 2000, p. 440). He looked into the different relationships between the sign vehicles and their context and included acknowledgements into the analysis (which Wouters [1999] had ignored): "References and acknowledgements, along with citations, are first cousins in an extended family of scholarly signs" (Cronin, 2000, p. 441) (for more on the interrelationship of these signs, see Desrochers, Paul-Hus, and Larivière, this volume). The essay shows how technical semiotic analysis can clarify the difference between different scholarly signs. For example, the reference embedded in the text is a different sign from the full bibliographic reference at the end of the scholarly article.

1 Sign Triads

The "sign triad" developed by Peirce is central in this mode of analysis (Gluck, 1997): "This triad allows us to examine references and citations in terms of three common dimensions: (i) the carrier of meaning (sign-vehicle); (ii) the meaning or concept referred to (interpretant); and (iii) the object pointed to (referent)" (Cronin, 2000, p. 443).

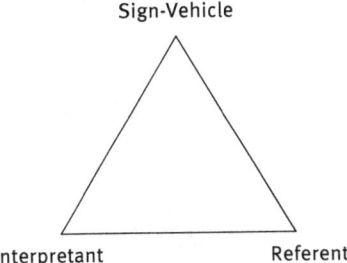

Fig. 1: Peirce's sign triad (after Gluck, [17]).

The triad makes visually clear the important differences between the embedded reference, acknowledgement statement, and individual citation as incorporated in the citation index and various forms of aggregated citations. The shape of the triad is identical, but the meaning of the three corners is different in different signs.

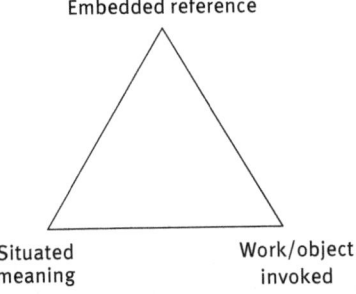

Fig. 2: Bibliographic reference sign triad.

In the case of the embedded reference, the sign vehicle is part of the citing text. Its interpretant is the concept flagged by the reference. This can be located in a specific part in the cited text (e.g., the methodology part), but it can also be more diffuse, such as when a complete book is cited. The embedded reference always

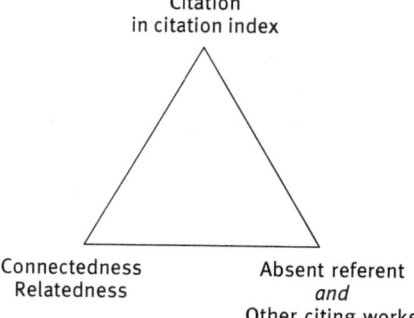

Fig. 3: Citation sign triad.

has two different referents: the full reference in the bibliography (or footnote) of the citing text and the cited text.

In the case of the individual citation, the triad is quite different. First of all, the sign vehicle is no longer to be found in the citing text, but in the citation index. It is produced from the reference in the citing text, albeit not from the embedded reference but from the references as far as they are visible in the bibliography (footnotes are still poorly processed). It also has dual referents: it points back to its "parent text" and, in addition, all the texts that are listed by the citation index as having invoked it are its collective referent. The interpretant is also distinct from the interpretant of the embedded reference. Basically, it denotes inter-textual linking interpreted by Cronin (2000) as connectedness or relatedness.

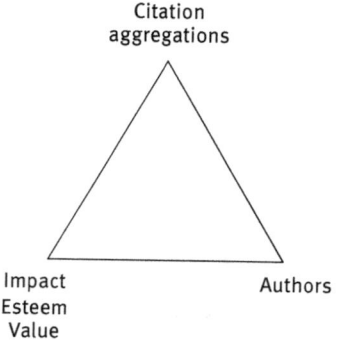

Fig. 4: Commodified citation sign triad.

The aggregated citation sign is a more important sign than the individual citation since a lone citation does not make much difference. It is in the aggregation that the power of citation analysis manifests itself (see also Day, 2014). Again, the sign vehicle is located in the citation indexes, not in the form of a bibliographic string, but rather as a calculated indicator. It can therefore also travel independently of the citation database proper, in the form of bibliometric reports or online bibliometric services. The referent relates to the unit of measurement at the specified level of aggregation. Cronin (2000) takes this to be the author, but of course this can also be the research group, the university, or the country as a whole. The interpretant is related to scientific impact as defined by the user of the citation analysis ("impact, esteem and/or value"). This can take subtly different formulations but the basic idea is that the more citations a work accrues, the bigger its scientific influence. In other words, the lower left corner of the commodified citation triad is the actual focus of evaluative bibliometrics.

Scientometricians have always examined the meaning and motivations underlying citations and the implications for citation analysis. However, since they have usually neglected to acknowledge the different configurations of the sign they were discussing, different realities have been collapsed into one another. In terms of the Peircean triads: the lower left corner of the embedded reference may be "situated meaning" and therefore able to explain why an author made the reference in the first place. Yet, in citation analysis, we are not dealing with embedded references but with the aggregated and commodified citations. Because the individual commodified citation is produced from the reference as listed in the bibliography, the original situated meaning of the embedded reference is lost in a two-step procedure. First, the embedded reference is transformed into the reference as listed in the bibliography. Then this list is inverted in the production of the citation index. Because the reference is decontextualized twice, the situated meaning cannot be aggregated and simply gets lost. This is why Wouters (1999) stressed that the resulting citation sign is in and of itself essentially meaningless. The application of citation analysis can no longer base itself on the original situated meaning of the embedded reference. A new theoretical foundation for citation analysis has to be created. This is the quest for the citation theory as conceived in the field of scientometrics (Leydesdorff, 1998; Nicolaisen, 2007).

According to Cronin (2000), the value of semiotics for the scientometric community lies primarily in its sensitivity to the variable interpretative possibilities of citations in the context of evaluative bibliometrics:

> Referencing is a complex phenomenon which can be analysed in terms of a set of sign systems (...). Furthermore, referencing and citation behaviours vary within and between disciplines, such that blanket criticism is misplaced.
> (Cronin, 2000, p. 445)

In addition, the processes of production and consumption of the relevant signs can be studied, which can be the basis for the study of the variation in the meaning attached to these signs. In this context, Cronin pointed to studies showing that referencing behavior is governed by epistemic and social norms and values demonstrating that patterns in references are not completely arbitrary (in a debate with the McRoberts critique of evaluative bibliometrics as basically meaningless (MacRoberts & MacRoberts, 1996; MacRoberts & MacRoberts, 2009)). In other words, Cronin (2000) addressed "the meaning of the citation" as the key problem for citation theory.

Cronin (2000) acknowledged that it might become possible, especially in the context of the UK national research assessment procedures (Research Assessment Exercise (RAE), now called Research Excellence Framework (REF), see http://www.ref.ac.uk/) for the symbolic citation exchange processes to have material consequences:

> More specifically, if an individual's, department's or university's ability to amass symbolic capital of this kind were to become the critical determinant of future research funding and career advancement, then it would not be difficult to imagine distortions creeping into the system, as players devised recruitment, publication, collaboration and citation harvesting stratagems to accelerate and maximise the accrual of symbolic capital.
>
> (Cronin, 2000, p. 450)

Note the strong moral orientation of this fairly accurate prediction of the future—"distortions creeping into the system" imply a negative view towards these developments. Moreover, the semiotic analysis that Cronin (2000) advocates to understand the meaning of the citation is not mobilized to understand the material implications of the increased use of citations in the reputational system. They merely appear as an afterthought.

This conception of semiotics as relevant for scientometrics is therefore by definition restricted to the classical Mertonian approach in which the relationship between sign systems and behavior is central. References and citations are seen as representations of real world relationships. Because of this focus, the analysis proposed by Cronin (2000) and Wouters (1999) remains firmly in the symbolic domain. Their semiotic citation analysis is completely intra- and inter-textual and the material world of knowledge production does not have a direct reference in this semiotic storyline.

As a consequence, it is not entirely clear what can actually be done with this refined perspective on the signs reference and citation. The mechanisms through which linguistic signs might affect the material world of knowledge creation are not specified. It is especially difficult to understand how the subtle difference between an embedded reference and a citation that is part of a citation index leads to the conclusion that the number of citations one gets would not be a more or less direct consequence of the choice of scientists to refer to ones work. Most people simply keep speaking about references and citations as more or less the same phenomenon. The details of the linguistic links seem no more than that: details that are only interesting for the person interested in the particularities of semiotic or linguistic theory. The semiotic approach was largely ignored by most researchers, including scientometricians dealing with citation analysis. It did impact the more theoretical discourse about citation theory, but even here its acceptance seems to have been limited to a small group of scholars. For example, in his comprehensive and well-documented review, Nicolaisen (2007) seems to conflate semantic and semiotic approaches.

At the same time, however, the practical application of citation analysis in the context of evaluation has taken off. Although the vast majority of "evaluation moments" are not recorded in a systematic way, it is clear that citation-based indicators have become available on a much larger scale than the inventors of the Science Citation Index could have predicted (Wouters, 2014). These indicators are used by managers as well as by researchers. It would be far too simplistic to assume that they are only management tools for which researchers can claim innocence. They have settled themselves firmly in the fabric of science and scholarship. In order to understand why and how this happened, we need an extended theoretical framework that is able to understand at a more fundamental level how the real world and semiotic signs like the citation and the reference actually interact.

2 Material Semiotics

This type of framework has already been developed, albeit outside of bibliometrics, and is called material semiotics. Material semiotics is not so much a unified theory as a family of attitudes and dispositions. They are relevant for the debate about the foundations of evaluative bibliometrics because they question the very distinction between the material and the symbolic. In order to understand how the sign system of the citation, produced by the citation indexer from the raw materials of the sign system of the reference delivered to the indexer by the research community, interacts with the material production of knowledge, we need an integrated way of thinking about, and acting with, both materiality and symbolism. The argument is succinctly formulated by the anthropologist Webb Keane:

> Efforts to bring theories of the sign into a full, robust articulation with accounts of human actions, self-consciousness, and social power are still commonly hampered by certain assumptions built into the lineage that runs from Saussure to post-structuralism. They tend still to demand that we divide our attention and choose between ideas and things. The re-

> sult is that even those who would study "things" too often turn them either into expressions or communications of "ideas," or relegate those ideas to an epiphenomenal domain. Those who would study "ideas" too often treat the associated material forms as transparent, taking their consequentiality to be suspect, and, at times, imputing implausible powers to human desires to impose meaning on the world. And this divide seems to give rise to what is still a common, if ill-informed, perception among social analysts, that "semiotics" is a species of idealism.
>
> (Keane, 2003, p. 410)

Keane is interested in the practical embodiments of semiotic ideologies in representational economies. This work is particularly relevant because research evaluation can be interpreted as an important moment in the exchange of reputation in the political economy of science and scholarship. He wants to draw attention to "the dynamic interconnections among different modes of signification at play within a particular historical and social formation" (Keane, 2003, p. 410). His research shows that how people handle and value material goods may be implicated in how they use and interpret words, and vice versa, reflecting certain underlying assumptions about the world and the beings that inhabit it (Keane, 2003, p. 410). His goal is to "open up social analysis to the historicity and social power of material things without reducing them either to being only vehicles of meaning, on the one hand, or ultimate determinants, on the other" (Keane, 2003, p. 411). He turns back to Peircean semiotics (in this sense his work is perhaps more linguistic in character than that of material semiotics in science and technology studies) because of its promise to overcome the radical sign-world dichotomy which is so characteristic for Saussurean analysis. Keane (2003) identifies two aspects of Peircean analysis as particularly important.

First, it is processual: "signs give rise to new signs, in an unending process of signification. This is important because, viewed sociologically, it can be taken to entail sociability, struggle, historicity, and contingency" (Keane, 2003, p. 413). It is striking how well this quote summarizes what has happened to citation indicators.

Second, it pays considerable attention to "the range of relationships not only between signifier (sign) and signified (interpretant) but between both of those and (possible) objects of signification" (Keane, 2003, p. 411). Keane argues that the nature of those relations between signifier and objects of signification needs to be grounded in the dynamics of the social relations. If we recall how Cronin (2000) used a triad to understand the difference between different forms of references and citations, it is clear that the anthropologist and the information scientist have found common ground, possibly without being aware of each other's existence. Keane's goal to "recognize how the cited materiality of signification is not just a factor for the sign interpreter but gives rise to and transforms modalities of action and subjectivity" (Keane, 2003, p. 411) resonates with Cronin (2000)'s goal to "develop greater sensitivity to the variable symbolic significance of the signs they routinely manipulate and treat as quasi-objective indicators of quality, impact and esteem."

Building on various critiques of modernist and realist philosophy of science, material semiotics has developed particularly strongly in the field of science and technology studies to understand how science is able to create new worlds and how the interactions between "representations" and "real objects" can be analyzed (Latour & Woolgar, 1986; Latour, 1988; Haraway, 1991; Berg & Mol, 1998; Mol, 2002; Law, 2004; Luukkonen, 1997). Material semiotics is a rather fundamental and radical alternative to the dominant epistemology in European and American thought.

Material semiotics is radical in that it refuses to accept the separation between epistemology and ontology. It is not interested in the conditions for knowing (a central problem in classical epistemology) but in the ways objects are handled in practice and consequently in the performative nature of knowledge (Mol, 2002, p. 5). Science and scholarship do not analyze and represent a reality "out-there", but engage in the creation of new worlds "in-here" (Law, 2004, pp. 54–55). This does not mean, inter alia, that material semiotics denies the existence of reality. On the contrary, it pays far more attention to how realities emerge than mainstream social science tends to do. Its practitioners are also more sensitive to the role of technology and materiality in social processes than our usual sociologist or psychologist. In actor network theory, one of the main embodiments of material semiotics, the concept of *construction* is central (Latour & Woolgar, 1986). The key idea is that science creates new objects that are unstable and contested in their infancy, but then gets hardened into facts. Latour calls this the Janus face of science: Science in the making still recognizes the uncertain nature of scientific facts, but science in the classroom discusses facts as if they are part of a stable nature (Latour, 1987). Mol (2002) prefers to speak of the *enactment* of realities rather than of their *construction*:

> The term 'construction' was used to get across the view that objects have no fixed and given identities, but gradually come into being. During their unstable childhoods their identities tend to be highly contested, volatile, open to transformation. But once they have grown up objects are taken to be stabilized.
>
> (Mol, 2002, p. 42)

She does not adopt this notion of stabilization; in her perspective a certain fluidity is a stable feature of reality:

> ... the idea that objects might not just gradually acquire an identity that they then hold on to has been pushed aside, or complemented, by this new idea. That maintaining the identity of objects requires a continuing effort. That over time they may change. (...) If an object is real this is because it is part of a practice. It is a reality *enacted*.
>
> (Mol, 2002, pp. 43–44)

This has an important consequence which is relevant to citation theory: reality is multiple rather than singular. In her study of the treatment of atherosclerosis[1] in a Dutch hospital, Mol shows that it is not simply one disease reality that patients and doctors are dealing with. The disease turns out to be quite different objects. Atherosclerosis in the walking therapy session is distinct from atherosclerosis under the microscope, and different again from atherosclerosis as operated on by the surgeon. The reality of the disease does not precede the diagnosis and treatment, but is intertwined with them. In the diagnosis and treatment, the disease gets its specific form that defines it (Mol, 2002, p. 96–97). We are not speaking of different perspectives on one underlying reality here—the material interactions are different in the ontological sense. Nor are they disconnected realities, as they can be present within a single patient:

> It is one of the great miracles of hospital life: there are different atheroscleroses in the hospital but despite the differences between them they are connected. Atherosclerosis enacted is more than one - but less than many. *The body multiple* is not fragmented. Even if it is multiple, it also hangs together. The question to be asked, then, is how this is achieved.
>
> (Mol, 2002, p. 55)

The question of how actors (human and non-human) achieve this hanging together dominates Mol's (2002) work. She exposes the variety of strategies by which reality is made coherent in the practical interaction between humans and objects. Making the multiple character of reality invisible is an aspect of these strategies.

This perspective diverges fundamentally from the way we commonly think about both our social and our physical reality. The recognition of reality as multiple, rather than singular, has fundamental implications for the role of methodologies in the social sciences. These consequences have been explored by Law (2004). He suggests the concept of a *fractional object*: "We are in a world where bodies, or organisations, or machines are more than one and less than many. In a *world* that is more than one and less than many. Somewhere in between" (Law, 2004, p. 62). According to Law, there are three options in ontology. The first op-

---

[1] Atherosclerosis is a disease that leads to thickened walls of the arteries, see http://en.wikipedia.org/wiki/Atherosclerosis

tion is to insist on singularity of the world. This means that those who perceive the world differently from ourselves are simply wrong. In social science, there is one best methodology to understand the world. The second option is to insist on pluralism and "the irreducibility of worlds, of knowledge, of ethical sensibilities, or of political preferences, to one another" (Law, 2004, p. 63). This is the relativist attitude. A large number of methodological choices in social science are now allowed, but the price we pay is that they are incommensurable. We have no criteria to decide whether a particular approach is better than another one. In contrast with these two options, Law advocates the third option which is in-between. Like Mol (2002), Law (2004) considers the world as fundamentally multiple. It is only through our active cohering of different practices and parts of realities that the world can develop as a coherent reality. This has an important consequence. The philosophical question on the nature of reality transforms into a political choice about how to live. Ontology is no longer in the first place a matter of *discovering* the real nature of reality, but a matter of making political choices as to which realities should be *created*. In terms of Law's and Mol's analysis: it is a matter of ontological politics. As a consequence, there is no general blueprint for social science, no generally valid methodology:

> There *is* no general world and there *are* no general rules. Instead there are only specific and enacted overlaps between provisionally congealed realities that have to be crafted in a way that responds to and produces particular versions of the good that can only ever travel so far. The general, then, disappears, along with the universal. The idea of the universal transportability of universal knowledge was always a chimera. But if the universal disappears then so too does the local - for the local is a subset of the general. Instead we are left with situated enactments and sets of particle connections, and it is to those that we owe our heterogeneous responsibilities.
>
> (Law, 2004, p. 155)

3 Semiotic Citation Theories

So what do these new developments in philosophy and material semiotics mean for the application of semiotics to the domain of citation theory? The step we need to take, which neither Cronin (2000) nor Wouters (1999) took, is to understand that the sign is not a representation of reality, however distorted, but an object in the real world of knowledge making. The differences between the embedded reference, the reference in the bibliography, the disembedded citation which is the in-between half-product hidden in the deep recesses of the citation index machinery, and the citation as part of the citation index, are not differences of *representation* of one and the same real world object, but *ontological* differences between objects. Each of them is a partially different but related object. This first conceptual step is not easy because it requires us to distance ourselves from the usual mainstream American/European epistemology. But we also need to take a second step. We need to accept that reality is multiple. Although this step is perhaps even more difficult, because of our common conceptual and ideological inertia, it solves a number of problems that have plagued eminent theorists who struggled with the problem of citation theory. If reality is multiple, we no longer need to search for one integrated theory that can explain the whole process of citing and citation. We can allow for a number of partly contradictory, and partly overlapping *sets* of citation theories, each emerging in a particular set of knowledge practices. The quest for a citation theory turns out to be the same type of chimera as the quest for universal transportable knowledge.

Let us delve into the details and reinterpret the process of citing and citation in these material semiotic terms. A scientist who cites a journal article or book written by another scientist creates by this very act a new object (different from the cited work). This object, the embedded reference, is tightly connected to the citing text. However, the scientist usually also creates another object as a consequence of his citing act: the reference in the bibliography. If she uses bibliographic software, this is done automatically. This second object is in principle still connected to the situated meaning of the first object but can be easily disconnected. This happens, for example, whenever another scientist copies the listed reference in his own bibliography or list of books to read. It is this second object which is the raw material for the citation indexer. In the indexing software, the reference is first inverted by sorting each citation according to the text that it cites, rather than by the citing texts from which it originated. This act of semiosis creates the third object, the individual citation (Wouters, 1999). Then, the citations are grouped together and counted. This results in the fourth citation object, the citation as part of the citation index. Note that the last two objects are not created by the citing scientist but by the citation indexing process. The citation indexes are sold commercially by the citation indexer or provided freely on the web as stand-alone products. They can also be sold or provided as part of more comprehensive research information systems. The citations thus provided are meaningful to the stakeholders involved, otherwise there would be no demand for them. But this meaning cannot be the situated meaning of the embedded reference since the citation objects have been created in a semiotic process that involves decontextualization. The original context has been lost. Therefore, the citation needs to be recontextualized in order to function as a social object. This happens in two different ways or modalities (see below) and it will no longer be a surprise that this means that actually two different types of citation objects are enacted in this process of recontextualization. And this increasing variety of citation objects all exist at the same time—they engage in complex interactions with each other, as well as with other active objects such as references, evaluation committees, deans, and researchers engaged in knowledge creation.

4 Citation Link Object

In the first modality, the citation enters into a one-to-one relationship with the cited text (the right hand side of the Peircean triad): the object is the link between the cited text and the citing text. Let us call it the citation link object. In this recontextualization, the citation is literally the inversion of the reference as part of the bibliography. This object can play a variety of roles and take on a variety of shapes. It can be an instrument for the cited author to locate the exact place at which his work has been cited by the citing author. This is a form of inverse snowball sampling and Eugene Garfield saw it as the main use of the citation index (Garfield, 1955). In this form, the citation is a novel bibliographic tool that enables scientists to go forward in time in searching for literature, rather than only backwards in time (as is the case in traditional snowball sampling using the bibliographies). Interestingly, this means that the citation link object can be used to retrieve the situated meaning of the embedded reference from which the citation link object emerged. This is an important cause of the possibility for the citation link object to appear as simply another format of the reference. In other words, because of this potential as a search tool, which was actively advertised by Garfield in the early years of the citation index (Garfield, 1955), the process of decontextualization which creates the citation from the reference is made invisible. The citation can pose as actually being nothing else but the reference and this has given a very strong boost to the process of naturalization of the sign citation. It has made this process almost seamless.

This citation link object can also be the building block for creating maps of science. In this endeavor, all publications in a given area are presented as nodes in a network and their configuration is determined by the patterns of links between the nodes. These links can be any kind of object: the authors, the references, shared terminology, publication years, and, since the emergence of citation indexes, also the citation relations. The direct citation link is the most basic citation link object, but it can easily morph into much more complicated citation objects. For example, co-citation links are links between two documents that are each cited by a common third document, although they may not have other types of links between them, e.g., they may not cite each other (Small, 1973). The inverse of the co-citation link object is bibliographic coupling which is to the listed reference in the bibliography what co-citation is to the single citation object (Kessler, 1963). Both direct citation links, co-citation links, as well as bibliographic coupling links are routinely used to create maps of science (Boyack, Klavans, & Börner, 2005; Small, 1977; Waltman, van Eck, & Noyons, 2010) (for more on science mapping, see Ginda, Scharnhorst and Börner, this volume).

5 Citation Number Objects

In the second modality, the citations to a cited text are aggregated and counted. The citation is now recontextualized not as the link between two texts, but as an attribute of the cited text. The cited text suddenly has a novel property: its citation frequency. The citation object is in other words recontextualized as metadata of the cited text. Moreover, it has now become a number and is therefore also recontextualized from the domain of textual strings and links into the domain of numbers and statistics. As a result, the possibilities of manipulation that the sign system of numbers has developed in the course of the last couple of centuries are now also available to the citation sign. Perhaps most importantly, the citation is thereby made commensurable and comparable. Cited texts can be compared in terms of their number of citations. These numbers can be added, leading to the number of citations of a particular oeuvre. As a result, the citation does not only become an attribute of the cited text, but also of the cited author. These aggregations can go on from author, to research group, institute, university, and country. At all levels of aggregation of the scientific system, we have a shadow reality of citations that hover over the actors (texts, knowledge creators, as well as institutions) as objects to which they can attach as well as detach. Practice, meaning, and context are intimately intertwined, they define each other, and it is therefore less fruitful to try to separate them into different domains of the symbolic representation and the real world. The reality of citation is indeed enacted within the double context of knowledge creation and research process evaluation.

6 Evaluative Bibliometrics

Evaluative bibliometrics as a field is the result of the emergence and enactment of this new citation reality as an added reflexive layer to the fabric of the scientific and scholarly system. Often, bibliometrics is seen as a data-driven field that has been "captured" by the creation of the Science Citation Index. This is a rather simple and poor explanation of the vastly richer semiotic reality that underlies the field of evaluative bibliometrics. If we take semiotics seriously as an analytical lens, we have a much better framework to understand the historical development of the field and the pervasive influence of the citation index on the way quality is defined in the scientific and scholarly system.

To understand this role of the citation, we must pay close attention to the subtle but important difference between the two modalities of the citation object. The first form, that of the link between the cited and citing text from the position of the cited text, is still only two steps removed from the situated meaning of the embedded reference. It can be used to retrieve this situated meaning. It can also be used to try to find similar locations of situated meaning in other texts. This use of the citation sign is often firmly embedded within the context of knowledge creation, for example when a researcher wishes to find traces in the literature of researchers working on the same topic or thinking along the same lines. In the second form (the number that has become an attribute of the cited text), the citation object is resolutely disconnected from the situated meaning of the embedded reference which was at the origin of its semiosis. It is not the specific meaning of the citing author to which it refers. As an object, it exclusively represents the fact that a certain author or a certain number of authors has cited the text. What that means is not prescribed by the citation object itself. In this sense, we can claim that the citation included in the citation index as such is still an under-defined object or perhaps better a proto-object. It will only become a fully-fledged functional socio-material object if it materializes into a *specific* citation object, such as a specific indicator (e.g., the normalized number of citations per paper). In other words, the citation object in its second modality (as number) can be compared to a *stemcell object* which has as its main function of morphing into one of a large variety of concrete citation objects within specific citation, evaluation, and knowledge creating contexts.

This means that the development of specific citation theories that can explain the structure and role of citation objects in their various forms requires the inclusion of the specific practices and institutional contexts that are co-enacted. It clearly does not make sense to justify citation counts in an evaluative context by claiming that the number of citations is like a vote by the scientific community about the value of a particular piece of work or of a particular author. What the citation means cannot be extracted from itself, because the citation object as number is a decontextualized and underdefined proto-object. At the same time, it is also not the case that the meaning of the citation is completely determined by the context of evaluation. The meaning of the citation is not completely arbitrary and it does make a difference whether the number is higher or lower in a particular context. The values and shapes that the citation object can adopt are constrained by the patterns among the references from which the citation objects emerge. Although the citation indexer is the producer of the citation objects, the citation indexer does not determine its values or shapes. In this sense, citation analysis is as objective as an analysis can be.

7 The Material Impact of Citation Objects

The system of citation has delivered key objects that are manipulated in this process of research evaluation and assessment. The development of the governance of research enabled and stimulated the uptake of these new objects (Wouters, 2014). The increased scale and specialization of scientific work as well as its increased role as a key instrument of production, reproduction, and distribution in current globalized capitalist economies have created a complex structure and introduced new dynamics into the management of science. The "social contract" that gave the scientific communities a relatively large amount of freedom (built on a combination of the notion of "academic freedom" in traditional academia and the promise of great economic and social progress—as well as profits—thanks to programmatic research) has been breaking down since the early 1970s. As a result, traditional forms of accountability and quality control in the form of various types of peer review have been supplemented as well as displaced by audits and accountability by science funders and stakeholders external to the scientific communities. The demand for more transparency in the organization of research than provided by traditional peer review forms has stimulated this development. These audits have created an increased demand for both quantitative and qualitative indicators as well as for forms of external expert review. The result is a complex dynamic of interactions between control by the relevant scientific communities and elites and control by various stakeholders. Who counts as a scientific expert or representative of a stakeholder community is not given a priori but is permanently redefined in these processes. Scientists play different roles in the interactions: as researchers, as experts, and as representatives of various stakeholder interests. How to combine these different roles and make them cohere is one of the challenges that researchers face in this complex science system.

National research systems have introduced a variety of performance based funding mechanisms, both based on peer review (such as the UK REF) and bibliometric evaluations (such as the Nordic bibliometric indicator) (Hicks, 2012). Currently, national systems vary in two dimensions: the tightness with which they couple performance assessment to funding and the degree to which they use metrics in addition to peer review (peer review based judgment is still the default). All combinations of these two dimensions occur. But even in systems without a direct or tight coupling between funding and assessment outcomes, assessments have direct material consequences as the reputation of a research group or senior researcher is related to the outcome of the assessment. The systems only vary with respect to the details of this feedback loop and the time it takes for this cycle to complete. Countries with a relatively larger share of block funding may allow researchers more time to recover from a low rating in the regular assessment, provided that the block funding itself is not directly related to assessment outcomes. But in the long run, researchers will have to have high scores or leave the scientific system. This means that indicators do not only influence the judgment of past work, but they indirectly shape the possibilities for future research via this feedback loop. In other words, by influencing the research agenda of tomorrow they have direct material consequences for researchers and for science in general. Therefore, it seems insufficient to analyze citation indicators only symbolically without attention to materiality and economics. This again underlines that the material turn in semiotics may be fruitfully employed in scientometrics.

What does this mean for the position of citation theories? The field of scientometrics has developed a variety of citation theories, all of them interesting, none of them completely satisfactory or uncontested. One of the main lines of argument has been that citations reflect the referencing behavior of researchers (see above) and that therefore the citation rate of a paper, an author, a research group, an institute, and a country reflect the use of, and response to, the work by the relevant scientific community. This response can then subsequently be seen as a proxy for either quality or scientific impact (this varies in different citation theories). A supporting argument has been that at the level of the individual paper many factors other than the quality of the paper may influence the choice of references by the author, but that these factors cancel out at higher levels of aggregation (van Raan, 1998). In a recent paper, we have shown that this expectation may be a belief that is sometimes unsubstantiated (Waltman, van Eck, & Wouters, 2013), but it is still implicitly used by most citation analysts. The inquiry of motivations and factors influencing the references in scientific papers is still an active line of research in the area of citation theories (Bornmann & Daniel, 2008). From a semiotic perspective, however, this line of attack is misdirected because it assumes that references and citations are identical whereas from a semiotic perspective it is clear that this cannot be the case.

By including the whole reputational cycle in research in a material semiotic analysis, an empirical analysis based on this theoretical framework would be akin to Lenoir and Ross (1996). Lenoir and Ross (1996) aim to understand the way science functions as a disunified enterprise with the help of historically grounded semiotics: "We intend to demonstrate that the power of a sign, a representation, or an interconnected set of representations to support scientific work is not merely a function of their own internal logic but also of their capacity to forge rhetorical links to representations in other domains by drawing upon metaphor as well as repertoires of tropes and narrative structures." Lenoir and Ross (1996) developed this to show how natural history museums are able to create artificially constructed sites to create a "meaningful nature". In the same vein, citation theory should analyze the main tropes and narrative structures in selected case studies of research evaluations (drawing on either documentary analysis or ethnographic field notes). Such an ethnographically grounded approach to the problem of citation theory would contribute to the work that aims to dismantle the artificial and unhelpful barrier between quantitative and qualitative work in scientometrics and science and technology studies (Wyatt et al., 2015).

Acknowledgment

I would like to thank the members of the EPIC workgroup as well as my colleagues at the Centre for Science and Technology Studies, Leiden University, for their creative response to, and comments on, earlier drafts of this chapter, in particular Rodrigo Costas, Thomas Franssen, Björn Hammarfelt, Tsjitske Holtrop, Wolfgang Kaltenbrunner, Joost Kosten, Thed van Leeuwen, Sarah de Rijcke, Alexander Rushforth, Clifford Tatum, and Ludo Waltman. I am also indebted to my colleagues Loet Leydesdorff and Jesper Schneider for their thoughtful comments and inspiring discussions. I thank the referees and editor for their helpful suggestions.

Cited References

Berg, M., & Mol, A. (1998). *Differences in Medicine: Unraveling Practices, Techniques, and Bodies.* Durham and London: Duke University Press.

Bornmann, L., & Daniel, H. D. (2008). What do citation counts measure? A review of studies on citing behavior. *Journal of Documentation, 64*(1), 45–80.

Boyack, K. W., Klavans, R., & Börner, K. (2005). Mapping the backbone of science. *Scientometrics, 64*(3), 351–374.

Cronin, B. (1984). The citation process. The role and significance of citations in scientific communication. *London: Taylor Graham, 1984, 1.*

Cronin, B. (2000). Semiotics and evaluative bibliometrics. *Journal of Documentation, 56*(4), 440–453.

Dahler-Larsen, P. (2013). Constitutive Effects of Performance Indicators: Getting beyond unintended consequences. *Public Management Review, 16*(7), 969–986.

Day, R. E. (2005). Poststructuralism and information studies. *Annual Review of Information Science and Technology, 39*(1), 575–609.

Day, R. E. (2014). "The Data—It Is Me!"("Les données—c'est Moi!"). *Beyond Bibliometrics: Harnessing Multidimensional Indicators of Scholarly Impact*, 67.

Eco, U. (1976). *A theory of semiotics* (Vol. 217). Indiana University Press.

Egghe, L., & Rousseau, R. (1990). Introduction to informetrics: Quantitative methods in library, documentation and information science.

Garfield, E. (1955). Citation indexes for science. A new dimension in documentation through association of ideas. *International journal of epidemiology*, 35(5), 1123–1127.

Gluck, M. (1997, August). Making sense of semiotics: privileging respondents in revealing contextual geographic syntactic and semantic codes. In *Proceedings of an international conference on Information seeking in context*(pp. 53–66). Taylor Graham Publishing.

Haraway, D. J. (1991). *Simians, cyborgs, and women: The reinvention of nature*. Routledge.

Hicks, D. (2012). Performance-based university research funding systems. *Research Policy*, 41(2), 251–261.

Irvine, J. T. (1989). When talk isn't cheap: Language and political economy. *American ethnologist*, 16(2), 248–267.

James, W. (1898). *Philosophical conceptions and practical results*. The University Press.

Keane, W. (2003). Semiotics and the social analysis of material things. *Language & Communication*, 23(3), 409–425.

Kessler, M. M. (1963). Bibliographic coupling between scientific papers. *American documentation*, 14(1), 10–25.

Latour, B. (1987). *Science in action: How to follow scientists and engineers through society*. Harvard University Press.

Latour, B. (1988). *The pasteurization of France*. Harvard University Press.

Latour, B., & Woolgar, S. (1986). *Laboratory life: The construction of scientific facts*. Princeton University Press.

Law, J. (2004). *After method: Mess in social science research*. Routledge.

Lenoir, T., & Ross, C. (1996). "The Naturalized History Museum." In *The Disunity of Science: Boundaries, Contexts, and Power*. Stanford: Stanford University Press: ,370–97.

Leydesdorff, L. (1998). Theories of citation?. *Scientometrics*, 43(1), 5–25.

Luukkonen, T. (1997). Why has Latour's theory of citations been ignored by the bibliometric community? Discussion of sociological interpretations of citation analysis. *Scientometrics*, 38(1), 27–37.

MacRoberts, M. H., & MacRoberts, B. R. (1996). Problems of citation analysis. *Scientometrics*, 36(3), 435–444.

MacRoberts, M. H., & MacRoberts, B. R. (2009). Problems of citation analysis: A study of uncited and seldom-cited influences. *Journal of the American Society for Information Science and Technology*, 61(1), 1–12.

Mol, A. (2002). *The body multiple: Ontology in medical practice*. Duke University Press.

Narin, F. (1976). *Evaluative bibliometrics: The use of publication and citation analysis in the evaluation of scientific activity* (pp. 206–219). Washington, D. C: Computer Horizons.

Nicolaisen, J. (2007). Citation analysis. *Annual review of information science and technology*, 41(1), 609–641.

Nicolaisen, J., & Frandsen, T. F. (2008). The reference return ratio. *Journal of Informetrics*, 2(2), 128–135.

Small, H. (1973). Co-citation in the scientific literature: A new measure of the relationship between two documents. *Journal of the American Society for information Science*, 24(4), 265–269.

Small, H. G. (1977). A co-citation model of a scientific specialty: A longitudinal study of collagen research. *Social studies of science*, 139–166.

van Raan, A. F. (1998). In matters of quantitative studies of science the fault of theorists is offering too little and asking too much. *Scientometrics*, *43*(1), 129–139.

Walker, J. A. (2014). Comments on Umberto Eco's Book "A Theory of Semiotics". *Leonardo*, 317–319.

Waltman, L., & van Eck, N. J. (2012). Source normalized indicators of citation impact: An overview of different approaches and an empirical comparison. *Scientometrics*, *96*(3), 699–716.

Waltman, L., van Eck, N. J., & Noyons, E. C. (2010). A unified approach to mapping and clustering of bibliometric networks. *Journal of Informetrics*, *4*(4), 629–635.

Waltman, L., van Eck, N. J., & Wouters, P. (2013). Counting publications and citations: Is more always better?. *Journal of Informetrics*, *7*(3), 635–641.

Wouters, P. (1998). The signs of science. *Scientometrics*, *41*(1), 225–241.

Wouters, P. (1999). The citation culture.

Wouters, P. (2014). The Citation: From Culture to Infrastructure. *Beyond Bibliometrics: Harnessing Multidimensional Indicators of Scholarly Impact*, 47.

Wyatt, S., Milojević, S., Lucio-Arias, D., Park, H. W., Šabanović, S., & Leydesdorff, L. (2015). Quantitative and Qualitative STS: The Intellectual and Practical Contributions of Scientometrics. *Available at SSRN 2588336*.

Christine L. Borgman
Data Citation as a Bibliometric Oxymoron

1 Introduction

"Data citation" is a broad construct that incorporates credit, attribution, and discovery of data. It has taken on a life of its own, quite apart from the theory and method of bibliometrics, informetrics, scientometrics, and other means to assess the flow of scholarly information via citations between published documents. International task groups have written hundreds of pages of reports. Manifestos abound. Principles and standards for data citation are being set and implemented in local practice (CODATA-ICSTI Task Group on Data Citation Standards and Practices, 2013; Crosas, Carpenter, Shotton, & Borgman, 2013; Datacitation Synthesis Group, 2014; Uhlir, 2012).

The argument for data citation is made most succinctly in the first of ten principles promulgated by a joint task group of CODATA (the Committee on Data of the International Council of Scientific Unions) and ICSTI (the International Council for Scientific and Technical Information):

> The Status Principle: Data citations should be accorded the same importance in the scholarly record as the citation of other objects (CODATA-ICSTI Task Group on Data Citation Standards and Practices, 2013; "International Council for Scientific and Technical Information," 2015; Lide & Wood, 2012).

The status principle puts data on equal footing with other objects that are cited in scholarly communication—but without defining what those are or establishing the basis for equal treatment. This equivalence raises a host of theoretical, methodological, and practical problems for bibliometrics. Historically, bibliometrics involves "written communication" (Pritchard, 1969, p. 348)—specifically, journals, periodicals, and books (Pritchard, 1969; Raisig, 1962). Bibliographic citation styles differ widely in the choice of data elements and citable units, as discussed further below. While the lack of agreement on bibliographic units for the purpose of citation remains problematic, at least these units usually can be aggregated into discrete documents such as journal articles or books. Of the many differences between data and written communication, the difficulty of defining citable units for data is the most problematic for bibliometrics.

Treating data citations as equivalent to bibliographic citations implies that data are publications, which in turn gives rise to the popular "data publication" metaphor. While "publication," strictly speaking, means only "to make public," publication in the sense of scholarly communication has a much higher bar. Scholarly publication normally requires peer review and dissemination in a venue with recognized status for credit and attribution (Borgman, 2007). Journals and books usually meet this standard of publication, whereas talks, blog posts, and objects posted on web pages generally do not. Reciprocal citation is a feature of bibliometrics and of related methods such as webometrics, scientometrics, and informetrics. Data are far more complex objects—if they are objects at all—than the entities to which bibliometrics applies. Units of data might receive citations, for example, but it is not clear that they can make references to other objects. The status principle for data citation and the data publication metaphor combine to muddy the waters of scholarly communication at a time when far more clarity about the characteristics of data is needed (Borgman, 2007, 2012, 2015; Parsons & Fox, 2013).

The leap from citing publications to citing data is a vast one, but if data are to be discovered, exchanged, reused, and repurposed, robust mechanisms for citation are necessary. Transferring bibliographic citation principles to data must be done carefully and selectively, lest the problems associated with citation practice be exacerbated and new ones introduced. Determining how to cite data is a non-trivial matter. Giving credit for data, which is among the arguments for data citation, also raises the complex ethical and policy issues associated with the use of bibliometrics for evaluating scholarship (Declaration on Research Assessment, 2013; Furner, 2014; Rafols, de Rijcke, & Wouters, 2014). This Festschrift chapter, which is informed by several decades of discussion with Blaise Cronin, explores the thorny relationships between citing publications and citing data, asking how theories of bibliometrics might be applied to the use of research data and vice versa.

In a Festschrift chapter for Eugene Garfield, edited some 15 years ago by Blaise Cronin and Helen Barsky Atkins (Borgman, 2000b), I expressed concerns about the slow uptake of bibliometrics to study scholarly communication and about the lack of understanding about how bibliometrics could be applied to electronic publishing. In the time since, the use of bibliometrics and webometrics to study scholarly communication in digital environments has blossomed. Theory and method in these areas is also far more mature (Almind & Ingwersen, 1997; Borgman, 1990; Borgman & Furner, 2002; Cronin & Sugimoto, 2014a, 2014b; Thelwall, Vaughan, & Bjorneborn, 2005). At this juncture, my concerns address how little is understood about the implications of data citation for the theory, method, and practice of bibliometrics—and conversely, how theories of bibliometrics can inform the design of citation mechanisms for data.

2 A Short History of Data Citation

The open access movement, writ large, is about facilitating the movement of publications, software code, government data, research data, and other intellectual content with minimal licensing restrictions and minimal costs (Kelty, 2008; "Open Knowledge Foundation," 2013; Suber, 2012). In the realm of scholarly communication, open access to publications and to data is being promoted or required by funding agencies, journals, universities, and other stakeholders. Adoption of these open access policies varies widely among fields, countries, institutions, and individuals. The biosciences, especially the "omics" fields, have adopted open data policies most fully. Genomic sequence data, for example, are submitted to repositories in concert with submitting articles for publication. Journals may require evidence of deposit, such as a record number, to consider the article for review. In most other fields, deposit of data is uneven at best, whether due to a lack of repositories, resources, skills, or incentives (Borgman, 2015; Fecher, Friesike, & Hebing, 2015; Kratz & Strasser, 2015; Wallis, Rolando, & Borgman, 2013).

Communities that value data as scholarly products to be shared, disseminated, recombined, and reused need ways to describe those data. The first method proposed, naively, was simply to map established mechanisms of bibliographic citation to data citation. The primary problem with this approach, as discussed below, is the lack of agreement on what constitutes data. A second problem, also discussed below, is the distinction between credit and attribution for data, hence the broader title of the research agenda workshop held by the U.S. National Academies of Science, "For Attribution—Developing Data Attribution and Citation Practices and Standards" (Uhlir, 2012). The workshop explicated a wide range of conceptual issues involved in the citation and attribution of data, allowing the work of the international CODATA-ICSTI Task Group to move forward. The report of that group promulgated a set of ten principles but did not establish an implementation plan. The diversity of constituencies and practices was deemed too great to be resolved by the Task Group alone (CODATA-ICSTI Task Group on Data Citation Standards and Practices, 2013). However, other parties joined the effort quickly. The several reports, in combination with a manifesto (Crosas et al., 2013), provided the foundation for the community to implement the recommendations. Members of the Task Group, most of whom were practitioners from libraries, archives, data repositories, policy and standards agencies, and publishers, joined other stakeholders to refine the ten principles into a more succinct list of eight (Datacitation Synthesis Group, 2014). These principles, now finalized and endorsed by many parties, are provided in full as a means to explore the comparisons between data and publications:

1. *Importance*: Data should be considered legitimate, citable products of research. Data citations should be accorded the same importance in the scholarly record as citations of other research objects, such as publications.
2. *Credit and Attribution*: Data citations should facilitate giving scholarly credit and normative and legal attribution to all contributors to the data, recognizing that a single style or mechanism of attribution may not be applicable to all data.
3. *Evidence*: In scholarly literature, whenever and wherever a claim relies upon data, the corresponding data should be cited.
4. *Unique Identification*: A data citation should include a persistent method for identification that is machine actionable, globally unique, and widely used by a community.
5. *Access*: Data citations should facilitate access to the data themselves and to such associated metadata, documentation, code, and other materials, as are necessary for both humans and machines to make informed use of the referenced data.
6. *Persistence*: Unique identifiers, and metadata describing the data, and its disposition, should persist—even beyond the life span of the data they describe.
7. *Specificity and Verifiability*: Data citations should facilitate identification of, access to, and verification of the specific data that support a claim. Citations or citation metadata should include information about provenance and fixity sufficient to facilitate verifying that the specific timeslice, version and/or granular portion of data retrieved subsequently is the same as was originally cited.
8. *Interoperability and Flexibility*: Data citation methods should be sufficiently flexible to accommodate the variant practices among communities, but should not differ so much that they compromise interoperability of data citation practices across communities.

These principles map to the general functions of bibliographic citation, with concerns for documenting evidence, accommodating variant practices among communities, identifying cited items unambiguously, and improving access to the cited objects. Two functional differences have notable ramifications for the theory, method, and practice of bibliometrics. One is the assumption that referencing and cited objects are in digital form and available online. A data citation is much more than descriptive metadata; it should support machine action (principle 4). The second, made most explicit in principle 7, is that a data citation should facilitate access to related objects. Data may be interpretable only in combination with contextual information, and perhaps with software code, instrumentation, and other technologies. In contrast, publications are presumed to be interpretable as independent units.

Working groups on the dissemination and implementation of the data citation principles were established under the auspices of *Force11*, "a community working together in support of the goal of advancing scholarly communication" (Force11, 2015). Data citation is but one of their topics of interest. This volunteer community has weekly conference calls and daily flows of email. Some of their activities overlap with that of *Research Objects for Scholarly Communication* (ROSC), a burgeoning eScience community established in 2014 under the auspices of the World Wide Web Consortium (Bechhofer, De Roure, Gamble, Goble, & Buchan, 2010; "Research Object for Scholarly Communication Community Group," 2014). The *Research Data Alliance* (RDA), a more formal organization that has funding from public agencies in the U.S., Europe, and Australia, has working groups, interest groups, and birds-of-a-feather groups that intersect with the concerns of Force11 and ROSC. RDA, established in 2013, has more than 1600 members from 70 countries. While the overlap in membership is considerable, RDA draws practitioners, technologists, and policy makers interested in building infrastructures for data management; Force11 is concerned with reforming scholarly communication generally; and Research Objects for Scholarly Communication is concerned with technical approaches for managing data, publications, software, and other objects created in scientific research.

Among the interests common to these groups, and to others within individual domains, are the desire to redesign scholarly communication for networked environments, the changing relationships among stakeholders, the changing criteria for evaluating scholarship, and the complexity of data management and stewardship. A critical mass of stakeholders now considers these to be urgent problems. Data citation is but one mechanism to address these issues, albeit a fairly central one to the extent that it facilitates credit, attribution, discovery, access, retrieval, management, use, and stewardship of scholarly content. These developments should be watched closely by bibliometricians, given the broad implications for scholarly communication; "Data citation" has become a catchword that encompasses a larger array of issues involved in managing the many digital objects that are created or used in research.

3 Theoretical Problems of Data Citation

Scholarly authors are expected to document their evidence by citing their sources. Bibliographic referencing, the traditional means to do so, matured in an era of print publication. Books, articles, and other scholarly products were stable entities. Once published, they stayed published. Given adequate bibliographic description, most cited documents could be located in research libraries, or perhaps in archives. As publication moved to digital formats, first as duplicates to print publication, later as a primary format, the stability of documents and citations no longer could be assumed.

Data are much different entities than publications, introducing many new features and requirements for citations. In turn, these different characteristics require a new set of theoretical premises for bibliometrics. Modeling the flows of data alone would be hard enough. To the extent that data are cited as objects on par with publications, bibliometric analyses will draw upon heterogeneous pools of cited entities. Thus it is useful to consider how citation practices differ between genres of publication and of data.

Generally speaking, authors cite sources that are accessible to their readers. In most cases, they cite other publications, providing enough information so that readers can locate those sources in a library or online. The publication to which a citation refers may exist in many copies. Metadata elements such as volume, issue, and page numbers usually suffice to identify the item uniquely, whether in a print issue or online. Even if the document was obtained online, citations may reference the page numbers of the printed copy. When cited objects are available only online, location information such as URLs, or unique and persistent identification such as digital object identifiers (DOI) that can resolve to a location, are required. Publications usually are assumed be static objects, which facilitates identity and location. In cases where cited objects are not assumed to be stable, a specific version can be cited. Although links to online publications may break fairly quickly, these objects tend to remain available somewhere, and discovery mechanisms are improving (Klein & Nelson, 2010; Van de Sompel et al., 2012; Van de Sompel, Nelson, & Sanderson, 2013)

Once outside the realm of formal publication, citations become less reliable means to locate sources of evidence. Authors may cite rare or original sources but not include the name and location of the archive in their bibliographic descriptions. Authors rarely provide bibliographic citations for their own data unless they are depositing those data in a place accessible to readers. Rather, most authors describe their methods and data to the degree expected by their field and publication venue, providing tables, figures, and supplementary materials as appropriate. In cases where a publication draws on data from external sources, such as those from an archive, repository, or colleague, those data may or may not be referenced. Data in repositories are most easily cited, as these institutions usually offer suggested citation formats that include unique and persistent identifiers. However, if external data were obtained to calibrate instruments or to "ground truth" a field site, they may not be cited because they were considered background to the research or implicit in the methods (Wallis et al., 2013; Wynholds, Wallis, Borgman, Sands, & Traweek, 2012). In other cases, authors might cite a "data paper" associated with a data release, as in astronomy (Ahn et al., 2012), an entire archive (e.g., Sloan Digital Sky Survey), or publisher of data sources (e.g., OECD). References to data often are informal, such as a URL, a footnote, a figure caption, or an oblique mention in a sentence (Pepe, Goodman, Muench, Crosas, & Erdmann, 2014). Links to data decay even more quickly than do links to publications, as researchers are much less likely to curate data for long periods of time. The eternal quest for bibliographic control (Borgman, 2000a) is even more ephemeral for data than for publications.

3.1 Stakeholders and Styles

A particular challenge in building bibliometric theory for data citation is the number of stakeholders involved. These include, for example, scholars, publishers, librarians, funders, repository managers, policy makers, and technologists. Each has different interests in the forms that data citation will take. Some would make credit and attribution the highest priorities; others would focus on data citation as a means to improve discovery and access. The diversity of publication manuals and bibliographic citation styles suggests that achieving unity in data citation is highly unlikely. Bibliographic referencing tools such as Zotero, Endnote, Refworks, and Mendeley provide style sheets that will render citations in the formats of individual journals, conferences, and publishers. For example, Zotero currently supports 7429 citation styles (Zotero, 2015). Only a few fields and journals have established citation styles for data.

The tensions are many. As discussed further below, scholars want credit for their scholarly work, but do not necessarily desire separate credit for their data. Most lack the skills, resources, and often motivation to invest in curating their own data well enough to make them citable. Search engines would like to add value to existing assets by making them more discoverable. Funding agencies may require that data resulting from projects they support be shared and reused, but few such agencies have been willing to invest heavily in data stewardship. Overall, better knowledge infrastructures are needed to manage, discover, and exploit research data and information (Borgman, 2015; CrossRef, 2013; Edwards et al., 2013).

Commercial interests see opportunities in hosting and providing access to data. Cloud computing services will host data, but do not wish to be in the curatorial business. Publishers may provide access to data as value-added services, but few are willing to host data except as a for-profit venture. Data repositories, which typically are non-profit consortial organizations, are concerned about their long-term ability to curate resources in the face of commercial competition that may have a shorter view. Universities seek better records of the scholarly output of their faculty, students, and research staff for use in promoting their reputations, managing their resources, and evaluating people and departments. Research libraries see a role in curating the data produced by researchers in their universities or other organizations, but may not wish to compete with repositories. Rather, libraries are more likely to apply their expertise in information organization, curation, and discovery of orphan data.

Each of these stakeholders addressed their concerns independently until 2005 or so. As interest grew in data management plans, data sharing, reuse, and citation, competing stakeholders began to see some common ground. Influential policy documents helped to lay foundations for further discussion (Atkins et al., 2003; Boulton et al., 2012; Bourne et al., 2011; CODATA-ICSTI Task Group on Data Citation Standards and Practices, 2013; Hey & Trefethen, 2005; National Science Board, 2005; Uhlir, 2012; Wood et al., 2010). Some of these documents were consensus reports; others resulted from conferences and workshops on several continents. Coalitions such as Force11 and RDA bring competing stakeholders to the same table to discuss the future of scholarly communication, including access to data (Borgman, 2015).

3.2 Defining Data

At the core of the data citation problem is the lack of agreement on what constitutes data. Despite the plethora of policies and press about data, big and small, little effort is devoted to defining these terms. This is not a new problem. As Rosenberg (2013) comments, histories of science and epistemology tend to mention data only in passing, if at all (Blair, 2010; Daston, 1988; Poovey, 1998; Porter, 1995). Foundational works on the making of meaning in science discuss facts, representations, inscriptions, and publications, with little attention to data per se (Bowker, 2005; Latour, 1987, 1988, 1993; Latour & Woolgar, 1979). Bibliometricians, as members of the information sciences, are well aware of the difficulties in defining "information" (Buckland, 1991; Case, 2002, 2012; Furner, 2010). Precise operational definitions of the units being cited are necessary for bibliometrics, and particularly for machine discovery of cited objects. Attempts to distinguish between data and datasets have not achieved much clarity, as notions of the identity of datasets pose other theoretical challenges (Agosti & Ferro, 2007; Renear & Dubin, 2003; Renear, Sacchi, & Wickett, 2010).

The definition proposed elsewhere is suitable for discussions of bibliometrics and data citation: *Data* refers to entities used as evidence of phenomena for the purposes of research or scholarship (Borgman, 2015). The advantages of this definition are several. It recognizes the degree to which data may exist in the eye of the beholder. One person's signal is another's noise. Thus, one set of entities could be used for evidence of different phenomena for different purposes. In scientific publications, authors may consider their data to be the tables and figures presented, the cleaned and analyzed data set from which those tables and figures were derived, the initial "raw" observations from the field or instrument—or all or none of these. Collaborators may reasonably disagree on what were the data from any given field site, experiment, or study (Borgman, Wallis, & Mayernik, 2012). Thence comes the problem of granularity. A data citation might refer to one or a few observations, to a dataset assembled over the course of a career, or anything in between. The essence of principle 7 is that citations can be made to whatever unit of data is appropriate evidence in a particular case. The citation should be unique, as stated in principle 4.

The granularity problem also arises in bibliographic citations. Scientific styles tend to cite entire documents, whereas humanities styles tend to cite individual page numbers or passages. Often these variant forms can be reconciled if enough metadata is provided; e.g., author, title, date, page numbers. While bibliometric analyses often aggregate documents by author, institution, journal, date range, or other elements, the unit of analysis is usually the cited document (Borgman, 1990). Similarly, most namespaces for publications are based on the publication as the basic unit—ISBN, LCCN, DOI, etc. As DOIs are assigned to articles, to data, and to individual tables and figures within articles, identification and retrieval are further complicated. Determining the "version of record" is ever more difficult in digital environments. The technological solution may be to reconcile "versions of the record" (Van de Sompel, 2013).

3.3 Provenance

Principles 4 and 5, on unique identification and access, and principle 8, on interoperability and flexibility, indicate the need for provenance information. Data citations can facilitate provenance, but may not be able to incorporate all the necessary content and context. Provenance is both more and less than metadata. It involves the origin and history of something, and documentation of the chain of evidence, custody, and relationships to other entities (Borgman, 2015; Buneman, Khanna, & Tan, 2001; Carata et al., 2014; Groth, Gil, Cheney, & Miles, 2012; Groth & Moreau, 2013).

Rarely can data be interpreted without provenance information such as research methods, protocols, and the software necessary to open a file or run the program. Data continue to change form and meaning as they are processed, mined, aggregated, and disaggregated. The farther that reusers are from the origins of data, whether in terms of time, theory, geography, domain, or other factors, the more reliant they may be on provenance documentation. Provenance records may provide the information necessary to interpret, trust, or determine the legal rights to reuse, repurpose, or combine datasets—the evidentiary chain. If data creators are to receive credit through citation, that credit must carry forward through subsequent reprocessing. Sustaining the provenance chain is a daunting technical challenge. Provenance chains will evolve over time as more relationships are accrued and as links break. Provenance may also pose the greatest theoretical challenge, as authors, readers, and later analysts encounter substantially different aggregations of objects over time (Pepe, Mayernik, Borgman, & Van de Sompel, 2010).

3.4 Releasing, Sharing, and Reusing Data

Authors cite evidence that is available to readers, so readers can evaluate that evidence. Thus, determining what data to cite is partly a function of what data are released and made publicly available. Little is understood about what data scholars choose to share or about how, when, and why they reuse data. Data sharing and reuse are topics ripe for research and theorizing (Borgman, 2012, 2015).

Theoretical questions persist about what objects scholars choose to cite in any given publication or about the meaning of individual citations, despite decades of empirical research and theoretical development (Cronin, 1981). Citation practices are more learned than taught. Publication manuals and "instructions to authors" in journals provide explicit instructions on how to cite sources in specific styles, but offer little guidance on what to cite. One commonality among data citation practice, data sharing, and reuse is that these are localized behaviors that are difficult to articulate.

Data sharing and reuse rest heavily on trust between the parties involved. Data repositories are intermediaries in the trust relationship between those who give data and those who receive. Data citation is one mechanism to document those relationships. Citing data already stored in repositories is the "low hanging fruit" for data citation, and a starting point for initiatives such as DataCite (DataCite, 2013). Unique and persistent identifiers, stable and persistent links between related digital objects, digital signatures that verify the integrity of digital objects, and similar mechanisms contribute to the trust fabric. No matter how sophisticated the technology, trust is based in the individuals and the social institutions involved (Blanchette, 2012).

The ability to share and reuse data rests on early decisions about how to describe and manage them. The earlier in the process that scholars document data in ways that make them reusable, the better they can represent them as citable objects. Data citation mechanisms can support these functions, although individual citations, per se, are unlikely to carry enough information to interpret data or to document provenance.

3.5 Credit

Assigning credit for data is even more problematic than is assigning credit for authoring publications. Contemporary authorship is negotiated with collaborators or determined by the policy of the parent organization. Policies of publishers and journals also may influence the designation of author or contributor roles. Notions of authorship credit appear to vary widely between domains, as Cronin has shown (Cronin, 1984, 1995, 1998, 2001, 2005, 2008; Davenport & Cronin, 2001). Policies at CERN, for example, are intended to provide authorship credit for early contributions to data collection, thus conflating credit for data and for publication (Mele, 2013). In space-based astronomy missions, decisions about what data to collect, how to collect them, and how to process them are made many years before researchers use those data in publications. Data papers and instrument papers are the means by which those involved early in the process get credit for their contributions. By the time those data are used by later astronomers, individuals responsible for creating the data may be invisible, anonymous, or departed (Borgman, 2015).

In smaller teams, authorship is negotiated, but credit for data is not usually part of the discussion. "Authorship" is not terminology that resonates with scholars when thinking about their data (Wallis, 2012; Wallis & Borgman, 2011). Data may not be released because the responsibility for data is so diffuse that no individual is empowered or motivated to do so. The larger the collaboration, the less familiarity the principal investigator (PI) may have with the specifics of the data collection, and the greater likelihood that the PI has the long-term responsibility for a diffuse organization. The students and post-doctoral fellows who have the most intimate knowledge of the data have the highest turnover rate as team members. The PI may be responsible for stewardship of the data, which deserves credit. Those who have the most intimate familiarity with the data possess tacit knowledge that is necessary for interpretation, which also deserves credit. Expertise, responsibility, and authorship are not equivalent with respect to data; it is unclear how credit should be allocated in each instance.

The workshop conducted by the National Academies and the CODATA-ICSTI Task Group sought input from many stakeholders about how to assign credit for data. While the starting assumption was that scholars cared the most about receiving credit for their data, it became clear over the two days of discussion that many other parties also wanted credit: funding agencies who supported the research; data repositories who acquire, curate, and release data; university research officers; and other data providers (Uhlir, 2012). Authors want credit for citations to their publications, as these are currency for hiring and advancement; thus, citing publications as surrogates for the data reported in them suits the interests of most authors. If datasets are cited instead of publications, authors may have disincentives for citing data. Researchers usually receive more credit for citations to peer-reviewed publications than for other activities such as teaching, editorial work, or service. Where citations to data, or to other non-peer-reviewed objects, fall on this credit spectrum is unknown, but it appears that any practice that risks diluting credit for publications may be viewed with suspicion.

3.6 Attribution of Sources

Attribution of the sources for data is equally problematic to credit. Agencies providing data commonly do so under licenses that constrain who can use the data, for what purposes, for how long, and with what attribution (Pearson, 2012). Researchers often place restrictions on the sharing and reuse of their data, whether by licensing or other means. They may require a specific citation to data. If they use Creative Commons licenses, they may specify whether the dataset (or other object) may be used only as a whole or whether in parts, for commercial or non-commercial purposes, and the form of attribution required (Creative Commons, 2013). While the desire for control is understandable, due to concerns for intellectual property, credit, and misuse or misinterpretation, attribution requirements complicate reuse considerably. Licensing also makes the process of combining and reusing data more complex, if attributions must be carried forward in provenance records (Guibault, 2013).

Due to these complications, many have argued for the open release of data without licensing restrictions, or for direct release into the public domain (Murray-Rust, Neylon, Pollock, & Wilbanks, 2010; Nielsen, 2011; Wilbanks, 2013). Releasing data openly without restrictions and without requiring credit or attribution certainly simplifies data sharing and reuse. However, it runs counter to the interests of most scholars. Documenting data for reuse often requires considerable investment of resources. Data can be assets to be controlled, protected, exchanged, and bartered for other resources, including academic posts (Borgman, 2015; Hilgartner & Brandt-Rauf, 1994; Latour, 1987; Latour & Woolgar, 1979). Credit and attribution may be insufficient rewards for scholars to relinquish those assets or to expose themselves to potential liabilities associated with reuse.

3.7 Discovery

While discovery is not mentioned explicitly in the data citation principles, it is implicit throughout. Describing data in sufficient detail to ensure unique identification, persistence, specificity, verifiability, and interoperability will improve their discovery. Discovery is a precondition for gaining access to the desired data or other objects (principle 5). Similar requirements apply in using bibliometrics to discover, locate, and retrieve publications (Cronin, 2014; Kousha & Thelwall, 2014). In principle 4, "machine actionability" implies that a citation should support machine discovery of data. Rather than a citation providing enough information to search the shelves of a library, it should have embedded links that allow direct access to the referenced object. Digital object identifiers (DOIs), in combination with technical standards such as OpenURL and publisher-led initiatives such as CrossRef, facilitate machine actionability from citations in online articles to cited articles. However, many such links, whether for publications or for data, lead to a landing page where a human can identify the object of interest. When the searcher is a computer, these discovery mechanisms fail (Van de Sompel, 2012). A goal for the next generation of search technologies, especially for data discovery, is to support machine actionable links for entire provenance chains (Bechhofer et al., 2010; CrossRef, 2009, 2014; Klein et al., 2014; Pepe et al., 2010; Sanderson & Van de Sompel, 2012; Simons, 2012; Van de Sompel, 2015; Van de Sompel, Hochstenbach, & Beit-Arie, 2000; Van de Sompel & Lagoze, 2009).

At present, most data discovery appears to be a fairly manual process. Individuals identify data of interest by reading papers or by searching repositories. Discovery can be improved by more extensive description of data, figures, tables, and other elements in publications. Such descriptions can be accommodated by open annotation systems that facilitate interoperability across systems, which includes synchronizing links to related resources (Ciccarese, Ocana, & Clark, 2012; Das et al., 2009; Foster & Moreau, 2006; Hunter, 2009; Van de Sompel et al., 2012). These approaches may be effective to the extent that document enrichment survives the publication process. Publishers tend to "flatten out" submitted documents by reducing them to portable document format (PDF), which is a proprietary standard, for ingest to their systems. In that process, they usually strip annotations, citation records stored in the document by bibliographic referencing tools, and other features that support machine actions. New platforms, unencumbered by legacy publishing systems, may enrich research objects in ways that support more robust discovery and more complex document structures.

Initiatives such as DataCite, Schema.org, and Object Reuse and Exchange are developing metadata schema for data. Search engines, which have largely ignored metadata and other forms of document enrichment, are implementing more structured methods. Provenance graphs are essential for data management at scale (DiLauro, 2013). Approaches that publish graphs of object relationships will aid both discovery and bibliometrics. Proprietary control of these graphs will hide those chains of evidence from other programs, users, and bibliometricians. To the extent that these metadata schema are adopted, and especially to the extent that graphs are open, they should aid in discovery of research data (DataCite, 2014; "Object Reuse and Exchange," 2014; Schema.org, 2012; World Wide Web Consortium (W3C), 2013). However, individual researchers tend to invest very little effort in providing metadata or other curatorial description to their data to make them usable for others. Labor and skill requirements to do so are high and incentives are low. Because digital data are far less self-describing than are textual objects such as publications, discovery depends heavily on metadata. Thus data citation is implicitly a means to improve the discovery of data (Borgman, 2015).

4 Discussion and Conclusion

Data are not equivalent to publications, hence data citation is not equivalent to bibliographic citation. However, theories of bibliographic citation are useful in thinking about what data citation is, or could be. The most fundamental distinction between bibliographic objects and data is the degree of independence. Bibliometrics—including scientometrics, informetrics, webometrics, altmetrics, and other variants—are used to model relationships between objects that can be treated as independent entities, whether web pages or tweets. Data, however, rarely can be interpreted as independent objects. Most are meaningless without links to contextual information, software, and related objects. The scope and identity of a dataset vary along multiple dimensions. Without agreements on what constitutes data in any given instance, it is difficult to count or compare the uses of those data. Empirical and theoretical work on what are data, how those data are used, how data are aggregated and disaggregated, and when and how they are cited as sources of evidence are avenues ripe for exploration at the intersection of scholarly communication and bibliometrics.

Blaise Cronin was among the first to call for a theory of citation behavior, as so little is understood about the purposes for which an object is cited (Cronin,

1981). Data citation exacerbates that theoretical challenge. References to articles are sometimes surrogates for citing the data within them. When data sets are accessible, those can be cited. Later authors who use those data may cite the dataset, a larger dataset or repository from which the data were drawn, articles in which the datasets were discussed, or some combination of these. Early efforts to classify the purposes for individual citations revealed that article citations are sometimes data citations (Lipetz, 1965; White, 1982). When data are cited, it is often not in the reference list, but buried in footnotes, URLs, or mentions in text. The difficulty of identifying citations to data is not new, but demands to standardize and promulgate data citation increase the urgency of addressing the problem.

Distinguishing between data citation and data use is another thorny theoretical challenge. The few studies on data reuse indicate that scientifically important uses of data may not be mentioned or cited in publications (Palmer, Weber, & Cragin, 2011; Wallis et al., 2013; Wynholds et al., 2012). The reasons for lack of citation are many. One is that data citation is not (yet) common scholarly practice. Another may be that many sources are used in research, but few are cited. Views, downloads, library reshelving statistics, and other measures of use tend not to correlate well with citations of those same items (Bollen, Van de Sompel, & Rodriguez, 2008; Haustein, 2014; Kousha & Thelwall, 2014; Thelwall, Haustein, Larivière, & Sugimoto, 2013). Again, it has long been known that reading, library use, and citation are different behaviors. How those differences translate to the use, reuse, and citing of data is unexplored territory.

Another opportunity for theory building in bibliometrics posed by data citation is the changing notion of authorship. While authorship was never a stable concept, as Blaise Cronin has shown (Cronin, 1981, 1995, 2001, 2003, 2005, 2008, 2013, 2014; Davenport & Cronin, 2000), practical concerns for credit and attribution have focused largely on the roles of individuals in scholarly communication. Some journals ask for precise descriptions of the contributions of each named author; e.g., writing, data collection, data analysis, instrumentation, and management (Committee on Publication Ethics, 2013; Harvard University and Wellcome Trust, 2012). The work associated with collecting, cleaning, analyzing, managing, and reporting data is essential to the conduct of scholarly research, but that work is not necessarily equivalent to authorship. How these roles should be credited in data citation, and how they should be weighted in contributions to scholarship are open questions. The labor associated with data management and software engineering tends to be lower in status than the scientific work that leads to peer-reviewed papers (Darch et al., 2015).

Lastly, the intersection of data citation and scholarly communication is an example of the uneasy fit between structure and process in scholarly communication. While research on process should inform research on structure, and vice versa, rarely do these approaches intersect (Lievrouw, 1990). Bibliometrics and their brethren address structural relationships in scholarly communication. The validity of these analyses rests on understanding the processes by which these structures arise and evolve. A better understanding of the processes associated with the creation, use, and reuse of data, should lead to the design of better data citation mechanisms.

Bibliometricians are in an ideal position to contribute to—and to learn from—the development of theory and practice in data citation. The caveat is in the title of this chapter. Bibliometrics, strictly speaking, are based on publications. Data are not publications, therefore data citation is something other than bibliometrics. However, data most certainly are objects exchanged in scholarly communication. Theoretical approaches to data citation must accommodate the ways in which data differ from publications. Data tend to be compound objects with unclear boundaries, whereas publications can be treated as independent objects with clear boundaries, at least for the purpose of bibliometrics. Data usually consist of multiple objects that are interdependent, with relationships that often are unstable and difficult to document. Theory and methods from bibliometrics, scientometrics, and webometrics can be used to study the characteristics of these relationships and how they evolve over time. The "catch-22" is that it will be difficult to model these relationships until units of data are sufficiently documented to be traceable. This is an opportune moment for those concerned with data, scholarly communication, knowledge infrastructures, and bibliometrics to explore common ground. Blaise Cronin has laid the foundation that allows this conversation to move forward.

Cited References

Agosti, M., & Ferro, N. (2007). A formal model of annotations of digital content. *ACM Transactions on Information Systems*, *26*(1). http://doi.org/10.1145/1292591.1292594

Ahn, C. P., Alexandroff, R., Allende Prieto, C., Anderson, S. F., Anderton, T., Andrews, B. H., ... Zinn, J. C. (2012). The Ninth Data Release of the Sloan Digital Sky Survey: First Spectroscopic Data from the SDSS-III Baryon Oscillation Spectroscopic Survey. *Astrophysical Journal*, *203*, 21. http://doi.org/10.1088/0067-0049/203/2/21

Almind, T. C., & Ingwersen, P. (1997). Informetric analyses on the world wide web: methodological approaches to "webometrics." *Journal of Documentation*, *53*(4), 404–426. http://doi.org/10.1108/EUM0000000007205

Atkins, D. E., Droegemeier, K. K., Feldman, S. I., Garcia-Molina, H., Klein, M. L., Messina, P., ... Wright, M. H. (2003). *Revolutionizing Science and Engineering through Cyberinfrastructure: Report of the National Science Foundation Blue-Ribbon panel on Cyberinfrastructure.*

Washington, DC: National Science Foundation. Retrieved from http://www.nsf.gov/cise/sci/reports/atkins.pdf

Bechhofer, S., De Roure, D., Gamble, M., Goble, C., & Buchan, I. (2010). Research Objects: Towards Exchange and Reuse of Digital Knowledge. *Nature Precedings*. http://doi.org/10.1038/npre.2010.4626.1

Blair, A. M. (2010). *Too Much to Know: Managing Scholarly Information before the Modern Age*. New Haven, CT: Yale University Press.

Blanchette, J.-F. (2012). *Burdens of Proof: Cryptographic Culture and Evidence Law in the Age of Electronic Documents*. Cambridge, MA: The MIT Press.

Bollen, J., Van de Sompel, H., & Rodriguez, M. A. (2008). Towards Usage-based Impact Metrics: First Results from the MESUR Project. In *JCDL '08: Proceedings of the 8th ACM/IEEE-CS Joint Conference on Digital Libraries* (pp. 231–240). Pittsburgh, PA: Association for Computing Machinery.

Borgman, C. L. (1990). Editor's introduction. In *Scholarly Communication and Bibliometrics* (pp. 10–27). Newbury Park, CA: Sage.

Borgman, C. L. (2000a). *From Gutenberg to the Global Information Infrastructure: Access to Information in the Networked World*. Cambridge, MA: MIT Press.

Borgman, C. L. (2000b). Scholarly communication and bibliometrics revisited. In *The Web of Knowledge: A Festschrift in Honor of Eugene Garfield* (pp. 143–162). Medford, NJ: Information Today.

Borgman, C. L. (2007). *Scholarship in the Digital Age: Information, Infrastructure, and the Internet*. Cambridge, MA: MIT Press.

Borgman, C. L. (2012). The conundrum of sharing research data. *Journal of the American Society for Information Science and Technology*, *63*(6), 1059–1078. http://doi.org/10.1002/asi.22634

Borgman, C. L. (2015). *Big Data, Little Data, No Data: Scholarship in the Networked World*. Cambridge MA: MIT Press.

Borgman, C. L., & Furner, J. (2002). Scholarly communication and bibliometrics. In *Annual Review of Information Science and Technology* (Vol. 36, pp. 3–72).

Borgman, C. L., Wallis, J. C., & Mayernik, M. S. (2012). Who's Got the Data? Interdependencies in Science and Technology Collaborations. *Computer Supported Cooperative Work*, *21*(6), 485–523. http://doi.org/10.1007/s10606-012-9169-z

Boulton, G., Campbell, P., Collins, B., Elias, P., Hall, W., Laurie, G., ... Walport, M. (2012). *Science as an Open Enterprise*. The Royal Society. Retrieved from http://royalsociety.org/policy/projects/science-public-enterprise/report/

Bourne, P. E., Clark, T., Dale, R., de Waard, A., Hovy, E. H., & Shotton, D. (Eds.). (2011). Force 11 Manifesto: Improving Future Research Communication and e-Scholarship. Retrieved from http://www.force11.org/white_paper

Bowker, G. C. (2005). *Memory Practices in the Sciences*. Cambridge, MA: MIT Press.

Buckland, M. K. (1991). Information as thing. *Journal of the American Society for Information Science*, *42*, 351–360.

Buneman, P., Khanna, S., & Tan, W.-C. (2001). Why and Where: A Characterization of Data Provenance. In J. V. den Bussche & V. Vianu (Eds.), *Database Theory—ICDT 2001* (Vol. 1973, pp. 316–330). Berlin: Springer.

Carata, L., Akoush, S., Balakrishnan, N., Bytheway, T., Sohan, R., Selter, M., & Hopper, A. (2014). A primer on provenance. *Communications of the ACM*, *57*(5), 52–60. http://doi.org/10.1145/2596628

Case, D. O. (2002). *Looking for Information: A Survey of Research on Information Seeking, Needs, and Behavior*. San Diego: Academic Press.

Case, D. O. (2012). *Looking for Information: a survey of research on information seeking, needs and behavior* (3rd ed.). Bingley, UK: Emerald Group Publishing.

Ciccarese, P., Ocana, M., & Clark, T. (2012). Open semantic annotation of scientific publications using DOMEO. *Journal of Biomedical Semantics, 3*(Suppl. 1), S1. http://doi.org/10.1186/2041-1480-3-S1-S1

CODATA-ICSTI Task Group on Data Citation Standards and Practices. (2013). Out of Cite, Out of Mind: The Current State of Practice, Policy, and Technology for the Citation of Data. *Data Science Journal, 12*, 1–75. http://doi.org/10.2481/dsj.OSOM13-043

Committee on Publication Ethics. (2013). [Home page]. Retrieved September 9, 2013, from http://publicationethics.org/

Creative Commons. (2013). Creative Commons License Choices. Retrieved October 2, 2013, from http://creativecommons.org/choose/

Cronin, B. (1981). The need for a theory of citing. *Journal of Documentation, 37*(1), 16–24. http://doi.org/10.1108/eb026703

Cronin, B. (1984). *The Citation Process: The Role and Significance of Citations in Scientific Communication*. London: Taylor Graham. Retrieved from http://garfield.library.upenn.edu/cronin/citationprocess.pdf

Cronin, B. (1995). *The scholar's courtesy: The role of acknowledgement in the primary communication process*. London: Taylor Graham. London: Taylor Graham.

Cronin, B. (1998). Metatheorizing citation. *Scientometrics, 43*(1), 45–55. http://doi.org/10.1007/BF02458393

Cronin, B. (2001). Hyperauthorship: A postmodern perversion or evidence of a structural shift in scholarly communication practices? *Journal of the American Society for Information Science and Technology, 52*(7), 558–569. http://doi.org/10.1002/asi.1097

Cronin, B. (2003). Scholarly communication and epistemic cultures. In *Scholarly Tribes and Tribulations: How Tradition and Technology are Driving Disciplinary Change*. Washington, DC: Association of Research Libraries. Retrieved from http://www.arl.org/scomm/disciplines/Cronin.pdf

Cronin, B. (2005). *The Hand of Science: Academic Writing and its Rewards*. Lanham, MD: Scarecrow Press.

Cronin, B. (2008). Toward a Rhopography of Scholarly Communication. *Studia Humaniora Ouluensis*.

Cronin, B. (2013). Self-plagiarism: An odious oxymoron. *Journal of the American Society for Information Science and Technology, 64*(5), 873–873. http://doi.org/10.1002/asi.22966

Cronin, B. (2014). Scholars and scripts, spoors and scores. In B. Cronin & C. R. Sugimoto (Eds.), *Beyond Bibliometrics: Metrics-Based Evaluation of Research* (pp. 3–21). Cambridge, MA: MIT Press.

Cronin, B., & Sugimoto, C. R. (2014a). *Beyond Bibliometrics: Metrics-Based Evaluation of Research*. Cambridge, MA: MIT Press.

Cronin, B., & Sugimoto, C. R. (Eds.). (2014b). *Scholarly Metrics Under the Microscope: Citation Analysis and Academic Auditing*. Medford, NJ: Information Today.

Crosas, M., Carpenter, T., Shotton, D., & Borgman, C. L. (2013). Amsterdam Manifesto on Data Citation Principles. Presented at the Force11: Beyond the PDF 2 Conference, Amsterdam. Retrieved from https://www.force11.org/AmsterdamManifesto

CrossRef. (2009). *The Formation of CrossRef: A Short History*. CrossRef. Retrieved from http://www.crossref.org/01company/02history.html
CrossRef. (2013). FundRef. Retrieved September 30, 2013, from http://www.crossref.org/fundref/
CrossRef. (2014). Home page. Retrieved May 26, 2014, from http://www.crossref.org/
Darch, P. T., Borgman, C. L., Traweek, S., Cummings, R. L., Wallis, J. C., & Sands, A. E. (2015). What lies beneath?: Knowledge infrastructures in the subseafloor biosphere and beyond. *International Journal on Digital Libraries*, 1–17. http://doi.org/10.1007/s00799-015-0137-3
Das, S., Girard, L., Green, T., Weitzman, L., Lewis-Bowen, A., & Clark, T. (2009). Building biomedical web communities using a semantically aware content management system. *Briefings in Bioinformatics*, *10*(2), 129–138. http://doi.org/10.1093/bib/bbn052
Daston, L. J. (1988). The Factual Sensibility. *Isis*, *79*(3), 452–467. http://doi.org/10.2307/234675
Datacitation Synthesis Group. (2014). Joint Declaration on Data Citation Principles - Final. Retrieved February 12, 2014, from http://www.force11.org/datacitation
DataCite. (2013). [Home page]. Retrieved September 10, 2013, from http://www.datacite.org/
DataCite. (2014). DataCite Schemas repository. Retrieved February 12, 2014, from http://schema.datacite.org/meta/kernel-3/index.html
Davenport, E., & Cronin, B. (2000). The citation network as a prototype for representing trust in virtual environments. In *The Web of Knowledge: A Festschrift in Honor of Eugene Garfield* (pp. 517–534). Medford, NJ: Information Today.
Davenport, E., & Cronin, B. (2001). Who dunnit? Metatags and hyperauthorship. *Journal of the American Society for Information Science and Technology*, *52*(9), 770–773. http://doi.org/10.1002/asi.1123
Declaration on Research Assessment. (2013). [Home page]. Retrieved May 24, 2013, from http://am.ascb.org/dora/
DiLauro, T. (2013). *Research data management experience at Johns Hopkins University Sheridan Libraries*. Retrieved from https://docs.google.com/file/d/0B1X7I2IVBtwzVTgxczJzVUFMMnM/edit
Edwards, P. N., Jackson, S. J., Chalmers, M. K., Bowker, G. C., Borgman, C. L., Ribes, D., ... Calvert, S. (2013). *Knowledge Infrastructures: Intellectual Frameworks and Research Challenges*. Ann Arbor: University of Michigan. Retrieved from http://deepblue.lib.umich.edu/handle/2027.42/97552
Fecher, B., Friesike, S., & Hebing, M. (2015). What Drives Academic Data Sharing? *PLoS ONE*, *10*(2), e0118053. http://doi.org/10.1371/journal.pone.0118053
Force11. (2015). Home page. Retrieved August 6, 2014, from https://www.force11.org/about
Foster, I., & Moreau, L. (2006). *Provenance and Annotation of Data*. Heidelberg: Springer Retrieved from http://www.w3.org/2011/prov/wiki/Connection_Task_Force_Informal_Report
Furner, J. (2010). Philosophy and information studies. *Annual Review of Information Science and Technology*, *44*(1), 159–200. http://doi.org/10.1002/aris.2010.1440440111
Furner, J. (2014). The ethics of evaluative bibliometrics. In B. Cronin & C. R. Sugimoto (Eds.), *Beyond Bibliometrics: Metrics-Based Evaluation of Research* (pp. 85–107). Cambridge, MA: MIT Press.
Groth, P., Gil, Y., Cheney, J., & Miles, S. (2012). Requirements for Provenance on the Web. *International Journal of Digital Curation*, *7*(1), 39–56. http://doi.org/10.2218/ijdc.v7i1.213
Groth, P., & Moreau, L. (2013). PROV-Overview. Retrieved April 14, 2014, from http://www.w3.org/TR/2013/NOTE-prov-overview-20130430/

Guibault, L. (2013). Licensing research data under open access conditions. In D. Beldiman (Ed.), *Information and Knowledge: 21st Century Challenges in Intellectual Property and Knowledge Governance*. Cheltenham: Edward Elgar.

Harvard University and Wellcome Trust. (2012). *International Workshop on Contributorship and Scholarly Attribution*. Retrieved from http://projects.iq.harvard.edu/files/attribution_workshop/files/iwcsa_report_final_18sept12.pdf

Haustein, S. (2014). Readership metrics. In B. Cronin & C. R. Sugimoto (Eds.), *Beyond Bibliometrics: Metrics-Based Evaluation of Research* (pp. 327–344). Cambridge, MA: MIT Press.

Hey, T., & Trefethen, A. (2005). Cyberinfrastructure and e-Science. *Science, 308*, 818–821. http://doi.org/10.1126/science.1110410

Hilgartner, S., & Brandt-Rauf, S. I. (1994). Data access, ownership and control: Toward empirical studies of access practices. *Knowledge, 15*, 355–372.

Hunter, J. (2009). Collaborative semantic tagging and annotation systems. In B. Cronin (Ed.), *Annual Review of Information Science and Technology* (Vol. 43, pp. 187–239).

International Council for Scientific and Technical Information. (2015). Retrieved February 17, 2015, from http://www.icsti.org/

Kelty, C. M. (2008). *Two Bits: the Cultural Significance of Free Software*. Durham, NC: Duke University Press.

Klein, M., & Nelson, M. L. (2010). Evaluating methods to rediscover missing web pages from the web infrastructure (p. 59). ACM Press. http://doi.org/10.1145/1816123.1816133

Klein, M., Van de Sompel, H., Sanderson, R., Shankar, H., Balakireva, L., Zhou, K., & Tobin, R. (2014). Scholarly Context Not Found: One in Five Articles Suffers from Reference Rot. *PLoS ONE, 9*(12), e115253. http://doi.org/10.1371/journal.pone.0115253

Kousha, K., & Thelwall, M. (2014). Web impact metrics for research assessment. In B. Cronin & C. R. Sugimoto (Eds.), *Beyond Bibliometrics: Metrics-Based Evaluation of Research* (pp. 289–306). Cambridge, MA: MIT Press.

Kratz, J. E., & Strasser, C. (2015). Researcher Perspectives on Publication and Peer Review of Data. *PLoS ONE, 10*(2), e0117619. http://doi.org/10.1371/journal.pone.0117619

Latour, B. (1987). *Science in Action: How to Follow Scientists and Engineers through Society*. Cambridge, MA: Harvard University Press.

Latour, B. (1988). Drawing things together. In M. E. Lynch & S. Woolgar (Eds.), *Representation in Scientific Practice* (pp. 19–68). Cambridge, MA: MIT Press.

Latour, B. (1993). *We Have Never Been Modern*. Cambridge, MA: Harvard University Press.

Latour, B., & Woolgar, S. (1979). *Laboratory life: The Construction of Scientific Facts*. Beverly Hills, CA: Sage.

Lide, D. R., & Wood, G. H. (2012). *CODATA @ 45 Years: 1966 to 2010*. Paris: CODATA. Retrieved from http://www.codata.org/about/CODATA@45years.pdf

Lievrouw, L. A. (1990). Reconciling structure and process in the study of scholarly communication. In *Scholarly Communication and Bibliometrics* (pp. 59–69). Newbury Park, CA: Sage.

Lipetz, B.-A. (1965). Improvement of the Selectivity of Citation Indexes to Science Literature through Inclusion of Citation Relationship Indicators. *American Documentation, 16*(2), 81–90.

Mele, S. (2013, May 23). Higgs Boson discovery at CERN: Physics and Publishing. Retrieved September 7, 2013, from http://www.oii.ox.ac.uk/events/?id=598

Murray-Rust, P., Neylon, C., Pollock, R., & Wilbanks, J. (2010). Panton Principles. Retrieved August 30, 2013, from http://pantonprinciples.org/

National Science Board. (2005). *Long-Lived Digital Data Collections*. Retrieved from http://www.nsf.gov/pubs/2005/nsb0540/

Nielsen, M. (2011). *Reinventing Discovery: The New Era of Networked Science*. Princeton, NJ: Princeton University Press.

Object Reuse and Exchange. (2014). Retrieved from http://www.openarchives.org/ore/

Open Knowledge Foundation. (2013). Retrieved July 22, 2013, from http://okfn.org/

Palmer, C. L., Weber, N. M., & Cragin, M. H. (2011). The analytic potential of scientific data: Understanding re-use value. *Proceedings of the American Society for Information Science and Technology, 48*(1), 1–10. http://doi.org/10.1002/meet.2011.14504801174

Parsons, M. A., & Fox, P. A. (2013). Is data publication the right metaphor? *Data Science Journal, 12*, WDS32–WDS46. http://doi.org/10.2481/dsj.WDS-042

Pearson, S. H. (2012). Three legal mechanisms for sharing data. In P. F. Uhlir (Ed.), *For Attribution—Developing Data Attribution and Citation Practices and Standards: Summary of an International Workshop* (pp. 71–76). Washington, DC: National Academies Press. Retrieved from http://www.nap.edu/openbook.php?record_id=13564&page=71

Pepe, A., Goodman, A., Muench, A., Crosas, M., & Erdmann, C. (2014). How Do Astronomers Share Data? Reliability and Persistence of Datasets Linked in AAS Publications and a Qualitative Study of Data Practices among US Astronomers. *PLoS ONE, 9*(8), e104798. http://doi.org/10.1371/journal.pone.0104798

Pepe, A., Mayernik, M. S., Borgman, C. L., & Van de Sompel, H. (2010). From artifacts to aggregations: Modeling scientific life cycles on the semantic web. *Journal of the American Society for Information Science and Technology, 61*, 567–582. http://doi.org/10.1002/asi.21263

Poovey, M. (1998). *A History of the Modern Fact: Problems of Knowledge in the Sciences of Wealth and Society*. Chicago: University of Chicago Press.

Porter, T. M. (1995). *Trust in Numbers: The Pursuit of Objectivity in Science and Public Life*. Princeton, NJ: Princeton University Press.

Pritchard, A. (1969). Statistical Bibliography or Bibliometrics. *Journal of Documentation, 25*(4), 348–9.

Rafols, I., de Rijcke, S., & Wouters, P. (2014). The Leiden Manifesto in the making. Retrieved October 30, 2014, from http://www.cwts.nl/News/

Raisig, L. M. (1962). Statistical Bibliography in the Health Sciences. *Bulletin of the Medical Library Association, 50*(3), 450–461. Retrieved from http://www.ncbi.nlm.nih.gov/pmc/articles/PMC197860/

Renear, A. H., & Dubin, D. (2003). Towards identity conditions for digital documents. In *Proceedings of the 2003 international conference on Dublin Core and metadata applications: supporting communities of discourse and practice*. Seattle, Washington: Dublin Core Metadata Initiative.

Renear, A. H., Sacchi, S., & Wickett, K. M. (2010). Definitions of dataset in the scientific and technical literature. In *Proceedings of the 73rd ASIS&T Annual Meeting on Navigating Streams in an Information Ecosystem* (Vol. 47, pp. 1–4). Medford, NJ: Information Today. http://doi.org/10.1002/meet.14504701240

Research Object for Scholarly Communication Community Group. (2014). Retrieved August 6, 2014, from http://www.w3.org/community/rosc/

Rosenberg, D. (2013). Data before the fact. In L. Gitelman (Ed.), *"Raw Data" is an Oxymoron* (pp. 15–40). Cambridge, MA: MIT Press.

Sanderson, R., & Van de Sompel, H. (2012). Cool URIs and dynamic data. *IEEE Internet Computing*, *16*(4), 76–79. http://doi.org/10.1109/MIC.2012.78

Schema.org. (2012). Describing Datasets with schema.org. Retrieved August 19, 2013, from http://blog.schema.org/2012/07/describing-datasets-with-schemaorg.html

Simons, N. (2012). Implementing DOIs for research data. *D-Lib Magazine*, *18*(5/6). http://doi.org/10.1045/may2012-simons

Suber, P. (2012). *Open Access*. Cambridge, MA: MIT Press.

Thelwall, M., Haustein, S., Larivière, V., & Sugimoto, C. R. (2013). Do Altmetrics Work? Twitter and Ten Other Social Web Services. *PLoS ONE*, *8*(5), e64841. http://doi.org/10.1371/journal.pone.0064841

Thelwall, M., Vaughan, L., & Bjorneborn, L. (2005). Webometrics. In *Annual Review of Information Science and Technology* (Vol. 39, pp. 81–135).

Uhlir, P. F. (Ed.). (2012). *For Attribution—Developing Data Attribution and Citation Practices and Standards: Summary of an International Workshop*. Washington, DC: National Academies Press.

Van de Sompel, H. (2012). The Web-Based Scholarly Record: Identification, Persistence, Actionability. *Libraries in the Digital Age (LIDA) Proceedings*, *12*(0). Retrieved from http://ozk.unizd.hr/proceedings/index.php/lida2012/article/view/60

Van de Sompel, H. (2013, April). *From the Version of Record to a Version of the Record*. Presented at the Coalition for Networked Information. Retrieved from http://www.youtube.com/watch?v=fhrGS-QbNVA&feature=youtube_gdata_player

Van de Sompel, H. (2015). hiberlink. Retrieved February 17, 2015, from http://hiberlink.org/

Van de Sompel, H., Hochstenbach, P., & Beit-Arie, O. (2000). OpenURL Syntax Description. Retrieved from http://www.exlibrisgroup.com/sfx_openurl_syntax.htm

Van de Sompel, H., & Lagoze, C. (2009). All Aboard: Toward a Machine-Friendly Scholarly Communication System. In T. Hey, S. Tansley, & K. Tolle (Eds.), *The Fourth Paradigm: Data-Intensive Scientific Discovery* (pp. 1–8).

Van de Sompel, H., Nelson, M. L., & Sanderson, R. (2013). HTTP framework for time-based access to resource states – Memento draft-vandesompel-memento-09. Retrieved September 30, 2013, from https://datatracker.ietf.org/doc/draft-vandesompel-memento/

Van de Sompel, H., Sanderson, R., Klein, M., Nelson, M. L., Haslhofer, B., Warner, S., & Lagoze, C. (2012). A perspective on resource synchronization. *D-Lib Magazine*, *18*(9/10). http://doi.org/10.1045/september2012-vandesompel

Wallis, J. C. (2012). *The Distribution of Data Management Responsibility within Scientific Research Groups* (PhD Dissertation). University of California, Los Angeles, Los Angeles, CA. Retrieved from http://escholarship.org/uc/item/46d896fm

Wallis, J. C., & Borgman, C. L. (2011). Who is responsible for data? An exploratory study of data authorship, ownership, and responsibility. *Proceedings of the American Society for Information Science and Technology*, *48*(1), 1–10. http://doi.org/10.1002/meet.2011.14504801188

Wallis, J. C., Rolando, E., & Borgman, C. L. (2013). If we share data, will anyone use them? data sharing and reuse in the long tail of science and technology. *PLoS ONE*, *8*(7), e67332. http://doi.org/10.1371/journal.pone.0067332

White, H. D. (1982). Citation analysis of data file use. *Library Trends*, *30*(2), 467–478. Retrieved from https://www.ideals.illinois.edu/handle/2142/7222

Wilbanks, J. (2013). Licence restrictions: A fool's errand. *Nature*, *495*(7442), 440–441. http://doi.org/10.1038/495440a

Wood, J., Andersson, T., Bachem, A., Best, C., Genova, F., Lopez, D. R., ... Hudson, R. L. (2010). *Riding the wave: How Europe can gain from the rising tide of scientific data*. Final report of the High Level Expert Group on Scientific Data. Retrieved from http://cordis.europa.eu/fp7/ict/e-infrastructure/docs/hlg-sdi-report.pdf

World Wide Web Consortium (W3C). (2013). WebSchemas/Datasets. Retrieved February 15, 2014, from http://www.w3.org/wiki/WebSchemas/Datasets

Wynholds, L. A., Wallis, J. C., Borgman, C. L., Sands, A. E., & Traweek, S. (2012). Data, data use, and scientific inquiry: two case studies of data practices. In *Proceedings of the 12th ACM/IEEE-CS joint conference on Digital Libraries* (pp. 19–22). New York: ACM. http://doi.org/10.1145/2232817.2232822

Zotero. (2015). Zotero Style Repository. Retrieved August 6, 2014, from https://www.zotero.org/styles

Part III: **Statistical theories**

Jonathan Furner
Type–Token Theory and Bibliometrics

1 Introduction

The terms "type" and "token" were introduced by the American pragmatist philosopher Charles Sanders Peirce (1839–1914) in 1906 (Peirce, 1906, pp. 505–506). Peirce's distinction has proven useful in various fields as a model of the supposedly pervasive relationship between repeatable, instantiable, abstract objects (such as the single word "the") and their concrete instances (such as the numerous individual occurrences of that word). While the importance of probability theory for quantitative analyses of people's document-handling activities—analyses, for example, of the productivity of authors, or the citedness of publications—has long been recognized, the common understanding that the probability distributions of values of bibliometric variables may be treated as distributions of sets of tokens over sets of types (i.e., publications over authors, or citations over publications) is a more recent phenomenon, dating back only to the 1980s. The goal of this paper is to examine critically the assumption that the application of type–token theory to bibliometrics is warranted.

In the second section, the metaphysical foundations of type–token theory are reviewed, and a distinction is made between two different, though possibly complementary understandings of the type–token relationship: one in which this relationship is conceived as roughly equivalent to that between kinds and individuals, and another in which occurrences are identified as forming a third category that consists of neither types nor tokens.

In the third section, the history is traced of attempts to apply type–token theory in empirical studies of language use (in the field of quantitative linguistics) and document use (in the field of quantitative bibliography, i.e., bibliometrics). This section begins with an overview of some of the assumptions made and notation used in the description of probability distributions in general, and power-law distributions in particular. The discovery (and regular rediscovery) of a power-law regularity in the distribution of word-tokens over word-types—usually known as Zipf's law of word frequency—is highlighted as one of the most important catalysts for the development of bibliometrics as a scientific endeavor.

Lastly, in the final section, the utility and impact of the application of type–token theory to bibliometrics is assessed, and the prospects for future developments evaluated. An analogy is drawn between the type–token distinction and a work–item distinction that is commonly made in the field of library cataloging.

The conclusion is reached that, while the importance of the type–token distinction for bibliometrics has at times been overplayed, a few opportunities for broadening the scope of type–token bibliometrics remain under-explored, not least in the analysis of the structure of large collections of bibliographic records.

2 Types and Tokens in Metaphysics

"The world is everything that is the case." How many words? Eight, if we're counting word-*tokens*; six, if we're counting word-*types*, since two of those word-types—"the" and "is"—occur twice. Each word-token stands for, signifies, represents, and denotes a particular word-type—viz., the type whose essential formal features are shared by the token. Tokens are said to instantiate types; they exemplify, embody, manifest, fall under, belong to types; they're occurrences, instances, members of types. Tokens are treated as individuals, singles, particulars, substances, objects; they're concrete, real, material. Types, on the other hand, are like sorts, kinds, forms, properties, classes, sets, universals; they're said to be abstract, ideal, immaterial.

The relationship between types and tokens is sometimes characterized as ontologically fundamental, in that the two categories are among those that comprise the basic elements of reality.[1] How is the type–token relationship precisely to be distinguished from other dichotomies said to be ontologically fundamental, such as the kind–individual relationship? The goal of this first section is to suggest one way in which types and tokens may be distinguished from properties and substances, kinds and individuals, abstracta and concreta, and universals and particulars. We begin by describing each of these dichotomies in turn.

2.1 Properties and substances

Some metaphysicians describe a world comprised of properties and substances. Typically, a thing X is said to be a *property* iff[2] there is something Y such that X is predicable of (i.e., is attributable to, is characteristic of) Y; X is a *substance* iff there is something Y such that Y is predicable of X. A few examples of properties

---

[1] See Wetzel (2006, 2009) for comprehensive overviews of philosophical approaches to the study of concepts of type and token.
[2] i.e., if and only if.

are redness, wisdom, and meaningfulness; those things that are red, wise, meaningful, etc. (i.e., that "have the property of" being red, wise, meaningful, etc.) are substances.

2.2 Kinds and individuals

Some metaphysicians describe a world comprised of kinds (a.k.a. categories, classes, sorts) and individuals. A thing X is a *kind* "iff there is something Y such that Y is an instance of X and Y is distinct from X"; while X is an *individual* "iff X is an instance of something Y (other than itself) and X itself has no instances (other than itself)" (Lowe, 1983, pp. 50–51). For example, the mountain kind is instantiated by individual mountains, the artifact kind by individual artifacts, the kind kind by individual kinds, and so on.

For any kind X—the mountain kind, the artifact kind, the kind kind, or any other kind—we may ask: What are the individually necessary and jointly sufficient *identity conditions* for instances of that kind? To put it this way is actually to conflate two separate questions:[3]

1. What properties individuate (i.e., serve to distinguish) all instances of that kind from all instances *of a different kind*? For example: On what criteria are mountains to be distinguished from non-mountains? Among the properties that have been suggested as such criteria are high elevation, high relative relief, steep slope gradient, large land volume, small summit area, and short inter-valley distance.[4]
2. What properties individuate any instance of that kind from any other instance *of the same kind*? For example: On what criteria is any one mountain to be distinguished from any other mountain (assuming we have already identified both as instantiations of the mountain kind)? The single property that is most commonly suggested as such a criterion is that of each instance's precise spatio-temporal coordinates (i.e., being located in a specific spatio-temporal position).

---

[3] Some authors make a distinction between *individuation conditions* (addressed by the first question) and identity conditions (addressed by the second question).
[4] See, e.g., Gerrard (1990, pp. 3–5); for the limitations of this approach, however, see Smith and Mark (2003).

2.3 Abstracta and concreta

Some metaphysicians describe a world comprised of *abstracta* (a.k.a. abstract objects) and *concreta* (a.k.a. concrete objects). Treating concreta as a kind—i.e., the concretum kind—we may ask: What are the individually necessary and jointly sufficient identity conditions for instances of that kind? Among the properties that are commonly said to distinguish instances of the concretum kind *from instances of other kinds* are the following: (a) *materiality*: i.e., being constituted by matter; (b) *spatio-temporality*: i.e., occupying space and persisting through time; (c) *causal efficacy*: i.e., having the capacity to enter into causal relationships; (d) *endurability*: i.e., having the capacity to undergo and survive change; and (e) *physical form*: i.e., having size, shape, and color. The single property that is most commonly said to distinguish individual concreta *from one another* is—as in the case of individuals—the precise *spatio-temporal coordinates* of each concretum.

2.4 Universals and particulars

It is no trivial matter to determine the precise nature of the relationships between the property–substance distinction, the kind–individual distinction, and the abstractum–concretum distinction. Are any two of these six purportedly fundamental categories identical? For example, are the categories of kinds and properties equivalent, such that X is a kind iff X is a property? At first, it might seem as if this situation would only be complicated further if we were to allow an additional distinction to be made between *universals* and *particulars*. It is rare, however, for the universal–particular distinction to be characterized in a uniquely different way from all others. Some metaphysicians define universals in the same way as they do properties, and particulars in the same way as substances; others define universals in the same way as they do kinds, and particulars in the same way as individuals. An anonymous contributor to a standard dictionary of philosophy takes the former approach, for example;[5] while Jonathan Lowe (2006) is one who takes the latter route, constructing a "four-category ontology" in which substantial universals (e.g., the mountain kind) are instantiated by substantial particulars (e.g., individual mountains), and non-substantial universals (e.g., redness) are instantiated by non-substantial particulars (e.g., the redness of my shirt).

---

5 "Things are particulars and their qualities are universals. So a universal is the property predicated of all the individuals of a certain sort or class. Redness is a universal, predicated of all red objects." (Flew 1979, p. 334).

2.5 Types and tokens

Again, adding the *type–token* distinction to the mix might appear to complicate the situation even further. Is the type kind identical to the property kind, the kind kind, the abstractum kind, and/or the universal kind? And is the token kind identical to the substance kind, the individual kind, the concretum kind, and/or the particular kind? To address these questions, it is instructive to turn to the originator of the type–token distinction in the form in which it has been understood since the early twentieth century.

Writing in 1906, Peirce introduced the terms *type, token, tone,* and *instance,* defining them in the following way:

> A common mode of estimating the amount of matter in a MS. or printed book is to count the number of words.[6] There will ordinarily be about twenty *the*s on a page, and of course they count as twenty words. In another sense of the word 'word,' however, there is but one word 'the' in the English language; and it is impossible that this word should lie visibly on a page or be heard in any voice, for the reason that it is not a Single thing or Single event. It does not exist; it only determines things that do exist. Such a definitely significant Form, I propose to term a *Type*. A Single event which happens once and whose identity is limited to that one happening or a Single object or thing which is in some single place at any one instant of time, such event or thing being significant only as occurring just when and where it does, such as this or that word on a single line of a single page of a single copy of a book, I will venture to call a *Token*. An indefinite significant character such as a tone of voice can neither be called a Type nor a Token. I propose to call such a Sign a *Tone*. In order that a Type may be used, it has to be embodied in a Token which shall be a sign of the Type, and thereby of the object the Type signifies. I propose to call such a Token of a Type an *Instance* of the Type. Thus, there may be twenty Instances of the Type 'the' on a page.
>
> (Peirce, 1906, pp. 505–506; emphases in original)

As might be expected, Peirce draws his examples of types and tokens from the domain of *semeiotic*, his theory of signs. Presentations of the concept of *sign,* frequently varying in some large or small respect, abound in his papers; but one recurrent idea is a model relating entities of three kinds—*objects, representamina,* and *interpretants*. A representamen is a sign standing for some object; and an interpretant is a separate sign, for the same object, that is created "in the mind of a person" by a representamen (Peirce, 1897/1932, p. 228). "Representamen," "interpretant," and "object" may be understood as corresponding loosely to "symbol" (or "term," "signal"), "thought" (or "concept," "sense"), and "referent," respectively, in later formulations of semiotic triangles by others.[7]

---

6 Peirce's footnote in the original: "Dr. Edward Eggleston originated the method."
7 See Cronin (2000) for discussion of a bibliometric application of Peirce's sign triad.

For Peirce, each word "on a single line of a single page of a single copy of a book" is a "Single" object. All "Single" (i.e., individual) objects or events are to be known as *tokens*; *types* are "definitely significant Form[s]" that "determine" (or are "embodied" by) tokens; and the type that a token embodies is the type of which that token is said to be an *instance*.[8] Both token and type are said to "signify": A token is a sign both of the type of which it is an instance, and of the "object" signified by the type. It may be tempting to infer from this that "token" and "type" should be understood merely as synonyms for "representamen" and "interpretant," respectively. Such a reading is undermined by at least two factors, however.

One relatively insignificant objection is that "object" seems to be used in at least two different ways in the quoted passage—to refer both to the kind of thing that a token is, and to the kind of thing that is signified by both token and type—whereas it is not the primary function of representamina to stand for themselves.

The second difficulty is more important to address. Peirce talks of "twenty Instances of the Type 'the' on a page," and of the multiple occurrences of words "on ... a single page of a single copy of a book." But he does not clarify how we should count the words on the pages of multiple copies of the same book. For example: Suppose we have two copies of the same page from the same book, each copy showing twenty instances of "the." Do we have forty instances of "the" in total, or still only twenty?[9]

The source of this difficulty is that there is a difference between instantiation-by-tokenization and instantiation-by-occurrence. In the case of the two copies of the same page from the same book, for example, we may count twenty tokens of the type "the," while simultaneously counting forty occurrences. The type–occurrence relationship would appear to correspond to the kind–individual relationship discussed earlier; the type–token relationship, on the other hand, is something new. To reduce ambiguity, then, "token" should be used as a name for the products of events of only one of these two kinds of instantiation, not both.

It would appear that Peirce's type–token distinction is orthogonal, rather than equivalent, to his representamen–interpretant distinction. In the quoted passage, the focus is on representamina, and on simple linguistic symbols in particular: strictly speaking, the definitions given are of "*word*-type" and "*word*-token." We should be alert to the possibility of the type–token distinction's applying not only to words, but also to (a) more-complex linguistic symbols such

---

[8] On other occasions, Peirce used "sinsign" instead of "token," and "legisign" instead of "type."
[9] Williams (1936) was one of the first to stress the significance of this ambiguity, but his resolution is different from the one presented here.

as sentences; (b) aggregates of linguistic symbols such as the full texts of books and other textual documents; (c) non-symbolic signs such as icons and indexes;[10] (d) interpretants—concepts, propositions, beliefs, and other mental states; and (e) objects or referents (including events, properties, relationships, and states of affairs)—both natural and artifactual.

In this light, the type–token relationship begins to look a little more like the kind–individual relationship. That there is a difference, however, is demonstrable if we return to the token–occurrence contrast noted above. The latter distinction makes sense only when applied to signs. We can distinguish sensibly among word-types, word-tokens, and word-occurrences, but not among bird-types, bird-tokens, and bird-occurrences. To extend the type–token distinction to referents in general would, it seems, be one step too far.

We are left, then, with one view of the world in which kinds (e.g., the bird kind) are instantiated by individuals (e.g., Alex the parrot, 1976–2007[11]); and another in which types (e.g., the word "bird," and the book *Bird by Bird* by Anne Lamott) are instantiated by tokens (e.g., the seventeenth word of this paragraph, and the 1994 edition of Lamott's work), which in turn are instantiated by occurrences (e.g., the set of ink marks on my print-out of this paper, and my copy of the book). These two views may easily be reconciled if we equate kinds and types, equate individuals and occurrences, and allow for intermediate tokenization of signs only.

We shall return to this interpretation after considering, in the next section, the role of the type–token distinction in statistical linguistics and statistical bibliography. As a preliminary to that discussion, it may be helpful first to review some theoretical, conceptual, and terminological aspects of the statistical approach.

---

10 Peirce (1911/1998, pp. 460–461) defined three main classes of sign: *icons*, "which serve to represent their objects only in so far as they resemble them in themselves"; *indices*, "which represent their objects independently of any resemblance to them, only by virtue of real connections with them"; and *symbols*, "which represent their objects, independently alike of any resemblance or any real connection, because dispositions or factitious habits of their interpreters insure their being so understood."
11 See http://en.wikipedia.org/wiki/Alex_(parrot).

3 Types and Tokens in Linguistics and Bibliometrics

3.1 Power-Law Distributions

The field of statistics is concerned with *random variables*, i.e., observable properties (of events, cases, etc.) whose values are not predictable. Random variables whose possible values may be specified in a list of finite length are known as *discrete*; those that can take any numerical value are known as *continuous*.

In statistics, a *probability distribution* is "a description of the possible values of a random variable, and of the probabilities of occurrence of these values" (Upton & Cook, 2008). Any probability distribution is specifiable by a function $p_X(x)$ that relates each possible value x to the probability of occurrence $P(X = x)$ of that value—a.k.a. a *probability mass function* (pmf) for discrete variables, or a *probability density function* (pdf) for continuous variables. For the discrete random variable X whose possible values are $x_1, x_2, x_3, \ldots, x_M$, where M_X is the total number of possible values, the pmf $p_X(x)$ may be given by $f_x = n_x/N_X$, where n_x is the *absolute frequency* of occurrences of the value x, N_X is the total number of events, and f_x is thus the *relative frequency* of occurrences of the value x. To visualize in graphical form the probability distribution specified by such a pmf, one might simply plot values of the variable X on the abscissa (x-axis) of a histogram, against the absolute frequencies of occurrence n_x of each value on the ordinate (y-axis).[12] This way of characterizing a probability distribution, however, says nothing about the properties of the relation between values of X and their expected frequencies of occurrence; as a result, a probability distribution function typically specifies such a relation explicitly. Some commonly instantiated types of probability distribution include the discrete *uniform* distribution (which describes, for example, the rolls of a fair die; pmf $p_X(x) = 1/M_X$), the *normal* or Gaussian distribution[13] (which describes, for example, people's heights), and the Pareto distribution[14] (which describes, for example, people's incomes).

A number of different methods of classifying general families of distributions have been defined by statisticians. Some distributions (e.g., the uniform and normal distributions) are symmetric; others (e.g., the Pareto distribution) are

---

[12] This presentation assumes the "frequency" interpretation of probability due to Venn (1876; see also Hájek, 2011), which defines a value's probability as the limit of its relative frequency in a large number of trials.
[13] Named for the German mathematician Carl Friedrich Gauss (1777–1855).
[14] Named for the Italian economist Vilfredo Pareto (1848–1923; see Pareto, 1895, 1896/1965).

asymmetric, a.k.a. *skewed*. Among the skew distributions, some (e.g., the Pareto distribution) are *heavy-tailed* (i.e., they have tails that are longer and/or fatter than the tail of an exponential distribution); while others are light-tailed (i.e., they have tails that are shorter and/or thinner). The *Zipf* (a.k.a. zeta) distribution (pmf $p_X(x) = c \cdot x^{-a}$, where a and c are constants whose values depend on context)[15]—like the skewed, heavy-tailed Pareto distribution of which it is the discrete version—is an example of a *power-law* distribution. In general, power-law distributions describe variables where events characterized by a large x are so rare, and events characterized by a small x are so common, that the probability of occurrence of a given value x is inversely proportional to a power (i.e., a in the pmf given above) of that value.

Power-law distribution functions can be fitted to empirical datasets on many different kinds of phenomena, both natural and social.[16] Power-law relationships have been observed not only in distributions of incomes of people, but also in distributions of magnitudes of earthquakes, populations of settlements, frequencies of occurrence of words, productivities of authors, and frequencies of occurrence of journal titles in bibliographic references or citations, among many others; see Table 1 for a summary.[17]

The last three in this list (again among others) have long been studied by *bibliometricians* interested in applying statistical techniques as a means of understanding people's document-related activities. Which words are used the most in German-language publications? Who in the field of biochemistry has been cited most often by philosophers? In which journals have papers about nanotechnology most frequently appeared? These are a small sample of the kinds of questions that may be answered simply by counting the number of times each value of a defined variable occurs in a given bibliographic dataset, and then comparing those counts to find the most frequently occurring values. Various bibliometric "laws", implying the existence of some sort of causal relationship between the values of a variable and their probabilities of occurrence, have been proposed as determinants of the distributions of probabilities—Zipf's law of word frequency (Zipf, 1929, 1932, 1935, 1949), Lotka's law of scientific productivity (Lotka, 1926), and Bradford's law of scattering (Bradford, 1934) are traditionally the "big three"— but it should always be borne in mind that here we are observing mere statistical

---

15 Named for the American linguist George Kingsley Zipf (1902–1950; see Zipf, 1929, 1932, 1935, 1949).
16 The degree of "goodness of fit" may be calculated by comparing the observed data with the data that would be expected if the function were accurate.
17 See Newman (2005) and Clauset, Shalizi, and Newman (2009) for comprehensive reviews of the properties of power-law distributions and their occurrence in the natural and social worlds.

regularity, or conformance to patterns, not the operation of laws in any way analogous to the laws of physics. In any case, it is even debatable which (if any) of these empirical datasets really are best-fitted by a power-law distribution, regardless of the values that are computed for its parameters. In some cases, the regularities observed are characteristic only of the middle range of the values of the defined variable, while some other distribution (e.g., the lognormal distribution) is a better fit for values in the upper or lower range.

Tab. 1: Some empirical phenomena that purportedly follow a power-law distribution.

Common name (if applicable)	Early sources	Classes	Events	Event-count
The Pareto law	Pareto (1895, 1896/1965)	Persons	Dollars	Wealth
The rank–size rule	Auerbach (1916)	Settlements	People	Population
Zipf's law	Estoup (1916); Condon (1928); Zipf (1929, 1932, 1935, 1949)	Words	Occurrences	Occurrence-count
The Willis–Yule distribution	Willis & Yule (1922)	Taxa	Subtaxa	Subtaxon-count
Lotka's law	Lotka (1926)	Authors	Publications	Productivity
Bradford's law	Bradford (1934, 1948); Vickery (1948)	Journals	Citations	Citedness
The Gutenberg–Richter law	Ishimoto & Iida (1938); Gutenberg & Richter (1944)	Earthquakes	Joules	Magnitude
The species abundance distribution (SAD)[18]	Corbet (1941)	Species	Individual organisms	Abundance
—	Fleming & Kilgour (1964)	Journals	Uses	Use-count

---

[18] The distribution of individual organisms over species was originally modeled as a geometric distribution (Motomura, 1932), and has since been modeled most frequently as either a logarithmic or a lognormal distribution.

3.2 Three Different Terminological Approaches

The terminology used to discuss power-law distributions in general, and the bibliometric laws in particular, varies in accordance with the writer's interpretation of the nature of these distributions' contexts.

One approach, as taken above, is to talk of sets of *events* (a.k.a. individuals, cases, or objects), each characterized by a particular categorical variable (a.k.a attribute, or property), which takes *classes* (a.k.a. kinds, or categories) as values. We might say, "A set of events is distributed over a set of classes," and tally the events that *constitute* (belong to, are members of) each class, in order to produce a set of class-specific event-counts that take numerical values n_x representing the *size* of each class.

An alternative is to speak of sets of *items*, each characterized by a particular categorical variable that takes *sources* as values. We might say, "A set of items is distributed over a set of sources," and tally the items *produced* (generated) by each source, in order to produce a set of source-specific item-counts that take numerical values n_x representing the *productivity* of each source.

Thirdly, the terminology of classes and events (or sources and items) can be mapped to types and tokens, so that we consider sets of *tokens*, each characterized by a particular categorical variable that takes *types* as values. We might say, "A set of tokens is distributed over a set of types," and tally the tokens that *signify* (stand for) each type, in order to produce a set of type-specific token-counts that take numerical values x representing the *incidence* (a.k.a. prevalence) of each type.

3.3 Two Different Conceptual Approaches

The possibility that any presentation of a given distribution may involve any or any combination of these terminological approaches is not the only potential source of confusion for students of bibliometrics. The class/event relationship manifested in any sample dataset can be represented by either or both of two plots: a (class-)*rank*–(class-)*size* plot,[19] in which classes of events are listed on the *x*-axis in rank order (from largest to smallest), and the frequency of events in each class plotted on the *y*-axis; and a (class-)*size*–(class-)*frequency* plot, in which the various sizes of classes are listed on the *x*-axis (from smallest to largest), and the frequency of classes of each size plotted on the *y*-axis.[20] The plots in Figures 1

---

[19] A.k.a. a (class-)*rank*–(event-)*frequency* plot.
[20] Rank–frequency and size–frequency plots are sometimes known as Zipfian and Lotkaian plots, respectively, after the authors with whom they were originally associated.

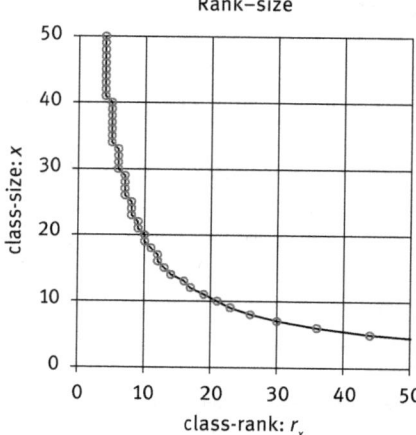

Fig. 1: A partial rank–size plot derived from the data in Table 2.

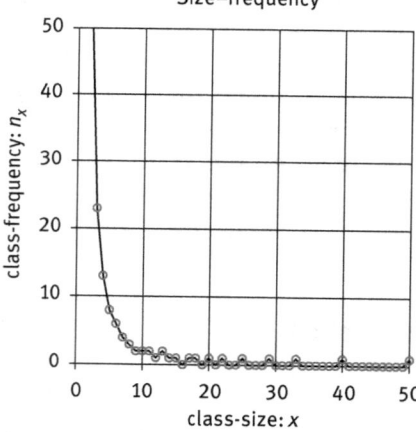

Fig. 2: A partial size–frequency plot derived from the data in Table 2.

and 2 are derived from the data presented in Table 2. It is important to recognize that the two plots "are not contradictory or competing descriptions; rather they are complementary ways of summarizing the same data" (Herdan, 1960, p. 87). In Figures 3 and 4, the same data is plotted on a double-log scale, producing the straight line that is typical of power-law distributions.

To take the example of a random variable X, each value x of which is a different word-form: in a rank–size plot (e.g., Figure 1), the word-forms are listed on the x-axis in descending order of frequency of occurrence (a.k.a. "size"), and the frequency of occurrence of each word-form plotted on the y-axis; whereas in a size–frequency plot, the various sizes of word-forms (i.e., the various frequen-

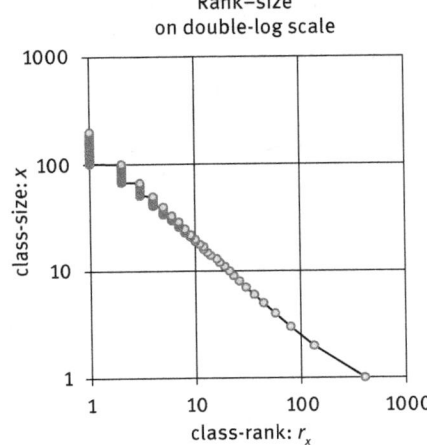

Fig. 3: The data from Figure 1 plotted on a double-log scale.

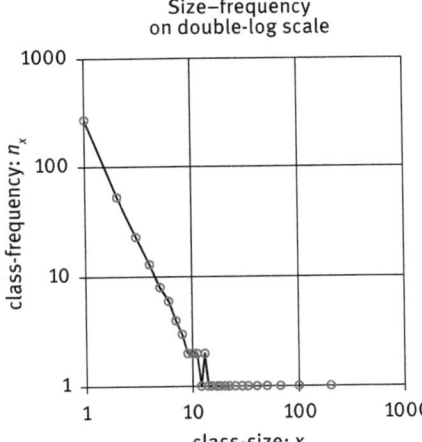

Fig. 4: The data from Figure 2 plotted on a double-log scale.

cies of occurrence) are listed on the x-axis, and the frequency of word-forms of each size plotted on the y-axis. In the case of the size–frequency plot (e.g., Figure 2), it is useful to think of class-sizes (e.g., the various possible frequencies of word-occurrence) as classes in their own right, and word-forms as the individual events in each class. In this way, we can conceive of the random variable X a little differently, such that each of its values x is a different class-size (e.g., a different frequency of word-occurrence).

Suppose, then, we are dealing with a population of N sources (e.g., word-forms), for each of which we can observe a value x of the random variable X, which

x	n_x	$x \cdot n_x$
1	271	271
2	53	106
3	23	69
4	13	52
5	8	40
6	6	36
7	4	28
8	3	24
9	2	18
10	2	20
11	2	22
12	1	12
13	2	26
14	1	14
15	1	15
17	1	17
18	1	18
20	1	20
21	1	21
22	1	22
25	1	25
29	1	29
33	1	33
40	1	40
50	1	50
67	1	67
100	1	100
200	1	200
Sum	**404**	**1374**

Tab. 2: Sample data consistent with a power-law distribution. Each value in the column headed *x* represents a different class-size, and each value in the column headed n_x is the number of classes that have the corresponding size *x*. We might imagine a text comprising 1374 word-occurrences, distributed over 404 word-forms, so that 271 of those word-forms occur once, 53 occur twice, and so on.

is equal to the number of items (e.g., word-occurrences) produced by that source, i.e., the source's productivity. In this context, we can make the following observations, using notation similar to that adopted by Burrell (1991), among others.

The number of sources that each have a productivity of *exactly x* is given by n_x; the combined productivity of those sources that each have a productivity of exactly *x* is given by $x \cdot n_x$; and the total productivity of all sources is given by $M = \sum x \cdot n_x$. The mean productivity (i.e., the average number of items per source) is given by $\mu = M/N$. The probability that a randomly selected source has a productivity of exactly *x* is given by $P(X = x) = f_x = n_x/N$; and the probability that a randomly selected item is the product of a source that has a productivity of exactly *x* is given by $g_x = x \cdot n_x/M$.

The rank of a source with a productivity of exactly x is given by r_x, and is equal to the number of sources that each have a productivity of *at least x*. The combined productivity of those sources that each have a productivity of at least x is given by R_x. The probability that a randomly selected source has a productivity of at least x is given by $P(X \geq x) = \Phi_x = r_x / N$, which is known as the *tail distribution function* (tdf) of X. The probability that a randomly selected item is the product of a source that has a productivity of at least x is given by $\Psi_x = R_x / M$, which is known as the *tail moment function* (tmf) of X. Plotting Φ_x against Ψ_x for all values of x produces a Leimkuhler curve[21] (see Figure 5).

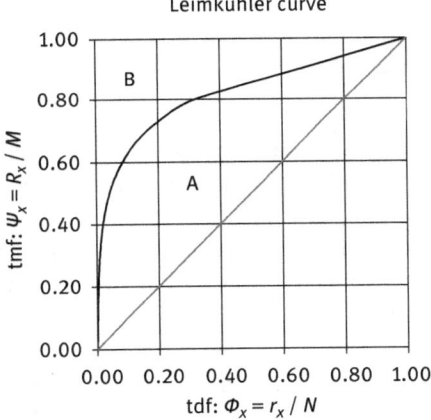

Fig. 5: The Leimkuhler curve derived from the data in Table 2.

The probability that a randomly selected source has a productivity of *at most x* is given by $P(X \leq x) = 1 - \Phi_x$, which is known as the *cumulative distribution function* (cdf) of X. The probability that a randomly selected item is the product of a source that has a productivity of at most x is given by $1 - \Psi_x$, which is known as the *cumulative moment function* (cmf) of X. Plotting $1 - \Phi_x$ against $1 - \Psi_x$ for all values of x produces a Lorenz curve[22] (see Figure 6).

The Leimkuhler and Lorenz curves are graphical representations of inequality (a.k.a., concentration, diversity, dispersion, richness). They allow us to find, for any given fraction of the total number of sources, what fraction of the total number of items are accounted for—i.e., to make statements like "the least-frequently occurring 50 % of word-forms account for only 20 % of word-occurrences," or

---

[21] Named for the American engineer Ferdinand F. Leimkuhler (b. 1928; see Leimkuhler, 1967).
[22] Named for the American economist Max Otto Lorenz (1876–1959; see Lorenz, 1905).

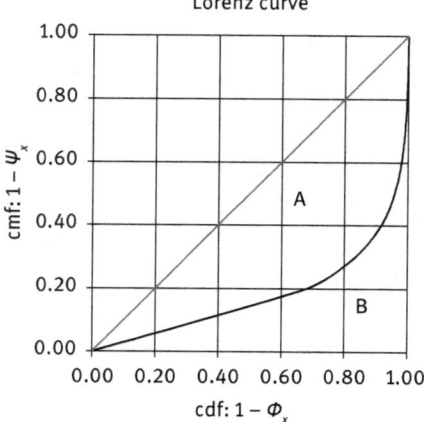

Fig. 6: The Lorenz curve derived from the data in Table 2.

"the most-frequently occurring 10% of word-forms account for 70% of word-occurrences." When $\Phi_x = \Psi_x$ (and $1 - \Phi_x = 1 - \Psi_x$) for all values of x, the amount of inequality is zero, and the curve is a straight line drawn from (0, 0) to (1, 1). The Gini index[23] G is a single-valued measure of the inequality of a probability distribution, given by the ratio of A (the area between the Leimkuhler [or Lorenz] curve and the 45° line of equality) to $A + B$ (the total area above [or below] that line).[24]

Having reviewed this statistical material, we are now ready to focus directly on the role played by type–token theory in the development of statistical approaches to linguistics and bibliography. We shall see that it is Zipf's work, not Peirce's, which has proved the more influential in both domains.

3.4 Zipf, Peirce, and Type–Token Theory: A Historical View

Zipf's law appears to have been first stated by the French stenographer Jean-Baptiste Estoup (1868–1950), in French, in 1916 (Estoup, 1916; see also Lelu, 2014), and first stated in English by E. U. Condon of Bell Telephone Labs in 1928. "While studying some data on the relative frequency of use of different words in the

---

[23] Named for the Italian statistician Corrado Gini (1884–1965; see Gini, 1914).
[24] The Gini index G (a.k.a. Gini coefficient) is equivalent to Herdan's "Lorenz factor" L (Herdan, 1960, pp. 48–50). Herdan points out (p. 50, emphasis in original) that "for the lognormal distribution the *Lorenz factor depends only upon the value of the logarithmic standard deviation*, σ and can be read off immediately from a numerical table giving values of L for specified values of σ," characterizing this result as one "of great importance" for quantitative linguistics.

English language," writes Condon (1928, p. 300), "I noticed a rather interesting functional relationship ..."

The Harvard linguist George Kingsley Zipf (1902–1950) developed the idea in a series of publications, beginning in 1929 with his doctoral dissertation, "Relative frequency as a determinant of phonetic change" (published as Zipf, 1929), in which, acknowledging the help of Estoup, he proposes (p. 4) a phonological "Principle of Frequency": the ease with which a word may be pronounced is "inversely proportionate to the relative frequency of that word ... among its fellow words ... in the stream of spoken language." In other words, "as usage becomes more frequent, form becomes ... more easily pronounceable." Zipf uses statistical data on the frequency of occurrence of words supplied by Godfrey Dewey's *Relativ* [sic] *Frequency of English Speech Sounds*,[25] in which Dewey analyzes 100,000 word-occurrences in English text (instantiating just over 10,000 different words), and presents further statistical data, including some on Chinese, purportedly in support of his phonological thesis, in *Selected Studies of the Principle of Relative Frequency in Language* (Zipf, 1932).

Zipf's next major work, *The Psycho-Biology of Language* (Zipf, 1935), presents "in full" the results of his decade-long study of "speech as a natural phenomenon ... investigated, in the manner of the exact sciences, by the direct application of statistical principles" (p. v). Here he argues not only that "the more complex any speech-element phonetically, the less frequently it occurs" (p. v), but also that "the length of a word ... is closely related to the frequency of its usage—the greater the frequency, the shorter the word" (p. v), and that "if the number of different words occurring once in a given sample is taken as x, the number of different words occurring twice, three times, four times, n times, in the same sample, is respectively $1/2^2, 1/3^2, 1/4^2, \ldots 1/n^2$ of x, up to, though not including, the few most frequently used words; that is, we find an unmistakable progression according to the inverse square, valid for well over 95 % of all the different words used in the sample" (p. vi). This evidence, Zipf says, "points quite conclusively to the existence of a fundamental condition of equilibrium between the form and function of speech-habits, or speech-patterns, in any language" (p. vi). By the time he came to write *Human Behavior and the Principle of Least Effort* (Zipf, 1949)—in which he again acknowledges the pioneering work of Estoup[26]—Zipf had gener-

---

[25] Godfrey Dewey's father was Melvil Dewey, the creator of the Dewey Decimal Classification. Another English "frequency dictionary" that came to be widely used was *The Teacher's Word Book of 30,000 Words* (Thorndike & Lorge, 1944).

[26] "The first person (to my knowledge) to note the hyperbolic nature of the frequency of word usage was French stenographer J.-B. Estoup who made statistical studies of French ..." (Zipf, 1949, p. 546).

alized from this idea to a general theory of all kinds of human behavior, not just linguistic behavior, purporting to explain such behavior by reference to a fundamental principle that people tend, when required to carry out a task, to expend the least possible effort that is consistent with an adequately effective performance.

Whatever has been made of the explanation that Zipf infers from the evidence (and contemporary reviews were not wholly kind[27]), only a few have denied that the empirical relationship that he establishes between word frequency and rank is something to be explained. Over the years, however, the reliability of the data used, and the validity of conclusions drawn, have been called into question. Gustav Herdan (1960), for example, mounts a sustained attack, arguing that not only is Zipf's "law" not a law in the theoretical sense,[28] but that it is not even empirically true.[29] Herdan asserts (pp. 33, 35) that "[i]t is difficult to understand why the Zipf law should have attained such notoriety, ... since it is not ... of much practical use to the linguist, and mathematically a triviality. ... [It] is the product of a period when quantitative methods were a novelty in linguistics. What was an achievement then is quite obsolete now." Herdan does allow (p. 38) that "the Zipf Law, although unsuitable for the scientific description of linguistic distributions, has its uses when it comes to the mechanical handling of word masses. ... [I]t is often sufficiently close to the actual distribution to be of service in the technology of language, and we may regard it as a useful technological device." But he then goes on to argue that, in any case, the lognormal distribution is a much closer fit than the Zipf distribution is to word-count data.

---

[27] See, for example, E. Prokosch's coruscating review of *Selected Studies* ...in *Language*: "An adequate review would consist in the two words 'utterly worthless,' and to say more seems waste of space. But ... [t]he censure should be directed not so much against him as against those ...who should have performed the duty of advising the Harvard University Press against accepting this book for publication. Zipf's book constitutes a disgrace to American scholarship ..." (Prokosch, 1933, p. 92).

[28] "That the decrease of frequency [of word-occurrences] should be related to an increase in rank [of word-forms] follows not from any natural property of language structure, but merely from the fact that the word with the highest frequency is given the lowest rank, and as the frequency decreases the words are given correspondingly higher ranks. Thus the inverse relation between frequency and rank which is at the basis of the so-called Zipf law is one of our own making" (Herdan, 1960, p. 35).

[29] "... [A]ll kinds of exceptions have had to be suggested to make the 'law' fit the actual observations. According to some investigators, it does not hold for high-frequency words, nor does it hold for the low-frequency words, but seems to fit only the distribution of words of intermediate frequency. Considering that no definition is given ...for high- and low-frequency ..., it is evident that we cannot speak here of a law. ... [T]he simple and straightforward relation between vocabulary and occurrence which it suggests [is] just not ... true" (Herdan, 1960, pp. 35–37).

Zipf did not use the terminology of "type" and "token" in his work, preferring instead simply to talk of the number of times words occur (or are used). The late 1930s and early 1940s saw the emergence of a research program in language behavior regarded as scientific by its proponents,[30] and the opportunity to relate Zipf's work to Peirce's gradually became apparent. One of the first to note the applicability of Peirce's terminology to discussions of Zipf's rank–frequency relationship was Wendell Johnson (Johnson, 1939), who discusses the *type–token ratio* (TTR)[31] and mentions that Zipf refrains from using the term—but Johnson does not cite Peirce. In a 1944 paper, Johnson notes that the effectiveness of the science-of-language program "depends upon the development of highly reliable and differentiating measures, by means of which specified aspects of language behavior might be systematically observed in relation to one another and to other variables" (Johnson, 1944, p. 1), and identifies the TTR as just such a measure. Even simpler, Johnson says, is the notion of *type frequency*, i.e., "the frequency of occurrence of each different word, or type" (p. 3)—but instead of compiling mere lists of the most-frequently occurring types in sample texts, à la Godfrey Dewey, the aim of the language behaviorists of the 1940s was to compare sets of type-frequency data for multiple individual language-users or group representatives, with a view to identifying characteristic patterns, group differences, changes over time, correlations with other variables, etc., while also distinguishing among types of different grammatical or semantic kinds.

In his overview of "highly reliable and differentiating measures," Johnson also discusses the concept of *proportionate vocabulary*: "How many different words or types make up 25, or 50, or 75 per cent of a given language sample?" (p. 4). He explains how to plot a curve representing the observed percentages of

---

30 See Sanford (1942) for an early review of research on "the existence, consistency, and significance of individual differences in the mode of verbal expression" (p. 811). Sanford draws attention to a development towards "a quantitative analysis and description of linguistic events …a quantitative science of language" (p. 813).

31 "This is a measure of vocabulary 'flexibility' or variability, designed to indicate certain aspects of language adequacy. It expresses the ratio of different words (types) to total words (tokens) in a given language sample. If in speaking 100 words (tokens) an individual uses 64 different words (types), his TTR would be .64." (Johnson, 1944, p. 1). The value of the TTR tends to decrease as the sample size increases. Johnson explains how a *cumulative TTR curve*—possibly helpful in predicting TTRs for larger samples (cf. Chotlos, 1944)—can be plotted "by computing successive TTRs as increments are added to the sample" (Johnson, 1944, p. 2). Chotlos (1944) finds that the *bilogarithmic TTR*—i.e., the ratio of the logarithm of the number of types to the logarithm of the number of tokens—is constant for samples of different sizes from the same text, and hence can be used as a single-valued characteristic of the style of a text. "This fact [is] one of the most remarkable in the field of quantitative linguistics …" (Herdan, 1960, p. 26).

types (x-axis) that account for certain percentages of tokens (y-axis), and notes (citing Zipf, 1935) that this curve can be expressed (a) mathematically, and (b) in terms of rank as well as in terms of frequency.[32]

John B. Carroll appears to have been one of the first to mention both Peirce and Zipf in the same work. In his study of psychological aspects of linguistic behavior,[33] Carroll (1944) draws on the work of the semiotician Charles Morris to define and focus on a category of *linguistic response* that is broader than that implied by "word" or "phoneme," encompassing "communicative habits which do not specifically involve the speech mechanism; namely, non-vocal gestures, expressive movements, and other conventionalized responses" (p. 104).[34] Carroll points out (p. 107) that "it is necessary to introduce a distinction between the terms *response* and *response-type*" that mirrors Peirce's type–token distinction.[35] However, Carroll cites Ogden and Richards (1936, Appendix D) as his source for Peirce's distinction.[36]

Meanwhile, in the course of his analysis of kinds of linguistic resource-types, Carroll (p. 113) describes his Phrase Completion Test, "in which the subject must give his first response to incomplete phrases like 'Hounds and _____'; 'And as for _____.'" He reports (p. 113) that "when a distribution is made of the responses to these items, it is found that two or three different responses constitute the majority of all the running responses, while a relatively large number of infrequent responses constitute the remainder of the responses," then notes (citing Zipf, 1935) that "in general these distributions, when frequency is plotted against descending rank order of frequency, follow roughly a Zipf-type curve."

---

32 "[A] curve that is fitted to word-frequencies as a function of rank, the most frequent word having the lowest rank number, 1, represents in an alternative way the same phenomenon that is discussed here in terms of proportionate vocabulary." (Johnson, 1944, p. 5).

33 "Our study is concerned, in the first instance, with the characteristics of verbal responses, the frequency with which these responses are emitted, the sequences in which they are patterned, and the general conditions of their occurrence." (Carroll, 1944, p. 102).

34 For Morris, semiosis is a process that involves three entities: the sign-vehicle, the designatum, and the interpretant (see Carroll, 1944, p. 106). Cf. Peirce's representamen, object, interpretant.

35 "The response-type is conceived here as an abstraction, a learned uniformity in linguistic behavior which has certain dynamic properties and which hence functions as a unit in behavior. In speaking of a linguistic response, on the other hand, we refer to a specific behavioral occurrence of a linguistic response-type. For example, the lexical form *dog* may be taken as a response-type, while a particular utterance of the sounds [dɔg] would constitute a linguistic response. This distinction is quite similar to C. S. Peirce's distinction between *token* and *type* ..., and is made in order to avoid the confusion between the specific and the generic usages of the term response often encountered in psychological writings." (Carroll 1944, p. 107).

36 A few years later, Osgood (1952) discusses the TTR, cites Zipf and Morris, and mentions (but does not cite) Peirce.

The Moravian statistician and linguist Gustav Herdan (1897–1968) made a series of major contributions to the emerging field of quantitative (a.k.a. statistical) linguistics in the 1950s and 1960s, including three pioneering textbooks (Herdan, 1956, 1960, 1966), one of which (1960) was called *Type–Token Mathematics*. The concept of type–token duality, mined later by Egghe (see, e.g., Egghe, 2003), was central to Herdan's view of the field; yet he preferred to cite the distinction made by the Swiss linguist Ferdinand de Saussure (1857–1913) between *langue* and *parole* (roughly, abstract linguistic rules and concrete speech acts) as historical precursor, rather than Peirce (see, e.g., Saussure, 1916/1983).

Charls Pearson and Vladimir Slamecka's *Semiotic Foundations of Information Science: Final Project Report* (1977), drawing on Pearson's research from 1974 onwards, appears to be the earliest work in library and information studies (LIS) to cite both Zipf and Peirce on types and tokens, and is followed by further elaborations by Pearson and by his erstwhile colleague Pranas Zunde (see, e.g., Zunde, 1984). LIS writers began to cite Herdan around the same time (see, e.g., Pratt, 1975), but did not straightaway pick up on the applicability of type–token theory to bibliometrics. Herdan's work was sufficiently well-known in bibliometric circles to be listed in J. Vlachý's bibliography of works relating to Lotka's law in volume 1, issue 1 of *Scientometrics* in 1978, and cited in J. J. Hubert's monumental review of "linguistic indicators" that appeared in 1980 (Hubert, 1980; see also Hubert, 1981).

By the late 1980s, Tague and Nicholls (1987, p. 155) were characterizing Zipf's law explicitly as "the distribution of a set of tokens over a set of types" (p. 155). Tague and Nicholls give several examples of other kinds of type–token pairs: author–publication, author–citation, publication–citation, and key–access (the last apparently indicating the distribution of search-term occurrences over search-term forms). From this time onwards, the terminology of types and tokens has become standard in bibliometrics. However, citations to Peirce's original work are still relatively rare.

3.5 Recent Developments

In a 1990 article summarizing the contributions made in his Ph.D. dissertation, Leo Egghe refers to the means by which sources such as authors, journals, etc., produce bibliographic items as "information production processes" (IPPs; Egghe, 1990, p. 17), and distinguishes one-dimensional bibliometrics—which "deal[s] with the sources or items separately (i.e., when they are not linked with each other)" (p. 18)—from two-dimensional or *dual* studies that examine the quantitative relationships between sources and items. Egghe asserts that every bibliometric problem can be addressed using either of two complementary approaches—"one looking at (sources, items), in that order, and the other looking at (items, sources), in the reverse order" (p. 19). Following Herdan (1960, pp. 14–15),[37] Egghe calls this "the *duality principle*," and compares it with the duality procedure in geometry, where "every time one obtains a theorem proving a relation between points and lines (in that order), one can formulate the dual theorem by interchanging the words lines and points" (p. 19). Egghe goes on to advocate for three- and even four-dimensional studies that involve more than one set of sources and/or more than one set of items (e.g., journals as well as authors and papers), and for examinations of the temporal aspects of IPPs.

By 2003, Egghe could write that "the dual approach" to bibliometrics—i.e., type–token (T/T), source–item, or Lotkaian bibliometrics—"is very well known" (Egghe, 2003, p. 603; see also Egghe, 2005). In the same paper, Egghe introduces, as a "more important" part of informetrics (p. 604), what he calls type/token–taken (T/T–T) informetrics, which "studies the *use* of items rather than the items [themselves]" (p. 603; emphasis added) by describing the source–item relationship "as it is experienced by users (information professionals as well as information seekers)" (p. 606). Egghe proposes that, rather than focus only on distributions of sets of items over sets of sources, and on (e.g.) finding the probability that a randomly-selected word-form occurs j times, we also consider distributions of sets of sources over sets of items, and (e.g.) finding the probability that a randomly-selected word-occurrence is the product of a word-form that occurs j times. His rationale is that, in doing so, we will be better able to understand the ubiquitous scenario in which, for every value of j, the probability that a given item is the product of a source with a productivity of at least j is greater than the probability that a given source has a productivity of at least j.

For Egghe, the "taken" (i.e., use) component of his T/T–T formulation is a "third level" (p. 605) that "has never been studied" (p. 604). Quentin Burrell, however, argues that Egghe's proposal "adds little new to the theoretical framework of informetrics" (Burrell, 2003, p. 1263). Burrell identifies two random variables whose distributions form the core of Egghe's proposal: the variable X, each value of which denotes the productivity of a randomly chosen source, and whose distribution is defined by $f(j)$; and the variable Y, each value of which denotes the productivity of the source from which a randomly selected item comes, and whose distribution is defined by $g(j)$. Burrell shows that, in fact, the distribution of vari-

---

[37] "This principle asserts for language that if in any valid proposition of language the words *type* (linguistic form, e.g., phoneme, morpheme) and *token* (frequency of occurrence, probability) are interchanged, the resulting proposition is also valid." (Herdan, 1960, p. 15).

able Y is "nothing more than the proportional tail-moment distribution of X" (p. 1261), while the relation between the distributions of X and Y "is illustrated by the familiar Leimkuhler curve of concentration" (p. 1261)—as we may confirm by comparing Egghe's definitions of $f(j)$ and $g(j)$ with the definitions of f_x and g_x given in the section on Two Different Conceptual Approaches, above.

4 Discussion and Conclusions

4.1 Not All Sources are Types

Bearing in mind the terminological distinctions noted above, we have now seen that to characterize as types and tokens the classes and events of interest to bibliometricians, and to other seekers of statistical regularities in human behavior, is a relatively recent phenomenon. It is also, we might conclude, a tactic that confuses rather than clarifies—for the simple reason that the type–token distinction is quite different from both the source–item distinction and the class–event (a.k.a. kind–individual) distinction. To take the example of authors and publications: it is no stretch to see how each author may be conceived as the source of each of the items they produce, nor to understand their publications as events that belong to the class of those that share the property of being authored by the same person. It is more difficult, however, to grasp the rationale for treating each author as a type that is tokenized by publications, in the same way in which word-forms are tokenized by word-occurrences. The kinds of things that we typically consider to be tokenizable are representamina (words, sentences, texts, etc.) and interpretants (concepts, propositions, works, etc.). The terms we use to talk about these kinds of things are essentially ambiguous: context may make our meaning clear, but if it does not, then we can clarify only by specifying whether our subject is type or token. No such issue arises with authors and publications: we seldom mistake the class for the event. So, for a bibliometrician to invoke, sweepingly, the type–token distinction that works for words, but not for birds, is misleading at worst, and simply unnecessary at best.

4.2 Not All Type–Token Relations are Power Laws

Mitzenmacher (2004) provides a comprehensive review of the various explanations that have been given over the years for the apparent prevalence of power-law (and lognormal) distributions in empirical data. He identifies three families of generative models for power-law distributions, each of which received particular attention in the 1950s before their later rediscovery: *preferential attachment* models (see, e.g., Simon, 1955), *optimization* models (see, e.g., Mandelbrot, 1953), and *multiplicative process* models (see, e.g., Champernowne, 1953). Almost half a century before Mitzenmacher's review, Herdan disputes the assumption that large numbers of heavy-tailed distributions can be explained by the same model: "Simon's claim [in Simon, 1955] to have provided a uniform mathematical explanation of these distributions rests upon an insufficient realization of the differences in form between the distributions, and suffers from a neglect of considering the relations between some of them which makes it highly unlikely, if not mathematically impossible, that one mathematical model should fit them all" (Herdan, 1960, p. 207). Herdan's view is not only that the contextual differences between, for example, the distribution of word-occurrences and the distribution of personal wealth are sufficiently significant to warrant a search for explanations of different kinds, but also that closer inspection of individual datasets reveals patterning that fits just as closely with a distribution of some other (non-power-law) kind entirely. Difficulties in distinguishing between instances of power-law and instances of lognormal distributions, especially, persist.

4.3 Not All Type–Token Relations Have Been Studied by Bibliometricians

The article in which Peirce originally presented his ideas on types and tokens was published to little notice from the wider philosophical community. It was the British philosopher Frank Ramsey (1903–30) who set the ball rolling in 1923 with his influential review of Ludwig Wittgenstein's *Tractatus Logico-Philosophicus*, in the course of which Ramsey uses the type–token distinction to explain aspects of Wittgenstein's picture theory of language (Ramsey, 1923; see also Nubiola, 1996, for a detailed account of Ramsey's role in the dissemination of Peirce's thought). Since then, the metaphysical status of types and tokens has been the subject of much philosophical work (see, e.g., Wetzel, 2009; Hilpinen, 2012), very little of which has been recognized as having implications for library and information science (LIS) in general or bibliometrics in particular.

One of the directions taken in philosophy of language, philosophy of literature, and philosophy of art has been to explore the ramifications of sentences, propositions, pictures, etc.—as well as aggregations of such phenomena at various levels—having type–token ambiguity (see, e.g., Stevenson, 1957; Jacquette, 1994; Howell, 2002). In LIS, meanwhile, a homegrown variation on type–token theory has emerged in the modeling of resource description data, where an analogous distinction between works and items is drawn in standards such as the *Functional Requirements for Bibliographic Records* (FRBR; IFLA, 1998). It is clear that the work carried out in philosophy is relevant to the ontology of bibliographic phenomena that forms the core of contemporary library cataloging and classification theory, and vice versa, but the connections have received little serious attention from either side. This is unfortunate, since it is not unreasonable to imagine philosophers' contributing especially usefully to debates about the supposed value of distinguishing not just between works and items, but among works, expressions, manifestations, and items (WEMI). Critics of FRBR, and of its instantiation in the library cataloging standard *RDA: Resource Description and Access*,[38] point to the existence of many sets of related bibliographic items that strongly resist WEMI modeling (see, e.g., Peponakis, 2012). A pluralist view of the bibliographic universe, in which different types of library materials (books, moving images, sound recordings, etc.) are modeled in different ways, may come to find stronger support among aestheticians than the uniformist view exemplified in FRBR.

Even more conspicuous by its absence is a bibliometric perspective on FRBR and related models. What probability distribution functions best describe empirical data on numbers of works, expressions, manifestations, and items, and what explanations can be given for the processes producing such distributions? Hickey and O'Neill (2005, pp. 243–245) present figures summarizing the distribution of manifestations over works in OCLC's WorldCat, as determined by the application of an algorithm, developed in OCLC's Office of Research, that identifies sets of works in very large collections of bibliographic records. Of the 37.8 million works identified, 36.3 million each had a single manifestation, 3.4 million each had two manifestations, 0.8 million each had three, and so on. It was never Hickey and O'Neill's goal to analyze such data further: understandably, they were more interested in the performance of their algorithm. But, given the relative ease with which such data may be collected, it is surprising how few others have attempted bibliometric analyses of the results of FRBRization.

4.4 Not All Bibliometricians Are Data Scientists (Yet)

It is already somewhat of a cliché that we live in an age of "big data". One upshot of the increasing scholarly interest in practical questions to do with the most effective means of managing large datasets has been a corresponding surge in the level

---

38 See http://www.rdatoolkit.org/

of attention given to philosophical questions about the nature of data, data models, database records, etc. (see Borgman, this volume). There is a long story that remains to be told about the development of standard database structures based on the modeling of entities and relationships, attributes and values, etc., against the backdrop of philosophical ideas about the ontological status of substances and properties, kinds and individuals, and—yes—types and tokens. The field of bibliometrics is both a participant in, and a contributor to the telling of this story. And there is much more to do than fitting power-law functions to distributions of links among websites. Bibliometricians are the natural pioneers of a science of *data* use (as well as *word* and *document* use) that applies type-token theory in as judicious a manner as did the language behaviorists three-quarters of a century previously.

Cited References

Auerbach, F. (1913). Das Gesetz der Bevölkerungskonzentration. *Petermann's Geographische Mitteilungen*, 59(1), 74–77.
Bradford, S. C. (1934). Sources of information on specific subjects. *Engineering*, 137(3550), 85–86.
Bradford, S. C. (1948). *Documentation*. London, England: Crosby Lockwood.
Burrell, Q. L. (1991). The Bradford distribution and the Gini index. *Scientometrics*, 21(2), 181–194.
Burrell, Q. L. (2003). Type/token-taken informetrics: Some comments and further examples. *Journal of the American Society for Information Science and Technology*, 54(13), 1260–1263.
Carroll, J. B. (1944). The analysis of verbal behavior. *Psychological Review*, 51(2), 102–119.
Champernowne, D. G. (1953). A model of income distribution. *Economic Journal*, 63(250), 318–351.
Chotlos, J. W. (1944). Studies in Language Behavior, IV: A statistical and comparative analysis of individual written language samples. *Psychological Monographs*, 56(2), 75–111.
Clauset, A., Shalizi, C. R., & Newman, M. E. J. (2009). Power-law distributions in empirical data. *SIAM Review*, 51(4), 661–703.
Condon, E. U. (1928). Statistics of vocabulary. *Science*, 68(1733), 300.
Corbet, A. S. (1941). The distribution of butterflies in the Malay Peninsula (Lepid.). *Proceedings of the Royal Entomological Society of London, Series A: General Entomology*, 16(10–12), 101–116.
Cronin, B. (2000). Semiotics and evaluative bibliometrics. *Journal of Documentation*, 56(4), 440–453.
Dewey, G. (1923). *Relativ [sic] frequency of English speech sounds*. Cambridge, MA: Harvard University Press.
Egghe, L. (1990). The duality of informetric systems with applications to the empirical laws. *Journal of Information Science*, 16(1), 17–27.

Egghe, L. (2003). Type–token/taken informetrics. *Journal of the American Society for Information Science and Technology, 54*(7), 604–610.

Egghe, L. (2005). *Power laws in the information production process: Lotkaian informetrics.* Bingley, England: Emerald.

Estoup, J.-B. (1916). *Gammes sténographiques: Méthode et exercices pour l'acquisition de la vitesse* (4th ed.). Paris, France: Institut Sténographique de France.

Fleming, T. P., & Kilgour, F. G. (1964). Moderately and heavily used biomedical journals. *Bulletin of the Medical Library Association, 52*(1), 234–241.

Flew, A. (Ed.). (1979). *A dictionary of philosophy.* London, England: Pan.

Gerrard, A. J. (1990). *Mountain environments: An examination of the physical geography of mountains.* London, England: Belhaven Press.

Gini, C. (1914). Sulla misura della concentrazione e della variabilità dei caratteri. *Atti del R. Istituto Veneto di Science, Letter ed Arti, 73*(2), 1203–1248.

Gutenberg, B., & Richter, C. F. (1944). Frequency of earthquakes in California. *Bulletin of the Seismological Society of America, 34*(4), 185–188.

Hájek, A. (2011). Interpretations of probability. In E. N. Zalta (Ed.), *Stanford Encyclopedia of Philosophy.* Stanford, CA: Metaphysics Research Lab, Center for the Study of Language and Information, Stanford University. http://plato.stanford.edu/entries/probability-interpret/

Herdan, G. (1956). *Language as choice and chance.* Groningen, The Netherlands: Noordhoff.

Herdan, G. (1960). *Type–token mathematics: A textbook of mathematical linguistics.* The Hague, The Netherlands: Mouton.

Herdan, G. (1966). *The advanced theory of language as choice and chance.* Berlin, West Germany: Springer.

Hickey, T. B., and O'Neill, E. T. (2005). FRBRizing OCLC's WorldCat. *Cataloging & Classification Quarterly, 39*(3–4), 239–251.

Hilpinen, R. (2012). Types and tokens: On the identity and meaning of names and other words. *Transactions of the Charles S. Peirce Society, 48*(3), 259–284.

Howell, R. (2002). Ontology and the nature of the literary work. *Journal of Aesthetics and Art Criticism, 60*(1), 67–79.

Hubert, J. J. (1980). Linguistic indicators. *Social Indicators Research, 8*(2), 223–255.

Hubert, J. J. (1981). General bibliometric models. *Library Trends, 30*(1), 65–81.

International Federation of Library Associations and Institutions. Study Group on the Functional Requirements for Bibliographic Records. (1998). *Functional requirements for bibliographic records.* Munich, Germany: K. G. Saur.

Ishimoto, M., and Iida, K. (1938). Observations sur les séismes enregistrés par le microsismographe construit dernièrement (I) [In Japanese]. *Bulletin of the Earthquake Research Unit, University of Tokyo, 17*(2), 443–478.

Jacquette, D. (1994). The type–token distinction in Margolis's aesthetics. *Journal of Aesthetics and Art Criticism, 52*(3), 299–307.

Johnson, W. (1939). *Language and speech hygiene: An application of general semantics; Outline of a course.* Chicago, IL: Institute of General Semantics.

Johnson, W. (1944). Studies in Language Behavior, I: A program of research. *Psychological Monographs, 56*(2), 1–15.

Lamott, A. (1994). *Bird by bird: Some instructions on writing and life.* New York, NY: Pantheon Books.

Leimkuhler, F. F. (1967). The Bradford distribution. *Journal of Documentation, 23*(3), 197–207.

Lelu, A. (2014). Jean-Baptiste Estoup and the origins of Zipf's law: A stenographer with a scientific mind (1868–1950) [In Spanish]. *Boletín de Estadística e Investigación Operativa*, *30*(1), 66–77. http://www.seio.es/BEIO/files/BEIOVol30Num1Feb2014-HyE.pdf

Lorenz, M. O. (1905). Methods of measuring the concentration of wealth. *Publications of the American Statistical Association*, *9*(70), 209–219.

Lotka, A. J. (1926). The frequency distribution of scientific productivity. *Journal of the Washington Academy of Sciences*, *16*(12), 317–325.

Lowe, E. J. (1983). Instantiation, identity, and constitution. *Philosophical Studies*, *44*(1), 45–59.

Lowe, E. J. (2006). *The four-category ontology: A metaphysical foundation for natural science*. Oxford, England: Oxford University Press.

Mandelbrot, B. (1953). An informational theory of the statistical structure of languages. In W. Jackson (Ed.), *Communication theory* (pp. 486–502). Woburn, MA: Butterworth.

Mitzenmacher, M. (2004). A brief history of generative models for power law and lognormal distributions. *Internet Mathematics*, *1*(2), 226–251.

Motomura, I. (1932). Statistical method in animal association [In Japanese]. *Dōbutsugaku Zasshi* [*Zoological Magazine*], *44*(2), 379–383.

Newman, M. E. J. (2005). Power laws, Pareto distributions and Zipf's law. *Contemporary Physics*, *46*(5), 323–351.

Nubiola, J. (1996). Scholarship on the relations between Ludwig Wittgenstein and Charles S. Peirce. In I. Angelelli and M. Cerezo (Eds.), *Studies on the history of logic: Proceedings of the III. Symposium on the History of Logic* (pp. 281–294). Berlin, Germany: Walter de Gruyter.

Ogden, C. K., and Richards, I. A. (1936). *The meaning of meaning: A study of the influence of language upon thought and of the science of symbolism* (4th ed.). London, England: Kegan Paul, Trench, Trübner.

Osgood, C. E. (1952). The nature and measurement of meaning. *Psychological Bulletin*, *49*(3), 197–237.

Pareto, V. (1895). La legge della domanda. *Giornale degli Economisti*, 2nd series, *10* (January), 59–68.

Pareto, V. (1896/1965). La courbe de la répartition de la richesse. In G. Busino (Ed.), *Écrits sur la courbe de la répartition de la richesse* (pp. 1–15). Genève, Switzerland: Librarie Droz.

Pearson, C. & Slamecka, V. (1977). *Semiotic foundations of information science: Final project report*. Atlanta, GA: School of Information and Computer Science, Georgia Institute of Technology.

Peirce, C. S. (1897/1932). On signs: Ground, object, and interpretant. In C. Hartshorne & P. Weiss (Eds.), *The collected papers of Charles Sanders Peirce, Volume 2: Elements of logic* (pp. 227–229). Cambridge, MA: Harvard University Press.

Peirce, C. S. (1906). Prolegomena to an apology for pragmaticism. *The Monist*, *16*(4), 492–546.

Peirce, C. S. (1911/1998). A sketch of logical critics. In The Peirce Edition Project (Ed.), *The essential Peirce: Selected philosophical writings, Volume 2 (1893–1913)* (pp. 451–462). Bloomington, IN: Indiana University Press.

Peponakis, M. (2012). Conceptualizations of the cataloging object: A critique on current perceptions of FRBR Group 1 entities. *Cataloging & Classification Quarterly*, *50*(5-7), 587–602.

Pratt, A. (1975). The analysis of library statistics. *Library Quarterly*, *45*(3), 275–286.

Prokosch, E. (1933). [Review of the book *Selected studies of the principle of relative frequency in language*, by G. K. Zipf]. *Language*, *9*(1), 89–92.

Ramsey, F. P. (1923). [Review of the book *Tractatus logico-philosophicus*, by L. Wittgenstein]. *Mind, 32*(128), 465–478.

Sanford, F. H. (1942). Speech and personality. *Psychological Bulletin, 39*(10), 811–845.

Saussure, F. de (1916/1983). *Course in general linguistics* (C. Bally & A. Sechehaye, Eds.; R. Harris, Trans.). London, England: Duckworth.

Simon, H. A. (1955). On a class of skew distribution functions. *Biometrika, 42*(3–4), 425–440.

Smith, B., & Mark, D. M. (2003). Do mountains exist? Towards an ontology of landforms. *Environment and Planning B: Planning and Design, 30*(3), 411–427.

Stevenson, C. L. (1957). On "What is a poem?" *Philosophical Review, 66*(3), 329–362.

Tague, J., & Nicholls, P. (1987). The maximal value of a Zipf size variable: Sampling properties and relationship to other parameters. *Information Processing & Management, 23*(3), 155–170.

Thorndike, E. L., & Lorge, I. (1944). *The teacher's word book of 30,000 words*. New York, NY: Teachers College, Columbia University.

Upton, G., & Cook, I. (Eds.). (2008). *A dictionary of statistics* (2nd ed.). Oxford, England: Oxford University Press. http://www.oxfordreference.com/view/10.1093/acref/9780199541454.001.0001/acref-9780199541454

Venn, J. (1876). *The logic of chance* (2nd ed.). London, England: Macmillan.

Vickery, B. C. (1948). Bradford's law of scattering. *Journal of Documentation, 4*(3), 198–203.

Vlachý, J. (1978). Frequency distributions of scientific performance: A bibliography of Lotka's law and related phenomena. *Scientometrics, 1*(1), 109–130.

Wetzel, L. (2006). Types and tokens. In E. N. Zalta (Ed.), *Stanford Encyclopedia of Philosophy*, Stanford, CA: Metaphysics Research Lab, Center for the Study of Language and Information, Stanford University. http://plato.stanford.edu/entries/types-tokens/

Wetzel, L. (2009). *Types and tokens: On abstract objects*. Cambridge, MA: MIT Press.

Williams, D. C. (1936). Tokens, types, words, and terms. *Journal of Philosophy, 33*(26), 701–707.

Willis, J. C., & Yule, G. U. (1922). Some statistics of evolution and geographical distribution in plants and animals, and their significance. *Nature, 109*(2728), 177–179.

Zipf, G. K. (1929). Relative frequency as a determinant of phonetic change. *Harvard Studies in Classical Philology, 40*, 1–95.

Zipf, G. K. (1932). *Selected studies of the principle of relative frequency in language*. Cambridge, MA: Harvard University Press.

Zipf, G. K. (1935). *The psycho-biology of language: An introduction to dynamic philology*. Boston, MA: Houghton Mifflin.

Zipf, G. K. (1949). *Human behavior and the principle of least effort*. Cambridge, MA: Addison-Wesley.

Zunde, P. (1984). Empirical laws and theories of information and software sciences. *Information Processing & Management, 20*(1–2), 5–18.

Ronald Rousseau and Sandra Rousseau
From a Success Index to a Success Multiplier

1 Introduction: The Success Index

Recently Kosmulski (2011) and Franceschini et al. (2012a) introduced the success index. This indicator, or better, family of indicators, is constructed as follows. One considers a set of articles and collects for each of these the number of citations received over a given citation window W. In a first step, a binary score (zero or one) is determined for each of these articles: the score is one if the citations received by a particular article reach a certain threshold value and it is zero otherwise. This threshold can be determined in a variety of ways (which is why we say that the success index is actually a family of indicators). In a next step the success index of this set of articles with respect to a particular threshold is defined as the number of publications that has reached the threshold, or stated otherwise: the sum of all binary scores.

Some variations of this index can be considered in which, for instance, time plays a role (Kosmulski, 2011). Among other proposals, the following thresholds could be used (Kosmulski, 2011; Franceschini et al., 2012a, b):
(a) The number of references (each publication's citations is compared with its own number of references). This is the original proposal by Kosmulski (2011).
(b) The mean or the median number of references in articles published in the same journal and year as the article under consideration.
(c) The mean or the median number of citations received by articles published in the same journal and year as the article under consideration, where citations are gathered over the same period W (Franceschini et al., 2012a,b). Kosmulski referred to this proposal as a modesty index, as it would reward publication of high-impact articles in lower impact journals (Kosmulski, 2012).

We note that, in general, an index can be defined as a number, derived from a formula, characterizing a property of a dataset. As such, this index is an indicator for a particular characteristic. In the case of a success index, the set of data is a set of articles and their citations, and its value is used as a proxy for the 'success'—the term visibility or popularity would be more to the point—of this dataset and the corresponding entity (scientist, department, journal). In this contribution we provide a short review of the family of success indices and introduce the success multiplier, a non-discrete version of the success index. The success multiplier is a number indicating to which extent citations reached or exceeded a threshold value. Examples are provided for articles published in the *Journal of the American Society for Information Science and Technology*, volumes 53 and 54 in 2002 and 2003. A simple statistical prediction exercise is performed for three success indices and the corresponding multipliers. Results are described as a function of variables such as the highest h-index of contributing authors, gender of the authors, content descriptors, and affiliation.

2 Overview of Relevant Indicators

In this section we provide an overview of several relevant indicator groups. First we look at the success index family, next we consider payback times and the success multiplier. Finally, we discuss some mathematical properties of these indicators.

2.1 The Success Index Family

Besides the three thresholds mentioned in the introduction, Franceschini et al. (2012a, b) also consider the following thresholds:
- The mean or the median number of references in articles belonging to a neighborhood of the article under consideration.
- The mean or the median number of citations received by articles belonging to a neighborhood of the article under consideration, where citations are gathered over the same period W.

In these cases there are many ways of defining a neighborhood of a given article. Consider the (directed) citation ego network of a given article A (Hu et al., 2011) and define a neighborhood of A as all articles at distance at most one, at most two, ... in the cited direction (or in the citing direction), or neglecting the direction.

Clearly, the amount of possible thresholds is limitless. One may, for instance, define a threshold by only considering citations in journals belonging to the first quartile in one of Thomson Reuters' JCR categories, or citations received from authors with a high h-index. Such approaches would operationalize the idea of "quality citations". Alternatively, one may consider only recent references.

In the examples presented thus far, we only considered received citations (or stated otherwise: different citing articles). Yet, instead of different citing articles, one can compute different citers (authors, journals, countries, etc.). In such cases the threshold must also be adapted as explained in Franceschini et al. (2014), where the problem is studied and examples are provided for citing authors.

Besides absolute success indices, one can also consider relative success indices of a set, defined as the success index of this set divided by the number of publications in the set under study. Finally, if all articles in a set are gauged with respect to the same threshold such as the average number of citations of the journal in which they are published (assuming that all articles in the set are all published in the same year and in the same journal), one may define the success index of a set of articles by comparing received citations and n (the number of articles in the set) times this threshold value. The result is again a success index which is either equal to one or to zero. Of course, this approach is not always meaningful, for instance if the set consists of all articles published in a given journal and year and the threshold is determined as its average number of citations. The success index has been studied in a Lotkaian framework by Egghe (2014), and further clarified by Rousseau (2014a).

2.2 Payback Times: A Variation on the Success Index

Instead of determining whether a given article has reached a certain threshold, a more dynamic approach can be considered by determining how long it takes for an article to reach the threshold. Actually, this idea precedes the concept of a success index. It was proposed by Liang and Rousseau (2008) for journals and is referred to as the yield period or the payback time. The phrase 'payback time' refers to the idea that a journal uses resources from the science system (as shown by its list of references) and that it takes a certain time to pay back (through received citations) to the science system what had been taken. Liang and Rousseau (2008) studied yearly issues of *Science* and *Nature*, leading to so-called yield sequences. They determined not only the time to reach a number of citations equal to the number of used references, but also the time to reach twice, thrice, ... this number. It was observed that payback times tended to become shorter over the years. Another variation on the success index and the idea of a payback time would be to consider the percentage of articles in a given set that already reached the threshold after a given time t.

2.3 The Success Multiplier

Instead of a binary score leading to a success index, we can also determine the fraction of the threshold reached by an article at any given moment. For instance, if the threshold is 10 citations and an article has obtained 7 citations, a value 0.7 can be associated with it.

Similarly, if an article received 15 citations, it receives a value of 1.5. The values 0.7 and 1.5 are then referred to as multipliers. An article's multiplier reflects the relative number of citations received by that article compared to the threshold value that is used.

The success multiplier of a set of articles is simply the sum of the scores of all articles in the set, generalizing the success index of a set of articles. When using success multipliers it is still possible to separate an elite set from the other ones, but this division is not as clear-cut as in the 0-1 case. Further, an average score is created by dividing this general score by the total number of articles. When the number of references is used as a threshold this leads to the formula

$$\frac{1}{n}\sum_{j=1}^{n}\frac{c_j}{r_j}. \qquad (1)$$

Here n is the number of publications under consideration, c_j is the number of citations received by article j (over a given citation window) and r_j is the number of references of article j. In case all articles' citations are compared with the same threshold, say T, then formula (1) becomes:

$$\frac{1}{n \cdot T}\sum_{j=1}^{n}c_j. \qquad (2)$$

This average score no longer has a theoretical upper limit. Note that the multiplier idea is not completely new. Yanovsky (1981) was likely the first to use a ratio of citations over references as a bibliometric indicator (his popularity factor and citation factor). Multipliers have also been proposed for scientific leadership by Matsas (2012) under the name of Normalized Impact Factor (NIF). The NIF of scientist A in the sense of Matsas is defined as:

$$\text{NIF}(A) = \frac{\sum_{j=1}^{n} a_j c_j}{\sum_{j=1}^{n} b_j r_j} = \frac{(\sum_{j=1}^{n} a_j c_j)/n}{(\sum_{j=1}^{n} b_j r_j)/n}. \qquad (3)$$

Here n is the number of publications written by scientist A, during a given period; c_j is the number of citations received by article j (again over a given citation window) and r_j is the number of references of article j. The numbers a_j and b_j are weighting factors. In the simplest case they are all equal to one. In a somewhat more complex setup, one may take $a_j = b_j = 1/$(the number of authors of article j); of course many other weighting factors are feasible. NIF(A) is the weighted average number of received citations divided by the weighted average number of references. Note that here we run across the well-known difference between ratios of averages and averages of ratios (Larivière & Gingras, 2011). In formula (1) we proposed an average of ratios (when dividing by the total number of articles in the set) while Matsas, formula (3), proposed a (weighted) ratio of averages.

Matsas' Normalized Impact Factor is very similar to the Reference Return Ratio (3R in short) for journals introduced by Nicolaisen and Frandsen (2008). This indicator for journal J is defined as:

$$3R(J) = \frac{\sum_{j=1}^{n} c_j}{\sum_{j=1}^{n} r_j},$$

where the numerator denotes the number of citations received during a given citation window by articles published during a given publication window (in the journal under consideration) and the denominator denotes the total number of references in those same articles (published during the publication window), where only references published during a given reference window are taken into account.

Besides using direct citations, one may also consider second-generation or higher forward generation effects (recall that second and higher generations may be defined in different ways as explained in Hu et al. [2011]) and calculate the multiplier for the first, second, or higher generation only.

2.4 Mathematical Properties

Bouyssou and Marchant (2011) represent an author by a mapping f from the natural numbers to the natural numbers, where $f(x)$ denotes the number of articles with exactly x citations, i.e., the frequency distribution of citations over articles in the author's publication set. We observe that in their discussion an author is actually represented by the set of his/her publications and hence the analysis in Bouyssou and Marchant (2011) applies to any set of articles.

We note that a success index is independent according to the terminology used by Bouyssou and Marchant. This means that if the value for set S_1 is larger than or equal to the value for set S_2, and one adds a publication with the same number of citations to each set, leading to sets S_1' and S_2' then the value of this success index for S_1' is larger than or equal to that for S_2'. Note that if the threshold value is determined by some external set (such as the median value of all articles in the same journal as those of the set S) then this threshold value must be the same for sets S_1 and S_2 for the previously mentioned property to hold. This property, though seemingly obvious, is not satisfied by the h-index. Clearly, success multipliers are also independent in this sense.

Moreover, Franceschini et al. (2014) showed that the union of two disjoint groups of publications with success indices su$^{(1)}$ and su$^{(2)}$ has success index

$su^{(1)} + su^{(2)}$ (with the same restriction for the thresholds). Again this addition property remains valid for success multipliers.

Clearly these properties are not satisfied by relative success indices or by relative success multipliers. Indeed, if set S_1 contains 3 articles of which 2 have reached the threshold value and set S_2 contains 30 articles of which 21 have reached the threshold value then the relative success index for S_1 is 2/3 which is smaller than the 21/30, the relative success index of S_2. Adding one publication that has reached the threshold to both sets, we obtain the new relative values $3/4 = 0.75$ and $22/31 \approx 0.71$. As a result, the relative success index of set S_1 becomes larger than that of S_2, contradicting the independence requirement. Yet, if S_1 and S_2 contain the same number of elements, the independence requirement is clearly satisfied.

Observing that, for instance $\frac{2}{7} + \frac{3}{7} \neq \frac{5}{14}$, suffices to show that also the addition property is not satisfied for relative success indices even if sets have the same number of elements. Considering now the case of success multipliers, we immediately assume that S_1 and S_2 have the same number of elements. It is clear that, using formula (1), if

$$\frac{1}{n}\sum_{j=1}^{n} \frac{c_j}{r_j} \leq \frac{1}{n}\sum_{j=1}^{n} \frac{c'_j}{r'_j} \quad \text{then also} \quad \frac{1}{n+1}\left(\sum_{j=1}^{n} \frac{c_j}{r_j} + \frac{c_{n+1}}{r_{n+1}}\right) \leq \frac{1}{n+1}\left(\sum_{j=1}^{n} \frac{c'_j}{r'_j} + \frac{c_{n+1}}{r_{n+1}}\right).$$

This property also holds when using formula (2). Yet, the property does not hold for formula (3), taking all weights equal to 1 for simplicity. Indeed:

$$\frac{5+4}{10+10} \leq \frac{1+2}{3+3}$$

but, adding one article with zero citations and two references yields:

$$\frac{5+4+0}{10+10+2} > \frac{1+2+0}{3+3+2}.$$

Finally, as the addition property is not satisfied for relative success indices, it is certainly not satisfied for relative success multipliers.

3 An Empirical Illustration

Next, we collected a dataset in order to have a closer look at success indices and success multipliers in practice. More specifically, we consider all publications in the *Journal of the American Society for Information Science and Technology* (JASIST) in the years 2002 and 2003. This set is restricted to those publications classified as *articles* in the Web of Science (WoS). The dataset contained 208 articles. Data collection took place during the first week of June 2014.

After defining and describing three success indices and three corresponding success multipliers, we performed a statistical analysis to identify factors that can be used to predict the different success indicators.

3.1 Examples: Success Indices

Three success indices for the articles in our dataset are determined by using three different thresholds. These indices are denoted by SU_1, SU_2 and SU_3, and defined as:

SU_1 = 1 if number of received citations ≥ number of references used,

SU_2 = 1 if number of received citations ≥ average number of references used in year of publication (in articles in JASIST), and

SU_3 = 1 if number of received citations ≥ average number of citations received by JASIST articles in the year of publication.

The average number of references and the average number of citations for our dataset is presented in Table 1. Articles published in 2002 were cited more frequently on average than articles published in 2003, while their average number of references was lower.

Tab. 1: Average number of references and citations per year.

	Average number of references	Average number of citations
2002	32.31	27.09
2003	34.35	22.71

We note that the indices SU_1 and SU_2 (corresponding to thresholds *a* and *b* of the introduction) have a static denominator and hence are non-decreasing, while the third one SU_3 (comparing with the average number of received citations) has a dynamic denominator if the citation window extends to the date of data collection. Hence the resulting index may fluctuate depending on the fact if the target publication receives citations faster or slower than the average of the set of publications under consideration.

The calculated values for the three indices are distributed as shown in Table 2. Clearly comparing the number of citations to an article to an article's own reference list and comparing to the average number of received citations yield very similar results, while comparing the number of citations to the average number of references makes it somewhat more difficult to be a successful article. Recall that these are citation values obtained after more than ten years (i.e., in June 2014).

Tab. 2: Percentages of successful JASIST articles, according to three success indices.

	No success	Success
SU_1	68.1 %	31.9 %
SU_2	74.0 %	26.0 %
SU_3	68.3 %	31.7 %

It is not because the percentages of successful articles for SU_1 and SU_3 are almost the same that these percentages necessarily refer to the same articles. We check this in Table 3. For most articles the values for SU_1 and SU_3 are identical. Still, for some 15 percent of the articles in this dataset the results for both indices differ.

Tab. 3: Overlap between SU_1 and SU_3.

	$SU_3 = 0$	$SU_3 = 1$	Total
$SU_1 = 0$	125	16	141
$SU_1 = 1$	16	51	67
Total	141	67	208

In addition, we note that the percentage of articles for which $SU_3 = 1$ is smaller than 0.5 (namely 0.317) as expected by the well-known skewness of citation distributions (Rousseau, 2014b). Figure 1 shows the citation distribution. Its skewness coefficient is 1.98; 44.23 % of the articles received between 0 and 10 (incl.) citations over a period of more than ten years.

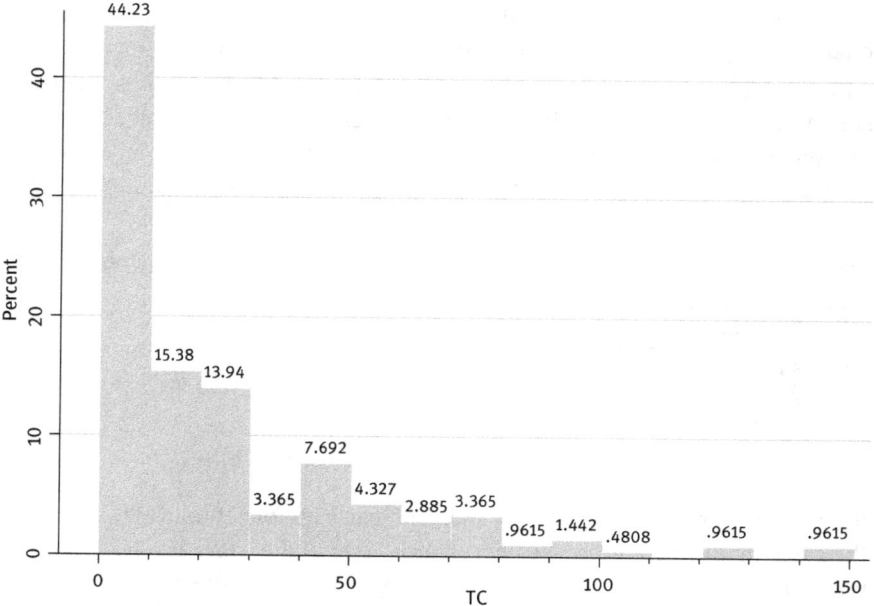

Fig. 1: Citation frequency distribution of articles published in JASIST (2002–2003); data collected in June 2014. TC stands for total number of citations.

3.2 Examples: Multipliers

Next, we calculated the multiplier values for the same articles. These are denoted $MULTI_1$, $MULTI_2$ and $MULTI_3$ and defined as:

$MULTI_1$ = number of received citations / number of references used,
$MULTI_2$ = number of received citations / average number of references used in year of publication (in articles in JASIST), and
$MULTI_3$ = number of received citations / average number of citations received by JASIST articles in the year of publication.

The distributions of these three multipliers are shown in Figures 2, 3, and 4.

The five articles with the highest values for $MULTI_1$, $MULTI_2$, $MULTI_3$, and number of received citations are shown in Tables 4 and 5. Note that, by definition, ranks according to $MULTI_2$, $MULTI_3$, and total number of received citations are the same. Coincidentally, there are more articles published in 2003 in these lists than articles published in 2002.

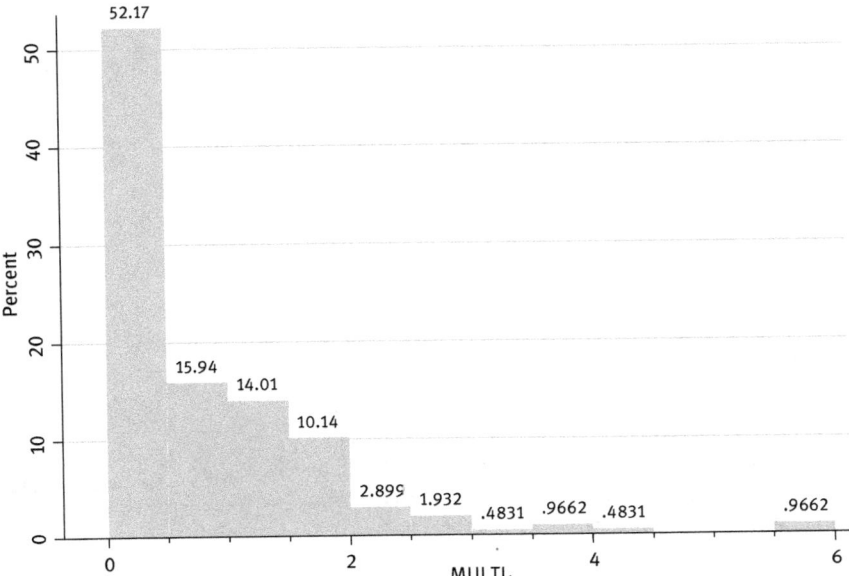

Fig. 2: Distribution of $MULTI_1$.

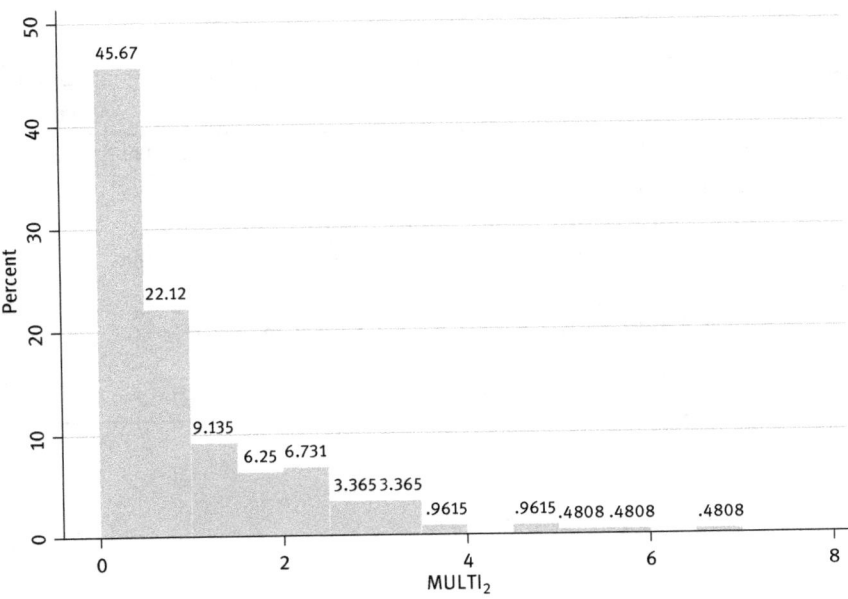

Fig. 3: Distribution of $MULTI_2$.

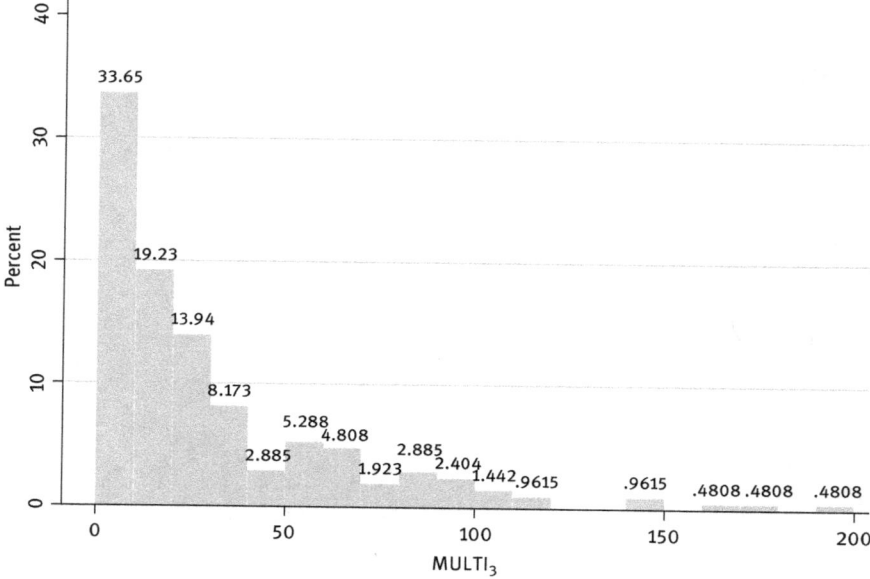

Fig. 4: Distribution of $MULTI_3$.

Tab. 4: The five articles with the highest $MULTI_1$ values.

Rank	Author(s)	# references	Volume - issue - year	Pages	$MULTI_1$ value
1	Pudovkin, AI; Garfield, E	15	53 - 13 - 2002	1113–1119	6.0
1	Garfield, E; Pudovkin, AI; Istomin, VS	7	54 - 5 - 2003	400–412	6.0
3	Ahlgren, P; Jarneving, B; Rousseau, R	35	54 - 6 - 2003	550–560	4.31
4	Morris, SA; Yen, G; Wu, Z; Asnake, B	15	54 - 5 - 2003	413–422	3.67
5	White, HD	20	54 - 13 - 2003	1250–1259	3.5

Tab. 5: The five articles with the highest numbers of received citations, $MULTI_2$ and $MULTI_3$ values.

Rank	Author(s)	Volume - issue - year	Pages	# received citations	$MULTI_2$ value	$MULTI_3$ value
1	Ahlgren, P; Jarneving, B; Rousseau, R	54 - 6 - 2003	550–560	151	6.06	4.53
2	Rieh, SY	53 - 2 - 2002	145–161	148	5.94	4.44
3	Wathen, CN; Burkell, J	53 - 2 - 2002	134–144	126	5.06	3.78
4	Borlund, P	54 - 10 - 2003	913–925	125	5.02	3.75
5	White, HD	54 - 13 - 2003	1250–1259	108	4.33	3.24

3.3 A Statistical Approach

As a small exercise we try to predict (certainly not explain) SU_1, SU_2, SU_3, $MULTI_1$, $MULTI_2$, $MULTI_3$, and the total number of received citations (TC) as a function of some predicting variables. For the continuous variables $MULTI_1$, $MULTI_2$, $MULTI_3$, and total citations (TC) we used OLS (ordinary least squares); while for the discrete cases, SU_1, SU_2, and SU_3, we used a logistic regression. From the literature (Deschacht & Engels, 2014; Didegah, 2014; Didegah & Thelwall, 2013) we know that possible predictors, at least for TC (we mention TC because, to the best of our knowledge, a regression analysis has never been performed for the success index), include: the journal's impact factor, the h-index of the authors, whether authors come from an English speaking country or not, the number of co-authors, the number of references, the number of countries in the address byline, the number of institutions involved in the research, the size of the field, the recency of references, the field, the specific topic, the type of document, the number of female authors, the length of the article, the length of the title, the readability of the article, etc.

Some of these factors clearly do not apply to the present situation such as the field, the journal's impact factor (all articles are published in JASIST), or the type of document (we only use the *article* type). Other factors were not constructed and therefore not applied, such as the recency of references or the readability of the article. Moreover, some factors were dichotomized such as number of authors (one or more), number of female authors (one or more), while others were somewhat adapted (see further). The gender of authors was determined manually by

Tab. 6: List of possible predictors.

Variable name	Definition (dummy variables are zero when they are not equal to 1)
MINREF	= 1 if the number of references is less than 15
MAXREF	= 1 if the number of references is 50 or more
Y2002	= 1 if the article has published in 2002
COUNTAUTHORS	Number of co-authors
DAUTHORS	= 1 if the article was written by more than 1 author
FEMALE	Number of female authors
DFEMALE	= 1 if at least one author is female
PAGES	Length of article expressed as number of pages
USA	= 1 if at least one of the affiliations is in the USA
ASIA	= 1 if at least one of the affiliations is in Asia (excl. Israel)
TEC	= 1 if at least one the affiliations has the letters 'tec' in its name
COMP	= 1 if at least one of the affiliations has the letters 'comp' in its name
KEYNR	Number of keywords
RETRIEVAL	= 1 if at least one of the keywords contains the word 'retrieval'
WEB	= 1 if at least one of the keywords contains one of the words 'www', 'internet', 'online' or 'world wide web'
HIRSCHMAX	The maximum h-index among all co-authors on January 1, 2003 according to the WoS
TIME	Time in days between date of acceptance and date of submission

searching for pictures on the Internet (at least in those cases where we did not know the author(s) personally). Finally we tried a few factors which may not have been studied before. The list of predictors is provided in Table 6.

Of course, some of the listed variables were never applied together, such as a variable and its dichotomized version. Furthermore, it turned out that some of these possible predictors were never significant or were not significant in combination with other highly significant ones.

We were not able to determine the gender of a few authors in the dataset. The corresponding six articles were thus removed from the analysis and the final analysis was done for 202 (or 201) articles. Indeed, it was not possible to calculate $MULTI_1$ for one article as it had no references, leading to 201 articles in the case where a division by the number of actual references had to be performed.

Finally, the following variables were at least once statistically significant at the 10 % level: Hirschmax, Pages, Female, Keynr, Web, Retrieval, Y2002, Tec, and Dauthors.

Results of our econometric estimation, performed in STATA, are presented in Table 7. For the OLS the adjusted R^2 is given, while for the logistic regression the pseudo R^2 is shown.

Tab. 7: Summary of obtained results.

predictors	Multipliers			Success indices			Total citations
	MULTI$_1$	MULTI$_2$	MULTI$_3$	SU$_1$	SU$_2$	SU$_3$	TC
Hirschmax	0.0656***	0.0376**	1.1398**	0.0607*	0.0826**	0.1046***	0.8912**
	(0.0125)	(0.0151)	(0.4633)	(0.0332)	(0.0360)	(0.0353)	(0.3740)
Pages	0.0098	0.0277	0.8443	−0.0198	0.0509	0.0883**	0.6714
	(0.0144)	(0.0174)	(0.5315)	(0.0421)	(0.0434)	(0.0427)	(0.4291)
Female	0.0736	0.1957**	5.9379**	0.4405**	0.3240	0.5462**	4.6537**
	(0.0764)	(0.0926)	(2.8314)	(0.2037)	(0.2299)	(0.2172)	(2.2860)
Keynr	0.0287	0.1382***	4.2574***	0.0964*	0.2180***	0.2118***	3.5014***
	(0.0213)	(0.0258)	(0.7888)	(0.0580)	(0.0616)	(0.0601)	(0.6369)
Web	0.0379	0.0177	0.5245	0.3941	0.9401**	0.9507**	0.3773
	(0.1725)	(0.2090)	(6.3948)	(0.4594)	(0.4629)	(0.4690)	(5.1632)
Retrieval	−0.2548*	−0.3650*	−11.1814*	−0.8446*	−0.4466	−0.3927	−9.0358*
	(0.1531)	(0.1855)	(5.6747)	(0.4447)	(0.4492)	(0.4409)	(4.5817)
Y2002	0.01557	0.0857	3.9913	0.9030***	1.0632***	0.4829	6.5797*
	(0.1198)	(0.1450)	(4.4357)	(0.3412)	(0.3945)	(0.3675)	(3.5814)
Tec	0.4016***	0.4185**	12.7473**	1.0767***	0.8524*	0.9994**	10.1159**
	(0.1511)	(0.1831)	(5.6012)	(0.4136)	(0.4609)	(0.4495)	(4.5224)
Dauthors	−0.1554	−0.1589	−4.7853	−0.0808	−0.2102	−0.7119*	−3.6635
	(0.1346)	(0.1630)	(4.9875)	(0.3817)	(0.4229)	(0.4159)	(4.0269)
constant	0.1667	−0.0734	−2.8463	−2.1061	−3.9657	−3.7294	−3.7658
	(0.2014)	(0.2416)	(7.3900)	(0.5981)	(0.7764)	(0.7112)	(5.9666)
Adj. R^2	0.1460	0.2087	0.2102	–	–	–	0.2169
Pseudo R^2	–	–	–	0.1147	0.1886	0.2142	–
# obs.	201	202	202	202	202	202	202
Prob. > F	0.0000	0.0000	0.0000	–	–	–	0.0000
Prob. > χ^2	–	–	–	0.0006	0.0000	0.0000	–

Estimated coefficient (standard error)
* significant at 10 % level; ** significant at 5 % level; *** significant at 1 % level

3.4 Discussion of the Regression Results

The majority of the results were expected; however, several require more discussion. The fact that the highest h-index of the co-authors is usually highly significant is not surprising and might be related to the Matthew Effect (see also Egghe et al., 2013; Glänzel & Schubert, this volume). A perhaps surprising result is the positive influence of the number of keywords. As JASIST did not have author keywords at that time, only KeyWords Plus are used. These are automatically generated by Thomson Reuters based on frequently occurring terms and phrases in the reference list. Still, the fact that these keywords are related—via references—to the content of the articles and are used for queries in the Web of Science seems to have its rewards, resulting in higher values for success indicators. The fact that a higher number of authors has no influence on the success indicators (or occasionally a negative one) is also not obvious. This result might be explained by the correlation between the number of authors and the number of female authors (Pearson correlation of 0.36). For this reason, we removed number of authors (but kept Dauthors). Still, having more than one author seems to influence the probability of being successful based on the SU_3-index negatively. In addition, there is some weak evidence that a longer article (more published pages) leads to more success as expressed by the SU_3-index. Moreover, one would expect that after more than ten years one year more of exposure would not have any influence on the success indicators, but see Table 1. While the variable Y2002 does not influence the success multipliers, it does make a difference with respect to the number of received citations and hence with respect to the success indices SU_1 and SU_2. Further, we find that topics and type of institute are of importance (at least for these data); technical institutes have a positive influence as do web discussions, while retrieval-related articles are less successful. Finally, female colleagues have a positive influence on the number of citations and hence on the success (however measured) of these articles. This observation differs from that made in earlier work (Cronin, 1996; Larivière et al., 2013). Yet, as we only studied one journal in the social sciences and a short publication period, this is, of course, no contradiction. Let us consider it an encouraging sign for female scientists.

4 Conclusion

The success index and its extension to rational numbers, the success multiplier, form a versatile family of research indicators. Some versions, such as SU_1, are not suitable for research evaluation as they are too easy to manipulate. Yet, the more difficult to manipulate (when comparing with a representative median number of citations, it becomes much more difficult to influence the result), the higher their potential in informetric studies. Our contribution provides only a small example (JASIST, volumes 53–54) of their use and thus more examples leading to a better appreciation of their advantages and disadvantages are required.

We note that some of the thresholds lead to an input-output system, thus the corresponding indicator can be considered an input-output indicator. Clearly, cases a and b, where the threshold is determined by references, fall within the input-output framework, while case c, for which the threshold is determined by citations received by related articles, does not. Related indicators such as Matsas' NIF and the 3R-indicator also are input-output indicators.

These input-output indicators treat articles as devices that create citations by using a certain amount of inputs (i.e., references). Such indicators, if applied in evaluation exercises would lead to a market-based strategy by which publication/citation maximization brings game players significant economic gains (Cronin, 1996). As such, input-output indicators reinforce the current culture of assessing academic success in terms of publications and citations, rather than stimulating original research as valuable in its own right. Success indices should hence be used to describe a current state and not to evaluate research or researchers. Furthermore, input-output indicators that are defined as ratios are not useful to help with decision making. Success multipliers rely on averages and as such tell an author nothing about the value of adding one more reference to a manuscript. Multipliers could provide a useful picture of the degree of internal linkage which exists in publication–citation networks.

Acknowledgment

The authors thank Cassidy Sugimoto and Domenico Maisano for helpful suggestions.

Cited References

Bouyssou, D., & Marchant, T. (2011). Ranking scientists and departments in a consistent manner. *Journal of the American Society for Information Science and Technology*, 62(9), 1761–1769.

Cronin, B. (1996). Rates of return to citation. *Journal of Documentation*, 52(2), 188–197.

Deschacht, N., & Engels, T. C. E. (2014). Limited dependent variable models and probabilistic prediction in informetrics. In Y. Ding, R. Rousseau, & D. Wolfram (Eds.) *Measuring Scholarly Impact: Methods and Practice*. Springer, p. 193–214.

Didegah, F. (2014). *Factors associating with the future citation impact of published articles: a statistical modelling approach*. Doctoral dissertation. University of Wolverhampton.

Didegah, F., & Thelwall, M. (2013). Determinants of research citation impact in nanoscience and nanotechnology. *Journal of the American Society for Information Science and Technology*, 64(55), 1055–1064.

Egghe, L. (2014). Impact coverage of the success-index. *Journal of Informetrics*, 8(2), 384–389.

Egghe, L., Guns, R., & Rousseau, R. (2013). Measuring co-authors' contribution to an article's visibility. *Scientometrics*, 95(1), 55–67.

Franceschini, F., Galetto, M., Maisano, D., & Mastrogiacomo, L. (2012a). The success-index: an alternative approach to the h-index for evaluating an individual's research output. *Scientometrics*, 92(3), 621–641.

Franceschini, F., Galetto, M., Maisano, D., & Mastrogiacomo, L. (2012b). Further clarifications about the success-index. *Journal of Informetrics*, 6(4), 669–673.

Franceschini, F., Maisano, D., & Mastrogiacomo, L. (2014). The citer-success-index: a citer-based indicator to select a subset of elite papers. *Scientometrics*, 101(2), 963–983.

Hu, XJ., Rousseau, R., & Chen, J. (2011). On the definition of forward and backward citation generations. *Journal of Informetrics*, 5(1), 27–36.

Kosmulski, M. (2011). Successful papers: a new idea in evaluation of scientific output. *Journal of Informetrics*, 5(3), 481–485.

Kosmulski. M. (2012). Modesty-index. *Journal of Informetrics*, 6(3), 368–369.

Larivière, V. & Gingras, Y. (2011). Averages of ratios vs. ratios of averages: an empirical analysis of four levels of aggregation. *Journal of Informetrics*, 5(3), 392–399.

Larivière, V., Ni, CQ., Gingras, Y., Cronin, B., & Sugimoto, C. R. (2013). Global gender disparities in science. *Nature*, 504(7479), 211–213.

Liang, LM., & Rousseau, R. (2008). Yield sequences as journal attractivity indicators: payback times for *Science* and *Nature*. *Journal of Documentation*, 64(2), 229–245.

Matsas, G. E. A. (2012). What are scientific leaders? The introduction of a normalized impact factor. *Brazilian Journal of Physics*, 42(5–6), 319–322.

Nicolaisen, J. & Frandsen, T. F. (2008). The reference return ratio. *Journal of Informetrics*, 2(2), 128–135.

Rousseau, R. (2014a). Comments on "Impact coverage of the success-index" by Leo Egghe. *Journal of Informetrics*, 8(3), 491–492.

Rousseau, R. (2014b). Skewness for citation curves. In E. Noyons (Ed.). *Context Counts: Pathways to Master Big and Little Data. Proceedings of STI 2014*, Leiden, Universiteit Leiden, p. 498–501.

Yanovsky, V. I. (1981). Citation analysis significance of scientific journals. *Scientometrics*, 3(3), 223–233.

Wolfgang Glänzel and András Schubert
From Matthew to Hirsch: A Success-Breeds-Success Story

1 Preamble: A Submicro-Level Bisociation Study

It was 50 years ago that James S. Coleman's *Introduction to Mathematical Sociology* was published (Coleman, 1964). The book has received more than 500 citations since then in Thomson Reuters' *Web of Science Core Collection* (and more than 1500 citations according to Google Scholar). One of these citations is found in a 1982 review by a young information scientist from London: Blaise Cronin (Cronin, 1982). Another one, two years later, was given by two authors from Budapest: Wolfgang Glänzel and András Schubert (Schubert & Glänzel, 1984). Although both papers have been cited above average (as they belong to the Hirsch-core of their respective authors), they have never been co-cited. As we might learn from Koestler (1964), some of the most remarkable instances of human creativity can be attributed to what he called *bisociation*: "the perceiving of a situation or idea in two self-consistent but habitually incompatible frames of reference". In his views, "creation" is making connection between two well-known, but yet unconnected entities. In bibliometric terms, bisociation is encountered whenever two frequently used but so far unconnected keywords co-occur, or when two frequently cited items are co-cited. In such cases, there are increased chances for outstanding achievements. For keyword bisociation, the conjecture was empirically supported by an inorganic chemistry example (Schubert & Schubert, 1997; Schubert, 2013). No systematic studies on co-citation bisociation presently exist. The present article may be considered a self-experiment in order to determine whether an unprecedented co-citation of Cronin (1982) and Schubert and Glänzel (1984) will lead to success. The result is the sole responsibility of the authors.

2 Introduction

In the present paper, an overview is given of statistical models of bibliometric distributions on the basis of the principle called "Matthew's principle", "cumulative advantage", or "success-breeds-success", among others. A general introduction is followed by the description of the model, the properties of a particular distribution derived from the model—the Waring distribution—and a family of apparently remote distributions all derivable from the model. In retrospect, the model can be considered a precursor of Barabási's celebrated "preferential attachment" network model resulting in power law-type distributions, and some relations with Hirsch's h-index are also revealed.

Skewness is one of the most conspicuous features of informetric distributions. Whether we refer to Pareto's 80/20 rule or any other specimen of unequal proportions, strong inequalities are readily illustrated on the distribution of publication productivity or citation impact. The skewness property is, however, only one of the common features of informetric distributions.

The mathematical models of these distributions are sometimes taken from the Gaussian distribution family, such as Poisson, negative binomial, etc., but more often—as in the case of the classical laws of bibliometrics: those of Lotka, Bradford, and Zipf—approximately follow an inverse power law (see Furner, this volume, for more on these and other power-law distributions). This is the second important feature of scientometric distributions: their heavy tail. The question about the usefulness of the two families of distributions in scientometrics has been discussed in detail, among others, by Brookes (1968) and Haitun (1982).

There is an apparent consensus that the generating mechanism of these distributions is some kind of positive feedback, what was called the Matthew principle by Merton (1968), "cumulative advantage" by Price and Gürsey (1976), reinforcement by Allison (1980), and "success-breeds-success" by Tague (1981).

From the mathematical viewpoint there are several ways of developing and describing such models. Proceeding from a simple point process, i.e., the random sum of independent exponentially distributed random variables, where all special properties of inequality, such as subject-specific peculiarities, the authors' social status, or academic age, etc., can be obtained via (1) *compound distributions* and stochastic processes, that is, by mixtures of random effects; (2) the *urn model* according to Pólya and Eggenberger (Eggenberger & Pólya, 1923), where success or failure might positively or negatively affect further trials; or (3) stochastic *birth-and-death processes* with particular transition rules controlling for the extent of cumulative advantage. All these models result in the same family of distributions and processes but highlight different aspects of the genesis of inequality properties like skewness and heavy tails.

A versatile model was proposed in the 1980's by Schubert and Glänzel (1984) based on a simple counting process using a deterministic birth model with immigration and emigration and a transition rate that is a linear function of the actual count. Depending on the supplementary conditions, the process may result in Poisson, negative binomial, geometric, or Waring distributions. Each of these distributions may be used to model bibliometric samples in certain conditions.

The model is based on the scheme of a simple Poisson process presented by Coleman (1964, p. 289). In his model, all transition rates are equal and independent of the previous counts. The more general model of a birth process can be obtained if the transition rates may change according to the previous counts and following particular rules (cf. Figure 1) (discussed in more detail later).

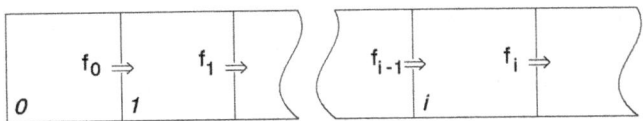

Fig. 1: Coleman's scheme of the Poisson process (with $f_i = a$ = const. for all $i \geq 0$).

In Coleman's brand loyalty example, "the states labelled 1, 2, 3, ... are the states of having bought brand A one, two, three, etc., times in succession."

Turning to bibliometrics, we can think about authors publishing 1, 2, 3, ... papers on a topic before getting into state 0 by changing topic (or ceasing to publish at all). In this simplest model there is no kind of "advantage", the chances of proceeding from the i-th state to the $(i + 1)$-th are equal independently of the present state (a).

3 The Schubert–Glänzel model

A somewhat modified and generalized version of Coleman's scheme was used in Schubert and Glänzel (1984). In order to build a (stochastic) birth process with the desired features to model informetric processes we first consider an infinite array of units or cells, indexed in succession by the non-negative integers, among which a certain substance is distributed. The content of the i-th cell is denoted by x_i; the (finite) content of all units or cells by x.

Obviously, $x = \sum_i x_i$. Then the fraction $y_i = x_i/x$ ($i \geq 0$) expresses the share of elements contained by the i-th cell. The change of content is postulated to obey the following rules.

Substance may enter the system from the external environment through the 0-th unit at a rate s; (1)

substance may be transferred unidirectionally from the i-th unit to the $(i + 1)$-th one at a rate f_i ($i \in \mathbf{N}_0$); and (2) substance may leak out from the i-th unit into the external environment at a rate g_i ($i \in \mathbf{N}_0$). (3)

The next step towards a stochastic model is to interpret the above ratios y_i as the (classical) probability with which an element is contained by the i-th unit. The stochastic process is then formed by the change of the content of the cells (or units), i.e., by the change of purchases or papers published by the authors, who have entered the system. The discrete random variable $X(t)$ denotes the (random) number of purchases or papers published at time t, $P(X(t) = i) = y_i$ its probability. In order to use an example from bibliometrics, $P(X(t) = i)$ might, for instance, be the probability that an author has published exactly i papers in the period from the time of his/her entrance into the system, denoted by 0, until time t. Figure 2 visualizes the scheme of substance flow of this process.

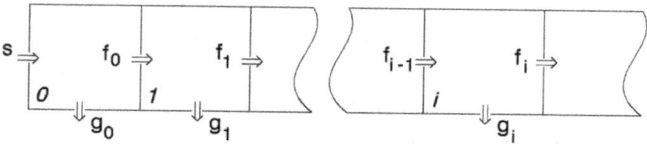

Fig. 2: Scheme of substance flow with immigration and emigration according to Schubert and Glänzel (1984).

According to Schubert and Glänzel, the following particular forms of the above rate terms are used:

$$s = \sigma \cdot x, \qquad (1^*)$$

$$f_i = (a + b \cdot i) \cdot x_i; \quad (i \geq 0), \qquad (2^*)$$

$$g_i = \gamma \cdot x_i; \quad (i \geq 0), \qquad (3^*)$$

where σ, a, b and γ are non-negative real values. The distribution of the substance over the units during time t can then be obtained as a solution of a relatively simple system of first order linear differential equations (cf. Schubert & Glänzel, 1984).

The relationship of this model with Price's author categorization bears mentioning. Price and Gürsey (1976) distinguished the following four categories of authors: *newcomers, continuants, transients,* and *terminators.* Within the framework of this model, s represents the group of newcomers, g_i terminators, g_1 transients and substance remaining in the system, i.e., $\sum_i f_i$ represents the group of continuants.

In addition, we would further like to mention that there is a certain relationship with the epidemic model according to Goffman and Nevill (Goffman & Nevill,

1964; Goffman, 1965), although the birth model with immigration and emigration does not explicitly assume the occurrence of any epidemic situation, and is, on the other hand, somewhat more complex as it differentiates the status of "infection" further by counting events. Goffman and Nevill introduced the theory of *intellectual epidemics as a model of scientific communication* in 1964. According to their model, which in turn is based on the classical Reed-Frost model, the diffusion of ideas in a population of scientists could be compared to the spreading of an influenza virus in a population of people, causing an epidemic. The population can at any time be subdivided into three groups of infected (I), resistant or immune (R), and infection sensitive, i.e., susceptible (S) animals or persons. Goffman and Nevill considered a published article on a specific topic an infection. Using this model as an analogon, we have S appearing in the Schubert–Glänzel scheme as the group (s) entering the system I corresponds to and group R to those who left the system ($\sum_i g_i$). But most notably, in this context the two main cases of the epidemic model are also obtained, particularly, if $\sigma = \gamma$ (with the further two subcases $\sigma = 0$ and $\sigma \neq 0$), or $\sigma \neq \gamma$, respectively. In the following section we will analyze these cases more in detail.

3.1 Two Special Cases: "Closed Systems" and "Equilibrium Systems"

For the entire population, we can derive $x(t) = x(0) \cdot \exp((\sigma - \gamma) \cdot t)$, i.e., the system is asymptotically time-invariant (stationary) if $\sigma = \gamma$, otherwise, if $\sigma > \gamma$ or $\sigma < \gamma$, it exponentially grows or decays, respectively. The distribution of the "substance" (purchases, publication productivity, etc.) can be exactly determined in two special cases using the notation of the Schubert–Glänzel scheme.

(i) In a "closed system" we assume $\sigma = \gamma = 0$, after (finite) time t.

In this case, the distribution of the substance will take a negative binomial distribution (Pólya distribution, in the terminology of Coleman [1964, p. 301]).

$$y_i = \binom{k+i-1}{i}\left(\frac{k}{\mu+k}\right)^k\left(\frac{\mu}{\mu+k}\right)^i, \qquad (4)$$

with a scale parameter $\mu = (a/b)(e^{bt} - 1)$, and a shape parameter $k = a/b$, where a and b are the two parameters of the transition rate, f_i. The first factor, $\binom{k+i-1}{i}$, is a binomial coefficient.

This model was successfully used by Allison (1980) in describing the publication productivity of a cohort of chemists in the first six years after the doctorate.

In the special case $b = 0$ (no cumulative advantage, as in Figure 1), we have $k \to \infty$, $\mu \to at$, and the distribution becomes Poisson.

$$y_i = \mu^i e^{-\mu}/i! . \tag{5}$$

(ii) In an "equilibrium system" we assume $\sigma = \gamma > 0$, and $t \to \infty$.

In this case, $b = 0$ (no cumulative advantage) leads to a geometric distribution.

$$y_i = q(1-q)^i , \tag{6}$$

with $q = \sigma/(\sigma + a)$.

This model describes the asymptotic steady state ("equilibrium") of the productivity distribution of an author community with a constant supply of newcomers and a constant "dropout" of authors (for whatever reason: retirement, death, topic change, leaving academia, etc.) independently of the productivity level reached so far, provided that there is no cumulative advantage effect.

In the cumulative advantage case, $b > 0$, the equilibrium distribution has a less well-known form, namely that of the Waring distribution (Schubert & Glänzel, 1984). In particular, we obtain the following limiting distribution.

$$\begin{aligned} y_i(\infty) &= \frac{\sigma(a+b)\ldots(a+b(i-1))}{(a+\sigma)(a+b+\sigma)\ldots(a+bi+\sigma)} \\ &= \frac{\alpha(N+1)\ldots(N+i-1)}{(N+\alpha)(N+\alpha+1)\ldots(N+\alpha+i)} , \end{aligned} \tag{7}$$

with parameters $\alpha = \sigma/b$, $N = a/b$.

3.2 Properties of the Waring Distribution

Although the closed-form definition of the Waring distribution looks a bit awkward, it obeys a rather simple recursive formula.

$$\begin{aligned} y_0 &= \alpha/(N+\alpha) , \\ &\vdots \\ y_i &= y_{i-1}(N+i-1)/(N+\alpha+i) . \end{aligned} \tag{8}$$

Also, the Waring distribution has some remarkable properties.
- It obeys Zipf's law:

$$y_i \approx i^{-(\alpha+1)} , \quad \text{as } i \text{ tends to infinity,} \tag{9}$$

i.e., the tail of the distribution follows an inverse power law. Due to the relation (8), the tail exponent can be estimated even from any two frequency values.
- The mean value of the Waring distribution has the very simple form:

$$\langle y \rangle = N/(\alpha - 1). \tag{10}$$

- The Waring distribution has a "self-similarity" property.

$$y_{-j} \equiv y_{i-j}(\alpha, N) = y_i(\alpha, N + j) \quad \text{for any } i \geq j, \tag{11}$$

i.e., a Waring distribution truncated from left at j and shifted back with j units, is again a Waring distribution with unchanged parameter α (as can be expected, since the asymptotic Zipf behavior must not change) and with a parameter N increased by j units. The geometric distribution, which is a limiting case of the Waring distribution, if $N, \alpha \to \infty$ and $N/\alpha = (1/q - 1) > 0$, has the "lack-of-memory property," that is, a geometric distribution truncated from left at j and shifted back with j units, is the identical geometric distribution with unchanged parameter.
- From equations (10) and (11) it follows, that

$$\langle y_{-j} \rangle = (N + j)/(\alpha - 1), \tag{12}$$

i.e., the mean value of the left-truncated and left-shifted Waring distribution is a linear function of the point of truncation. This property is a characterization: the linear relation holds if and only if the distribution is Waring. This characterization is a special case of a more general characterization theorem (Glänzel et al., 1984).

3.3 Applications of a Characterization Theorem

The linear relation (12) can be used as the basis of an effective statistical test and extrapolation tool. Plotting the series of truncated mean values $\langle y_{-0} \rangle$, $\langle y_{-1} \rangle$, $\langle y_{-2} \rangle$, ... against the point of truncation, 0, 1, 2, ... a straight line should be obtained indicating the subsistence of a Waring distribution. A statistical test has been elaborated and presented on a linguistic example by Telcs et al. (1985).

If one happens to have a left-truncated set of frequency data, the same straight line may help to extrapolate to the missing region. Most typically, publication frequency data start with 1, i.e., do not account for the "silent majority": those researchers who happen not to publish within the framework studied. The number of these researchers can be estimated using the Waring model. A successful attempt has been reported by Schubert and Telcs (1987) on the example of estimating the size of "publication-worthy" researcher community ("publication potential") of U.S. states. Furthermore, the method has been adapted to evaluate research institutions in Sweden, and induced heated science policy debates that have not yet been settled (Koski, 2013).

Another interesting consequence of the linear relation (12) is connected with the so-called "Characteristic Scores and Scales" (CSS) method (Glänzel & Schubert, 1988). This is a method for marking thresholds to divide a sample into classes according to the value of a random variable ξ. While, e.g., in case of quantiles, the classes are defined to contain equal number of elements, CSS classes adjust themselves according to the nature of the distribution. CSS thresholds originated from iteratively truncating samples at their mean value and recalculating the mean of the truncated sample until the procedure is stopped or no new scores are obtained. This procedure is briefly described in the following.

After putting $b_0 = 0$, the sample mean is chosen as the first threshold, denoted now as b_1.

$$b_1 = E(\xi). \tag{13}$$

Further thresholds are defined recursively.

$$b_k = E(\xi \mid \xi \geq b_{k-1}). \tag{14}$$

That is, the second threshold, b_2, is equal to the mean value of all sample elements equal to or greater than the overall sample mean, and so on. The classes are then defined by the pairs of the corresponding threshold values, particularly on the basis of the half-closed intervals $[b_{k-1}, b_k)$ with $k \geq 0$. Depending on the sample size and the nature of the distribution, three to five classes are usually sufficient for a practical classification task.

Taking into account that in the above-average region Zipf's law (Eq. (9)) begins to come into force, the linear relation (12) leads to the following approximation (Glänzel, 2013):

$$b_k \approx b_1(a^k - 1)/(a - 1), \tag{15}$$

where $a = \alpha/(\alpha - 1)$, α being the tail exponent, which is identical with the corresponding parameter of the Waring distribution (cf. Eq. (9)). Approximate thresholds can, therefore, be calculated from estimations of the mean value and the tail exponent even if the full distribution of the variable is not available.

3.4 Another Special Case

The $a = 0$ case (here a denotes the coefficient in the transfer rate of the above model according to Schubert and Glänzel) seems to lead to a trivial solution.

Eq. (2*) reduces to a formula often associated with "Gibrat's law"[1] (Gibrat, 1931):

$$f_i = bix_i, \qquad (16)$$

consequently, $f_0 = 0$, thus no substance reaches beyond cell 0: $y_0 = 1$, $y_i = 0$ for all $i > 0$. If, however, the limiting distribution is sought for $i > 0$, $a \to 0$, a non-trivial solution is found both in the "closed-system" and the "equilibrium-system" case.

In a closed system, we have

$$y_i = q(1-q)^{i-1}. \qquad (17)$$

This is a geometric distribution analogous to equation (6), but in this case $q = e^{bt}$. In this case the geometric distribution emerges as a special case of the zero-truncated negative binomial distribution. This case is treated in (Coleman, 1964, p. 307).

In an equilibrium system the same procedure leads to a Yule distribution (see, e.g., Price, 1976).

$$y_i = \alpha B(\alpha + 1, i), \qquad (18)$$

where $B(\cdot, \cdot)$ denotes the beta function. The Yule distribution is a prototype of distributions obeying Zipf's law (Eq. (9)); remarkably, Simon (1955) derived it from Gibrat's law. In this case, extrapolation to zero is meaningless; there is an infinite pool of zero-elements behind the apparent distribution.

3.5 A Summary of Distributions Emerging from the Schubert–Glänzel Model

Table 1 summarizes the distributions emerging from the model outlined in Figure 2 and equations (1)–(3) under various conditions.

The most striking feature is that while the 'closed-system' solutions are Gaussian in nature (i.e., have an exponential tail), the 'equilibrium' solutions are Zipfian (have a power-law tail). The special appeal of the model is that both of these classes, sometimes considered antagonistic, can be derived from it. The geometric distribution, which is a degenerate case of both classes has its generating scheme in both columns.

---

[1] en.wikipedia.org/wiki/Gibrat's_law

Tab. 1: Distributions emerging from the Schubert–Glänzel model.

	Closed system	Equilibrium system
General case	Negative binomial (Pólya); Eq. (4)	Waring; Eq. (7)
$b = 0$ (no cumulative advantage)	Poisson; Eq. (5)	Geometric; Eq. (6)
$a \to 0, i > 0$	Geometric; Eq. (14)	Yule; Eq. (15)
$i \to \infty$	Exponential	Inverse power (Zipf); Eq. (9)

4 An Alternative Explanation: Heterogeneity

It is important to note that the same distribution patterns can be explained without the cumulative advantage hypothesis. We may assume that any given researcher has a constant probability to publish the next paper independently of the number of papers already published (i.e., $b = 0$), yet a set of researchers may have a productivity distribution given in Table 1. This is possible, if the population is heterogeneous, namely, if a (constant for each single researcher) has a gamma distribution. A Poisson distribution with a gamma distributed parameter, μ, provides a negative binomial distribution, while a geometric distribution with gamma distributed parameter, q, results in a Waring distribution.

As Coleman (1964) notes:

> It is impossible to choose between a contagious[2] interpretation and a heterogeneity interpretation merely on the basis of the empirical distribution itself, no matter how well it fits a theoretical distribution. What are required in addition are over-time data, which can show the development of contagion if it exists.
>
> (p. 301)

In two rare cases of such longitudinal studies, Huber and Wagner-Döbler (2001a, b) found that in two fields: mathematical logic and physics, heterogeneity rather than cumulative advantage is responsible for the observed empirical productivity distributions.

---

2 In Coleman's terminology, "contagion" is analogous with cumulative advantage.

5 Network Aspects

Given the fact that scientific publications are increasingly the result of collaborative authorship (see, e.g., Glänzel & Schubert, 2004)—or hyperauthorship (Cronin, 2001), it seems obvious to seek cumulative advantage patterns in co-authorship distributions as well. At the time of elaborating the cumulative advantage publication productivity models, attempts to extend the idea to co-author networks were largely hindered by the lack of a proper mathematical theory. The Erdős-Rényi model of random graphs led to a Poisson distribution, and the cumulative advantage element could not be included into the model.

An alternative approach was found by Barabási and his group at the turn of the millennium. The scale-free network concept (Barabási & Albert, 1999) was inspired by well-tested physical models, and was successfully applied for such popular examples as the Internet and the network of movie actors. They coined the term "preferential attachment" for the cumulative advantage phenomenon. The applicability of the model to co-author networks has been demonstrated (Newman, 2001; Barabási et al., 2002) and became milestone papers of the topic.

6 The Hirsch-Connection

Shortly after Hirsch (2005) let the h-index genie out of the bottle, Glänzel (2006) attempted to find the position of the index in the framework of statistical theory. He found that it is closely connected with Gumbel's theory of characteristic extreme values. For distributions having inverse power tail (obeying Zipf's law), he could relate the h-index to traditional statistical parameters of the sample with the following formula:

$$h \approx x^{\alpha/(\alpha+1)} n^{1/(\alpha+1)}, \qquad (19)$$

where h is the h-index, x is the sample mean, n is the sample size, and α is the tail exponent.

The formula found widespread empirical support, among others, on the example of h-indices of journals (Schubert & Glänzel, 2007) and countries (Csajbók et al., 2007).

7 Network-based *h*-indices

Far beyond the scope of bibliometrics, in general, and research evaluation, in particular, the *h*-index raised interest in network/graph research. Eppstein and Spiro (2009) interpreted it as a graph invariant used in constructing dynamic graph algorithms particularly efficient for scale-free networks. Korn et al. (2009) used it under the name of lobby-index as a centrality measure characterizing the network's capability for efficient communication. Its use as a measure of coherence in a community of researchers (authors) was demonstrated by Schubert et al. (2009).

An interesting Hirsch-type index characterizing social networks was defined by Schubert (2012a) and amended by Rousseau (2012). Actually, the index is a special case of an idea of Zhao et al. (2011). The partnership ability index, φ, can be defined for arbitrary actions and actors as follows: An actor is said to have a partnership ability index φ, if with φ of his/her n partners had at least φ joint actions each, and with the other $(n - \varphi)$ partners if they had no more than φ joint actions each. In the original paper, the index was exemplified on a co-authorship sample, but it proved to be applicable also in a network of jazz musicians (Schubert, 2012b).

Although the indicator is meaningful for networks of any structure, for scale-free networks Glänzel's relation (19) is supposed to hold. Indeed, both mentioned studies supported the validity of this approximation, similarly to a study on a large co-author sample reported by Cabanac (2013).

The reader should be reminded that, similarly to the empirical distribution in the case of publication productivity models, the network properties (e.g., the inverse power tail of the degree distribution) is not a sufficient basis for inferring to the generating mechanism. Cumulative advantage (preferential attachment) is a reasonable possibility, but other mechanisms (e.g., heterogeneity) cannot be excluded.

8 Conclusion

Success is an extremely multifaceted concept. In scientific and scholarly research, success is the creation and communication of new knowledge. In informetrics, publication output and citation impact are considered the main measurable aspects of success. In both aspects, success appears to be 'contagious': success breeds success, advantages cumulate. Theories of informetrics should give an account of this feedback mechanism—that is what our model attempted, and maybe not quite unsuccessfully achieved.

A particular recipe for success is attributed to Mark Tyson: "Confidence breeds success and success breeds confidence ...Confidence applied properly surpasses genius."[3] As a net result, in this 'model', as well, success seems to breed success and, although the mechanisms can be disputed, Matthew's truth still prevails. And as it could be seen from the overview compiled in this paper, success-breeds-success is not only a successful way to reach success in publication and citation terms, but also a fruitful and successful topic of bibliometric modeling.

Cited References

Allison, P. D. (1980). Estimation and testing for a Markov model of reinforcement. *Sociological Methods & Research*, 8, 434–453.

Barabási, A.-L., & Albert, R. (1999). Emergence of scaling in random networks. *Science* 286(5439), 509–512.

Barabási, A. L., Jeong, H. Néda, Z., Ravasz, E., Schubert, A. & Vicsek, T. (2002). Evolution of the social network of scientific collaborations. *Physica A*, 311(3–4), 590–614.

Brookes, B. C. (1968). The derivation and application of the Bradford-Zipf distribution. *Journal of Documentation*, 24(4), 247–265.

Cabanac, G. (2013). Experimenting with the partnership ability φ-index on a million computer scientists. *Scientometrics*, 96(1), 1–9.

Coleman, J. S. (1964). Introduction to Mathematical Sociology. New York: Free Press.

Cronin, B. (1982). Invisible-colleges and information-transfer – A review and commentary with particular reference to the social sciences. *Journal of Documentation*, 38(3), 212–236.

Cronin, B. (2001). Hyperauthorship: A postmodern perversion or evidence of a structural shift in scholarly communication practices? *Journal of the American Society for Information Science and Technology*, 52(7), 558–569.

Csajbók, E., Berhidi, A., Vasas, L., & Schubert, A. (2007). Hirsch-index for countries based on essential science indicators data. *Scientometrics*, 73(1), 91–117.

Eggenberger, F., & Pólya, G. (1923). Über die Statistik verketer Vorgänge, *Zeitschrift für Angewandte Mathematik und Mechanik*, 1, 279–289.

Eppstein, D., & Spiro, E. S. (2009). The h-Index of a Graph and Its Application to Dynamic Subgraph Statistics. Algorithms and Data Structures. *Lecture Notes in Computer Science*, 5664, 278–289

Gibrat, R. (1931). *Les Inégalités Économiques*. Paris: Librairie du Recueil Sirey.

Glänzel, W. (2006). On the h-index - A mathematical approach to a new measure of publication activity and citation impact. *Scientometrics*, 67(2), 315–321.

Glänzel, W. (2013). High-end performance or outlier? Evaluating the tail of scientometric distributions. *Scientometrics*, 97(1), 13–23.

Glänzel, W., & Schubert, A. (1988). Characteristic scores and scales in assessing citation impact. *Journal of Information Science*, 14(2), 123–127.

---

[3] http://mmaquotes.blogspot.hu/2014/04/confidence-breeds-success-and-success.html

Glänzel, W., & Schubert, A. (2004). Analyzing scientific networks through co-authorship, In: H. F. Moed et al. (eds.), *Handbook of Quantitative Science and Technology Research*, pp. 257–276.

Glänzel, W., Telcs, A., & Schubert, A. (1984). Characterization by truncated moments and its application to Pearson-type distributions. *Probability Theory and Related Fields* (at the time of publication: Zeitschrift für Wahrscheinlichkeitstheorie und Verwandte Gebiete), 66(2), 173–183. (Correction: *Probability Theory and Related Fields*. 74 (1987) 317.)

Goffman, W. (1965). An epidemic model in an open population, *Nature*, 205, 831.

Goffman W., & Nevill, V. A. (1964). Generalization of epidemic theory. *Nature*, 204, 225.

Haitun, S. D. (1982). Stationary scientometric distributions. I-II-III. *Scientometrics*, 4(1), 5–25; 4(2), 89–104; 4(3), 181–194.

Hirsch, J. E. (2005). An index to quantify an individual's scientific research output. *Proceedings of the National Academy of Sciences of the United States of America*. 102(46), 16569–16572.

Huber, J. C., & Wagner-Döbler, R. (2001a). Scientific production: A statistical analysis of authors in mathematical logic. *Scientometrics*, 50(2), 323–337.

Huber, J. C., & Wagner-Döbler, R. (2001b). Scientific production: A statistical analysis of authors in physics, 1800–1900. *Scientometrics*, 50(3), 437–453.

Koestler, A. (1964). *The Act of Creation*, Dell: New York.

Korn, A., Schubert, A., & Telcs, A. (2009). Lobby index in networks. *Physica A-Statistical Mechanics and its Applications*, 388(11), 2221–2226.

Koski, T. (2013). *On the Waring distribution, the Glänzel-Schubert model and their applications – a historiett*. Retrieved from http://www.math.kth.se/~tjtkoski/goranwaring.pdf

Merton, R. K. (1968). The Matthew Effect in Science. *Science*, 159(3810), 56–63.

Newman, M. E. J. (2001). The structure of scientific collaboration networks. *Proceedings of the National Academy of Sciences of the United States of America*. 98(2), 404–409.

Price, D. De Solla (1976). A general theory of bibliometric and other cumulative advantage processes. *Journal of the American Society for Information Science*, 27(5), 292–306.

Price, D. D., & Gürsey, S. (1976). Studies in scientometrics. Part 1. Transience and continuance in scientific authorship. *Internation Forum on Information and Documentation*, 1, 17–24.

Rousseau, R. (2012). Comments on "A Hirsch-type index of co-author partnership ability". *Scientometrics*, 91(1), 309–310.

Schubert, A. (2012a). A Hirsch-type index of co-author partnership ability. *Scientometrics*, 91(1), 303–308.

Schubert, A. (2012b). Jazz discometrics: a network approach. *Journal of Informetrics*, 6(4), 480–484.

Schubert, A. (2013). A follow-up study of title word bisociations in Inorganica Chimica Acta. *ISSI Newsletter*, 9(3), 54–55.

Schubert, A., & Glänzel, W. (1984). A dynamic look at a class of skew distributions – A model with scientometric applications. *Scientometrics*, 6(3), 149–167.

Schubert, A., & Glänzel, W. (2007). A systematic analysis of Hirsch-type indices for journals. *Journal of Informetrics*, 1(3), 179–184.

Schubert, A., Korn, A., & Telcs, A. (2009). Hirsch-type indices for characterizing networks. *Scientometrics*, 78(2), 375–382.

Schubert, A. P., & Schubert, G. A. (1997). Inorganica Chimica Acta: its publications, references and citations. An update for 1995–1996, *Inorganica Chimica Acta*, 266(2), 125–133.

Schubert, A., & Telcs, A. (1989). Estimation of the publication potential in 50 U.S. states and in the District of Columbia based on the frequency distribution of scientific productivity. *Journal of the American Society for Information Science*, *40*(40), 291–297.

Simon, H. A. (1955). On a class of skew distribution functions, *Biometrika*, *42*(3–4), 425–440.

Tague, J. (1981). The success-breeds-success phenomenon and bibliometric processes. *Journal of the American Society for Information Science*, *32*(4), 280–286.

Telcs, A., Glänzel, W., Schubert, A. (1985). Characterization and statistical test using truncated expectations for a class of skew distributions. *Mathematical Social Sciences*, *10*(2), 169–178.

Zhao, S. X., Rousseau, R. & Ye, Y. (2011). h-degree as a basic measure in weighted network. *Journal of Informetrics*, *5*(4), 668–677.

David Bawden and Lyn Robinson
Information's Magic Numbers: The Numerology of Information Science

1 Introduction

Two themes were presented at the Libraries in the Digital Age (LIDA) conference, held in Zadar, Croatia, in June 2014. The first, chaired by David Bawden, focused on "qualitative assessment". Blaise Cronin chaired the second theme, focused on "altmetrics". They, as well as several other conference speakers, emphasized the complementary nature of qualitative and quantitative methods; while quantitative data is of unarguable importance, it must be interpreted insightfully and used with care.[1] Applying numbers sensibly has always been a major concern for Blaise Cronin, as is attested by his publication list. His academic webpage[2] notes that "much of his research focuses on collaboration in science, scholarly communication, citation analysis, the academic reward system and cybermetrics—the intersection of information science and social studies of science", while his Wikipedia entry[3] describes him as being jointly an "information scientist and bibliometrician". Despite this strong informetric focus, Cronin has had a long-standing concern about the potential descent of this aspect of the information science discipline into a "new age of numerology," due to over-use and misuse and of bibliometrics and altmetrics; see, for example, Cronin (1998; 2000), Cronin and Sugimoto (2015), and Priego (2012). It is therefore appropriate to include in this volume a chapter on the numerology of information science; to ask to what extent we are able to identify a few numbers which may helpfully encapsulate important aspects of the subject.

Numerology, roughly the belief that numbers in general, and integers in particular, have their own nature and properties, and can of themselves influence events, is rather out of favor nowadays, being regarded as a pseudoscience. The impeccable scientific belief that the regularities of nature can be captured by simple mathematical relationships is a long way from Blair's (1976, p. 81) notion that "numbers, quite distinct from their empirical use, become a language, as full of

---

[1] The presentations may be found on the conference website at http://ozk.unizd.hr/proceedings/index.php/lida
[2] http://www.soic.indiana.edu/all-people/profile.html?profile_id=4
[3] http://en.wikipedia.org/wiki/Blaise_Cronin

metaphor and dimension as poetry". However, before sneering at the idea that numbers in themselves can have a significance, we should remember that the long-standing, and still influential, Platonic tradition within science views numbers as having their own objective existence, and indeed that the physical universe and everything in it is, at root, a mathematical structure made of numbers (see Tegmark [2014] for a recent and accessible account of this position).

As well as numbers *per se*, numerology is often taken, usually critically, to mean an enthusiasm for simple numerical formulae, usually involving integers, capturing some significant aspect of reality. These have been seen in both the sciences and the social sciences: notoriously, the British physicist and astronomer Sir Arthur Eddington spent many years seeking simple integer relationships as the clue to the universe (Kilmister, 2005). It is clear that there are strong relations between numbers, the physical world and cultural issues, as is clearly shown by the sequence of "kissing numbers", the number of spheres which in any space exactly bound a further identical sphere (Weisstein, n.d.); two points on a one dimensional line bound a third point, six circles circumscribe a seventh, and twelve balls circumscribe a thirteenth. The resultant sequence of "kissing number plus one"— three, seven, thirteen—captures the principal significant/lucky/unlucky numbers in numerous cultures, and is numerologically present in the 'leader with twelve followers' meme of Christ, Osiris, King Arthur, and others (Blair, 1976).[4] Therefore, despite the dangers of slipping into a facile numerology, simple numbers and integer relations may still be worth investigating.

There are, in fact, relatively few such simple numbers and number relations in information science, and what exists was imported from adjacent disciplines. In truth, they are not all very simple: one is very large, some have alternatives, one is a sequence, and one is infinite. These numbers encapsulate a variety of issues: how much information there is, or could be; the optimal size of communicating groups; the structure of information networks; the distribution of information activities; and the limits to the growth of knowledge. We find that sometimes, but not always, the actual number is less important than the theoretical perspective to which it points. We begin by considering the big picture: how much information there is, or could be, in the human context and in the universe. Then we move to the smallest scale, the information associated with the conscious attention of a single person. From there, we move up the scale, to information associated with

---

4 It would have been nice if the four-dimensional kissing number, which was not known until 2003 (Pfender & Ziegler, 2004) and cannot be intuitively grasped like the small dimension equivalents, had also related to some culturally significant number. Disappointingly, it was shown to be 24, and 25 does not appear to have significance in any culture.

groups, with networks, and with disciplines; and finally up to the largest scale, to the infinity of possible recorded information.

2 The Universal Number: 8×10^{21}

The most fundamental number-related question we can ask about information is simply: *How much information is there?* This leads to a spin-off question: *How much information could there be?* Both, perhaps not surprisingly, are difficult to answer accurately. Attempts to answer such questions have been reviewed by Bawden and Robinson (2012a), Gleick (2011), Davis and Shaw (2011), and Floridi (2014).

Before the advent of widespread digital information, the "How much information is there?" question was generally answered in terms of counts of documents: how many books, articles, reports, etc. had been published. For example, Jinha (2010) suggested that the total number of scholarly articles had reached fifty million. More recent attempts have had to include the much larger amount of born-digital information—an intrinsically more difficult process—with results that can only be approximate.

The first attempt in the digital era to address this question in a rigorous way was the "How much information?" study from the School of Information Management and Systems at University of California Berkeley, United States (U.S.), first carried out in 2000, and repeated in 2003 (SIMS, 2003). The study estimated that approximately 12 exabytes of information had been recorded by humanity before the general use of computers, but was being dwarfed by the amounts now being generated and stored. About 5 exabytes of new information was stored during 2002; equal to 37,000 times the information in the Library of Congress, or 800 megabytes/30 feet (10 metres) of bookshelf content per person on the planet. However, more than three times this amount of information was communicated through electronic channels but never stored.

Later studies (Hilbert & Lopez 2011; Ganz & Reinsel 2011; Hilbert, 2014) have suggested that the amount of information broadcast each year, in increasingly varied formats, was approaching 2 zetabytes by 2007, that current capacity of all information storage devices approaches 300 exabytes, and that the total grew to over 1600 exabytes between 2007 and 2011. Floridi (2014, p. 13) points out that this amounts to enough information being generated each day to fill all the libraries in the U.S. eight times over, and that the figure is likely to grow threefold every four years, so that there may be expected to be 8 zetabytes (8 times 10^{21} bytes) of information by 2015; this figure is taken as 'the number' for this section.

One consequence of this, as Floridi (2014) points out, is that since 2007 information has been produced at a faster rate than have storage devices to handle it; this despite Kryder's Law, which shows that the capacity of storage devices is increasing at an even faster rate than is processing capability, the latter obeying Moore's Law. That we cannot therefore store all our information arguably does not, in fact, matter; the great proportion now is data generated by machines and used by machines, without any need for longer-term storage for human intervention or reflection.

The actual value of these numbers is immaterial—what is of importance is their scale and order of magnitude, and the ways in which they are changing, to create what Floridi (2014) terms the "infosphere," an entirely new form of information environment.

The second question, how much information could there be, is answered by considering the capacity of the physical universe to hold bits of information; a rough estimate, subject to many approximations, is reported by Gleick (2011) to be about 10^{90} bits. This figure, though of no practical significance for information science, reminds us that information is always physically instantiated, and its processing is limited by the constraints of the physical universe. Of course, there are those who would go further, and say that information is physical *per se*, but that is a topic for a different discussion; see, for instance, Bawden and Robinson (2013), the contributors to Davies and Gregersen (2010), and Hjørland (2007).

3 The Personal Number: 7 (or 4)

One of the most cited papers in the human sciences is American psychologist George Miller's "Magical number 7, plus or minus 2" (Miller, 1956). This paper drew attention to the significance of the number in human information processing. The main finding was that the number of concepts of items which an adult can hold in conscious attention, or short-term memory, at one time is about seven. Miller, an early enthusiast for the application of information theory in psychology, used information theory concepts to speculate about what this meant for the mechanism of memory. This limit has been widely tested, and was generally regarded as correct. However, more recent studies, summarized by Cowan (2001), have suggested that the limit may be lower, between three and five rather than between five and nine. On the basis of these findings, Cowan recommends a "magical number 4".

Whatever the exact number may be, it is clearly small, and has implications for the way in which information is handled and should be presented. However, there seems to have been relatively little explicit recognition of this in information science. It is tempting to ascribe to this factor the well-known tendency for users of search engines to attend only to the items presented on the first page. This seems likely to be more a matter of disinclination to spend the time necessary to consider more items, rather than an inability to hold them in conscious attention at once; but it may be that some underlying mechanism, associated with the number limit, accounts for both factors.

Knowledge organization systems appear to respect this feature. Decimal classifications may be guided to their ten main sections by a desire for a pleasing notation, and others, most notably the Library of Congress Classification, follow the twenty six letters of the Roman alphabet. But the general tendency, following Ranganathan's five fundamental facets (Hedden, 2010; Broughton, 2006), to have between four and ten main sections or facets in the great majority of taxonomies and thesauri may be seen as an unconscious recognition that this is a number which enables the user, or at least the compiler, to hold the whole structure in mind. Miller's number holds up at more detailed levels of taxonomy design: "A popular rule of thumb is to go only three levels deep and have only six to eight concepts per level. These numbers are based on user experience tests, which have shown that users have the patience to click down only to a third level and can scan only six to eight term entries at once" (Hedden, 2010, p. 236). This, of course, reflects the similar experience with search engines noted above.

4 The Group Number: 150

The group number stems from the work of the British evolutionary psychologist Robin Dunbar, initially inspired by the study of the correlation between brain size and the size of social groups in primates. This led to the idea that there is a natural group size for humans; stable communicative relationships can be maintained with about 150 people (Dunbar, 1993; Dunbar, 2008; Dunbar, 2012). The number derived from the correlation was actually 148, but it has generally, and sensibly, been rounded to 150. This idea is of evident importance for information science, since it is well-known that close acquaintances are a major source of information in most, if not all, contexts (Case, 2012). Further, shared knowledge is a major factor in the maintenance of social groups (Dunbar, 2012; McPherson, Smith-Lovin, & Cook, 2001).

Dunbar argues that the size of the group of communicative relationships which can be maintained at any one time is constrained in part by cognitive factors, and hence ultimately by some aspect of brain size and structure, and partly by available time. Direct evidence in humans is provided by correlations of individual differences in social network size and volumes of social cognition areas in the cortex and amygdala brain structures (Kanai, Bahrami, Roylance, & Rees, 2012; Bickart, Wright, Dautoff, Dickerson, & Feldman Barrett, 2011; Powell, Lewis, Roberts, García-Fiñana, & Dunbar, 2012). Empirically, this has been tested by the observations of groupings in a wide variety of contexts, including hunter-gatherers, farming communities, military formations, industrial and commercial workforces, Christmas card lists, online social networks, and academic disciplines (Dunbar, 1992; Dunbar, 2008; Hill & Dunbar, 2003; Roberts, Dunbar, Pollet, & Ruppens, 2009).

Objections to the 150 value have been raised by those who argue that groupings of around 30–50 people are commonly found in hunter-gatherer populations, arguably the most "natural" form of human grouping (de Ruiter, Weston, & Lyon, 2011). Others have suggested that the number must be much larger because of the evidence that many people have several hundred contacts on social media (Wellman, 2012). However, as Dunbar (2012, p. 2195) asserts, "there is now considerable evidence that groupings of this size [around 150 individuals] occur frequently in human social organization, and that this is the normative limit on the size of personal social networks among adults."

A more nuanced viewpoint, rather than seeking to insist on a single number to encapsulate the complexities of social interaction, is to see a series of numbers, reflecting different strengths of social ties, and of shared knowledge and perspectives. These groups exhibit the kind of "small world" network structure and behavior which will discussed later. Typically, these represent groups with rough sizes 5, 15, 50, 150, 500, 1500, which can be seen as circles, each including those inner, with a scaling factor of about three (Dunbar, 2012; Hamilton, Milne, Walker, Burger, & Brown, 2007; Roberts, Dunbar, Pollet, & Ruppens, 2009; Zhou, Sornette, Hill, & Dunbar, 2005). Groups of these sizes may be characterized roughly as follows:

- **5:** a core social group, or "support clique," to whom an individual would refer very frequently for support, assistance, information and advice;
- **15:** a "sympathy group," with whom there are special ties and frequent contact;
- **50:** typically a temporary grouping, formed for a particular period or task;
- **150:** the stable inter-communicating group, with regular interaction and knowledge sharing;
- **500:** the "megaband," again typically a temporary or pragmatic grouping; and
- **1500:** the "tribe"—acquaintances at best, with whom any relationship, or communication of information, is typically one-way, and there is no little or no sharing of knowledge.

Of these, the 5 and 150 levels seem particularly significant: 150 for the reasons set out by Dunbar, supported by a good deal of evidence, and in keeping with Shirky's (2003, n.p.) recommendation for effective online group size (i.e., "larger than a dozen, smaller than a few hundred"); five because it appears to be a natural small group equivalent, related to the idea that spontaneous conversation and information sharing almost always occurs in groups of not more than four individuals (Dunbar, Duncan, & Nettle, 1995).

It seems evident that an understanding of this group interaction structure, if indeed it is valid and omnipresent, is important for several areas within information science, perhaps most notably in knowledge management. However, there seems to have been little examination of the significance of this group structure with respect to the communication of information. Studies have established that the smaller, and more information-intensive and knowledge-sharing, groups require an investment of time, and ideally substantial face-to-face contact, if their members are not to slip into the larger, and less effective groupings (Dunbar, 2012; Roberts, Dunbar, Pollet, & Ruppens, 2009). This seems to be a warning against reliance on purely digital information sharing, particularly with an assumption that its scale can be increased by technological means, and typifies the value that such theoretical concepts can bring to information practice.

5 The Linking Number: 6

The idea that everyone in the world is connected to everyone else by no more than "six degrees of separation" has become entrenched in popular consciousness through newspaper and magazine articles, plays, TV series, films, and games (Six degrees of separation, n.d.). The concept was introduced by the Hungarian writer Frigyes Karinthy (1929), in his short story *Láncszemek* (*Chains*), but became well-known only with the classic paper of American psychologist Stanley Milgram (1967). This initiated a research program in what became known as "small world" phenomena; for a detailed review, from Karinthy onwards, see Schnettler (2009).

In Milgram's study, randomly chosen participants in the Midwest (U.S.), were asked to try to send a printed message to a target in New England (U.S.), by sending it to a person with whom they were personally acquainted, asking that it be forwarded in the same way. Only about 30 % succeeded, and those that did varied between two and ten intermediaries, with a median of five. This was the basis for the idea of "six degrees of separation," although Milgram did not use this phrase in his paper. Focusing on the number of nodes, rather than links, in the chain, he wrote of "five circles of acquaintances" (Milgram, 1967, p. 65). The rather more memorable "six degrees of separation" phrase was introduced two decades later, in a play with that name (Guare, 1990).

Some limited empirical research in the social sciences investigated this idea over the next thirty years, until the subject was revitalized by formal mathematical modeling of network connectivity in all kinds of contexts, not just social (Caldarelli & Catanzaro, 2012; Mitchell 2009; Schnettler, 2009). The formal modeling results tend to support empirical studies in various contexts, in confirming commonly occurring short paths through extensive networks, though they do not support the idea that there is anything special about the number six (or five); median chain lengths can vary from three to fifteen, according to the nature of the network. However, a study aiming to replicate Milgram's work on a much larger scale using e-mail gave quite similar results, of between five and seven steps for the minority of messages which were completed, suggesting that this may be a natural scale for social information networks (Dodds, Muhamad, & Watts, 2003).

As Stock and Stock (2013, p. 384–385) note, the "six degrees of separation" concept has become synonymous with the idea of "small worlds". This expresses, in the social context, the idea that "people are not only linked to their immediate friends, family, and acquaintances, but they are embedded in a larger structure of direct and indirect contacts" (Schnettler, 2009, p. 166). More formally, the "small-world effect" denotes the fact that most nodes in most networks are joined by relatively small paths; a specific "small-world network" has been identified as one with a structure intermediate between highly regular and totally random, with nodes highly clustered, as in regular graphs, and yet with a short path length between any two nodes, as is typical in random graphs (Schnettler, 2009; Watts & Strogatz, 1998).

However, despite this theoretical support for short paths, empirical work on social networks, typically carried out in the sociology domain, have tended to show that, although extended chains of social contacts were available, they were used infrequently for finding information (Schnettler, 2009). For example, in a study of how people found information about job prospects, most used one intermediary, or none, and no chain was more than four links (Granovetter, 1995). The only example of longer chains, with up to nine links and a median of five, was found in a study of women in the U.S. seeking a doctor willing to perform an abortion at a time when legal abortion was severely restricted (Lee, 1969).

Björneborn and Ingwersen (2001, p. 74) noted that small world metrics were potentially relevant to several topics within information science including webometrics, citation analysis, semantic networks, and thesauri, but that there was a lack of research in these areas. Since then there has been some usage in webometric studies, a typical example being the demonstration that the typical path link between sites in the United Kingdom (U.K.) academic web network is three or four (Björneborn, 2006), and in bibliometrics, for example, a study of the co-occurrence of keywords in databases, where the number reflects the distance between papers measured by the keywords in common (Zhu, Wang, Hassan & Haddawy, 2013). The only specific mentions of the "six degrees" idea in the recent information science literature appears to be James' (2006) reflections on the relevance of the idea to information literacy instruction, and Dennie and Cuccia's (2014) application to a chemical literature search assignment.

While considerable research has been carried out within information science using the "small worlds theory", this has largely been detailed qualitative studies of information interactions between groups and networks in limited spaces, physical or virtual (Savolainen, 2009). Concepts such as 'density' from network theory may be applied (see, for example, Huotari & Chatman, 2001), but generally in an informal and semi-quantitative way. Even within these caveats, Schultz-Jones (2009, p. 626) found that "library and information service settings [are] a largely undeveloped context for the application of social network theory and social network analysis." It may be that there is scope for better integration of qualitative and quantitative methods, as Schnettler (2009) advocates in general for small world research, and for a greater focus on contexts closer to our own (disciplinary) home. The number, whether it be 6 or not, is not, in this case, as important as the "network thinking" (Mitchell 2009) to which it points.

Finally, we might note that the "six degrees of separation" idea has launched metrics such as the Bacon number, the closeness of the Hollywood actor Kevin Bacon to any other actor, based on the actors who have worked with actors who have worked with Kevin Bacon, and, perhaps more seriously, the Erdös number, based on how many links of co-authorship link anyone to the Hungarian mathematician Paul Erdös (Grossman, 2014). Perhaps we should establish an analogous Cronin number: one of us [DB] would be 2, since he has not co-authored with Cronin, but has co-authored with at least one person who has, LR would have a Cronin number of 3, on the same basis.

6 The Network Number: 59

As we have just seen, experiments have shown that messages across small world networks fail to get through a majority of the time. This may be due to a variety of context-specific factors, depending on the nature of the network, and the pattern and strength of its connections (Dodds, Muhamad & Watts, 2003; Schnettler, 2009). Milgram (1967) noted a specific, and fairly obvious, point that two groups within a network may be cut off, if there is no link path joining them, so that there is no possibility of information passing between them. Mathematical analysis of networks by the American complexity scientist Stuart Kauffman has shed an interesting light on network behavior in this respect.

Kauffman has shown that, for any network of nodes which are all initially isolated, adding links randomly between nodes causes a pattern of connections to build up, steadily and linearly, so that linked groups are created within the overall network. This may be seen as an instantiation of Ramsey theory, which posits the unavoidable emergence of regularity in large structures, such as networks. It is often expressed as the 'party problem'; how many guests must be invited to a party (or people invited to link to a social media site) so that a minimum number (the "Ramsey Number") will know each other (Gould, nd).

Kauffman shows that when 59 % of the nodes are linked to at least one other, the pattern suddenly and dramatically changes, and the great majority of the nodes are connected. This is referred to as a network phase transition. An accessible account of the phenomenon is given by Kauffman (1996), and its significance is described for computer networks, such as the World Wide Web (Tetlow, 2007) and for social networks such as the financial system (Beinhocker, 2006).

The importance of this number for information science is that it should instill an awareness that the behavior of information networks of all kinds may change, suddenly and dramatically, as their interconnectivity increases. It is easy to assume that overall connectivity within a network, and hence the ability to pass information between any two of its nodes, will increase in a regular manner, as more individual interconnections are added, depending on the number of connected nodes. This is the basis for "laws" relating the value of a network, specifically a computer network, to the number of nodes connected. Metcalfe's Law, for example, states that the value of a network increases as the square of the numbers of nodes connected (Floridi, 2014), while a variant due to Briscoe, Odlyzko, and Tilly (2006) argue for a less rapid growth of n(log n), with n nodes connected. Kauffman's number shows us that this kind of continuous growth in network value is only valid up to a point. Beyond this, rather precisely specifiable, point, a qualitative change in the nature, and value, of the network occurs, leading to an essentially new information environment.

7 The Distribution Numbers: 90, 9, and 1

The numbers 90-9-1 have been found to represent the distribution of activity among users of social media sites, including microblogs, such as Twitter, and wikis, most notably Wikipedia. For every regular contributor, or "superuser", there are nine occasional contributors, and ninety "lurkers", who take information but do not contribute with any regularity; as an example, see van Mierlo (2014). This is an instantiation of a very widespread distribution in information areas. From our days as information practitioners, we recall it being an article of faith, stated anecdotally though never written down so far as we know, that in any complex search for information requiring high recall it was easy to get 90 % of the material, very difficult to get 99 % and impossible to get 100 %.

These are examples of the ubiquitous power law distributions that govern the information world, including those of Bradford, Lotka, Pareto, and Zipf (Bawden & Robinson 2012a; Egghe, 2005; Rousseau, 2010). As such, they are better known within the information science community than the other numbers described in this chapter, and need less exposition. An appreciation of these laws, and the numbers which come from them, informs practice in areas such as collection management, information retrieval, institutional bibliometrics, and the assessment of impact of social media; see, as examples, Corby (2003), Nicolaisen and Hjørland (2007), Bhavnani and Peck (2010), Åström and Hansson (2012), and Hoffman and Doucette (2012). These are thus among the few "magic numbers" which are used widely and directly in the practice of the information disciplines, and particularly in scientometrics.

8 The Knowledge Number: ∞

The knowledge number is generally termed the Champernowne number, after the British mathematician David Champernowne, who derived and published it while still an undergraduate student before going on to a career as an economics professor (Champernowne, 1933; Pickover, 2012, p. 364–365). While he derived his number simply as a mathematical curiosity, it has interesting implications for the information world (von Baeyer, 2003, p. 101–102).

We first choose a base for our number, say binary or decimal. Then we enumerate all the symbols that constitute that number set, then all the pairs, then all the triplets, and so on, for as long as we wish. In decimal base 10, as Champernowne originally presented it, we would write 0.12345678910111213141516 ... or, in the binary system, we would write 0 1 00 01 10 11 000 001 010 100 ... Since we can always continue adding to this number, it must necessarily be infinite in magnitude.

Then we choose a code to convert the number to characters—something like ASCII or Unicode—and convert our potentially infinite number to a potentially long infinite text string. In this infinite character string there will be found everything that has ever been written using the chosen character set, embedded in the (literally) infinitely larger set of everything could be written. We will find the text of Shakespeare's *Midsummer Night's Dream*, in all its editions, in all possible languages, and with all possible misprints and errors. We will find a copy of this paper, with all these variants, and a copy of all the works which Blaise Cronin has written, or might have written. This is an instantiation of Borges' (1998) Library of Babel,

> [Whose] bookshelves contain all possible combinations of [symbols] – that is, all that is able to be expressed, in every language. *All* – the detailed history of the future, the autobiographies of the archangels, the faithful catalog of the Library, thousands and thousands of false catalogs, the proof of the falsity of those false catalogs, a proof of the falsity of the *true* catalog, the Gnostic gospel of Basilides, the commentary upon that gospel, the commentary on the commentary on that gospel, the true story of your death, the translation of every book into every language, the interpolations of every book into all books, the treatise Bede could have written (but did not) on the mythology of the Saxon people, the lost books of Tacitus.
> (Borges, 1998, p. 115)

And Champernowne gives us this in a number.

The number is of no practical value, but it is a striking formal indication of the idea that creativity, and growth of knowledge, are unlimited. While our first number indicated that the amount of information that can be held within the physical universe must be finite, creativity is unlimited, and knowledge can grow indefinitely (see, for example, Deutsch, 2011; Kauffman, 2010).

9 Conclusions

It is difficult to state concisely where these numbers fit into our understanding of the information world, and more specifically in our understanding of informetrics and scholarly communication; though it would be difficult to deny their potential significance. All these numbers are interesting, and some are of immediate use for practice; they take us into the areas where the information sciences overlap with the human sciences, especially psychology, with the physical sciences, and even with philosophy. It is not evident that there is any metatheory which could encapsulate them all, and it may be unrealistic to think of anything of the sort. However, the links between the numbers, for example between Dunbar's social groups and Milgram's small world networks, may serve as a basis for building a modest theoretical framework.

It is still more unrealistic to seek for a single magic number for information. Though, if we had to do so, it would probably be 5, since this appears in several contexts, including cognitive scope, small world links, and optimal group size for information exchange. The numbers measure attributes of people and groups, cognition and networks, collections and activities; all three of Popper's Worlds, for those who like that ontology as a basic for the subject (Bawden, 2002; Bawden & Robinson, 2012B).

The numbers themselves appear rather fluid, and usually their exact value does not matter. It is the general magnitude that is important; it does not matter exactly what volume of information is produced daily, but it does matter, for practical purposes, that it is very large, and getting much larger very rapidly. Nor does it matter, for our purposes, whether the optimal group size for information interaction is exactly Dunbar's 150; though it does matter that it is about 150 rather than the suggested alternative values of 30 or 500.

We may do better to forget numerological relations, and think of qualitative patterns, with the numbers acting as a kind of aide-memoire: "statistical regularities, observed in a context where social influences play an important role", as Rousseau (2010, p. 2747) puts it. Or we may take the numbers as a clue, or introduction, to new theoretical perspectives, in the same way that Milgram's small world of 6 connections opens the way to the much wider idea of scale-free networks following power laws (Mitchell, 2009).

In their LIDA2014 presentations, both Blaise Cronin and David Bawden cited a quotation about the limitations of metrics. His quotation was Albert Einstein's remark that "not everything that can be counted counts, and not everything that counts can be counted," while David's mentioned Václav Havel's recommendation that we should have "a humble reverence for everything that we shall never measure". They amount to the same thing. Numbers will never tell the whole story, in information or in any other context. But that should not prevent us from continuing to seek for numbers, magic or otherwise, which capture the structures and patterns of the information world.

Cited References

Åström, F. & Hansson, J. (2012). How implementation of bibliometric practice affects the role of academic libraries. *Journal of librarianship and information Science*, 45(4), 316–322.

Bawden, D. (2002). The three worlds of health information. *Journal of Information Science*, 28(1), 51–62.

Bawden, D., & Robinson, L. (2012A). Informetrics. In D. Bawden and L. Robinson, *Introduction to information science* (pp. 163–185). London: Facet.

Bawden, D., & Robinson, L. (2012B). Basic concepts of information science. In D. Bawden and L. Robinson, *Introduction to information science* (pp. 63–89). London: Facet.

Bawden, D. & Robinson, L. (2013). "Deep down things": in what ways is information physical, and why does it matter for LIS?. *Information Research*, *18*(3), paper C03. Retrieved from http://InformationR.net/ir/18-3/colis/paperC03.html

Beinhocker, E. D. (2006). *The origin of wealth: evolution, complexity, and the radical remaking of economics*. Cambridge, MA: Harvard Business School Press.

Bhavnani, S. K., & Peck, F.A (2010). Scatter matters: Regularities and implications for the scatter of healthcare information on the Web. *Journal of the American Society for Information Science and Technology*, *61*(4), 659–676.

Blair, L. (1976). *Rhythms of Vision*, St. Albans: Paladin.

Bickart, K. C., Wright, C. I., Dautoff, R. J., Bradford, C. D., & Feldman Barratt, L. (2011). Amygdala volume and social network size in humans. *Nature Neuroscience*, *14*(2), 163–164.

Björneborn, L. (2006). "Mini small worlds" of shortest link paths crossing domain boundaries in an academic Web space. *Scientometrics*, *68*(3), 395–414.

Björneborn, L. & Ingwersen, P. (2001). Perspectives of webometrics. *Scientometrics*, *50*(1), 65–82.

Borges, J. L. (1998), The Library of Babel. In J. L. Borges, *Collected fictions*, London: Allen Lane, pp. 112–118.

Briscoe, B., Odlyzko, A., & Tilly, B (2006). Metcalfe's Law is wrong. *IEEE spectrum*, July 2006, pp. 26–31. Retrieved from http://spectrum.ieee.org/computing/networks/metcalfes-law-is-wrong

Broughton, V. (2006). The need for a faceted classification as the basis of all methods of information retrieval. *Aslib Proceedings*, *58*(1/2), 49–72.

Caldarelli, G. & Catanzaro, M. (2012). *Networks: a very short introduction*. Oxford: Oxford University Press.

Case, D. O. (2012). *Looking for information: a survey of research on information seeking, needs and behavior (3rd ed.)*, Bingley: Emerald.

Champernowne, D. G. (1933). The construction of decimals normal in the scale of ten. *Journal of the London Mathematical Society*, *8*(4), 254–260.

Corby, K. (2003), Constructing core journal lists: mixing science and alchemy. *portal: Libraries and the academy*, *39*(2), 207–217.

Cowan, N. (2001). The magical number 4 in short-term memory: a reconsideration of mental storage capacity. *Behavioural and Brain Sciences*, *24*(1), 87–114.

Cronin, B. (1998). New Age numerology: a gloss on Apostol. *Science Tribune*, June 1998. Retrieved 1 July 2014 from http://www.tribunes.com/tribune/art98/cron.htm

Cronin, B. (2000). Bibliometrics and beyond: some thoughts on webometrics and influmetrics. *Biomed central*. Retrieved 1 July 2014 from http://www.biomedcentral.com/meetings/2000/foi/transcripts/cronin

Cronin, B., & Sugimoto, C. R. (Eds.). (2015). *Scholarly metrics under the microscope: From citation analysis to academic auditing*. Medford, NJ: Information Today, INC/ASIST, pp. 976.

Davies, P. & Gregersen, N. H. (2010). *Information and the nature of reality: from physics to metaphysics*. Cambridge: Cambridge University Press.

Davis, C. H. & Shaw, D. (eds.) (2011). *Introduction to information science and technology*. Medford NJ: Information Today.

de Ruiter, J., Weston, G., & Lyon, S. M. (2011). Dunbar's Number: group size and brain physiology in humans re-examined. *American Anthropologist*, *113*(4), 557–568.

Dennie, D. & Cuccia, L. A. (2014). "Six degrees of separation"—Revealing a "small-world phenomenon" through a chemistry literature search activity. *Journal of Chemical Education*, 91(4), 546–549.

Deutsch, D. (2011). *The beginnings of infinity: explanations that transform the world*. London: Allen Lane.

Dodds, P. S., Muhamad, R. & Watts, D. J. (2003). An experimental study of search in global social networks. *Science*, 301(5634), 827–829.

Dunbar, R. I. M. (1993). Coevolution of neocortex size, group size and language in humans. *Behavioral and Brain Sciences*, 16(4), 681–684.

Dunbar, R. I. M. (2008), Mind the gap: or why humans aren't just great apes. *Proceedings of the British Academy*, vol. 154 (2007 lectures), 403–423.

Dunbar, R. I. M. (2012), Social cognition on the Internet: testing constraints on social network size. *Philosophical transactions of the Royal Society B*, 367(1599), 2192–2201.

Dunbar, R. I. M., Duncan, N. & Nettle, D. (1995), Size and structure of freely forming conversational groups. *Human Nature*, 6(1), 67–78.

Egghe, L. (2005). *Power laws in the information production process: Lotkaian informetrics*. Amsterdam: Elsevier.

Floridi, L. (2014). *The 4th revolution: how the infosphere is reshaping human reality*. Oxford: Oxford University Press.

Ganz, J. & Reinsel, D. (2011). Extracting value from chaos. Retrieved 30 June 2014 from http://uk.emc.com/collateral/analyst-reports/idc-extracting-value-from-chaos-ar.pdf

Gleick, J. (2011). *The information: a history, a theory, a flood*. London: Fourth Estate.

Gould, M. (nd). Ramsey theory. Retrieved 12 September 2014 from http://people.maths.ox.ac.uk/~gouldm/ramsey.pdf

Granovetter, M. S. (1995). *Getting a job: a study of contacts and careers (2nd ed.)*. Chicago IL: University of Chicago Press.

Grossman, J. (2014). The Erdös number project. Oakland University. Retrieved 12 September 2014 from http://www.oakland.edu/enp

Guare, J. (1990). *Six degrees of separation*. New York NY: Vintage.

Hamilton, M. J., Milne, B. T., Walker, R. S., Burger, O., & Brown, J. H. (2007). The complex structure of hunter-gatherer social networks. *Proceedings of the Royal Society B*, 274(1622), 2195–2202.

Hedden, H. (2010). *The accidental taxonomist*. Medford NJ: Information Today.

Hilbert, M. (2014). What is the content of the world's technologically mediated information and communication capacity: how much text, image, audio and video? *The Information Society*, 30(2), 127–143.

Hilbert, M. & Lopez, P. (2011). The world's technological capacity to store, communicate and compute information. *Science*, 332(6025), 60–65.

Hill, R. A. and Dunbar, R. I. M. (2003). Social network size in humans. *Human Nature*, 14(1), 53–72.

Hjørland, B. (2007). Information: objective of subjective/situational? *Journal of the American Society for Information Science and Technology*, 58(10), 1448–1456.

Hoffman, K. & Doucette, L. (2012), A review of citation analysis methodologies for collection management. *College and Research Libraries*, 73(4), 321–335.

Huotari, M-L. & Chatman, E. (2001), Using everyday life information seeking to explain organizational behaviour, *Library and Information Science Research*, 23(4), 351–366.

James, K. (2006), Six degrees of information seeking: Stanley Milgram and the small world of the library, *Journal of Academic Librarianship, 32*(5), 527–532.

Jinha, A. (2010). Article 50 Million: an estimate of the number of scholarly articles in existence. *Learned Publishing, 23*(3), 258–263.

Kanai, R., Bahrami, B., Roylance, R., & Rees, G. (2012). Online social network size is reflected in human brain structure. *Proceedings of the Royal Society B, 279*(1732), 1327–1334.

Karinthy, F. (1929). Láncszemek (Chains). In F. Karinthy. *Minden másképpen van (Everything is different)*. Budapest: Atheneum Press. Reprinted in English in M. E.J Newman, A. Barabási & D. J. Watts. *The structure and dynamics of networks*. Princeton NJ: Princeton University Press, 2006, pp. 21–26.

Kauffman, S. (1996), *At home in the universe: the search for laws of self-organization and complexity*. Oxford: Oxford University Press.

Kauffman, S. (2010), *Reinventing the sacred: a new view of science, reason and religion*, New York NY: Basic Books.

Kilmister, C. W. (2005). *Eddington's search for a fundamental theory: a key to the universe*. Cambridge: Cambridge University Press.

Lee, N. H. (1969). *The search for an abortionist*, Chicago IL: University of Chicago Press.

McPherson, M., Smith-Lovin, L., & Cook, J. M. (2001). Birds of a feather: homophily in social networks. *Annual Review of Sociology, 27*, 415–444.

Milgram, S. (1967). The small world problem. *Psychology Today, 1*(1), 61–67.

Miller, G. A. (1956). The magical number 7 plus or minus 2: some limits on our capacity for processing information. *Psychological Review, 63*(2), 81–97.

Mitchell, M. (2009). *Complexity: a guided tour*. New York NY: Oxford University Press.

Nicolaisen, J. & Hjørland, B. (2007). Practical potentials of Bradford's Law: a critical examination of the received view. *Journal of Documentation, 63*(3), 359–377.

Pfender, F., & Ziegler, G. M. (2004). Kissing numbers, sphere packings and some unexpected proofs. *Notices of the American Mathematical Society, 51*(8), 873–883.

Pickover, C. A. (2012). *The math book*. New York NY: Sterling.

Powell, J., Lewis, P. A., Roberts, N., García-Fiñana, M., & Dunbar, R. I. M. (2012). Orbital prefrontal cortex volume predicts social network size: an imaging study of individual differences in humans. *Proceedings of the Royal Society B, 279*(1736), 2157–2162.

Priego, E. (2012). Insights from "The Numbers Game", lecture by Blaise Cronin. *Altmetric blog*. Retrieved 1 July 2014 from http://www.biomedcentral.com/meetings/2000/foi/transcripts/cronin

Roberts, S. B. G., Dunbar, R. I. M., Pollet, T., & Ruppens, T. (2009). Exploring variations in active network size: constraints and ego characteristics. *Social Networks, 31*(2), 138–146.

Rousseau, R. (2010). Informetric laws, *Encyclopedia of library and information sciences* (3rd ed.). London: Taylor and Francis, 1:1, 2747–2754.

Savolainen, R. (2009), Small world and information grounds as contexts of information seeking and sharing. *Library and Information Science Research, 31*(1), 38–45.

Schnettler, S. (2009). A structured overview of 50 years of small-world research. *Social Networks, 31*(3), 165–178.

Schultz-Jones, B. (2009). Examining information behaviour through social networks: an interdisciplinary review, *Journal of Documentation, 65*(4), 592–631.

Shirky, C. (2003). A group is its own worst enemy. *Clay Shirky's writings about the Internet*. Retrieved 1 July 2014 from http://www.shirky.com/writings/group_enemy.html

Six degrees of separation. (n.d). In *Wikipedia*. Retrieved 29 June 2014 from http://en.wikipedia.org/wiki/Six_degrees_of_separation

SIMS (2003). *How much information?* School of Information Management and Systems, University of California Berkeley. Retrieved June 30 2014 from http://www2.sims.berkeley.edu/research/projects/how-much-info-2003

Stock, W. G., & Stock, M. (2013). *Handbook of information science*. Berlin: Walter de Gruyter.

Tegmark, M. (2014). *Our mathematical universe*, London: Allen Lane.

Tetlow, P. (2007). *The Web's awake: an introduction to the field of web science and the concept of web life*. Hoboken NJ: Wiley.

van Mierlo, T. (2014). The 1% rule in four digital health social networks: an observational study. *Journal of Medical Internet Research*, *16*(2), e33. Retrieved 30 June 2014 from http://www.jmir.org/2014/2/e33

von Baeyer, H. C. (2003). *Information: the new language of science*. London: Weidenfeld & Nicolson.

Watts, D. J., & Strogatz, S. H. (1998), Collective dynamics of 'small world' networks. *Nature*, *393*(6684), 440–442.

Wiesstein, E. W. (n.d.). Kissing number. *Mathworld*. Retrieved 1 July 2014 from http://mathworld.wolfram.com/KissingNumber.html

Wellman, B. (2012). Is Dunbar's number up?. *British Journal of Psychology*, *103*(2), 174–176.

Zhou, W-X., Sornette, D., Hill, R. A., & Dunbar, R. I. M. (2005). Discrete hierarchical organization of social group sizes. *Proceedings of the Royal Society B*, *272*(1561), 439–444.

Zhu, D., Wang, D., Hassan, S., & Haddawy, P. (2013). Small-world phenomenon of keywords network based on complex network. *Scientometrics*, *97*(2), 435–442.

Part IV: **Authorship theories**

Howard D. White
Authors as Persons and Authors as Bundles of Words

1 Introduction

In 2002 Blaise Cronin and Debora Shaw published "Identity-creators and image-makers: Using citation analysis and thick description to put authors in their place". This article was, to my knowledge, the first to adopt the "ego-centered" style of citation analysis I had put forward in White (2000, 2001a, 2001b)—"ego" implying not egotism but an individual whose links to others ("alters") in a network are the focus of research interest (Wasserman & Faust, 1994). In my work, "ego" is an author's name used to retrieve terms that co-occur with it in the records of a bibliographic database. It is thus a seed term to which the co-occurring terms (the "alters") bear a fixed relation (e.g., "co-author-with"). When rank-ordered by their co-occurrence counts with the seed, these other terms, especially the high-ranked ones, characterize the seed economically and aptly. The characterizations are superficial, but as rapidly-formed synopses, they can aid in browsing and searching literatures and in gratifying curiosity about author-centered fields of study.

Of particular interest among co-occurring terms are other authors related to the seed in some way by citation. Cronin and Shaw's "identity-creators" and "image-makers," which I will explain, are relations of this sort. However, authors' names are an unusual unit of analysis, in that the same name can simultaneously mean both a person and a body of writings. This fact bears on some major features of ego-centered bibliometric distributions described in sections below. I will first introduce the framework into which the Cronin and Shaw article fits—a framework for bibliometric distributions in general. That will lead to an explanation of ego-centered ones, which involves the relative ease with which terms in them can be associated.

2 Bibliograms

Authors, editors, and indexers routinely use terms of various kinds to identify and describe the writings that constitute literatures. Over time, such terms appear with differing frequencies in bibliographies, just as they appear with differing frequencies in the full-text writings themselves. When ranked by their frequencies, the terms form bibliometric distributions. In White (2005a, b) I proposed "bibliogram" as a name for these distributions as verbal constructs. Bibliograms consist of (1) a seed term that sets a linguistic context, (2) terms of a fixed kind that co-occur with the seed across a database of bibliographic records, and (3) counts of term co-occurrences with the seed by which the terms can be ordered high to low. With appropriate changes, the same definition can be extended to non-bibliographic records, such as the texts of one or more items of discourse.

In return for merely knowing a seed term, bibliograms provide new information. The top terms in them can be visualized as word clouds, for example. Seeds of various kinds may be used to obtain various kinds of co-occurring terms. A classic Bradford distribution takes a subject term as seed and ranks the journals that co-occur with it by how many articles in the journals are indexed with that subject term. A classic Lotka distribution takes a subject term as seed and ranks the authors that co-occur with it by how many papers they have contributed to the literature it designates. Moving beyond bibliographic sources, a classic Zipf distribution takes an extended text as seed (e.g., Joyce's *Ulysses*) and ranks the words that co-occur with its title by their frequencies in body text. If the last list is stripped of high-ranking function words (like "the" and "of"), the remaining content words often have thematic or stylistic interest.

For decades, information scientists have labeled such distributions by the mathematical or statistical properties of their counts, calling them skewed, empirical-hyperbolic, scale-free, power-law, size-frequency, reverse-J, core-and-scatter, and so on (see, in this volume, Furner, and Glänzel and Schubert). The point of adding "bibliogram" as a new designator is simply to emphasize semantic and other features of the ranked terms no less than their counts. The counts are content-neutral, but the ranked terms associated with a seed make a verbal object that is content-laden. As numbers people, many bibliometricians focus chastely on the counts, whereas the verbal object invites word people to interpret *why* the terms come together as they do—an instance of Geertz's (1973) "thick description". Until White (2005a, b), that object had no name.[1]

---

[1] Bibliograms have analogues in fields allied to bibliometrics, such as webometrics and altmetrics. They also have an interesting parallel in word association lists from psycholinguistics. In White (2005a, b, and 2011) I call the latter "associograms" to bring out the parallel.

3 CAMEOs

The acronym CAMEO stands for Characterizations Automatically Made and Edited Online (White, 2001a). "Online" in White (2001a) refers to the now-defunct Dialog search system, whose Rank command could rapidly create CAMEOs in many databases. However, a similar command has been and could yet be implemented in other systems. The discussion here presumes Dialog's near-instant response time in retrieving the terms that co-occur with a seed.

A CAMEO is a specific type of bibliogram—one in which an *author's name* as seed retrieves a rank-ordered list of terms associated with the author's publications. The terms characterize the author personally. When the list indicates subject matter, a CAMEO is a profile in the librarian's sense of a customer's subject interests expressed in indexing terms. (This of course plays on the *Webster's New Collegiate Dictionary* sense of CAMEO as "a small medallion with a profiled head in relief.") White (2001a), for instance, used two scientists' names as seeds to rank the INSPEC and Ei Compendex descriptors applied to their papers. It also used the name of a famous Victorian author and artist, William Morris, as a seed to profile him by means of the Library of Congress subject headings applied to his books. (The idea can be expanded from one author's books to multiple authors' books combined, as in Ginda et al., this volume.)

Notably, however, White (2000) and (2001a) show how "ego" authors as seeds can be profiled in terms of their co-occurring "alter" authors in the citation databases of Thomson Reuters. This was done by exploiting four retrieval strategies that Dialog software made possible in these databases. (Dialog had tools not in the Web of Science, Scopus, Google Scholar, or CiteSeer.) Using the tags AU for *author* and CA for *cited author*, four different ego-alter relations could be revealed. Dialog's Select command formed a set of documents defined by the seed, while its Rank command rank-ordered terms by their frequency of occurrence in the set. The four relations are given in Table 1.

These CAMEOs are drawn from bibliographic records only, because their tagged fields keep the relation between the seed and the co-occurring terms constant. That is, when a seed from one field is used to generate a CAMEO of co-occurring terms from the same or a different field, the tags will yield a single relation, as seen in the AU and CA combinations of Table 1. In associating names, a seed is *active* as a co-author or citer; *passive*, as a citee or co-citee. The individual

Tab. 1: Four types of CAMEOs.

Co-authors	Select AU = seed author forms the set of papers by the seed. Then *Rank AU* ranks by frequencies the seed plus all other persons *with bylines in this set*. This is the *co-author* relation.
Identity	Select AU = seed author forms the set of papers by the seed. Then *Rank CA* ranks the authors in this set *by the frequencies with which the seed has cited them*. I call this relation the seed author's *citation identity*. It includes (removable) self-citations.
Image	Select CA = seed author forms the set of papers in which the seed author is cited. Then *Rank CA* ranks the authors in this set *by the frequencies with which they and the seed have been cited together*. This is the co-citation relation, which I call the seed's *citation image*. (Self-citation is again present, but removable.)
Image-makers	Select CA = seed author forms the set of papers in which the seed author is cited. Then *Rank AU* ranks the authors in this set by the frequencies of papers in which they cite the seed. I call these authors the seed's *image-makers*, since they create the seed's image through co-citation. (The seed can be one of them through self-citation.)

citer's identity is the basic citation relation, because it is from citers' identities that the counts for the image-makers and the image are aggregated.[2]

Co-authorships differ from the other relations, in that the data come solely from bylines rather than reference lists. (Co-authors frequently cite their own past collaborations, as well as each other; they are also frequently co-cited.) As one would expect, co-authorships are strongly influenced by geographic proximity (cf. Katz, 1994), but with contemporary communications technology, they no longer depend on it.

The CAMEOs in Cronin and Shaw (2002) present three seed authors: Cronin himself, Stephen Harter, and Rob Kling, all at the time at Indiana University. The relations displayed and analyzed are, first, their identities (authors they frequently cite) and, second, their image-makers (authors who frequently cite them). In Table 2, I give examples of all four relations, using as seeds Eugene Garfield (from White, 2000) and Belver Griffith (White, 2001a). For brevity, the distributions are severely truncated to show only the top four names from each ranking—that is, the inmost core of core-and-scatter distributions that are hun-

---

[2] Retrievals based on *bibliographic coupling* strength—the number of references any two papers share—are possible in Web of Science and Scopus, but were not possible in Dialog. In any case, they are not part of the ego-centered CAMEO framework presented here.

Tab. 2: Top names in four CAMEO types, with Eugene Garfield and Belver Griffith as seeds.

	Co-authors			Identity			Image			Image-makers
1264	Garfield E		815	Garfield E		3630	Garfield E		846	Garfield E
7	Welljams-Dorof A		78	Merton RK		520	Price DJD		52	Vlachy J
6	Small H		76	Price DJD		295	Small H		26	Braun T
3	Cawkell AE		67	Zuckerman H		285	Narin F		22	Small H
	Co-authors			Identity			Image			Image-makers
36	Griffith BC		11	Griffith BC		368	Griffith BC		17	McCain KW
7	Drott MC		9	Price DJD		207	Small H		15	Garfield E
6	White HD		9	Small H		147	Price DJD		15	Griffith BC
2	McCain KW		4	Garvey WD		130	Garfield E		13	Small H

dreds of names long. The data come mainly from Social Scisearch (in its surname-and-initials format). They are not current, merely illustrative.[3]

What stands out in the discussions of these CAMEOs, whether by Cronin and Shaw or myself, is our almost automatic tendency to treat the authors in them as persons—that is, as agents who write and cite on the basis not only of intellectual ties, but of social ties and geographic proximity (see Ekbia, this volume, for more on the somatics of science). Cronin and Shaw can do "thick description" of their seed authors because they have extensive knowledge of them as persons. In my own studies I used the Institute for Scientific Information's Garfield and Drexel University's Griffith for the same reason. For example, because of my non-bibliographic knowledge of the people involved, I can say that the seed authors in Table 2 are or were personally acquainted with every other author listed. Moreover, in its columns I see collegial ties, mentor-student ties, employer-employee ties, co-authorships, trusted assessorships, friendships, rivalries—the dense interpersonal linkages that research specialties typically exhibit. Many of these ties must be read into the data from one's mental encyclopedia, but some, such as an adviser-author tie, may be formally acknowledged in publications (Cronin, 1995). *If* one has considerable domain knowledge of this sort, interpreting citation CAMEOs is easy, and there is much to say. Without it, there may seem little to write about.

---

[3] I have used Small H (rather than Small HG) for Henry Small and chosen Cawkell AE and McCain KW from among co-authors who had tied counts with the seed. Garfield's self-citation count of 815 in his identity differs from the 846 in his image-makers column; Griffith correspondingly has 11 as against 15. These discrepancies in the ISI data are at least partially explained in White (2000, 2001a).

Recall, however, that any author's name in a CAMEO can also mean an oeuvre, which connotes subject matter. This opens up wholly different analytic possibilities on two levels. On the primary level, an oeuvre consists of one or more full texts—a bundle of retrievable words and their verbal contexts. On the secondary (or meta-data) level, an oeuvre consists of the bibliographic records representing those works, and they, too, are a bundle of retrievable words. It is these word-bundles that allow us to document *intellectual* ties between authors. Intellectual ties pre-eminently include subjects shared within and across oeuvres. They are frequently signaled by exact or partial term-matches and by other easy-to-see terminological relations (e.g., synonyms, hypernyms, hyponyms) from work to work. Citation indexes contain millions of connections of this sort (see Stock, this volume, for the relationship between informetrics and knowledge organization systems). Aggregated in the Thomson Reuters databases on Dialog, they became a form of collaborative tagging.

4 Intellectual Ties and CAMEO Structure

A shallow but important connection is semantic closeness in title terms. For example, "Ritchie (2009)" is a journal article. Data from its bibliographic record in Social Scisearch include its author, AU = L. David Ritchie, and its title, TI = Relevance and Simulation in Metaphor. Among its 39 cited references (CR =) are a book, a handbook chapter, and a *Mind & Language* article. Abbreviated Thomson Reuters-style, they are:

```
SPERBER D, 1996, RELEVANCE COMMUNICAT
WILSON D, 2004, HDB PRAGMATICS, P607
WILSON D, 2006, MIND LANG, V21, P404
```

Table 3 spells out the works that Ritchie is actually citing. They obviously map onto his own title. The 2006 article matches Ritchie's in two key terms. The 1996 book and the 2004 book chapter match his on one, but by moving from the bibliographic level to passages in full text, it will be found that they, too, discuss metaphor. As Ritchie cites, he is actually indexing his own article *topically* with other works.

This indexing process feeds into the CAMEOs seen here. The authors' names in them were extracted from the CR strings designating works, as in the Sperber and Wilson examples above. Technically, an author's name becomes a metonym for the works in his or her oeuvre; that is, it can be substituted for them—or, more

Tab. 3: Three works cited in Ritchie (2009).

Authors	Titles
Dan Sperber and Deirdre Wilson	Relevance: Communication and Cognition
Deirdre Wilson and Dan Sperber	Relevance Theory
Deirdre Wilson and Robyn Carston	Metaphor, Relevance and the 'Emergent Property' Issue

hazily, for their subject matter—because of its frequent association with them in bibliographic and full-text sources (Falkum, 2011, ch. 6). Through the metonymic process, for example, the names Dan Sperber, Deirdre Wilson, and Robyn Carston have all come to stand for relevance theory, a major specialty in linguistic pragmatics. (Sperber and Wilson (S&W) created it, and Carston is probably now their foremost exponent.) At the bibliographic level, Ritchie's own title and the works he cites suggest that his name, too, connotes S&W's relevance theory to the knowledgeable reader, and the full text of his article confirms it.

Intellectual ties—broadly, shared specializations, shared journals, shared topical relationships—are even more fundamental than social ties in binding learned literatures together (White et al., 2004). As stated earlier, authors often have (or had) social ties with the people, living and dead, they cite. But they also know countless people they do not cite, just as they cite people they do not know. The latter include living persons with whom they have never communicated, but also, in many cases, the dead known only through reading. The tie underlying all these possibilities is an intellectual one—the relevance of one work to another, which frequently implies one or more topics in common.

However—and it is a big however—the relevance of one work to another *varies* in how obvious it is, prior to reading. At one extreme, it may immediately manifest itself on Cronin's (1994) "opus" level, which is also the bibliographic level of titles, subject indicators, and abstracts. At the other, it must be traced to Cronin's "quantum" level in body text—the passages actually cited—and it may not be obvious even then. I reproduce Cronin's full list of levels, with his headings and examples, in Table 4.

Present readers can probably think of many ways in which the authors in Table 2 are connectable through their articles and books: it is no great stretch to get from, e.g., Garfield to Small, or Merton to Price, or Griffith to McCain through topically similar publications, even when the authors' technical vocabularies differ. But what of a case like White (2000), in which I co-cited two papers by Garfield with poems by Walt Whitman and W. H. Auden? For someone not knowing my context, that *is* a stretch; the ties between Whitman, Auden, Garfield, and my chapter are neither obvious nor presumably strong.

Tab. 4: Tiered citation typology from Cronin (1994).

Focus	Scope	Level
Oeuvre (works of Freud)	Compound	V
Motif (punishment in Foucault; writers on sex)	Macromolecular	IV
Opus (Belkin's article)	Molecular	III
Chunk (the discussion section; chapter 3; opening paragraph)	Atomic	II
Quantum (formula; phrase; chemical compound; method; result)	Subatomic	I

As it happens, Garfield's image—his CAMEO as a co-cited author—conveys as much. Price, Small, and Narin are his top co-citees. The fact that citers refer to works by him and these authors in many different contexts suggests that their interrelatedness is easy to see. In contrast, authors like Auden and Whitman, whose works have no apparent connection with Garfield's, rank down in the tail of his image's frequency distribution. Moreover, like the vast majority of low-ranked names in citation images, they will *stay* in the tail, because they and Garfield do not jointly have rich implications for citers. There are no burgeoning Auden-Garfield or Whitman-Garfield studies. Put simply, citers see Price, Small, and Narin as vastly more relevant to Garfield than Auden or Whitman.

The same observation holds for citation identities, which are interpreted much like citation images. For example, because I cited Auden and Whitman once each in White (2000), they are in my identity, but they are among the many names in the tail of the distribution. My top-ranked names include several of the authors in Table 2—McCain, Small, Griffith, Garfield—and have for many years. My identity will continue to evolve, but none of the names in it are likely to change much in their rankings—certainly not Auden and Whitman.

The overarching lesson at this point is that the ease of associating the seed's name with other authors' names can be crudely measured by their co-occurrence frequencies over time. Table 5 recasts the CAMEOs of Table 1 in terms of this idea. If ease of association is linked to *relevance*, one must ask: what makes authors' works relatively easy or hard to associate and therefore of varying degrees of relevance to each other? I have already sketched an answer here and there, but it will be laid out more fully later.

Tab. 5: Hypothetical ease of association in four types of CAMEOs.

Seed as co-author	A seed author knows some other potential authors. *Co-authors* shows the relative ease with which the seed has been able to publish new works with them.
Seed as citer	A seed author knows some written works. *Citation identity* shows the relative ease with which the seed, in his or her own new publications, has cited their authors.
Seed as citee	Many citers know a seed author's works. *Citation image-makers* shows the relative ease with which these citers, in their own new publications, have cited anything by the seed.
Seed as co-citee	Many citers know not only works by a seed author but works by others. *Citation image* shows the relative ease with which these citers, in their own new publications, have co-cited anything by the seed with anything by others.

5 Inference

The names in Table 2 connote oeuvres linked by subject matter, and the reader may also be able to interpret individual author's names as implicit subject headings on the basis of their writings (e.g., Derek Price = Citation Networks, William Garvey = Communication in Science, Belver Griffith = Co-citation Mapping). Consider, then, a *global* subject heading for *all* the names in Table 2: what would it be? (Or if multiple global labels are allowed for subsets of names, what would they be?) This, of course, is the problem of labeling clusters of authors in a co-citation map, or factors of authors in a factor analysis. The same problem occurs if one is clustering or factor-analyzing research publications or journals.

I do not propose a label here myself; many readers will be able to supply at least one. Rather, I would point out that deciding on any label involves inference. The reader starts with existing assumptions about information science as a field and then is given as new input the names (i.e., the oeuvres) in Table 2. By combining the new input with the existing assumptions, one or more global labels are inferred as a new conclusion. Once the proposed labels are all in view, further inferences might be drawn as to their quality. "Information Science" and "Communication in Science" are too broad, "Co-citation Analysis" is too narrow, and so on.

The larger point is that *every* act of connecting scholarly and scientific texts involves inferences. As another example, take Table 6. These are the top names in Richard Smiraglia's citation image—the authors with whom he had been co-cited

11 or more times in Social Scisearch as of 2009.[4] Given this input, where does he fit in information science? What thematic threads can be inferred from the data? Let me imagine one response that you, the reader, as an information scientist, might make: "I don't see bibliometrics or information retrieval or even information behavior in these names; in fact, I can't make much of them at all." Since Table 6 failed to interact with any of your existing assumptions about information science, it is largely or wholly *irrelevant* to you, like an unknown foreign language.

Tab. 6: Citation image for Richard Smiraglia.

Count	Name
105	*Smiraglia RP*
23	Svenonius E
21	Wilson P
20	Tillett BB
16	Carlyle A
16	Yee MM
15	Gorman M
15	Hjorland B
14	Leazer GH
14	Lubetzky S
13	Buckland MK
13	Vellucci SL
12	Cutter CA
12	O'Neill ET
12	Smiraglia R
12	Taylor AG
11	Chan LM

A very different response to Table 6 would be: "It obviously represents the kinds of things that people in the International Society on Knowledge Organization write about—bibliographic control, bibliographic organization, works as cataloguing entities, conceptual foundations of cataloguing and indexing ... Smiraglia edits the ISKO journal ... His counts with Pat Wilson and Elaine Svenonius show he's a theory guy ... In fact, I see theorists from long ago—Charles Ammi Cutter from the 19th century and Seymour Lubetzky—which is a sign of humanities-type re-

---

[4] Social Scisearch on Dialog counted the *papers* in which co-citations occurred. At the time, exclusive of co-citation, Smiraglia had been cited with his middle initial in 105 papers and without it in 12. All the other counts reflect co-citation; for example, 23 papers cited at least one of his works with at least one by Elaine Svenonius.

search ... A practical cataloguer like Lois Mai Chan is lower down ... All these people are pretty library-oriented ... They're more qualitative than quantitative in style ... Greg Leazer was Smiraglia's doctoral student ..." A babbling-brook response like this would indicate that Table 6 is at least somewhat relevant to you, in that you can readily interpret it. In other words, as a new input, it interacts with your existing assumptions—items of domain knowledge—to produce many new inferences, which you then communicate. (More discussion on domain knowledge and inference in scientometrics can be found in Hjørland, this volume.)

Your existing assumptions further suggest you are at least somewhat interested in the various topics that the names in Table 6 imply. From what you know of their works, it is possible that you yourself might find contexts for citing them in a work of your own. In that event, knowledge of your own work-in-progress is part of your existing assumptions, and recollection or discovery of a related work is a new input. Combining the two, you infer new conclusions, such as: "Pat Wilson's paper reinforces what I'm saying here. But if I adopt his terminology, I've got to cite him." In so doing, you document the connection between your work and a previous one. Your motives for citing may be various, but one is constant across citers—a wish to observe the norm that use of other works will be documented. By citing, you intend that your readers, too, will experience the "proper documentation" effect, along with others having to do with your substantive claims. You may believe, for instance, that the earlier work provides evidence for your own argument, or negates someone else's, or supports a witty insight; there are numerous possibilities. In any case, you trust that your citations will produce in your audience the cognitive effects you intend. As a general principle, citers who intend readers to draw certain conclusions from their citations must first have reached those conclusions themselves.

Here, I have been imagining inferences by present readers, but surely the seed authors in Table 2 also drew inferences about the relevance of certain works to their own as they created their citation identities. In turn, their image-makers drew inferences about these same authors' works as they created their citation images. From cognitive and communicative processes along these lines, the entire edifice of citation is built.

6 Relevance Theory

Some may recognize that my discussions of "inferences" and "ease of association" have been informed by Sperber and Wilson's (1995) relevance theory, a tendency I now want to make explicit. In the article that introduced relevance theory (RT) to information science, Harter (1992, p. 614) wrote: "The act of citing is the statement of an historical relevance relationship, captured for all time in a published article." He was speculating about whether data from bibliometrics and citation analysis could help information scientists understand relevance as a dynamic cognitive process in S&W's sense, as opposed to how it is commonly understood in retrieval system evaluations (relevance = a query-document match in topic). In the spirit of Harter, I will use RT to explain core and scatter in citation CAMEOs. My argument is developed much more fully in White (2011), and so the treatment of RT here will be brief and highly selective. I will relate it to CAMEOs in later sections.

The First Principle of RT is that "Human cognition tends to be geared to the maximisation of relevance" (Sperber and Wilson, 1995, p. 260). This is a cognitive universal, reached through evolution. Wilson and Sperber (2004, p. 608) ask, when is an input relevant?

> Intuitively, an input (a sight, a sound, an utterance, a memory) is relevant to an individual when it connects with background information he has available to yield conclusions that matter to him: say, by answering a question he had in mind, improving his knowledge on a certain topic, settling a doubt, confirming a suspicion, or correcting a mistaken impression. In relevance-theoretic terms, an input is relevant to an individual when its processing in a context of available assumptions yields a positive cognitive effect. A positive cognitive effect is a worthwhile difference to the individual's representation of the world—a true conclusion, for example. False conclusions are not worth having. They are cognitive effects, but not positive ones.
>
> (Sperber & Wilson, 1995, 3.1–3.2)[5]

Wilson and Sperber (2004) proceed to define *the relevance of an input to an individual*:

a. Other things being equal, the greater the positive cognitive effects achieved by processing an input, the greater the relevance to the individual at that time.
b. Other things being equal, the greater the processing effort expended, the lower the relevance of the input to the individual at that time.

(p. 610)

Cognitive effects occur when newly presented information interacts with someone's context of existing assumptions. "Context" in RT is thus a *psychological* notion, and existing assumptions are the thoughts, beliefs, perceptions, and knowl-

---

[5] Wilson and Sperber (2004) introduce RT at chapter length. The summary of S&W's ideas in Yus (2011) may be especially useful for present readers because it applies RT to Web-based communications, including document retrieval. Clark's (2013) lucid book on RT is one of the Cambridge Textbooks in Linguistics.

edge (including knowledge of textual contexts—"co-texts") that an individual can access in making sense of new inputs. Such inputs produce effects by (1) *strengthening* an existing assumption, (2) *contradicting and eliminating* it, or by (3) *combining with it to yield a new conclusion*—one derived from neither the new information alone, nor the context alone, but from both together.

S&W hold that, while human beings constantly receive inputs from many sources, they automatically heed those with the greatest relevance for them at a given time—that is, they heed the inputs that produce the greatest effects for the least effort. This in RT is defined as "maximal relevance." Since the two factors operate simultaneously, one way of expressing them is as a ratio:

Relevance = cognitive effects / processing effort

Relevance thus varies directly with effects and inversely with effort (White, 2007, 2010a, 2011). But S&W also deny that effects and effort can be measured on ratio scales; the numerical values are not available to us either through introspection or by instrument. Human beings can only measure relevance *comparatively*—that is, by sensing it as a matter of degree. This dovetails with information scientists' ubiquitous use of *ordinal*-level scales to measure the relevance of documents in retrieval system evaluations: one document will be more relevant to a query than another, but the difference between them cannot be gauged in exact units. Also, a document could be called "more relevant" than another either because it has greater cognitive effects for the same processing effort or because it has about the same effects as the other but costs less effort to process.[6]

As part of linguistic pragmatics, RT is primarily oriented toward spoken communication—toward explaining how hearers infer speakers' intended meanings from what they actually say. Hearers automatically expect a speaker addressing them to be relevant, and speakers tend to comply, since they want their utterances to be understood. For hearers of an utterance, writes Clark (2013, p. 68), the relevance-theoretic comprehension procedure is:

> Follow a path of least effort in deriving cognitive effects.
> Consider interpretations in order of accessibility.
> Stop when expectations of relevance are satisfied.

---

[6] In RT, effort is mainly discussed as it affects the spontaneous processing of utterances *at sentence level*. Larger units of processing, such as paragraphs or whole texts, and intuitions of future processing costs, as opposed to present ones, have received relatively little attention. A relevance theorist who does discuss the non-spontaneous interpretation of literary texts, as opposed to ordinary talk, is Furlong (1995, 2007).

For example, a wife says "It's late" to her husband at a party, by which she means—and he understands—"It's time to leave." Later, on the train platform, he says to her, "It's late," by which he means, and she understands, "The train is past due." The hearer in each case understands what is meant through inference—that is, a new input, the speaker's utterance, combines with a context of assumptions readily available to the hearer to produce a new conclusion as a cognitive effect. Out of the various meanings an utterance *could* have, hearers automatically seek the interpretation that, in context, has the greatest cognitive effects for the least effort. Moreover, they stop at the *first* interpretation that meets these criteria as the *only* one, which allows talk to proceed without endless parsing of what was meant. (This eliminates consideration of "It's late" as possibly meaning, e.g., "It's hours after sundown" in the above example.) Nevertheless, hearers' interpretations are merely hypotheses, and they can be wrong. Speakers, too, can be wrong (or deceitful), and so cognitive effects are by no means necessarily "positive."

RT is not only a theory of interpersonal communication, however; it is also a theory of cognition and can accommodate processes that go on in a single head, such as a citing author's. New inputs, that is, can come from an author's perceptions or memories or trains of inference rather than talk. In White (2011), I wrote:

> Citations in a sense are responses to stimuli that authors themselves have created. It is as if the speaker-hearer pairs typical of RT are no longer separate individuals …but are lodged within each author. An internal speaker proposes possible utterances by recording them; an internal hearer acts like an editor or critic who accepts some utterances as maximally relevant while rejecting others. Such deliberations presumably account for the redraftings of documents, including the citations in them that depend on authorial reflection rather than reader input or feedback.
>
> (p. 3348)

As noted, Harter (1992) called each citation "a statement of an historical relevance relationship"—in other words, it explicitly shows that an author judged a particular work to be relevant enough to cite, implying that, for the author, it produced acceptably high effects and cost acceptably low effort in a particular context. Any such judgment involves a bundle of inferences on the citer's part—inferences in which the citing work sets a context of assumptions and the cited work is a new input.

In information science we sometimes read citers' minds as to what these inferences may have been (cf. Clark, 2013, p. 349–351). By examining the prose in which citations appear, we infer *why* an author cited at that point (as in studies of citer motivations) or *what* a citation contributes to the argument at that point (as in studies of citation functions). Authors themselves sometimes explain why they cited something. In any case, before readers ever see a citation, it will have had cognitive effects on the citer. It will also have been easy enough for the citer to process; otherwise, it would not occur. (Citations considered but dropped are thick on the ground.)

Table 7 presents some relevance judgments that are open to (pedestrian) mind-reading. Zhao and Strotmann (2008) cited both Schneider et al. (2007) and Zhao (2006). Zhao cites her own 2006 article not only because of its high cognitive accessibility, but also because its topic bears directly on her new topic and shows her developing a "research stream" within her oeuvre. Moreover, as she states, Schneider et al. (2007) themselves built on—and cited—Zhao (2006), and their title is a topical bridge between that article and Zhao and Strotmann (2008). Admittedly, I have chosen titles whose topical relation to each other is very plain, but then so did she.

Tab. 7: Titles in a citing-cited chain.

Year	Citing authors	Title
2008	Zhao & Strotmann	Comparing all-author and first-author co-citation analyses of information science

Year	Cited Authors	Titles
2007	Schneider, Larsen, & Ingwersen	Comparative study between first and all-author co-citation analysis based on citation indexes generated from XML data
2006	Zhao	Towards all-author co-citation analysis

Zhao is citing the earlier articles on Cronin's (1994) "opus" level; they are relevant as entire works. When she sets up linkages like this, she implicitly justifies her present research in terms of research already published. She intends this justification to be inferred by readers—it is what RT calls an implicature—but it rests on her own inference that the prior articles strengthen her argument and should be discussed. These citer inferences occur whether the connections between citing and cited works will be obvious to readers (as in Table 7) or initially obscure (as in my linking Garfield to Auden and Whitman).

7 Explaining Core and Scatter

As Harter (1992) remarks, once a citation is made, the relevance judgment it represents is fixed over time. In contrast, citation CAMEOs are based on *aggregates* of citations that gradually change over time. Furthermore, unlike individual citations, they facilitate comparisons of data. Take the citation identity. As an author's publications accumulate, it will develop the core-and-scatter, power-law shape of a bibliogram. Relatively few authors will be recited frequently, forming the core. Increasingly many authors will be recited less and less frequently, forming the scatter, which ends in a long tail of authors cited only once.

Looking only at the ranked counts, network physicists explain the power-law shape of citation bibliograms probabilistically, under such names as "cumulative advantage" (Price, 1976) or "preferential attachment" (Barabási & Albert, 1999). As glossed by Newman (2005):

> ... the probability of a paper getting a new citation is proportional to the number it already has. In many cases this seems like a natural process. For example, a paper that already has many citations is more likely to be discovered during a literature search and hence more likely to be cited again.
>
> (p. 341)

But the depersonalized account of the physicists ignores the verbal *content* of the distribution that makes it a bibliogram. A relevance-theoretic explanation of this content at the level of individuals is compatible with the content-neutral probabilistic explanation at the level of citers in general.

By hypothesis, the shape of citations identities is determined by processing effort, in the RT sense. Recall that an identity ranks citees by the number of papers in which a seed author has cited them. The ranks of citees indicate their cognitive accessibility to the seed—that is, the effort it costs to associate his or her works with theirs—over years or decades of authorship. Authors as citers reduce this effort by stopping at certain names that spring to mind in the context of new writings. (Citation counts in identities are counts of these writings after publication.) The more frequently certain names have been cited in the past, the less effort is required to use them again. Names easy to process form the *core* of citation identities. Other, more numerous names cited in the past do *not* spring to mind in the context of new writings. The less frequently they have been cited in the past, the more effort required to process them again. They form the *scatter* in citation identities.

Wilson (2007, n.p.) notes that *frequency of use* is among the psychometric factors that affect an individual's effort in understanding utterances in conversations: "The more often a word, a concept, a sound, a syntactic construction or a contextual assumption is used, the less effort is required to process it." S&W (1995, p. 77) extend this observation to use of items held in long-term memory: "... as a result of some kind of habituation, the more a representation is processed, the more accessible it becomes. Hence, the greater the amount of processing involved in the formation of an assumption, and the more often it is accessed thereafter, the greater its accessibility." The effortful habituation that forms certain assumptions I take to include instances of intensive reading, writing, social interaction, and thought. But one devotes such effort to relatively few works, which thereby become more accessible than others.

The verbal content of citation identities indicates *which* names (and associated works) are more accessible in memory. Some key evidence comes from *authors as persons*:
- Disproportionate self-citation;
- Disproportionate citation of selected acquaintances (including co-authors);
- Disproportionate citation of selected orienting figures (non-acquaintances) from the citer's reading;
- Disproportionate citation of works *not* highly cited by others (*pace* Newman);
- Disproportionate citation of familiar works—personal anthologies—as opposed to those that must be newly read.

Evidence that certain *works* are easier for citers to process comes from *authors as bundles of words*:
- Repeated agreement in vocabulary in the full texts of citing and cited works;
- Repeated instances of matching or semantically close terms in citing-cited titles and abstracts;
- Repeated citation of the same works to symbolize the same concepts;
- Repeated citation of works in certain journals and from certain named specialties and disciplines.

This account grounds core-and-scatter citation distributions in the psychology of individual citers—the "natural process" that Newman and other network physicists explain probabilistically at a higher level of abstraction. White (2011) gives examples of several of the bulleted points above, including evidence from Newman's own citation record (e.g., his personal anthology). Ideally, the bulleted points should be considered hypotheses that would be tested with massive amounts of data. That is not presently feasible, but readers can test them against what they know of citation practices. Readers can also test such hypotheses against the examples in the next sections.

The notion of "personal anthologies" was introduced in White (2011). Table 8 displays a typical one—the works I myself cited five or more times through 2009. The bulleted list above was based on other data, but mine show the predicted features: frequent recitation of relatively few works, heavy self-citation, recitation of acquaintances (McCain, Small), recitation of orienting non-acquaintances (Baldi, Harter, Schvaneveldt), and re-use of works to symbolize concepts (Schvaneveldt on Pathfinder networks; Small on "concept symbols" as an idea).

Tab. 8: Top works in Howard D. White's personal anthology.

Count	Works
9	WHITE HD, 1989, V24, P119, ANNU REV INFORM SCI
8	WHITE HD, 1981, V32, P163, J AM SOC INFORM SCI
8	WHITE HD, 1997, V32, P99, ANNU REV INFORM SCI
8	WHITE HD, 1998, V49, P327, J AM SOC INFORM SCI
6	BALDI S, 1998, V63, P829, AM SOCIOL REV
6	MCCAIN KW, 1990, V41, P433, J AM SOC INFORM SC
6	WHITE HD, 1990, P84, SCHOLARLY COMMUNICAT
5	HARTER SP 1992, V43, P602, J AM SOC INFORM SC
5	SCHVANEVELDT RW, 1990, PATHFINDER ASS NETWO
5	SMALL HG, 1978, V8, P327, SOC STUD SCI
5	WHITE HD, 1982, V38, P255, J DOC
5	WHITE HD, 1986, V5, P93, INFORM TECHNOL LIBR
5	WHITE HD, 2000, P475, WEB KNOWLEDGE FESTSC

Count	Titles
9	Bibliometrics
8	Author cocitation: A literature measure of intellectual structure
8	Visualization of literatures
8	Visualizing a discipline: An author co-citation analysis of information science, 1972–1995
6	Normative versus social constructivist processes in the allocation of citations: A network-analytic model
6	Mapping authors in intellectual space: A technical overview
6	Author cocitation analysis: Overview and defense
5	Psychological relevance and information science
5	Pathfinder associative networks: Studies in knowledge organization
5	Cited documents as concept symbols
5	Authors as markers of intellectual space: Cocitation in studies of science, technology and society
5	Cocited author retrieval
5	Toward ego-centered citation analysis

Very few authors know they can be profiled in this way. Citation CAMEOs and personal anthologies reveal patterns that citers themselves do not monitor or see reported. As my own anthology grew over time, I was largely unaware of it. Having seen it, I am not surprised; it is a window into a long-term cognitive dynamic I recognize. But I did not intend to create this anthology as such; like every other citer, I was simply behaving. However, I *do* intend this chapter's tables as overt communications, and so, for readers, they fall under the cognitive effects / processing effort formula of RT. They do not convey single, sharp implicatures on the order of "It's late" = "It's time to leave." Rather, they convey an indeterminate number of what RT calls "weak implicatures"—various meanings they *could* be taken to have (as in the case of Smiraglia's image above). In this, as relevance theorists might point out, they resemble poems.

The strings identifying works in Table 8 reappear in the lower part as bundles of words—titles again. Certain terms explicitly link works, and there are many implicit linkages. Clearly, global *topical* relevance is a binding force here; Harter (1992) was wrong to dismiss it summarily (cf. Bean & Green, 2001, pp. 120–121). But he was right that there is far more to relevance than inferences about whether topics match. For instance, no one would infer that the topics "Bibliometric Distributions" and "Marketing" are even remotely similar, yet the former is highly relevant to the latter once the case is made, as in Chris Anderson's (2006) book *The Long Tail*.

8 Identities, Images, and Effort

The examples below focus on cores in citation identities and images, which reflect citers' past cognitive processes. But CAMEOs are also verbal constructs for present readers to interpret. Readers can judge degrees of accessibility and processing effort in specialties they know, because they have the same cognitive mechanism as citers: Relevance = cognitive effects / processing effort. By hypothesis, readers with domain expertise will find names in core easier to relate to a seed than names in scatter. If core and scatter are divided into zones, the descending zones of scatter will tend to be progressively harder to interpret. In other words, readers will be able to give reasonably quick and accurate accounts of what a set of top-ranked names implies. By contrast, bottom-ranked names, taken together, will mean little or nothing to them (cf. White, 2011). Interpretations of top-ranked names are themselves hypotheses that can be tested for accuracy by examining further bibliographic or full-text data. For example, a domain expert might be able to look at the names of an ego-alter pair in a citation image and correctly predict the exact *works* of theirs that are being co-cited.

Table 9 presents 30 names from the information scientist Peter Ingwersen's citation identity in 2010. His name is italicized as the seed. At left are authors he has cited in eight or more papers. At right are alphabetically selected authors he has cited in one paper each. I discussed the core of this identity at some length in White (2010b). Here, let me simply recapitulate a few points.

Although I recognize several names in the scatter column, they seem virtually meaningless as a group. Core names, in contrast, are vividly suggestive. Ingwersen's interests as a citer put him at the center of the last few decades of in-

Tab. 9: Peter Ingwersen's identity: Names from top core and bottom scatter.

Core		Scatter	
Ingwersen P	41	Abraham RH	1
Wormell I	17	Babbie ER	1
Belkin NJ	16	Calza L	1
Garfield E	11	Dahlberg I	1
Saracevic T	11	East H	1
Bates MJ	10	Fagan JL	1
Christensen F	10	Gaillard J	1
Cronin B	10	Hahn U	1
Jones KS	9	Jacob EK	1
Rousseau R	9	Kaplan D	1
Brookes BC	8	Larsen HL	1
Croft WB	8	Machlup F	1
De Mey M	8	Nance RE	1
Ellis D	8	Oddy RN	1
Pejtersen AM	8	Paice CD	1

formation science—the intersection of informetrics (Wormell, Garfield, Cronin, Rousseau,); cognitive information science (Belkin, Saracevic, Brookes, De Mey, Ellis); experimental information retrieval (Croft, Jones); and online interactive behavior (Bates, Christensen, Petjersen). The Festschrift editors independently drew much the same conclusion about Ingwersen as an integrator of information science fields (Larsen et al., 2010). His identity also bears out claims from the bulleted list above, such as disproportionate self-citation and disproportionate citation of works not highly cited by others. His social ties are evident as well: Wormell (his wife), Christensen and Pejtersen (workplace colleagues), and just about everyone else (friends and acquaintances).

Another kind of test, which appears in White (2010b, 2011), involves comparing a seed author's citation identity with his or her citation image. I have claimed that names in the core of an identity are relatively easy for the seed to cite. It would strengthen this assumption, however, if the seed's image-makers frequently *co-cited* the seed with at least some of the same names. For example, Blaise Cronin might cite certain authors heavily for both intellectual and social reasons. If those authors are also repeatedly *co-cited* with him, it confirms that names he finds easy to relate to his work are similarly easy for his image-makers. But the image-makers need not consider Cronin's social ties, if any, with his co-citees—with authors as persons. They can base their co-citations on intellectual ties between oeuvres—on authors as bundles of words.

Tab. 10: Top cores in identity and image for Blaise Cronin.

Identity		Image	
Cronin B	106	**Cronin B**	1237
Davenport E	21	Garfield E	308
Garfield E	20	Small H	192
Merton RK	18	**Merton RK**	132
Small H	18	**White HD**	132
White HD	16	Rousseau R	128
Chubin DE	15	Price DJD	121
McCain KW	14	Borgman CL	116
Kling R	11	**Ingwersen P**	112
MacRoberts MH	11	van Raan AFJ	112
Porter ME	11	Oppenheim C	108
Ingwersen P	10	Harter SP	106
Machlup F	10	Egghe L	99
Meadows AJ	10	**MacRoberts MH**	96
Mullins NC	10	Glanzel W	95
Porat MU	10	Moed HF	94
Swanson DR	10	Leydesdorff L	92
Toffler A	10	**McCain KW**	90
Edge D	9	Thelwall M	89
Hyland K	9	Bar-Ilan J	88
Latour B	9	**Chubin DE**	88
Shapin S	9	Lancaster FW	83

Table 10 has the identity-image comparison for Cronin, with counts as of 2009. The identity displays authors he has cited at least eight times, an arbitrary core of 21 names plus his own. Accordingly, his top 21 co-citees are also shown, and identity-image matches are bolded. Unboldfaced names from his identity could be matched in lower ranks of his image; even so, the top names show considerable overlap.[7]

Both matched and unmatched names in Table 10 are open to interpretations that are applicable, I believe, to many other seeds (Cronin, 1981). Particulars first. The bolded names in Cronin's identity imply that he specializes in citation theory and analysis. By co-citing him heavily with these same names, his image-makers reveal that the same associations are obvious to them as well, which supports the

---

[7] Cronin's identity in Cronin and Shaw differs somewhat from the one here. If Dialog were available, I could probably reduce the differences. For example, Derek Price should be above the threshold in my data. He is not, because his count is fragmented among his various name-forms in ranks I excluded in my 2009 retrieval.

ease-of-processing hypothesis. Cronin and Shaw (2002, p. 36) call Cronin's specialty "citation analysis," but note that he has other strings to his bow. The first—"social studies of science"—is attested in Table 10 by Meadows, Mullins, Edge, Latour, and Shapin; the second—"business strategy"—by Porter. The remaining unboldfaced names in Cronin's identity suggest his wide-ranging interests in information science as a discipline.

These additional interests, however, are not the most salient ones for Cronin's image-makers. They pigeonhole him among citationists and bibliometricians, including mathematical ones (Egghe, Rousseau, Glänzel) that he, as a non-mathematician, is less inclined to cite. If asked to convert his name to a subject heading, as I did with some authors earlier, his image-makers would probably just say "Citation Analysis." In effect, they tend to *stereotype* him (called *typecasting* in White, 2010b). Identities generally imply the grounds for the stereotype—"the author as subject-heading"—while also picking up a seed author's idiosyncratic choices. They reveal the seed's own reading, as opposed to what is widely read by the image-makers.

Stereotyped associations, like clichés, spring to mind with relatively little effort. They abound in research fields (as elsewhere) because they speed interpretation. Above, I described RT's stopping rule for conversations:

> ... hearers automatically seek the interpretation that, in context, has the greatest cognitive effects for the least effort. Moreover, they stop at the *first* interpretation that meets these criteria as the *only* one, which allows talk to proceed without endless parsing of what was meant.

For individual citers, the first and only interpretation of an author—the one they stop at—is defined by relatively few works. This allows them to cite without endlessly considering possibilities from an author's oeuvre. Moreover, they tend to converge on the *same* works, suggesting an economy of attention. Cronin as a very big bundle of words is thereby reduced to a much smaller bundle of words, such as *The Citation Process* (1984), which is cited repeatedly and hence co-cited repeatedly. Out of hundreds of works he has written, that book and 10 or so of his other top-ranked items account for about a third of his citations (as of mid-2014) in Google Scholar. The content of his most cited works helps to determine the top co-citees in his citation image. RT, in which maximal relevance goes up as processing effort goes down, allows us to make sense of these phenomena.

9 Conclusion

To summarize, the foregoing remarks illustrate two broad claims, based on my reading of RT. Suitably adapted, they apply to all bibliograms, but I will confine them to citation CAMEOs:
- CAMEOs *store cognitive effects*—the associations that authors have inferred among cited works.
- CAMEOs *reflect processing effort*—the ranked frequencies with which authors have made those associations.

Hypothetically, as authors write, their effort varies with the cognitive accessibility of terms—the ease with which the mind supplies them in particular contexts. Authors as citers reduce processing effort by citing people, works, journals, and vocabulary that are relatively accessible to them over time. In CAMEOs, more accessible terms will appear more frequently and become cores; less accessible terms will appear more rarely and become scatter. Determinants of accessibility are what citers know of their citees as persons and as useful bundles of words.

At the same time, CAMEOs are intentional communications for readers to interpret. Those excerpted above are meant to lead readers to certain inferences I myself have drawn, and perhaps to other inferences I have not foreseen. This is merely to say that they permit my claims from relevance theory to be intuitively tested.

While Dialog-based CAMEOs were possible only from 1992 (when Dialog got the Rank command) to 2013, CAMEOs remain instructive bibliometric displays. Practically speaking, their creation has been limited to a few people who could search Dialog through institutional accounts. The underlying programming, however, has turned up in various document retrieval systems since the days of NASA's RECON system in the 1960s (cf. White, 1990, pp. 453–454; White, 1996, pp. 244–245). The idea of featuring CAMEOs within citation-bearing databases, such as a future Web of Science or Scopus, is therefore not entirely far-fetched. Meanwhile, WoS can rank co-authors or image-makers, but cannot do a seed's identity, image, personal anthology, or co-cited works. It seems unlikely that these constructs, especially their cores, have lost their interest. Rather, they have not yet been made easy enough for enough people to generate.

Finally, I would add that segments of bibliograms, such as those seen here, are examples of the *citation objects* that Wouters, this volume, discusses in the last three sections of his chapter on semiotics. They are constructs that can exist only through the retrieval and reorganization of data from citation indexes, and their whole *raison d'être* is to be interpreted as numerically conjoined names or words. Although they are closely related to the raw data that underlie the maps of science Wouters mentions, they are themselves interesting objects. If explicated, they can make the abstractions of semiotics more concrete. (One can even make testable predictions about their contents.) I have focused on grounding them in what I take to be citers' psychological processes, but that is not the only line of semiotic analysis they can support. Likening them to poems, above, was mainly tongue-in-cheek. But not altogether.

Cited References

Anderson, C. (2006). *The Long Tail: Why the Future of Business Is Selling Less of More*. New York: Hyperion.
Barabási, A., & Albert, R. (1999). Emergence of scaling in random networks. *Science, 286*, 509–512.
Bean, C. A., & Green, R. (2001). Relevance relationships. In *Relationships in the Organization of Knowledge*. Dordrecht, The Netherlands: Kluwer. 115–132.
Clark, B. (2013). *Relevance Theory*. Cambridge, UK: Cambridge University Press.
Cronin, B. (1981). The need for a theory of citing. *Journal of Documentation, 37*, 16–24.
Cronin, B. (1984). *The Citation Process: The Role and Significance of Citations in Scientific Communication*. London: Taylor Graham.
Cronin, B. (1994). Tiered citation and measures of document similarity. *Journal of the American Society for Information Science, 45*, 537–538.
Cronin, B. (1995). *The Scholar's Courtesy: The Role of Acknowledgement in the Primary Communication Process*. London: Taylor Graham.
Cronin, B., & Shaw, D. (2002). Identity-creators and image-makers: Using citation analysis and thick description to put authors in their place. *Scientometrics, 54*, 31–49.
Falkum, I. L. (2011). *The Semantics and Pragmatics of Polysemy: A Relevance-Theoretic Account*. PhD dissertation, University College London.
Furlong, A. (1995). *Relevance Theory and Literary Interpretation*. PhD dissertation, University College London.
Furlong, A. (2007). A modest proposal: Linguistics and literary studies. *Canadian Journal of Applied Linguistics, 10*, 323–345.
Geertz, C. (1973). Thick description: Toward an interpretive theory of culture. In *The Interpretation of Cultures: Selected Essays*. New York: Basic Books.
Harter, S. P. (1992). Psychological relevance and information science. *Journal of the American Society for Information Science, 43*, 602–615.
Katz, J. S. (1994). Geographic proximity and scientific collaboration. *Scientometrics, 31*, 31–43.
Larsen, B., Schneider, J. W., & Ångström, F. (2010). Foreword. In *The Janus Faced Scholar: A Festschrift in Honour of Peter Ingwersen. E-Newsletter of the International Society for Scientometrics and Informetrics*, v. 6-S: 7–9.
Newman, M. E. J. (2005). Power laws, Pareto distributions and Zipf's law. *Contemporary Physics, 46*, 323–351.

Price, D. de S. (1976). A general theory of bibliometric and other cumulative advantage processes. *Journal of the American Society for Information Science, 27*, 291–306.

Ritchie, L. D. (2009). Relevance and simulation in metaphor. *Metaphor and Symbol, 24*, 249–262.

Schneider, J. W., Larsen, B., & Ingwersen, P. (2007). Comparative study between first and all-author co-citation analysis based on citation indexes generated from XML data. *Proceedings of the 11th International Conference of the International Society for Scientometrics and Informetrics* (pp. 696–707), Madrid, Spain, June 25–27, 2007.

Sperber, D., & Wilson, D. (1995). *Relevance: Communication and Cognition.* 2nd ed. Oxford: Blackwell. (1996). *Ibid.* Cambridge, MA: Harvard University Press.

Wasserman, S., & Faust, K. (1994). *Social Network Analysis: Methods and Applications.* Cambridge, UK: Cambridge University Press.

White, H. D. (1990). Profiles of authors and journals in information science: Some trials of ORBIT's Get command. *Proceedings of the Eleventh National Online Meeting.* Medford, NJ: Learned Information. 453–459.

White, H. D. (1996). Literature retrieval for interdisciplinary syntheses. *Library Trends, 45*, 239–264.

White, H. D. (2000). Toward ego-centered citation analysis. In *The Web of Knowledge: A Festschrift in Honor of Eugene Garfield,* Blaise Cronin and Helen Barsky Atkins, eds. Medford, NJ: Information Today. 475–496.

White, H. D. (2001a). Author-centered bibliometrics through CAMEOs: Characterizations automatically made and edited online. *Scientometrics, 51*, 607–637.

White, H. D. (2001b). Authors as citers over time. *Journal of the American Society for Information Science, 52*, 87–108.

White, H. D. (2005a). On extending informetrics: An opinion paper. *Proceedings of ISSI 2005,* the 10th International Conference of the International Society for Scientometrics and Informetrics. Stockholm, Sweden: Karolinska University Press. Vol. 2: 442–449.

White, H. D. (2005b). Bibliogram. In *Wikipedia, the Free Encyclopedia.*

White, H. D. (2007). Combining bibliometrics, information retrieval, and relevance theory: Part 1. First examples of a synthesis. *Journal of the American Society for Information Science and Technology, 58*, 536–559

White, H. D. (2010a). Some new tests of relevance theory in information science. *Scientometrics, 83*, 653–667.

White, H. D. (2010b). Ingwersen's image and identity compared. In *The Janus Faced Scholar: A Festschrift in Honour of Peter Ingwersen. E-Newsletter of the International Society for Scientometrics and Informetrics,* v. 6-S: 219–227.

White, H. D. (2011). Relevance theory and citations. *Journal of Pragmatics, 43*, 3345–3361.

White, H. D., Wellman, B., & Nazer, N. (2004). Does citation reflect social structure? Longitudinal evidence from the 'Globenet' interdisciplinary research group. *Journal of the American Society for Information Science and Technology, 55*, 111–126.

Wilson, D. (2007). Relevance: The cognitive principle. Lecture 3 in Pragmatic Theory [PLIN 2002], an online course of the Department of Phonetics and Linguistics, University College London. [Unpaginated; no longer available online.]

Wilson, D., & Carston, R. (2006). Metaphor, relevance and the 'emergent property' issue. *Mind & Language, 21*, 404–433.

Wilson, D., & Sperber, D. (2004). Relevance theory. In *The Handbook of Pragmatics.* Oxford, UK: Blackwell. 607–632.

Yus, F. (2011). *Cyberpragmatics: Internet-Mediated Communication in Context*. Amsterdam/Philadelphia: Benjamins.
Zhao, D. (2006). Towards all-author co-citation analysis. *Information Processing & Management, 42*, 1578–1591.
Zhao, D., & Strotmann, A. (2008). Comparing all-author and first-author co-citation analyses of information science. *Journal of Informetrics, 2*, 229–239.

Nadine Desrochers, Adèle Paul-Hus, and Vincent Larivière
The Angle Sum Theory: Exploring the Literature on Acknowledgments in Scholarly Communication

1 Introduction

"The authors would like to thank" and other variations on this formulation are one of many conventions by which researchers bestow their gratitude upon the individuals, organizations, or funding agencies that help research come to fruition as published works. However, beyond niceties, these often formulaic sentences are also the markers of a clear division in academic standing: those who have obtained the status of author, as established by varying and often unclear parameters (International Committee of Medical Journal Editors, 2006; 2013; Pontille, 2004), and those who are denied such status. There are also individuals whose names appear in reference lists. References bestow yet another status upon the individuals they name—and they do so whether the referenced work is alluded to, praised, questioned, or critiqued.

Thus emerge the three statuses that have come to form the "reward triangle" (Cronin & Weaver-Wozniak, 1993) of science: author, person cited, person thanked. Merton's (1973) work on the structure of the scientific community and, more specifically, on cumulative advantages in science (i.e., the Matthew Effect), shed light on the process by which an individual moves from being an accessory to becoming an author—and back again, although with more prestige, through the accumulation of citations or by being acknowledged for his or her contribution to a work. In this way, acknowledgments place the highly regarded alongside those who have not yet attained recognition.

Blaise Cronin began studying the dynamics of scientific acknowledgments in the 1990s, quickly placing his work among the few models in existence or in development at the time (Mackintosh, 1972; McCain, 1991; in Cronin, 1995). He revived his interest for this topic at various moments in his career and with various collaborators, creating an unrivalled body of work on acknowledgments in scholarly communication. In recent years, the relationship between those who thank and those—individuals or organizations—who are thanked has been studied theoretically and empirically.

This chapter maps the landscape of research on scientific acknowledgments which has appeared relatively regularly in the literature since the 1970s. Analyses of the role and value of acknowledgments are often isolated by discipline or methodological approach, and present data-specific models or adaptations of previous models as premises for new analyses. We provide here an analytical review of the literature on acknowledgments in scholarly communication in order to gauge how this phenomenon has been studied. This is not a systematic review in the methodological sense; rather, we triangulate qualitative analysis and quantitative descriptions to paint a portrait of the acknowledgement literature in terms of approaches, theories, contributions, trends, and limitations.

2 Triangulating the Rewards of Science

The social sciences' penchant for figures and the geometric schematization of concepts is served well by the notion of a "reward triangle." This turn of phrase represents the basic premise upon which acknowledgments research is built. In 1995, Cronin posited that, "authorship and citation do not tell the whole story," and situated acknowledgments as "another vector" in the assessment of scholarship (p. 14). Three years earlier, he had underlined the intrinsic value of certain types of acknowledgments by qualifying them as "closet citations" (Cronin, 1992, p. 25). Twenty years prior to that, however, Mackintosh had been even more categorical: "[L]ack of interest in acknowledgements does not necessarily indicate their complete irrelevance as rewards in science, or, if it does, then citations of one's published work by others must fall at the same stroke" (p. 70).

The "reward triangle" phrase itself was coined in 1993 by Cronin and Weaver-Wozniak: "If authorship and citedness are to be counted, so ought acknowledgments. By admitting acknowledgments, the Reward Triangle is closed" (p. 94). This image, reintroduced by the same authors two years later (Cronin & Weaver, 1995; Cronin, 1995, p. 27), featured prominently in the title of a recent paper by Costas and van Leeuwen (2012) in which the authors cite Cronin and Weaver (p. 1648), thereby revealing sustained interest in this imagery.

The perception of the fruits of scholarly pursuits as "rewards" allows for an easy stretch towards Mertonian and later Bourdieusian perspectives which have had either stated or indirect influences in acknowledgments literature. Acknowledgments research has long been anchored in the conceptual framework of a "reward system of science" (Mackintosh, 1972, p. 16;[1] McCain, 1991, p. 495). Cronin integrated both theoretical perspectives in his corpus, at times in tandem, for ex-

---

[1] Mackintosh cited Merton, but not Bourdieu—likely because the first English translations of Bourdieu's works were not published until the late 1970s.

ample in *The Hand of Science: Academic Writing and its Rewards* (2005). This book offers, in itself, a framework for the study of the "reward system of science, understood in terms of an economy of attention" (p. 5). Therefore, we can argue for a triumvirate of theoreticians in the study of the reward triangle: Cronin, Bourdieu, and Merton.

Acknowledgments have a dubious reputation. This is due, first, to their "subtler" (Cronin, 1992, p. 128), and more "personal" (Hyland, 2003, p. 243) nature; second, to the fact that they are unruly, and not "as frequent or as standardized" as citations (Cronin, 2014, p. xvii); and third, to their perceived propensity to be, at least in certain cases, "self-serving gestures, [... that are] by no means innocent" (Coates, 1999, p. 255). Perhaps given these very characteristics, acknowledgments offer insight into both the scientific field and the incarnation of that field in the very person of the scientist (see Bourdieu, 2001, pp. 84–85)—the "*homo academicus*" (Bourdieu, 1984). The practice of acknowledgments, its forms, its purposes, and its evolution are of course deeply rooted in the scholar's *habitus*, and it goes without saying that the set of dispositions which form this *habitus* answers to both the broader field of scholarly production and disciplinary paradigms. Again because of their nature, acknowledgments participate in the *illusio* upon which the scientific field, like all others (Bourdieu, 1996, p. 228) is built: the premise whereby adhering to the rules of the game supposes, ipso facto, that one deems this game relevant and, more importantly, worth one's time, effort and, as is often the case for academics, livelihood. Bourdieu (1988) insists on this: without *illusio*, "there would be no stakes to play for, nor even any game" (p. 56).[2]

As stated above, acknowledgments can also testify to the ebb and flow of legitimization (often provided by authorship) and consecration (intrinsic to citation), which are key in the construction of symbolic capital—the "accumulation" of which "is a driving force of academic life" (Cronin, 2005, p. 139). Finally, acknowledgments differ from authorship or citations in that they can satisfy the two sets of values that underlie symbolic goods: the obvious symbolic values of contribution and intellectual indebtedness, but also the economic value, often decried, yet obviously intrinsic to all fields where funds are involved. Such is the role of funding acknowledgments or the identification of paid services, facilities, and institutions.

This chapter presents a review of the literature on acknowledgments in scholarly communication, demonstrating the significance of acknowledgements in the

---

[2] Interestingly, the English translation omitted part of the sentence here; the original French text is more specific, since it qualifies the *illusio* as "an adherence to the cultural arbitrary that is the very foundation of the group" (1984, p. 80, our translation).

reward system of science. In doing, so, we will show that the interactions between the three elements of the triangle (authorship-citations-acknowledgments) play a fundamental role in the *illusio* that shapes the sociology of science.

3 Finding the Literature

We searched the following bibliographic databases to retrieve items pertaining to acknowledgments in scholarly communication: Web of Science (WoS) citation indexes (Science Citation Index Expanded, Social Sciences Citation Index, Arts & Humanities Citation Index, Conference Proceedings Citation Index-Science and Conference Proceedings Citation Index); Library and Information Sciences Abstracts (LISA); Library, Information Science & Technology Abstracts (LISTA); Library Literature & Information Science Index; Dissertation & Theses (ProQuest); FRANCIS; and Sociological Abstracts. Keyword[3] and controlled-vocabulary searches were used, as well as pearl-growing techniques (Bopp & Smith, 2011, p. 112). We then examined and mined the reference lists of relevant items, which were identified through a preliminary assessment of abstracts or a summary reading. The dataset was considered "open," as new items could always be added, no matter their means of discovery. As stated, this was an exploratory analysis of the existing literature, rather than a systematic review. A total of 115 items were identified and selected for analysis.

Two researchers independently read the retrieved documents in order to ascertain the relevance of these items to acknowledgments research and to assign initial classification tags to each of them. Only one item caused a tagging conflict, which was resolved through discussion.

The following rounds of analysis were qualitative and inductive. Researchers jointly validated the original tags assigned to each document and identified 71 documents for deeper, qualitative analysis. 10 documents were excluded (this was validated by both researchers) and reasons for exclusion were: false positives, format (presentation notes or abstracts of work published elsewhere in more complete form); book reviews; documents not written in English or French;[4] and

---

[3] Keywords searched in title, keyword and abstract fields: acknowledgement*, acknowledgment*, author*, subauthorship OR sub-author*, credit*, contribution*, reward*, gratitude and courtes*.

[4] While we did not actively search for French-language texts, we did not exclude the ones that came to our attention, since we were capable of analyzing them; nevertheless, it goes without saying that studying the literature from other languages and cultures might yield other interesting findings.

documents not secured before the end of the analysis process—these items were deemed, upon evaluation of the abstracts, as having little potential impact on the findings. The remaining documents were classified as "peripheral," meaning that they informed the research in some way, but were not part of the "core" dataset.

Due to the preliminary nature of analysis, the coding that ensued was, of course, "data-driven" (Schreier, 2012, p. 88), but did not begin with a tabula rasa. Rather, it was directed by the premise emanating from the framework presented above and the aspect of the *illusio* it supports: that acknowledgments are worth studying. While such a stated theoretical bias is, of course, quite acceptable in directed qualitative research, it can make it "more likely" for researchers "to find evidence that is supportive rather than nonsupportive of a theory" (Hsieh & Shannon, 2005, p. 1283). Given the fact that our stated goal was to provide the reader with a foray into the current state of the literature, we wished to target certain aspects, and so had some "predetermined" categories (Hsieh & Shannon, 2005, p. 1282), such as the discipline of the sample (where applicable), the methods used, the presentation of a model, etc. However, aside from these broad axes, the rest of the codes emerged from the iterative readings of the texts. Nevertheless, while the overview presented here is analytical in nature, it does not have the pretension to be a full content analysis of the textual data contained in the documents that were examined.

These limitations notwithstanding, some validations and verification measures were put into place throughout the process, in a manner that befits the review approach and the methodology used, in accordance with the flexibility (White & Marsh, 2006) and contextual principles (Morse et al., 2002) of qualitative studies. Treating the whole document as the unit of analysis, one coder (C1) used an initial subset of 10 texts to create a first codebook; the coding scheme was then used on the same 10 documents by the second coder (C2). The two coders met and discussed their respective coding. The codebook was then refined and a new version was proposed. All the coding for the original subset of 10 was imported to the revised codebook; the two coders reconciled all conflicting codes and made sure that they were in agreement regarding any coding change resulting from the revision of the codebook.

The analysis continued in parallel with open discussions between the two coders throughout the process as they each coded different texts. If the creation of a new code was deemed necessary, or if a coder questioned the application of a code, the case was discussed and resolved. The creation of a new code was always accompanied by the decision to recode any texts that may be affected by this addition. As a measure of verification, after the coding of all documents was completed, C2 recoded 10 of C1's documents; a few conflicts arose, but were resolved through discussion. During the process, memos were kept to document each step;

furthermore, various notes and comments on the content of the papers were inserted in the coding spreadsheet itself. More reading led to more discoveries, and, by the end of the process, 80 items had been analysed.

Ultimately, what we propose is a classification of the body of work on acknowledgments, in the hopes that it will guide others in their own research; we encourage this namely through the lists presented in Appendix 1 which contain the full references of the documents we analyzed and which form the core dataset of 80 documents; these include: 66 journal articles, 9 book chapters, 2 books, 2 conference proceedings papers and 1 doctoral dissertation.

4 Assessing the Trends in the Literature

The 80 documents form a foundation for anyone aiming to research acknowledgments in scholarly communication from the "rewards of science" perspective, as represented in Figure 1. Of these, 59 can be considered acknowledgment-centric. This includes 11 documents that pertain to acknowledgments in theses and dissertations (T&D), which are treated as specific types of academic output and perceived as having an acknowledgment culture of their own.

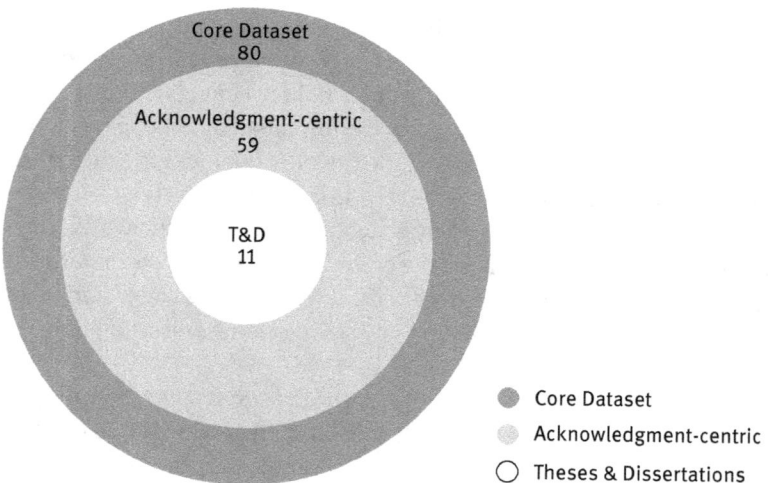

Fig. 1: Core dataset of documents considered in the analysis.

4.1 Bibliometric characteristics

As shown in Figure 2, the publication years of the 80 documents indicate a clear rise of the interest in the topic in the 1990s, with waxing and waning in the following decades creating a pendulum effect.

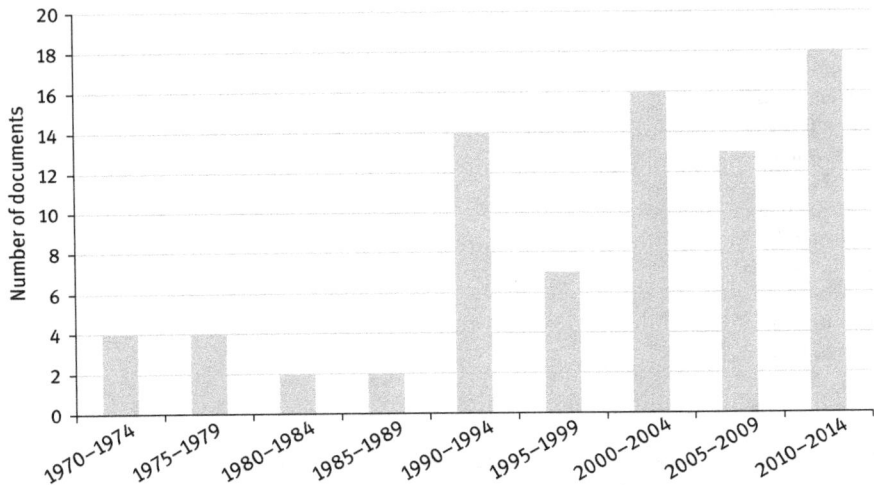

Fig. 2: Evolution of the number of documents published on acknowledgments, 1970–2014.

Table 1 presents the authors who contributed more than one item to the core dataset, whether as sole author or as co-authors. It clearly shows that Cronin's work is the unequivocal cornerstone of research on the topic. Some of his work builds on or presents other angles of previously published research; this pattern of iterative analysis and the important (not to mention humble) realization that "one's perspective changes over time" (Cronin, 2005, p. 15) are just some of the factors that have shaped Cronin's corpus as authoritative.[5]

Given the formats of the documents, establishing the fields that have taken an interest in acknowledgments research is slightly more complex. Limiting our analysis to the journal articles and using the Web of Science "Research Areas" classification of journals (Web of Science, 2012), we identified the field of publication of the 52 journal articles from our corpus that were indexed in WoS (where

---

[5] A bibliometric analysis could be performed, in further studies, to show the progression and influence of Cronin's acknowledgment-centric work through the years.

Tab. 1: Authors of acknowledgments research corpus.

Author	Number of documents
Cronin, Blaise	23
Salager-Meyer, Françoise	4
Weaver (Wozniak), Sherrill*	4
Alcaraz-Ariza, María Ángeles	3
Berbesí, Maryelis Pabón	3
Giannoni, Davide Simone	3
Hyland, Ken	3
McKenzie, Gail*	3
Shaw, Debora*	3
Tiew, Wai Sin	3
Chubin, Daryl. E.	2
Costas, Rodrigo	2
Heffner, Alan. G.	2
Rubio, Lourdes*	2
Sen, B. K.	2
van Leeuwen, Thed N.	2
Verner, Dima	2
Yang, Wenhsien	2
(60 other authors)	(1)

* Collaborators of Cronin. To our knowledge, these authors did not contribute to acknowledgments research beyond the publications co-authored with Cronin.

there were more than one category assigned, we favored disciplinary categories such as "Information Science & Library Science" over broader categories such as "Social Sciences"). To this, we added, as shown in Table 2, the 14 journal articles not indexed in WoS but whose journal titles or editorial mission clearly situates them in a given discipline.

Granted, our search strategies may have created a bias towards Information Science and Library Science; nevertheless, we harnessed a strong output of Linguistics contributions, as well as articles from other fields. However, Tables 2 and 3 clearly show the preponderance of Information Science and Library Science (including bibliometrics) contributions to the acknowledgments research corpus.

These disciplinary boundaries may yet be seen as arbitrary and, in many respects, they are, because other systems may classify academic disciplines differently. Interestingly, the complexity that accompanies the notion of "discipline" (Abbott, 2001) allows us what we hope to be an eloquent leap into our findings, in which such boundaries certainly play an important part.

Tab. 2: Number of articles by "Research areas".

Research areas	Number of journal articles
Information Science & Library Science	37
Linguistics	11
History & Philosophy of Science	3
Astronomy	2
Education	2
Literature	2
Psychology	2
Anthropology	1
Business & Economics	1
Communication	1
Medical Ethics	1
Science & Technology	1
Social Issues	1
Sociology	1

Tab. 3: Number of articles by journal.

Journal	Number of journal articles
Journal of the Association for Information Science and Technology*	11
Journal of Documentation	6
Social Science Information	3
Social Studies of Science	2
The Messenger	2
Scientometrics	2
Malaysian Journal of Library & Information Science	2
Journal of Scholarly Publishing	2
(36 other journals)	(1)

* Previously known as the *Journal of the American Society for Information Science and Technology* and the *Journal of the American Society for Information Science*.
Only journals with more than one article are named.

4.2 Conceptual characteristics

Let us begin by noting that our dataset contains items that do not present original empirical research but whose conceptual or theoretical contributions help shape the acknowledgments research landscape. We have already mentioned the importance of Cronin's *The Hand of Science* (2005). To this, we add Cronin's 1992

"Opinion" paper in the *Bulletin of the American Society for Information Science*, Cronin's 2012 comparison of artistic and scientific collaboration in *Information & Culture*, and Cronin's foreword to the book *Examining Paratextual Theory and its Applications in Digital Culture* (co-edited by one of this chapter's authors; 2014).

Other texts contribute to the topic by proposing theoretical and critical views of acknowledgments as representative of the field-made-man, to revive the Bourdieusian image evoked earlier (2001, pp. 84–85). This can help contextualize the dichotomous reputation of acknowledgments as valuable tools for insight into the field and excessively self-serving academic fluff. Some authors even offer comic relief. Hollander (2002) notes, for instance, that "Never do we come upon an author who does not wholeheartedly embrace criticism" (p. 64); he even describes the self-portraits of scientific acknowledgments as "disarmingly humble, self-effacing, even self-deprecating, sometimes bordering on confessions of incompetence" (p. 65). Such tone puts a great deal of weight on those the literature has come to call "trusted assessors" (see for example Mullins & Mullins, 1973, pp. 21, 32; Chubin, 1975b, pp. 363, 365; Cronin, 1991; Cronin, 1995, p. 18; Cronin, 2005, p. 56). The sometimes incongruous humanity shown through the acknowledgments' looking-glass is epitomized in the fictitious want-ad derived by Corey Coates from his 1999 analysis of acknowledgments of spouses in English Studies monographs:

> WANTED: Wife for scholar. Duties: general help—researching, proofing, typing/wordpro, indexing, style advice. Good humour and cheer necessary. Patience and endurance essential. Hours: many, variable. Remuneration in form of short acknowledgment.
>
> (pp. 258–259)

On the more serious side, reading conceptual pieces can help contextualize empirical works by providing the backdrop against which these studies were conducted. In that sense, Chubin (1975) helps contextualize early research like that of Mackintosh (1972); likewise, Caesar (1992) complements the work of McCain (1991) and the early Cronin studies.

Perspectives, of course, vary. We found that 34 of the 80 items included some analysis of the attributes of the acknowledgments themselves (length, placement, form, structure, wording, etc.) and some also performed a linguistics move-pattern analysis. In certain cases (such as Al-Ali, 2010 and Gesuato, 2004), acknowledgments were the central focus of a detailed text-based analysis. In other cases, like some early Cronin pieces, the discussion on style was brief, mentioned almost in passing, and used mostly as a means of outlining the importance of the actual wording in studying acknowledgments. This might be done, for example, with respect to the language used to thank certain people (Cronin, 1992b,

p. 131), through a look at language trends by discipline (Cronin, McKenzie, & Rubio, 1993, p. 41), or by mentioning the difficulties wording can create in the analysis (Cronin, McKenzie, & Stiffler, 1992, p. 112). Another trend was research by comparison. Comparative findings by such variables as journals, researchers, disciplines, countries, types of documents, or time-period were found in 51 items (including different papers based on the same studies).

Finally, there is a clear propensity in the literature for suggesting typologies of acknowledgments. However, this is not as straightforward as might appear. We looked at this qualitatively and coded for an angle to the research that would address the questions "who gets thanked for what?," "who gets thanked instead of being an author?," or "what are the roles, functions, or statuses of the people and organizations being thanked?;" we took into consideration occurrences of typologies presented in text, whether as findings or as models. This allowed us to identify 50 documents that could be analyzed further to draw comparisons and establish potential trends in terms of how acknowledgments are constructed, why they are included in a publication, as well as any proposed typologies or models. It should be noted that this is a very heterogeneous set. In some cases, following Hyland's 2004 model, the purpose (such as "Thanking for academic assistance") is presented as a subcategory of a structural analysis (p. 308); Al-Ali (2010) presents an adaptation of this model (p. 8) while Yang (2012) uses it as a framework for quantitative descriptions. In Basthomi's (2008) analysis, the focus is placed on *how* people are thanked; yet its method yields a list of *who* gets thanked (p. 4) as a necessary by-product. The reporting style of the aforementioned Coates (1999) does not afford him a typology, but one could certainly be derived from a qualitative content analysis of his findings.

Of course, Cronin's typologies are presented as central frameworks in Library and Information Science; this is true of the original six-part typology (1991, p. 231), which he built before encountering Mackintosh's 1972 work and simultaneously with McCain's 1991 work (1995, p. 41). It is also true of the subsequent typologies he developed with other collaborators, namely Weaver, between 1992 and 1995. These foundational classifications are sometimes presented in a continuum with other models (e.g., Tiew & Sen, 2002, p. 45; Rattan, 2013); they are also adapted, tweaked, or augmented, either slightly or significantly (e.g., Salager-Meyer, Alcaraz-Ariza, Berbesí, & Zambrano, 2006; Salager-Meyer, Alcaraz-Ariza & Berbesí, 2009; Weber & Thomer, 2014).

4.3 Limitations

The aim of the analytical review presented in this chapter is to provide insight into the acknowledgments research literature from the reward triangle perspective. Its limitations are obvious: the research strategy had a strong LIS and social sciences bias, given the fact that the bulk of the research was done in databases which favor journals over monographs. We did try to remedy this through bibliography mining, which made the dataset both richer and more complete. Furthermore, our qualitative content analysis was exploratory and used the document as its unit of analysis.

Other avenues could be pursued, including an analysis of the papers that pertain strictly to funding acknowledgments (FA); these were excluded from our analysis since they were seen as lying outside our reward triangle paradigm. We nevertheless flag this as a fast-growing field, namely thanks to the addition in the Web of Science databases of three funding acknowledgments or FA-related fields (Web of Science, 2009). As noted above, a review of the literature in other languages would be another important addition to this landscape.

Finally, the literature on acknowledgments in the context of editorial standards or guidelines should also be considered. As the interest for authorship and acknowledgments has been growing in the past decades, the editorial and opinion pieces that have been published since Kassirer and Angell (1991) raised the issue of the proliferation of acknowledgments in scientific articles would certainly warrant attention and add depth to the discussion.

5 Summing Up the Reward Triangle

We have already anchored our review in the reward triangle paradigm proposed by Cronin and Weaver-Wozniak (1993) and Cronin and Weaver (1995). The triangle figure was also used by Cronin in *The Hand of Science* to illustrate the aptly named "triadic sign systems" of references, acknowledgments, and citations through a semiotic lens (2005, pp. 147–151). We have chosen to expand upon this imagery.

Although none of the Cronin (1995) or Cronin and Weaver (1995; and as Weaver-Wozniak, 1993) articles, nor the Costas and van Leeuwen (2012) article offer an actual visualization of the reward triangle, an instinctive reading might lead to something like what is presented in Figure 3.

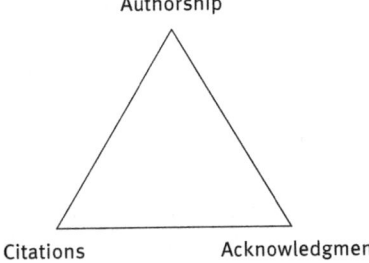

Fig. 3: The reward triangle: A classic interpretation.

However, through the help of the literature reviewed here, we now have an opportunity to visualize this triangle differently and to further its use by looking *inside* in more detail, all the while examining the relationships created between the three constitutive elements.

The angle sum theorem is a basic geometric paradigm: the sum of the measures of the interior angles of any given triangle is 180°. Building on this Euclidian truth, we propose an angle sum theory of the reward triangle in the scientific field. To do this, we moved the three constitutive elements from the vertices (understood here in the mathematical sense as all intersections), to the sides, as shown in Figure 4.

Fig. 4: The reward triangle: An angle sum theory interpretation of the literature, with the distribution of the relevant dataset numbers.

The apex of the triangle is where authorship meets citations. Scholarly performance is often assessed by both measures: "[t]o set the reward register ringing, all a scholar has to do is feature as an author or co-author and/or have his work cited by another" (Cronin & Weaver, 1995, p. 173). Indeed, if becoming an author grants legitimization, becoming a *cited* author grants consecration, in a field where one of the objectives, according to Bourdieu (1988), is to "make a name for oneself" (p. 2). In other words, the apex of the figure is not just authorship, but the intersection of authorship and intellectual influence—the intersection of an author's "productivity" and an author's "productive impact" (Cronin, 1995, pp. 14–15). This is the cornerstone of the scientific reward system. While the literature solely devoted to these two features was not included in our corpus, this angle has been studied thoroughly by a large body of literature and is at the core of the bibliometrics field; hence the right angle, fixed and enduring, to represent the body of research pertaining to the authorship-citation relationship.

The hypotenuse of the triangle, opposite the right angle, represents acknowledgments. It is the broader base. It is foundational because collaboration is key to producing high-impact knowledge (Larivière et al., 2014). It is broad because acknowledgments remain, for the most part, elective textual testimonies that manifest in a myriad of ways reflective of the myriad contents, forms, and even purposes they espouse.

While the right angle illustrates the strongest connection, the angle at the intersection of acknowledgments and citations constitutes the least studied portion of the triangle, with only 8 documents in our corpus addressing this relationship without much, if any, attention to authorship issues. The connection between acknowledgments and authorship has been the subject of a broader subset—our dataset includes 22 documents that discuss these two issues conjointly, with only a contextual, if any, reference to citations. Finally, the full reward triangle formed by authorship, citations, and acknowledgments was addressed in 17 documents.

In other words, to truly understand how the scientific community views and apprehends the reward triangle as both a set of independent elements and a set of relationships, one has to look not only at the center of the figure, but also at the angles that reflect the attention given to the various relationships between the three constitutive elements. When considered along with the literature that focuses on only one of the three elements of the reward triangle, this will provide an even more complete view; it will also reveal where imbalances lie. This, in itself, is telling in terms of the values granted to each relationship as a vector of symbolic capital in the scientific field.

6 Conclusion and Outlook

The findings presented herein show that acknowledgments research is not an emerging field, even though it is as eclectic as acknowledgments themselves. Flattening this landscape too quickly would be reductive to the collective knowledge it has contributed to the study of the reward system of science. The scientific field, with its "high degree of codification of entry into the game" (Bourdieu, 1996, p. 226), ensures the legitimization of its members; their consecration, however, is ruled by aspects of the *illusio* that the sociology of science has labelled *recognition* after Merton (1973), *capital* after Bourdieu, or the *reward triangle* after Cronin.

There are other views, of course, but these are the ones that led us to sum up, quite literally, the literature on acknowledgments research. Acknowledgments, like authorship and citations, testify to the fact that "[w]riting, in short, does not take place in a sociocognitive vacuum" (Cronin, 2005, p. 109). We now partake in more of the *illusio* by ending this co-authored chapter with acknowledgments and references of our own. In so doing, we are drawing the reward triangle, for ourselves and for other players in the game, from apex to hypothenuse, with every angle in-between.

Acknowledgment

The authors acknowledge the support of the Social Sciences and Humanities Research Council of Canada (Insight Development grants).

Cited References

Abbott, A. D. (2001). *Chaos of disciplines*. Chicago, IL: University of Chicago Press.
Al-Ali, M. N. (2010). Generic patterns and socio-cultural resources in acknowledgements accompanying arabic Ph.D. dissertations. *Pragmatics, 20*(1), 1–26.
Basthomi, Y. (2008). Interlanguage discourse of thesis acknowledgements section: Examining the terms of address. *Philippine Journal of Linguistics, 39*(1), 55–66.
Bopp, R. E., & Smith, L. C. (2011). *Reference and information services: an introduction*. Santa Barbara, CA: Libraries Unlimited.
Bourdieu, P. (1984). *Homo academicus*. Paris: Les Éditions de Minuit.
Bourdieu, P. (1988). *Homo academicus*. Stanford, CA: Stanford University Press.
Bourdieu, P. (1996). *The rules of art: Genesis and structure of the literary field*. Stanford, CA: Stanford University Press.
Bourdieu, P. (2001). *Science de la science et réflexivité*. Paris : Éditions Raisons d'agir.
Caesar, T. (1992). On Acknowledgements. *New Orleans Review, 19*(1), 85–94.
Chubin, D. E. (1975). Trusted assessorship in science: A relation in need of data. *Social Studies of Science, 5*(3), 362–367. doi:10.1177/030631277500500307
Coates, C. (1999). Interpreting academic acknowledgements in English studies: Professors, their partners, and peers. *English Studies in Canada, 25*(3–4), 253–276.
Costas, R., & van Leeuwen, T. N. (2012). Approaching the "reward triangle": General analysis of the presence of funding acknowledgments and "peer interactive communication." in scientific publications. *Journal of the American Society for Information Science and Technology, 63*(8), 1647–1661.
Cronin, B. (1991). Let the credits roll: A preliminary examination of the role played by mentors and trusted assessors in disciplinary formation. *Journal of Documentation, 47*(3), 227–239. doi:10.1108/eb026878

Cronin, B. (1992a). Acknowledged but ignored: Credit where credit's due. *Bulletin of the American Society for Information Science, 18*(3) 25.
Cronin, B. (1992b). The hidden influencers: An examination of the role played by mentors and trusted assessors in the evolution of information science. In P. Vakkari & B. Cronin (Ed.), *Conceptions of library and information science?: Historical, empirical and theoretical perspectives.* (p. 126–134). London: Taylor Graham.
Cronin, B. (1995). *The scholar's courtesy?: The role of acknowledgement in the primary communication process.* London: Taylor Graham.
Cronin, B. (2005). *The hand of science: Academic writing and its rewards.* Lanham, MD: Scarecrow Press.
Cronin, B. (2012). Collaboration in Art and in Science: Approaches to attribution, authorship, and acknowledgment. *Information & Culture, 47*(1), 18–37.
Cronin, B. (2014). Foreword: The penumbral world of the paratext. In N. Desrochers & D. Apollon (Eds.), *Examining paratextual theory and its applications in digital culture.* Hershey, PA: IGI Global. Retrieved February 5, 2015, from http://www.igi-global.com/pdf.aspx?tid=122526&ptid=97342&ctid=15&t=foreword
Cronin, B., & Weaver, S. (1995). The praxis of acknowledgement: from bibliometrics to influmetrics. *Revista española de documentación científica, 18*(2), 172–177.
Cronin, B., & Weaver-Wozniak, S. (1992). An online acknowledgment index: Rationale and feasibility. In D. Raitt (Ed.), *Online Information 92: Proceedings of the 16th International Online Information Meeting, London, 5-10 December 1992* (p. 281–290). Oxford: Learned Information.
Cronin, B., & Weaver-Wozniak, S. (1993). Online access to acknowledgements. In Williams, M. E. (Ed.), *Proceedings of the 14th National Online Meeting 1993* (p. 93–98). Medford, NJ : Learned Information.
Gesuato, S. (2004). Acknowledgments in PhD dissertations: The complexity of thanking. In C. Taylor Torsello, M. Grazia Bùsa, & S. Gesuato (Eds.), *Lingua inglese e mediazione linguistica. Ricerca e didattica con supporto telematico* (p. 273–318). Padova: Unipress.
Hollander, P. (2001). Acknowledgments: An academic ritual. *Academic Questions, 15*(1), 63–76. doi:10.1007/s12129-001-1056-x
Hsieh, H. F., & Shannon, S. E. (2005). Three approaches to qualitative content analysis. *Qualitative Health Research, 15*(9), 1277–1288. doi:10.1177/1049732305276687
Hyland, K. (2003). Dissertation acknowledgements: The anatomy of a Cinderella genre. *Written Communication, 20*(3), 242–268. doi:10.1177/0741088303257276
Hyland, K. (2004). Graduates' gratitude: The generic structure of dissertation acknowledgements. *English for Specific Purposes, 23*(3), 303–324. doi:10.1016/S0889-4906(03)00051-6
International Committee of Medical Journal Editors. (2006). Uniform requirements for manuscripts submitted to biomedical journals. Retrieved on August 1, 2014, from http://www.ncbi.nlm.nih.gov/pmc/articles/PMC3142758/
International Committee of Medical Journal Editors. (2013). Recommendations. Retrieved on August 1, 2014, from http://www.icmje.org/recommendations/
Kassirer, J. P., & Angell, M. (1991). On authorship and acknowledgments. *The New England Journal of Medicine, 325*(21), 1510–2. doi:10.1056/NEJM199111213252112
Larivière, V., Sugimoto, C. R., Tsou, A., & Gingras, Y. (2014). Team size matters: Collaboration and scientific impact since 1900. *Journal of the American Society for Information Science and Technology.*

Mackintosh, S. H. (1972). *Acknowledgment patterns in sociology* (Doctoral dissertation). Retrieved from ProQuest Dissertations and Theses (Accession Order No. 7228159).

McCain, K. W. (1991). Communication, competition, and secrecy: The production and dissemination of research-related information in genetics. *Science, Technology & Human Values, 16*(4), 491–516. doi:10.1177/016224399101600404

Merton, R. K. (1973). *The sociology of science: Theoretical and empirical investigations.* Chicago, IL: Chicago University Press.

Moore, R. (2004). Cultural capital: Objective probability and the cultural arbitrary. *British Journal of Sociology of Education, 25*(4), 445–456. doi:10.1080/0142569042000236943

Morse, J. M., Barrett, M., Mayan, M., Olson, K., & Spiers, J. (2008). Verification strategies for establishing reliability and validity in qualitative research. *International Journal of Qualitative Methods, 1*(2), 13–22.

Mullins, N. C., & Mullins, C. J. (1973). *Theories and theory groups in contemporary American sociology.* New York, NY : Harper and Row.

Pontille, D. (2004). *La signature scientifique: Une sociologie pragmatique de l'attribution.* Paris: CNRS Éditions.

Rattan, G. K. M. (2013). Acknowledgement patterns in Annals of Library and Information Studies 1999–2012. *Library Philosophy and Practice, e-journal* (Paper 989). Retrieved on August 1, 2014 from http://digitalcommons.unl.edu/libphilprac/989/

Salager-Meyer, F., Alcaraz-Ariza, M. Á., & Berbesí, M. P. (2009). "Backstage solidarity" in Spanish- and English-written medical research papers: Publication context and the acknowledgment paratext. *Journal of the American Society for Information Science and Technology, 60*(2), 307–317. doi:10.1002/asi.20981

Salager-Meyer, F., Alcaraz-Ariza, M. Á., Berbesí, M. P., & Zambrano, N. (2006). Paying one's intellectual debt: Acknowledgments in conventional vs. complementary/alternative medical research. In M. Gotti & F. Salager-Meyer (Eds.), *Advances in Medical Discourse Analysis: Oral and Written Contexts* (p. 407–430). Bern: Peter Lang.

Schreier, M. (2012). *Qualitative content analysis in practice.* London; Thousand Oaks, CA: Sage Publications.

Tiew, W. S., & Sen, B. K. (2002). Acknowledgement patterns in research articles: A bibliometric study based on Journal of Natural Rubber Research 1986–1997. *Malaysian Journal of Library & Information Science, 7*(1), 43–56.

Weber, N., & Thomer, A. (2014). Paratexts and documentary practices: Text mining authorship and acknowledgment from a bioinformatics corpus. In N. Desrochers & D. Apollon (Ed.), *Examining paratextual theory and its applications in digital culture.* Hershey, PA: IGI Global. Retrieved February 5, 2014, from http://www.igi-global.com/book/examining-paratextual-theory-its-applications/97342

Web of Science. (2009). *Funding Acknowledgements.* Retrieved August 3, 2014 from http://wokinfo.com/products_tools/multidisciplinary/webofscience/fundingsearch/

Web of Science. (2012). *Web of Science Help: Research Areas.* Retrieved August 3, 2014 from http://wokinfo.com/products_tools/multidisciplinary/webofscience/fundingsearch/

White, M. D., & Marsh, E. E. (2006). Content analysis: A flexible methodology. *Library Trends, 55*(1), 22–45. doi:10.1353/lib.2006.0053

Yang, W. (2012). A genre analysis of PhD dissertation acknowledgements across disciplinary variations. *LSP Journal—Language for special purposes, professional communication, knowledge management and cognition, 3*(2), 51–70.

Appendix 1

Core Dataset

Acknowledgments and Co-authorship Literature (22)

Bing, J., & Ruhl, C. (2008). It's all my fault! The pragmatics of responsibility statements. *Journal of Pragmatics, 40*(3), 537–558. doi:10.1016/j.pragma.2007.04.010

Birnholtz, J. P. (2006). What does it mean to be an author? The intersection of credit, contribution, and collaboration in science. *Journal of the American Society for Information Science and Technology, 57*(13), 1758–1770. doi:10.1002/asi.20380

Chubin, D. E. (1975). Trusted Assessorship in science: A relation in need of data. *Social Studies of Science, 5*(3), 362–367. doi:10.1177/030631277500500307

Cronin, B. (2001). Hyperauthorship: A postmodern perversion or evidence of a structural shift in scholarly communication practices? *Journal of the American Society for Information Science and Technology, 52*(7), 558–569. http://doi.org/10.1002/asi.1097

Cronin, B., & Franks, S. (2006). Trading cultures: Resource mobilization and service rendering in the life sciences as revealed in the journal article's paratext. *Journal of the American Society for Information Science and Technology, 57*(14), 1909–1918. doi:10.1002/asi.20407

Cronin, B., Martinson, A., & Davenport, E. (1997). Women's studies: Bibliometric and content analysis of the formative years. *Journal of Documentation, 53*(2), 123–138. doi:10.1108/EUM0000000007196

Cronin, B., Shaw, D., & La Barre, K. (2003). A cast of thousands: Coauthorship and subauthorship collaboration in the 20th century as manifested in the scholarly journal literature of psychology and philosophy. *Journal of the American Society for Information Science and Technology, 54*(9), 855–871.

Díaz-Faes, A. A., & Bordons, M. (2014). Acknowledgments in scientific publications: Presence in Spanish science and text patterns across disciplines. *Journal of the Association for Information Science and Technology.* doi:10.1002/asi.23081

Hartley, J. (2003). Single authors are not alone: Colleagues often help. *Journal of Scholarly Publishing, 34*(2), 108–113.

Heffner, A. G. (1979). Authorship recognition of subordinates in collaborative research. *Social Studies of Science, 9*(3), 377–384. doi:10.1177/030631277900900305

Heffner, A. G. (1981). Funded research, multiple authorship, and subauthorship collaboration in four disciplines. *Scientometrics, 3*(1), 5–12. doi:10.1007/BF02021860

Laudel, G. (2002). What do we measure by co-authorships? *Research Evaluation, 11*(1), 3–15. doi:10.3152/147154402781776961

Mackintosh, S. H. (1972). *Acknowledgment patterns in sociology* (Doctoral dissertation). Retrieved from ProQuest Dissertations and Theses (Accession Order No. 7228159).

Patel, N. (1973). Collaboration in the professional growth of American sociology. *Social Science Information, 12*(6), 77–92.

Pontille, D. (2001). L'auteur scientifique en question: Pratiques en psychologie et en sciences biomédicales. *Social Science Information, 40*(3), 433–453. doi:10.1177/053901801040003004

Salager-Meyer, F., Alcaraz-Ariza, M. Á., & Berbesí, M. P. (2009). "Backstage solidarity" in Spanish- and English-written medical research papers: Publication context and the acknowledgment paratext. *Journal of the American Society for Information Science and Technology, 60*(2), 307–317. doi:10.1002/asi.20981

Salager-Meyer, F., Alcaraz-Ariza, M. Á., Berbesí, M. P., & Zambrano, N. (2006). Paying one's intellectual debt: Acknowledgments in conventional vs. complementary/alternative medical research. In M. Gotti & F. Salager-Meyer (Eds.), *Advances in Medical Discourse Analysis: Oral and Written Contexts* (p. 407–430). Bern: Peter Lang.

Seeman, J. I., & House, M. C. (2010). Influences on authorship issues: An evaluation of giving credit. *Accountability in research, 17*(3), 146–169. doi:10.1080/08989621003791986

Spiegel, D., & Keith-Spiegel, P. (1970). Assignment of publication credits: Ethics and practices of psychologists. *American Psychologist, 25*(8), 738–747. doi:10.1037/h0029769

Sugimoto, C. R., & Cronin, B. (2012). Biobibliometric profiling: An examination of multifaceted approaches to scholarship. *Journal of the American Society for Information Science and Technology, 63*(3), 450–468. doi:10.1002/asi.21695

Suls, J., & Fletcher, B. (1983). Social comparison in the social and physical sciences: An archival study. *Jounal of Personality and Social Psychology, 44*(3), 575–580.

Weber, N., & Thomer, A. (2014). Paratexts and documentary practices: Text mining authorship and acknowledgment from a bioinformatics corpus. In N. Desrochers & D. Apollon (Eds.), *Examining paratextual theory and its applications in digital culture*. Hershey, PA: IGI Global. Retrieved February 5, 2014, from http://www.igi-global.com/book/examining-paratextual-theory-its-applications/97342

Acknowledgments and Citations Literature (9)

Cronin, B. (1992a). Acknowledged but ignored: Credit where credit's due. *Bulletin of the American Society for Information Science, 18*(3), 25.

Cronin, B. (1992b). The hidden influencers: An examination of the role played by mentors and trusted assessors in the evolution of information science. In P. Vakkari & B. Cronin (Eds.), *Conceptions of library and information science?: historical, empirical and theoretical perspectives.* (p. 126–134). London: Taylor Graham.

Cronin, B. (1995). *The scholar's courtesy?: The role of acknowledgement in the primary communication process*. London: Taylor Graham.

Cronin, B. (2001).

Cronin, B. (2014). Foreword: The penumbral world of the paratext. In N. Desrochers & D. Apollon (Eds.), *Examining paratextual theory and its applications in digital culture*. Hershey, PA: IGI Global. Retrieved February 5, 2015, from http://www.igi-global.com/pdf.aspx?tid=122526&ptid=97342&ctid=15&t=foreword

Cronin, B., McKenzie, G., Rubio, L., & Weaver-Wozniak, S. (1993). Accounting for influence: Acknowledgments in contemporary sociology. *Journal of the American Society for Information Science, 44*(7), 406–412.

Cronin, B., McKenzie, G., & Stiffler, M. (1992). Patterns of acknowledgement. *Journal of Documentation, 48*(2), 107–122.

Giles, C. L., & Councill, I. G. (2004). Who gets acknowledged: Measuring scientific contributions through automatic acknowledgment indexing. *Proceedings of the National Academy of Sciences of the United States of America, 101*(51), 17599–17604. doi:10.2307/3374014

McCain, K. W. (1991). Communication, competition, and secrecy: The production and dissemination of research-related information in Genetics. *Science, Technology & Human Values, 16*(4), 491–516. doi:10.1177/016224399101600404

Weigert, A. J. (1970). The immoral rhetoric of scientific sociology. *The American Sociologist, 5*(2), 111–119.

Reward Triangle Literature (17)

Bazerman, C. (1988). Theoretical integration in experimental reports in twentieth-century physics: Spectroscopic articles in Physical Review, 1893–1980. In *Shaping written knowledge: The genre and activity of the experimental article in science* (p. 153–186). Madison, WI : University of Wisconsin Press.

Costas, R., & van Leeuwen, T. N. (2012). Approaching the " reward triangle ": General analysis of the presence of funding acknowledgments and " peer interactive communication " in scientific publications. *Journal of the American Society for Information Science and Technology, 63*(8), 1647–1661.

Cronin, B. (1991). Let the credits roll: A preliminary examination of the role played by mentors and trusted assessors in disciplinary formation. *Journal of Documentation, 47*(3), 227–239. doi:10.1108/eb026878

Cronin, B. (2005). *The hand of science: Academic writing and its rewards.* Lanham, MD.: Scarecrow Press.

Cronin, B. (2012). Collaboration in art and in science: Approaches to attribution, authorship, and acknowledgment. *Information & Culture, 47*(1), 18–37.

Cronin, B., & Overfelt, K. (1994). The scholar's courtesy: A survey of acknowledgement behaviour. *Journal of Documentation, 50*(3), 165–196. doi:10.1108/eb026929

Cronin, B., & Shaw, D. (2007). Peers and spheres of influence: Situating Rob Kling. *The Information Society, 23*(4), 221–233. doi:10.1080/01972240701444147

Cronin, B., Shaw, D., & Barre, K. L. (2004). Visible, less visible, and invisible work: Patterns of collaboration in 20th century chemistry. *Journal of the American Society for Information Science and Technology, 55*(2), 160–168. doi:10.1002/asi.10353

Cronin, B., & Weaver, S. (1995). The praxis of acknowledgement: From bibliometrics to influmetrics. *Revista española de documentación científica, 18*(2), 172–177.

Cronin, B., & Weaver-Wozniak, S. (1992). An online acknowledgment index: Rationale and feasibility. In D. Raitt (Ed.), *Online Information 92: Proceedings of the 16th International Online Information Meeting, London, 5-10 December 1992* (p. 281–290). Oxford: Learned Information.

Cronin, B., & Weaver-Wozniak, S. (1993). Online access to acknowledgements. In Williams, M. E. (Ed.), *Proceedings of the 14th National Online Meeting 1993* (p. 93–98). Medford, NJ : Learned Information.

Giannoni, D. S. (1998). The genre of journal acknowledgments: Findings of a cross-disciplinary investigation. *Linguistica e Filología, 6*, 61–84.

Giannoni, D. S. (2002). Worlds of gratitude: A contrastive study of acknowledgement texts in English and Italian research articles. *Applied Linguistics, 23*(1), 1–31. doi:10.1093/applin/23.1.1

Laband, D. N., & Tollison, R. D. (2000). Intellectual collaboration. *Journal of Political Economy, 108*(3), 632–662. doi:10.1086/262132

Roa-Atkinson, A., & Velho, L. (2005). Interactions in knowledge production: A comparative case study of immunology research groups in Colombia and Brazil. *Aslib Proceedings, 57*(3), 200–216. doi:10.1108/00012530510599172

Tiew, W. S. (1998a). Journal of Malaysian Branch of the Royal Asiatic Society (JMBRAS) 1987–1996: A ten-year bibliometric analysis. *Malaysian Journal of Library & Information Science, 3*(2), 49–66.

Tiew, W. S. (1998b). Journal of Natural Rubber Research 1987–1996: A ten-year bibliometric study. *IASLIC Bulletin, 43*(2), 49–57.

Other (32)

Al-Ali, M. N. (2010). Generic patterns and socio-cultural resources in acknowledgements accompanying Arabic Ph.D. dissertations. *Pragmatics, 20*(1), 1–26.

Basthomi, Y. (2008). Interlanguage discourse of thesis acknowledgements section: Examining the terms of address. *Philippine Journal of Linguistics, 39*(1), 55–66.

Ben-Ari, E. (1987). On acknowledgments in ethnographies. *Journal of Anthropological Research, 43*(1), 63–84.

Brown, R. (2009). How scholars credit editors in their acknowledgements. *Journal of Scholarly Publishing, 40*(4), 384–398. doi:10.3138/jsp.40.4.384

Caesar, T. (1992). On acknowledgements. *New Orleans Review, 19*(1), 85–94.

Cheng, S. W. (2012). A contrastive study of Master thesis acknowledgements by Taiwanese and North American students. *Open Journal of Modern Linguistics, 2*(1), 8–17. doi:10.4236/ojml.2012.21002

Chubin, D. E. (1975). The journal as a primary data source in the sociology of science?: With some observations from sociology. *Social Science Information, 14*(1), 157–168. doi:10.1177/053901847501400114

Coates, C. (1999). Interpreting academic acknowledgements in English studies: Professors, their partners, and peers. *English Studies in Canada, 25*(3–4), 253–276.

Costas, R., & van Leeuwen, T. N. (2012). New indicators based on the 'Funding Acknowledgement' information in the Web of Science: Analysis of the effect of peer review over the impact of scientific journals. In É. Archambault, Y. Gingras, & V. Larivière (Eds.), *Proceedings of 17th International Conference on Science and Technology Indicators* (p. 193–205). Montréal: Science-Metrix and OST.

Cronin, B. (2001). Acknowledgement trends in the research literature of information science. *Journal of Documentation, 57*(3), 427–433.

Cronin, B., McKenzie, G., & Rubio, L. (1993). The norms of acknowledgement in four social sciences disciplines. *Journal of Documentation, 49*(1), 29–43. doi:10.1108/eb026909

Davis, C. H., & Cronin, B. (1993). Acknowledgments and intellectual indebtedness: A bibliometric conjecture. *Journal of the American Society for Information Science, 44*(10), 590–592. doi:10.1002/(SICI)1097-4571(199312)44:10<590::AID-ASI5>3.0.CO;2-U

Gesuato, S. (2004). Acknowledgments in PhD dissertations: The complexity of thanking. In C.Taylor Torsello, M. Grazia Bùsa and S. Gesuato (Eds.), *Lingua inglese e mediazione linguistica. Ricerca e didattica con supporto telematico* (p. 273–318). Padova: Unipress.

Giannoni, D. S. (2006a). Book acknowledgements across disciplines and texts. In K. Hyland & M. Bondi (Eds.), *Academic discourse across disciplines* (p. 151–176). Bern: Peter Lang.

Giannoni, D. S. (2006b). Evidence of generic tension in academic book acknowledgements. In V. K. Bhatia & M. Gotti (Eds.), *Explorations in specialized genres* (p. 21–42). Bern: Peter Lang.

Hollander, P. (2001). Acknowledgments: An academic ritual. *Academic Questions*, *15*(1), 63–76. doi:10.1007/s12129-001-1056-x

Hyland, K. (2003). Dissertation acknowledgements: The anatomy of a Cinderella genre. *Written Communication*, *20*(3), 242–268. doi:10.1177/0741088303257276

Hyland, K. (2004). Graduates' gratitude: the generic structure of dissertation acknowledgements. *English for Specific Purposes*, *23*(3), 303–324. doi:10.1016/S0889-4906(03)00051-6

Hyland, K., & Tse, P. (2004). "I would like to thank my supervisor". Acknowledgements in graduate dissertations. *International Journal of Applied Linguistics*, *14*(2), 259–275. doi:10.1111/j.1473-4192.2004.00062.x

Koley, S., & Sen, B. K. (2013). Acknowledgements in research papers in electronics and related fields: 2008–2012. *SRELS Journal of Information Management*, *50*(5), 619–627.

Lasaky, F. G. (2011). A contrastive study of generic organization of doctoral dissertation acknowledgements written by native and non-native (Iranian) students in applied linguistics. *The Modern Journal of Applied Linguistics*, *3*(2), 175–199.

Rattan, G. K. M. (2013). Acknowledgement patterns in Annals of Library and Information Studies 1999–2012. *Library Philosophy and Practice*, *e-journal* (Paper 989). Retrieved on August 1, 2014 from http://digitalcommons.unl.edu/libphilprac/989/

Salager-Meyer, F., Alcaraz-Ariza, M. Á., & Berbesí, M. P. (2010). Hidden influencers and the scholarly enterprise: a cross-linguistic/cultural analysis of acknowledgments in medical research papers. In M. F. Ruiz-Garrido, J. C. Palmer-Silveira, & I. Fortanet-Gomez (Eds.), *English for Professional and Academic Purposes*. Castellón, Spain: Universitat Jaume I.

Salager-Meyer, F., Alcaraz-Ariza, M. Á., Luzardo Briceño, M., & Jabbour, G. (2011). Scholarly gratitude in five geographical contexts: A diachronic and cross-generic approach of the acknowledgment paratext in medical discourse (1950–2010). *Scientometrics*, *86*(3), 763–784. doi:10.1007/s11192-010-0329-y

Scrivener, L. (2009). An exploratory analysis of History students' dissertation acknowledgments. *The Journal of Academic Librarianship*, *35*(3), 241–251. doi:10.1016/j.acalib.2009.03.004

Tiew, W. S., & Sen, B. K. (2002). Acknowledgement patterns in research articles: A bibliometric study based on Journal of Natural Rubber Research 1986–1997. *Malaysian Journal of Library & Information Science*, *7*(1), 43–56.

Tokdemir Demirel, E., & Shahriari Ahmadi, H. (2013). Lexical bundles in research article acknowledgments: A corpus comparison. *Hacettepe Universitesi Egitim Fakultesi Dergisi-Hacettepe University Journal of*, *28*(2), 457–468.

Verner, D. (1992). Astronomy acknowledgement index 1991. *The Messenger*, *67*, 61–62.

Verner, D. (1993). Astronomy acknowledgement index 1992. *The Messenger*, *71*, 59.

Woolf, P. (1975). The second messenger: Informal communication in Cyclic AMP research. *Minerva*, *13*(3), 349–373.

Yang, W. (2012a). A genre analysis of PhD dissertation acknowledgements across disciplinary variations. *LSP Journal - Language for special purposes, professional communication, knowledge management and cognition*, *3*(2), 51–70.

Yang, W. (2012b). Comparison of gratitude across context variations: A generic analysis of dissertation acknowledgements written by Taiwanese authors in EFL and ESL contexts. *International Journal of Applied Linguistics & English Literature*, *1*(5), 130–146.

Hamid R. Ekbia
The Flesh of Science: Somatics and Semiotics

1 Introduction: Content, Context, and Structure

Scientists are human beings, too. This innocuous statement might strike us as trivially true, banally evident, conditionally valid, or despicably demeaning, depending on our perspective on science and scientists. Versions of each of these interpretations did, in fact, emerge in the second half of the twentieth century, after science turned into an object of inquiry in the hands of sociologists, anthropologists, and historians of science. Although the language and conceptual framing applied varied across studies and schools of thought—institutional norms (Merton, 1973), paradigms and ab/normal science (Kuhn, 1962), deviance and explanatory symmetry (Zuckerman, 1977; Barnes & Edge, 1982), token manipulation (Latour & Woolgar, 1979), boundary objects (Star & Griesmer, 1989), epistemic cultures (Knorr-Cetina, 1999), to name but a few—the shared motif, broadly speaking, was to find social, cultural, or historical *mechanisms* and *processes* that enable scientists or prevent them from going about the business of "constructing" truth claims about the physical, biological, and psychological worlds.

The *processual* perspective (Becker, 2003) behind these studies was one of the features that differentiated them from works of philosophers of science who had traditionally focused on the *products* of science, making sure that they meet the standards and metrics derived from one or other foundational philosophical framework—logic and rationality in logical empiricism, evidential adequacy in verificationism, falsifiability in Popper's objectivism, and so forth. The type of processes that were studied, however, varied according to the theoretical framing behind the specific account, as a brief overview will demonstrate.

2 Science Studies: The Quest for Realism

2.1 1st Wave Institutionalism: Scientists follow norms

The strategy adopted by social scientists was "to distinguish the behavior of scientists *as* scientists from the details of their 'output'" (Storer, 1973, xvii). This strategy, however, found two different interpretations or orientations among sociologists. The first orientation, focusing on the social *context* in which scientific inquiry takes place, sought to delineate the boundaries of the scientific community. This is roughly the strategy that Thomas Kuhn pursued in his seminal work on scientific paradigms, although he sought to identify the social parameters that can explain the formal organization of scientific knowledge. The second orientation, largely associated with Robert Merton's work, focused on the (internal) social *structure* of science, postulating norms that allegedly govern the behavior of scientists as they engage in the production of scientific knowledge: universalism, communism, organized skepticism, and disinterestedness (Merton 1973). This second orientation, which provided a meaningful strategy for separating content from context, is considered the founding moment of sociology of science as an area of inquiry.

Scientists, according to this institutional and structural perspective, are like the rest of us in that they follow the norms specific to their community. What makes them different from others is in the character of the norms to which they adhere. This was a powerful and defensible position, given the dominant thinking in social sciences of the time, except that it faced the challenge of explaining "deviant behavior" among scientists. One such controversial case was that of the geologist and amateur archaeologist Charles Dawson who, in 1912, presented a fossil as the skull of what came to be known as the Piltdown Man, which allegedly predated all human fossils found until then—e.g., the Java Man or the Heidelberg Man. Disagreements over the genuineness of Dawson's claim were finally resolved when new X-ray techniques showed that some of the "fossil" teeth have been artificially ground down, leading to the conclusion that the evidence was forged (Zuckerman, 1977). Cases such as this illustrate that the norms postulated by sociologists do not protect scientists against error, forgery, and deception, as rare and unlikely as these behaviors might be.

2.2 2nd Wave Institutionalism: Scientists also deviate from norms

To deal with such instances of deviant behavior, along with many other cases of explicit and implicit error, sociologists of science proposed a distinction between cognitive (technical) norms, on the one hand, and moral norms, on the other. Harriet Zuckerman, a student (and later spouse) of Merton, describes these two sets of norms as, respectively, those that "specify what should be studied and how" and "prescriptions, proscriptions, preferences, and permissions concerning the attitudes and behaviors of scientists in relation to one another and their research" (Zuckerman, 1977, p. 89). Both sets of norms, according to Merton, "are binding, not only because they are procedurally efficient, but because they are believed right and good" (Merton, 1973, p. 270). The empirical analysis of multiple cases of fraud and error by marginal as well as prominent scientists leads Merton, Zuckerman, and others to conclude that science is not "special or even unique among social institutions in having the same normative and social conditions pressing for deviant behavior and for its disclosure" (Zuckerman, 1977, p. 131). In other words, as with Durkheim's famous hypothesis on crime and punishment, the same reward mechanisms (e.g., reputation) that encourage deviant behavior among scientists also exert social control over them by imposing high costs to non-conforming behavior.

2.3 Strong Programme: Scientists adhere to the principles of science itself

The interest in 2nd-wave institutionalism in deviance and in "the blind alleys entered by science" (Ben-David, 1971, p. 11) did not sit well with those sociologists who sought after a "strong programme" for the Sociology of Scientific Knowledge (SSK)—namely, one that would explain the success stories of science as much as its failures; a *symmetric* account, in other words, that can provide a sociological explanation for the truth of "our culture's most highly valued form of knowledge" (Shapin, 1995, p. 292). These sociologists found a strong ally and a useful insight in Thomas Kuhn and his idea that science itself provides the principles that regulate scientists' conduct. By emphasizing the collective and distributed character of knowledge and of the processes that give rise to it, they sought to put SSK on the right sociological footing, avoiding individualistic philosophies that only give credence to direct experiential observations. In their place, they proposed social mechanisms of trust, authority, and morality as guarantors of the collective creation of valid knowledge (Barnes, 1985), and highlighted customs and conventions as the means to propagate it beyond its situated sites of production (Bloor, 1982). Simultaneously, these authors did not question the realism of scientific claims, iterating that "[t]here is indeed one world, one reality, 'out there'" (Bloor, 1992, p. 33). The robust realism, which arose from this combination of natural and sociological realism, is often contrasted with rationalist thinking that is grounded in rules of method (Shapin, 1995, p. 303).

2.4 Laboratory Studies: Scientists are as worldly as the rest of us

SSK's realism, however, was challenged on a number of fronts by a broad array of commentators from within science studies itself, from those who took an interest in the rhetorical and persuasive devices of scientific discourse (e.g., Woolgar, 1976) to those who highlighted the embodied and physical character of knowledge-making in science (Collins, 1992; Lynch, 1991). Most radical among these critiques perhaps was the so-called "laboratory studies" line of work, inaugurated famously by Latour and Woolgar (1979)'s *Laboratory Life*, which portrayed a very mundane image of the scientific enterprise as heavily involved in the production of signs and symbols. Following an anthropological approach, and portraying themselves as "foreign observers," these authors described scientists in a lab as a "strange tribe" of "compulsive and manic writers ... who spend the greatest part of their day coding, marking, altering, correcting, reading, and writing" (Latour & Woolgar, 1979, pp. 48–9).[1]

2.5 Semiotics of Science: Scientists are cyborgs, like the rest of us

Laboratory studies, and the diverse body of work that followed from it—e.g., the studies of the epistemic machinery and cultures of science (Knorr-Cetina, 1999)—led further down the road to the influential work in actor-network theory (ANT) and beyond. With its strong post-humanist impulse, ANT injected a discourse with a new dimension of symmetry between human and nonhuman actors. In so doing, it turned scientists, like the rest of us, into cyborgs—with technologically augmented brains and bodies, but presumably not much feeling.

In navigating the narrow strait between naïve realism and social constructivism, actor-network theorists took extreme pain to show that their account of science provides a more "realistic" image of science and scientists than the earlier alternatives. To that end, they distanced themselves from, among others, phenomenology that provides "much talk about the real, fleshy, pre-reflexive world, but...[that] leaves us with the most dramatic split in this whole sad story"—namely, the split between the "cold" world of science and the lived world of humans. ANT sought to eliminate this split by presenting a "modernist settlement," which brings four seemingly independent spheres together: "'out there,'

---

[1] Having been trained in the natural sciences, I clearly remember the deeply deflating and depressing impact that reading Latour and Woolgar's book had on me the first time I read it.

'nature'; 'in there,' the mind; 'down there,' the social; 'up there,' God" (Latour 1999, p. 14). What was missing from this settlement, however, was "deep there"—the body.

3 Somatics of Science: Scientists are made of flesh, like the rest of us

This brief overview of the development of perspectives and theories in science studies illustrates some of the seminal moments and "turns" in the history of the field and in how it has looked at science and scientists, in their relationship to each other and to the broader socio-cultural and historical context. The overview also reveals a certain gap, an unspoken dimension of scientific life, in all of these accounts that seems to have escaped, by and large, the attention of science studies scholars. The multifaceted character of this dimension makes it difficult to give it an encompassing label but I propose to call it the "somatics of science".[2] To distinguish some of these facets, I now turn to Cronin's work which has been partly oriented toward this dimension.

3.1 Paratext: A Window to the Invisible

Blaise Cronin's oeuvre, broadly speaking, is grounded in scientometrics, with its established theories and methods, which tend to be conveniently aligned with quantitative techniques. The quantitative bent of the tradition, however, has not occluded his view to those aspects of science and scientific work that seem to be more amenable to qualitative methods such as ethnography. To the contrary, he has shrewdly and effectively used the so-called quantitative methods as a window *and* a support to understand and explicate "the messy materiality of science in the raw" (Cronin, 2008b)—a feat that deserves intellectual nod but that also casts great doubt on the meaningfulness of the commonly accepted dichotomy between quantitative and qualitative work.

---

[2] By "somatics" I mean that which has to do with the soma, broadly understood. This goes beyond the more specific meaning of the term as, for instance, used by Hanna (1986), where soma is defined as the body as perceived from within by first-person perception. I use the term to also refer to relationships between bodies.

One example of this approach is Cronin's work on "paratext": acknowledgments, dedications, forewords, and the like, which he once described as "the goat droppings of scholarly communication" (Cronin, 2008b, p. 43)—trivial and banal on first sight but revealing and informative on closer examination. Through a series of studies, using novel techniques, Cronin identified patterns of authorship, crediting, and trading among research groups and scientific labs but also hidden tessellations of proximity, co-location, and friendship among individual scientists (Cronin, 2008a). These kinds of ties, hidden and unnoticed as they were, turn out to be as significant in the day-to-day practice of science as more rigorous "academic" measures such as credentials, specialty, and ranking. Location and proximity, for instance, turn out to be key determining parameters in the selection of collaborators, highlighting a facet of place other than its role in the construction of truth, which has been the focus of some science studies scholars (Gieryn, 1999).

3.2 Rhopography: Deconstruction of an Historical Myth

Acknowledgments and other forms of implicit crediting, however, form the tip of a bigger iceberg—namely, the broad range of contributions from unacknowledged contributors such as technicians, apprentices, suppliers, experimenters, analysts, and, of course, students who carry the bulk of the daily work of science but who have remained unnoticed and underappreciated since the beginning of modern science and, for that matter, art (Cronin, 2012). Cronin has borrowed the term "rhopography" (from the Greek "rhopos" meaning "petty wares") from the realm of art—another key interest of his—to refer to a new kind of accounting in scientific work. In contrast to "megalography"—the dominant narrative style in the history of sciences and the arts, which gives most or all of the credit to Big Minds—rhopography can provide an historical corrective, where Little Hands would also get credit for what they, in fact, contribute to the practice of science and the production of scientific knowledge.

The migration of a large portion of science communication to the digital medium, according to Cronin, will facilitate this historical shift toward the recognition of Little Hands. Customs and traditions, however, have proven to be stubborn, and there are as yet no promising indications to corroborate this optimism, as in the case of citizen science, for instance (Kouper et al., forthcoming).

3.3 Warm Bodies and Cool Minds: Science in the Flesh

Opening up scholarly inquiry to these hidden dimensions of scientific work does not, and perhaps should not, stop here. If physical proximity matters in the choice of colleagues and collaborators, one might ask, what about more sublime forms of affinity and association? What about friendships, romantic relations, and fleeting moments of flirtation? In fact, the history of science is witness to many instances where these kinds of relationships seem to have, indeed, left their print on the real practice of science. It has been known, for instance, that a relatively large proportion of female scientists—e.g., 70 % and 80 %, respectively, of women physicists and mathematicians—marry or partner with other scientists (Blaser, 2008). This pattern seems to still be in place, perhaps with an overall upward trend of "more husband-wife teams" (Anonymous, 2008). How can this be explained sociologically? Marriage with peers in the 19th century could provide women scientists an entry point to a male-dominated academe, but is this still the case in the 21st century (Creamer, 2001)? Or does the "greedy institution" of science (Grant, Kennelly & Ward, 2000) or its need for "collegial roles" (Reskin, 1978) drive this in order to facilitate the interweaving of family and professional lives among scientists—e.g., in the form of invisible labor, spouses discussing or reviewing each others' work, or simply an environment of productive trust and proximity (Creamer, 2001)? What kinds of concepts and theories do we need to investigate the place of romance, affect, and friendship in science?

The official history of science, ironically, has been less attentive to these relationships and their effects and more focused on rivalries and competitions among major figures, theorizing them in concepts such as "concurrent discovery". The not-so-novel facets and dimensions of science discussed above, however, suggest we need more inquiries into the scientific enterprise of the kind that Cronin has pursued throughout his career. For reasons that should be clear by now, I propose to call this line of inquiry "the somatics of science", which can be broadly understood as a subfield of science studies that would take into account the effects on the practice of science of bodily relationships—from physical proximity to friendships and romantic attachment.

Whether we are concerned with realism (natural or social), symmetry, or "context", I argue, the somatics of science seems to be an integrated aspect of its conduct.

4 Conclusion: For a Somatics of Science

Science studies has been historically haunted by an inner tension and dilemma between "symmetry" and "realism". On the one hand, driven by the sociological impulse to understand science as a socio-cultural institution, it seeks to put science in its proper place, understanding it symmetrically beyond modernist dualisms such as nature-culture, mind-body, and self-society. The pursuit of symmetry, however, comes to clash with the realism and the realistic idiom that science studies, embedded as it is in modernism, has to adopt as a baseline. Hence, "saying that science ought to be understood as a typical form of culture is, of course, not the same thing as saying that it is no different from other forms of culture" (Shapin, 1995, p. 305). This is what gives rise to the somewhat defensive avowal that the ultimate goal of science studies is to "*add*[ed] reality to science" (Latour, 1999, p. 2). It is this dilemma perhaps that explains why historians and sociologists of science have, by and large, shied away from engaging with the somatics of science.

There is, however, a deeper conceptual reason for the paucity of work in this area, and that has to do with the impoverished understanding of "embodiment" in the analytic tradition:

> Disengagement and disembodiment were ancient tropes of value. Removing knowledge-making from the polis was seen as a technique for transcendence. Accordingly, to say that knowledge was produced in and through mundane interactions between people, as well as between people and reality, was taken to say that its truth, objectivity, universality, and power were compromised. So far as genuine philosophical knowledge was concerned, the polity was a pollutant.
> (Shapin, 1995, p. 299)

While phenomenologists such as Merleau-Ponty have provided deep insights into the multifaceted nature of embodiment, Anglo-Saxon analytic philosophy has been reluctant to incorporate them into its thinking. The semiotic tradition is science studies, on the other hand, which, in principle, could have provided an accommodating milieu for phenomenological insights, leaned toward a more Heideggerian and technological understanding of embodiment. The emphasis in actor-network theory on the agential symmetry between human and non-human actants is emblematic of this trend, which came at the expense of the more biological aspects of embodiment. The time might be ripe for an adjustment, turning our attention to the somatics of science and beyond.

Cited References

Anonymous. (2008). The Cost of a Genuine Collaboration. *Science, 320,* 859.

Barnes, B. (1985). *About Science.* Oxford: Blackwell.

Barnes, B. & Edge, D. (eds.) (1982). *Science in Context: Readings in Sociology of Science.* Milton Keynes: Open University Press.

Becker, H. (2003, April). New Directions in Sociology of Art. Paper Presented at the Meeting of the European Sociological Association, Paris.

Ben-David, J. (1971). *The Scientist's Role in Society: A Comparative Study.* University of Chicago Press.

Blaser, B. (2008) More than Just Lab Partners: Women Scientists and Engineers Married to or Partnered with other Scientists and Engineers. Doctoral Dissertation, Department of Women Studies, University of Washington.

Bloor, D. (1982). Duhem and Mauss Revisited: Classification and Sociology of Knowledge. *Studies in the History and Philosophy of Science, 13,* 267–297.

Creamer, E. (2001). Knowledge Production, Publication Productivity, and Intimate Academic Relationships. *Journal of Higher Education, 70,* 261–277.

Collins, H. (1992). *Changing Order: Replication and Induction in Scientific Practice.* Chicago University Press.

Cronin, B. (2005). Warm bodies, cold facts: The embodiment and emplacement of knowledge claims. *Proceedings of ISSI Volume, 1.*

Cronin, B. (2008a) The Sociological Turn in Information Science. *Journal of Information Science, 34*(4), 465–475.

Cronin, B. (2008b). Toward a rhopography of scholarly communication. *Studia Humaniora Ouluensis, 8,* 37–51.

Cronin, B. (2012). Collaboration in art and in science: Approaches to attribution, authorship, and acknowledgement. *Information & Culture: A Journal of History, 47*(1), 18–37.

Davenport, E. (eds.) *From Information Provision to Knowledge Production.* Proceedings of the International Conference for the Celebration of the 20th Anniversary of Information Science. Oulu, Finland.

Gieryn, T. F. (1999). *Cultural Boundaries of Science: Credibility on the Line.* Chicago University Press.

Grant, L., Kennelly, I. & Ward, K. B. (2000). Revisiting the Gender, Marriage, and Parenthood Puzzle in Scientific Careers. *Women's Studies Quarterly, 28,* 62–85.

Hanna, T. (1986). What is Somatics? *SOMATICS: Magazine-Journal of the Bodily Arts and Sciences, 5*(4). Retrieved from http://somatics.org/library/htl-wis1

Knorr-Cetina, K. (1999). *Epistemic Cultures: How the Sciences Make Knowledge.* Cambridge: Harvard University Press.

Kouper, I., Qarooni-Fard, D., Ghazinejad, A., and Ekbia, H. (forthcoming). Public Participation in Science: Labor, Reward, and Expertise.

Kuhn, T. S. (1962). *The Structure of Scientific Revolution.* Cambridge, MA: Harvard University Press.

Latour, B. (1999). *Pandora's Hope: Essays on the Reality of Science.* Cambridge: Harvard University Press.

Latour, B. & Woolgar, S. (1979). *Laboratory Life: The Construction of Scientific Facts.* Beverley Hills: Sage Publications.

Lynch, M. (1991). Laboratory Space and the Technological Complex: An Investigation of Topical Contextures. *Science in Context*, 4, 51–78.

Merton, R. (1973). *The Sociology of Science: Theoretical and Empirical Investigations*. The University of Chicago Press.

Reskin, B. F. (1978). Sex Differentiation and the Social Organization of Science. *Sociological Inquiry*, 48, 6–36.

Shapin, S. (1995). Here and Everywhere: Sociology of Scientific Knowledge. *Annual Review of Sociology*. 21, 289–321.

Star, S. L. & Griesmer, J. R. (1989). Translations and Boundary Objects: Amateurs and Professionals in Berkeley's Museum of Vertebrate Zoology. *Social Studies of Science*, 19, 387–420.

Woolgar, S. (1976). Writing an Intellectual History of Discovery Accounts. *Social Studies of Science*, 6, 395–422.

Zuckerman, H. (1977). Deviant Behavior and Social Control in Science. In E. Sagarin (ed.). *Deviance and Social Change*. Beverly Hills: Sage Publications. pp. 87–138.

Part V: **Knowledge organization theories**

Wolfgang G. Stock
Informetric Analyses of Knowledge Organization Systems (KOSs)

1 Introduction

For many evaluation models, an important indicator of the quality of an information service is the quality of its content. In our Information Service Evaluation (ISE) model (Schumann & Stock, 2014), Content Quality is a sub-dimension of the main dimension of Information Service Quality (see Figure 1). The content quality concentrates on the knowledge that is stored in the system (DeLone & McLean, 1992; DeLone & McLean, 2003; Jennex & Olfman, 2006). Knowledge in regard to information services consists of two aspects, namely the knowledge of the documents (the knowledge authors put into their publications) and knowledge of the surrogates (the knowledge indexers put into the document's metadata). In turn, the knowledge of the surrogates has two dimensions: the quality of indexing (applying the right concepts to describe the document's knowledge; Stock & Stock, 2013, p. 817–825) and the quality of the Knowledge Organization System (KOS), which is deployed for indexing (Stock & Stock, 2013, p. 809–816). A KOS is an order of concepts which is used to represent (in most cases: scientific or other specialized) documents. Common types of KOSs include nomenclatures, classification systems, thesauri, and ontologies. KOSs are applied in professional information services which support scholarly communication by the provision of specialized literature. While there is a vast number of studies on indexing quality and its indicators (e.g., indexing depths including indexing exhaustivity of a surrogate and indexing specificity of the attributed concepts, indexing effectiveness of the concepts, and indexing consistency of the surrogates), there are in information science only a few works on the quality of the KOSs.

Information services for science and technology (e.g., *Medline* for medicine, *Chemical Abstracts Service* for chemistry, or *Inspec* for physics) and information services in the context of corporate knowledge management in many cases apply so-called "controlled vocabularies" or "documentation (or documentary) languages" for the purposes of information indexing and information retrieval. Such vocabularies organize the concepts and the semantic relations between the concepts of a specific knowledge domain in a "Knowledge Organization System" (KOS).

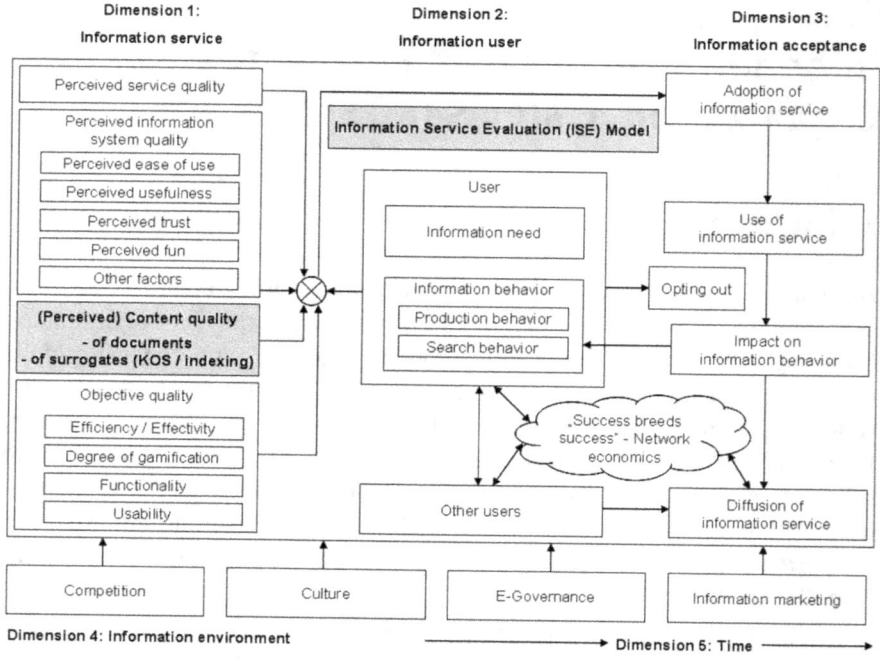

Fig. 1: The Content Quality Dimension in the Information Service Evaluation (ISE) Model. *Source:* Schumann & Stock, 2014, p. 8 (modified).

The aim of this chapter is to underline the importance of the evaluation of KOSs as part of empirical information science, i.e., informetrics. According to Tague-Sutcliffe (1992), informetrics is "the study of the quantitative aspects of information in any form ...and in any social group" (Tague-Sutcliffe, 1992, p. 1). Wolfram divides informetrics in two aspects, namely "system-based characteristics that arise from the documentary content of IR systems and how they are indexed, and usage-based characteristics that arise from the way users interact with system content and the system interfaces that provide access to the content" (Wolfram, 2003, p. 6). Stock and Weber (2006) distinguish three subjects and accordingly three research areas of informetrics: (1) information users and information usage (with the area of user/usage research); (2) information itself including special information (e.g., science information) and Web information (with the research areas of bibliometrics, scientometrics, and webometrics); and, (3) information systems (with the research area of evaluation and technology acceptance studies). The informetric analysis of KOSs is part of Wolfram's system-based characteristics and of Stock and Weber's information systems evaluation research.

Evaluation studies are able to answer two questions (Drucker, 1963): Do we do the right things (leading to an evaluation of effectiveness), and do we do the things in a right way (this time leading to an evaluation of efficiency)? Concerning KOS evaluation, effectiveness means the construction of right KOS, and efficiency the appropriate construction of the KOSs (adequately employed funds, speed of implementation, optimal software tools, etc.) (Casellas, 2009, p. 597). We focus on effectiveness and ignore efficiency. Our research question is: *How can we informetrically analyze the effectiveness of KOSs?* Quantitative informetric indicators allow for the empirical description, for comparative analyses as well as for evaluation of KOSs and their quality. Indicators of KOS analyses and evaluation are off the beaten path of mainstream informetrics and thus "beyond bibliometrics" (Cronin & Sugimoto, 2014). With the empirical investigation of KOSs we break new ground in the theories of informetrics.

In the next paragraph, we describe briefly Knowledge Organization Systems as systems of concepts and semantic relations. Hereafter, an overview on the state of the art of the description and evaluation of KOSs will follow. In the chapter's core paragraph, we present measures and indicators for the informetric evaluation of KOSs. The aim is not only to present a synthesis of a large number of approaches of KOS evaluation, but also to propose a solution for a comprehensive set of basic KOS structure measures and of KOS assessment criteria. For KOS developers, these measures and indicators should provide useful hints to construct good nomenclatures, thesauri, classification systems, and ontologies.

2 Concepts and Semantic Relations

Knowledge Organization Systems consist of both concepts as well as semantic relations between the concepts with respect to a knowledge domain (Stock, 2010). A "concept" is a class containing certain objects as elements where the objects have certain properties. The linguistic expression of a concept is a "word." Concepts do not exist independently of one another, but are interlinked. We will call relations between concepts "semantic relations" (Khoo & Na, 2006; Storey, 1993). Apart from folksonomies, semantic relations in KOSs always are "paradigmatic" relations, i.e., relations which are valid independently of documents (in contrast to syntagmatic relations, which depend on co-occurrences of concepts in documents). In KOSs, the following semantic relations are important:
- Equivalence (synonymy, quasi-synonymy, or gen-identity between concepts);
- Hierarchy (hyponymy, meronymy, and instance); and,

– as a residual class, Further relations ("see also" as association relation, or specific relations such as usefulness or has_subsidiary_company in an enterprise KOS).

We define knowledge organization systems via their cardinality for expressing concepts and semantic relations. The three "classical" methods in information science and practice—nomenclature, classification, thesaurus—are supplemented by folksonomies and ontologies. Folksonomies represent a borderline case of KOSs, as they do not have a single paradigmatic relation (Peters, 2009).

Nomenclatures (keyword systems) distinguish themselves mainly by using the equivalence relation and ignoring all forms of hierarchical relation. In classification systems, the (unspecifically designed) hierarchy relation is added. Thesauri also work with hierarchy; some use the unspecific hierarchy relation, others differentiate via hyponymy ("is-a" relation) and meronymy ("part-of" relation). In thesauri, a generally unspecifically designed associative relation ("see also") is necessarily added. Ontologies make use of all the paradigmatic relations mentioned above. They are modeled in formal languages, where terminological logic is also accorded its due consideration. Compared to other KOSs, ontologies categorically contain instances (individual concepts). Most ontologies work with precisely defined, further relations. The fact that ontologies directly represent knowledge (and not merely the documents containing the knowledge) allows the syntagmatic relations to disappear in this case.

Tab. 1: Knowledge Organization Systems (KOSs) and the Relations They Use. *Source:* Stock, 2010, p. 1965 (modified).

	Folksonomy	Nomenclature	Classification	Thesaurus	Ontology
	Tag	Keyword	Notation	Descriptor	Concept
Equivalence	–	yes	yes	yes	yes
Synonymy	–	yes	yes	yes	yes
Gen-identity	–	yes	–	–	yes
Hierarchy	–	–	yes	yes	yes
Hyponymy	–	–	–	yes	yes
Meronymy	–	–	–	yes	yes
Instance	–	–	–	as req.	yes
Further relations	–	–	–	yes	yes
"See also"	–	as req.	as req.	yes	yes
Specific relations	–	–	–	–	yes
Syntagmatic relation	yes	yes	yes	yes	no

3 State of the Art of the Evaluation of KOSs

Most of the evaluation studies found in the literature are about ontologies (for overview articles, see Brank, Grobelnik, & Mladenić, 2005; Gangemi, Catenacci, Ciaramita, & Lehmann, 2005; Gómez-Pérez, 2004a; Hartmann et al., 2005; Kehagias, Papadimitriou, Hois, Tzovaras, & Bateman, 2008; Obrst, Ceusters, Mani, Ray, & Smith, 2007; Pak & Zhou, 2011; Vrandečić, 2009). The first article on KOS evaluation—by Gómez-Pérez in 1995— was on ontologies as well. Our scope is broader and covers all kinds of KOSs. There are a few evaluation studies about other kinds of KOSs. Vogel (2002) developed a set of quality criteria for classification systems and thesauri deployed in his retrieval system *Convera*. Applying parameters such as usability, scope, recall, and precision, Owens and Cochrane (2004) worked out methods of thesaurus evaluation. Wang, Khoo and Chaudhry (2014) evaluated the navigation effectiveness of a classification system.

Gómez-Pérez, Fernández-López, and Corcho (2004) distinguish between KOS verification and KOS validation. While verification is focused on the correct (formal as well as informal) representation of concepts and semantic relations (with aspects like consistency, completeness, and redundancy; Lovrenčić & Čubrillo, 2008), KOS validation refers to the "real world", i.e., the comparison between the content of the KOS and its "real" counterpart in the corresponding knowledge domain (Lovrenčić & Čubrillo, 2008).

Based on the definition given by Sabou and Fernandez (2012, p. 194), KOS evaluation is the determination of the quality of a KOS against a frame of reference. In this definition, there are two crucial concepts. What is the definition of "quality" and to what does "frame of reference" refer? *Quality criteria* define a "good" KOS. Vrandečić (2009, p. 295–296) provides us with a list of such quality criteria, among others: accuracy (Does the KOS correctly represent its knowledge domain?), adaptability (Does the KOS anticipate its use?), completeness (Is the knowledge domain appropriately covered?), consistency (Is the KOS logically coherent?), and commercial accessibility (Is the KOS easy to access and to deploy?). But all these quality criteria are "desiderata, goals to guide the creation and evaluation of the ontology. None of them can be directly measured" (Vrandečić, 2009, p. 296). It is important to bear in mind that we cannot always work with *quality measures*, but only with *quality indicators*. There are several frames in the literature concerning the *frame of reference* (Brank, Grobelnik, & Mladenić, 2005; Sabou & Fernandez, 2012, p. 197 ff.), namely primitive metrics (as, e.g., the number of concepts), data-driven frames (comparisons of the KOS with its knowledge domain), KOS to KOS comparisons, frameworks concerning the syntactic and semantic structures of the KOS and, finally, user-driven frames (experiments with users and questionnaires or interviews). For all frames of reference, we present illustrative examples from the literature.

3.1 Primitive Metrics

Simple evaluation metrics—better known as description metrics—are based on counting concepts and relations in KOSs. For Huang and Diao (2006, p. 133), the "Concept Quantity evaluation is to count the number of concepts in the ontology," and the "Property Expectation evaluation provides an overview of the abundance of relations between concepts." Tartir and Arpinar (2007) distinguish between inheritance relationships (relations, in which the concepts' properties become inherited to the concepts' narrower terms such as the hyponymy) and other relations (as, e.g., the association relation) and count both kinds of relations. Additionally, Tartir and Arpinar (2007, p. 187) count instances, otherwise known as concepts in the KOS, which represent individuals. Yang, Zhang, and Ye (2006, p. 165) work with the average number of relations per concept. A more subtle indicator is the "tree balance" of the KOS (Huang & Diao, 2006, p. 133): "If a tree is balanced, all its sub-trees have the same structure."

3.2 KOSs and Their Knowledge Domains

Does a KOS represent its knowledge domain adequately? Brewster, Alani, Dasmahapatra, and Wilks (2004) re-define the well-known recall and precision metrics with regard to KOSs:

> One would like *precision* to reflect the amount of knowledge correctly identified (in the ontology) with respect to the whole knowledge available in the ontology. One would like to define *recall* to reflect the amount of knowledge correctly identified with respect to all the knowledge that it should identify.
>
> (Brewster et al., 2004, p. 1)

For the authors, "knowledge" refers to "concepts", as represented linguistically by words. They developed a corpus of typical documents for the knowledge domain and compared the words in the texts with the words in the KOS. For Brewster and colleagues the ontology "can be penalized for terms present in the corpus and absent in ontology, and for terms present in the ontology but absent in the corpus" (Brewster et al., 2004, p. 3). While it is not difficult to identify the words in a KOS, it is a bold venture to collect typical (or even all) documents of the given knowledge domain.

3.3 KOS and Other KOSs

To indicate the uniqueness of a KOS, it is necessary to compare it with other KOSs. The simple research question here is: "So, how may we measure the similarity of ontologies or of ontology parts?" (Maedche & Staab, 2002, p. 251). But the answer is by no means as simple as the question. In the literature, there are two approaches to study similarity between KOSs: one approach based on common words and concepts in the vocabulary (Maedche & Staab, 2002; Obrst et al., 2007, p. 146–147; Brank, Grobelnik, & Mladenić, 2005), and another that works with indexed documents in the case of polyrepresentation (i.e., applying different KOSs to index the same documents) (Haustein & Peters, 2012).

3.4 Syntactic and Semantic Structure of KOSs

The evaluation of the syntactical structure is targeted at the correct use of a formal language. For ontologies assigned for application in the semantic web, the Web Ontology Language (OWL) and Resource Description Framework (RDF) are used. Much more important is the evaluation of the semantic structure of a KOS. Fahad and Abdul Qadir (2008) distinguish between redundancy, incompleteness (which is similar to the data-driven approach of recall and precision), and inconsistency. Redundancy occurs when certain information is inferred more than once in the KOS, for example, when a concept is located twice in the KOS at two different positions. Inconsistency is mainly the consequence of circularity errors (a concept is defined as a broader term or as a narrower term of itself) and partition errors (wrong decompositions of a concept into narrower terms). Fahad, Abdul Qadir, and Noshairwan (2007) determine that "the main reason for these errors is that ontologists do not classify the concepts properly" (p. 286).

3.5 User-driven Approaches

Noy (2004) calls indicators like completeness, consistency, and correctness "objective" evaluation criteria: "Although all these evaluation types or comparison methods are necessary, none are helpful to *ontology consumers*, who need to discover which ontologies exist and, more important, which one would be suitable for their tasks at hand" (Noy, 2004, p. 80). To get a user-driven impression of the quality of KOSs, some authors conducted experimental studies with test persons or interviewed users with the aid of questionnaires or guides.

Casellas (2009) evaluated a KOS through usability measures. He offered two questionnaires, one with questions concerning concepts, definitions, instances, and relations of the KOS, and a second one with more general items (as, e.g., "I found the ontology easy to understand," or "I thought there was too much inconsistency in this ontology."). The questionees were experts in the knowledge domain of the KOS. They were asked to express their opinions on a scale between 0 and 5 (first questionnaire) and 1 and 10 (second questionnaire).

Suomela and Kekäläinen (2006) evaluated an ontology as a query construction tool. Wang, Khoo, & Chaudhry (2014) evaluated the navigational effectiveness of a classification system. Both studies worked with experiments (task-based test method) as well as with interviews (Wang, Khoo, & Chaudhry, 2014) or questionnaires (Suomela & Kekäläinen, 2006).

4 Measures and Indicators of the Evaluation of KOSs

In this section, we introduce informetric measures and indicators of KOS evaluation. Based upon the literature review and the chapter on evaluation of KOSs in our *Handbook of Information Science* (Stock & Stock, 2013), we introduce one set of measures of the structure of KOSs and four indicators of KOS quality (completeness, consistency, overlap, and use).

4.1 Basic Structure Measures

Several simple parameters can be used to analyze the structure of a KOS (Gangemi, Catenacci, Ciaramita, & Lehmann, 2006). These parameters relate both to the concepts and to the semantic relations. We will introduce the following structural measures:
– Number of concepts;
– Semantic expressiveness (number and kind of semantic relations);
– Granularity (average number of semantic relations per concept);
– Number of hierarchy levels;
– Fan-out factor (number of top terms);
– Groundedness (number of bottom terms);
– Tangledness (degree of polyhierarchy); and
– Precombination degree (average number of partial terms per concept).

An initial base value is the number of concepts in the KOS. Here the very opposite of the dictum "the more the better" applies. Rather, the objective is to arrive at an optimal value of the number of terms that adequately represent the knowledge domain and the documents contained therein, respectively. If there are too few terms, not all aspects of the knowledge domain can be selectively described. If a user does not find "his/her" search term, this will have negative consequences for the recall, and if he/she does find a suitable hyponym, the precision of the search results will suffer. If too many concepts have been admitted into the KOS, there is a danger that users will lose focus and that only very few documents will be retrieved for each concept. When documents are indexed via the KOS (which—with the exception of ontologies—is the rule), the average number of documents per concept is a good estimate for the optimal number of terms in the KOS. Of further interest is the number of designations (synonyms and quasi-synonyms) per concept. The average number of designations (e.g., non-descriptors) of a concept (e.g., of a descriptor) is a good indicator for the use of designations in the KOS.

Analogously to the concepts, the number of different semantic relations used provides an indicator for the structure of a KOS (semantic expressiveness). The total number of relations in the KOS is of particular interest. Regarded as a network, the KOS's concepts represent the nodes while their relations represent the lines. The size of relations is the total number of all lines in the KOS (without the connections to the designations, since these form their own indicator). A useful derived parameter is the average number of semantic relations per concept, i.e., the terms' mean degree. The indicators for size of concepts and size of relations can be summarized as the "granularity of a KOS".

Information concerning the number of hierarchy levels as well as the distribution of terms throughout these individual levels is of particular interest. Also important are data concerning the number of top terms (and thus the different facets) and bottom terms (concepts on the lowest hierarchy level), each in relation to the total number of all terms in the KOS. The relation of the number of top terms to the number of all terms is called the "fan-out factor", while the analogous relation to the bottom terms can be referred to as "groundedness". "Tangledness" in turn measures the degree of polyhierarchy in the KOS. It refers to the average number of hyperonyms for every concept. By counting the number of hyponyms for all concepts that have hyponyms (minus one), we glean a value for each concept's average number of siblings.

Soergel (2001) proposes measuring the degree of a term's precombination. A KOS's degree of precombination is the average number of partial terms per concept. The degree of precombination for *Garden* is 1, for *Garden Party* it is 2, for *Garden Party Dinner* 3, etc. For English-language KOSs, it is (more or less) easy to count the words forming a term, for other languages, e.g., German with many

Tab. 2: Basic KOS Structure Measures. *Source:* Stock & Stock, 2013, p. 815 (modified).

Dimension	Informetric Measure	Calculation
Granularity	Size of concepts	Number of concepts (nodes in the network)
	Size of relations	Number of relations between concepts (lines in the network)
	Semantic expressiveness	Number of different semantic relations
	Documents per concept	Average number of documents per concept (for a given information service)
	Use of denotations	Average number of denotations per concept
Hierarchy	Depth of hierarchy	Number of levels
	Hierarchical distribution of concepts	Number of concepts on the different levels
	Fan-out factor	Quotient of the number of top terms and the number of all concepts
	Groundedness factor	Quotient of the number of bottom terms and the number of all concepts
	Tangledness factor	Average number of hyperonyms per concept
	Siblinghood factor	Average number of co-hyponyms per concept
Precombination	Degree of precombination	Average number of partial concepts per concept

compounds (*Garten*: 1; *Gartenfest*: 2; *Gartenfestessen*: 3), we have to apply compound decomposition in the first place and then to count for every KOS entry its number of partial terms. Table 2 presents an overview of the multitude of basic KOS structure measures.

4.2 Completeness Indicator

Completeness refers to the degree of terminological coverage of a knowledge domain. If the knowledge domain is not very small and easily grasped, this value will be very difficult to determine. Yu, Thorn, and Tam (2009, p. 775) define completeness via the question: Does the KOS "have concepts missing with regards to the relevant frames of reference?" Portaluppi (2007) demonstrates that the completeness of thematic areas of the KOS can be estimated via samples from indexed documents. In the case study, articles on chronobiology were researched in *Medline*. The original documents were acquired, and the allocated MeSH concepts ("Medical Subject Headings", which is a thesaurus for medical terminology) were analyzed in the surrogates. Portaluppi (2007, p. 1213) reports, "By reading each article, it was ... possible to identify common chronobiologic concepts not yet associated with specific MeSH headings." The missing concepts thus identified might be present in MeSH and may have been erroneously overlooked by the indexer (in which case it would be an indexing error), or they are simply not featured in the KOS. In the case study, some common chronobiological concepts are "not to be associated with any specific MeSH heading" (Portaluppi, 2007, p. 1213), so that MeSH must be deemed incomplete from a chronobiological perspective.

If one counts the concepts in the KOS's thematic subset and determines the number of terms that are missing from a thematic point of view, the quotient of the number of missing terms and the total number of terms (i.e., those featured in the KOS plus those missing) results in an estimated value of completeness or recall (in the sense of Brewster, Alani, Dasmahapatra, & Wilks, 2004) with regard to the corresponding knowledge subdomain.

4.3 Semantic Indicators

The consistency of a KOS relates to five aspects:
- Semantic inconsistency;
- Circularity error;
- Skipping hierarchical levels;
- Redundancy; and
- the "tennis problem".

Inconsistencies are particularly likely to arise when several KOSs (that are consistent in themselves) are unified into a large KOS. In the case of semantic inconsistency, terms have been wrongly arranged in the semantic network of all concepts. Consider the following descriptor entry:

Fish
BT: Marine animals
NT: Salt-water fish
NT: Freshwater fish.

BT (broader term) and NT (narrower term) span the semantic relation of hyponymy in the example. In this hierarchical relation, the hyponyms inherit all characteristics of their hyperonyms. The term *Marine animals*, for instance, contains the characteristic "lives in the ocean". This characteristic is passed on to the hyponym *Fish* and onward to its hyponyms *Salt-water fish* and *Freshwater fish*. The semantic inconsistency arises in the case of *Freshwater fish*, as these do not live in the ocean.

Circularity errors occur in the hierarchical relation when one concept appears more than once in a concept ladder (Gómez-Pérez, 2004a): "Circularity errors ... occur when a class is defined as a specialization or generalization of itself" (p. 261). Suppose that two KOSs are merged. Let KOS 1 contain the following set of concepts:

Persons
NT: Travelers

whereas KOS 2 formulates

Travelers
NT: Persons

When both KOSs are merged, the result is a logical circle (example taken from Cross & Pal, 2008).

Skipping errors are the result of hierarchy levels being left out. This error is well described by Aristotle in his *Topics* (2005, Book 6, Ch. 5, p. 479–480). Here, too, we can provide an example:

Capra
NT: Wild goat
NT: Domestic Goat
Wild goat
NT: Domestic goat.

In the biological hierarchy, *Capra* is the broader term for *Wild goat* (Capra aegagrus). *Wild goat*, in turn, is the broader term for *Domestic goat* (Capra hircus). By establishing a direct relation between *Capra* and *Domestic goat*, our KOS skips a hierarchy level. The cause of the skipping error is the erroneous subsumption of NT *Domestic goat* within the concept *Capra*.

A KOS is redundant when a concept appears more than one time in the KOS. Such an error can occur when the concept is integrated in several contexts. In a thesaurus, *Cherry* may be hyponym of *Fruit tree* and hyperonym of *Sour cherry* and *Sweet cherry*. In another facet of the same thesaurus, *Cherry* is a narrower term of

Fruit brandy and a broader term of *Cherry brandy*. In this example, the second variant is erroneous. *Cherry* has to be removed from the *Brandy*-facet. Instead of this descriptor, an association link between *Cherry* and *Cherry brandy* should be established.

For ontology evaluation, Hartmann et al. (2005, p. 17) mention the so called "tennis problem". This is a phenomenon "where related words could occur in two completely different parts of the ontology with no apparent link between them, e.g., "ball boy" could occur as a descendant of 'male child' and 'tennis ball' as a descendant of 'game equipment,' despite an obvious semantic relation." Indeed, if a KOS only consists of hierarchy, the tennis problem gives ontology engineers a headache. However, every KOS that allows for the use of the association relation is able to relate both concepts:

Ball boy *SEE ALSO* Tennis ball

(and vice versa). The task for the evaluator is to locate concepts in the KOS with close semantic relations which are not linked via short paths.

4.4 Overlap with Other KOSs

An approach to study the similarity between KOSs is to count common words and concepts in two KOSs. On the word level, Maedche and Staab (2002, p. 254) use the Levenshtein distance (i.e., the number of edit steps between two strings). Words with low numbers of editing steps are considered similar. If KOS 1 has the entry "TopHotel" and KOS 2 "Top_Hotel", the Levenshtein distance is 1 (one insertion operation) and the words are therefore similar. But this method is prone to failure. The Levenshtein distance between "Power" and "Tower" is 1 as well despite their dissimilarity. On the concept level, the comparison is even more challenging. Obrst et al. (2007) describe this problem:

> To say that two concepts have similar semantics ... means roughly that they occupy similar places in their lattices. A problem with the above is, however, clear: ontology alignment is defined in terms of correspondence (equivalence, sameness, similarity) of concepts. But how, precisely, do we gain access to concepts in order to determine whether they stand in a relation correspondence?
>
> (p. 146)

Obrst et al. (2007) found that the majority of studies are based on the vocabulary (i.e., the words—with the above-mentioned problems) or on the structure of the KOS (e.g., similar broader terms and similar narrower terms). Counting common words and common concepts is a good idea on a theoretical level, but when it comes to practical application, a problem arises.

Fortunately, there is an alternative method. In the case of polyrepresentation (Ingwersen & Järvelin, 2005, p. 346), different methods of knowledge representation as well as different KOSs are used to index the same documents. Haustein and Peters (2012) compare the tags (i.e., in the sense of folksonomies, the readers' perspective), subject headings of *Inspec* (the indexers' perspective), *KeyWords Plus* (as a method of automatic indexing) as well as author keywords and the words from title and abstract (the authors' perspective) of over 700 journal articles. The authors are particularly interested in the overlap between folksonomy-based tags and other methods of knowledge representation. Of course, one can also compare several KOSs with each other, as long as they have been used to index the same documents. The value g represents the number of identical concepts of different KOSs per document, a is the number of unique concepts from KOS 1 per document, and b the number of unique concepts from KOS 2 per document. The similarity of KOS 1 and KOS 2 can be calculated by the Cosine.

The Haustein-Peters method can be used to comparatively evaluate different KOSs in the context of polyrepresentation. When the similarity measurements between two KOSs are relatively low, this points to vocabularies that complement each other—which is of great value to the users, as it provides additional access points to the document. If similarities are high, on the other hand, one of the two KOSs will probably become redundant in practice.

4.5 Use

We have learned from Noy (2004) that it is essential for KOS evaluation to consider the KOS users' view. Accordingly, the KOS evaluation has to be embedded into a broader frame, which includes the service, the user, his/her acceptance, the environment, and time (Schumann & Stock, 2014). Aspects of user-driven methods include indicators of perceived service quality (captured, e.g., by the SERVQUAL method), perceived system quality with the sub-dimensions of perceived ease of use, usefulness, trust, fun, usability, and further factors (applying the Technology Acceptance Model).

For evaluating the perceived service quality we propose to use SERVQUAL (Parasuraman, Zeithaml, & Berry, 1988). SERVQUAL works with two sets of statements: those that are used to measure expectations about a service category in general (EX) and those that measure perceptions (PE) of the category of a particular service. Each statement is accompanied by a seven-point scale ranging from "strongly disagree" (1) to "strongly agree" (7). For the expectation value, one might note that "in a KOS in economics it is useful to have the relation *has_subsidiary_company* when formulating queries", and then ask the test subject to express this numerically on the given scale. The corresponding statement for registering the perception value would then be: "In the KOS X, the relation *has_subsidiary_company* is useful when formulating queries." Here, too, the subject specifies a numerical value. For each item, a difference score Q = PE − EX is defined. If, for instance, a test subject specifies a value of 1 for perception after having noted a 4 for expectation, the Q value for system X with regard to the attribute in question will be 1 − 4 = −3.

When evaluating perceived KOS quality, questionnaires are used. The test subjects must be familiar with the system in order to make correct assessments. For each subdimension, a set of statements is formulated that the user must estimate on a 7-point scale (from "extremely likely" to "extremely unlikely"). Davis (1989, p. 340), for instance, posited: "using system X in my job would enable me to accomplish tasks more quickly" (to measure perceived usefulness), and "my interaction with system X would be clear and understandable" (for the aspect of perceived ease of use).

Usable KOSs are those that do not frustrate the users. A common procedure in usability tests according to Nielsen (1993) is task-based testing. Here, an examiner defines representative tasks that can be performed using the KOS and which are typical for such KOSs. Such a task for evaluating the usability of a KOS in economics might be as follows: "Look for concepts to prepare a query on the Fifth Kondratiev cycle!" Test subjects should be "a representative sample of end users" (Rubin & Chisnell, 2008, p. 25). The test subjects are presented with the tasks and are observed by the examiner while they perform the prescribed tasks. It is useful to have test subjects speak their thoughts when performing the tasks ("thinking aloud"). In addition to the task-based tests, it is useful for the examiner to interview the subjects on the KOS (e.g., on their overall impression of the KOS, on completeness, and semantic consistency). In Table 3, all mentioned KOS quality indicators are listed.

5 Conclusion

Is KOS evaluation a new research problem (Cronin, 1991), leading to valuable scientific results? Our parameters in the group of "Basic Structure" are simple measures, which can be made automatically available by the system. Indeed, it is a quality aspect of every KOS construction and maintenance software to provide such basic structure data (Vogel, 2002). Completeness, semantic consistency, the

Tab. 3: KOS Quality Indicators. *Source:* Stock & Stock, 2013, p. 815 (modified).

Dimension	Informetric indicator	Calculation/method
Completeness	Completeness of knowledge subdomain	Quotient of the number of missing concepts and the number of all concepts (in the KOS and the missing ones) regarding the subdomain
Semantics	Semantic inconsistency	Number of semantic inconsistency errors
	Circularity	Number of circularity errors
	Skipping hierarchical levels	Number of skipping errors
	Redundancy	Number of redundancy errors
	Tennis problem	Number of missing links between associated concepts
Multiple KOSs	Degree of polyrepresentation	Overlap
Use	Perceived KOS quality	SERVQUAL questionnaires
	KOS acceptance	Technology acceptance surveys
	Usability	Task-based tests

overlap with other KOSs, and user-based data are quality indicators, which "will remain a task for a human level intelligence" (Vrandečić, 2009, p. 308).

Next steps in KOSs evaluation research should include the analysis of the different evaluation methods. Gómez-Pérez (2004b, p. 74) mentions research questions such as "How robust are ontology evaluation methods?" or "How do ontology development platforms perform content evaluation?"

The focus of this chapter was to draw information scientists' attention to a widely neglected aspect of informetrics: the informetric description and evaluation of KOSs. As a basis for further discussion, we described the state of the art of KOS evaluation and introduced suggestions for measures as well as indicators of the quality of KOSs. We thereby expand the theory of informetrics by introducing evaluation methods of KOSs.

Cited References

Aristotle (2005). *Topics*. Sioux Falls, SD: NuVision.
Brank, J., Grobelnik, M., & Mladenić, D. (2005). A survey of ontology evaluation techniques. In *Conference on Data Mining and Data Warehouses*. Ljubljana, Slovenia, October 17, 2005.
Brewster, C., Alani, H., Dasmahapatra, S., & Wilks, Y. (2004). Data driven ontology evaluation. In *International Conference on Language Resources and Evaluation (LREC-2004)*. Lisbon, Portugal, 24–30 May 2004.
Casellas, N. (2009). Ontology evaluation through usability measures. An experiment with the SUS scale in the legal domain. *Lecture Notes in Computer Science, 5872*, 594–603.
Cronin, B. (1991). When is a problem a research problem? In L. S. Estabrook (Ed.), *Applying Research to Practice: How to Use Data Collection and Research to Improve Library Management Decision Making* (pp. 117–132). Urbana-Champaign, IL: Graduate School of Library and Information Science (Allerton Park Institute Proceedings; 33).
Cronin, B., & Sugimoto, C. R., Eds. (2014). *Beyond Bibliometrics. Harnessing Multidimensional Indicators of Scholarly Impact*. Cambridge, MA: MIT Press.
Cross, V., & Pal, A. (2008). An ontology analysis tool. *International Journal of General Systems, 37*(1), 17–44.
Davis, F. D. (1989). Perceived usefulness, perceived ease of use, and user acceptance of information technology. *MIS Quarterly, 13*(3), 319–340.
DeLone, W. H., & McLean, E. R. (1992). Information systems success. The quest for the dependent variable. *Information Systems Research, 3*(1), 60–95.
DeLone, W. H., & McLean, E. R. (2003). The DeLone and McLean model of information systems success. A ten-year update. *Journal of Management Information Systems, 19*(4), 9–30.
Drucker, P. F. (1963). Managing for business effectiveness. *Harvard Business Review, 41*(May/June), 53–60.
Fahad, M., & Abdul Qadir, M. (2008). A framework for ontology evaluation. In *16th International Conference on Conceptual Structures (ICCS 2008)* (pp. 149–158). Toulouse, France.
Fahad, M., Abdul Qadir, M., & Noshairwan, M. W. (2007). Semantic inconsistency errors in ontology. In *2007 IEEE International Conference on Granular Computing* (pp. 283–286). Los Alamitos, CA: IEEE Computer Society.
Gangemi, A., Catenacci, C., Ciaramita, M., & Lehmann, L. (2005). A theoretical framework for ontology evaluation and validation. In *Proceedings of SWAP 2005, the 2nd Italian Semantic Web Workshop*. Trento, Italy, December 14–16, 2005.
Gangemi, A., Catenacci, C., Ciaramita, M., & Lehmann, L. (2006). Modelling ontology evaluation and validation. *Lecture Notes in Computer Science, 4011*, 140–154.
Gómez-Pérez, A. (1995). Some ideas and examples to evaluate ontologies. In *Proceedings of the 11th Conference on Artificial Intelligence for Applications* (pp. 299–305). Los Alamitos, CA: IEEE Computer Society.
Gómez-Pérez, A. (2004a). Ontology evaluation. In S. Staab & R. Studer (Eds.), *Handbook on Ontologies* (pp. 251–273). Berlin, Germany: Springer.
Gómez-Pérez, A. (2004b). Evaluating ontology evaluation. *IEEE Intelligent Systems, 19*(4), 74–76.
Gómez-Pérez, A., Fernández-López, M., & Corcho, O. (2004). *Ontological Engineering*. London, UK: Springer.

Hartmann, J., Spyns, P., Giboin, A., Maynard, D., Cuel, R., Suárez-Figueroa, & Sure, Y. (2005). *Methods for Ontology Evaluation* / Knowledge Web Consortium (EU-IST Network of Excellence IST-2004-507482 KWEB).

Haustein, S., & Peters, I. (2012). Using social bookmarks and tags as alternative indicators of journal content description. *First Monday, 17*(11).

Huang, N., & Diao, S. (2006). Structure-based ontology evaluation. In *Proceedings of the IEEE International Conference on e-Business Engineering (ICEBE-2006)* (pp. 132–137). Los Alamitos, CA: IEEE Computer Society.

Ingwersen, P., & Järvelin, K. (2005). *The Turn. Integration of Information Seeking and Retrieval in Context*. Dordrecht, NL: Springer.

Jennex, M. E., & Olfman, L. (2006). A model of knowledge management success. *International Journal of Knowledge Management, 2*(3), 51–68.

Kehagias, D. D., Papadimitriou, I., Hois, J., Tzocaras, D., & Bateman, J. (2008). A methodological approach for ontology evaluation and refinement. In *ASK-IT International Conference*. Nürnberg, Germany, 26–27 June, 2008.

Khoo, C. S. G., & Na, J. C. (2006). Semantic relations in information science. *Annual Review of Information Science and Technology, 40*, 157–228.

Lovrenčić, S., & Čubrillo, M. (2008). Ontology evaluation. Comprising verification and validation. In *Central European Conference on Information and Intelligent Systems (CECIIS-2008)*. Zagreb, Croatia, September 24–26, 2008.

Maedche, A., & Staab, S. (2002). Measuring similarity between ontologies. *Lecture Notes in Computer Science, 2473*, 251–263.

Nielsen, J. (1993). *Usability Engineering*. Cambridge, MA, London, UK: Academic Press.

Noy, N. F. (2004). Evaluation by ontology consumers. *IEEE Intelligent Systems, 19*(4), 80–81.

Obrst, L., Ceusters, W., Mani, I., Ray, S., & Smith, B. (2007). The evaluation of ontologies. In C. J. O. Baker & K.-H. Cheung (Eds.), *Semantic Web. Revolutionizing Knowledge Discovery in the Life Sciences* (pp. 139–158). Berlin, Germany: Springer.

Owens, L. A., & Cochrane, P. A. (2004). Thesaurus evaluation. *Cataloging & Classification Quarterly, 37*(3–4), 87–102.

Pak, J., & Zhou, L. (2011). A framework for ontology evaluation. *Lecture Notes in Business Information Processing, 52*, 10–18.

Parasuraman, A., Zeithaml, V. A., & Berry, L. L. (1988). SERVQUAL: A multiple-item scale for measuring consumer perceptions of service quality, *Journal of Retailing, 64*(1), 12–40.

Peters, I. (2009). *Folksonomies. Indexing and Retrieval in Web 2.0*. Berlin, Germany: De Gruyter Saur. (Knowledge & Information. Studies in Information Science.)

Portaluppi, E. (2007). Consistency and accuracy of the Medical Subject Headings thesaurus for electronic indexing and retrieval of chronobiologic references. *Chronobiology International, 24*(6), 1213–1229.

Rubin, J., & Chisnell, D. (2008). *Handbook of Usability Testing*. 2nd Ed. Indianapolis, IN: Wiley.

Sabou, M., & Fernandez, M. (2012). Ontology (network) evaluation. In M. C. Suárez-Figueroa et al. (Eds.), *Ontology Engineering in a Networked World* (pp. 193–212). Berlin, Germany: Springer.

Schumann, L., & Stock, W. G. (2014). The Information Service Evaluation (ISE) model. *Webology, 11*(1), art. 115.

Soergel, D. (2001). Evaluation of knowledge organization systems (KOS). Characteristics for describing and evaluation KOS. In *Workshop „Classification Crosswalks: Bringing Commu-*

nities Together" at the First ACM + IEEE Joint Conference on Digital Libraries. Roanoke, VA, USA, June 24–28, 2001.

Stock, W. G. (2010). Concepts and semantic relations in information science. *Journal of the American Society for Information Science and Technology, 61*(10), 1951–1969.

Stock, W. G., & Stock, M. (2013). *Handbook of Information Science*. Berlin, Germany, Boston, MA: De Gruyter Saur.

Stock, W. G., & Weber, S. (2006). Facets of informetrics. *Information – Wissenschaft und Praxis, 57*(8), 385–389.

Storey, V. C. (1993). Understanding semantic relationships. *VLDB Journal, 2*(4), 455–488.

Suomela, S., & Kekäläinen, J. (2006). User evaluation of ontology as query construction tool. *Information Retrieval, 9*(4), 455–475.

Tague-Sutcliffe, J. (1992). An introduction to informetrics. *Information Processing & Management, 28*(1), 1–4.

Tartir, S., & Arpinar, I. B. (2007). Ontology evaluation and ranking using OntoQA. In *International Conference on Semantic Computing (ICSC-2007)* (pp. 185–192). Los Alamitos, CA: IEEE Computer Society.

Vogel, C. (2002). *Quality Metrics for Taxonomies*. Vienna, VA: Convera.

Vrandečić, D. (2009). Ontology evaluation. In S. Staab & R. Studer (Eds.), *Handbook on Ontologies* (pp. 293–313). Berlin, Germany: Springer.

Wang, Z., Khoo, C. S. G., & Chaudhry, A. S. (2014). Evaluation of the navigation effectiveness of an organizational taxonomy built on a general classification scheme and domain thesauri. *Journal of the Association for Information Science and Technology, 65*(5), 948–963.

Wolfram, D. (2003). *Applied Informetrics for Information Retrieval Research*. Westport, CO, London, UK: Libraries Unlimited.

Yang, Z., Zhang, D., & Ye, C. (2006). Evaluation metrics for ontology complexity and evolution analysis. In *Proceedings of the IEEE International Conference on e-Business Engineering (ICEBE-2006)* (pp. 162–169). Los Alamitos, CA: IEEE Computer Society.

Yu, J., Thorn, J. A., & Tam, A. (2009). Requirements-oriented methodology for evaluating ontologies. *Information Systems, 34*(8), 766–791.

Loet Leydesdorff
Information, Meaning, and Intellectual Organization in Networks of Inter-Human Communication

1 Introduction

Due to the salience of citations in bibliometrics, there have been periodic calls for a theory of citation (e.g., Amsterdamska & Leydesdorff, 1989; Cozzens, 1989; Cronin, 1981, 1984, 1998; Garfield, 1979; Kaplan, 1965; Leydesdorff, 1998; Leydesdorff & Amsterdamska, 1990; Luukkonen, 1997; Nicolaisen, 2007; Woolgar, 1991; Wouters, 1998, 1999). Theories about citations tend to emphasize the relational aspect—that is, citation *relations* among authors and/or documents. Relations can also be aggregated into networks and the citation networks can be analyzed using social network analysis (e.g., Hummon & Doreian, 1989; Otte & Rousseau, 2002). However, neither meaning nor knowledge is purely relational. Meaning, rather, is provided positionally, not relationally.

Unlike Shannon-type information—that is, the uncertainty in a probability distribution (Shannon, 1948, p. 10)—meaning can only be provided with reference to a system for which "the differences make a difference" (MacKay, 1969; Bateson, 1972, p. 315). I shall argue that systems can be considered as sets of relations that are the results of first-order relations. However, the sets relate at the systems level not in terms of individual relations, but in terms of *correlations*. Because of potentially spurious correlations among two distributions of relations given a third one, uncertainty can also be reduced in the case of interactions among three (or more) sources of variation (Strand & Leydesdorff, 2013; cf. Garner & McGill, 1956). This communication at the systems level can be expressed as mutual information in the overlap among the sets—or with the opposite sign as reduction of uncertainty because of mutual redundancies.

On top of the information and meaning exchanges, discursive knowledge develops by relating meanings reflexively on the basis of cognitive codes that remain mentally and socially constructed (Callon et al., 1986). The specification of the role of citations in the development of discursive knowledge thus first requires that the relational perspective be extended with a positional one. Positions make it possible to develop perspectives (Leydesdorff & Ahrweiler, 2014). Translations among perspectives provide a third layer of the exchange on top of information processing in relations and the redundancy generated when meanings are shared.

2 Meaning, Meaningful Information, and the Codification of Meaning

One can provide the Shannon-type information contained in relations with a variety of meanings from different perspectives. A perspective, however, presumes a position. In the case of a reflecting agent, each position is defined in terms of the vector space that is spanned—as an architecture—by the set(s) of relations (Leydesdorff, 2014a). When a distributed network reflects (e.g., discursively), the positioning contains uncertainty since different (and potentially orthogonal) perspectives can be used at the same time, but from different positions. The meaning of the information for the receiving system can then no longer be identified unambiguously, but can only be hypothesized with reference to a virtual domain of possible relations and meanings. Giddens (1979, p. 64) called this virtual structure "an absent set of differences". The latent dimensions can be considered as providing perspectives that allow for sharing or not-sharing meaning(s) when information is positioned in a network.

For example, a perspective can be used to develop discursively a rationalized system of expectations, and thus to generate knowledge by codifying specific meanings. The codification provides an additional selection mechanism: perspectives thus add a third layer by potentially codifying communication on top of the information and meaning processing. In this context, the notion of "double contingency" (Parsons, 1968, p. 436; Parsons & Shills, 1951, p. 16) can be extended to a "triple contingency" (Strydom, 1999, p. 12). Meaningful information can first be selected from the Shannon-type information fluxes on the basis of codes that are further developed in the communications. The three layers operate in parallel.

The construction of this triple-layered system is bottom-up, but—using a cybernetic principle—control can increasingly be top-down as the feedback layers are further developed (Ashby, 1958). Whereas the three contingencies can be expected to develop in parallel, this assumption enables us to hypothesize a hierarchy among the layers that can be expected for analytical reasons. Let me stepwise extend the single-layered and linear Shannon-model (Figure 1 below) into such a triple-layered model, as depicted in Figure 2.

3 Extensions of the Shannon-Weaver Model

As is well known, Shannon (1948, p. 3) first focused on information that was not (yet) meaningful: "Frequently the messages have *meaning*; that is they refer to or are correlated to some system with certain physical or conceptual entities." According to Shannon (1948, p. 3), however, "(t)hese semantic aspects of communication are irrelevant to the engineering problem."

It is less well known that Shannon's co-author Warren Weaver argued that Shannon's distinction between information and meaning "has so penetratingly cleared the air that one is now, for the first time, ready for a real theory of meaning" (Shannon & Weaver, 1949, p. 27). Weaver (1949, p. 26) proposed to insert another box with the label "semantic noise" into the Shannon model between the information source and the transmitter, as follows (Figure 1):

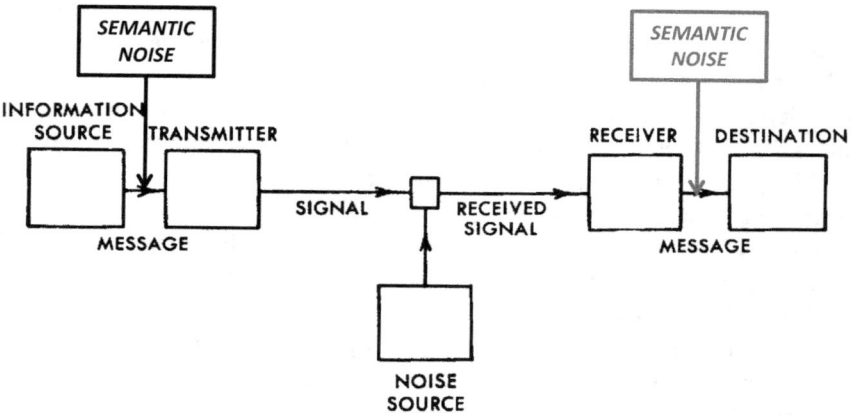

Fig. 1: Schematic diagram of a general communication system. Source: Shannon (1948, p. 380); with Weaver's box of "semantic noise" first added (to the left) and then further extended with a second source of "semantic noise" between the receiver and the destination (to the right).

What if one adds a similar box to the right side of this figure between the receiver and the destination of the message (added in grey to Figure 1)? The two sources of semantic noise may be correlated; for example, when the sender and receiver of the message share a language or, more generally, a code of communication. I propose to distinguish between "language" as the natural—that is, undifferentiated—code of communication versus codes of communication which can be symbolically generalized and then no longer require the use of language (Luhmann, 2002; 2012, pp. 120 ff.). For example, instead of negotiating about the price of a commodity, one can simply pay the market price using money as a symbolically generalized medium of communication. One is able to translate reflexively among codes of communication by elaborating upon the different meanings of the information in language (Bernstein, 1971).¹

Thus, one arrives at the following model (Figure 2):

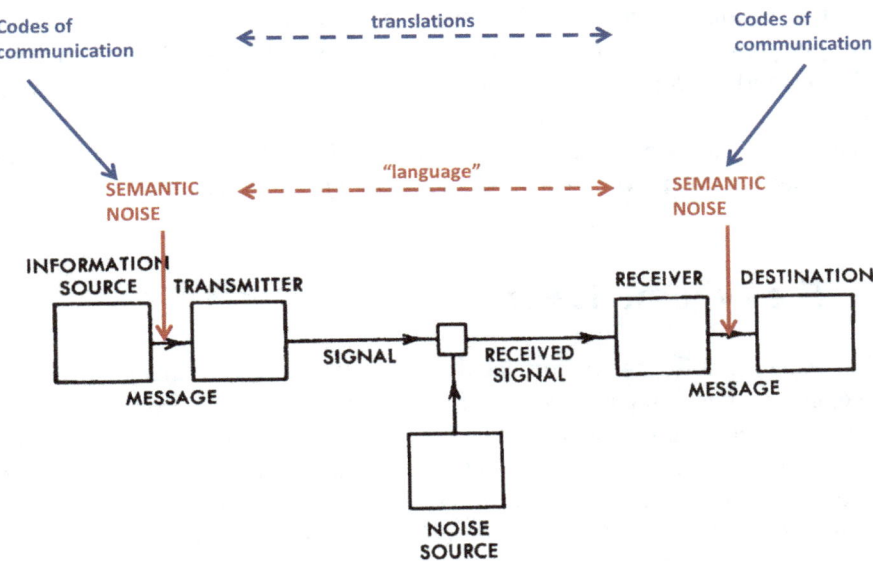

Fig. 2: Three mutual contingencies in the dynamics of codified knowledge.

Contrary to Shannon's counterintuitive definition of information as uncertainty, MacKay (1969) proposed to define information as "a distinction which makes a difference," and Bateson (1972, p. 315) followed by defining information as "a difference which makes a difference" to which he added "for a later event" (p. 381). In my opinion, a difference can only make a difference for a system of reference receiving the information. This latter system may be able to provide a relevant part of the Shannon-type information with meaning from the perspective of hindsight—that is, at a later moment. Meaningful (Bateson-type) information can no longer be considered as Shannon-type information, since it is a selection from the uncertainty that prevails. Bateson-type information may add to the uncertainty, but it can also be "informative" and thus reduce uncertainty for the receiving system (Brillouin, 1962).

---

1 I deviate here from Luhmann's theory. In his theory, the sub-systems of communication are operationally closed and communications cannot be transmitted reflexively from one system into another (cf. Callon, 1998; Leydesdorff, 2006, 2010a).

In other words, one can distinguish between "meaningful information"—potentially reducing uncertainty—and Shannon-type information that is by definition equal to uncertainty (Hayles, 1990, p. 59). Shannon (1948) chose his formulas so that uncertainty could be measured as probabilistic entropy in bits of information. The mathematical theory of communication thus provides us with entropy statistics that can be used in different domains (Bar-Hillel, 1955; Krippendorff, 1986; Theil, 1972). Meaning is provided to the information from the perspective of hindsight (of the "later event"—that is, a system of reference). However, the measurement of "meaningful information" in bits or otherwise had remained heretofore without an operationalization (cf. Dretske, 1981).

4 The Cybernetic Perspective

The semantic noises can be correlated when the semantics are shared, for example, in a common language. Various forms of semiotics have been developed to study the processing of signs in inter-human communication (e.g., Fiske, 2011, pp. 37–60; Nöth, 2014). The focus of this contribution, however, remains on the shaping of discursive knowledge using cybernetic and information-theoretical perspectives. Can the effects of the codification in scholarly exchanges also be measured?

The sharing of meaning is far from error-free, and thus other uncertainty can be generated at this later moment, but the selective operation is analytically different from the generation of variation: some differences are selected as making a difference—a signal—whereas other differences (bits) are discarded as noise. A second contingency is thus added reflexively to the relational uncertainty in the communication of information.

The relations are "contingent"—and not necessary or transcendent—because a variation could also have been different. Secondly, the relational information may mean something different for the sender and the receiver, but this is again contingent because it depends on the respective positions in the networks of relations. However, both analysts and participants are able to specify an *expectation* about this meaning, given codes of communication, insofar as the codes have emerged as densities (eigenvectors) in the networks of communications at the two lower levels of relational information processing and positional meaning-sharing (Leydesdorff, 1998).

Parsons (1951, p. 10 f.) elaborated "double contingency" as a basic condition for inter-human interactions, but he presumed a normative—that is, relatively stable—binding of mutual expectations in a symbolic order (Deacon, 1997).

However, different horizons of meaning can always be invoked (Husserl, 1962; Luhmann, 1990, p. 27 and 1995, p. 69). This third layer of codes in the communication emerges as a source of friction—and thus contingency—when differences become manifest in historical encounters such as misunderstandings. Normative integration is then no longer sufficient, and differentiation among the codes of communication can become functional. For example, while concerned about "truth," science is not involved in the pursuit of religious truth. "Truth-finding" in a criminal investigation is differently coded from heuristics in theoretical contexts.

The symbolic order among the codes of communication is not a given, but a construct that can be reconstructed reflexively by using another code such as another alphabet or language. Luhmann (1995) added that symbolically generalized codes of communication can be functionally different. Whereas normative integration was presumed in understanding at the second level—using a common language—differentiation operates against the integrative tendency of normative learning by developing cognitive learning in parallel. When this differentiation prevails, the fluxes of communication can no longer be integrated historically into organizations, but tend to "self-organize."

Against Luhmann's reification of these tendencies (Habermas, 1987; Leydesdorff, 2006, 2010a), I propose considering the self-organizing dynamic as a third contingency (Strydom, 1999): a triple contingency can thus be expected to operate in inter-human communications, but the processing at different levels remains historically contingent since socially constructed. The self-organizing tendencies have the status of hypotheses; the codes can be expected to enable both participants and analysts to specify expectations (Leydesdorff, 2012).

In other words, inter-human communication first requires a historical medium in which probabilistic entropy (Shannon-type information) is generated, but this first-order proliferation of differences can be provided with meaning at both the sending and receiving ends. Meaning can be provided to the communication from the perspective of hindsight, but also differently using other perspectives and codes with reference to self-organizing "horizons of meaning" (Husserl, 1962; Luhmann, 1995, pp. 60 ff.; cf. Borch, 2011, p. 41).

Note that the codes of communication can be considered as second-order variables, that is, variables that are attributed as eigenvectors to the communications as first-order variables (Von Foerster, 2003).[2] Consequently, the coded dimensions

---

[2] Luhmann indicates the latent dimensions with the word "eigenvalue". Technically, the eigenvalue of an eigenvector is the factor by which the eigenvector is scaled when multiplied by the matrix.

of the communication can no longer be attributed to the communicating agents; they are attributes of the communications and the analysis thus becomes more abstract and layered: not only can the agents interact, but also their interactions can be expected to interact. The next-order interactions among interactions provide the lower-level structures of first-order interactions with new degrees of freedom in feedback loops.

In summary, this model—based on and inspired by Luhmann (1995)—follows Herbert Simon's (1973) model of complex systems, but with modifications. One assumes both horizontal and vertical differentiation in the communication. Vertical differentiation was visualized in Figure 2 and can be labeled as (1) *interactions* at the bottom providing variation, (2) *organization* of the communication when the different codes of communication are historically interfaced, and (3) *self-organization* of the codes of communication spanning horizons of meaning (Luhmann, 1975).

Horizontally, the codes of communication can be expected to operate in parallel; they can be considered as the evolving units and are modeled as "genotypical." Because the codes are not material ("phenotypical"), they can develop with a higher frequency than the historical realizations. Expectations proliferate faster than actions (Weinstein & Platt, 1969). In this respect, the model is different from Simon's model where the higher the level, the lower the frequencies. The additional feed forward of the communication under the condition of horizontal differentiation among the codes enables the communication to process more complexity. When the normative order among the codes is broken, differentiation can evolve into another degree of freedom in the system's capacity (Leydesdorff, 2014b).

The uncertainty can be reduced by the specification of expectations in highly codified communications such as systems of rationalized expectations or, in other words, scholarly discourses. Translations from one code into another require integration into elaborate discourse in a historical context (at the second level), but not necessarily at the same moment. The historical organization can thus be considered as a synchronizing retention mechanism of the otherwise self-organizing dynamics. While these mechanisms can be distinguished analytically, they operate in parallel and can be expected to "overflow" (Callon, 1998) into one another because of the ongoing generation of uncertainty in all historical processes.

5 Relevance for the Study of Organized Knowledge Production in the Sciences

The distinction between organization and self-organization of communication enables us to operationalize distinctions that were made in science studies, but could at the time not yet be operationalized in communication-theoretical terms. In the sociology of science, for example, Whitley (1984) distinguished between the social and intellectual organization of the sciences or, in other words, between the "field"-level and the "group"-level (Rip, 1981). In the philosophy of science, Popper ([1935] 1959) introduced the distinction between the locally contingent context of discovery and the trans-local context of justification (cf. Lakatos & Musgrave, 1970). The field-level, the intellectual organization, and the context of justification are evolutionary and self-organizing (Popper, 1972); whereas the group-level, the social organization, or the contexts of discovery are historically organized. The two levels co-evolve and are co-constructed, but the direction of the arrows is reversed (Campbell, 1960).

For example, when the peer-review process is organized in terms of editors and referees at the journal level, this is a social process, but the intellectual organization is supposed to take control in terms of the codes of the communication. The codes of communication are needed for the context of justification in order to function, but the material conditions also need to be organized. The social organization of science is sensitive to funding, but the intellectual organization in terms of self-organizing codes of communication can be expected to resist such steering of the scientific enterprise (van den Daele & Weingart, 1975). The intellectual self-organization operates as a latent feedback mechanism. Under certain conditions, this feedback can come to fruition into a feed-forward, and the field can auto-catalytically develop its code(s) of communication (Figure 3).

Figure 3 elaborates on Ulanowicz's (2009, p. 1888) model of auto-catalysis (cf. Padgett & Powell, 2012): a third code—that is, meaning providing system or perspective—can auto-catalyze the relation between the other two. However, the rotation can be clockwise or counter-clockwise (Ivanova & Leydesdorff, 2014, p. 930). Whereas the one dynamic can be appreciated as a feed-forward from

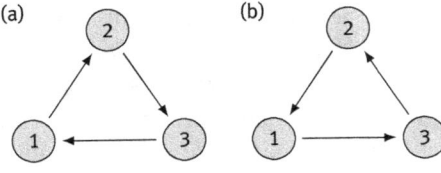

Fig. 3: Circulation and feedback in cycles in both directions.

organization at each moment of time to self-organization over time, the reverse dynamic retains historical organization at each moment of time. Since both dynamics can be expected to operate in parallel but opposite directions, one can assume a balance or trade-off between them: is intellectual self-organization leading at the field-level or historical organization at the institutional level? Note that one can only observe the historical instantiations; the self-organization remains a theoretically-informed hypothesis about an evolutionary (that is, suprahistorical) dynamic.

In another context—that of the Triple Helix of university-industry-government relations—I proposed mutual information in three (or more) dimensions as an indicator of this trade-off between historical organization (in networked university-industry-government relations) versus the evolutionary self-organization of synergy in terms of functionalities such as—in the case of Triple-Helix relations—(*i*) novelty production through the development of science and technology, (*ii*) economic wealth generation, and (*iii*) normative control by governance (Leydesdorff & Zawdie, 2010; cf. Ulanowicz, 1986, p. 143). The historical relations cannot be the sole purpose of a Triple Helix, but one rather aims at the fruition of these relations into synergy at a systems level. Under what historical conditions can the loops among the three juxtaposed coordination mechanisms flourish and blossom auto-catalytically?

$$T_{123} = H_1 + H_2 + H_3 - H_{12} - H_{13} - H_{23} + H_{123} \qquad (1)$$

Mutual information in three dimensions (Eq. (1)) can be used to model the trade-off between organization and self-organization because this measure can be positive or negative. The equation can be derived from the Shannon formulas (e.g., Abramson, 1963; McGill, 1954; cf. Jakulin, 2005; Yeung, 2008), but T_{123} can no longer be considered as a Shannon entropy because it can also be negative (Krippendorff, 2009a). Shannon's model (Figure 1), however, excluded feedback loops and thus developments against the arrow of time—in accordance with Shannon's aim to discard meaning-processing as not relevant to the engineering problem.

Leydesdorff and Ivanova (2014) showed that the mutual information in three (or more) dimensions can also be considered as a measure of mutual redundancy—that is, overlap among "pure sets" (*ibid.*, p. 391). An overlap among sets is then appreciated twice (or more times) by considering both overlapping systems as systems of reference. It could then be shown that the mutual redundancy $R_{12} = -T_{12}$ in the case of two systems, while in the case of three systems $R_{123} = T_{123}$ (with the opposite sign). The choice of sign warrants consistency with Shannon's (1948) mathematical theory of communication, so that the values can be expressed in bits of information (Leydesdorff, 2010b). Negative values of *R* indicate reduction of uncertainty because of synergy in the configuration of relations.

Given space constraints, I will not repeat this argument, but instead use the mutual redundancy in three dimensions as a possible operationalization for the distinction between (self-organizing and hypothesized) intellectual versus historical organization in texts using, on the special occasion of this *Festschrift*, the work of Professor Blaise Cronin. This œuvre provides an example of a historically organized set of documents in which intellectual organization operates reflexively to the extent that it can be expected to prevail over the historical organization of the texts.

To what extent are these documents organized intellectually in terms of title words, cited references, and/or the title words of the papers citing them? Can one use the concepts of latent variables (factors or eigenvectors) of the matrices of documents versus words to uncover this trade-off between intellectual self-organization over time and social or semantic organization at specific moments of time? I operationalize the three layers specified above as follows: (1) relations in terms of co-occurrences of title words, (2) the positions of these words in the vector-space spanned by these relations, and (3) the mutual redundancies among the three main (factor-analytic) dimensions of this vector-space in each set.

6 Data

Given the character of this *Festschrift* for Professor Cronin, it seemed reasonable to illustrate the above arguments empirically by focusing on this author's œuvre insofar as available using the Web of Science (WoS) data provided by Thomson-Reuters. Since there are several authors under "B Cronin" in WoS, the download was limited to "au = Cronin B* and ci = Bloomington". Cronin has published at this address since 1991. Thus, 164 documents were retrieved from the database on April 23, 2014. I use these data and the 949 articles citing these 164 documents at this same date. Table 1 provides descriptive statistics.

The sets of documents are used as samples to pursue an analysis analogous to the evaluation of aggregated journal-journal citations (Leydesdorff, 2011a) and of title words in a single journal—namely, *Social Science Information* (Leydesdorff, 2011b).

Tab. 1: Descriptive statistics of the downloads under study, including the number of cited and citing documents.

	N	Times Cited	Cited References
Article	65	1113	2314
Article; Proceedings Paper	7	151	187
Biographical Item	2	9	2
Book Review	36	1	78
Discussion	1	0	0
Editorial Material	35	36	51
Letter	7	17	16
Meeting Abstract	1	0	0
Note	4	72	75
Review	6	42	780
	164	1441*	3503

* These 1441 citations—based on aggregating the field "times cited" of the 164 documents—were carried by 949 citing documents (including self-citations).

7 Methods

Three matrices are central to the analysis:
1. The asymmetrical word/document matrix based on the 164 documents authored by Cronin as cases, and the 57 title words in these documents that occurred more than twice in this set (after correction for stopwords, using a list of 429 stopwords)[3];
2. The asymmetrical word/document matrix based on the 949 documents citing one of these 164 documents (1441 times) versus the 108 words that occurred more than ten times in the titles of these citing documents (after a similar correction for stopwords); and,
3. Parsing the 3526 cited references in the first document set[4], 398 cited source names could be retrieved, of which 109 (27.4 %) matched with the abbreviations for journal names used in the *Journal Citation Index* 2012 of WoS.[5] These

---

[3] Provided at http://www.lextek.com/manuals/onix/stopwords1.html
[4] Table 1 provides the number of 3503 cited references based on cross-tabulation in Excel, and using the field "N of references" (NRef) in the WoS output.
[5] Using automatic matching, the *Journal of the American Society for Information Science* (*JASIS*) is not matched because it is included in JCR 2012 as the *Journal of the American Society for Information Science and Technology* (*JASIST*). However, 163 references in the set refer to this old title. We will use this set as an additional control in the discussion section.

109 journal names were used as variables to the 164 documents as cases for the construction of a third matrix.

Co-occurrence matrices and cosine matrices were derived from each of these three matrices for further analysis and visualization using Pajek (v. 3.11).[6] The three matrices can be used for drawing semantic maps, both in terms of relations and in terms of cosine-normalized relations in the vector space.[7] Moreover, the asymmetrical word/document matrices can be imported in SPSS (v. 21) for factor analysis. Factor loadings on the three main components (after orthogonal rotation using Varimax) are used for visualizing the variables (vectors) in relation to the first three eigenvectors and also for the analysis of mutual redundancy using dedicated software.

8 Results

8.1 The Document Set Authored by Cronin (*N* = 164)

As noted, 164 documents were downloaded on April 23, 2014, using the search string "au = Cronin B* and ci = Bloomington". These documents contain 57 title words which occur more than twice after correction for stopwords. Figure 4 shows the *relational* network among 56 of these words colored according to the partitioning using Blondel *et al.*'s (2008) algorithm for community-finding, and Kamada and Kawai's (1989) algorithm for the layout.

A relational map of co-occurring words in the same subject area can always be provided with an interpretation because the words are grouped and placed in relation to one another. Frequently used words will tend to be central (e.g., "Science," "Society," "Library"). In this set, for example, "Bibliometrics" is placed in this central set, but in a grouping different from words which are commonly used in bibliometrics such as "Author," "Journal," and "Citation."

---

[6] Pajek is a program for network analysis and visualization; available for download at http://pajek.imfm.si/doku.php?id=download
[7] The cosine can be considered as the non-parametric equivalent of the Pearson correlation; as against the latter, the distribution is not first z-normalized with reference to the mean (Ahlgren *et al.*, 2003).

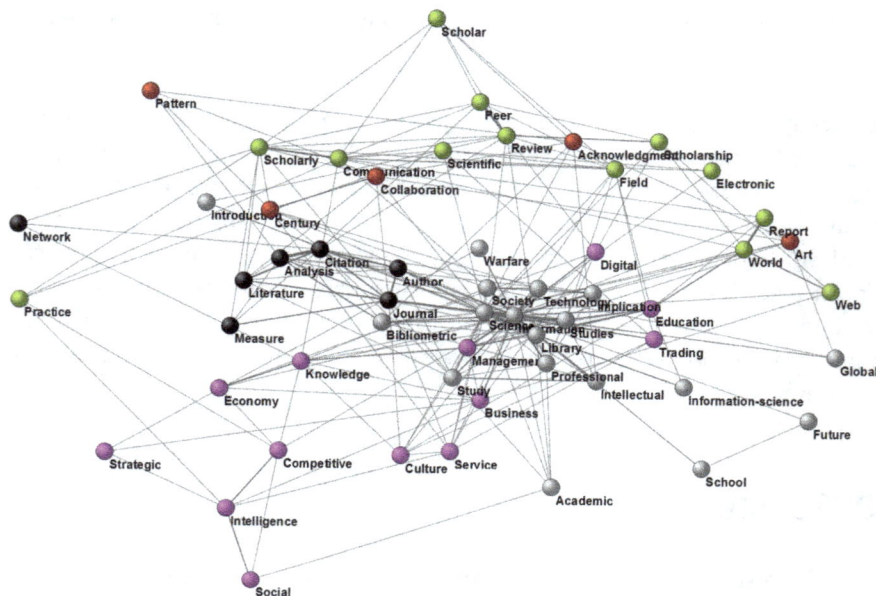

Fig. 4: 56 (of the 57) words connected in the largest component of the network of title-words occurring more than twice in the set. $Q = 0.359$; N of Clusters = 5.

After cosine-normalization and setting a threshold of cosine > 0.2, one obtains a systems perspective on Cronin's œuvre. Fifty-three of the title words form a largest component (Figure 5); five communities are indicated using the algorithm of Blondel *et al.* (2008)[8] with a modularity $Q = 0.542$. The modularity of this network is enhanced because of the threshold; the words are now grouped in the vector space (Leydesdorff, 2014a). The grouping indicates the structure in the set of relations.

Thus, we have moved from a relational to a positional perspective on the structure in this data (Burt, 1982; Leydesdorff, 2014a). The topology is different: we no longer study the network of *relations* among words in terms of co-occurrences ("co-words"; Callon *et al.*, 1983), but the *correlations* among the distributions of words over the documents under study. The grouping of words in Figure 5 indicates the latent dimensions of the network as a system of words (Leydesdorff, 2014a).

---

8 This algorithm is used because the algorithm of VOSviewer indicated three more communities.

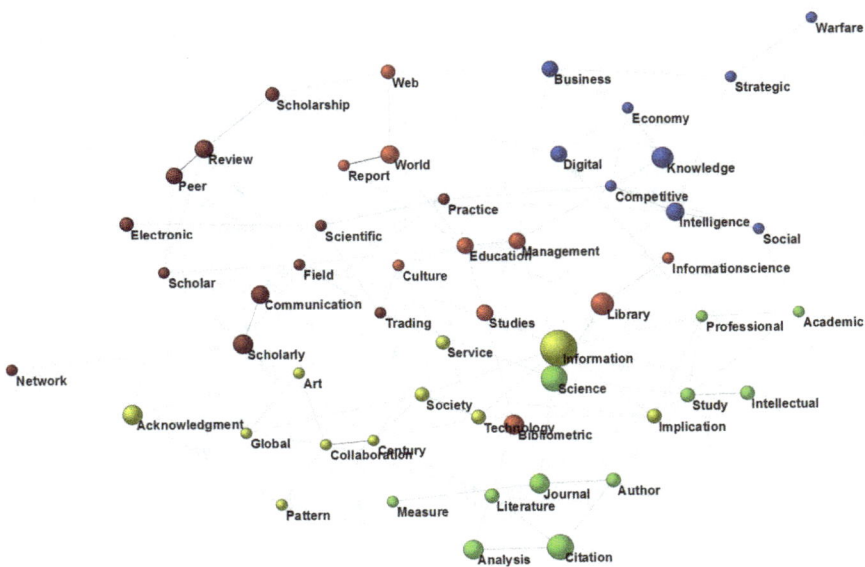

Fig. 5: 53 words organized in five communities forming a largest component using 164 documents (cosine > 0.2).

In Figure 5, for example, "Bibliometrics," "Library Studies," "Education," and "Management" are grouped (using pink) as different from bibliometric terminology such as "Citation," "Analysis," "Measure," "Author," and "Journal." The differences between Figures 4 and 5, however, are, in this case, not so large.

Figure 6 uses a different input: it visualizes the three-factor matrix based on the same set (Vlieger & Leydesdorff, 2011). For reasons of presentation, I have removed the negative (dotted) lines from the visualization and also the nine words which thus became isolates. All 57 words and their factor loadings were used in the further analysis of the mutual redundancy in three dimensions. Whereas these dimensions could be induced from Figure 5, I now force the three (latent) dimensions to become center stage. As noted, the choice for three is made for reasons of parsimony, but one can also extend this to more than three dimensions.

Factor 1 groups the words in bibliometrics; factor 2 the words focusing on scholarly communication; and factor 3 more general terminology. The three factors can be considered as the latent dimensions (eigenvectors) of the word/document matrix.

Eq. (1) can be used for the computation of the mutual redundancy among these three dimensions (Leydesdorff, 2010b). The (binned) factor loadings of the 57 words as variables provide a mutual redundancy of –1888.9 mbits of informa-

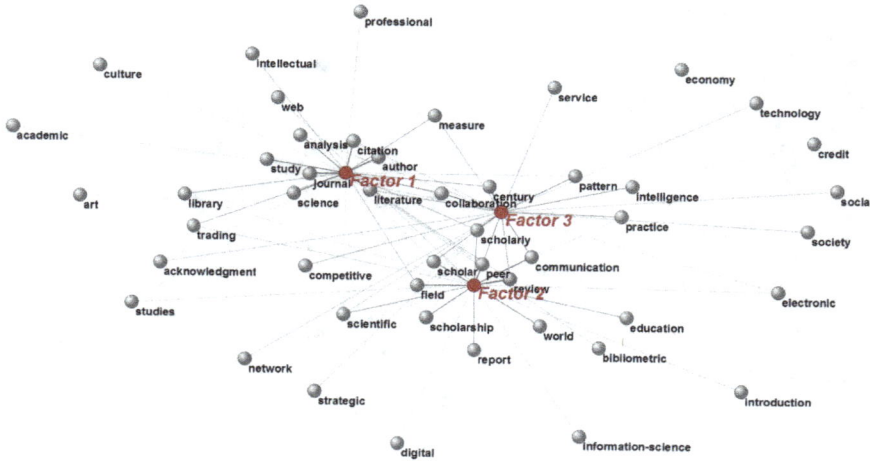

Fig. 6: 48 words with positive loadings on three factors in a matrix of 164 documents and 57 variables (words).

tion. In other words, the uncertainty in this textual domain is reduced by almost two bits by the intellectual organization of the words in the three main (latent) dimensions.

8.2 Citing Papers (*N* = 949)

Using the 949 documents that could be retrieved as citing at least one of the 164 documents authored by Cronin, a similar procedure was followed. Figure 7 shows 92 of the 108 words occurring more than ten times in these documents with at least one (among three) *positive* factor loadings, similarly to Figure 6.

Figure 7 shows the structure in the vocabulary of Cronin's (citing) audiences. Bibliometric terminology loads on a second factor after a first one with a focus on academia; factor 3 indicates concerns of library and education.

Following an analogous procedure, the mutual redundancy among the three main dimensions in this matrix of 949 documents versus 108 title words is −70.1 mbits of information. This is only 3.7 % of the synergy retrieved from the word distributions in the 164 cited documents that were authored by Cronin himself.

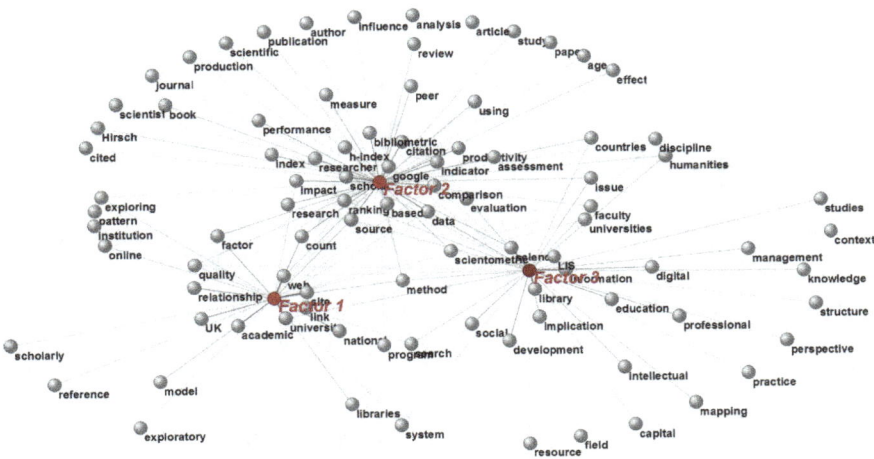

Fig. 7: 92 (of the 108) words occurring more than ten times in the 949 citing documents in relation and positive factor loading on at least one of the three factors.

8.3 Cited References

The document set of 164 documents authored by Cronin is not only cited, but also citing. As noted, the documents contain 3526 cited references. Since the cited references in WoS do not contain title words, I used the subfield of the abbreviated journal titles in the references as variables to the 164 documents. This can be considered as a representation of the knowledge bases of Cronin's articles (Leydesdorff & Goldstone, 2014).

Among the 3526 cited references, 398 unique sources can be counted,[9] of which 109 sources could be matched to the journal abbreviations provided by the Journal Citation Reports for 2012. One can thus construct two matrices: one with 398 cited sources as variables and another with 109 matched sources that occur in 1223 (34.3%) of the cited references.

Figure 8 shows the map of the factor matrix of 96 of these 109 journals based on 91 documents carrying these references.[10] Factor 2 is recognizable as a group of information-science journals, but the designation of the other two factors is less obvious except that Factor 1 includes general-science journals such as *Nature, The*

---

9 A referenced journal has to be included more than once into the set so that two journals are related by the document as the observational unit.
10 The 3526 cited references to 398 sources were counted in 111 documents.

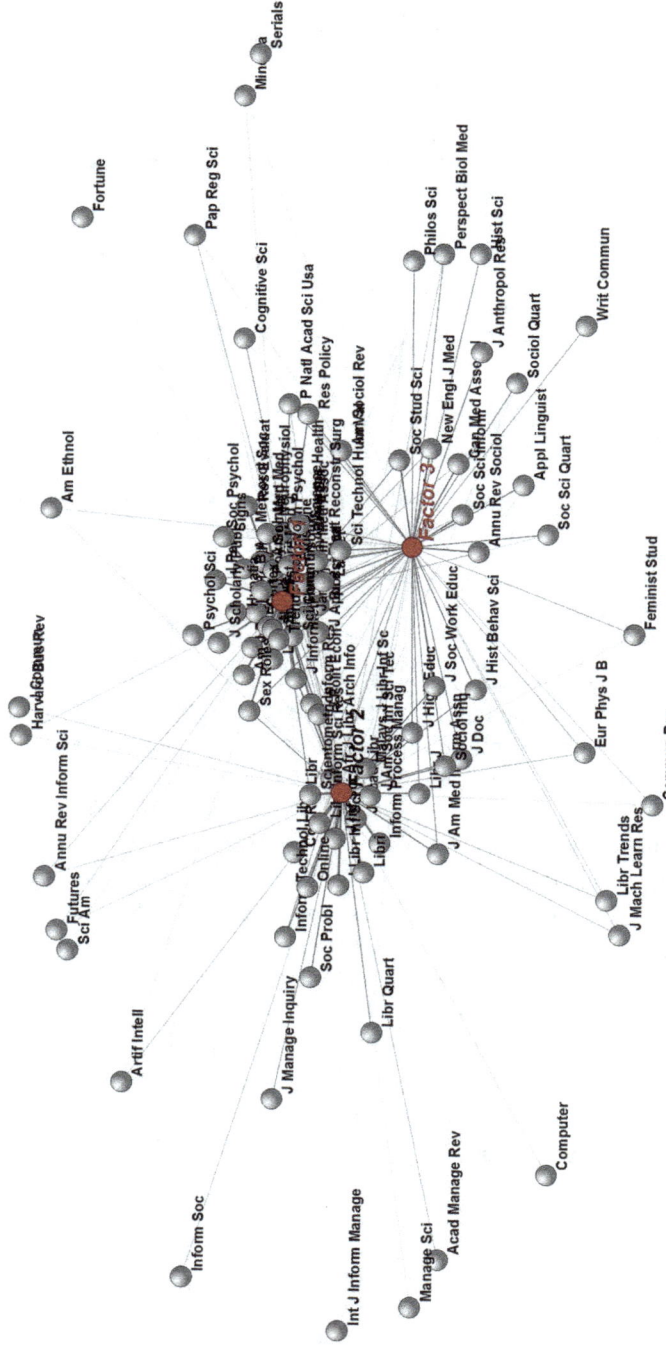

Fig. 8: 96 of the 109 journal abbreviations with positive factor loadings.

Lancet, and the *American Economic Review*, whereas Factor 3 is composed mainly of specialist journals in the social sciences and the humanities.

The mutual redundancies are +14.2 mbit for the larger set of 398 cited sources versus –160.4 mbit for the references to journals active in the WoS database. Thus, these more codified references contribute to the synergy, while the larger set tends to be more incidental and contingently organized. Table 2 summarizes the findings for the four analyses discussed above.

Tab. 2: Mutual redundancy among the three main dimensions of the four document/word matrices compared (in mbits of information).

	Mutual redundancy in mbits
164 documents authored by Blaise Cronin	–1888.9
949 citing documents	–70.1
398 cited sources	+14.2
109 cited sources that match with JCR	–160.4

9 Discussion

As noted, I performed a similar analysis in a contribution on the occasion of the 50th volume and publication year of *Social Science Information* (SSI) using title words in the volumes between 2005 and 2009 (Leydesdorff, 2011b). Using 69 title words occurring three or more times in a set of 149 titles, the mutual redundancy among the three main dimensions of this matrix added +50.6 mbits to the uncertainty. These 149 documents were cited by 187 other documents; for the title words in these citing journals I obtained a mutual redundancy of –106.2 mbits. In this case, the citing journals provide windows on different (self-organizing) literatures, whereas the articles published in the journal were intellectually a heterogeneous set that was organized historically.

In the case of Cronin's publications, the original documents are all authored by him and thus the title words are intellectually organized to a degree much larger than the citing documents. The latter show a synergy comparable to that of the set of citing papers in the case of *SSI* (–70.1 versus –106.2 mbits). When the non-source references are included in the analysis of Cronin's set, the synergy disappears, while it remains when the analysis is restricted to the set of references to indexed journals.

We note another possible control: Adding the abbreviation "*J AM SOC INFORM SCI*", that is, the name of *JASIST* before 2001 (but no longer included in

JCR and therefore not matched above), another 163 references can be included (1223 + 163), and the journal set is extended to (109 + 1 =) 110. The mutual redundancy is in this case further increased to −179.5 mbits. This result accords with the expectation that references to *JASIS* contribute to the intellectual organization of the set.

10 Conclusions

Luhmann's sociological theory of communication and Shannon's mathematical one can be considered two almost orthogonal perspectives. On the one hand, Luhmann (1995, p. 67) defined information as a selective operation and stated that "all information has meaning." Thus, the measurement of communication (e.g., in bits of information) remains external to this theoretical perspective. On the other hand, Shannon (1948, p. 3) excluded "meaning" as not relevant to his theory of communication. The crucial question, in my opinion, is how meaning is generated in communication of information and then also codified. Can the one perspective be translated into the other or are these theories fully incommensurable?

Weaver's (1949, p. 27) call for a "real theory of meaning" based on Shannon's distinction between meaning and information can be elaborated both theoretically and then also empirically. We have begun to develop instruments such as semantic maps for the positioning of information, and mutual redundancy for the measurement of the relations among codes in the communication. These operationalizations have been illustrated empirically.

The first step in how meaning is generated in communicative relations is articulated in the operation of *semantic* mapping. The aggregate of relations allows for a systems perspective since an architecture is shaped by the network which can also be analyzed in terms of correlations and latent dimensions. The relational analysis can thus be complemented with a positional one (see Leydesdorff, 2014a). Meaning is provided in terms of positions, that is, with reference to a system. The system(s) of reference position the incoming information and thus appreciate uncertainty as noise or signal. Over time, this positioning may either increase or decrease uncertainty within the system. Brillouin (1962) introduced the concept of "negentropy" in this context.

Negative entropy can be generated when the redundancy increases more rapidly than uncertainty, given that the maximum entropy—that is the sum of the redundancy and uncertainty—can also evolve in dynamic systems (Brooks & Wiley, 1986, p. 43). As Krippendorff (2009b, p. 676) formulated: "Note that *interactions with loops entail positive or negative redundancies, those without loops do not*. Loops can be complex, especially in systems with many variables."

Using Weaver's (1949, p. 26) loophole of "semantic noise", next-order loops can be related to the Shannon model. Using the sociological progression from Parsons' assumption of normative integration in the first next-order loop to Luhmann's option of functional differentiation in a second-order loop of codes of communication, a model with both horizontal and vertical differentiation (Luhmann's social or systems differentiations, respectively) could thus be developed in terms that allow for empirical operationalization.

The codes of communication provide a superstructure that operates evolutionarily (as "genotypes"), and thus becomes historically manifest only as a source of structural reduction of uncertainty (i.e., redundancy). When different codes of communication operate, the same information may redundantly be provided with different meanings and thus appreciated twice or more times. In the case of three or more codes, two rotations are possible (Figure 3 above), of which one can be considered as feed forward and the other as feedback. Using the example of Cronin's publications, we have suggested that mutual redundancy can be used as a measure of intellectual versus historical (in this case, textual) organization.

Unlike the organization of articles in journal issues, the single author adds intellectual organization to his texts. The titles are not a bag of words which can be co-occurring or not, but their organization can be made visible as meaningful using a semantic map, and then further be analyzed in terms of the synergy among the latent dimensions of the vector space spanned by the distributions of words as variables in relation to their textual organization—that is, with the historical documents as the cases (Hesse, 1980, p. 103; Law & Lodge, 1984; Leydesdorff, 1997). The author organizes this vector space intellectually by more than an order of magnitude when compared with the cited references or the documents that cite his œuvre.

Acknowledgment

I thank Cassidy Sugimoto, Lutz Bornmann, and an anonymous referee for comments on a previous version.

Cited References

Abramson, N. (1963). *Information Theory and Coding*. New York, etc.: McGraw-Hill.

Ahlgren, P., Jarneving, B., & Rousseau, R. (2003). Requirements for a Cocitation Similarity Measure, with Special Reference to Pearson's Correlation Coefficient. *Journal of the American Society for Information Science and Technology, 54*(6), 550–560.

Amsterdamska, O., & Leydesdorff, L. (1989). Citations: Indicators of Significance? *Scientometrics 15*(5–6), 449–471.

Ashby, W. R. (1958). Requisite variety and its implications for the control of complex systems. *Cybernetica, 1*(2), 83–99.

Bar-Hillel, Y. (1955). An Examination of Information Theory. *Philosophy of Science, 22*, 86–105.

Bateson, G. (1972). *Steps to an Ecology of Mind*. New York: Ballantine.

Bernstein, B. (1971). *Class, Codes and Control, Vol. 1: Theoretical studies in the sociology of language*. London: Routledge & Kegan Paul.

Blondel, V. D., Guillaume, J. L., Lambiotte, R., & Lefebvre, E. (2008). Fast unfolding of communities in large networks. *Journal of Statistical Mechanics: Theory and Experiment, 8*(10), 10008.

Borch, C. (2011). *Niklas Luhmann*. London and New York: Routledge.

Brillouin, L. (1962). *Science and Information Theory*. New York: Academic Press.

Brooks, D. R., & Wiley, E. O. (1986). *Evolution as Entropy*. Chicago/London: University of Chicago Press.

Burt, R. S. (1982). *Toward a Structural Theory of Action*. New York, etc.: Academic Press.

Callon, M. (1998). An essay on framing and overflowing: economic externalities revisited by sociology. *The Laws of the Market* (pp. 244–269). Oxford and Malden, MA: Blackwell.

Callon, M., Courtial, J.-P., Turner, W. A., & Bauin, S. (1983). From Translations to Problematic Networks: An Introduction to Co-word Analysis. *Social Science Information 22*(2), 191–235.

Callon, M., Law, J., & Rip, A. (Eds.). (1986). *Mapping the Dynamics of Science and Technology*. London: Macmillan.

Campbell, D. T. (1960). Blind variation and selective retentions in creative thought as in other knowledge processes. *Psychological review, 67*(6), 380.

Cozzens, S. E. (1989). What do citations count? The rhetoric-first model. *Scientometrics, 15*(5), 437–447.

Cronin, B. (1981). The need for a theory of citing. *Journal of Documentation, 37*(1), 16–24.

Cronin, B. (1984). *The citation process. The role and significance of citations in scientific communication*. London: Taylor Graham.

Cronin, B. (1998). Metatheorizing citation. *Scientometrics, 43*(1), 45–55.

Deacon, T. W. (1997). *The Symbolic Species: The co-evolution of language and the brain*. New York/London: W. W. Norton & Company.

Dretske, F. I. (1981). *Knowledge and the flow of information*. Cambridge MA: MIT Press.

Fiske, J. (2011). *Introduction to communication studies* (3rd ed.). New York: Routledge.

Garfield, E. (1979). *Citation Indexing: Its Theory and Application in Science, Technology, and Humanities*. New York: John Wiley.

Garner, W. R., & McGill, W. J. (1956). The relation between information and variance analyses. *Psychometrika, 21*(3), 219–228.

Giddens, A. (1979). *Central Problems in Social Theory*. London, etc.: Macmillan.

Habermas, J. (1987). Excursus on Luhmann's Appropriation of the Philosophy of the Subject through Systems Theory *The Philosophical Discourse of Modernity: Twelve Lectures* (pp. 368–385). Cambridge, MA: MIT Press.

Hayles, N. K. (1990). *Chaos Bound; Orderly Disorder in Contemporary Literature and Science* Ithaca, etc.: Cornell University.

Hesse, M. (1980). *Revolutions and Reconstructions in the Philosophy of Science*. London: Harvester Press.

Hummon, N. P., & Doreian, P. (1989). Connectivity in a citation network: The development of DNA theory. *Social Networks, 11*(1), 39–63.

Husserl, E. ([1935/36] 1962). *Die Krisis der Europäischen Wissenschaften und die Transzendentale Phänomenologie*. Den Haag: Martinus Nijhoff.

Ivanova, I. A., & Leydesdorff, L. (2014). Redundancy Generation in University-Industry-Government Relations: The Triple Helix Modeled, Measured, and Simulated. *Scientometrics, 99*(3), 927–948.

Jakulin, A. (2005). *Machine learning based on attribute interactions* (Vol. http://stat.columbia.edu/~jakulin/Int/jakulin05phd.pdf). Ljubljana: University of Ljubljana.

Kamada, T., & Kawai, S. (1989). An algorithm for drawing general undirected graphs. *Information Processing Letters, 31*(1), 7–15.

Kaplan, N. (1965). The norms of citation behavior: Prolegomena to the footnote. *American Documentation, 16*(3), 179–184.

Krippendorff, K. (1986). *Information Theory. Structural Models for Qualitative Data*. Beverly Hills, etc.: Sage.

Krippendorff, K. (2009a). W. Ross Ashby's information theory: a bit of history, some solutions to problems, and what we face today. *International Journal of General Systems, 38*(2), 189–212.

Krippendorff, K. (2009b). Information of Interactions in Complex Systems. *International Journal of General Systems, 38*(6), 669–680.

Lakatos, I., & Musgrave, A. (Eds.). (1970). *Criticism and the Growth of Knowledge* Cambridge: Cambridge University Press).

Law, J., & Lodge, P. (1984). *Science for Social Scientists*. London, etc.: Macmillan.

Leydesdorff, L. (1997). Why Words and Co-Words Cannot Map the Development of the Sciences. *Journal of the American Society for Information Science, 48*(5), 418–427.

Leydesdorff, L. (1998). Theories of Citation? *Scientometrics, 43*(1), 5–25.

Leydesdorff, L. (2006). The Biological Metaphor of a (Second-order) Observer and the Sociological Discourse. *Kybernetes, 35*(3/4), 531–546.

Leydesdorff, L. (2010a). Luhmann Reconsidered: Steps towards an empirical research program in the sociology of communication. In C. Grant (Ed.), *Beyond Universal Pragmatics: Essays in the Philosophy of Communication* (pp. 149–173). Oxford: Peter Lang.

Leydesdorff, L. (2010b). Redundancy in Systems which Entertain a Model of Themselves: Interaction Information and the Self-organization of Anticipation. *Entropy, 12*(1), 63–79.

Leydesdorff, L. (2011a). "Structuration" by Intellectual Organization: The Configuration of Knowledge in Relations among Scientific Texts. *Scientometrics 88*(2), 499–520.

Leydesdorff, L. (2011b). "Meaning" as a sociological concept: A review of the modeling, mapping, and simulation of the communication of knowledge and meaning. *Social Science Information, 50*(3–4), 1–23.

Leydesdorff, L. (2012). Radical Constructivism and Radical Constructedness: Luhmann's Sociology of Semantics, Organizations, and Self-Organization. *Constructivist Foundations, 8*(1), 85–92.

Leydesdorff, L. (2014a). Science Visualization and Discursive Knowledge. In B. Cronin & C. Sugimoto (Eds.), *Beyond Bibliometrics: Harnessing Multidimensional Indicators of Scholarly Impact* (pp. 167–185). Cambridge MA: MIT Press.

Leydesdorff, L. (2014b). Niklas Luhmann's Magnificent Contribution to the Sociological Tradition: The Emergence of the Knowledge-Based Economy as an Order of Expectations. In T. Bakken & M. Tzaneva (Eds.), *Nachtflug der Eule: 150 Stimmen zum Werk von Niklas Luhmann* (Vol. 2, pp. 470–484). Berlin: Lidi Verlag.

Leydesdorff, L., & Ahrweiler, P. (2014). In search of a network theory of innovations: Relations, positions, and perspectives. *Journal of the Association for Information Science and Technology, 65*(11), 2359–2374.

Leydesdorff, L., & Amsterdamska, O. (1990). Dimensions of Citation Analysis. *Science, Technology & Human Values, 15*(3), 305–335.

Leydesdorff, L., & Goldstone, R. L. (2014). Interdisciplinarity at the Journal and Specialty Level: The changing knowledge bases of the journal *Cognitive Science*. *Journal of the Association for Information Science and Technology 65*(1), 164–177.

Leydesdorff, L., & Ivanova, I. A. (2014). Mutual Redundancies in Inter-human Communication Systems: Steps Towards a Calculus of Processing Meaning. *Journal of the Association for Information Science and Technology, 65*(2), 386–399.

Leydesdorff, L., & Zawdie, G. (2010). The Triple Helix Perspective of Innovation Systems. *Technology Analysis & Strategic Management, 22*(7), 789–804.

Luhmann, N. (1975). Interaktion, Organisation, Gesellschaft: Anwendungen der Systemtheorie. In M. Gerhardt (Ed.), *Die Zukunft der Philosophie* (pp. 85–107). München: List.

Luhmann, N. (1990). Meaning as Sociology's Basic Concept. In N. Luhmann (Ed.), *Essays on Self-Reference* (pp. 21–79). New York / Oxford: Columbia University Press.

Luhmann, N. (1995). *Social Systems*. Stanford, CA: Stanford University Press.

Luhmann, N. (2002). How Can the Mind Participate in Communication? In W. Rasch (Ed.), *Theories of Distinction: Redescribing the Descriptions of Modernity* (pp. 169–184). Stanford, CA: Stanford University Press.

Luhmann, N. (2012). *Theory of Society, Vol. 1*. Stanford, CA: Stanford University Press.

Luukkonen, T. (1997). Why has Latour's theory of citations been ignored by the bibliometric community? Discussion of sociological interpretations of citation analysis. *Scientometrics, 38*(1), 27–37.

MacKay, D. M. (1969). *Information, Mechanism and Meaning*. Cambridge and London: MIT Press.

McGill, W. J. (1954). Multivariate information transmission. *Psychometrika, 19*(2), 97–116.

Nicolaisen, J. (2007). Citation analysis. *Annual review of information science and technology, 41*(1), 609–641.

Nöth, W. (2014). Human Communication from the Semiotic Perspective. In T. Dousa & F. Ibekwe-SanJuan (Eds.), *Theories of Information, Communication and Knowledge* (pp. 97–119). Dordrecht: Springer.

Otte, E., & Rousseau, R. (2002). Social network analysis: a powerful strategy, also for the information sciences. *Journal of Information Science, 28*(6), 441–453.

Padgett, J. F., & Powell, W. W. (2012). The Problem of Emergence. *The Emergence of Organizations and Markets* (pp. 1–32). Princeton, NJ: Princeton University Press.

Parsons, T. (1951). *The Social System*. New York: The Free Press.
Parsons, T. (1968). Interaction: I. Social Interaction. In D. L. Sills (Ed.), *The International Encyclopedia of the Social Sciences* (Vol. 7, pp. 429–441). New York: McGraw-Hill.
Parsons, T., & Shils, E. A. (1951). *Toward a General Theory of Action*. New York: Harper and Row.
Popper, K. R. ([1935] 1959). *The Logic of Scientific Discovery*. London: Hutchinson.
Popper, K. R. (1972). *Objective Knowledge. An Evolutionary Approach*. Oxford: Oxford University Press.
Rip, A. (1981). A cognitive approach to science policy. *Research Policy, 10*(4), 294–311.
Shannon, C. E. (1948). A Mathematical Theory of Communication. *Bell System Technical Journal, 27*, 379–423 and 623–656.
Shannon, C. E., & Weaver, W. (1949). *The Mathematical Theory of Communication*. Urbana: University of Illinois Press.
Simon, H. A. (1973). The Organization of Complex Systems. In H. H. Pattee (Ed.), *Hierarchy Theory: The Challenge of Complex Systems* (pp. 1–27). New York: George Braziller Inc.
Strand, Ø., & Leydesdorff, L. (2013). Where is Synergy in the Norwegian Innovation System Indicated? Triple Helix Relations among Technology, Organization, and Geography. *Technological Forecasting and Social Change, 80*(3), 471–484.
Strydom, P. (1999). Triple Contingency: The theoretical problem of the public in communication societies. *Philosophy & Social Criticism, 25*(2), 1–25.
Theil, H. (1972). *Statistical Decomposition Analysis*. Amsterdam/ London: North-Holland.
Ulanowicz, R. E. (1986). *Growth and Development: Ecosystems Phenomenology*. San Jose, etc.: toExcel.
Ulanowicz, R. E. (2009). The dual nature of ecosystem dynamics. *Ecological modelling, 220*(16), 1886–1892.
van den Daele, W., & Weingart, P. (1975). Resistenz und Rezeptivität der Wissenschaft—zu den Entstehungsbedingungen neuer Disziplinen durch wissenschaftliche und politische Steuerung. *Zeitschrift für Soziologie, 4*(2), 146–164.
Vlieger, E., & Leydesdorff, L. (2011). Content Analysis and the Measurement of Meaning: The Visualization of Frames in Collections of Messages. *The Public Journal of Semiotics, 3*(1), 28.
Von Foerster, H. (2003). On Self-Organizing Systems and Their Environments *Understanding Understanding: Essays on Cybernetics and Cognition* (pp. 1–19). New York: Springer.
Weaver, W. (1949). Some Recent Contributions to the Mathematical Theory of Communication. In C. E. Shannon & W. Weaver (Eds.), *The Mathematical Theory of Communication* (pp. 93–117.). Urbana: University of Illinois Press.
Weinstein, F., & Platt, G. M. (1969). *The Wish to be Free: Society, Psyche, and Value Change*. Berkeley: University of California Press.
Whitley, R. D. (1984). *The Intellectual and Social Organization of the Sciences*. Oxford: Oxford University Press.
Woolgar, S. (1991). Beyond the citation debate: towards a sociology of measurement technologies and their use in science policy. *Science and Public Policy 18*(5), 319–326.
Wouters, P. (1998). The signs of science. *Scientometrics, 41*(1), 225–241.
Wouters, P. (1999). *The Citation Culture*. Amsterdam: Unpublished Ph.D. Thesis, University of Amsterdam.
Yeung, R. W. (2008). *Information Theory and Network Coding*. New York, NY: Springer.

Michael Ginda, Andrea Scharnhorst, and Katy Börner
Modeling the Structure and Dynamics of Science Using Books

1 Introduction

Scientific research is a major driving force in a knowledge-based economy. Income, health, and well-being depend on scientific progress. The better we understand the inner workings of the scientific enterprise, the better we can prompt, manage, steer, and utilize scientific progress. Diverse indicators and approaches exist to evaluate and monitor research activities—from calculating the reputation of a researcher, institution, or country to analyzing and visualizing global brain circulation. However, there are very few predictive models of science that are used by key decision makers in academia, industry, or government interested in improving the quality and impact of scholarly efforts.

Other scientific communities rely extensively on predictive models to simulate events such as weather, seismic hazards (UNAVCO Facility, 2010), or epidemics (Colizza et al., 2006). Recent efforts have sought to forecast science and technology in the form of an "innovation accelerator" (Van Harmelen et al., 2012). However, the heterogeneous and proprietary datasets required to model science remain scattered, cultures of algorithm and model sharing are slow to evolve, and a unified theory that interlinks validated models of science does not yet exist.

According to the Oxford English Dictionary (2002), the term model may function as: a representation of structure or system; an object of imitation; and a type and design. The latter two definitions of model are used to indicate an object's status as an exemplar meant to be imitated or a prototype to be copied and are irrelevant for what is discussed in this chapter. The first function, i.e., a representative model, is the focus here and may either describe a targeted system or phenomena (e.g., a science model); represent a broader theoretical interpretation of the laws, axioms, and models of a discipline (e.g., a model of science); or perform both functions simultaneously (Frigg & Stephan, 2012).

In this chapter—building on prior work (Scharnhorst et al., 2012)—we define a model of science as "a systematic description of an object or phenomenon that shares important characteristics with its real-world counterpart and supports its detailed investigation" (Börner et al., 2012a, p. 1). Models of science put forward a theoretical and/or empirical understanding with predictive power and are validated based on the accuracy of their predictions. Focusing on scientific models of science, we purposefully exclude anecdotal evidence and narratives, e.g., the analysis of science fiction literature to identify possible future developments (Steinmueller, 2010). Instead, we focus on models of science that explain and help to predict the activities of scholars (also called authors, researchers, scientists) because they are the generators of ideas and innovation—papers don't write papers, authors do (Cronin, 2005)—and it is scholars who collaborate and read and write papers leading to the diffusion of ideas, knowledge, innovations, and the "making of science" (Cronin, 2008).

The remainder of the chapter is organized as follows. The next section discusses challenges and opportunities when attempting to delineate and map the space of existing models of science. Subsequently, we present a novel "bibliographic-bibliometric" analysis which we apply to a large collection of books relevant for the modeling of science—we explain the data collection together with the results of the data analyses and visualizations. In the final section we discuss how the analysis of books that describe different modeling approaches can inform the design of new models of science.

2 Prior Work: Context and Focus

Models of science are developed in many scientific disciplines and use different (mathematical) approaches and terminology that are difficult, if not impossible, to align across disciplinary boundaries.

Descriptive models of science can be found in philosophy of science, history of science, sociology of science, and science and technology studies—in short, in all those areas of social sciences and humanities which have knowledge production as their object of study. Bernal's encyclopedic work, "The Social Function of Science" (1939, 1967), has influenced many of those reflecting about science in a systematic manner (Garfield, 2007). Since 1981, the Society for Social Studies of Science[1] awards the *John Desmond Bernal Prize* annually to scholars that have made a distinguished contribution to the field. The first three award recipients were Derek de Solla Price (1981), Robert K. Merton (1973), and Thomas S. Kuhn and their books—*Little Science, Big Science* (Price, 1963), *The Sociology of Science* (Merton, 1973), and *The Structure of Scientific Revolutions* (Kuhn, 1962)—are included in this analysis.

Predictive models of science (computational and mathematical) are developed in scientometrics, bibliometrics, system dynamics, physics, mathematics, and, more recently, in a new branch of philosophy of science and cognition

---

[1] http://4sonline.org/

(Payette, 2012). One of the first predictive models was introduced by Goffman—he used a model originally developed to predict the spread of diseases to describe the spreading of ideas (Goffman & Nevill 1964; Goffman 1966; Harmon 2008). The so-called SIR model orders researchers in three categories: the number of researchers 'susceptible' to a new idea but not yet infected with it (S), the number of 'infected' researchers (I), and the number of 'recovered' researchers (R) who lost interest and will not return to the idea. The model presumes that boundaries of scientific fields and/or invisible colleges (Crane, 1972) can be defined. Goffman's work showcases the complex relationship between mathematical and theoretical models, and empirical validation. Using Goffman's model, it is possible to define the probability that a researcher will become 'infected' with an idea and the predicted growth rate of a new scientific field can be compared with the actual growth rate (Wagner-Döbler, 1999) (see also Lucio-Arias and Scharnhorst [2012] for a review). However, case studies have demonstrated that it is difficult to validate all processes inscribed in Goffman's model (Burger & Bujdoso, 1985).

There are very few comparisons of existing models or attempts to combine multiple models to arrive at a more holistic understanding of the structure and dynamics of science. The isolation of mathematical models was demonstrated in an empirical study of journals using Lotka (1926), Price (1965; 1976), and Goffman (1966) as models (Lucio-Arias & Scharnhorst, 2012). Textbooks that provide an overview of different types of models can only be written if an acknowledged and shared body of validated models exists—which is not yet the case, though an inventory of models in certain domains has been attempted, e.g., see Scharnhorst et al. (2012) and Schulze (2014).

As with any system, there are many different ways one can study and model the science system: e.g., from the perspective of the cognitive structure (Collins, 1988); political-economic base (Nowotny et al., 2005); institutions, politics, and social actors (Gibbons et al. 1994); or communications (Kaufer & Carley 1993). Those cognizant of the problems of studying science are scattered across multiple domains, all of which have their own epistemological and methodological emphases. There are few who try to bridge between different epistemic perspectives, and even fewer who reflect about science in a wider historic context of knowledge production. Among them, Blaise Cronin stands out as a scholar able to play on all strings of the harp of scientific reflection about science. He looks at current forms of scholarly communication from a macro perspective which encompasses scholarship from the Enlightenment to Force11 (Cronin & Sugimoto, 2014). His early book *The Citation Process* (1984) called for a study of science as a social system taking into account "norms and values which guide and constrain the actions of individual scientists" (p. 1).

It is from a broad perspective that we evaluate and describe the relationships among books on the topic of models of science. World Cat data[2] of library catalog records and subject headings plus library classification codes were used to identify a set of relevant books, to identify major topical clusters, and to show interlinkages. The resulting semantic networks were then explored to determine the spheres of influence, relevance, and context around specific sets of books on models of science, subject headings, and library classification codes.

3 Bibliographic-Bibliometric Data Collection and Analysis

Currently there exists neither a "Models of Science" handbook nor a comprehensive annotated bibliography. A search for "models of science", "models of science dynamics", "modeling processes of science", "modeling of scholarly communication", or similar phases using any major citation index is of limited value when aimed at identifying relevant literature. Our starting point is the collection *Models of Science Dynamics* (Scharnhorst et al., 2012), which presents a review of major types of and applications for models of science. While this book does not claim to cover all relevant works across the landscape of science, the authors of each chapter reviewed a specific branch of models of science developed in different areas of science. Using references to books on modeling science, library classification data and subject headings can be retrieved and used to map the evolving topical space in which models of science are researched and developed.

3.1 Identification of Relevant Books

To map the concept "model of science", a book list was generated using the references from the *Models of Science Dynamics* (Scharnhorst et al., 2012). Using a bibtex file that captured all 589 references cited in the book, 196 citations were identified as book references. Two additional books were added: the *Models of Science Dynamics* (2012) book itself and the book *The Web of Knowledge: A Festschrift*

---

[2] World Cat is a database managed by the Online Computer Library Center (OCLC) that collects library catalog records from around the world into a single information resource discovery system. http://www.worldcat.org

in Honor of Eugene Garfield (2000), edited by Blaise Cronin and Helen Barsky Atkins.

3.2 Identification of Associated World Cat Subject Headings

The resulting list of 198 books was then searched in World Cat to collect all English language subject terms and to determine the accuracy of the document type. Twenty-one titles were removed from the seed list for three reasons: (a) the citation was not a book [e.g., conference proceedings that were not published as a book, and therefore not cataloged (9), journal articles (3), or self-published program instruction manuals (4)]; (b) the book reference lacked subject headings in English (4); or (c) the book reference duplicated a book in the data (1). For the frequency distribution of the final 177 titles by type—*book, ebook, incollection,* and *inproceedings*[3]—see Table 1.

For a distribution of all 198 book titles and the 177 final books references per publication year (binned by 5-years) see Figure 1. Most of the cited books in *Models of Science Dynamics* were published between 2001 and 2005 (bin label 2005). This age-distribution for cited work is in line with other studies on obsolescence of literature (Lariviére et al., 2008), but could also signal the relative youth of the domain of science modeling.

Tab. 1: Number of reference types of book titles.

Initial Reference Types		Final Reference Types	
article	3	Book	147
book	151	Ebook	1
ebook	1	Incollection	18
electronic (handbook)	1	inproceedings	11
incollection	21		
inproceedings	21		
Grand Total	**198**		**177**

---

[3] Each citation collected for this analysis had a bibtex category assigned that defined its genre. The categories include: *article* indicates that a citation is an article published in a *book* and *ebook* that indicate that a citation is either a book or an electronic book without a print publication; *electronic (handbook)* indicates that a citation is for software tool handbooks; *inproceedings* indicates that a citation was published in a conference proceeding rather than a book; last, the category *incollection* indicates that a citation is chapter included a multi-author or edited book.

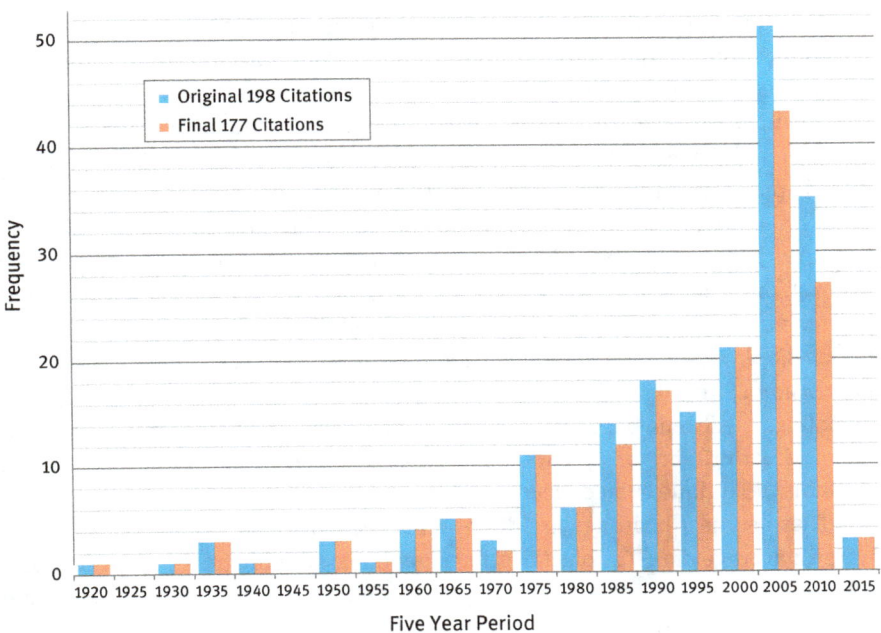

Fig. 1: Number of initial 198 (blue) and final 177 book titles (red) per publication year.

The bibliographic record for books in World Cat contains, among others, a field called *subject*. This field contains the *subject headings, genre terms and forms, and unindexed subject keywords* attributed to a book by a librarian or cataloguer when the book is purchased and added to the collection of a library. Modern information systems may allow librarians to identify already attributed subject headings for a work, and wide-spread bibliographic classification systems as Dewey, Unified Decimal Classification, and Library of Congress lead to some standardization. Still, libraries have idiosyncratic classification schemes and indexing practices, whereby a number of distinct subject headings can be assigned to the same item.

To harvest the various subject headings, we selected "View all editions and formats" in the publically displayed bibliographic records on World Cat. Collecting from all unique editions of a book allowed us to gather the full variety and scope of subjects assigned by catalogers around the globe. This method provided a substantial number of different subject headings for each book and all distinct terms per book were identified using a semi-automatic process.

The collected subject headings were then normalized for spelling, topicality, and relevance. The initial list of 1313 subject headings for all 177 books was consolidated into a list of 876 unique subject headings after removing duplicate occurrences. The unique subject headings were refined a second time to combine related topics and remove extraneous headings. Subject headings were *combined* if: the subject varied in spelling or punctuation (e.g., *Biology – Mathematical models*[4] also includes *Biology/Mathematical model*); the subject heading contained a designation of the type of material (e.g., *Biology – Mathematical models – Textbooks* would appear under *Biology – Mathematical models*), geographic region (e.g., *Alcoholism and crime – Wales – Cardiff* is grouped with *Alcoholism and crime*), or temporally (e.g., *Economic history – 16th century* would appear under *Economic history*); or the subject headings were topically similar enough that a work could be found using the chosen variant (e.g., *Biophysics/Biomedical Physics* is grouped under *Biophysics*; *Comprehension (Theory of knowledge)* is grouped under *Comprehension*). Subject headings were *removed* if they described the materiality of a book (e.g., electronic book), a geographic place without a proceeding topic (e.g., Japan, Great Britain), or were the name of a researcher (e.g., Lotka). The final list contains 675 unique subject headings.

These subject headings are distributed unevenly over the 177 books: there were an average of 6.31 subject headings per book, ranging from 1 to 31. A book's set of subject headings indicate the topics that indexers and catalogers determine are coextensive to the work, i.e., the concepts that most accurately represent a book's subject. Coextensive subject headings indicate a co-occurrence relationship between concepts. The co-occurrence of subject headings have been used to identify inter-index consistency and to map concept-spaces based on indexer perceptions of subject headings (Olson & Wolfram, 2008; Gabel & Smiraglia, 2009). Within this analysis, the co-occurrence of subject headings across multiple books is used as a proxy measure of the relationships between science domains.

3.3 Identification of Associated Library of Congress Classification Codes

Using the Library of Congress online catalog,[5] the Library of Congress Classification (LCC) shelf numbers[6] were collected for 171 books (six books did not have LCC such numbers). The number of books and the number of subject headings for each of the nine LCC classes is given in Table 2. For example, seven of the

---

[4] Throughout the text, book subject heading are *italicized;* subject heading domains groups are **bold**.
[5] Library of Congress Online Catalog http://catalog.loc.gov/vwebv/searchAdvanced
[6] Library of Congress Classification codes http://www.loc.gov/catdir/cpso/lcc.html

Tab. 2: Library of Congress Classifications and Respective Book and Subject Heading Counts.

Library of Congress Classification	Book Count	Subject Heading Count
B – Philosophy, Psychology, Religion	**7**	**36**
B – Philosophy – General	2	12
BF – Psychology	2	12
BC – Logic	1	7
BD – Speculative philosophy	1	4
BJ – Ethics	1	1
H – Social Science	**63**	**429**
HM – Sociology	18	155
HB – Economic Theory, Demography	15	75
H – Social Sciences – General	9	52
HD – Industries, Land use, Labor	8	68
HC – Economic history and conditions	4	30
HV – Sociology – Social pathology ...	3	21
HQ – Sociology – The family ...	2	8
HA – Statistics	2	6
HF – Commerce	1	9
HG – Finance	1	5
J – Political Science	**1**	**10**
JN – Political Institutions ...	1	10
L – Education	**2**	**25**
LC – Special Aspects of Education	2	25
Q – Science	**77**	**563**
Q – Science – General	38	253
QH – Natural History, biology	15	141
QA – Mathematics	13	98
QC – Physics	7	50
QP – Physiology	2	13
QD – Chemistry	1	4
QL – Zoology	1	4
R – Medicine	**2**	**23**
RC – Internal Medicine	1	12
RA – Public Aspects of medicine	1	11
T – Technology	**10**	**121**
T – Technology – General	5	42
TK – Electrical Engineering ...	4	65
TA – Engineering – Civil Engineering	1	14
U – Military Science	**1**	**8**
UG – Military Engineering, Air forces	1	8
Z – Bibliography. Library Science ...	**8**	**63**
Z – Books (General), Writing ...	7	56
ZA – Information resources	1	7
Books without LCC Codes	**6**	**27**
Total	**177**	**1305**

171 books have been classified under **B – Philosophy, Psychology, Religion**. How these seven books and their subject headings distribute over the next level in the classification is also shown in the table. That is, the table interlinks LCC classes to books and subject headings. Note that different subject headings might appear simultaneously in different LCC classes.

LCC numbers were then used to define a crosswalk of LCC classes to a wider scientific domain coding system (Table 3). We use the thirteen major scientific disciplines identified in the UCSD Map of Science (Börner, et al., 2012b) as a proxy for upper-level knowledge organization. For example, **QH, QP, QL** are assigned to **Biology**. Four domains from the UCSD map did not appear in the LCC codes: **Health Professionals, Infectious Diseases, Biotechnology**, and **Earth Sciences**. **Earth Sciences** was given a code because it could not be subsumed under a secondary code; **Biotechnology** was grouped with **Biology, Health**

Tab. 3: LCC class and science domain code crosswalk, with related book counts.

Code	Domain	LCC Class	Book Count	Notes
0	Science General	Q	37	Subjects that can be applied across domains.
1	Biology	QH, QP, QL	18	UCSD domain Biotechnology grouped here.
2	Medical Specialties	R (all)	2	UCSD domains Health Professionals grouped here.
3	Engineering	T, TA, UG	5	LCC class T is split between code 3 and 6.
4	Chemistry	QD	1	
5	Earth Science	–	0	
6	Electrical Engineering & Computer Science	T, TK, Z, ZA	14	Library and Information Science included
7	Brain Research	BC	1	Cognitive Science and Psychology
8	Humanities	B, BD, BF, BJ, LC	8	History, Philosophy, Education
9	Math & Physics	QA, QC	20	
10	Social Sciences	H (all), JN	65	Sociology, Economics, Business, etc. UCSD Infectious Diseases grouped here.

Professionals with **Medicine**, and infectious diseases with **Epidemiology** in the **Social Sciences**. A **Science General** category was also added to categorize subjects that either could be applied across domains (e.g., the subject heading Research is coded zero) or relates a specific domain's study of science broadly (e.g., **Science – social aspects** is coded zero and twelve to indicate connection between social science and the general study of science).

The division of domains within LCC classes does not align cleanly with the domains identified in the UCSD map. In particular, **Social Science** books are dispersed across and combined within LCC class divisions, while works related to modern technology are classified within the general **Technology** class. This is not unusual—classification and knowledge organization systems have a history within, and moreover are tailored towards, the collection for which they are designed (Smiraglia, 2014).

We then applied the same domain coding system to assign the book subject headings a scientific domain using a common code book. Each subject heading was assigned one to two of the eleven domain codes shown in Table 3. A subject heading's domain code was identified by analyzing its topic coverage and the LCC number(s) assigned to the book(s) using the particular subject heading. The goal of coding subject headings in this manner is to see where topics (as expressed by subject headings broadly) overlap across domains and disciplines. We treat subject headings as terms of a controlled vocabulary. Individually, or in combination with one another, they characterize a topic. Domain codes were applied in an as needed fashion; some subject headings have only one associated domain and secondary domain codes were only made when the subject is studied across multiple domains. Subject headings with broad application were mapped into the domain code zero. The resulting code matrix is unbalanced because some subject headings were given both a primary code for a domain most associated with a subject and a secondary code indicating the second domain associated with a subject. Likewise, many subjects were not coded twice.

The result of these multiple mappings is a co-occurrence of domains by the number of subject headings associated with both domains related to books on modeling science (Table 4).

Of the 675 unique subject headings, 317 subjects were coded with one domain. Conversely, 358 subject headings were assigned two domain codes as they were either complex subject headings, multiple concepts and domains imbedded in them (e.g., the subject heading *Science – Psychological aspects* would be coded for **Science (General)** and **Psychology**) or a subject heading topic was associated with multiple domains (e.g., the subject *Social Networks* is a methodology used within the **Electrical Engineering & Computer Science** and **Social Sciences** domains). The subject *Communication in science – Data processing* was coded **Science (Gen-**

Tab. 4: Cross tabulation of domain codes assigned to book subject headings.

Domain Name	Domain Code	0	1	2	3	4	6	7	8	9	10	Single Domain Code	Grand Total
Science (General)	0		1			1			2	6	15	17	42
Biology	1	2		3		3			4	13	3	23	51
Medicine	2	4							2	4		3	13
Engineering	3					1			2	5	6	5	19
Chemistry	4		1	2						3		6	12
Earth Science	5	3								2		0	5
Elect. Eng. & Comp. Science	6	3			6				1	23	29	56	118
Brain Research	7	1	7			1			5	2	24	9	49
Humanities	8	2	1			3				1	15	10	32
Math & Physics	9	2	4	1	7	2	14		1		10	61	102
Social Sciences	10	5	5				23	1	50	21		127	232

eral) and **Electrical Engineering & Computer Science** because *Communication in science* could refer to research by any number of domains, while the secondary topic *Data processing* is a topic most relevant to **Information and Computer Science**.[7]

The domains of **Social Sciences** (sociology, economics), **Math & Physics**, and **Computer and Information Science** are most strongly associated with subject headings from the 171 books, followed by **Biology, Psychology**, and general science domains. Domains with the most domain intersections are bolded in Table 4: **Social Sciences** and **Humanities** (50); **Electrical Engineering & Computer Science** and **Social Sciences** (29); **Brain Research** and **Social Sciences** (24); **Electrical Engineering & Computer Science** and **Math & Physics** (23); **Social Sciences** and **Electrical Engineering & Computer Science** (23); **Social Sciences** and **Math & Physics** (21). Please note that these intersections are created by the content of our specific set of books. In other words, books relevant to modeling science combine knowledge between social sciences, mathematics

---

[7] Throughout the text, book subject heading are *italicized*; subject heading domains groups are **bold**.

(and physics), computer and information science. This also suggests that to be able to study models of science, readers and authors needs to be familiar with several areas of research.

4 Topical Space of Books Relevant for Modeling Science

Using the data detailed in the previous section, different topical spaces can be extracted, analyzed, visualized, and interpreted.

4.1 Major Subject Headings Linked to Books

To understand the topical space of books and subject headings, a bipartite network of the 177 books and their 675 subject headings was extracted. The resulting network has 852 nodes—too many to depict in a network layout in letter size. Using the Science of Science tool (Sci2)[8] and the Gephi[9] graph visualization platform, the network was analyzed to identify all subject nodes with an out-degree (i.e., number of linked books) greater than five, and all their associated books. The resulting network has 19 subject nodes and was laid out in a two dimensional space using a force-directed layout (Figure 2).

Subject heading nodes are colored pink and labeled by subject headings; the nodes for the 177 books are green and labeled with book titles. For the 19 subject heading nodes, node and label size increases and color darkens as the out-degree increases from six to 21. For book title nodes, the node and label size and the color are scaled according to the number of unique subject headings associated with a book title in the original network. Node labels are truncated to improve the readability of the graph.

Overall, the network shows that the high-degree subject headings and associated books cover a wide range of modeling approaches developed in diverse disciplines of science. *Science* characterizes many of the books, and its subcategories *Science – Social Aspects* and *Science – Philosophy* play a major role. We also see "Mathematics" and "Mathematical models". Specific areas in mathematical modeling emerge: *System Theory*, *Game Theory*, models of *Evolution* and *Social Networks*. Another set of subject headings describes research areas that inspired

---
8 http://sci2.cns.iu.edu
9 http://gephi.org

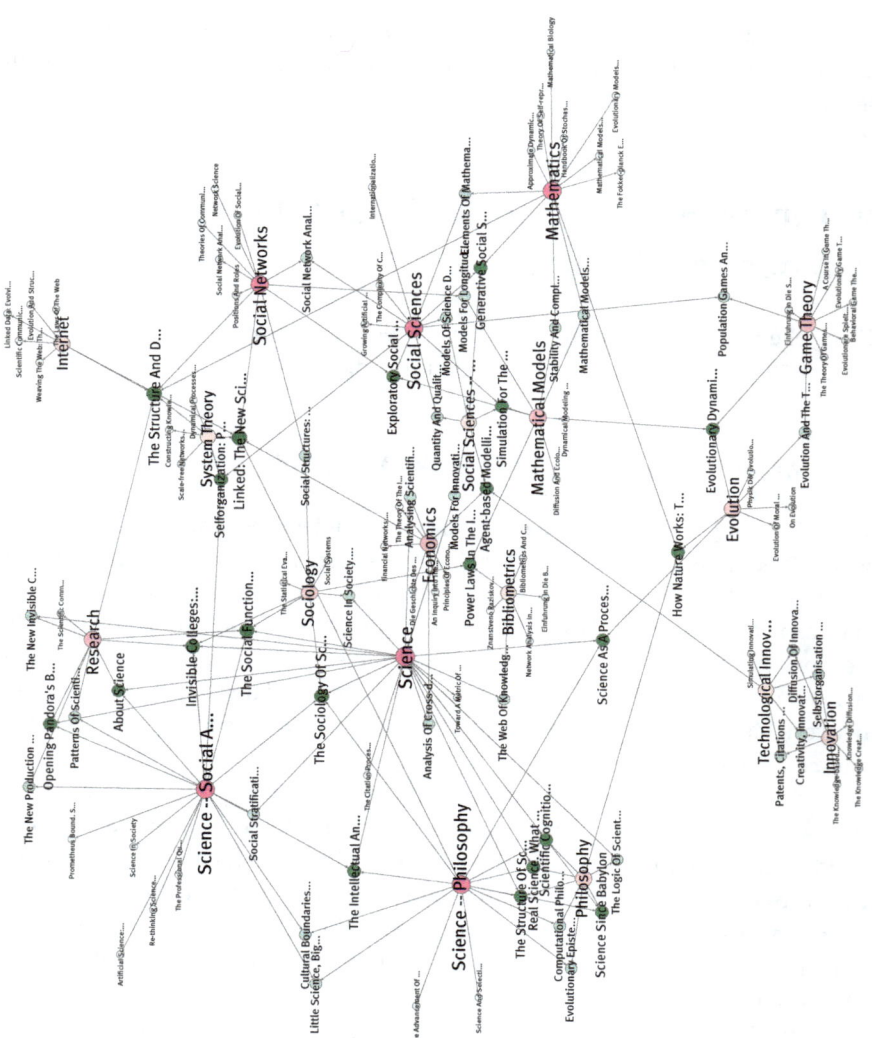

Fig. 2: Bimodal network of high-degree subject heading nodes (in pink) linked to associated book nodes (in green). See website at http://cns.iu.edu/2015-ModSci.html for a high-resolution, searchable pdf file.

new mathematical models of science to answer questions related to the process of knowledge production, e.g., *Innovation, Communication, Internet,* and *Bibliometrics*. While most books are associated with only one subject heading, some books are associated with many areas. Among them is *The Structure and Dynamics of Networks* (Newman et al., 2006) which introduces the highly interdisciplinary, emerging area of network science to a broad audience. Usually, books belonging to the same epistemic thread are connected to the same subject headings. For instance, Per Bak's *How Nature Works* (1996) is linked to the subject node *Evolution* which contains other books that discuss evolution from the perspective of physics (physics of self-organization), game theory (evolutionary game theory), or biology. One of them is the German title *Physik der Evolutionsprozesse* (Ebeling et al., 1990)—a linkage that would be difficult to identify using linguistic analysis or citation-based analysis. Those two books belong to one research stream within statistical physics. Some titles do not deal with science specifically, but describe methods that can be applied to describe and model complex phenomena such as the science system itself. Only a close inspection of the content of the books can reveal this similarity, yet subject headings and library classification codes can be used to identify key linkages.

Figure 3 shows the same network using the very same node positions. However, the Blondel community detection[10] algorithm (Blondel et al., 2008) was applied randomly using a resolution parameter of 0.9. The networks modularity was measured to be 0.643. The communities detected in this network represent the major areas of research on models of science discussed in *Modelling Science Dynamics* (Scharnhorst et al., 2012), including, philosophy of science and knowledge (teal), science studies (yellow), innovation and communication in science (pink), economics and social sciences (purple), mathematical models (lime green), bibliometrics and information science (Kelly green), evolution and game theory (light blue), and computer science (blue).

The science studies community encompasses books from science and technology studies, such as the *New Production of Knowledge* by Gibbons et al. (1994), the classics *Invisible Colleges* by Crane (1972) from the sociology of science, as well as *The New Invisible College* by Wagner (2008) from bibliometrics. Also "Science" as general subject heading is put into this community. Note that *The Web of Knowledge: A Festschrift in Honor of Eugene Garfield*, edited by Blaise Cronin and Helen Barsky Atkins (2000) (indicated by a red dotted frame) bridges two major communities relevant to study science: the community of science studies "Science" and the community of "Bibliometrics".

---

10 The Blondel community detection algorithm partitions a network into communities based on the density of links in a network. A node's membership in a Blondel community is determined by its relationship to other nodes. Nodes are more likely to link to members within their community, than link to those outside of their communities. The algorithm detects and partitions communities based on the relative density of the relationship between nodes in a given network.

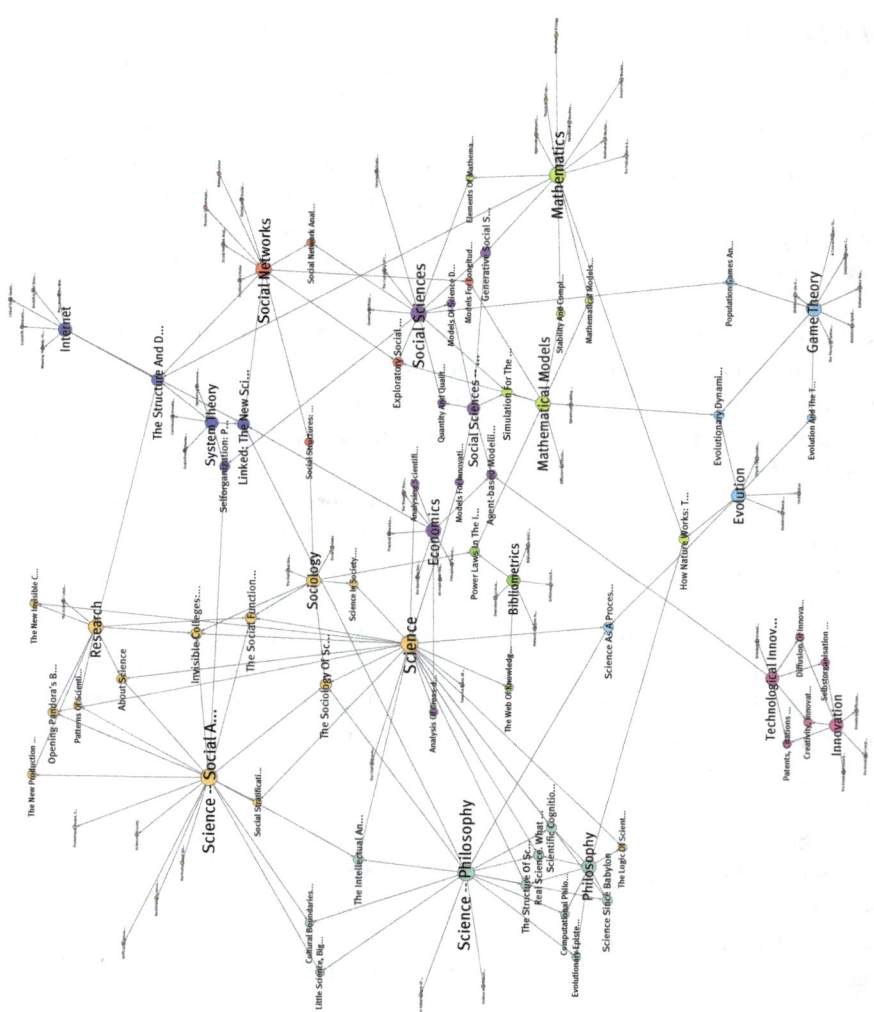

Fig. 3: Bimodal network of high-degree subject heading nodes linked to associated book nodes and colored by Blondel communities. See website at http://cns.iu.edu/2015-ModSci.html for a high-resolution, searchable pdf file.

As in Figure 2, the different subject headings are grouped by *disciplines*, *methods*, and *perspectives*. The community detection algorithm and coloring groups different subject headings, e.g., *Science – Philosophy* and *Philosophy*. It also makes visible how aggregations of subject headings are interlinked, e.g., *Mathematical Models* and *Mathematics* are closely interlinked with *Social Sciences*.

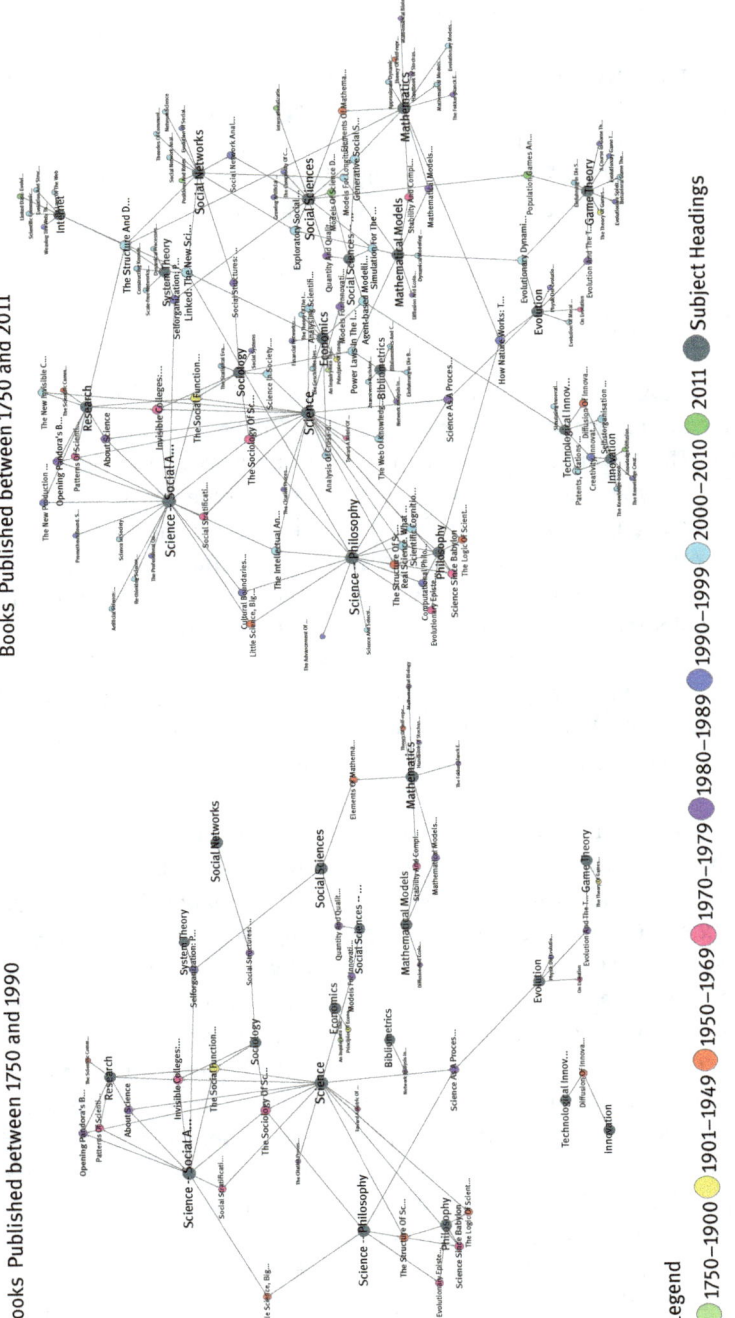

Fig. 4: Temporal comparison of networks by book publication date for period between 1990 and 2011. See website at http://cns.iu.edu/2015-ModSci.html for a high-resolution, searchable pdf file.

Figure 4 shows how the topic space of models of science has developed over time. We use the publication date of the different books (first print) and color coded book nodes by binned years. Books published between 1750 and 1990 are given on the left-hand side. 18 of the 19 subject headings are shown—only *Internet* is missing. Several books are not yet published. The full network is given on the right hand side—with book nodes colored by year bins. Early books in yellow and later books in cyan and green can be easily identified.

5 Limitations

A closer examination of *Models of Science Dynamics* (Scharnhorst et al., 2012) reveals some limitations of the present approach. The book is divided into three major parts: The "Foundations" includes two introductory chapters; the "Exemplary Model Types" part introduces three different types of models such as epidemics models, agent-based models, and game theoretic models; the "Exemplary Model Applications" section showcases the application of different models to study collaboration and citation networks. The chapters are written by author teams from different scientific disciplines and they cite different areas of work. Fourteen books are cited in more than one chapter or in the Foreword (FW) or Preface (PF) (Table 5). Among the books listed in Table 3, Kuhn's *Structure of Scientific Revolution* (1962) stands out, followed by Price *Little Science, Big Science* (1963). Although written in the 1960s, both still inspire today's modeling science efforts.

Figures 2–4 present only nine of the listed books as the other five are not connected to the highly interlinked 19 subject headings. For example, the *Atlas of Science* (Börner, 2010) has subject headings: *Classification of sciences – Atlases, Science – Atlases, Communication in science – Data processing, Digital mapping*. Only *Science – xxx* occurs in the network shown in Figures 2–4. However, the subject *Science – Atlas* was not merged under the term Science in the initial subject heading aggregation process and hence the book does not show in the figures.

Subject headings indicate multiple aspects of the topics covered in a work. Complex subject headings may be used to combine multiple topical subjects into one or to combine topical subjects with a specific methodology; temporal period and era; the material, format, and genre; or geographic regions and languages of a work. Many subject heading schemes have a hierarchical structure, e.g., a subject term has parent and child terms, or is a composite of two parent terms with two facets of co-equal status. In other words, there are relationships between subjects, books and classification schemes that are currently not utilized in this initial anal-

Tab. 5: Listing of books that are cited by more than one chapter, the Foreword, or Preface.

Title of the book (authors)	Year	Chapters*
The Theory of Games and Economic Behaviour (Von Neumann, Morgenstern)	1944	2,5
Human Behaviour and the Principle of Least-Effort (Zipf)	1949	1,3
The Structure of Scientific Revolutions (Kuhn)	1962	FW,PF,1,2,3,6
Little Science, Big Science and Beyond (Price)	1963	FW,PF,1,3,4,6
Invisible colleges: Diffusion of knowledge in scientific communities. (Crane)	1972	FW,1,6
The sociology of science: Theoretical and empirical investigations (Merton)	1973	PF,1,6
Matematicheskie modeli v issledovanii nauki (Yablonsikii)	1986	PF,FW
Introduction to informetrics: quantitative methods in library, documentation and information science (Egghe & Rousseau)	1990	FW,2,3
The New Production of Knowledge. The Dynamics of Science and Research in Contemporary Societies. (Gibbons et al.)	1994	1,6
Social network analysis: Methods and applications (Wasserman & Faust)	1994	6,7
Growing artificial societies: social science from the bottom up (Epstein & Axtell)	1996	2,4
Linked: The New Science of Networks (Barabási)	2002	PF,2,6
Evolution and structure of the Internet: A statistical physics approach (Pastor-Satorras & Vespignani)	2004	2,7
Atlas of Science: Visualizing What We Know (Börner)	2010	FW,PF,8

* PF = Preface, FW = Foreword

ysis. A follow-up study could refine links between books, classification schemes, and domains by using both topical and methodological subject headings.

There are also problems connected with the context-richness of subject headings. One problem is the vagueness of compound subject terms. Subjects headings like "Data processing", "Methodology", and "Research" can describe many ideas and techniques. However, compound subjects can allow for the collection of thematically related materials for later comparison. More specific methodological subjects, like network analysis, may be used to compare the use of a method or technique across disciplines.

While the bibliographic-bibliometric method proposed and exemplified here benefits from the collective wisdom of indexers, it also comes with its own caveats.

However, the resulting analyses and visualizations can be used to gain a new, more comprehensive understanding of the richness of scientific disciplines, methods, and perspectives as captured in books.

6 Conclusions

The edited book *Models of Science Dynamics* provided a review of major models of science for an expert audience (Scharnhorst et al., 2012). This chapter introduced and exemplified a novel means to construct the topical or concept space in which works on models of science are situated by using key books, library subject headings, and classification codes. Specifically, this chapter *extends* existing methods of bibliometric analysis of classification systems to subject headings, which come from multiple controlled vocabularies. We implemented a method to identify and classify both LC classifications and subject headings within a common framework of scientific domains to facilitate comparative analysis.

Our method, as applied to subject headings, is unique in that it reveals a degree of cross-domain pollination of concepts and method that is not captured with LCC numbers. While LCC numbers reveal the most unique domain associated with a work, our analysis of subject headings reveal the interlocking domains used to create models of science.

The bibliographic-bibliometric analysis of existing models of science provides a first depiction of major *disciplines*, *methods*, and *perspectives*. The study also highlights challenges and opportunities that arise when books, cataloging data, and subject headings are used in delineating and mapping a domain. It is our hope that this study inspires future reviews, exemplifications, and discussions of models of science developed in different scientific disciplines. Future work might expand this bibliographic-bibliometric analysis beyond books, e.g., to journal publications, course content, and/or encyclopedias. It might attempt to generate cross-walks between science, engineering, education, and other classification systems and taxonomies that define and organize different model types. Likely, challenges encountered in the work presented here will persist—document titles and author names are non-unique, the terminology used differs considerably among the different disciplines, and among catalogers.

Most relevant to the present volume, this work depicts the landscape of models of science by identifying key works and visualizing the relationships among these works. Starting with the references in one book on models of science (Scharnhorst et al., 2012), a landscape unfolds as diverse and broad as the table of contents in Bernal's book (Bernal, 1939). However, a comparison of the headings of Bernal's book and the dominant subject headings in Figure 3 reveals an important difference. The structure of Bernal's book reads like a *what-to-be-modeled* list. Examples are organization (*The existing organization of research in Britain*), scientific practices (*The efficiency of scientific research*), scientific careers (*The training of the scientist*), and globalization (*International science*). In turn, the dominant subject headings form a checklist of necessary dimensions or ingredients for a *good* model of science, a *how-to-model* list. Such a model would need to address the epistemic foundations of science (*Science Philosophy*), its social structure (*Science Social*), its relations to innovations and economic growth (*Innovation*), and aspects of its networked nature (*Systems theory, Social Networks, Internet*). Taken together, these depictions provide science modelers with holistic orientation to begin their work.

Acknowledgment

We would like to thank Cassidy Sugimoto for inspiring and editing this Festschrift and for her editorial comments. We thank David Kloster for his help collecting and coding subject heading data. Allyson Carlyle, Alexander Petersen, Richard Smiraglia, and Nicolai Vitanov provided expert comments on an earlier version of this chapter. The Sci2 Tool used in this study was developed by Chin Hua Kong, Adam Simpson, Steven Corenflos, Joseph Biberstine, Thomas G. Smith, David M. Coe, Micah W. Linnemeier, Patrick A. Phillips, Chintan Tank, and Russell J. Duhon. The Sci2 Tool uses the Cyberinfrastructure Shell (http://cishell.org) developed at the Cyberinfrastructure for Network Science Center (http://cns.iu.edu) at Indiana University. This work was partially funded by the National Institutes of Health under awards NIA P01AG039347 and U01 GM098959; and partly funded by the COST Action TD1210 KnowEscape.

Cited References

Bak, P. (1996). *How nature works: The science of self-organized criticality*. Copernicus, New York, NY.

Barabási, A. L. (2002) *Linked: The new science of networks*. Perseus Publishing, Cambridge, MA.

Bernal, J. D. (1939, 1967). *The social function of science*. Cambridge: MIT Press.

Blondel, V., Guillaume, J., Lambiotte, R., & Lefebvre, E. (2008). Fast Unfolding of Communities in Large Networks. *Journal of Statistical Mechanics* P10008. DOI:10.1088/1742-5468/2008/10/P10008

Börner, K. (2010). *Atlas of science: Visualizing what we know*. Cambridge, MA: MIT Press.

Börner, K., Boyack, K., Milojevic, S., & Morris, S. (2012a). An Introduction to Modeling Science: Basic Model Types, Key Definitions, and a General Framework for the Comparison of Process Models. In *Models of Science Dynamics: Encounters between Complexity Theory and Information Sciences*, edited by Scharnhorst, Andrea, Katy Börner, and Peter van den Besselaar, Ch. 1. Springer Verlag.

Börner, K., Klavans, R., Patek, M., Zoss, A., Biberstine, J., Light, R., Larivière, V., & Boyack, K. (2012b). Design and Update of a Classification System: The UCSD Map of Science. *PLoS ONE*, 7(7), e39464. DOI:10.1371/journal.pone.0039464

Carrington, P. J., Scott, J., & Wasserman, S. (2005). *Models and Methods in Social Network Analysis*. Cambridge University Press.

Colizza, V., Barthélemy, M., & Vespignani, A. (2006). The Role of the Airline Transportation Network in the Prediction and Predictability of Global Epidemics. *PNAS*, 103(7), 2015–2020.

Collins, R. (1998). *The sociology of philosophies: A global theory of intellectual change*. Cambridge, Massachusetts; London, England: The Belknap Press of Harvard University Press.

Crane, D. (1972). *Invisible colleges: Diffusion of knowledge in scientific communities*. Chicago, IL: University of Chicago Press.

Cronin, B. (1984). *The citation process: The role and significance of citations in scientific communication*. London: T. Graham.

Cronin, B. (2005). *The hand of science: Academic writing and its rewards*. Lanham, MD: Scarecrow Press.

Cronin, B. (2008). The sociological turn in information science. *Journal of Information Science*, 34(4), 465–475. DOI:10.1177/0165551508088944

Cronin, B. & Atkins, H. B. (2000). *The web of knowledge: A festschrift in honor of Eugene Garfield*. Medford, NJ: Information Today.

Cronin, B. & Sugimoto, C. R. (Eds.) (2014). *Beyond bibliometrics: Harnessing multidimensional indicators of scholarly impact*. Cambridge, MA: The MIT Press.

Ebeling, W., Engel, A., & Feistel, R. (1990). *Physik der Evolutionsprozesse*. Akademie-Verlag, Berlin.

Egghe, L., Rousseau, R. (1990) *Introduction to informetrics: Quantitative methods in library, documentation and information science*. Elsevier Science Publishers, Amsterdam.

Epstein, J. M. & Axtell R. (1996) *Growing artificial societies: Social science from the bottom up*. Complex Adaptive Systems. Brookings Institution Press, Washington, DC; Cambridge, MA: MIT Press.

Frigg, R. & Stephan, H. (2012). Models in Science. *The Stanford Encyclopedia of Philosophy* (2012 ed.). (Reprinted from: Fall 2012).

Gabel, J. & Smiraglia, R. P. (2009). Visualizing similarity in subject term co-assignment. In M. Breitenstein and C. L. Loschko (Eds.), *Bridging Worlds, Connecting People: Classification Transcending Boundaries—Proceedings of the 20th SIG/Classification Research Workshop, November 7, 2009*. Retrieved from https://journals.lib.washington.edu/index.php/acro/article/download/12886/11382

Garfield, E. "Tracing the influence of J. D. Bernal on the World of Science through Citation Analysis" Paper presented at the British Association for Crystal Growth/Irish Association for Crystal Growth Conference & Bernal Symposium on Protein Crystallization, University College Dublin, Belfield, Ireland. September 3–4, 2007. Unpublished manuscript, on-line

http://garfield.library.upenn.edu/papers/bernaldublin0907.pdf. Accessed January 27, 2015.
Gibbons, M., Limoges, C., Nowotny, H., Schwartzman, S., Scott, P., & Trow, M. (1994). *The new production of knowledge: the dynamics of science and research in contemporary societies.* London: Sage.
Goffman, W. & Newill, V. A. (1964). Generalization of epidemic theory: An application to the transmission of ideas. *Nature, 204*(4955):225–228 (DOI: 10.1038/204225a0)
Goffman, W. (1966). Mathematical approach to the spread of scientific ideas – the history of mast cell research. *Nature,* 212(5061), 449–452. DOI: 10.1038/212449a0.
Harmon, G. (2008). Remembering William Goffman: Mathematical information science pioneer. *Information Processing & Management, 44*(4), 1634–1647. DOI: 10.1016/j.ipm.2007.12.004
Kaufer, D. S. & Carley, K. M. (1993). *Communication at a distance: The influence of print on sociocultural organization and change.* Hillsdale, NJ: Lawrence Erlbaum Associates.
Kuhn, T. S. (1962). *The structure of scientific revolutions.* Chicago: University of Chicago Press.
Larivière, V., Archambault, É., & Gingras, Y. (2008). Long-term variations in the aging of scientific literature: From exponential growth to steady-state science (1900–2004). *Journal of the American Society for Information Science and Technology, 59*(2): 288–296. http://lariviere.ebsi.umontreal.ca/Publications/JASIST_Aging.pdf
Lotka, A. J. (1926). "The frequency distribution of scientific productivity". *Journal of the Washington Academy of Sciences, 16*(12), 317–324.
Lucio-Arias D. & Scharnhorst A. (2012). Mathematical approaches to modeling science from an algorithmic-historiography perspective. In: Scharnhorst A, Börner K, van den Besselaar P (eds) *Models of science dynamics.* Springer, Berlin, Ch. 2, pp. 23–66.
Merton, R. K. (1973). *The sociology of science: Theoretical and empirical investigations.* Chicago: University of Chicago Press.
Newman, M. E. J., Barabasi, A. L., & Watts, D. J. (2006). *The structure and dynamics of networks.* Princeton Studies in Complexity. Princeton, NJ: Princeton University Press.
Nowotny, H., Pestre, D., Schmidt-Assman, E., Schulze-Fielitz, H., & Trute, H. (2005). *The public nature of science under assault: Politics, markets, science and the law.* Berlin: Springer.
Olson, H. A. & Wolfram, D. (2008). Syntagmatic relationships and indexing consistency on a larger scale. *Journal of Documentation, 64*(4), 602–615.
Oxford English Dictionary. (2002). *"model, n. and adj.":* Oxford University Press.
Pastor-Satorras, R., & Vespignani, A. (2004). *Evolution and structure of the Internet: A statistical physics approach.* Cambridge University Press, Cambridge (DOI: 10.1017/CBO9780511610905).
Payette, N. (2012). Agent-based models of science. In: Scharnhorst A, Börner K, van den Besselaar P (eds) *Models of science dynamics.* Springer, Berlin, Ch 4, pp. 127–158.
Price, D. (1965). Networks of scientific papers. Science 149(3683):510–515. (DOI:10.1126/science.149.3683.510). Reprinted in: Price DJ de Solla (1986) *Little science, big science ... and beyond.* Columbia University Press, New York, NY, pp. 103–118.
Price, D. J. S. (1963). *Little science, big science and beyond.* New York: Columbia Univ. Press.
Price, D. J. S (1976). A general theory of bibliometric and other cumulative advantage processes. *J Am Soc Inf Sci* 27(5):292–306 (DOI: 10.1002/asi.4630270505), also available online at the URL: http://www.asis.org/Publications/JASIS/Best_Jasist/1976pricejasistarticle.pdf

Scharnhorst, A., Börner, K., & Besselaar, P. (Eds.). (2012). *Models of Science Dynamics: Encounters between Complexity Theory and Information Science*. Springer Verlag.

Schulze, F. (2014). Classification and development of mathematical models and simulation for industrial ecology. *Open Access Master's Theses*. University of Rhode Island. Paper 367. http://digitalcommons.uri.edu/theses/367

Smiraglia, R. (2014). *The Elements of Knowledge Organization*. Berlin: Springer.

Steinmüller, K. (2010). Science Fiction – Eine Quelle von Leitbildern für Innovationsprozesse und ein Impulsgeber für Foresight. In: Hauss, K.; Ulrich, S.; Hornbostel, S. (Eds) (2010). *Foresight – between science and fiction*. iFQ Working paper No. 7, Bonn 2010. Available http://www.forschungsinfo.de/publikationen/Download/working_paper_7_2010.pdf

UNAVCO Facility. (2014). *Jules Map Server Home Page*. Accessed September 5, 2014. http://jules.unavco.org

Van Harmelen, F., Kampis, G., Börner, K., van den Besselaar, P., Schultes, E., C. Goble, C., P. Groth, P., B. Mons, B., Anderson, S., Decker, S., Hayes, C., Buecheler, T., & Helbing, D. (2012). Theoretical and technological building blocks for an innovation accelerator. *EPJ Special Topics* 214: 183–214.

Von Neumann J. & Morgenstern O. (1944). *Theory of games and economic behavior*. Princeton, NJ: Princeton University Press.

Wagner, C. S. (2008). *The new invisible college: Science for development*. Washington, DC: Brookings Institution Press.

Wagner-Döbler, R. (1999). William Goffman's "Mathematical approach to the prediction of scientific discovery" and its application to logic, revisited. *Scientometrics*, 46(3), 635–645. DOI: 10.1007/BF02459617

Wasserman S. & Faust K. (1994). *Social network analysis: Methods and applications*. Structural Analysis in the Social Sciences, Vol. 8. Cambridge University Press, Cambridge.

Yablonskii, A. I. (1986). *Matematicheskie modeli v issledovanii nauki*. Moscow: Nauka.

Zipf, G. K. (1949). *Human behavior and the principle of least effort: An introduction to human ecology*. Cambridge, MA: Addison-Wesley Press.

Appendix A

Amann, E. (1999). *Evolutionäre Spieltheorie: Grundlagen und neue Ansätze*. Studies in Contemporary Economics. Physica-Verlag, Heidelberg.

Axelrod, R. (1997). *The complexity of cooperation: Agent-based models of conflict and cooperation*. Princeton Studies in Complexity. Princeton University Press, Princeton, NJ.

Bak, P. (1996). *How nature works: The science of self-organized criticality*. Copernicus, New York, NY.

Barabasi, A. L. (2002). *Linked: The new science of networks*. Perseus Publishing, Cambridge, MA.

Barnes, B. (1985). *About Science*. Oxford: Basil Blackwell. Oxford.

Barrat, A., Barthélemy, M., Vespignani, A. (2008). *Dynamical processes on complex networks*. Cambridge University Press, Cambridge (DOI:10.1017/CBO9780511791383).

Barro, R. J., Sala-i-Martin, X. (2004). *Economic growth*. 2nd ed. MIT Press, Cambridge, MA.

Bartholomew, D. J. (1982). *Stochastic models for social processes*. 3rd ed. Wiley Series in Probability and Mathematical Statistics. Applied Probability and Statistics. Wiley, Chichester.

Becker, G. S. (1996). *Accounting for tastes*. Harvard University Press, Cambridge, MA.

Berg, C. (2005). *Vernetzung als Syndrom. Risiken und Chancen von Vernetzungsprozessen für eine nachhaltige Entwicklung*. Campus: Forschung, Vol. 883. Campus Verlag, Frankfurt am Main.

Bernal, JD. (1939). *The social function of science*. George Routledge & Sons, London.

Berners-Lee, T., Fischetti, M. (1999). *Weaving the web: The original design and ultimate destiny of the World Wide Web by its inventor*. Harper, San Francisco, SF.

Börner, K. (2010). *Atlas of science: Visualizing what we know*. The MIT Press, Cambridge, MA.

Bourdieu, P. (1986). Forms of capital. In: Richardson JG (Ed) *Handbook of theory and research for the sociology of education*. Greenwood, New York, NY, pp. 241–258.

Brauer, F., Castillo-Chavez, C. (2001). *Mathematical models in population biology and epidemiology*. Texts in Applied Mathematics, Vol. 40. Springer, New York, NY.

Bryman, A. (1988). *Quantity and quality in social research*. Contemporary Social Research Series, Vol. 18. Unwin Hyman, London.

Bucchi, M. (2004). *Science in society: An introduction to social studies of science*. Routledge, London. Revised and expanded ed. of: Bucchi, M. (2002). *Scienza e Società: Introduzione alla sociologia della scienza*. Il Mulino, Bologna.

Budd, T. (2003). *Alcohol related assault*. London: Home Office.

C. T. J. Flood-Page (Ed.). (2003). *Crime in England and Wales 2001/2002: Supplementary Volume*. Home Office Statistical Bulletin 01/03. London: Home Office.

Caldarelli, G. (2007). *Scale-free networks: Complex webs in nature and technology*. Oxford Finance Series. Oxford University Press, Oxford.

Camerer, C. (2003). *Behavioral game theory experiments in strategic interaction*. New York [u. a.]: Russell Sage [u. a.].

Campbell, D. T. (1974). Evolutionary epistemology. In: Schilpp, P. A. (Ed.) *The philosophy of Karl Popper*. The Library of Living Philosophers, Vol. 14. Open Court Publishing, La Salle, IL.

Carrington, P. J., Scott, J., & Wasserman, S. (2005). Models and Methods in Social Network Analysis. Cambridge University Press.

Carruthers, P., Stich, S., Siegal, M. (Eds.) (2002). *The cognitive basis of science*. Cambridge University Press, Cambridge, pp. 285–299 (DOI: 10.1017/CBO9780511613517.016).

Chapman, R. N. (1931). *Animal ecology*. McGraw Hill, New York, NY, pp. 409–448.

Cole, S. & Cole, J. R. (1973). *Social stratification in science*. University of Chicago Press, Chicago, IL.

Coleman, J. S. (1964). *An introduction to mathematical sociology*. Free Press, New York, NY; Collier-Macmillan, London.

Committee on Network Science for Future Army Applications NRC. (2005). *Network science*. The National Academies Press, Washington, DC, available online at the URL: http://www.nap.edu/catalog.php?recordid=11516

Crane, D. (1972). *Invisible colleges: Diffusion of knowledge in scientific communities*. University of Chicago Press, Chicago, IL.

Cressman, R. (2003). *Evolutionary dynamics and extensive form games*. Economic Learning and Social Evolution, Vol. 5. MIT Press, Cambridge, MA.

Cronin, B. (1984). *The citation process. The role and significance of citations in scientific communication*. Taylor and Graham, London.

Cronin, B., & Atkins, H. B. (2000). *The web of knowledge: A festschrift in honor of Eugene Garfield*. Medford, N.J: Information Today.

Dasgupta, P. & Stoneman, P. (Eds.). (1987). *Economic policy and technological performance*. Cambridge University Press, Cambridge.

Davis, J. B. (2003). *The theory of the individual in economics: Identity and value*. Routledge Advances in Social Economics. Routledge, London (DOI: 10.4324/9780203457689).

De Bellis, N. (2009). *Bibliometrics and citation analysis: From the Science Citation Index to cybermetrics*. Scarecrow Press, Lanham, MD.

Dolfsma, W. (2008). *Knowledge economies: Organization, location and innovation*. Routledge Studies in Global Competition, Vol. 39. Routledge, London.

Dopfer, K. (2001). *Evolutionary economics: program and scope*. Kluwer Academic Publishers, Boston.

Doreian, P. & Stokman, F. N. (Eds.). (1997). *Evolution of social networks*. Gordon and Breach, Amsterdam; Routledge, London.

Doreian, P., Batagelj, V., Ferligoj, A. (2005). *Generalized blockmodeling*. Structural Analysis in the Social Sciences, Vol. 25. Cambridge University Press, Cambridge (DOI: 10.1017/CBO9780511584176).

Douvan, E. & Adelson, J. (1966). *The Adolescent Experience*. New York: John Wiley & Sons, Inc.

Durkheim, E. (1947). *The Division of Labor in Society*. Glencoe, IL: Free Press.

Ebeling, W. & Parthey, H. (Eds.). (2009). Selbstorganisation in Wissenschaft und Technik. Wissenschaftsforschung Jahrbuch 2008. Verlag Berlin, Berlin.

Ebeling, W., Engel, A., Feistel, R. (1990). *Physik der Evolutionsprozesse*. Akademie-Verlag, Berlin.

Edelstein-Keshet, L. (1988). *Mathematical models in biology*. The Random House/Birkhäuser Mathematics Series. Random House, New York, NY.

Edmonds, B., Troitzsch, K. G., Iglesias, C. H. (Eds.). (2007). *Social simulation: Technologies, advances and new discoveries*. IGI Global, Hersey, PA.

Egghe, L. & Rousseau, R. (1990). *Introduction to informetrics: Quantitative methods in library, documentation and information science*. Elsevier Science Publishers, Amsterdam.

Egghe, L. (2005). *Power laws in the information production process: Lotkaian informetrics*. Library and Information Science, Vol. 5. Elsevier Academic Press, Amsterdam, available online at the URL: http://www.emeraldinsight.com/books.htm?issn=1876-0562&volume=05

Elkana, Y., Lederberg, J., Merton, R. K., Thackray, A. (Eds.). (1978). *Toward a metric of science: The advent of science indicators*. Science, Culture and Society. Wiley, New York, NY.

Epstein, J. M. & Axtell, R., (1996) *Growing artificial societies: Social science from the bottom up*. Complex Adaptive Systems. Brookings Institution Press, Washington, DC; MIT Press, Cambridge, MA.

Epstein, J. M. (1997). *Nonlinear dynamics, mathematical biology, and social science*. Santa Fe Institute Studies in the Sciences of Complexity. Lecture Note Volume 4. Addison-Wesley, Reading, MA.

Epstein, J. M. (2006). *Generative social science: Studies in agent-based computational modeling*. Princeton Studies in Complexity. Princeton University Press, Princeton, NJ.

Etzkowitz, H. & Leydesdorff, L. (Eds.). (2001). *Universities and the global knowledge economy: A triple helix of university-industry-government relations*. Science, Technology and the International Political Economy. Pinter, London.

Field, R. J., Burger, M. (Eds.). (1985). *Oscillations and traveling waves in chemical systems*. Wiley, New York, NY, pp. 565–604.

Fladung, R. B. (2007). *Scientific Communication. Economic Analysis of the Electronic Journal Market* Ibidem Press.

Foray, D. (2004). *The economics of knowledge.* MIT Press, Cambridge, MA. Revised and extended translation of: Foray D (2000) *L'conomie de la connaissance.* La Decouverte, Paris.

Freeman, L. C. (2004). *The Development of Social Network Analysis: A Study in the Sociology of Science.* Empirical Press, London.

Fuchs, S. (1992). *The professional quest for truth: A social theory of science and knowledge.* Albany: State University of New York Press.

Gardiner, C. W. (1983). *Handbook of stochastic methods for physics, chemistry and the natural sciences.* Springer Series in Synergetics, Vol. 13. Springer-Verlag, Berlin.

Garfield, E. (1979). *Citation indexing: Its theory and application in science, technology, and humanities.* Information Sciences Series. John Wiley, New York, NY.

Gause, G. F. (1934). *The struggle for existence.* Williams and Wilkins, Baltimore, MD.

Gibbons, M., Limoges, C., Nowotny, H., Schwartzman, S., Scott, P., Trow, M. (1994). *The new production of knowledge: The dynamics of science and research in contemporary societies.* Sage Publications, London.

Gieryn, T. F. (1999). *Cultural Boundaries of Science: Credibility on the Line.* Chicago, IL: University of Chicago Press.

Gilbert, G. N. & Mulkay, M. J. (1984). *Opening Pandora's Box: A sociological analysis of scientists' discourse.* Cambridge University Press, Cambridge.

Gilbert, G. N. & Troitzsch, K. G. (2005). *Simulation for the social scientist.* 2nd ed. Open University Press, Maidenhead.

Glimcher, W. P. (2009). *Neuroeconomics: Decision making and the brain* (1 ed.). Amsterdam: Academic Press.

Greiner, W. (1989a). *Quantum Mechanics.* Springer. Berlin.

Greiner, W. (1989b). *Thermodynamics and Statistical Physics.* Springer. Berlin.

Hadzikadic, M. & Carmichael, T. (Eds.). (2009). *Complex adaptive systems and the threshold effect: Views from the natural and social sciences: Papers from the AAAI Fall Symposium, November 5 7, 2009, Arlington, Virginia.* AAAI Technical Report FS-09-03. The AAAI Press, Menlo Park, CA.

Hagstrom, W. (1965). *The Scientific Community.* New York: Basic Books.

Hargens, L. L. (1975). *Patterns of scientific research.* American Sociological Association.

Havemann, F. (2009). *Einführung in die Bibliometrie.* Gesellschaft für Wissenschaftsforschung, Berlin, available online at the URL: http://edoc.hu-berlin.de/oa/books/reMKADKkid1Wk/PDF/20uf7RZtM6ZJk.pdf

Hayashi, N., Jajima, K., Bock, H. H., Ohsumi, N., Tanaka, Y., Baba, Y. (Eds.). (1998). *Data science, classification, and related methods: Proceedings of the fifth conference of the International Federation of Classification Societies (IFCS-96), 3 Kobe, Japan, March 27–30, 1996.* Studies in Classification, Data Analysis, and Knowledge Organization. Springer, Tokyo.

Heath, T. & Bizer, C. (2011). *Linked data: Evolving the web into a global data space.* Synthesis Lectures on the Semantic Web: Theory and Technology, Vol. 1. Morgan & Claypool, San Rafael, CA (DOI: 10.2200/S00334ED1V01Y201102WBE001).

Heise, D. R. (Ed.). (1975). *Sociological methodology 1976.* Jossey-Brass Publishers, San Francisco, CA.

Helbing, D., Herrmann, H. J., Schreckenberg, M., Wolf, D. E. (Eds.). (2000). *Traffic and granular flow' 99. Social, traffic and granular dynamics.* Springer, Berlin. Hodgson, G. M. (1993).

Economics and Evolution: Bringing Life back into Economics. The University of Michigan Press, Ann Arbor.

Hodgson, G. M. (1993). *Economics and Evolution: Bringing Life back into Economics*. The University of Michigan Press, Ann Arbor.

Hogg, A. (Ed.) (2003). Social identity sociological and social psychological perspectives. Washington, DC: American Sociological Assoc.

Holland, J. H. (1975). *Adaptation in natural and artificial systems: An introductory analysis with applications to biology, control, and artificial intelligence*. University of Michigan Press, Ann Arbor, MI.

Hornbostel, S. (1997). *Bewertungen in der Wissenschaft. Wissenschaftsindikatoren*. Westdeutscher Verlag, Opladen.

Huberman, B. A. (2001). The laws of the Web. MIT Press.

Hull, D. L. (1988). *Science as a process: An evolutionary account of the social and conceptual development of science*. Science and Its Conceptual Foundations. University of Chicago Press, Chicago, IL.

Hull, D. L. (2001). *Science and selection: Essays on biological evolution and the philosophy of science*. Cambridge Studies in Philosophy and Biology. Cambridge University Press, Cambridge.

Jaffe, A. B. & Trajtenberg, M. (Eds.). (2002). *Patents, citations and innovations: A window on the knowledge economy*. MIT Press, Cambridge, MA.

Joos, E., Zeh, H. D., Kiefer, C., Giulini, D., Kupsch, J., & Stamatescu, I. O. (2003). *Decoherence and the Appearance of a Classical World in Quantum Theory*. Springer.

Kagel, J. H., & Roth, A. E. (1995). *Handbook of Experimental Economics*. Princeton University Press.

Keynes, J. M. (1930). *A treatise on money*. 2 Volumes. Harcourt, Brace and Co., New York, NY. Reprinted in: Keynes, J. M. (1971, 1989 – 2nd ed.). *The collected writings of John Maynard Keynes: Volume V: A treatise on money: In two volumes: 1. The pure theory of money, Volume VI: A treatise on money: In two volumes: 2. The applied theory of money*. Macmillan, London.

Kitcher, P. (1995). *The Advancement of Science: Science Without Legend, Objectivity Without Illusions*. Oxford University Press US.

Krohn, W., Küppers, G., & Nowotny, H. (1990). *Selforganization: portrait of a scientific revolution*. Kluwer Academic, Dordrecht.

Krug, E. G., Dahlberg, L. L., Mercy, J. A., Zwi, A. B., & Lozano, R. (2002). World report on violence and health. Geneva: World Health Organization.

Kuhn, M., & Weidemann, D. (Eds.). (2010). *Internationalization of the Social Sciences*. Verlag, Bielefeld.

Kuhn, T. S. (1962). *The structure of scientific revolutions*. University of Chicago Press, Chicago, IL.

Latour, B., Woolgar, S. (1986). *Laboratory life: The social construction of scientific facts*. Princeton University Press, Princeton, NJ.

Leydesdorff, L. (1995). *The challenge of scientometrics: The development, measurement, and self-organization of scientific communications*. Science Studies/Wetenschapsstudies. DSWO Press, Leiden University, Leiden.

Leydesdorff, L. (2006). *The knowledge-based economy: Modeled, measured, simulated*. Universal Publishers, Boca Raton, FL.

Liotta, G. (Ed.). (2004). *Graph drawing: 11th international symposium, GD 2003, Perugia, Italy, September 21–24,2003: Revised papers*. Lecture Notes in Computer Science, Vol. 2912. Springer, Berlin.

Lotka, A. J., & James, A. (1956). *Elements of mathematical biology*. Dover Publications.

Luhmann, N. (1990). *Die Wissenschaft der Gesellschaft*. Suhrkamp, Frankfurt am Main.

Luhmann, N. (1995). *Social systems*. Stanford University Press, Stanford, CA. Translation of: Luhmann, N. (1984). *Soziale Systeme: Grundriß einer allgemeinen Theorie*. Suhrkamp, Frankfurt am Main.

Luke, S. (2010). *Essentials of metaheuristics*. Lulu, available online for free at the URL: http://cs.gmu.edu/sean/book/metaheuristics

Ma, Z. & Li, J. (Eds.). (2009). *Dynamical modeling and analysis of epidemics*. World Scientific, Singapore, available online at the URL: http://ebooks.worldscinet.com/ISBN/9789812797506/9789812797506.html

Maguire, M. & Nettleton, H. (2003). *Reducing alcohol-related violence and disorder: an evaluation of the "TASC" project*. London: Home office Research, Development and Statistics Directorate.

Mahajan, V. & Peterson, R. A. (1985). *Models for innovation diffusion*. Quantitative Applications in the Social Sciences, Vol. 48. Sage Publications, Beverly Hills, CA.

Malthus, T. R. (1798). *An essay on the principle population as it affects the future improvement of society with remarks on the speculations of Mr. Godwin, M. Condorcet and other writers*. Johnson, London.

Marshall, A. (1920). *Principles of economics: An introductory volume*. 8th ed. McMillan, London, available online ((1907) 5th ed.) at the URL: http://www.archive.org/details/principlesofecon01marsuoft

Matthew, D. (2005). *Science in society*. Palgrave Macmillan, Basingstoke.

Matthies, M., Malchow, H., Kriz, J. (Eds.). (2001). *Integrative systems approaches to natural and social dynamics*. Springer, Berlin.

May, R. M. (1974). *Stability and complexity in model ecosystems*. 2nd ed. Monographs in Population Biology, Vol. 6. Princeton University Press, Princeton, NJ.

McClelland, J. L. & Rumelhart, D. E. (1987). *Parallel distributed processing: Explorations in the microstructure of cognition. Volume 2: Psychological and biological models*. Computational Models of Cognition and Perception. A Bradford book. MIT Press, Cambridge, MA.

Merton, R. K. (1973). *The sociology of science: Theoretical and empirical investigations*. Chicago: University of Chicago Press.

Moed, H. F., Glänzel, W., Schmoch, U. (Eds.). (2004). *Handbook of quantitative science and technology research: The use of patent and publication statistics in studies on S&T systems*. Kluwer Academic Publishers, Dordrecht.

Monge, P. R. & Contractor, N. S. (2003). *Theories of communication networks*. Oxford University Press, USA.

Morone, P. & Taylor, R. (2010). *Knowledge diffusion and innovation: Modelling complex entrepreneurial behaviours*. Edward Elgar Publishing Inc., Northampton, MA.

Murray, J. D. (1989). *Mathematical biology*. Biomathematics, Vol. 19. Springer, Berlin.

Nagurney, A. & Siokos ,S. (1999). *Financial networks: Statics and dynamics*. Advances in Spatial Science. Springer, Berlin.

Newman, M. E. J., Barabasi, A. L., Watts, D. J. (2006). *The structure and dynamics of networks*. Princeton Studies in Complexity Princeton University Press, Princeton, NJ.

Nicolis, G. & Prigogine, I. (1977). *Self-organization in nonequilibrium systems: From dissipative structures to order through fluctuations*. John Wiley, New York, NY.

Nonaka, I. & Takeuchi, H. (1995). *The knowledge creating company: How Japanese companies create the dynamics of innovation*. Oxford University Press, Oxford.

Nooy, W. de, Mrvar, A., & Batagelj, V. (2005). *Exploratory Social Network Analysis with Pajek*. Cambridge: Cambridge University Press.

Nowotny, H., Scott, P., Gibbons, M. (2001). *Re-thinking science: Knowledge and the public in an age of uncertainty*. Polity Press, Cambridge.

Odum, E. P. (1959). *Fundamentals of Ecology*. W. B. Saunders, Philadelphia, PA.

Okubo, A. (1980). *Diffusion and ecological problems: Mathematical models*. Biomathematics, Vol. 10. Springer, Berlin. Extended translation of: Okubo, A. (1975). *Seitaigaku to kakusan*. Tukijishokan, Tokyo.

Osborne, M. J., & Rubinstein, A. (1994). *A course in game theory*. MIT Press, Cambridge, Massachusetts.

Pach, J. (Ed.). (2005). *Graph drawing: 12th international symposium, GD 2004, New York, NY, USA, September 29-October 2, 2004: Revised selected papers*. Lecture Notes in Computer Science, Vol. 3383. Springer, Berlin.

Pastor-Satorras, R, Vespignani, A. (2004). *Evolution and structure of the Internet: A statistical physics approach*. Cambridge University Press, Cambridge (DOI: 10.1017/CBO9780511610905).

Plesk, P. E. (1997). *Creativity, innovation and quality*. ASQ Quality Press, Milwaukee, WI.

Popper, K. R. (1959). *The logic of scientific discovery*. Hutchison, London. Translation of: Popper, K. (1935). *Logik der Forschung: Zur Erkenntnistheorie der modernen Naturwissenschaft*. Schriften zur Wissenschaftlichen Weltauffassung, Vol. 9. Julius Springer, Wien.

Powell, W. B. (2007). *Approximate dynamic programming: Solving the curses of dimensionality*. Wiley Series in Probability and Statistics. Wiley-Interscience, Hoboken, NJ.

Price, D. J. de Solla. (1961). *Science since Babylon*. Yale University Press, New Haven, CT.

Price, D. J. de Solla. (1963). *Little science, big science*. Columbia University Press, New York, NY.

Putnam, R. D., Leonardi, R., Nanetti, R. Y. (1993). *Making democracy work: Civic transitions in modern Italy*. Princeton University Press, Princeton, NJ.

Pyka, A. & Scharnhorst, A. (Eds.). (2009). *Innovation Networks. New Approaches in Modelling and Analyzing*. Springer Complexity: Understanding Complex Systems. Springer, Dordrecht.

Pyka, A. Küppers, G. (Eds.). (2002). *Innovation networks: Theory and practice*. New Horizons in the Economics of Innovation. Edward Elgar Publishing, Cheltenham.

Reboiras, F. D., Varneda, P. V., & Walter, P. (2002). Arbor scientiae: Der Baum des Wissens von Ramon Lull: Akten des Internationalen Kongresses aus Anlass des 40-jährigen Jubiläums des Raimundus-Lullus-Institut der Universität Freiburg i. Br. Brepols.

Rennard, J.(Ed.). (2007). *Handbook of research on nature-inspired computing for economics and management*. Idea Group Reference, Hershey, PA.

Risken, H. (1984). *The Fokker-Planck equation: Methods of solution and applications*. Springer Series in Synergetics, Vol. 18. Springer-Verlag, Berlin.

Robertson, P. L. (Ed.). (1999). *Authority and control in modern industry: Theoretical and empirical perspectives*. Routledge Studies in Business Organization and Networks, Vol. 10. Routledge, London.

Rogers, E. (1962). *Diffusion of innovations*. The Free Press, New York, NY; Collier-MacMillan, London.

Romer, D. (1996). *Advanced macroeconomics*. McGraw-Hill, New York, NY.
Ruse, M. (Ed.) (2008). *Oxford Handbook on the Philosophy of Biology*. Oxford University Press, Oxford.
Sandholm, W. H. (2010). *Population games and evolutionary dynamics*. Economic Learning and Social Evolution. MIT Press, Cambridge, MA.
Savage, L. J. (1954). *The foundations of statistics*. Wiley.
Scharnhorst, A., Börner, K., & Besselaar, P. (Eds.). (2012). *Models of Science Dynamics: Encounters between Complexity Theory and Information Science*. Springer Verlag.
Schlee, W. (2004). *Einführung in die Spieltheorie: Mit Beispielen und Aufgaben*. Fried. Vieweg & Sohn Verlag, Wiesbaden.
Scott, J. P. (2000). *Social Network Analysis: A Handbook*. SAGE Publications. Retrieved from http://www.amazon.com/exec/obidos/redirect?tag=citeulike07-20&path=ASIN/076196339
Scott, J. P., Carrington (Eds.). (2011). Sage Handbook of Social Network Analysis. London: Sage, London.
Shrum, W., & Mullins, N. (1988). *Network analysis in the study of science and technology*. (A. van Ran, Ed.). Amsterdam: Elsevier.
Simon, H. A. (1957). *Models of man: Social and rational: Mathematical essays on rational human behaviour in a social setting*. John Wiley & Sons, New York, NY; Chapman & Hall, London.
Smith, A. (1776). *An inquiry into the nature and causes of the wealth of nations*. Strahan and Cadell, London. Reprint in Oxford University Press, Oxford 1993.
Smith, A. (2000). *The theory of moral sentiments*. Amherst, NY: Prometheus Books.
Smith, J. M. (1972). *On Evolution*. Edinburgh University Press, Edinburg.
Smith, J. M. (1982). *Evolution and the theory of games*. Cambridge University Press, Cambridge.
Sobel, M. E., Becker, M. P. (Eds.). (2001). *Sociological methodology: Volume 31: 2001*. Blackwell, Boston, MA.
Söllner, F. (2001). *Die Geschichte des ökonomischen Denkens*. Springer, Berlin.
Sorčan, S., Demšar, F., Valenci, T. (2008). *Znanstveno raziskovanje v Sloveniji?: primerjalna analiza. Ljubljana?*: Javna agencija za raziskovalno dejavnost Republike Slovenije.
Steuer, E. (1986). *Multiple Criteria Optimization: Theory, Computations, and Application*. Wiley Series in Probability and Mathematical Statistics John Wiley & Sons, Inc., New York, NY.
Sun, R. (2002). *Duality of the mind: A bottom-up approach toward cognition*. Lawrence Erlbaum Associates, Mahwah, NJ.
Tesfatsion, L., Judd, K. L. (Eds.). (2006). *Handbook of computational economics, Volume 2: Agent-based computational economics*. Handbooks in Economics, Vol. 13. North-Holland, Amsterdam.
Thagard, P. & Holyoak, K. (1985). Discovering the wave theory of sound: Inductive inference in the context of problem solving. In *Proceedings of the Ninth International Joint Conference on Artificial Intelligence* (pp. 610–612).
Thagard, P. (1993). *Computational philosophy of science*. A Bradford book. MIT Press, Cambridge, MA.
Tiit, E. M., Kollo, T., Niemi, H. (Eds.). (1995). New Trends in Probability and Statistics (Vol. 3, pp. 221–227). Vilnius, Lithuania: TEV and Utrecht, The Netherlands.
Toulmin, S. (1972). *Human understanding: The collective use and evolution of concepts*. Princeton University Press, Princeton, NJ.

van Kampen, N. G. (1981). *Stochastic processes in physics and chemistry*. North Holland Publishing Company, Amsterdam.
von Neumann, J. & Morgenstern, O. (1944). *Theory of games and economic behavior*. Princeton University Press, Princeton, NJ.
von Neumann, J. (1932). *Mathematische Grundlagen der Quantenmechanik*. Springer.
von Neumann, J. (1966). *Theory of self-reproducing automata*. (A. W. Burks, Ed.). University of Illinois Press.
Wagner, C. S. (2008). *The new invisible college: Science for development*. Brookings Institution Press, Washington, DC.
Wallerstein, I. (1974). *The Modern World System: Capitalist Agriculture and the Origins of the European World-Economy in the Sixteenth Century*. New York: Academic.
Wasserman, S. & Faust, K. (1994). *Social network analysis: Methods and applications*. Structural Analysis in the Social Sciences, Vol. 8. Cambridge University Press, Cambridge.
Watts, D. J. (2003). *Six degrees: The science of a connected age*. 1st ed. W. W. Norton & Company, New York, NY.
Weibull, J. (1995). *Evolutionary game theory*. The MIT Press, Cambridge, MA.
Wellman, B., & Berkowitz, S. D. (Eds.). (1988). *Social Structures: A Network Approach*. Cambridge: Cambridge University Press.
Whitley, R. (1984). *The intellectual and social organization of the sciences*. Oxford University Press, Oxford.
Yablonskiĭ, A. I. (1986). *Matematicheskie modeli v issledovanii nauki*. Nauka, Moscow.
Youniss, J. & Smollar, J. (1985). *Adolescent relations with mothers, fathers, and friends*. Chicago: University of Chicago Press.
Ziman, J. (1994). *Prometheus bound: Science in dynamic steady state*. Cambridge University Press, Cambridge.
Ziman, J. (2000). *Real science: What it is, and what it means*. Cambridge University Press, Cambridge (DOI: 10.1017/CBO9780511541391).
Zipf, G. K. (1949). *Human behavior and the principle of least effort: An introduction to human ecology*. Addison-Wesley Press, Cambridge, MA.

Part VI: **Altmetric theories**

Michael Thelwall
Webometrics and Altmetrics: Home Birth vs. Hospital Birth

1 Introduction

Almost two decades ago it became apparent that scientometric techniques that had been developed for citation databases could also be applied to the web. This triggered two reactions: optimism and pessimism. On the one hand, a number of optimistic articles were written by Ray Larson, Tomas Almind, Josep-Manuel Rodríguez-Gairín, Peter Ingwersen, Blaise Cronin, Judit Bar-Ilan, Isidro Aguillo, Lennart Björneborn, Alastair Smith, and Ronald Rousseau that described or developed new ways in which the web could be used for scientometrics. On the other hand, more critical articles were written by Anthony van Raan and Leo Egghe that focused on the problems that webometric methods were likely to face. This chapter argues that these two approaches represented different theoretical perspectives on scientometrics and that time has shown both to be valid. This chapter concludes by contrasting the academic literature that gave birth to webometrics with the coherent set of goals that announced altmetrics on a public website.

2 The Birth of Webometrics

Webometrics is an information science research field concerned with quantitative analyses of web data for various purposes. It was born from scientometrics, the quantitative analysis of science, with the realization that, using commercial search engines, some standard scientometric techniques could, and perhaps should, be applied to the web. The basic idea for webometrics apparently dawned on several people at almost the same time (Aguillo, 1998; Almind & Ingwersen, 1997; Cronin, Snyder, Rosenbaum, Martinson, & Callahan, 1998; Larson, 1996; Rodríguez-Gairín, 1997), although the most developed concept was that of Almind and Ingwersen (1997), who explicitly compared the web to traditional citation indexes and coined the term *webometrics*.

The idea driving the birth of webometrics was that many scientometric studies had analyzed information about sets of scientific documents extracted from a publication database or citation index, and that the same methods could be adapted for the web. For example, the productivity of one or more departments could be assessed by counting the number of documents produced by them, as recorded in an international scientific database, but on the web the number of web pages produced by them could also be counted, either directly or using an appropriate search engine query. Perhaps more usefully, evaluative scientometric studies often assessed the impact of the documents produced by one or more researchers by counting citations to them. On the web, the impact of collections of documents could be assessed to some extent by counting the number of hyperlinks pointing to them (Ingwersen, 1998). In addition, new types of study of scientific impact were possible with the web because of the increasingly many activities that were recorded online, such as for education, public engagement, and talks. Hence, for example, it might be possible to trace the wider impact of individual academics by counting and analysing how often they were mentioned online (Cronin et al., 1998).

There were two different reactions to the emergence of webometrics: enthusiasm and scepticism. The enthusiastic perspective described the range of studies that might be possible with webometrics and concentrated on its potential applications and strengths (Björneborn, & Ingwersen, 2001; Borgman, & Furner, 2002; Cronin, 2001; Leydesdorff, & Curran, 2000); the critical perspective instead emphasized the problems inherent in web data and focused on the limitations that webometric methods would necessarily face (Björneborn, & Ingwersen, 2001; Egghe, 2000; van Raan, 2001). Drawing from both strands, webometrics emerged as an empirical field that sought to identify limitations with web data, to develop methods to circumvent these limitations, and to evaluate webometric methods through comparisons with related offline sources of evidence (e.g., comparing counts of hyperlinks to journal websites with counts of citations to the associated journals), when possible (Bar-Ilan, 1999; Rousseau, 1999; Smith, 1999).

3 Webometric Theories

Like the mother field scientometrics, webometrics has not succeeded in creating a single unifying theory for its main tasks but it has produced a few theoretical contributions and one specific new theory. Within scientometrics, a detailed theory to deal with the practice of citation analysis has long been needed (Cronin, 1981), but has not been produced. Instead, practicing scientometricians draw upon a range of different theories (e.g., Merton, 1973; de Solla Price, 1976) and empirical evidence (Oppenheim, & Renn, 1978) about why people cite and the biases in citation analysis (e.g., Cronin, 1984) in order to effectively process and interpret citation data (van Raan, 1998). Within webometrics and altmetrics there are speculations about why people cite in the web as well as some empirical evidence, but both are weaker than for citation analysis.

Although early webometric papers were mainly quite theoretical in terms of discussing the potential for webometrics, the first major clearly articulated theoretical contribution to the mature field was an article that gave it a formal definition as "the study of the quantitative aspects of the construction and use of information resources, structures and technologies on the Web drawing on bibliometric and informetric approaches" (Björneborn 2004, p. vii), placed the name of the field within a research taxonomy, systematically named the main objects of study for link analysis, and introduced a standard diagram style for link networks (Björneborn & Ingwersen, 2004).

While no article has attempted to create a unifying theory of hyperlinks (or any other aspect of webometrics), a third article proposed a unifying "theoretical framework" for link analysis by specifying the stages that an effective link analysis would have to include, as follows:

1. Link interpretation is required in any link analysis exercise if conclusions are to be drawn about underlying reasons for link creation. An exception would be made for evaluative link analysis if it could be consistently demonstrated that inlink counts correlate with the phenomenon desired to be evaluated.
2. No single method for link interpretation is perfect. Method triangulation is required, ideally including a direct method and a correlation testing method.
3. Fundamental problems, including the "rich get richer" property of link creation and web dynamics, mean that definitive answers cannot be given to most research questions. As a result, research conclusions should always be expressed cautiously.
4. Extensive interpretation exercises are not appropriate because of the reasons given in point 3 above. (Thelwall, 2006)

The purposes of the above theoretical framework were to create a consensus about the minimum requirements for a published link analysis study and to ensure that the conclusions drawn from future studies would always be tied to the evidence provided in them. In this sense it copies the earlier work of van Raan (1998). Although no new link analysis theories have been proposed since the above, more powerful link analysis methods have been developed (e.g., Seeber, Lepori, Lomi, Aguillo, & Barberio, 2012) and the field has continued to progress.

Within webometrics, link analysis' younger sibling is search engine evaluation, the analysis of properties of commercial web search engines. This area of study was conceived from its parent fields—scientometrics and informetrics—when it became apparent that link analysis could not survive alone because the results that web search engines gave for queries were inconsistent and sometimes illogical. Search engine evaluation studies attempted to cure this childhood disease by identifying strategies for extracting information that was as reliable as possible (e.g., Bar-Ilan, 2001; Bar-Ilan, 2004), such as by conducting multiple searches and aggregating the results (Rousseau, 1999). In addition, by understanding and mapping the extent of the problem of search engine reliability (e.g., Vaughan & Thelwall, 2004), the results of link analysis studies could be interpreted with an appropriate degree of caution. From a theoretical perspective, this is a very odd type of information science research because the object of study is a computer system (Google, Bing etc.) created by a small number of humans (mainly computer scientists) that is, in theory, perfectly understandable to researchers. Nevertheless, the exact details of the functioning of all the major commercial search engines are proprietary secrets, thus necessitating empirical analysis. This area of research has generated no formal theories at all, perhaps because it seems illogical to theorize about a very small number of complex computer systems. To fill this gap, here are some new theoretical hypotheses about commercial search engines. These are consistent with the history of search engines over the past decade but are clearly not directly testable until one of them fails:

- *Incompleteness hypothesis*: No major commercial search engine will ever be designed to give an accurate and complete set of matches to a user's search.
- *Unknown ranking hypothesis*: No major commercial search engine will ever fully specify its ranking algorithm.
- *Instability hypothesis*: No major commercial search engine will ever cease to make continual changes to its core ranking and retrieval algorithms.
- *Unknown coverage hypothesis*: No search engine will ever crawl the entire web, with any reasonable definition of "the entire web".

Although the majority of early webometric studies focused on either hyperlinks or search engine evaluation, later studies investigated new types of website, such as blogs, and attempted to engage a wider social science audience. This led to a proposed new definition for webometrics as "the study of web-based content with primarily quantitative methods for social science research goals using techniques that are not specific to one field of study" (Thelwall, 2009, p. 6). Therein we find the theoretical contribution of webometrics: a big data theory that casts information scientists as proactive data librarians for the web. *Information Centred Research* (ICR) theory proposes that information science as a discipline should take on the roles of evaluating new sources of web data and helping to ensure that it was used, and used effectively, by researchers in disciplines for which it would be most useful (Thelwall, Wouters, & Fry, 2008). The background to ICR was the realization that when a new web service arises (e.g., blogs, social network sites, Twitter), many researchers from different fields naturally investigate it to see whether it could provide new evidence to shed light on field-specific problems (e.g., perhaps public tweets about research could give insights into the topics found to be most interesting). ICR argued that a more efficient approach would be for information scientists to investigate the new web service and target research fields for which the data could be useful (e.g., if tweets tended to be about politicians then politics researchers should be targeted to research it but not family researchers).

In terms of the theoretical basis of webometrics, although the foundations of the field lay within scientometrics and its theoretical basis and goals overlap with those of scientometrics, its theoretical contributions seem to have mainly come from within webometrics rather than externally. The main exception is the theorizing about the position of webometrics with respect to bibliometrics, scientometrics, and informetrics (Björneborn & Ingwersen, 2004), which explicitly extends similar prior work (Tague-Sutcliffe, 1992). Webometrics research has mostly been concerned with developing and evaluating methods and hence many of its theoretical contributions are formulated as methodological rather than theoretical and have typically been web-specific and generated to fill a gap that prior scientometrics research not had to address. The above theoretical framework for link analysis and ICR theory are exceptions to the atheoretical methods focus of much webometrics, but these are both clearly about methods, albeit at a more general level than in most webometric research. It is interesting to contrast this with another theoretical contribution, the alternative document model formulation (Thelwall, 2002), which suggested new methods for counting hyperlinks by aggregating all links from the same source and target website into one. This idea was theoretical in the sense that it hypothesized, for example, that the website could be the real single "document" of the web rather than the web page, in the same way that academic publications are counted by article rather than by page. Nevertheless, the purpose was to generate improved methods for counting links. The alternative document model idea was later expressed in a more theoretical abstract mathematical way (Thelwall & Wilkinson, 2008) but has since become methodologically less relevant[1]. In summary, it seems that while webometrics has drawn freely upon theory from other fields its own theories have tended to be internally generated in order to fill gaps that existing theories have not needed to address.

---

[1] This is because commercial search engines now try to avoid returning too many matches from a single website, reducing the importance of the problem that the alternative model concept was introduced to solve.

4 The Birth of Altmetrics

Although not originally at the heart of webometrics, counts of various forms of web citations to individual academic publications began to dominate webometric research, starting with a seminal paper on web citation counting that used commercial search engine queries to identify and count web pages citing academic articles (Vaughan & Shaw, 2003). Although initially targeted at whole journals (by aggregating citation counts to individual articles), web citation counting was later applied to evaluate individual articles in many different ways, providing broader evidence of the impact of academic articles than that obtainable from scholarly citations alone (e.g., Kousha, Thelwall, & Rezaie, 2010).

Despite the empirical success of web citation counting in webometrics, it requires significant human labour to identify citations on a large scale. It also became expensive to do this as commercial search engines withdrew permission for researchers to run large-scale free web searching. Altmetrics was conceived, or at least launched, by a few people that identified a new source of data for individual article webometrics: the social web—complete with, in many cases, free, large-scale, automated web access.

In contrast to the home birth of webometrics, emerging from several different similar articles published around the world in an apparently uncoordinated fashion, altmetrics was born wide awake and screaming with its own website proclaiming an apparently carefully thought-out and well-articulated manifesto of its potentials and aims (Priem, Taraborelli, Groth, & Neylon, 2010) (see also, Moed, this volume, for an extract). It recognized that parts of the social web, such as Twitter and the reference sharing site Mendeley, were practical and useful sources of article-level metrics. They were practical because they had free Applications Programming Interfaces (APIs) that allowed the automatic large-scale harvesting of citation-like information (e.g., counts of "readers" in Mendeley and counts of tweets with links to articles in Twitter). They were useful because they could provide both broader evidence of impact (like webometrics) and earlier evidence of impact than hyperlinks or citations, broadly speaking, since articles could be "read" or mentioned in the social web shortly after publication, whereas citations from scholarly publications take years to accumulate as evidence of impact. Taken together, this meant that altmetrics had the potential to be used by *publishers* to help guide readers to the most important recently published articles, which never seemed be a realistic goal for webometrics. This idea has greatly enhanced the value of altmetrics by making it potentially relevant to all scientists, rather than just to science evaluators. This importance has been reflected in the publicity that altmetrics has generated (Cronin, 2013), which already far exceeds that of webometrics.

5 Altmetric Theories

Unlike webometrics, altmetrics has not produced any clearly named theories (Priem, 2014) but was born with theoretical analyses of its possibilities, as discussed above. In addition, almost all empirical altmetric studies have drawn upon theoretical analyses from scientometrics in order to justify correlating citations with altmetrics (or using other statistical tests of association) as a first step towards assessing whether the latter have value (Bornmann & Leydesdorff, 2013; Costas, Zahedi, & Wouters, 2014; Eysenbach, 2011; Shema, Bar-Ilan, & Thelwall, 2014; Li, Thelwall & Giustini, 2012; Thelwall, Haustein, Larivière, & Sugimoto, 2013; Waltman & Costas, 2014; Zahedi, Costas, & Wouters, 2014). This approach relies upon the dual beliefs that citation counts have some value and that a statistical relationship with them is partial evidence of a related value. At the very minimum, such a relationship shows that altmetrics are not completely random. Moreover, the stronger the relationship, the closer the connection between citations and metrics, and the more likely they are to reflect similar aspects of the impact of articles (Sud & Thelwall, 2014). Most studies covering multiple fields have also drawn upon a range of other types of theoretical knowledge that is common within scientometrics, such as the importance of disciplinary differences and the likelihood that indicators vary between fields in utility and meaning (e.g., Kousha & Thelwall, in press; Mohammadi & Thelwall, 2014).

Another strand of altmetric research is descriptive but could be used to build future theories. This strand involves analyses of the sources and content of altmetric data in order to understand more about what is created and by whom (Priem, 2014), or detailed analyses of individual groups of users (e.g., Haustein, Bowman, Holmberg, Peters, & Larivière, 2014). Such information would presumably be necessary for any future altmetric theory. Content analyses have also been popular in webometric studies (e.g., Holmberg, 2010) but there do not seem to have been substantial investigations into the creators of the webpages involved.

An important theoretical contribution to altmetrics was an analysis of the purposes for which a range of existing websites delivering altmetric data could be used (Wouters & Costas, 2012). This argued that the existing websites did not give high enough quality data to be used for "control" purposes, such as for evaluations of researchers, but that they could be used by individual researchers for self-evaluation purposes (or "narcissism", but without a pejorative overtone), and for "users" in the sense of those using altmetrics to help them to discover important articles. This theoretical perspective seems to be particularly helpful for those seeking to argue that altmetrics can have value in some contexts but should not be used in evaluations without extreme care being taken to guard against abuse.

Finally, although altmetrics is still controversial and is perhaps not yet fully established as providing clear value to publishers and scientists, it is making good progress (Adie & Roe, 2013) and the expertise of its careful delivery to the world in the well-constructed hospital of altmetrics.org attests to the safety of web metrics research in the hands of the next generation of information scientists.

Cited References

Adie, E., & Roe, W. (2013). Altmetric: enriching scholarly content with article-level discussion and metrics. *Learned Publishing, 26*(1), 11–17.

Aguillo, I. F. (1998). STM information on the Web and the development of new Internet R&D databases and indicators. In *Online Information-International Meeting* (pp. 239–244). Learned Information Ltd.

Almind, T. C., & Ingwersen, P. (1997). Informetric analyses on the world wide web: methodological approaches to 'webometrics'. *Journal of Documentation, 53*(4), 404–426.

Bar-Ilan, J. (1999). Search engine results over time—a case study on search engine stability. *Cybermetrics, 2*(3), 1.

Bar-Ilan, J. (2001). Data collection methods on the Web for infometric purposes—A review and analysis. *Scientometrics, 50*(1), 7–32.

Bar-Ilan, J. (2004). The use of Web search engines in information science research. In: Cronin B, ed. *Annual Review of Information Science and Technology, 38*, 231–288.

Björneborn, L. (2004). Small-world link structures across an academic Web space: A library and information science approach. Doctoral dissertation, Royal School of Library and Information Science, Copenhagen, Denmark.

Björneborn, L., & Ingwersen, P. (2001). Perspectives of webometrics. *Scientometrics, 50*(1), 65–82.

Björneborn, L., & Ingwersen, P. (2004). Toward a basic framework for webometrics. *Journal of the American Society for Information Science and Technology, 55*(14), 1216–1227.

Borgman, C. L., & Furner, J. (2002). Scholarly Communication and Bibliometrics. In: Cronin B, ed. *Annual Review of Information Science and Technology* (ARIST), 36, 3–72.

Bornmann, L., & Leydesdorff, L. (2013). The validation of (advanced) bibliometric indicators through peer assessments: A comparative study using data from InCites and F1000. *Journal of Informetrics, 7*(2), 286–291.

Costas, R., Zahedi, Z., & Wouters, P. (2014). Do altmetrics correlate with citations? Extensive comparison of altmetric indicators with citations from a multidisciplinary perspective. arXiv preprint arXiv:1401.4321

Cronin, B. (1981). The need for a theory of citing. *Journal of Documentation, 37*(1), 16–24.

Cronin, B. (1984). *The citation process. The role and significance of citations in scientific communication*. London: Taylor Graham.

Cronin, B. (2001). Bibliometrics and beyond: some thoughts on web-based citation analysis. *Journal of Information Science*, 27(1), 1–7.

Cronin, B. (2013). Metrics à la mode. *Journal of the American Society for Information Science and Technology*, 64(6), 1091–1091.

Cronin, B., Snyder, H. W., Rosenbaum, H., Martinson, A., & Callahan, E. (1998). Invoked on the Web. *Journal of the American Society for Information Science*, 49(14), 1319–1328.

de Solla Price, D. (1976). A general theory of bibliometric and other cumulative advantage processes. *Journal of the American Society for Information Science*, 27(5), 292–306.

Egghe, L. (2000). New informetric aspects of the Internet: some reflections-many problems. *Journal of Information Science*, 26(5), 329–335.

Eysenbach, G. (2011). Can tweets predict citations? Metrics of social impact based on Twitter and correlation with traditional metrics of scientific impact. *Journal of Medical Internet Research*, 13(4), e123.

Haustein, S., Bowman, T. D., Holmberg, K., Peters, I., & Larivière, V. (2014). Astrophysicists on Twitter: An in-depth analysis of tweeting and scientific publication behavior. Aslib Journal of Information Management, 66(3), 279–296.

Holmberg, K. (2010). Co-inlinking to a municipal Web space: A webometric and content analysis. Scientometrics, 83(3), 851–862.

Ingwersen, P. (1997). The calculation of web impact factors. *Journal of Documentation*, 54(2), 236–243.

Kousha, K., Thelwall, M., & Rezaie, S. (2010). Using the web for research evaluation: the integrated online impact indicator. *Journal of Informetrics*, 4(1), 124–135.

Kousha, K. & Thelwall, M. (in press). Can Amazon.com reviews help to assess the wider impacts of books? *Journal of the Association for Information Science and Technology*.

Larson, R. R. (1996). Bibliometrics of the World Wide Web: An exploratory analysis of the intellectual structure of cyberspace. In *Proceedings of The Annual Meeting-American Society For Information Science* (Vol. 33, pp. 71–78).

Leydesdorff, L., & Curran, M. (2000). Mapping university-industry-government relations on the Internet: the construction of indicators for a knowledge-based economy. *Cybermetrics*, 4(1), 1–17.

Li, X., Thelwall, M., & Giustini, D. (2012). Validating online reference managers for scholarly impact measurement. *Scientometrics*, 91(2), 461–471

Merton, R. K. (1973). *The sociology of science: Theoretical and empirical investigations*. Chicago: University of Chicago Press.

Mohammadi, E. & Thelwall, M. (2014). Mendeley readership altmetrics for the social sciences and humanities: Research evaluation and knowledge flows. *Journal of the Association for Information Science and Technology*, 65(8), 1627–1638.

Oppenheim, C., & Renn, S. P. (1978). Highly cited old papers and the reasons why they continue to be cited. *Journal of the American Society for Information Science*, 29(5), 225–231.

Priem, J. (2014). Altmetrics. In: B. Cronin, C. Sugimoto, Beyond Bibliometrics: Harnessing multidimensional indicators of scholarly impact. Cambridge, MA: MIT Press (pp. 263–287).

Priem, J., Taraborelli, D., Groth, P., & Neylon, C. (2010). *Altmetrics: A manifesto*. http://altmetrics.org/manifesto/

Rodríguez i Gairín, J. M. (1997). Valoración del impacto de la información en Internet: AltaVista, el Citation Index de la red. *Revista Española de Documentación Científica*, 20(2), 175–181.

Rousseau, R. (1999). Daily time series of common single word searches in AltaVista and NorthernLight. *Cybermetrics*, 2(3), 1.

Seeber, M., Lepori, B., Lomi, A., Aguillo, I., & Barberio, V. (2012). Factors affecting web links between European higher education institutions. *Journal of Informetrics*, 6(3), 435–447.

Shema, H., Bar-Ilan, J., & Thelwall, M. (2014). Do blog citations correlate with a higher number of future citations? Research blogs as a potential source for alternative metrics. *Journal of the Association for Information Science and Technology*, 65(5), 1018–1027.

Smith, A. G. (1999). A tale of two web spaces: comparing sites using web impact factors. *Journal of Documentation*, 55(5), 577–592.

Sud, P. & Thelwall, M. (2014). Evaluating altmetrics. *Scientometrics*, 98(2), 1131–1143.

Tague-Sutcliffe, J. (1992). An introduction to informetrics. *Information Processing & Management*, 28(1), 1–3.

Thelwall, M. (2002). Conceptualizing documentation on the Web: An evaluation of different heuristic-based models for counting links between university Web sites. *Journal of the American Society for Information Science and Technology*, 53(12), 995–1005.

Thelwall, M. (2006). Interpreting social science link analysis research: A theoretical framework. *Journal of the American Society for Information Science and Technology*, 57(1), 60–68.

Thelwall, M. (2009). *Introduction to webometrics: Quantitative web research for the social sciences*. San Rafael, CA: Morgan & Claypool.

Thelwall, M., Haustein, S., Larivière, V. & Sugimoto, C. (2013). Do altmetrics work? Twitter and ten other candidates. *PLoS ONE*, 8(5), e64841.

Thelwall, M. & Wilkinson, D. (2008). A generic lexical URL segmentation framework for counting links, colinks or URLs. *Library and Information Science Research*, 30(2), 94–101.

Thelwall, M., Wouters, P., & Fry, J. (2008). Information-Centred Research for large-scale analysis of new information sources, *Journal of the American Society for Information Science and Technology*, 59(9), 1523–1527.

van Raan, A. F. (1998). In matters of quantitative studies of science the fault of theorists is offering too little and asking too much. *Scientometrics*, 43(1), 129–139.

van Raan, A. F. (2001). Bibliometrics and Internet: Some observations and expectations. *Scientometrics*, 50(1), 59–63.

Vaughan, L., & Shaw, D. (2003). Bibliographic and web citations: what is the difference? *Journal of the American Society for Information Science and Technology*, 54(14), 1313–1322.

Vaughan, L., & Thelwall, M. (2004). Search engine coverage bias: evidence and possible causes. *Information Processing & Management*, 40(4), 693–707.

Wouters, P., & Costas, R. (2012). Users, narcissism and control: tracking the impact of scholarly publications in the 21st century. In: E Archambault, Y Gingras, V Larivière *Proceedings of 17th International Conference on Science and Technology Indicators*, Montréal: Science-Metrix and OST, Vol. 2 (pp. 847–857).

Waltman, L., & Costas, R. (2014). F1000 Recommendations as a potential new data source for research evaluation: a comparison with citations. *Journal of the Association for Information Science and Technology*, 65(3), 433–445.

Zahedi, Z., Costas, R., & Wouters, P. (2014). How well developed are altmetrics? A cross-disciplinary analysis of the presence of 'alternative metrics' in scientific publications. *Scientometrics*, 101(2), 1491–1513.

Lutz Bornmann
Scientific Revolution in Scientometrics: The Broadening of Impact from Citation to Societal

1 Introduction

In recent decades, scientometrics has developed into a distinct research field with its own journals, conferences, academic chairs, and prizes. In this research field, a widely accepted taxonomy has been established for the investigation of particular research questions by the use of publication and citation data. Taxonomy is understood here to mean a widely accepted framework for the community of scientometricians to pursue research and application (Wray, 2011). Following Kuhn (1962), we can regard scientometrics of recent decades as a normal science in a field of research, in which refinements, revisions, and extensions may take place, but without fundamental alterations of the taxonomy. Thus, for example, scientometrics regularly applies indicators in the evaluation of research which are normalized for subject category and publication year (Bornmann & Marx, 2013). Discussion is taking place in scientometrics about, *inter alia*, whether the "rate of averages" or the "averaging of rates" (Gingras & Larivière, 2011) should be calculated, or whether percentiles should be used instead of mean citation rates (Leydesdorff, Bornmann, Mutz, & Opthof, 2011); but hardly a scientometrician would dispute that a field and time normalization of citation impact is necessary (Cronin & Sugimoto, 2014).

Scientific revolutions, in the Kuhnian sense (Kuhn, 1962), can be characterised as taxonomic changes in a research field. An example of a taxonomic change is the Copernican revolution (further examples of revolutionary changes can be found in Wray, 2011): Whereas Ptolemaic astronomers did not consider the earth to be a planet, Copernican astronomers did. According to Kuhn (1962), when competing taxonomies do not categorize phenomena in the same way and the meanings of key terms are incompatible, a revolution in the field replaces one taxonomy with another (Wray, 2011). Recently, Bornmann (2014) claimed that scientometrics is now in a phase of a change of taxonomy and thus a revolution. The most important key term in scientometrics is "scientific impact", which is typically measured by citations in literature databases (such as Web of Science, Thomson Reuters, or Scopus, Elsevier). In recent years, however, the operationalization of impact has widened and is interpreted not only in the context of science, but in all areas of society.

This chapter expands on Bornmann's (2014) assertions regarding taxonomy change and discusses its effect on the measurement of, and theory construction around, scientific impact. Parallel to this epistemological view there is a second dimension, the psychological or sociological view (Kvasz, 2014), which is not the object of this chapter. Rather, the chapter follows the argumentation of Wray (2011) and treats scientific revolutions as taxonomic changes.

2 Measuring of Societal Impact

Historically, the measurement of scientific impact revolved exclusively around the impact of research on academia and scientific knowledge—it concerned the impact of science on science. It was assumed that society could best profit from science which was pursued at the highest level. Since the end of the 1990s, the relationship between science and societal value has been challenged. Science must now prove its worth: "Research that is highly cited or published in top journals may be good for the academic discipline but not for society" (Nightingale & Scott, 2007, p. 547). Impact is increasingly understood in a broader sense which implies not only scientific but also many other kinds of impact. This alters the meaning of the key term "scientific impact," which no longer relates only to a section of society (science) but to almost all areas. The scope of research evaluations then broadens (Hanney, Packwood, & Buxton, 2000; van der Meulen & Rip, 2000), as societal use (i.e., societal references) and societal benefits (i.e., changes in society) of research come into scope (Mostert, Ellenbroek, Meijer, van Ark, & Klasen, 2010).

The measurement of societal impact (especially use, but also changes) generally involves the measurement of (1) social, (2) cultural, (3) environmental, and (4) economic returns (impact and effects) from results or products of publicly funded research (Donovan, 2011; European Commission, 2010; Lähteenmäki-Smith, Hyytinen, Kutinlahti, & Konttinen, 2006). In this chapter, (1) social benefits refers to the contribution of research to the social capital of a nation (e.g., stimulating new approaches to social issues, informed public debate and improved policy-making); (2) cultural benefits are contributions to the cultural capital of a nation (e.g., understanding how we relate to other societies and cultures, contributing to cultural preservation and enrichment); (3) environmental benefits contribute to the natural capital of a nation (e.g., reduced waste and pollution, uptake of recycling techniques); and (4) economic benefits signify contributions to the economic capital of a nation (e.g., enhancing the skills base, improved productivity) (RQF development advisory group, 2006).

3 Incommensurabilities of Key Terms

Wray (2011) calls changes in the meaning of key terms—such as the change of impact measurement—"meaning-incommensurabilities" (p. 71) between two different taxonomies. In scientometrics, change of meaning of key terms naturally leads to changes in the practice of impact measurement: There will be differences in the methodology of the measurement, which Wray (2011) calls topic-incommensurability. Scientometricians in the 1990s would have relied upon citations to measure science. However, citations cannot be used to measure scientific impact in all areas of society. Contemporary scientometricians will therefore have to increasingly concern themselves with different kinds of societal impact measurement. In this measurement, an important role will be played by new tools (besides other options of impact measurements), which are often subsumed under the heading "altmetrics" (Priem, 2014):

> Activities outside classic publication channels such as scientific journals are rarely considered in official evaluations of scientists' impact and scope. Yet, with the growing importance of using the Internet in scientific communication, there is a need for discussing combinations of scientometric and webometric indicators. So far, the most notable effort to promote and discuss alternative scientometric indicators for Web environments has been the altmetrics initiative.
>
> (Weller & Peters, 2012, p. 210)

Data providers, such as ImpactStory[1] or Altmetric[2], claim to measure the impact of scientific papers beyond the area of science (Wouters & Costas, 2012). Altmetrics has already been included in the Snowball Metrics Recipe Book (Colledge, 2014). Snowball Metrics, which is owned by several research-intensive universities around the globe, is a list of metrics from which a selection can be made to analyse institutional strengths and weaknesses (see http://www.snowballmetrics.com/). A current overview of the data which are used by this and other providers (e.g., tweets) can be found in Costas, Zahedi, and Wouters (2014). Torres-Salinas, Cabezas-Clavijo, and Jimenez-Contreras (2013) have categorized altmetric data as follows: (1) social bookmarking and digital libraries (e.g., Mendeley), (2) mentions

---

[1] http://impactstory.org/
[2] http://www.altmetric.com/

in social networks (e.g., Twitter and ResearchGate), (3) mentions in blogs (e.g., Wordpress and *Nature* Blogs), (4) mentions in encyclopedias (e.g., Wikipedia), and (5) mentions in new promotion systems (e.g., Faculty of 1000). As the classifications of ImpactStory in Table 1 show, the different altmetrics can be divided into scholarly and public metrics.

Tab. 1: Altmetrics classification of ImpactStory (ImpactStory, 2014).

	Scholars	Public
Recommended	Citations by editorials, F1000	Press article
Cited	Citations, full-text mentions	Wikipedia mentions
Saved	CiteULike, Mendeley	Delicious
Discussed	Science blogs, journal comments	Blogs, Twitter, Facebook
Viewed	PDF downloads	HTML downloads

In order to improve the flow of information from science into society (which could then be measured by altmetrics), the output of science should be widened. For example, Bornmann and Marx (2014) propose that scientists write so-called assessment reports summarizing the state of research on a particular topic. Such a summary should be expressed in appropriately general terms so as to be comprehensible to people outside the specialist area or science in general. These assessment reports could be regarded as belonging to the secondary scientific literature, which was previously fed by review journals, monographs, handbooks, and textbooks (the primary literature consists of the publications of the original research literature) (Ziman, 2000). As the proposal of Bornmann and Marx (2014) shows, the alteration of the key term "impact" will likely lead to an alteration of the key term scientific "output" or "productivity". Productivity won't only be measured by number of publications or external funds received, but by products (e.g., assessment reports or training for lay people) producing impact outside the sciences.

There are a number of studies available which have investigated the use of metrics for societal impact measurement (e.g., Bornmann, 2012, 2013). In 2005, Godin and Dore (2005) saw the general state of research into the possibilities of societal impact measurement at the stage where the measurement of research and development (R&D) was in the early 1960s. There has been, in recent years, an increasing emphasis on the assessment of societal impact, particularly in health and medical fields (Hanney et al., 2000; Holbrook & Frodeman, 2010). For example, a special issue of *Research Evaluation* was published with a collection of papers presented on a workshop on 'State of the Art in Assessing Research Impact' (Donovan, 2011). However, notions of societal impact remain ambiguous and contentious. Research into scientometrics should now—after a revolutionary phase with alterations in key terms—come into a phase of normal science in which established methods for societal impact measurement are developed, which can be generally applied and continuously developed further in the community.

Even more than with the measurement of impact on science, the measurement of societal impact urgently demands research effort from scientometricians. Societal impact is significantly more difficult to measure than impact on science. There may be no indicators corresponding to citation counts in the area of scientific impact measurement which can be applied across subjects and institutions and made easily accessible in database format (Martin, 2011). In addition, the societal impact of research is often revealed after many years, and it is difficult in many cases to establish a causal connection between a particular piece of research and a particular effect.

4 Theories of Citations

What significance does the change in the meaning of the key term "scientific impact" have on theory construction in scientometrics?

Two competing theories of citing behavior have been developed, both of them situated within broader social theories of science. One is often denoted as (1) the normative theory of citing behavior, and the other as (2) the social constructivist view of citing behaviour (see Small, this volume, for extensive treatment of these theories; see Haustein, Bowman, and Costas for the application of these theories to altmetrics).

The *normative theory*, following Merton's (1973) sociological theory of science, states that scientists give credit to colleagues whose work they use by citing that work. Thus, citations represent intellectual or cognitive influence on scientific work. Merton (1988) expressed this aspect as follows:

> The reference serves both instrumental and symbolic functions in the transmission and enlargement of knowledge. Instrumentally, it tells us of work we may not have known before, some of which may hold further interest for us; symbolically, it registers in the enduring archives the intellectual property of the acknowledged source by providing a pellet of peer recognition of the knowledge claim, accepted or expressly rejected, that was made in that source.
> (p. 622, see also Merton, 1957; Merton, 1968)

According to Small (1978, 1982), the cognitive symbol, or the content concept, that links citing scientists to a particular work can be studied through content analysis of the citation context. Over a set of citing documents, the percent uniformity (the degree to which citing scientists demonstrate consensus on the nature of the cited concept) can be calculated to identify the ideas symbolized by the cited work (Cronin, 1984).

If we were to regard the measurement of societal impact from the point of view of normative theory, then mentions in social media would mean societal credit for the scientists and papers named. These mentions demonstrate that a scientist was successful in producing results which are relevant to society and are thus transferred as reliable knowledge from research into society. Assessment reports written by scientists for lay people would facilitate the uptake of this knowledge. The problem with the measurement of societal impact with altmetrics is that it is not clear what the individual altmetrics actually measure. The symbolic meaning of a piece of research can vary significantly (Cronin & Sugimoto, 2014): A paper can appear on a private Facebook page in one context or in an important government publication in another context. With citations in papers there are also differences in the significance of citations—citations with or without content-related discussions of a paper (Bornmann & Daniel, 2008)—but the differences could be exacerbated with altmetrics. It seems particularly important within the realm of altmetrics to determine the cognitive symbol (or symbols) of a publication beyond its being named in various contexts, in order to determine its value for society (or for various parts of society). The measurement of impact which does not consist solely of a count of mentions, but also involves a content analysis of the mentions, seems to be significantly more important in the use of altmetrics than with the use of citations in scientific papers: What is the actual value of a piece of research for the various subgroups of society?

The *social constructivist* view on citing behaviour is grounded in the constructivist sociology of science (see, e.g., Collins, 2004; Knorr-Cetina, 1981; Latour & Woolgar, 1979). This view casts doubt on the assumptions of normative theory and questions the validity of evaluative citation analysis. Constructivists argue that the cognitive content of papers has little influence on how they are received. Scientific knowledge is socially constructed through the manipulation of political and financial resources and the use of rhetorical devices (Knorr-Cetina, 1991). For this reason, citations cannot be satisfactorily described uni-dimensionally through the intellectual content of the paper. Scientists have complex citing motives that are variously socially constructed. The varying motivations for citing have long been acknowledged in the field. In the 1960s, Garfield (1962)—the Founder and Chairman Emeritus of the Institute for Scientific Information (now Thomson Reuters)—listed fifteen possible motivations for citing (p. 85):

1. Paying homage to pioneers;
2. Giving credit for related work (homage to peers);
3. Identifying methodology, equipment, etc.;
4. Providing background reading;
5. Correcting one's own work;
6. Correcting the work of others;
7. Criticizing previous work;
8. Substantiating claims;
9. Alerting to forthcoming work;
10. Providing leads to poorly disseminated, poorly indexed, or uncited work;
11. Authenticating data and classes of fact (physical constants, etc.);
12. Identifying original publications in which an idea or concept was discussed;
13. Identifying original publication or other work describing an eponymous concept or term (...);
14. Disclaiming work or ideas of others (negative claims);
15. Disputing priority claims of others (negative homage).

Taylor (2013) considers all these motivations as relevant to mentions of papers in social media in 2013 as they were to mentions of papers in papers in 1962. To this list, Taylor (2013) added the following six motivations which are especially relevant for mentions of papers in social media (p. 20):

16. Building a network of related researchers;
17. Building a reputation as a good networker;
18. Paying visible homage to a senior researcher;
19. Seeking the attention of a senior researcher;
20. Demonstrating that one's reading is up to date;
21. Intimidating critics with the breadth of one's reading.

With mentions of research in social media, as with references in scientific publications, we can assume that it is not only the intellectual content of the paper which has an influence—in this area too there will be complex motives for mentioning a particular piece of research.

Bornmann (2015b) argues that the existence of a couple of motives for citing should be interpreted in the context of the normative theory. The social constructivist view cannot only be reduced to the existence of these motives—this view is more complex and radical. According to Merton's (1938) theory of deviant behavior scientists do not follow norms of citing (i.e., scientists cite when they were influenced by important publications) and have other motives, for example, if metrics are over-stressed in research assessments.

Using impact measurement based on social media data, there will be great danger of manipulation in the measurement of societal impact. The more important these measurements will be in future, the greater the danger of manipulation. According to the NISO Alternative Assessment Metrics Project (2014), "one important aspect of data quality is the potential for gaming metrics, e.g., behavior that is meant to unfairly manipulate those metrics, generally for one's benefit. Many alternative assessment metrics are more prone to gaming compared to traditional citations" (p. 9). Citation impact measurement may be influenced to some extent by manipulative factors (for example by excessive self-citation); but with societal impact measurement, deliberate manipulation can occur much more simply and more effectively: "It is well-known that mentions on the Internet or in other electronic communication media are very sensitive to manipulations: just ask any businessman how to manipulate large crowds on a public forum" (Rousseau & Ye, 2013, p. 3289).

According to Greenhow and Gleason (2014), "social media practices can embody social constructivist values of knowledge as decentralized, accessible and co-constructed among a broad base of users; 'knowledge' may become 'collective agreement' that 'combines facts with other dimensions of human experience' (i.e., opinions, values)" (p. 394). Studies on social media practices indicate that scholarly blogging is used to construct a "personal thinking space" in which ideas are developed, disseminated, and discussed with colleagues (Kjellberg, 2010). Thus, blogging is a kind of "knowledge construction in the context of being a researcher" (Kjellberg, 2010, para. 7). Bloggers create a certain image of themselves which can be called their online identity. An interviewee of Kjellberg (2010) expresses this point as follows: "It is like all writing, you develop yourself by writing" (para. 52). Whereas the results of Kjellberg (2010) might be also true for micro-blogging (using, e.g., Twitter), it can be questioned whether it is true for other social media platforms. Saving a paper on Mendeley or posting it on Facebook seems to be a more technical process than a process of self-construction.

5 Summary

This chapter presents and further develops Bornmann's (2014) assertion that scientometrics is now in a state of scientific revolution. This statement is justified by there being (or having been) a change in the taxonomy of scientometrics. Impact is no longer understood as impact on science (which can be measured by citations), but as impact on society. Alterations in impact measurements will also lead to alterations in the delivered products of science. As noted by Kurtz and Bollen (2010):

... bibliometrics is undergoing a renaissance; novel types of data are being combined with powerful new mathematical techniques to create a substantial change. The new techniques are being developed across a wide range of scholarly disciplines, from evolutionary genetics to theoretical physics. Central to the new bibliometrics is the study of usage and usage patterns. Collections of article level usage event records have existed for only about a decade and their applications are not yet at the level of commonplace acceptance that was long ago reached by article counts and citations.

(p. 51)

There have been many developments in scientometrics in recent years—besides the changes in the key term—which have received much attention. The development of the *h*-index (Hirsch, 2005) can be interpreted as a high profile event in scientometrics (Bornmann & Daniel, 2007). The introduction of this indicator led to an enormous amount of research (e.g., Cronin & Meho, 2006); yet, as distinct from the change of the key term "impact", the introduction of the *h*-index was not associated with a basic taxonomic change in scientometrics. The *h*-index merely combined two things that were previously treated separately (output und citation impact). According to Wray (2011), changes in techniques and practices can be significant contributions to a field, but we need not treat all these changes as revolutionary.

Contemporary scientometricians are facing the question of how to conceptualize and oeprationalize "societal impact" (Bornmann, 2012, 2013; Bornmann & Marx, 2014; Grant, Brutscher, Kirk, Butler, & Wooding, 2009). Scientometrics now needs a phase of "normal science", to arrive, after years of research, at a similarly set of advanced methods for the measurement of societal impact as now exists for the measurement of impact on science. At the moment, the case study approach is regarded favorably in the measurement of societal impact. However, this results in a lack of generalizability and comparability. Altmetrics offer large volumes of attractive data for societal impact measurement; however, it is not yet clear what the individual metrics are measuring. Most of the studies which have empirically investigated altmetrics focus on correlations between citations and altmetrics (Bornmann, 2015a; Costas, et al., 2014; Torres-Salinas, et al., 2013). The resulting small to medium correlation coefficients provide evidence that both metrics are not completely independent, but measure more or less different dimensions—depending on the kind of altmetrics studied (see, e.g., Haustein, Peters, Sugimoto, Thelwall, & Larivière, 2014). Scientometric research should work on evaluating these novel data to enable the determination of the concept symbol of a piece of research for society. Since a large volume of altmetrics data covering various areas is available from a range of data sources, it should be possible to determine validly and reliably the contribution of a piece of research for the various subunits of society.

Until scientometric research has developed robust and reliable methods for societal impact measurements in a phase of normal science, it certainly makes sense initially to have the societal relevance of research qualitatively assessed with the help of expert panels: "Just as peer review can be useful in assessing the quality of academic work in an academic context, expert panels with relevant experience in different areas of potential impact can be useful in assessing the difference that research has made" (Rymer, 2011, p. 12).

In a phase of normal science in scientometric research, not only robust and reliable methods for societal impact measurements should be developed, but the connection between these measurements and sociological theories, theories of informetrics, and theories of scholarly communication should be extensively studied.

Cited References

Bornmann, L. (2012). Measuring the societal impact of research. *EMBO Reports, 13*(8), 673–676.

Bornmann, L. (2013). What is societal impact of research and how can it be assessed? A literature survey. *Journal of the American Society of Information Science and Technology, 64*(2), 217–233.

Bornmann, L. (2014). Is there currently a scientific revolution in scientometrics? *Journal of the Association for Information Science and Technology, 65*(3), 647–648.

Bornmann, L. (2015a). Alternative metrics in scientometrics: A meta-analysis of research into three altmetrics. *Scientometrics, 103*(3), 1123–1144.

Bornmann, L. (2015b). Letter to the Editor: On the conceptualisation and theorisation of the impact caused by publications. *Scientometrics, 103*(3), 1145–1148. doi: 10.1007/s11192-015-1588-4.

Bornmann, L., & Daniel, H.-D. (2007). What do we know about the h index? *Journal of the American Society for Information Science and Technology, 58*(9), 1381–1385. doi: 10.1002/asi.20609.

Bornmann, L., & Daniel, H.-D. (2008). What do citation counts measure? A review of studies on citing behavior. *Journal of Documentation, 64*(1), 45–80. doi: 10.1108/00220410810844150

Bornmann, L., & Marx, W. (2013). How good is research really? Measuring the citation impact of publications with percentiles increases correct assessments and fair comparisons. *EMBO reports, 14*(3), 226–230. doi: 10.1038/embor.2013.9

Bornmann, L., & Marx, W. (2014). How should the societal impact of research be generated and measured? A proposal for a simple and practicable approach to allow interdisciplinary comparisons. *Scientometrics, 98*(1), 211–219.

Colledge, L. (2014). *Snowball Metrics Recipe Book*. Amsterdam, the Netherlands: Snowball Metrics program partners.

Collins, H. (2004). *Gravity's shadow: the search for gravitational waves*. Chicago, IL, USA: The University of Chicago Press.

Costas, R., Zahedi, Z., & Wouters, P. (2014). Do altmetrics correlate with citations? Extensive comparison of altmetric indicators with citations from a multidisciplinary perspective. Retrieved February 11, from http://arxiv.org/abs/1401.4321

Cronin, B. (1984). *The citation process: The role and significance of citations in scientific communication*. Oxford, UK: Taylor Graham.

Cronin, B., & Meho, L. (2006). Using the h-index to rank influtential information scientists. *Journal of the American Society for Information Science & Technology, 57*(9), 1275–1278.

Cronin, B., & Sugimoto, C. R. (2014). *Scholarly metrics under the microscope: from citation analysis to academic auditing*. Medford, NJ, USA: Information Today Inc.

Donovan, C. (2011). State of the art in assessing research impact: introduction to a special issue. *Research Evaluation, 20*(3), 175–179.

European Commission. (2010). *Assessing Europe's university-based research. Expert group on assessment of university-based research*. Brussels, Belgium: Publications Office of the European Union.

Garfield, E. (1962). Can citation indexing be automated? *Essays of an information scientist, 1*, 84–90.

Gingras, Y., & Larivière, V. (2011). There are neither "king" nor "crown" in scientometrics: comments on a supposed "alternative" method of normalization. *Journal of Informetrics, 5*(1), 226–227. doi: 10.1016/j.joi.2010.10.005

Godin, B., & Dore, C. (2005). *Measuring the impacts of science; beyond the economic dimension, INRS Urbanisation, Culture et Société*. Paper presented at the HIST Lecture, Helsinki Institute for Science and Technology Studies, Helsinki, Finland. http://www.csiic.ca/PDF/Godin_Dore_Impacts.pdf

Grant, J., Brutscher, P.-B., Kirk, S., Butler, L., & Wooding, S. (2009). *Capturing research impacts*. Cambridge, UK: RAND Europe.

Greenhow, C., & Gleason, B. (2014). Social scholarship: Reconsidering scholarly practices in the age of social media. *British Journal of Educational Technology, 45*(3), 392–402. doi: 10.1111/bjet.12150

Hanney, S., Packwood, T., & Buxton, M. (2000). Evaluating the benefits from health research and development centres: a categorization, a model and examples of application. *Evaluation, 6*(2), 137–160.

Haustein, S., Peters, I., Sugimoto, C. R., Thelwall, M., & Larivière, V. (2014). Tweeting biomedicine: An analysis of tweets and citations in the biomedical literature. *Journal of the Association for Information Science and Technology, 65*(4), 656–669. doi: 10.1002/asi.23101

Hirsch, J. E. (2005). An index to quantify an individual's scientific research output. *Proceedings of the National Academy of Sciences of the United States of America, 102*(46), 16569–16572. doi: 10.1073/pnas.0507655102

Holbrook, J. B., & Frodeman, R. (2010). *Comparative Assessment of Peer Review (CAPR). EU/US workshop on peer review: assessing "broader impact" in research grant applications*. Brussels, Belgium: European Commission, Directorate-General for Research and Innovation.

ImpactStory. (2014). A new framework for altmetrics. Retrieved September 1, from http://blog.impactstory.org/31524247207/

Kjellberg, S. (2010). *I am a blogging researcher: Motivations for blogging in a scholarly context*.

Knorr-Cetina, K. (1981). *The manufacture of knowledge: an essay on the constructivist and contextual nature of science*. Oxford, UK: Pergamon Press.

Knorr-Cetina, K. (1991). Merton sociology of science: the first and the last sociology of science. *Contemporary Sociology, 20*(4), 522–526.

Kuhn, T. S. (1962). *The structure of scientific revolutions* (2. ed.). Chicago, IL, USA: University of Chicago Press.

Kurtz, M. J., & Bollen, J. (2010). Usage Bibliometrics. *Annual Review of Information Science and Technology, 44*, 3–64.

Kvasz, L. (2014). Kuhn's Structure of Scientific Revolutions between sociology and epistemology. *Studies in History and Philosophy of Science Part A, 46*, 78–84.

Lähteenmäki-Smith, K., Hyytinen, K., Kutinlahti, P., & Konttinen, J. (2006). *Research with an impact evaluation practises in public research organisations*. Kemistintie, Finland: VTT Technical Research Centre of Finland.

Latour, B., & Woolgar, S. (1979). *Laboratory life: the social construction of scientific facts*. London, UK: Sage.

Leydesdorff, L., Bornmann, L., Mutz, R., & Opthof, T. (2011). Turning the tables in citation analysis one more time: principles for comparing sets of documents. *Journal of the American Society for Information Science and Technology, 62*(7), 1370–1381.

Martin, B. R. (2011). The Research Excellence Framework and the 'impact agenda': are we creating a Frankenstein monster? *Research Evaluation, 20*(3), 247–254.

Merton, R. K. (1938). Social structure and anomie. *American Sociological Review, 3*(5), 672–682.

Merton, R. K. (1957). Priorities in scientific discovery: a chapter in the sociology of science. *American Sociological Review, 22*(6), 635–659. doi: 10.2307/2089193.

Merton, R. K. (1968). The Matthew effect in science. *Science, 159*(3810), 56–63.

Merton, R. K. (1973). *The sociology of science: theoretical and empirical investigations*. Chicago, IL, USA: University of Chicago Press.

Merton, R. K. (1988). The Matthew effect in science, II: cumulative advantage and the symbolism of intellectual property. *ISIS, 79*(4), 606–623.

Mostert, S., Ellenbroek, S., Meijer, I., van Ark, G., & Klasen, E. (2010). Societal output and use of research performed by health research groups. *Health Research Policy and Systems, 8*(1), 30.

Nightingale, P., & Scott, A. (2007). Peer review and the relevance gap: ten suggestions for policy-makers. *Science and Public Policy, 34*(8), 543–553. doi: 10.3152/030234207x254396

NISO Alternative Assessment Metrics Project. (2014). NISO Altmetrics Standards Project White Paper. Retrieved July 8, 2014, from http://www.niso.org/apps/group_public/document.php?document_id=13295&wg_abbrev=altmetrics

Priem, J. (2014). Altmetrics. In B. Cronin & C. R. Sugimoto (Eds.), *Beyond bibliometrics: harnessing multi-dimensional indicators of performance*. Cambridge, MA, USA: MIT Press.

Rousseau, R., & Ye, F. Y. (2013). A multi-metric approach for research evaluation. *Chinese Science Bulletin, 58*. doi: 10.1007/s11434-013-5939-3

RQF development advisory group. (2006). *Research quality framework: assessing the quality and impact of research in Australia. Research Impact (report by the RQF development advisory group)*. Canberra, Australia: Department of Education.

Rymer, L. (2011). *Measuring the impact of research - the context for metric development*. Turner, Australia: The Group of Eight.

Small, H. G. (1978). Cited documents as concept symbols. *Social Studies of Science, 8*(3), 327–340.

Small, H. G. (1982). Citation context analysis. In B. J. Dervin & M. J. Voigt (Eds.), *Progress in communication sciences* (Vol. 3, pp. 287–310). Norwood, NJ, USA: Ablex.

Taylor, M. (2013). Towards a common model of citation: some thoughts on merging altmetrics and bibliometrics. *Research Trends*(35), 19–22.

Torres-Salinas, D., Cabezas-Clavijo, A., & Jimenez-Contreras, E. (2013). Altmetrics: new indicators for scientific communication in Web 2.0. *Comunicar, 41*, 53–60.

van der Meulen, B., & Rip, A. (2000). Evaluation of societal quality of public sector research in the Netherlands. *Research Evaluation, 9*(1), 11–25.

Weller, K., & Peters, I. (2012). Citations in Web 2.0. In A. Tokar, M. Beurskens, S. Keuneke, M. Mahrt, I. Peters, C. Puschmann, T. van Treeck & K. Weller (Eds.), *Science and the Internet* (pp. 209–222). Düsseldorf. Germany: Düsseldorf University Press.

Wouters, P., & Costas, R. (2012). *Users, narcissism and control – tracking the impact of scholarly publications in the 21st century*. Utrecht, The Netherlands: SURFfoundation.

Wray, K. B. (2011). *Kuhn's evolutionary social epistemology*. Cambridge, UK: Cambridge University Press.

Ziman, J. (2000). *Real science. What it is, and what it means*. Cambridge, UK: Cambridge University Press.

Henk F. Moed
Altmetrics as Traces of the Computerization of the Research Process

1 Introduction

In the Altmetrics Manifesto published on the Web in October 2010, the concept of "Altmetrics" is introduced as follows:

> In growing numbers, scholars are moving their everyday work to the web. Online reference managers Zotero and Mendeley each claim to store over 40 million articles (making them substantially larger than PubMed); as many as a third of scholars are on Twitter, and a growing number tend scholarly blogs. These new forms reflect and transmit scholarly impact: that dog-eared (but uncited) article that used to live on a shelf now lives in Mendeley, CiteULike, or Zotero–where we can see and count it. That hallway conversation about a recent finding has moved to blogs and social networks–now, we can listen in. The local genomics dataset has moved to an online repository–now, we can track it. This diverse group of activities forms a composite trace of impact far richer than any available before. We call the elements of this trace altmetrics.
>
> (Priem et al., 2010)

Online reference managers, social networking tools, scholarly blogs, and online repositories are highlighted as technological inventions, and their use by the scientific community or even the wider public leaves traces of impact of scientific activity.

A leading commercial provider of such data, Altmetric.com, distinguishes four types of altmetric data sources (Altmetric.com, 2014):
- Social media such as Twitter and Facebook, covering social activity;
- Reference managers or reader libraries such as Mendeley or ResearchGate covering scholarly activity;
- Various forms of scholarly blogs reflecting scholarly commentary;
- Mass media coverage, for instance, daily newspapers or news broadcasting services, informing the general public.

This paper is based on a keynote lecture presented by the author at Altmetrics'14, Indiana University, Bloomington, USA, 23 June 2014.

I distinguish three drivers of development of the field of altmetrics.[1] *Firstly*, in the policy or political domain, there is an increasing awareness of the multi-dimensionality of research performance, and an increasing emphasis on societal merit, an overview of which can be found in Moed and Halevi (2015a) (see also Bornmann, this volume). A typical example of this awareness is the ACUMEN project (Academic Careers Understood through Measurement and Norms) funded by the European Commission, aimed at "studying and proposing alternative and broader ways of measuring the productivity and performance of individual researchers" (Bar-Ilan, 2014). The reader is referred to Bar-Ilan (2014) for an overview of this project and the role of altmetrics therein.

In the domain of technology, a *second* driver is the development of information and communication technologies (ICTs), especially websites and software in order to support and foster social interaction. The technological inventions mentioned in the Altmetrics Manifesto are typical examples of this development. It seems appropriate to link the Altmetrics manifesto to the notion of a "computerization movement". Elliot and Kraemer (2009) define a computerization moment as "... a type of movement that focuses on computer-based systems as the core technologies which their advocates claim will be instruments to bring about a new social order. These advocates of computerization movements spread their message through public discourse in various segments of society such as vendors, media, academics, visionaries, and professional societies" (p. 3). A further positioning of the Altmetrics ideas as a computerization movement falls outside the scope of this chapter, even though there is a vast amount of literature on computerization movements, of which Elliot and Kraemer give an overview. I am inclined to conceive the Altmetrics Manifesto as a proclamation of a computerization movement, but a very special one, appealing to basic ideals of science and scholarship. What is important in this chapter is to characterize the type of ideals that inspires the altmetrics movement. I believe they can best be associated with a *third* driver, primarily emerging from the scientific community itself, namely the Open Science movement. Open Science is conceived as:

> The movement to make scientific research, data and dissemination accessible to all levels of an inquiring society, amateur or professional. It encompasses practices such as publishing open research, campaigning for open access, encouraging scientists to practice open notebook science, and generally making it easier to publish and communicate scientific knowledge.
>
> ("Open Science", n.d.)

---

[1] Practitioners increasingly use the new term "alternative metrics" rather than "altmetrics". In this contribution I use the original term.

The increasing importance of altmetrics is also reflected in the foundation of the NISO Altmetrics Standards Project. The National Information Standards Organization (NISO) is a United States non-profit organization that develops, maintains and publishes technical standards related to publishing, bibliographic, and library applications. Funded by the Alfred P. Sloan Foundation, NISO established a project to identify standards and/or best practices related to altmetrics, as an important step towards the development and adoption of new *assessment metrics*. The NISO Project Group published a White Paper in June 2014 (NISO, 2014).[2]

In the NISO Project mentioned above and also in sessions of scientific conferences, altmetrics is increasingly linked to—and often limited to—social media references, and to research performance assessment. Empirical studies of altmetrics have focused nearly exclusively on these as well. In the following section, I will propose a much broader, multi-dimensional conception of altmetrics, namely as *traces of the computerization of the research process*. "Computerization" should be conceived in its broadest sense, including all recent developments in ICT and software, taking place in society as a whole. I distinguish four aspects of the research process: the collection of research data and development of research methods; scientific information processing; communication and organization; and, last but not least, research assessment. I will argue that in each aspect, computerization plays a key role, and metrics are being developed to describe this process. I propose to label the total collection of such metrics as "Altmetrics". I then provide a theoretical foundation of altmetrics, based on notions developed by Michael Nielsen in his monograph *Reinventing Discovery: The New Era of Networked Science* (Nielsen, 2011).

To the extent that altmetrics are used as research assessment tools, I underline a series of basic theoretical distinctions, which are not only valid in the case of "classical" metrics such as those based on citation analysis, but also, and, perhaps, even more so, in the case of new metrics such as those based on social media references or electronic document usage patterns. These are as follows: the distinction between scientific-scholarly and societal impact; scientific opinion and scientific fact; peer reviewed versus non-peer reviewed manuscripts; immediate and delayed response or impact; intended and unintended consequences of particular behaviors; and, lastly, a distinction between the various domains of science and scholarship, for instance, between natural, technical, formal, biological and medical, social sciences, and humanities.

---

[2] A project headed by Vincent Larivière, Stefanie Haustein, and Cassidy Sugimoto is being currently funded by the Sloan foundation, to investigate the meanings and motivations of social media metrics. In a way, this activity is a follow-up to the NISO project (Sugimoto, 2014).

I conclude that altmetrics can provide tools not only to reflect this process passively, but, even more so, to design, monitor, improve, and actively facilitate it. From this perspective, altmetrics can be conceived as tools for the practical realization of the ethos of science and scholarship in a computerized or digital age.

2 The Computerization of the Research Process

I distinguish four aspects of the research process. In this section, I briefly explain these aspects by giving typical outcomes of metrics-based studies of these aspects. The purpose of these examples is to illustrate an aspect, rather than give a detailed account of it. *Firstly,* at the level of the everyday research practice, there is the *collection of research data and the development of research methods.* A "classical" citation analysis in Scopus of articles published during 2002–2012 and cited up until March 2014, generated per discipline a list of the most frequently cited articles. A subject classification of journals was used to classify these into 26 research disciplines. It was found that in many disciplines, computing-related articles are the most heavily cited (Halevi, 2014). Table 1 presents nine such articles. The term "computing-related" is used in a broad sense. Most articles describe software packages for data analysis, digital imaging, and simulation techniques. Interestingly, the most frequently cited article in social sciences is about user acceptance of information technology.

The *second* aspect relates to *scientific information processing.* There is a long history of research in the field of information science on information seeking behavior; since this behavior occurs increasingly online, a digital trace of it can be readily identified. A topic of rapidly increasing importance is the study of searching, browsing, and reading behavior of researchers, based on an analysis of the electronic log files recording the usage of publication archives such as Elsevier's ScienceDirect or an Open Access archive such as arxiv.org. Comparison of citation counts and full text downloads of research articles may provide more insight both into citation practices and in usage behavior (Kurtz et al., 2005; Kurtz & Bollen, 2010; Gorraiz, Gumpenberger, & Schlögl, 2013; Guerrero-Bote & Moya-Anegón, 2014). Table 2 summarizes the main sources of differences between these two types of counts (Moed & Halevi, 2015b). Usage and citation leaks, bulk downloading, differences between reader and author populations in a subject field, the type of document or its content, differences in obsolescence patterns between downloads and citations, and different functions of reading and citing in the research process, all provide possible explanations of differences between download and citation distributions.

Tab. 1: Computer science-related top cited articles in Scopus.

# Cites	Discipline	Article Title
17 171	Agr & Biol Sci, Mol Biol; Medicine	MEGA4: Molecular Evolutionary Genetics Analysis (MEGA) software version 4.0 (2007)
4 335	Social sciences; business, managemt	User acceptance of information technology: Toward a unified view (2003)
5 325	Chemistry	UCSF Chimera – A visualization system for exploratory research and analysis (2004)
15 191	Computer Sci; Eng	Distinctive image features from scale-invariant keypoints (2004)
1 335	Energy	Geant4 developments and applications (2006) [software for simulating passage of particles through matter]
7 784	Engineering; Math	A fast and elitist multi-objective genetic algorithm: NSGA-II (2002)
4 026	Environm Sci	GENALEX 6: Genetic analysis in Excel. Population genetic software … (2006)
4 404	Materials Science	The SIESTA method for ab initio order-N materials simulation (2002)
10 921	Physics & Astron	Coot: Model-building tools for molecular graphics (2004)

Tab. 2: Ten important factors differentiating between downloads and citations.

1	Usage leak: Not all downloads may be recorded.
2	Citation leak: Not all citations may be recorded.
3	Downloading the full text of a document does not mean that it is read.
4	The user (reader) and the author (citer) population may not coincide.
5	Distribution # downloads less skewed than that of # cites, and depends upon the type of document differently.
6	Downloads and citations show different obsolescence functions.
7	Downloads and citations measure distinct concepts.
8	Downloads and citations may influence one another in multiple ways.
9	Download counts are more sensitive to manipulation.
10	Citations are public, usage is private.

Communication and organization is a *third* group of aspects. These two elements are distinct, from an altmetric point of view, to the extent that the first takes place via blogs, Twitter, and similar social media, whereas the second occurs for instance in scholarly tools as Mendely or Zotero. In this paper, the two aspects will be discussed jointly. The analysis of the use of online tools such as social media, reference managers, and scientific blogs perhaps constitutes the core of studies of the computerization in this domain. Many altmetric studies cover this aspect. In a recent special altmetrics issue of the journal *Research Trends*, Thelwall gives an historical overview of the study of social web services using altmetrics, focusing on Mendeley and Twitter (Thelwall, 2014). He underlines the need to further validate altmetrics, by investigating the degree at which they correlate with—or predict—citation counts and other traditional measures. In the same issue, Shema presents an additional, and state of the art, altmetric data source: scholarly blogs (Shema, 2014). The studies focusing on this aspect aim to deepen our understanding of the ways in which researchers communicate and organize themselves, and how the new technologies not only influence communication and organization, but also how they could improve these processes.

The use of altmetrics—or metrics in general—in *research assessment* is a *fourth* aspect of the computerization of the research process. Mentions of authors and their publications in social media like twitter, in scholarly blogs and in reference managers form the basis of the exploration of new impact measures. In his historical overview, Thelwall concludes that "altmetrics [also] have the potential to be used for impact indicators for individual researchers based upon their web presences, although this information should not be used as a primary source of impact information since the extent to which academics possess or exploit social web profiles is variable" and that, "more widely, however, altmetrics should not be used to help evaluate academics for anything important because of the ease with which they can be manipulated" (Thelwall, 2014).

Moed and Halevi (2015a) underline that indicators that are appropriate in one context may be invalid or useless in another. The decision as to which indicators should be used in a particular assessment depends upon (a) what units have to be assessed; (b) which aspect of research performance is being assessed; and (c) what constitutes the overall objective of the assessment. The authors introduce the notion of a "meta-analysis" of the units under assessment, in which metrics are not used as tools to evaluate individual units, but rather to reach policy inferences regarding the objectives and general set-up of an assessment process. For instance, publication counts and average journal impact factors of a group's publications are hardly useful in a relative assessment of research active groups with a strong participation in international networks, but they may be very useful in a context in which there is solid evidence that a substantial number of groups is hardly research active or publishing mainly in national journals (Moed & Halevi, 2015a).

3 A Theoretical Foundation: Michael Nielsen's "Reinventing Discovery"

Fully capturing the notion of the ethos of science and scholarship and tracing back its history requires a full essay, the presentation of which reaches far beyond the scope of the current chapter and also exceeds the competency of its author. Perhaps it is appropriate to refer to Francis Bacon and his proposal "for an universal reform of knowledge into scientific methodology and the improvement of mankind's state using the scientific method" ("Francis Bacon", n.d.).

It must be noted that Bacon is generally conceived of as the founder of the positive, empirical sciences. But the ethos I seek to capture does not merely relate to this type of science, but to science and scholarship in general, including, for instance, hermeneutic scholarship. In any case, Bacon's proposal develops *two* base notions, namely the notion that science can be used to improve the state of mankind, and that it is governed by a strict scientific-scholarly methodology. Both dimensions, the practical and the theoretical-methodological, are essential in his idea.

A key contemporary issue is how the ethos of science and scholarship, admittedly outlined so vaguely above, must be realized in the modern, computerized, or digital age. The state of development of information and communication technology (ICTs) creates enormous possibilities for the organization of the research process, as well as for society as a whole. I believe that it is against this background that the emergence and potential of altmetrics should be considered.

Michael Nielsen's (2011) monograph presents a systematic, creative exploration of the actual and potential value of the new ICT for the organization of the research process. The aim of the remaining part of this section is to summarize some of the main features of this thinking. I believe it provides an adequate framework in which altmetrics can be positioned and further developed, without claiming that alternative frameworks are of no value.

In scaffolding his ideas, Nielsen borrows concepts from several disciplines, and uses them as building blocks or models. A central thesis is that online tools can and should be used in science to amplify collective intelligence. Collective intelligence results from an appropriate organization of collaborative projects. In order to further explain this, he uses the concept of "diversity", borrowed perhaps from biology, or its sub-branch, ecology, but in the sense of cognitive diversity, as he states: "To amplify cognitive intelligence, we should scale up collaborations, increasing cognitive diversity and the range of available expertise as much as possible" (Nielsen, 2011, p. 32).

As each participant can give only a limited amount of attention in a collaboration, there are inherent limits to size of the contributions that participants can make. At this point the genuine challenge of the new online tools comes into the picture: they should create an "architecture of attention", and in my view one of the most intriguing notions in Nielsen's work, "that directs each participant's attention where it is best suited—i.e., where they have maximal competitive advantage" (Nielsen, 2011, p. 33).

In the ideal case, scientific collaboration will achieve what he terms as "designed serendipity", so that a problem posed by someone who cannot solve it finds its way to one with the right micro expertise. Using a concept stemming from statistical physics, namely, critical mass, he further explains that "conversational critical mass is achieved and the collaboration becomes self-stimulating, with new ideas constantly being explored" (Nielsen, 2011, p. 33).

One of the ways to optimize the collaboration is by modularizing it. Here Nielsen adopts the open source software development as a model. Actually, he speaks of open source collaboration, in which participants work in a modular way, make small contributions, and have easy reuse of earlier work. And, last but not least, this type of collaboration uses signaling mechanisms (e.g., scores, or metrics) to help people to decide where to direct attention.

Also, he uses the concept of "data web", being defined as "a linked web of data that connects all parts of knowledge", and "an online network intended to be read by machines". He underlines that data driven intelligence is controlled by human intelligence and amplifies collective intelligence. Nielsen highlights the potential of the new online tools to stimulate interaction and even collaboration between professional researchers and the wider public, and the role this public can play for instance in data collection processes using crowdsourcing techniques.

My proposal is to use Michael Nielsen's set of creative ideas as a framework in which altmetrics can be positioned. Their role would not merely be that of rather passively descriptors, but, actively, or proactively, as tools to establish and optimize Nielsen's "architecture of attention", a configuration that combines the efforts of researchers and technicians on the one hand, and the wider public and the policy domain on the other. I will further discuss this issue later in the chapter. In the next section I will highlight a series of distinctions that are crucial when discussing the potential and limits of altmetrics in the assessment of research performance.

4 Useful Distinctions

To further explore the potential and limitations of altmetrics, I believe it is useful to highlight a series of distinctions that are often made in the context of the use of "classical" metrics and publishing, but that are, in my view, highly relevant in connection with altmetrics.

First of all, a distinction is that between *scientific-scholarly and societal merit and impact*. These two aspects do not coincide. In the previous section, speaking of the ethos of science, two dimensions were highlighted: a practical and a theoretical-methodological: science potentially improves the state of mankind, and is governed by strict scientific-scholarly methodology. I defend the position that these methodological rules are essential to the scientific method. These rules are constitutive for science and scholarship, and discriminate between what is a justified scientific-scholarly knowledge claim and what is not.

Societal merit of scientific–scholarly research is in my view a legitimate and valuable aspect, not only in connection with motives and strivings of individual researchers, but also related to funding and assessment criteria. But it cannot be assessed in a politically neutral manner. To be successful, the project proposed by Bacon and so many others requires a certain distance and independence from the political domain, and most of all, a strong, continuous defense of proper methodological rules when making knowledge claims and examining their validity.

A next distinction is perhaps even more difficult to make, namely between *scientific opinion and scientific fact*. In journal publishing, many journals distinguish between research articles on the one hand, and opinion pieces, discussion papers, or editorials on the other. At least in the empirical sciences, the first type ideally reports on the outcomes of empirical research conducted along valid methodological lines and discusses their theoretical implications. The second type is more informal, normally not peer-reviewed, and speculative. The two types have, from an epistemological point of view, a different status. I believe it is crucial to keep this in mind when exploring the role of altmetric data sources containing scholarly commentaries, such as scientific-scholarly blogs. It is also important to distinguish between speculations or opinion pieces related to scientific-scholarly issues, and those primarily connected with political issues. I believe it is in the interest of the ethos of science to be especially alert to a practice in which researchers make political statements using their authority as scientific-scholarly experts. Such practices should be rigorously unmasked whenever they are detected.

Intended versus unintended consequences of particular behavior is the next distinction. During the past ten years or so, the general debate on the application of "classical" metrics based on publication and citations, especially their large-scale use in national research assessment exercises, strongly focused on the effects that the actual use of such metrics have upon researchers, and on the degree of manipulability of the metrics (a discussion of these systemic effects can be found in Cronin and Sugimoto's [2015] compilation). These were among the main topics of the discussions on the organization of national research assessment exercises in the United Kingdom and Australia. This debate is equally relevant as regards the use of altmetrics based on social media. But, as indicated in the previous section, Thelwall warns that the problem of manipulability is much larger in case of altmetrics than it is in the application of citation indices (Thelwall, 2014).

Finally, it is also crucial to distinguish the *various domains of science and scholarship*—for instance, natural, technical, formal, biological, medical, social sciences, and humanities. Although such subject classifications suffer from a certain degree of arbitrariness, it is important to realize that the research process, including communication practices, reference practices, and orientation towards social media, may differ significantly between one discipline and another.

In this context one of the limitations of the model Michael Nielsen proposes in his monograph *Reinventing Discovery* should be highlighted: the use of the open source software development as a model of collaboration may fit the domain of the formal sciences rather well, but may be less appropriate in many subject fields in humanities and social sciences. In other passages in his monograph he is aware that this organizational model may not be appropriate in all domains of science and scholarship.

5 Concluding Remarks

What then are the main conclusions of this chapter? I propose a broad conception of altmetrics. Altmetrics is more than measuring attention in social media to scientific-scholarly artifacts, but should be conceived as metrics of the computerization of the research process in general. I propose the set of ideas developed by Michael Nielsen as a framework within which altmetrics can be positioned and further explored. His work represents a thorough, systematic account of the potential of online tools in the research process, and, in this way, articulates the practical realization of the ethos of science and scholarship in the computerized or digital age. He shows how the new online tools support open science, the notion that is in my view one of the pillars, perhaps even the most important one, of the altmetrics manifesto.

Many proponents of altmetrics may, either as a first impression, or after reflection, not be happy with my proposal—after all, the demarcation between altmetrics and "classical" metrics is rather vague. Citation indexes are also the product of the ICT development, be it in an earlier phase than the current one. Moreover, citation indices are even used to illustrate the computerization of the research process (for more on the relationship between high quality knowledge organization systems and informetrics, see Stock, this volume). Therefore, in a sense, classical metrics are altmetrics as well. Both classical metrics and altmetrics are subjected to the same danger, namely, that their utility is limited to a few very specific cases, and both types of metrics do have in principle the same potential.

In the same way that classical citation metrics are often uniquely linked to the use of journal impact factors for assessing individual researchers—although many other citation-based metrics and methodologies have been developed, applied to different aggregations and with different purposes—altmetrics runs perhaps a danger of being too closely linked with the notion of assessing individuals by counting mentions in Twitter and related social media, a practice that may provide a richer impression of impact than citation counts do, but that clearly has its limitations as well (e.g., Cronin, 2014).

Altmetrics and science metrics, or indicators in general, are much more than that. Apart from the fact that much more sophisticated indicators are available than journal impact factors or Twitter counts, these indicators do not have a function merely in the evaluation of research performance of individuals and groups, but also in the study of the research process. In this way, in terms of a distinction developed in Geisler (2000), these indicators are used as process indicators rather than outcome measures. Also, like science metrics in general, altmetrics does not merely provide reflections of the computerization of the research process, but can, in fact, develop into a set of tools tool to further shape, facilitate, design, and conduct this process.

Cited References

Altmetric.com (2014). www.altmetric.com.
Bar-Ilan, J. (2014). Evaluating the individual researcher – adding an altmetric perspective. *Research Trends*, 37. Retrieved from http://www.researchtrends.com/issue-37-june-2014/evaluating-the-individual-researcher/
Cronin, B. (2014). Meta Life. *Journal of the American Society for Information Science and Technology*, 65(3), 431–432.
Cronin, B. & Sugimoto, C. R. (Eds.) (2015). *Scholarly metrics under the microscope: From citation analysis to academic auditing*. Medford, NJ: Information Today, Inc./ASIST, pp. 976.
Elliott, M. S. & Kraemer, K. L. (2009). Computerization Movements and the Diffusion of Technological Innovations. In M. Elliott & K. Kraemer (Eds.), Computerization Movements and

Technology Diffusion: From Mainframes to Ubiquitous Computing (p. 3–41), Medford, New Jersey: Information Today, Inc.

Francis Bacon. (n.d.) In *Wikipedia*. Retrieved August 25, 2014 from http://en.wikipedia.org/wiki/Francis_Bacon

Geisler, E. (2000). *The Metrics of Science and Technology*. Westport, CT, USA: Greenwood Publishing Group.

Gorraiz, J., Gumpenberger, C., & Schlögl, C. (2013). Differences and similarities in usage versus citation behaviours observed for five subject areas. In Proceedings of the 14th ISSI Conference Vol. 1, 519–535. http://www.issi2013.org/Images/ISSI_Proceedings_Volume_I.pdf.

Guerrero-Bote, V. P., & Moya-Anegón, F. (2014). Relationship between Downloads and Citations at Journal and Paper Levels, and the Influence of Language. *Scientometrics, 101*(2), 1043–1065.

Halevi, G. & Moed, H. (2014). 10 years of research impact: top cited papers in Scopus 2001–2011. *Research Trends, 38*. Retrieved from http://www.researchtrends.com/issue-38-september-2014/10-years-of-research-impact/

Kurtz, M. J., Eichhorn, G., Accomazzi, A., Grant, C., Demleitner, M., Murray, S. S., Martimbeau, N., & Elwell, B. (2005). The bibliometric properties of article readership information. *Journal of the American Society for Information Science and Technology, 56*, 111–128.

Kurtz, M. J., & Bollen, J. (2010). Usage Bibliometrics. *Annual Review of Information Science and Technology, 44*, 3–64.

Moed, H. F. & Halevi, G. (2015a). The Multidimensional Assessment of Scholarly Research Impact. *Journal of the Association for Information Science and Technology*, to be published.

Moed, H. F. & Halevi, G. (2015b). On full text download and citation distributions in scientific-scholarly journals. *Journal of the Association for Information Science and Technology*, to be published.

Nielsen, M. (2011). *Reinventing Discovery: The New Era of Networked Science*. Princeton University Press.

NISO (National Information Standards Organization) (2014). NISO Altmetrics Standards Project White Paper. Retrieved from http://www.niso.org/apps/group_public/download.php/13295/niso_altmetrics_white_paper_draft_v4.pdf

Open Science. (n.d.) In *Wikipedia*. Retrieved August 22, 2014 from http://en.wikipedia.org/wiki/Open_science

Priem, J., Taraborelli, D., Groth, P. & Neylon, C. (2010). Altmetrics: A Manifesto. Retrieved from http://altmetrics.org/manifesto/

Shema, H., Bar-Ilan, J. & & Thelwall, M. Scholarly blogs are a promising altmetric source. *Research Trends, 37*. Retrieved from http://www.researchtrends.com/issue-37-june-2014/scholarly-blogs-are-a-promising-altmetric-source/

Sugimoto, C. (2014). Private communication.

Thelwall, M. (2014). A brief history of altmetrics. *Research Trends, 37*. Retrieved from http://www.researchtrends.com/issue-37-june-2014/a-brief-history-of-altmetrics/

Stefanie Haustein, Timothy D. Bowman, and Rodrigo Costas
Interpreting 'Altmetrics': Viewing Acts on Social Media through the Lens of Citation and Social Theories

1 Introduction

More than 30 years after Blaise Cronin's seminal paper (Cronin, 1981), the metrics community is once again in need of a new theory, this time one for so-called 'altmetrics'. Altmetrics, short for alternative (to citation) metrics—and as such a misnomer—refers to a new group of metrics based (largely) on social media events relating to scholarly communication. The term originated on September, 29, 2010 in a tweet by Jason Priem in which he uttered his preference for the word *altmetrics* in the context of various metrics provided for PLOS journal articles: "I like the term #articlelevelmetrics, but it fails to imply *diversity* of measures. Lately, I'm liking #altmetrics" (Priem, 2010). Although Priem is responsible for coining the term, the idea of measuring broader scientific impact through the web had been discussed by Cronin and others (e.g., Almind & Ingwersen, 1997; Cronin, Snyder, Rosenbaum, Martinson, & Callahan, 1998; Cronin, 2001; see also Thelwall, this volume) in the context of webometrics years before:

> Scholars may be cited formally, or merely mentioned en passant in listservs and others electronic discussion fora, or they may find that they have been included in reading lists or electronic syllabi. Polymorphous mentioning is likely to become a defining feature of Web-based scholarly communication.
>
> (Cronin et al., 1998, p. 1320)

> There will soon be a critical mass of web-based digital objects and usage statistics on which to model scholars' communication behaviors—publishing, posting, blogging, scanning, reading, downloading, glossing, linking, citing, recommending, acknowledging—and with which to track their scholarly influence and impact, broadly conceived and broadly felt.
>
> (Cronin, 2005b, p. 196)

Priem—co-author of the altmetrics manifesto (Priem, Taraborelli, Groth, & Neylon, 2010) and co-founder of ImpactStory,[1] an online tool aggregating various metrics on the individual researcher level— and colleagues argued that metrics based on "traces" of use and production of scholarly output on social media plat-

---

[1] https://impactstory.org/

forms could help to improve scholarly communication and research evaluation. The term *altmetrics* was introduced out of the need to differentiate these new metrics from traditional citation-based indicators, which the altmetrics movement seeks to replace or use as an alternative. The altmetrics manifesto and other work by Priem and colleagues call on the scientific community and research managers to "value all research products" (Piwowar, 2013, p. 159), not just journal articles, and to measure impact in a broader sense by looking at more than just citations. The manifesto lists various sources of new metrics that would complement and replace traditional forms of publication, peer review, and citation analysis (Priem et al., 2010). Priem (2014) claimed that with scholarship moving online, former invisible aspects of scholarly communication—such as reading, discussing, and recommending scientific papers—leave traces that can be collected earlier and easier than citations and would thus provide an alternative to citations. The idea of altmetrics resonated with scholars, academic librarians, publishers, and (particularly) with research managers and funders, who were attracted by the idea of measuring the impact of research on the broader non-scientific community as a return on their investment (Adie, 2014). Within the bibliometric community, the examination of social bookmarking data as indicators of readership was one of the early examinations of altmetrics (Haustein & Siebenlist, 2011). Bornmann (2014a) even argued that scientometrics was undergoing a scientific revolution (Kuhn, 1962) due to taxonomy changes regarding the definition of impact (i.e., from scientific to a broader concept of impact) (see Bornmann, this volume, for more on this taxonomic change).

Although hopes are high that these new metrics are able to capture research impact earlier or more broadly than citations, they are limited by the technological ecosystems from which they are captured as they often measure what is technically feasible instead of what is sensible (Taylor, 2014; see also, Moed, this volume, on altmetrics as a computerization movement). While there is a debate among scholars on how to properly define these new metrics, they are considered by some university administrators, librarians, publishers, funders, and others to evaluate and assess scholarly output. In the context of the Research Excellence Framework (REF), the Higher Education Funding Council for England (HEFCE) requests metrics that demonstrate "all kinds of social, economic and cultural benefits and impacts beyond academia" (HEFCE, 2011, p. 4). This has introduced a certain level of social pressure for scholars to understand, participate in, and manage their use of computer-mediated environments, as there is the possibility that their events within these contexts will be recorded and made available to others for evaluation. The new metrics purportedly provide insight into measuring societal impact, as they are able to track events outside the scientific community revolving around scholarly output (Priem et al., 2010; Priem, 2014).

Just as there is a need for citation theory, there is also a strong need to define the meaning of the various indicators grouped under the term altmetrics. As depicted in Cronin (1981), the search for the meaning of citations was pervasive in the early days of citation analysis. Similar to Gilbert (1977, p. 114), who stated that "we do not yet have any clear idea about what exactly we are measuring when we analyze citation data", the question "What do they actually mean?" has been a recurring one in research on altmetrics. At the same time, the study of various roles and functions of citations (i.e., their 'polymorphous' nature) as well as theoretical discussions of the citation process with regard to the meaning and validity of citation metrics are still part of the current scientometrics research agenda (see for example Bertin, Atanassova, Gingras, & Larivière, 2015; Hjørland, this volume; Wouters, this volume).

Several parallels can be drawn between the early days of citation analysis and today's search for the meaning and need for a theoretical framework of social media metrics. What is considerably different, however, is that altmetrics capture events on platforms that are highly dynamic and whose use and user communities are new, diverse, and not entirely understood, while the act of citing (although not always being counted) has existed since the early days of modern science. While social rules and norms exist within the scientific community of how, when, and what to cite, these norms are currently lacking with regard to social media.

2 Defining and classifying social media events and metrics

Although altmetrics are generally understood as metrics that measure impact beyond citations and define scholarly output in a broader sense than restricting it to peer-reviewed journal articles, there is no common, agreed-upon definition or understanding of altmetrics except for that they "capture very different things" (Lin & Fenner, 2013, p. 20). The only unifying concept is that they stand in opposition to "traditional" bibliometrics and common practices in research evaluation, especially citations (Priem, 2014). Altmetrics include download and article usage statistics, although these have been available much longer than social media applications (Borghuis, 1997; Kaplan & Nelson, 2000; Luther, 2001; Glänzel & Gorraiz, 2014). Priem (2014, p. 266) defines altmetrics as the "study and use of scholarly impact measures based on activity in online tools and environments" and thus situates it as a subset of webometrics (see Thelwall, this volume). As a pragmatic attempt at a suitable definition for altmetrics, one could say that these metrics are: *events on social and mainstream media platforms related to scholarly* content or scholars, which can be easily harvested (i.e., through APIs) and measured, and are not the same as the more 'traditional' concept of citations.

The criticism for the term *alt*metrics has grown as more empirical studies have found that most social media based indicators are complements and not alternatives to citation-based indicators. Rousseau and Ye (2013, p. 3289) stated that altmetrics was "a good idea but a bad name" and proposed *influmetrics*—initially introduced by Elisabeth Davenport and discussed by Cronin and Weaver (1995) in the context of acknowledgements and webometrics (Cronin, 2001)—as an alternative term to "suggest diffuse and often imperceptible traces of scholarly influence – to capture the opportunities for measurement and evaluation afforded by the new environment" (Cronin, 2005b, p. 176). Haustein and colleagues (Haustein, Larivière, Thelwall, Amyot, & Peters, 2014a) used *social media metrics* to emphasize the platforms from which the metrics were obtained without attempting to describe intent or meaning and to better differentiate new indicators from more traditional ones (i.e., citation and downloads). Although *social media metrics* seems a better fit as an umbrella term because it addresses the social media ecosystem from which they are captured, it fails to incorporate the sources that are not obtained from social media platforms (such as mainstream newspaper articles or policy documents) that are collected (for instance) by Altmetric.com. As current definitions of altmetrics are shaped and limited by active platforms, technical possibilities, and business models of aggregators such as Altmetric.com, ImpactStory, PLOS, and Plum Analytics—and as such constantly changing—this work refrains from defining an umbrella term for these highly heterogeneous new metrics.

Rather, a framework is presented that describes *acts* leading to (online) events on which the metrics are based. These acts refer to activities occurring in the context of social media, such as discussing on Twitter or saving to Mendeley, as well as downloading and citing. The framework groups various types of acts into three categories—accessing, appraising, and applying—and provides examples of actions that lead to visibility and traceability online. These are the *polymorphous mentions* Cronin and colleagues (1998, p. 1320) anticipated. In order to discuss the traces that these acts leave online, the following generic terms —as agreed upon at the 2014 PLOS ALM workshop (Bilder, Fenner, Lin, & Neylon, 2015)— have been adopted:
- **research object:** a scholarly object, for which an event can be recorded;
- **event:** a recorded activity or action which relates to the research object;
- **host:** the place where research objects are made available and exposed to potential events;
- **source:** a platform where events are available;
- **consumer:** a party that collects and/or uses events related to research objects

- *aggregator*: a type of consumer who collects and provides events to research objects with a specific methodology;
- *end user* or *audience*: a type of consumer who uses and applies events in a specific context and intention.

As acts and recorded events will differ whether they focus on, for example, a journal article or a researcher, this framework distinguishes between *scholarly agents* and *scholarly documents* as two particular categories of research objects. Agents (Bourdieu, 1975) include individual scholars, research groups, departments, universities, funding organizations, and others entities acting within the scholarly community. Following Otlet's (1934, p. 6) broad definition of a document as "a set of facts or ideas presented in the form of a text or image",[2] this category includes traditional scholarly publications (e.g., journal articles, book chapters, conference proceedings, monographs, theses, reports, and other types of grey literature), patents, presentations and lectures, as well as blog posts, datasets, software code, and other forms of scholarly work and output. This dichotomy between agent and document demonstrates that 'altmetrics' can appear not only as article-level metrics,[3] but can also be applied to a broad spectrum of research objects.

In order to differentiate between various acts leading to online events on different sources in relation to the document or agent, we propose a framework that classifies these acts into three categories (Figure 1). We argue that these three categories—*access, appraise,* and *apply*—capture various stages and facets of use and interactions with research objects. The framework is designed to incorporate all main act types leading to events related to scholarly documents and agents. Although it does not claim to be exhaustive as to include all types of possible events, particularly in terms of future changes regarding technology and affordance[4] use, it is assumed that the categories should be broad enough to incorporate new developments when required. A framework is proposed in this instance because it allows one to consider the "system of concepts, assumptions, expectations, be-

---

[2] Translated by the authors from: "un ensemble de faits ou d'idées présentés sous forme de texte ou d'image" (Otlet, 1934, p. 6).

[3] It should also be noted that from an indicator perspective, events related to a particular research object can also be aggregated. For example, if the act of saving a journal article to Mendeley leads to a recorded number of Mendeley readers, these event counts can be aggregated for all documents of a particular agent associated with the documents (e.g., author, journal, discipline, country). However, even though the indicator refers to the agent, the recorded event relates to the research object as the smallest level of analysis, in this case the document and not the particular agent.

[4] Affordances are observed qualities of an object within a context that allow for some type of action (Gibson, 1977).

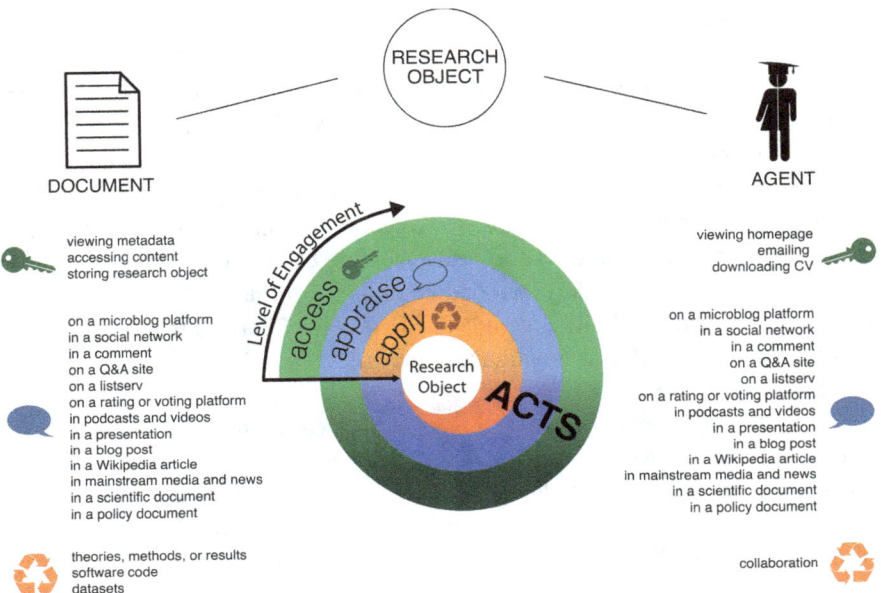

Fig. 1: Framework of categories and types of acts referring to research objects (scholarly documents and agents).

liefs, and theories that supports and informs" (Maxwell, 2009, p. 222) the problem. It is thought to improve the understanding of the various heterogeneous acts that relate to different research objects.

As shown in Figure 1, each of the three act categories, *access*, *appraise*, and *apply*, includes various types of acts, which differ slightly depending on the research object. For example, *applying* a document would comprise reusing and building upon theories, software, or datasets, while for an agent the act of *applying* refers to collaboration. Emphasized by the spiral layout, it is generally assumed that the level of engagement increases as one moves across categories of acts from *accessing* over *appraising* to *applying* (i.e., inwards across layers in Figure 1), as well as across types of acts within categories (i.e., clock-wise along the spiral). For example, acts related to engagement with a journal article increase within the *access* category as one moves from viewing a paper title to storing it in a reference manager or within the *appraise* category as one moves from a quick mention on Twitter to a mention in a policy document. It is also important to note that the boundaries between specific categories and types are permeable, as they can vary and overlap based on use or context.

2.1 Access

This category refers to acts that involve accessing and showing interest in the research object. In the case of scholarly documents this includes *viewing metadata*, which involves viewing the title, abstract, or description of, for example, a paper or book, presentation slides, datasets, or software. *Accessing content* includes viewing and downloading the entire document, while *storing the research object* implies making it available for future use. Online events that currently capture these acts include view and download counts on various platforms and repositories (e.g., journal websites, Dryad, FigShare, SlideShare, Github) and reader and bookmarking counts on reference managers such as BibSonomy, CiteULike, Mendeley, and Zotero.

Focusing on agents as research objects, the access category includes, for example, *viewing* a university's or scholar's homepage or user profile on platforms such as ResearchGate or Academia.edu, *accessing* the agent through electronic means (e.g., email, messaging, Skype, etc.), and *storing* their information for future use, for example by downloading a scholar's CV or 'friending' or 'following' them on a social media platform such as Twitter, ResearchGate, or Academia.edu.

2.2 Appraise

The category of appraising includes the act of mentioning the research object on various platforms such as a microblogs, in a social network, in a comment, on a Q&A site, listserv, or rating or voting platform, as well as in a podcast or video, presentation, review, blog post, Wikipedia article, mainstream media and news, or scientific or policy document. These appraisal acts are almost identical for both types of research objects except for particular technical differences and affordance use, which can be different for agents and documents. For example, mentioning a scholarly paper on Twitter usually implies linking to it via a URL or document identifier (e.g., http://dx.doi.org/10.1038/504211a), while mentioning a researcher implies using the "@" symbol followed by a Twitter handle (e.g., @csugimoto to mention the Twitter user Cassidy R. Sugimoto).[5] With increasing level of engagement, appraising a scholarly document or agent can range from a brief mention in a post on Twitter or Facebook to a citation in a policy document. Various acts

---

5 Of course, mentions of scholars, as well as scholarly documents, occur on Twitter without the use of these particular affordances (e.g., "Cassidy R. Sugimoto", "Sugimoto's latest paper in JASIST"), but they are not recognized as such by Twitter and their proper identification requires more sophisticated tools.

of appraisal can be expressed in a comment, on rating and voting systems (which are usually crowd-sourced and quantitative) such as rating functions on Reddit, Upworthy, or RateMyProfessor.com, or as brief discussions and more extensive and qualitative (peer) judgment, typically carried out by an expert (e.g., on F1000, Pubpeer, and ResearchGate).

2.3 Apply

In terms of scholarly documents, we define apply as actively using significant parts of, adapting, or transforming the research object. This occurs in the form of applying theories, frameworks, methods, or results from a scientific document, software code, or dataset(s) as a foundation to create new work. In scholarly documents, applying the content of other documents (and to a lesser extent datasets and software code) is usually indicated through a citation, in which case the distinction between the event categories "mentioning" and "applying" may become blurry. However, applying suggests a much higher degree of engagement with the original content than is found in the access or appraise categories. This mirrors the different functions of citations as reflected in the distribution of references across scientific articles: a few influential papers are cited in the method section, while a large number of references are briefly mentioned in the introduction (Bertin, Atanassova, Gingras, & Larivière, 2015). Examples of types of applying acts include the thorough discussion of an article's content in a blog, the use of a scholarly document for self-study, the adaptation of the content of an article for a lecture, the modification or improvement of a dataset or software, or even the use of scholarly output for commercial purposes. Regarding agents, the apply category refers to the act of collaboration. The scholar's knowledge, experience, and reputation are applied to formulate something that did not exist before. It may also refer to the participation of the scholar in Q&A sites (such as ResearchGate) where their involvement helps to answer questions.

3 Introducing potentially relevant theories

To improve the understanding of the acts resulting in online events from which metrics are collected, select citation and social theories are used below to interpret the phenomena being measured. Citation theories are used because the new metrics based on these events were proposed to replace or complement citations as indicators of impact. Social theories, on the other hand, are discussed because there is an inherent social aspect to the measurements and because scholars are increasingly facing pressures to ensure their work has societal impact (e.g., HEFCE, 2011).

3.1 Citation theories

Knowledge about citing behavior and the symbolic characteristics of citations is essential to determining whether it makes sense to use citation analysis in various areas of application, particularly in the context of impact metrics and research evaluation. However, a complete theory of citations is lacking (Cronin, 1981; Leydesdorff, 1998). The increasing use of social media in scholarly communication comes with the same demand, as theories and frameworks are required to assess meaning and to validate new indicators as performance and impact metrics (Wouters & Costas, 2012). Citation theories discussed here are the *normative theory*, the *social constructivist theory*, and *concept symbols*.[6] The normative and social constructivist approaches can be considered as two of the most important (and opposing) facets of citation theory (Cronin, 2005a) that are still discussed and tested today (Riviera, 2015). In addition, Small's (1978) concept symbol theory has been intensively discussed in the literature, particularly in the context of "obliteration by incorporation" (Merton, 1968a) and for the study of the "socio-cognitive location" of scholars (Costas & Van Leeuwen, 2012; Moed, 2005), and has been considered in recent conceptual discussions in the field of scientometrics (Guns, 2013).

3.1.1 Normative theory

According to the normative theory, citations are indirect indicators of intellectual influence, reflecting norms and values of science through which scholars are expected to acknowledge the use of the cited work (Kaplan, 1965). Merton (1973) defined the *ethos of science* (i.e., the set of norms and values that rule science) in terms of four basic norms: communism, universalism, disinterestedness, and organized skepticism. As the basis of normative citation theory, Merton's "sociology of science provides the most coherent theoretical framework available" (Small, 2004, p. 72). Although the normative citation theory is based on the as-

---

6 There are other theoretical approaches that have been used for citation theories. Examples are the "reflexive theory" by Wouters (Wouters, 1999) or the 'handicap principle' (Nicolaisen, 2007), as well as network theories (de Solla Price, 1965; Newman, 2005).

sumption that referencing behavior is guided by these norms, it does not claim that authors always strictly adhere to it (De Bellis, 2009; Moed, 2005). In Merton's words, the *communism norm* refers to the "nontechnical and extended sense of common ownership of goods" (Merton, 1973, p. 273). In the context of citations, the well-known idea of "giving credit where credit is due" is attributed to this norm, as authors acknowledge the value of a colleague's work by citing it. *Universalism*, as defined by Merton, "finds immediate expression in the canon that truth-claims, whatever their source, are to be subjected to pre-established impersonal criteria" (Merton, 1973, p. 210). Thus, this norm ascertains that all scientists can contribute to science and are expected to evaluate the works of others regardless of non-scientific characteristics such as race, nationality, culture, or gender. Merton (1988, p. 621) argued that "symbolically, [the reference] registers in the enduring archives the intellectual property of the acknowledged source by providing a pellet of peer recognition of the knowledge claim". Thus, according to the normative theory, citations are the rewards in the science system indicating fair cognitive and intellectual influence.

That scientists should act for the benefit of a common scientific enterprise, rather than professional gain, is expressed by the *disinterestedness norm*. In Merton's (1973, p. 276) words "a passion for knowledge, idle curiosity, altruistic concern with the benefit to humanity, and a host of other special motives have been attributed to the scientist". In the context of citation analysis, Nicolaisen (2007, p. 617) argues that "it assumes that scientists are disinterested and do not seek to gain personal advantages by flattering others or citing themselves". According to the *organized skepticism norm*, scientific claims must be exposed to critical scrutiny before being accepted. From a citation analysis perspective, this is directly related with the publication process of scientific results and new knowledge, as scientists must treat any new claim with skepticism, including their own contributions. Frequently, the *norm of originality* is also included (Ziman, 2000) among the Mertonian norms of science because this norm requires that scientific claims contribute something new, whether a new problem, a new approach, new data, a new theory, or a new explanation.

3.1.2 Social constructivist theory

The focal point of this theory is that works are cited for a variety of factors, many of which have nothing to do with intellectual debt as explained by the normative theory. This implies that the foundation of science originates from social actors engaging in a negotiation process in which one party convinces the other through persuasion. Thus, citations are sometimes seen as "mere persuasion"

(Gilbert, 1977); accordingly, citations are merely attempts at persuading readers of the goodness of an author's claims. In essence, the social constructivist theory opposes the normative theory as it suggests that there are different motivations for citing, many of them influenced by cognitive style and personality and not necessarily by universalistic reasons. Citations are activities based on social psychological influences and are not free of personal bias or social pressures and are not always made for the same reasons. The following describes four main sources of distortion or biases: persuasion hypothesis, perfunctory citations, Matthew effect, and negational citations.

The *persuasion hypothesis* considers citations as 'tools of persuasion' to persuade the scientific community of the value of the work. According to White (2004), persuasion is achieved by logical arguments and inference detailed within the body of the work and by selecting important (authoritative) and adequate papers to convince readers of the importance and validity of the results resulting in a kind of "logical" persuasion, which aligns with the universalism norm. However, White also talks about "dark" persuasion that would be in line with the social constructivist theory. Within this "dark" persuasion there are two types: "persuasion by distortion" that occurs when "citers often misrepresent the works they allude to" (White, 2004, p. 96) and "persuasion by name-dropping" that can be linked to the disproportionate citation of works by established authorities to gain credibility through association. *Perfunctory citations*,[7] according to Murugesan and Moravcsik (1978), are citations that describe alternative approaches not utilized in the citing paper, references that are merely used to compare certain results or conclusions, references that are used to indicate the fact that a certain method employed is routine in the literature, and references that merely contribute to the chronological context of the citing paper. In other words, perfunctory citations are nonessential, superficial, redundant, or even wrong citations.

According to Merton (1968b, p. 58) the *Matthew effect* can be defined as the "accruing of greater increments of recognition for particular scientific contributions to scientists of considerable repute and withholding of such recognition from scientists who have not yet made their mark". Thus, scientists who are rich in recognition find it easier to get more recognition (and resources), which causes "the rich [to] get richer at a rate that makes the poor become relatively poorer" (Merton, 1968b, p. 62). Price (1976) demonstrated the Matthew effect mathemat-

---

[7] Perfunctory citations are opposed to "Organic" citations which are references to those from which concepts or theories are taken to lay the foundations of the citing paper, or papers from which certain results (including numerical ones) are taken to develop the ideas in the citing paper, or papers which help to better understand certain concepts in the citing paper (Murugesan & Moravcsik, 1978).

ically for publications and citations and referred to it as *cumulative advantage* or *success breeds success*, showing that the probability of being cited increases with the number of citations already obtained (for more on success indicators, see Glänzel and Schubert [this volume] and Rousseau and Rousseau [this volume]). This self-reinforcing effect for citations has also been shown to apply to countries (Bonitz, Bruckner, & Scharnhorst, 1997) and papers published in journals with high impact factors (Larivière & Gingras, 2010). In network theory, the Matthew effect is referred to as *preferential attachment*, where nodes in a network accumulate new edges proportionally to their number of edges, leading to power law distributions (Barabási, 1999; Newman, 2001). *Obliteration by incorporation* is a variant of the cumulative advantage and was also suggested by Merton (1968a), but it takes the point of view that there is an underestimation of mentions through the obliteration of the sources by their incorporation in currently accepted knowledge (Merton, 1988). In essence, papers that have become well known are no longer formally cited. *Negational (or negative) citation* is a citation that "describes the situation when the author of the citing paper is not certain about the correctness of the cited paper" (Murugesan & Moravcsik, 1978, p. 297). In other words, these are citations to papers that may have been challenged or contradicted in other (or the citing) work.

3.1.3 Concept symbols theory

The *concept symbols* theory (Small, 1978) considers the citation as symbolic of the idea expressed in the paper. The basic idea is that a citation is a symbolic act of authors associating particular ideas (i.e., concepts, procedures, or kind of data) with particular documents and is thus based on Garfield's (1964) notion of citations as descriptors in subject indexing. By using this theory one can consider citations as private symbols (cited by only one or a few authors) or standard symbols (highly cited). With a document that is repeatedly cited the citers engage in a dialogue on the document's significance, thus the meaning is conferred through this iterative activity, while at the same time the meaning of the document becomes limited through the capsulizing of a complex text into a few standard sentences (Small, 1978). This may result in the distortion or oversimplification of the original text and cause the symbolic meaning to change over time.

3.2 Social theories

Researchers investigating actors and output in specific computer-mediated environments have interpreted interaction and communication using a variety of theories including theories from economics, psychology, anthropology, and sociology. In this section a select few theories will be considered in order to improve the understanding of the acts resulting in online events from which metrics are collected. These include the theories of social capital, attention economics, and impression management.

3.2.1 Social capital

Social capital is a theory that has garnered much interest from a variety of disciplines. The theory stipulates that humans are social creatures and thus need to be connected to others in close-knit groups; these connections are treated as two-way investments that are maintained through reciprocal support and re-investment. Bourdieu (1985) was the first sociologist to distinguish social capital as one of three types of capital in social relations: economic, cultural, and social. Social capital can be thought of as a source of power that can be accrued through connections in a social network; actors in networks establish and maintain relationships with other actors in the hope that they may benefit in some way from these relationships. The relationships can be strong or weak (Granovetter, 1973) and this measure can have an impact on the return that an actor derives from either type including emotional support, the exchange of information, or mobilization toward a common goal. Bozionelos (2014, p. 288) used social capital theory to examine career paths in the Greek academic system and found that social capital "determines careers within that system." In social media research, several researchers (Hofer & Aubert, 2013; Steinfield, Dimicco, Ellison, & Lampe, 2009; Valenzuela, Park, & Kee, 2008) have used social capital theory to discuss aspects of interaction on various platforms.

Many other definitions in multiple disciplines have been suggested since Bourdieu's discussion of social capital (see Adler & Kwon, 2002; Portes, 1998 for summaries) including two prominent definitions from Coleman (1988, 1990) and Putnam (1995, 2000). The concept has become (in a sense) a catchall term that captures aspects of social interaction that have been studied through the lens of other concepts. Outside the arena of information communication technologies (ICT), social capital has been used to study youth behavior problems, families, schooling, public health, education, political action, community, and organizational issues such as job and career success, innovation, and supplier relations

(Adler & Kwon, 2002). Social capital has become "one of the most popular exports from sociological theory into everyday language" (Portes, 1998, p. 2).

3.2.2 Attention economics

The theory of attention economics (Davenport & Beck, 2001) considers the costs and benefits of finding useful information. Simon (1971) was one of the first to postulate that the world is full of information and that this takes the attention of the information consumer. When considering the theory of attention economics it is necessary to think of the growing amount of information available as a scenario in which human attention becomes increasingly valuable because there is a limited amount to be utilized. Franck (2002, p. 9) argued that scientists are "entrepreneurs who allocate time and effort so as to maximize the attention received from other scientists" and it is this view that allows one to consider the ways in which scientists use tools and technologies to minimize the amount of attention they spend on sifting through the never-ending output of material to locate relevant and useful information.

Researchers have used this theoretical framework to analyze behavior within social media platforms. For example, Rui and Whinston (2011, p. 322) examined approximately 3 million Twitter users and found that social media environments are a "marketplace where people contribute information to attract attention and contribute attention while consuming information." The attention economy framework has also been used to evaluate novelty and popularity in social networks (Huberman, 2013) and to examine pedagogical strategies for retaining the attention of law students in the technology-rich environment of today's classroom (Matthews, 2012). The attention level of an audience member is determined by their "attention capacities and on the total volume of signals to which they are exposed" (Falkinger, 2003, p. 4), and today's environment exposes scholars to an unconscionable amount of information suggesting that it is extremely important to consider how they manage and conserve attention (see Bawden, this volume, for more on the escalating size of available information and psychological attention).

3.2.3 Impression management

The dramaturgical framework put forth by Erving Goffman (1959) describes activities termed self-presentation and impression management. Impression management is a process that takes place as humans interact with one another and is motivated by the need to avoid shame and embarrassment, while self-presentation is the act of presenting information about oneself to an audience. Goffman described these processes using dramaturgical concepts which include actors, audience, and stage, and argued that when people interact with one another they act out a role for their audience and are required to maintain the impression of that role through the entirety of the interaction; if the impression is broken and the audience loses faith in the presentation of the role, the actor will be shamed and embarrassed.

The concepts of impression management and self-presentation have been defined in the literature in many ways, with most building upon Goffman's description. Gosling and colleagues (Gosling, Gaddis, & Vazire, 2007) examined the accuracy of impressions on Facebook finding that personality impressions were limited in accuracy and that authors did enhance their own self-presentations. When comparing impressions made on Facebook with impressions made in face-to-face meetings, Weisbuch and colleagues (2009) found that they were very similar. With regards to Twitter, Gilpin (2011, p. 234) writes that tweeting plays an important role in impression formation, "as followers will primarily draw conclusions based on the contents of tweet messages as well as indications of the intended recipients of those messages."

4 Applying theories to selected acts

Using the framework in Figure 1 to describe, define, and distinguish various acts related to research objects, we discuss the citation and social theories introduced above. Due to space restrictions, this work will focus solely on applying these theories to acts related to the scientific journal article[8] as the most common and important type of scholarly documents (and the focus of most currently captured altmetrics). Future work should consider discussing acts related to other types of documents, as well as to scholarly agents. In order to simplify the discussion and provide more room for detail, the focus will be on some of the most popular acts in terms of number of captured online events to scholarly papers as well as researched events in the current altmetrics setting.[9] These include the acts of

---

[8] In this context, the journal article as the research object may also refer to other versions of the original publication such as the preprint/eprint on repositories, which may or may not be considered as one single research object.
[9] See for example Bornmann (2014b); Costas, Zahedi, and Wouters (2014); Haustein, Costas, and Larivière (2015b); Haustein et al. (2014a); Holmberg and Thelwall (2014), Mohammadi and Thelwall (2013) and Waltman and Costas (2014).

saved in Mendeley, for the *access* category; *mentioned in a tweet*, and *reviewed on F1000* for *appraise*; and *cited in a blog post* for a specific case of *applying* the content of a scientific journal paper. Mendeley reader counts and tweets have been shown to be the most prevalent online events currently captured for scientific papers;[10] Mendeley reader counts account for two thirds of recent journal articles and tweets mention approximately one fifth of recent journal articles. Reviews on F1000 and blog citations occur much less due to their selectivity and higher level of engagement, but are discussed as they represent particular forms of acts regarding journal articles (Bornmann, 2014b; Costas, Zahedi, & Wouters, 2014; Haustein, Costas, & Larivière, 2015b; Haustein et al., 2014a).

4.1 Access: Saved in Mendeley

A Mendeley readership count for a particular document (at present) indicates that a Mendeley user has added the document to his or her Mendeley library.[11] Users of Mendeley are assumed to have an interest in organizing bibliographic metadata to keep track of and manage scientific documents either for citing or using them in a professional or educational context (which could include teaching and self-teaching). However, each document added to a Mendeley user library is not necessarily read (Mohammadi, 2014) and there is no guarantee that a user adds all documents he or she has (read or cited (or intents to read or cite) to their Mendeley library.

According to previous research (Mohammadi, Thelwall, Haustein, & Larivière, 2015; Mohammadi, 2014), most Mendeley users are students, postdocs, and researchers and as such it is assumed that Mendeley readership counts are a reflection of interest by a scholarly audience beyond the community of citing authors. It is not known whether the approximately three million Mendeley users (Haustein & Larivière, 2014) are representative of the entire readership of scientific documents and whether certain biases exist regarding disciplines, academic age, or countries. Among the currently captured social media metrics related to scientific documents, Mendeley reader counts have the highest correlations with

---

10 It should be noted that due to current technical constraints, the scholarly document being tracked is (in most cases) a peer-reviewed journal article with a DOI or comparable identifier (e.g., arXiv id or PMID).
11 Technically, a user can save a document either online or in the desktop version of the reference manager. Bibliographic information is typically extracted directly from the document or the metadata is harvested from the website where the document is located. This may lead to errors in the bibliographic data that can be manually corrected by the user.

citations, ranging from medium to high values (e.g., Mohammadi et al., 2015; Mohammadi & Thelwall, 2014; Zahedi, Costas, & Wouters, 2014), which implies a certain similarity between the two metrics. This suggests that citation theories may be of value to understand what is happening in the Mendeley environment.

Opposed to citing, where the different norms of communism, universalism, disinterestedness, and organized skepticism (and originality) are expected to apply, Mendeley users may not necessarily adhere to these norms when adding documents to their libraries – in fact, norms regarding literature management do not exist. Students and young scientists presumably are not (yet) taught that they are supposed to save and organize all relevant documents in reference management software. When saving papers, the principle of *giving credit where credit is due* does not necessarily apply because documents are often added before they are actually read, which implies that Mendeley user libraries do not only include the most influential and relevant documents, but also include those without actual value to the user. The act of saving a document to Mendeley is assumed to be more general than the act of citing, because more documents are saved and read than cited. Moreover, saving to Mendeley may not only be due to utilitarian reasons of saving and organizing, intended reading, highlighting, and annotating, which would imply a certain level of giving credit to authors, but also due to (self-)marketing.

However, if the act of *saving to Mendeley* is considered *use* of the document— including various facets from mere saving to intense reading, annotating, and citing—then Merton's communism, as well as universalism, could apply because authors receive Mendeley reader counts when their papers are saved to Mendeley. If users added all documents they read to their Mendeley libraries, Mendeley readership would give credit to the sources upon which their knowledge is based without distinguishing to what extent these documents were relevant or required to fulfill the library owner's information needs. In this regard, the act of saving to Mendeley as reflected in reader counts could be considered as a 'pellet of peer recognition' similar to citations, although certainly on a different level of engagement and without any quality control or space restrictions[12] of peer-reviewed journal articles. However, a survey among 679 Mendeley users found that only 27 % of users had read all of the documents in their libraries (Mohammadi, 2014). It can be argued that the disinterestedness norm applies to saving to Mendeley, but more as an unconscious act given that saving to Mendeley is essentially anonymous;[13]

---

[12] Note that technical limitations such as available space in user libraries could still apply.
[13] It should be note that the link between user and document is visible on other platforms (e.g., CiteULike).

this is in contrast to the act of citing, which can be considered "a private process with a public face" (Cronin, 1981, p. 16). The norm of organized skepticism does not apply to the act of saving to Mendeley because documents are often added before they are read, thus they are added without being considered "skeptically". Organized skepticism could only apply if a document was scrutinized by the user and then removed from their Mendeley library.

Empirical user studies have yet to show whether and to what extent users adhere to norms when saving documents to Mendeley in order to determine whether Mendeley reader counts might signify influence (albeit in a broader sense than citations). Even if the normative theory does not yet apply to the act of saving to Mendeley due to the current lack of equivalent norms regarding the use of reference managers, norms regarding literature management could be introduced in the future to establish *saving to Mendeley* (or any other reference manager) as an inherent part of the scholarly communication process.

The value of the social constructivist theory to interpret this event would stem from its ability to interpret the act in terms of its pre-citation role and, indeed, a survey among Mendeley users found that the main reason to save documents to Mendeley was to cite them in the future (Mohammadi, 2014). It is, however, difficult to expect that someone would simply save a document in Mendeley for persuasive reasons given the anonymous nature of the act on Mendeley. Saving a document as a negative example would conceptually be possible, although identifying this kind of negative use is currently not possible.

The Matthew effect could apply to Mendeley in a manner similar to citations. Considering the cumulative advantage within the platform, documents that have already been saved to Mendeley libraries are more likely to be added by other users because they appear in Mendeley search results and when browsing the Mendeley website. Applying the Matthew effect in a more general sense, considering various aspects of scientific and social capital, Mendeley users would be prone to save more documents from renowned authors and high impact journals. Findings by Costas, Zahedi, and Wouters (2015) note that articles published in high-impact journals such as *Nature* or *Science* account for a substantial amount of reader counts suggesting that some kind of Matthew effect applies when documents are saved to Mendeley.

Apart from the pre-citation context—saving a document to Mendeley in order to cite it—the idea of concept symbols could be applied to tagging or summarizing a document in Mendeley and thus make it a particular symbol for the Mendeley user. However, this would be more in line with appraising than accessing a Mendeley document.

Using the theory of social capital to interpret why a user saves a document in Mendeley can also be useful. Users may save their publications into the system with hope that it will increase their worth by increasing the visibility of their own work. As social network connections are seen to be of value, it is clear that increasing the visibility of one's work has the potential of increasing one's social capital in that network.

When examining this act from the perspective of attention economics, this social theory is well suited to explain why a user saves documents in Mendeley. He or she is making use of Mendeley (such as searching, storing, and organizing) to reduce the amount of attention they will need to utilize it in the future. Saving a publication to Mendeley allows the user to reduce the amount of time and effort they spend on information sifting so that they may spend their valuable attention on other matters.

If one applies impression management theory to the act of saving a document in Mendeley, it becomes clear that a user may save their own publication to Mendeley (and thus the publications appear in the Mendeley search or when browsing the Mendeley website) in order to impress upon others that they are accomplished in their area of study or that they are merely meeting certain impressions others (such as their colleagues, students, or administrators) have of them.

4.2 Appraise: Mentioned in a tweet

Due to the 140-character limitation of a tweet, a scientific document has to be referred to by a commonly used unique identifier or URL.[14] Perhaps the most important difference between citations and tweets is that the former is a standardized and codified type of mention, while in Twitter the norms surrounding the mentions are rather different. Many documents are highly tweeted not due to their scientific merits (Haustein, Peters, Sugimoto, Thelwall, & Larivière, 2014b), but instead because they reflect "ephemeral (or prurient) interest[s], the usual trilogy of sex, drugs, and rock and roll" (Neylon, 2014, para. 6), which discredits Merton's notion of valuing knowledge claims. Twitter users do not seem to (and they are not expected to) concern themselves with whether or not the document is original, if it is of high quality, if they are rewarding the authors, etc., instead the Twitter environment appears to be mostly free of these expectations (or at least not intrinsically based on the Mertonian norms). It could still be argued that some

---

[14] Mentions of scientific papers on Twitter are currently captured if they include the publisher URL or common document identifiers such as DOI, PMID, or arXiv ID. Formal or informal citations such as Cronin, B. (1981). *The need for a theory of citing. Journal of Documentation, 37(1), 16–24* or Cronin's paper in *JDoc* are not captured.

degree of communism, universalism, or disinterestedness apply to a specific subset of tweets, if researchers use Twitter to discuss, debate, or contrast scientific ideas. Findings regarding bot accounts, which automatically tweet links to scientific documents, are another example of the limitations of Mertonian norms to this type of act (Haustein, Bowman, Holmberg, Tsou, Sugimoto, & Larivière, 2015a), as automated diffusion cannot be considered a social act.

Finding aspects of social constructivism in tweets mentioning scientific publications is hampered by the 140-character restriction. However, it can be argued that some forms of persuasion might be attributed to Twitter users when mentioning a scientific document. Perfunctory tweets, for example wrongful mentions of papers linked to unrelated topics or presenting authoritative references for invalid arguments, are possible. However, these might instead be considered misunderstandings or "misframings" (Goffman, 1974) by their users instead of a conscious act of manipulation of the counts of publications with superficial or wrong mentions. The findings that retracted publications tend to receive more Twitter mentions than regular papers (Haustein et al., 2015b) supports the idea that negative mentions of scientific papers on Twitter occur, but initial studies (Friedrich, Bowman, Stock, & Haustein, 2015; Thelwall et al., 2013) suggest that they might be as rare as negative citations in the natural sciences and medicine (Murugesan & Moravcsik, 1978).

The Matthew effect might play an important role in the accumulation of tweets for scientific documents, for example within the platform itself through affordances like the retweet function. A (re)tweeted paper would increase its Twitter visibility and accrue more (re)tweets as an effect of its previous (re)tweets. Twitter users receive push notifications if a particular number of users they follow has retweeted the same tweet (Satuluri, 2013), which might produce further tweets. Another Twitter-specific aspect related to the cumulative advantage is the number of followers. A paper mentioned by an account with a large number of followers can be expected to be visible to a larger audience, thus increasing its potential to receive more tweets. This might, for example, be the case when official Twitter accounts of scientific journals tweet their papers (Haustein et al., 2014b). The Matthew effect can be argued to apply in a more general sense; for example, when a paper is frequently mentioned on Twitter due to the academic capital (Bourdieu, 1984) of the authors or the journal in which it was published. It is likely that success on Twitter is bred by a mix of social capital and impression management within the platform—profile information, number of (re)tweets and followers, etc.—as well as in the scientific community (e.g., reflected by the citation impact, funding success, or awards). This is supported by the finding that the highest number of tweets are obtained by papers published in journals such as *Nature*, *Science*, *New England Journal of Medicine* and *Lancet*, which belong to the most prestigious scientific journals and, at the same time, promote their content through official Twitter accounts with many followers (Costas, Zahedi, & Wouters, 2015; Haustein et al., 2014b).

The fast and brief nature of tweeting promotes obliteration by incorporation in so far as users might avoid linking to the original paper due to space limitations. This could lead to an undervaluation of certain documents.

The concept symbols theory has a special fit for the act of tweeting about scientific papers. The short nature of tweets strongly supports the narrowing of meaning stipulated by this theory, as the meaning of (or engagement of the Twitter users with) the publication has to be encapsulated in 140 characters. Also, the association of publications with hashtags (which can be signs or signifiers referring to ideas or concepts) supports the idea that mentions of documents on Twitter are concept symbols. Similarly, when a document is repeatedly tweeted and Twitter users engage in a discussion about the value of the document, the meaning of the tweets is conferred through the symbolic usage of the publications (similar to the use of citations as symbols). This narrowing of meaning and the fact that many of the users are not necessarily experts on the paper's topic may result in the distortion or oversimplification of the original text (similar to citations), a phenomenon that has been already discussed for altmetrics (Colquhoun, 2014).

Approaching the act of mentioning on Twitter using social theory can provide additional insight. Users may have many different motivations for mentioning a scientific document in a tweet, yet the theory of social capital suggests that one of these motivations will be to establish a connection between the tweeter and the publication (and in return the author(s) of the document). When a scholar tweets about a scientific document, they are making a weak connection in the network between themselves and the other. If the tweeter continues to tweet about publications from the same author(s), the connection between the two (or more) can become stronger creating a potential form of revenue that can be later converted into benefits such as a collaboration or a letter of reference.

When examining the Twitter mention from the perspective of attention economics, the tweeter will use Twitter-specific affordances (such as the URL, an @ symbol, favoriting, and/or a #hashtag) to reduce the amount of attention they and others will need to access and understand the article, as the searching and organization in the Twitter environment is facilitated by the use of these affordances.

Looking at this act through the lens of impression management allows one to interpret the act as an attempt to impress upon others that he or she is up to date on the work in their field, that they present themselves as one who can be trusted to spread relevant documents, or that they are simply reinforcing their identity as an expert in a specific domain.

4.3 Appraise: Reviewed on F1000Prime

Faculty of 1000 (F1000Prime or F1000[15]) is a commercial online post-publication peer review and recommendation service for biological and medical research launched in 2002. More than 5000 peer-nominated researchers and clinicians, referred to as F1000 faculty members, produce the reviews. Faculty members are requested to select the most interesting publications they read and to provide reviews of these publications. A review of a publication consists of a recommendation ("good", "very good", or "exceptional") along with an explanation of the strengths (and possibly also the weaknesses) of the publication. Faculty members can choose to review any primary research article from any journal without being limited to recent publications or publications indexed in any given database (Waltman & Costas, 2014). Papers are not only rated in F1000, but they are also reviewed and labeled in order to indicate such things as the appropriateness for changes to clinical practice, suitability for new drugs, or usability for teaching (Mohammadi & Thelwall, 2013).

Given the scholarly nature of F1000 reviews, the normative theory can apply in a similar manner as to citations. F1000 faculty are expected to behave according to the "ethos of science" when selecting and reviewing their publications for F1000, as "they must sign a statement to indicate that the article has been selected for inclusion in F1000Prime's Article Recommendations entirely on its scientific merit and that they have not been influenced directly or indirectly in the selection of articles by the authors or any third party".[16] The F1000 post-publication peer review system shares advantages as well as some disadvantages and biases—e.g., subjectivity, lack of consensus and biases of referees, cost and time issues, and difficulty to scale (e.g., King, 1987; Lee, Sugimoto, Zhang, & Cronin, 2013)—with traditional 'blind' peer review, which makes the normative theory highly applicable. In addition to the traditional pre-publication review, recommendations on F1000 are attributed and linked to referees and there are various steps of quality control, such as monitoring by section heads and the possibility for faculty members to disagree with recommendations,[17] which should further encourage referees to behave according to Mertonian norms.

---

[15] See http://f1000.com/prime
[16] http://f1000.com/prime/about/whatis
[17] http://f1000.com/prime/about/whatis

For the same reasons, persuasive and perfunctory reviews and recommendations are quite unlikely and negative reviews are technically not possible on F1000,[18] although constructive criticism is encouraged.[19] Although publications from all types of sources and authors are expected to be reviewed, the higher accumulation of reviews in high impact journals (Waltman & Costas, 2014) points to a form of the "Matthew effect" in the selection and review of documents by F1000 similar to what Larivière and Gingras (2010) found for citations. The cumulative advantage taken in a stricter sense, in that papers with many F1000 recommendations are likely to accrue even more within the same platform, is less likely to apply because F1000 functions as a filter where experts supposedly choose the most important articles from their research area. This assumption is supported by findings that the vast majority of reviewed publications have only one review and less than 2.5 % receive more than three recommendations (Waltman & Costas, 2014).

The concept symbol theory applies in so far that faculty members choose and recommend documents for particular reasons that are indicated by particular tags, such as *new findings, controversial,* or *good for teaching* or in the recommendation text in the form of concrete statements about the content, interest, and usefulness of the documents. A recommended document could thus be considered a private symbol of the reviewer, who distills the meaning of the original text in his or her review. The idea of standard symbols is less likely to apply, as most documents are only recommended by one faculty member.

When a scholar reviews an article he or she is establishing a (weak) connection between his or her review and the paper itself, and subsequently the venue in which the paper occurs, the content of the article, and potentially the author(s) of the document. This connection can be of value to the reviewer at a later time as they can list this service on their CV or they can help establish trends in research areas by reviewing (what they consider) quality documents, thus supporting the interest of the social capital theory in the understanding of F1000 recommendations.

From another perspective, attention economics might suggest that a reviewer would choose to participate in this act to reduce the amount of information they need to search by focusing on documents relevant to their own work. This would reduce the amount of documents they would need to examine when trying to find information in the future.

---

[18] It should be noted that negative reviews are possible on other platforms (e.g., Publons or Pubpeer).

[19] http://f1000.com/prime/about/whatis

If one were to use impression management to examine this act, it is clear that the reviewer may be looking to create a new impression of himself or herself as someone who can be relied upon to act as a gatekeeper of science or to reinforce an existing impression. The affordances of the platform allows for the establishment of a reviewer as a "global expert"[20] thus allowing them to present a self that contributes to the impression others have of them.

4.4 Apply: Cited in a blog post

Among current social media activity, the act of citing in blogs is believed to be the most similar to citing in scientific documents, because research blogs allow for and provide the space to discuss and analyze scientific content (Shema, Bar-Ilan & Thelwall, 2014). The findings that blogs have moderate correlations with citations (Costas, Zahedi, & Wouters, 2014; Haustein et al., 2015b; Shema et al., 2014) support this assumption. As a result, citation theories are more likely to apply to blog citations than mentions on Twitter. However, even in the case of *applying* a scientific document to a blog (e.g., building upon and reusing results, methods, and theories of a scientific documents[21]) particular differences between scientific peer-reviewed documents and blog posts limit the applicability of citation theory; this can be caused by blogs not having the same scholarly nature as scientific publications as they lack the gatekeeping and quality control present in academic work: anyone can publish a blog on their homepage, posts are typically not peer-reviewed, and some blog posts simply announce the publication of interesting articles. It should be noted, however, that some blog aggregator platforms (such as ResearchBlogging.org) have bloggers agree to specific guidelines[22] to ensure that the posts of bloggers on the platform discuss peer-reviewed research that they have fully read, understood, and formally cited, while adding original content.

The normative theory could thus be applied to mentions in blogs, if one would expect bloggers and science journalists to cite according to similar "norms" as scholars. However, given the more open and less controlled nature of blogs, it is reasonable to think that the application of these rules would be less strict than in scholarly contexts.

---

[20] As indicated on the F1000 website (http://f1000.com/about-and-contact).
[21] This seems plausible, as reported by Fausto and colleagues (Fausto et al., 2012) the number of citations per blog is increasing but with values of citations per blog post between 1.38 to 1.48.
[22] http://researchblogging.org/news/?p=53

From another perspective, persuasion is indeed a driving force in blogging and scientific journalism by frequently discussing scholarly information and presenting the viewpoints of their authors on scientific issues (Shema et al., 2014; Shema, Bar-Ilan, & Thelwall, 2015). However, it could be debated whether the value of name-dropping and perfunctory mentions have the same incidence in blog posts as in scholarly publications. Considering that bloggers and science journalists do not share the same reward system as scholars, it is arguable that the presence of these types of persuasions may be less frequent in this environment, although the possibility still exists that other types of rewards (e.g., followers, visitors of their blogs, commenters, etc.) may play a role in influencing bloggers' behaviors (e.g., by distorting the content of scientific documents in order to support their views or to mention publications from esteemed journals or authors). The Matthew effect is also applicable for blog posts, as it is plausible that bloggers and scientific journalists primarily focus on well-established, famous, and popular authors or journals (Shema et al., 2015). Finally, the existence of important blogging activities around retracted publications (Haustein et al., 2015b) supports the idea that negative mentions are also important in the consideration of blog mentions.

The concept symbols theory can be applied to blog mentions in a similar manner as to citations; being reinforced by the open-natured and laymen-authored activity of typical blogs, which allows for the narrowing of the document's original meaning.

Social capital, attention economics, and impression management all provide useful insight into why a blogger or journalist may cite a scholarly document in their blog. For instance, the blogger establishes a weak connection between her blog and the scholarly document (and subsequently the author(s) and/or the journal) that can become stronger by the continued use of other documents by the same author(s), thus providing social capital to the blogger by creating a connection between her and the author(s) of the documents, or by simply driving traffic to her blog. The creation of blogs around scientific documents also allows the blogger (and his or her users) to keep a record of "useful" (or not useful) academic work that can be easily filtered through the typical blogging affordances of searching, tagging, and storing posts, thus decreasing the attention needed to find these documents in the future. Finally, impression management may explain why a blogger might cite a specific scholarly document, as the blogger must be concerned about the impression he or she is creating by applying the document. Thus the blogger may be attempting to create an impression that implies they understand and have expertise on the cited material.

5 Conclusions and Outlook

In the current debate around so-called altmetrics, some argue that these *polymorphous mentions* (Cronin et al., 1998, p. 1320) can be a good proxy for societal impact (Bornmann, 2014b), early scientific impact (Eysenbach, 2011), attention, and educational and practical use (Mohammadi et al., 2015; Zahedi, Costas, & Wouters, 2013), while others argue that they reflect nothing but buzz, popularity, or simply increasing visibility (Colquhoun, 2014). The answer is probably that the new metrics are all of the above and the extent to which each of these occurs depends on the particular platform, its uptake and users, as well as on the research topic, the unit of analysis, and the context of the metric.

It is important to keep in mind that these new metrics may be influenced by "noise" (i.e., all mentions that are not meaningful or deviate from the intended meanings such as "automated" mentions, self-mentions, data errors, etc.) and that this noise can introduce doubt as to how to properly interpret the significance of the acts leading to these captured metrics. In addition, the technology and its affordances are constantly changing so that the acts themselves are being affected, which in turn can bring new challenges and issues to the understanding of these metrics. In general, what is lacking is a concrete set of frameworks, models, and theories that can help to support interpretations and uses of these new metrics.

This chapter provides a conceptual framework that can be applied to the acts leading to (online) events underlying these metrics in the context of scholarly communication. In order to better comprehend these heterogeneous acts, the framework identifies three broad categories of acts related to scholarly documents and agents: accessing, appraising, and applying. Common citation and social theories are introduced to discuss whether they can be used to explain the acts underlying the various indicators referred to as altmetrics. The reason to begin theoretical discussions by applying normative, social constructivist, and concept symbols theories to social media metrics is based on the strong, albeit antagonistic, relationship of altmetrics to citations (Priem et al., 2010; Priem, 2014). In addition to these citation theories, three social theories were used to interpret these events including social capital, attention economics, and impression management because of the inherent social nature of these platforms. Focusing on the journal articles as the most common form of scholarly documents, these theories were applied to the acts of saving to Mendeley, mentioning on Twitter, reviewing on F1000, and citing in a blog post in order to determine their applicability.

Due to the heterogeneity of various types and categories of acts (i.e., access, appraise, and apply), the discussed citation theories are more or less suitable. Similar to Hogan and Sweeney (2013) who discussed the limited fitting of Mertonian norms to the new social media, this work found that Mertonian norms fit quite well with the act of reviewing and recommending on F1000, to a lesser extent with being cited in blogs, and that the norms did not apply to mentions on Twitter. In the context of saving to Mendeley, the normative theory is more likely to apply only in the pre-citation context, i.e., when it is linked to the act of citing.

In terms of social constructivist theories, the Matthew effect idea has the strongest potential for most of the discussed acts and can, to a certain extent, explain the concentration and skewness of social media events across publications. This might be attributed to the networked nature of these platforms. Thus, platforms such as Mendeley and Twitter support the necessary processes most often associated with the Matthew effect and preferential attachment, as documents with more events get higher visibility within the platforms through different mechanisms (e.g., re-tweets, number of followers, or Mendeley filtering tools). For F1000 reviews, as well as blogs, the higher presence of papers from prestigious journals suggests that the Matthew effect could apply from the point of view of the concentration of events around specific agents (e.g., prominent authors, journals, etc.) represented in the system. The presence of the Matthew effect may have important implications for the potential consideration of acts in social media metrics with regard to the reward and communication systems of science.

Concept symbols are more likely to apply to the act of tweeting documents in so far as Twitter could serve as a language system with particular symbols (e.g., hashtags linked to publications) indicating a particular idea or concept in relation to the document. The applicability of this theory would conceptually support the notion of tweeted papers being used as concept symbols by an audience broader than the scientific community. Thus, it would be reasonable to use Twitter as a tool to capture the public perception of science, particularly if these concepts regarding scientific documents differ from those of the scientific community.[23] To a lesser extent than Twitter, the theory of concept symbols could also be applied to the acts of blog mentions and F1000 reviews.

Three social theories were used to interpret these acts: social capital, attention economics, and impression management. Each of these theoretical viewpoints allows one to interpret the specific acts described above using different lenses. From a purely social perspective, social capital explains how the use of these platforms benefits the scholars by providing them with a network of

---

[23] For example, a common criticism is that Twitter users do not understand scientific publications and therefore they mention them for other reasons than their scientific merit. Identifying these different symbolic connections generated by the general public would help to develop mechanisms to improve the understanding of research results outside the scientific community.

potential resources to mine and utilize when necessary. From a pragmatic view, attention economy is useful as it discusses the benefits of using social media to decrease the time spent both finding and attending to information sources. Finally, impression management describes the ways in which scholars must actively maintain their presentation of self as they navigate the blurring boundaries of the public/private nature of social media.

The theories discussed in this chapter cannot fully explain social media acts related to scholarly communication. Empirical research—such as content analyses along the lines of Shema et al. (2015), as well as user surveys like Mohammadi (2014)—is needed to further investigate user motivations behind these acts and support (or not) the use of altmetrics in research evaluation. This chapter provides the scaffolding for such research. It represents a very much needed step towards understanding the various outputs and impacts of research in the digital age.

Acknowledgment

The authors would like to thank Vincent Larivière for fruitful discussions on the topic and helpful comments on an earlier version of the manuscript. SH acknowledges funding from the Alfred P. Sloan Foundation Grant # 2014-3-25 and TBD from the Canada Research Chair on the Transformations of Scholarly Communication.

Cited References

Adie, E. (2014). Taking the alternative mainstream. *El Profesional de La Informacion*, *23*(4), 349–351.

Adler, P. S., & Kwon, S. (2002). Social capital: Prospects for a new concept. *Academy of Management Preview*, *27*(1), 17–40.

Almind, T. C., & Ingwersen, P. (1997). Informetric analyses on the world wide web: methodological approaches to "webometrics." *Journal of Documentation*, *53*(4), 404–426. doi:10.1108/EUM0000000007205

Barabási, A. (1999). Emergence of scaling in random networks. *Science*, *286*(5439), 509–512. doi:10.1126/science.286.5439.509

Bertin, M., Atanassova, I., Gingras, Y., & Larivière, V. (2015). The invariant distribution of references in scientific articles. *Journal of the Association for Information Science and Technology*. doi:10.1002/asi.23367

Bilder, G., Fenner, M., Lin, J., & Neylon, C. (2015). *ALM Workshop 2014 Report*. doi:10.6084/m9.figshare.1287503

Bonitz, M., Bruckner, E., & Scharnhorst, A. (1997). Characteristics and impact of the Matthew effect for countries. *Scientometrics*, *40*(3), 407–422. doi:10.1007/BF02459289

Borghuis, M. G. M. (1997). User feedback from electronic subscriptions: The possibilities of logfile analysis. *Library Acquisitions: Practice & Theory*, *21*(3), 373–380. doi:10.1016/S0364-6408(97)00066-5

Bornmann, L. (2014a). Is there currently a scientific revolution in scientometrics? *Journal of the Association for Information Science and Technology*, *65*(3), 647–648. doi:10.1002/asi.23073

Bornmann, L. (2014b). Validity of altmetrics data for measuring societal impact: A study using data from Altmetric and F1000Prime. *Journal of Informetrics*, *8*(4), 935–950. doi:10.1016/j.joi.2014.09.007

Bourdieu, P. (1975). The specificity of the scientific field and the social conditions of the progress of reason. *Social Science Information*, *14*(6), 19–47. doi:10.1177/053901847501400602

Bourdieu, P. (1984). *Distinction: A Social Critique of the Judgement of Taste*. London: Routledge.

Bourdieu, P. (1985). The forms of capital. In J. G. Richardson (Ed.), *Handbook of theory and research for the sociology of education* (pp. 241–258). New York: Greenwood.

Bozionelos, N. (2014). Careers patterns in Greek academia: social capital and intelligent careers, but for whom? *Career Development International*, *19*(3), 264–294. doi:10.1108/CDI-01-2014-0011

Coleman, J. (1988). Social capital in the creation of human capital. *American Journal of Sociology*, *94*, S95–S120.

Coleman, J. (1990). *Foundations of Social Theory*. Cambridge: Harvard University Press.

Colquhoun, D. (2014). Why you should ignore altmetrics and other bibliometric nightmares. *DC's Improbable Science*. Retrieved February 09, 2015, from http://www.dcscience.net/2014/01/16/why-you-should-ignore-altmetrics-and-other-bibliometric-nightmares/

Costas, R., & Van Leeuwen, T. N. (2012). Referencing patterns of individual researchers: Do top scientists rely on more extensive information sources? *Journal of the American Society for Information Science and Technology*, *63*(12), 2433–2450. doi:10.1002/asi.22662

Costas, R., Zahedi, Z., & Wouters, P. (2014). Do altmetrics correlate with citations? Extensive comparison of altmetric indicators with citations from a multidisciplinary perspective. *Journal of the Association for Information Science and Technology*, *66*(10), 2003–2019. doi:10.1002/asi.23309

Costas, R., Zahedi, Z., & Wouters, P. (2015). The thematic orientation of publications mentioned on social media: Large-scale disciplinary comparison of social media metrics with citations. *Aslib Journal of Information Management*, *67*(3), 260–288. doi:10.1108/AJIM-12-2014-0173

Cronin, B. (1981). The need for a theory of citing. *Journal of Documentation*, *37*(1), 16–24. doi:10.1108/eb026703

Cronin, B. (2001). Bibliometrics and beyond: Some thoughts on web-based citation analysis. *Journal of Information Science*, *27*(1), 1–7. doi:10.1177/016555150102700101

Cronin, B. (2005a). A hundred million acts of whimsy? *Current Science*, *89*(9), 1505–1509.

Cronin, B. (2005b). *The Hand of Science: Academic Writing and Its Rewards*. Lanham: Scarecrow Press.

Cronin, B., Snyder, H. W., Rosenbaum, H., Martinson, A., & Callahan, E. (1998). Invoked on the Web. *Journal of the American Society for Information Science*, *49*(14), 1319–1328. doi:10.1002/(SICI)1097-4571(1998)49:14<1319::AID-ASI9>3.0.CO;2-W

Cronin, B., & Weaver, S. (1995). The praxis of acknowledgement: from bibliometrics to influmetrics. *Revista Española de Documentación Científica, 18*(2), 172–177. Retrieved from http://cat.inist.fr/?aModele=afficheN&cpsidt=3638277

Davenport, T. H., & Beck, J. C. (2001). *The Attention Economy: Understanding the New Currency of Business.* Harvard Business Press.

De Bellis, N. (2009). *Bibliometrics and Citation Analysis. From the Science Citation Index to Cybermetrics.* Lanham: Scarecrow Press.

De Solla Price, D. J. (1965). Networks of scientific papers. *Science, 149*(3683), 510–515.

Eysenbach, G. (2011). Can tweets predict citations? Metrics of social impact based on Twitter and correlation with traditional metrics of scientific impact. *Journal of Medical Internet Research, 13*(4), e123. doi:10.2196/jmir.2012

Falkinger, J. (2003). Attention economies. *Journal of Economic Theory, 133*(1), 266–294.

Fausto, S., Machado, F. A., Bento, L. F. J., Iamarino, A., Nahas, T. R., & Munger, D. S. (2012). Research blogging: indexing and registering the change in science 2.0. *PLOS ONE, 7*(12), e50109. doi:10.1371/journal.pone.0050109

Franck, G. (2002). The scientific economy of attention: A novel approach to the collective rationality of science. *Scientometrics, 55*(1), 3–26.

Friedrich, N., Bowman, T. D., Stock, W. G., Haustein, S. (2015). Adapting sentiment analysis for tweets linking to scientific papers. In *Proceedings of the 15th International Conference on Scientometrics and Informetrics*, Istanbul, Turkey. (pp. 107–108). Retrieved from: http://www.issi2015.org/files/downloads/all-papers/0107.pdf

Garfield, E. (1964). "Science Citation Index"-A new dimension in indexing. *Science, 144*(3619), 649–654.

Gibson, J. J. (1977). The Theory of Affordances. In R. Shaw & J. Bransford (Eds.), *Perceiving, Acting, and Knowing: Toward an Ecological Psychology* (pp. 127–143). Lawrence Erlbaum.

Gilbert, G. N. (1977). Referencing as Persuasion. *Social Studies of Science, 7*(1), 113–122. doi:10.1177/030631277700700112

Gilpin, D. (2011). Working the Twittersphere: Microblogging as professional identity construction. In Z. Papacharissi (Ed.), *A networked self: Identity, community and culture on social network sites* (pp. 232–250). New York: Routledge.

Glänzel, W., & Gorraiz, J. (2014). Usage metrics versus altmetrics: confusing terminology? *Scientometrics*, 102(3), 2161–2164. doi:10.1007/s11192-014-1472-7

Goffman, E. (1959). *The Presentation of Self in Everyday Life* (1st ed.). Anchor.

Goffman, E. (1974). *Frame Analysis: An Essay on the Organization of Experience* (p. 586). Boston: Northeastern University Press. doi:10.4135/9781412952552.n110

Gosling, S. D. S. D., Gaddis, S., & Vazire, S. (2007). Personality Impressions Based on Facebook Profiles. In *International Conference on Weblogs and Social Media* (pp. 1–4). Boulder.

Granovetter, M. S. (1973). The strength of weak ties. *American Journal of Sociology, 78*(6), 1360–1380.

Guns, R. (2013). The three dimensions of informetrics: a conceptual view. *Journal of Documentation, 69*(2), 295–308. doi:10.1108/00220411311300093

Haustein, S., Bowman, T. D., Holmberg, K., Tsou, A., Sugimoto, C. R., & Larivière, V. (2015a). Tweets as impact indicators: Examining the implications of automated bot accounts on Twitter. *Journal of the Association for Information Science and Technology.* doi: 10.1002/asi.23456

Haustein, S., Costas, R., & Larivière, V. (2015b). Characterizing social media metrics of scholarly papers: the effect of document properties and collaboration patterns. *PLOS ONE*, 10(3): e0120495. doi:10.1371/journal.pone.0120495

Haustein, S., & Larivière, V. (2014). Mendeley as the source of global readership by students and postdocs? In *IATUL Conference, Espoo, Finland, June 2–5 2014*. Retrieved from http://docs.lib.purdue.edu/cgi/viewcontent.cgi?article=2033&context=iatul

Haustein, S., Larivière, V., Thelwall, M., Amyot, D., & Peters, I. (2014a). Tweets vs. Mendeley readers: How do these two social media metrics differ? *It – Information Technology*, 56(5), 207–215. doi:10.1515/itit-2014-1048

Haustein, S., Peters, I., Sugimoto, C. R., Thelwall, M., & Larivière, V. (2014b). Tweeting biomedicine: an analysis of tweets and citations in the biomedical literature. *Journal of the Association for Information Science and Technology*, 65(4), 656–669. doi:10.1002/asi.23101

Haustein, S., & Siebenlist, T. (2011). Applying social bookmarking data to evaluate journal usage. *Journal of Informetrics*, 5(3), 446–457. doi:10.1016/j.joi.2011.04.002

Higher Education Funding Councils Funding Council of England. (2011). *Decisions on assessing research impact. Research Excellent Framework (REF) 2014*. Retrieved from http://www.ref.ac.uk/media/ref/content/pub/decisionsonassessingresearchimpact/01_11.pdf

Hofer, M., & Aubert, V. (2013). Perceived bridging and bonding social capital on Twitter: Differentiating between followers and followees. *Computers in Human Behavior*, 29(6), 2134–2142. doi:10.1016/j.chb.2013.04.038

Holmberg, K., & Thelwall, M. (2014). Disciplinary differences in Twitter scholarly communication. *Scientometrics*, 101(2), 1027–1042. doi:10.1007/s11192-014-1229-3

Huberman, B. A. (2013). Social computing and the attention economy. *Journal of Statistical Physics*, 151(1–2), 329–339. doi:10.1007/s10955-012-0596-5

Kaplan, N. (1965). The norms of citation behavior: Prolegomena to the footnote. *American Documentation*, 16, 179–184. doi:10.1002/asi.5090160305

Kaplan, N. R., & Nelson, M. L. (2000). Determining the publication impact of a digital library. *Journal of the American Society for Information Science*, 51(4), 324–339. doi:10.1002/(SICI)1097-4571(2000)51:4<324::AID-ASI3>3.0.CO;2-B

King, J. (1987). A review of bibliometric and other science indicators and their role in research evaluation. *Journal of Information Science*, 13, 261–276.

Kuhn, T. S. (1962). *The Structure of Scientific Revolutions*. Chicago: University of Chicago Press.

Larivière, V., & Gingras, Y. (2010). The impact factor's Matthew Effect: A natural experiment in bibliometrics. *Journal of the American Society for Information Science and Technology*, 61(2), 424–427.

Lee, C. J., Sugimoto, C. R., Zhang, G., & Cronin, B. (2013). Bias in peer review. *Journal of the American Society for Information Science and Technology*, 64(1), 2–17. doi:10.1002/asi.22784

Leydesdorff, L. (1998). Theories of citation? *Scientometrics*, 43(1), 5–25. doi:10.1007/BF02458391

Lin, J., & Fenner, M. (2013). Altmetrics in evolution: Defining and redefining the ontology of article-level metrics. *Information Standards Quarterly*, 25(2), 20–26. Retrieved from http://www.niso.org/apps/group_public/download.php/11273/IP_Lin_Fenner_PLOS_altmetrics_isqv25no2.pdf

Luther, J. (2001). *White Paper on Electronic Journal Usage Statistics*. Washington, DC. Retrieved from http://www.clir.org/pubs/reports/pub94/pub94.pdf

Matthews, A. F. (2012). Managing distraction and attention in diverse co-horts: 21st century challenges to law student engagement. *Queensland University of Technology Law and Justice Journal, 12*(1), 45–65.

Maxwell, J. a. (2009). Designing a Qualitative Study. In L. Bickman & D. J. Rog (Eds.), *The SAGE Handbook of Applied Social Research Methods* (pp. 214–253). London: SAGE Publications.

Merton, R. K. (1968a). *Social Theory and Social Structure*. New York: The Free Press.

Merton, R. K. (1968b). The Matthew Effect in Science. *Science, 159*(3810), 56–63.

Merton, R. K. (1973). *The sociology of science: Theoretical and empirical investigations*. Chicago: University of Chicago Press.

Merton, R. K. (1988). The Matthew effect in science, II: Cumulative advantage and the symbolism of intellectual property. *Isis, 79*, 606–623.

Moed, H. F. (2005). *Citation analysis in research evaluation*. Dordrecht: Springer.

Mohammadi, E. (2014). *Identifying the Invisible Impact of Scholarly Publications: A Multi-disciplinary Analysis Using Altmetrics*. University of Wolverhampton.

Mohammadi, E., & Thelwall, M. (2013). Assessing non-standard article impact using F1000 labels. *Scientometrics, 97*(2), 383–395. doi:10.1007/s11192-013-0993-9

Mohammadi, E., & Thelwall, M. (2014). Mendeley readership altmetrics for the social sciences and humanities: Research evaluation and knowledge flows. *Journal of the Association for Information Science and Technology, 65*(8), 1627–1638. doi:10.1002/asi.23071

Mohammadi, E., Thelwall, M., Haustein, S., & Larivière, V. (2015). Who reads research articles? An altmetrics analysis of Mendeley user categories. *Journal of the Association for Information Science and Technology, 66*(9), 1832–1846. doi: 10.1002/asi.23286

Murugesan, P., & Moravcsik, M. J. (1978). Variation of the nature of citation measures with journals and scientific specialties. *Journal of the American Society for Information Science, 29*(3), 141–147. doi:10.1002/asi.4630290307

Newman, M. E. J. (2001). Clustering and preferential attachment in growing networks. *Physical Review E, 64*(2), 025102. doi:10.1103/PhysRevE.64.025102

Newman, M. E. J. (2005). Power laws, Pareto distributions and Zipf's law. *Contemporary Physics, 46*(5), 323–351.

Neylon, C. (2014). Altmetrics: What are they good for? *PLOS Opens*. Retrieved from http://blogs.plos.org/opens/2014/10/03/altmetrics-what-are-they-good-for/.

Nicolaisen, J. (2007). Citation Analysis. *Annual Review of Information Science and Technology, 41*, 609–641.

Otlet, P. (1934). *Traité de documentation. Le Livre sur le Livre: Théorie et Pratique*. Bruxelles: D. Van Keerberghen & fils.

Piwowar, H. A. (2013). Altmetrics: Value all research products. *Nature, 493*(7431), 159. doi:10.1038/493159a

Portes, A. (1998). Social capital: Its origins and applications in modern Sociology. *Annual Review of Sociology, 24*, 1–24.

Price, D. J. D. S. (1976). A general theory of bibliometric and other cumulative advantage processes. *Journal of the American Society for Information Science, 27*(5), 292–306. doi:10.1002/asi.4630270505

Priem, J. (2010). I like the term #articlelevelmetrics, but it fails to imply *diversity* of measures. Lately, I'm liking #altmetrics. *21 September 2010, 3:28 a.m. Tweet*.

Priem, J. (2014). Altmetrics. In B. Cronin & C. R. Sugimoto (Eds.), *Beyond bibliometrics: harnessing multi-dimensional indicators of performance* (pp. 263–287). Cambridge: MIT Press.

Priem, J., Taraborelli, D., Groth, P., & Neylon, C. (2010). Alt-metrics: a manifesto. *October*. Retrieved from http://altmetrics.org/manifesto/

Putnam, R. D. (1995). Bowling alone: America's declining social capital. *Journal of Democracy*, 6(1), 65–78.

Putnam, R. D. (2000). *Bowling Alone: The Collapse and Revival of American Community*. New York: Simon & Schuster.

Riviera, E. (2015). Testing the strength of the normative approach in citation theory through relational bibliometrics: The case of Italian sociology. *Journal of the Association for Information Science and Technology*, 66(6), 1178–1188. doi:10.1002/asi.23248

Rousseau, R., & Ye, Y. (2013). A multi-metric approach for research evaluation. *Chinese Science Bulletin*, 58(26), 3288–3290. doi:10.1007/s11434-013-5939-3

Rui, H., & Whinston, A. (2011). Information or attention? An empirical study of user contribution on Twitter. *Information Systems and E-Business Management*, 10(3), 309–324. doi:10.1007/s10257-011-0164-6

Satuluri, V. (2013). Stay in the know. *Twitter blog post 24 September 2013*. Retrieved from https://blog.twitter.com/2013/stay-in-the-know

Shema, H., Bar-Ilan, J. and Thelwall, M. (2014). Do blog citations correlate with a higher number of future citations? Research blogs as a potential source for alternative metrics. *Journal of the Association for Information Science and Technology*, 65(5), 1018–1027. doi: 10.1002/asi.23037

Shema, H., Bar-Ilan, J. and Thelwall, M. (2015). How is research blogged? A content analysis approach. *Journal of the Association for Information Science and Technology*, 66(6), 1136–1149. doi: 10.1002/asi.23239

Simon, H. A. (1971). Designing organizations for an information-rich world. In M. Greenberger (Ed.), *Computers, Communications, and the Public Interest* (pp. 37–72). John Hopkins Press.

Small, H. (1978). Cited documents as concept symbols. *Social Studies of Science*, 8, 327–340. doi:10.1177/030631277800800305

Small, H. (2004). On the shoulders of Robert Merton: Towards a normative theory of citation. *Scientometrics*, 60(1), 71–79. doi:10.1023/B:SCIE.0000027310.68393.bc

Steinfield, C., Dimicco, J. M., Ellison, N. B., & Lampe, C. (2009). Bowling Online?: Social Networking and Social Capital within the Organization. In *4th International Conference on Communities and Technologies* (pp. 245–254). University Park, Pennsylvania: ACM Press.

Taylor, M. (2014). Towards a common model of citation: some thoughts on merging altmetrics and bibliometrics. *Research Trends* (35). Retrieved from http://www.researchtrends.com/issue-35-december-2013/towards-a-common-model-of-citation-some-thoughts-on-merging-altmetrics-and-bibliometrics/

Thelwall, M., Shema, H., & Bar-Ilan, J. (2012). Research blogs and the discussion of scholarly information. *PLoS ONE*, 7(5), e35869. doi:10.1371/journal.pone.0035869

Thelwall, M., Tsou, A., Weingart, S., Holmberg, K., & Haustein, S. (2013). Tweeting links to academic articles. *Cybermetrics: International Journal of Scientometrics, Informetrics and Bibliometrics*, 1–8. Retrieved from http://cybermetrics.cindoc.csic.es/articles/v17i1p1.html

Valenzuela, S. S., Park, N., & Kee, K. F. (2008). Lessons from Facebook: The Effect of Social Network Sites on College Students' Social Capital. In *9th International Symposium on Online Journalism* (pp. 1–4). Austin, Texas. Retrieved from: https://online.journalism.utexas.edu/2008/papers/Valenzuela.pdf

Waltman, L., & Costas, R. (2014). F1000 recommendations as a potential new data source for research evaluation: A comparison with citations. *Journal of the Association for Information Science and Technology, 65*(3), 433–445. doi:10.1002/asi

Weisbuch, M., Ivcevic, Z., & Ambady, N. (2009). On being liked on the web and in the "real world": Consistency in first impressions across personal webpages and spontaneous behavior. *Journal of Experimental Social Psychology, 45*(3), 573–576. doi:10.1016/j.jesp.2008.12.009

White, H. D. (2004). Reward, persuasion, and the Sokal Hoax: a study in citation identities. *Scientometrics, 60*(1), 93–120.

Wouters, P. (1999). *The Citation Culture*. University of Amsterdam.

Wouters, P., & Costas, R. (2012). *Users, narcissism and control – tracking the impact of scholarly publications in the 21st century*. (M. Van Berchum & K. Russell, Eds.) *Image Rochester NY*. SURFfoundation.

Zahedi, Z., Costas, R., & Wouters, P. (2013). What is the impact of the publications read by the different Mendeley users? Could they help to identify alternative types of impact? *PLoS ALM Workshop*. San Francisco. Retrieved from http://article-level-metrics.plos.org/files/2013/10/Zahedi.pptx

Zahedi, Z., Costas, R., & Wouters, P. (2014). How well developed are altmetrics? cross-disciplinary analysis of the presence of "alternative metrics" in scientific publications. *Scientometrics, 101*(2), 1491–1513. doi:10.1007/s11192-014-1264-0

Ziman, J. (2000). *Real Science: what it is, and what it means*. Cambridge: Cambridge University Press.

Biographical information for the editor and contributors

Editor

Cassidy R. Sugimoto is Associate Professor in the School of Informatics and Computing at Indiana University Bloomington and Visiting Professor of Information Science at the University of Wolverhampton. She researches within the domain of scholarly communication and scientometrics, examining the formal and informal ways in which knowledge producers consume and disseminate scholarship. She has co-edited two volumes with Blaise Cronin (Beyond Bibliometrics, MIT Press; Scholarly Metrics Under the Microscope, ITI/ASIST) and has published more than 60 journal articles in the area of informetrics and scholarly communication. Her work has received funding from the National Science Foundation, the Institute for Museum and Library Services, and the Sloan Foundation, among other agencies. Sugimoto is the President of ISSI (the International Society for Scientometrics and Informetrics), Associate Editor of the *Journal of the Association of Information Science and Technology*, and on the editorial board of *Scientometrics*. Sugimoto has an undergraduate degree in music performance, a MS in library science, and a PhD in information and library science from the University of North Carolina at Chapel Hill.

Contributors

David Bawden is Professor of Information Science at City University London, and editor of *Journal of Documentation*. His main interests are information theories and philosophies, digital literacy, and information history. He is co-author of Facet's best-selling 'Introduction to Information Science' text and co-editor of Facet's 'Foundations of the Information Sciences' monograph series.

Christine L. Borgman is Distinguished Professor and Presidential Chair in Information Studies at UCLA and the author of more than 200 publications in information studies, computer science, and communication. Her newest book, *Big Data, Little Data, No Data: Scholarship in the Networked World*, was published by MIT Press in January 2015. Prior books, *Scholarship in the Digital Age: Information, Infrastructure, and the Internet* (MIT Press, 2007) and *From Gutenberg to the Global Information Infrastructure: Access to Information in a Networked World* (MIT Press, 2000), each won the Best Information Science Book of the Year award from the American Society for Information Science and Technology (ASIST). In 2012–2013, Prof. Borgman was the Oliver Smithies Visiting Fellow at Balliol College, University of Oxford, and a Visiting Fellow at the Oxford Internet Institute and at the Oxford eResearch Centre. She is a Fellow of the American Association for the Advancement of Science and of the Association for Computing Machinery, and a recipient of the Paul Evan Peters Award from the Coalition for Networked Information, Association for Research Libraries, and EDUCAUSE, and the Research in Information Science Award from ASIST. She is a member of the Board of Directors of the Electronic Privacy Information Center, U.S. Co-Chair of the CODATA-ICSTI Task Group on Data Citation and Attribution, and previously served on the U.S. National Academies' Board on Research Data and Information and the U.S. National CODATA.

Katy Börner is the Victor H. Yngve Professor of information science in the Department of Information and Library Science in the School of Informatics and Computing, Adjunct Professor at the Department of Statistics in the College of Arts and Sciences, Core Faculty of Cognitive Science, Founding Director of the Cyberinfrastructure for Network Science Center at Indiana University Bloomington, and Visiting Professor at the Royal Netherlands Academy of Arts and Sciences (KNAW) in The Netherlands. She is a curator of the international *Places & Spaces: Mapping Science* exhibit. She holds a MS in Electrical Engineering from the University of Technology in Leipzig, 1991 and a PhD in Computer Science from the University of Kaiserslautern, 1997.

Lutz Bornmann is a sociologist of science at the Division for Science and Innovation Studies in the Administrative Headquarters of the Max Planck Society in Munich (Germany). Since the late 1990s, he has been working on issues in the promotion of young academics and scientists in the sciences and on quality assurance in higher education. His current research interests include research evaluation, peer review, bibliometrics, and altmetrics.

Timothy D. Bowman is a research professional examining altmetrics and scholarly communication in online environments at the University of Montreal. He holds a PhD in information science from Indiana University Bloomington (2015). He has has over 7 years of experience examining aspects of social interaction, impression management, and scholarly communication in online environments. The main focus of his research concerns impression management, framing, and affordance use by scholars in social media. In addition, he is interested in the management of personal and professional communications in online environments.

Rodrigo Costas is an experienced researcher in the field of information science and bibliometrics. With a PhD in Library and Information Science obtained at the CSIC in Spain, Rodrigo has been working at CWTS (Leiden University, the Netherlands) since 2009. His lines of research cover a broad scope of topics, including the development of new bibliometric tools and indicators as well as tools for the study of research activities based on quantitative data, having a particular focus on the analysis of individual scholars through bibliometric methodologies. Rodrigo recently started novel research lines at CWTS including the study of 'altmetrics' and the possibilities of funding acknowledgments in order to expand the analytical possibilities of scientometrics. At CWTS Rodrigo also coordinates several projects for different scientific organizations worldwide.

Blaise Cronin is Rudy Professor Emeritus of Information Science at Indiana University. He has published extensively on scientometrics and related subjects. He is Editor-in-Chief of the *Journal of the Association for Information Science and Technology* and for 10 years was Editor of the *Annual Review of Information Science and Technology*. He holds an MA from Trinity College Dublin, and both a PhD and DSSc from the Queen's University of Belfast. He received a DLitt (*honoris causa*) from Queen Margaret University, Edinburgh in 1997; the Award of Merit from the American Society for Information Science and Technology in 2006; the Derek de Solla Price Award and Medal in 2013; the Jason Farradane Award in 2014.

Nadine Desrochers is Assistant Professor at the Université de Montréal's École de bibliothéconomie et des sciences de l'information. She holds an MLIS from the University of Western Ontario and a PhD in French Literature from the University of Ottawa. Her work has been published in *Information Research*, the *Canadian Journal of Information and Library Science*, and

Library & Information Science Research. She is the co-editor of *Examining Paratextual Theory and its Applications in Digital Culture* (with Daniel Apollon; IGI Global, 2014).

Hamid Ekbia is Associate Professor in the School of Informatics and Computing, Program in Cognitive Science, and School of Global and International Studies at Indiana University Bloomington, where he also directs the Center for Research on Mediated Interaction. His research interests focus on how technologies mediate interactions among people, organizations, and communities. He has written about technology and mediation in work organizations, healthcare environments, user groups, and scholarly and design communities. His book *Artificial Dreams: The Quest for Non-Biological Intelligence* (Cambridge University Press, 2008) is a critical-technical analysis of AI. He is a co-editor of a forthcoming volume titled *Big Data Is Not a Monolith: Problems, Practices, and Policies* (MIT Press, 2015).

Jonathan Furner (M.A. Cambridge 1990, PhD Sheffield 1994) is Professor and Chair of the Department of Information Studies at the University of California, Los Angeles. He studies the history and philosophy of cultural stewardship, and teaches classes on the representation and organization of archival records, library materials, and museum objects. He has published over fifty papers on these and related topics, frequently using conceptual analysis to evaluate the theoretical frameworks, data models, and metadata standards on which information access systems rely.

Michael Ginda is Data Analyst for the Cyberinfrastructure for Network Science Center (CNS) at Indiana University Bloomington. He holds a diploma in political science from Temple University in Philadelphia and a Masters in Library Science from Indiana University. His research focuses on applications of statistical modelling and information visualization to areas of library and information science, online education, and learning analytics.

Wolfgang Glänzel is Full Professor at KU Leuven (Belgium) and Director of the Centre for R&D Monitoring. He is also Senior Scientist in the Department of Science Policy & Scientometrics at the Library of the Hungarian Academy of Sciences in Budapest (Hungary). Wolfgang Glänzel studied mathematics in Budapest and holds a doctorate in mathematics from Eötvös Lorand University as well as a PhD in Social Sciences from University Leiden (Netherlands). He worked for twenty years at the Library of the Hungarian Academy of Sciences and was an Alexander von Humboldt Fellow for two years in Germany. Wolfgang Glänzel is Editor-in-Chief of the international journal *Scientometrics*, Academic Editor of the journal *PLoS ONE*, and Secretary-Treasurer of the *International Society for Scientometrics and Informetrics* (ISSI). Wolfgang Glänzel is author, co-author, or co-editor of several books and more than 300 publications in international journals and conference proceedings. He has published in probability theory and mathematical statistics, computer science and various topics in quantitative science studies, scientometrics and informetrics. In 1999 he received the international *Derek deSolla Price Award* for outstanding contributions to the quantitative studies of science.

Stefanie Haustein is a post-doctoral researcher at the Canada Research Chair on the Transformations of Scholarly Communication at the University of Montreal. Her current research focuses on social media in scholarly communication and making sense of so-called "altmetrics" and is supported by a grant from the Alfred P. Sloan Foundation. Stefanie holds a Master's degree in history,

American linguistics, and literature and information science and a PhD in information science from Heinrich Heine University Düsseldorf, Germany. She has previously worked as a research analyst at Science-Metrix in Montreal, Canada and in the bibliometrics team at Forschungszentrum Jülich, Germany. Stefanie is a visiting lecturer in the Department of Information Science at Heinrich Heine University. She frequently presents her work at international conferences and has published in journals such as *JASIST*, *Scientometrics*, *Journal of Informetrics*, and *PLoS ONE*.

Birger Hjørland is Professor of knowledge organization at the Royal School of Library and Information Science in Copenhagen (since 2001) and was previously Professor at the University College in Borås (2000–2001). He holds an M.A. in psychology from the University of Copenhagen and PhD in library and information science from the University of Gothenburg. He was a research librarian and coordinator of computer based information services at the Royal Library in Copenhagen (1978–1990) and taught information science at the Department of Mathematical and Applied Linguistics at the University of Copenhagen (1983–1986). He is chair of ISKO's Scientific Advisory Council and a member of the editorial boards of, among other journals, *Knowledge Organization*, *Journal of the Association for Information Science and Technology*, and *Journal of Documentation*. In the field of information science he introduced and is continuing to develop "the domain-analytic approach".

Vincent Larivière holds the Canada Research Chair on the Transformations of Scholarly Communication at the Université de Montréal, where he is Associate Professor of information science. He is also scientific director of the Érudit journal platform, associate scientific director of the Observatoire des sciences et des technologies (OST), and a regular member of the Centre interuniversitaire de recherche sur la science et la technologie (CIRST).

Loet Leydesdorff (PhD Sociology, M.A. Philosophy, and M.Sc. Biochemistry) is Professor at the Amsterdam School of Communications Research (ASCoR) of the University of Amsterdam. He is Honorary Professor of the Science and Technology Policy Research Unit (SPRU) of the University of Sussex, Visiting Professor of the Institute of Scientific and Technical Information of China (ISTIC) in Beijing, Guest Professor at Zhejiang University in Hangzhou, and Visiting Professor at the School of Management, Birkbeck, University of London. He has published extensively in systems theory, social network analysis, scientometrics, and the sociology of innovation. He received the Derek de Solla Price Award for Scientometrics and Informetrics (2003) and, 2005, held "The City of Lausanne" Honor Chair at the School of Economics, Université de Lausanne.

Henk F. Moed has been senior staff member and Full Professor in research assessment methodologies in the Center for Science and Technology Studies at Leiden University from 1981 until February 2010. After that, he was senior scientific adviser and director of an informetric research group at Elsevier in Amsterdam until November 2014. He has published over 100 research articles in peer-reviewed journals in the field of quantitative science studies and research assessment, co-authored a handbook in 2004, and published *Citation Analysis in Research Evaluation* (Springer, 2005), one of the few textbooks in the field. At present he is a visiting professor at the Sapienza University of Rome.

Adèle Paul-Hus is a doctoral student in information science at the Université de Montréal's École de bibliothéconomie et des sciences de l'information, under the joint-supervision of Vincent Larivière and Nadine Desrochers. Her doctoral research focuses on acknowledgement functions within scholarly communication. She holds Master's degrees in Information Science and in Anthropology from the Université de Montréal.

Lyn Robinson is Reader in Library and Information Science at City University London, and author of Facet's 'Understanding Healthcare Information'. Her main interests are the history and theory of information and documents, new forms of document and collection, information behavior, and digital culture. She is co-author of Facet's best-selling 'Introduction to Information Science' text, and co-editor of Facet's 'Foundations of the Information Sciences' monograph series.

Ronald Rousseau is the former President of ISSI, the International Society for Scientometrics and Informetrics (2007–2015). He is a guest professor at the Catholic University of Louvain (KU Leuven) and a guest professor at Antwerp University, School for Library and Information Science. He holds a doctorate in Mathematics and one in Library and Information Science. After obtaining the doctoral degree in mathematics he became a Dr. habil. He received the Prize of the Belgian Academy of Science for his mathematical work and the Derek J. de Solla Price award (2001) for his work in scientometrics. He holds Honorary Professorships from Zhejiang University and from Henan Normal University (China).

Sandra Rousseau is Associate Professor in environmental economics and head of the Research Center for Economics and Corporate Sustainability (CEDON) of the Faculty of Economics and Business at the KU Leuven, Brussel campus. She holds a PhD in economics from KU Leuven. The main focus of her research concerns the design, implementation, and evaluation of environmental policy and policy instruments. In addition, she is interested in the evaluation of research output and research activities.

Andrea Scharnhorst is Head of Research and Innovation at the Data Archiving and Network Services institute (DANS) in The Hague and scientific coordinator of the Computational Humanities programme at the eHumanities group at the Royal Netherlands Academy of Arts and Sciences in Amsterdam. She holds a diploma in physics and a PhD in philosophy of science, both from the Humboldt University Berlin. She has published about modelling, simulating, and visualising the emergence of innovations, new ideas, and classification systems. Currently, she chairs the European COST network TD1210 KnoweScape with more than 100 researchers from 29 countries. In KnoweScape, insights from complexity theory and knowledge organization are combined to improve the understanding of the collective, self-organized nature of human knowledge production and to create interactive knowledge maps for a better navigation through large information spaces.

András Schubert is with the Library of the Hungarian Academy of Sciences since the late 1970's as one of the pioneers of scientometrics in Hungary. He is Editor of the journal *Scientometrics*, winner of the 1993 Derek de Solla Price Medal and became in 2001 the first representant of scientometrics in ISI's Highly Cited Authors List. He is an ardent clarinet player and the author of children's books.

Henry Small is a research scientist with SciTech Strategies. He received a joint PhD in Chemistry and the History of Science from the University of Wisconsin with a dissertation on the history of atomic theory. At the Center for History and Philosophy of Physics of the American Institute of Physics he worked on a project to document the history of nuclear physics and began using bibliometric methods. Joining the Institute for Scientific Information in 1972 (later Thomson Reuters), he introduced a number of citation analysis methods and products. His 1973 paper on co-citation (designated a Citation Classic) led to numerous papers on the mapping of science and specialty studies. In 1987 he received the Derek J. de Solla Price Medal from the journal *Scientometrics*, and in 1998 the Award of Merit from the American Society for Information Science and Technology. He is a Fellow of the AAAS and of the National Federation of Abstracting and Indexing Services, and a past president of the International Society for Scientometrics and Informetrics. His current research interests include the analysis of citation contexts, theories of referencing, and specialty emergence.

Wolfgang G. Stock is Professor of information science and Head of the Information Science Department of the Heinrich Heine University Düsseldorf, Germany. His research activities und lectures include information retrieval, knowledge representation, informetrics, informational cities, social media, and the markets of digital information. He is author of about 275 articles and some basic text books in information science. Additionally he is editor of the book series "Knowledge & Information. Studies in Information Science" (De Gruyter Saur).

Mike Thelwall is Professor of information science and Head of the Statistical Cybermetrics Research Group at the University of Wolverhampton in the UK. He is also a research associate at the Oxford Internet Institute, and a docent in the Department of Information Studies, Åbo Akademi University. He is an associate editor of the *Journal of the Association for Information Science and Technology* and a member of the editorial boards of the *Journal of Informetrics*, *Scientometrics*, and the *Journal of Information Science*. He researches altmetrics, webometrics, scientometrics, sentiment analysis, social media, and web-based social science research methods.

Howard D. White is Professor Emeritus at Drexel University's College of Computing and Informatics, which he joined in 1974, after taking his PhD in librarianship at the University of California, Berkeley. He authored *Brief Tests of Collection Strength* (Greenwood, 1995) and co-authored *For Information Specialists: Interpretations of Reference and Bibliographic Work* with Marcia Bates and Patrick Wilson (Ablex, 1992). He has published extensively on bibliometrics and co-citation analysis, innovative online searching, and literature retrieval for meta-analysis and interdisciplinary studies, among other topics. He won the Research Award of the Association for Information Science and Technology (ASIST) for distinguished contributions in his field (1993) and the Award of Merit, ASIST's highest honor for career achievement (2004). In 2005, the International Society for Scientometrics and Informetrics honored him with the Derek de Solla Price Memorial Medal for contributions to the quantitative study of science.

Paul Wouters is Director of the Centre for Science and Technology Studies at Leiden University, professor of scientometrics in Leiden, visiting professor of Cybermetrics at the University of Wolverhampton, and chair of the Dutch national Graduate School *Science, Technology and Modern Culture*. He has published on the history of the Science Citation Index, on scientometrics, and on the way the criteria of scientific quality have been changed by citation analysis.

In this area, theories of citation in relation to the sociology of evaluation are his main current concerns, particularly how performance criteria and rankings influence research agendas and scientific careers. Wouters was PI of the European project ACUMEN on research careers and evaluation of individual researchers. He is also interested in the role of information and information technologies in the creation of new scientific and scholarly knowledge. He publishes a website about the future of research www.researchdreams.nl and a blog about citation cultures http://citationculture.wordpress.com (with Sarah de Rijcke). His most recent book is *Virtual Knowledge*, a collection edited in collaboration with Anne Beaulieu, Andrea Scharnhorst, and Sally Wyatt (MIT Press, 2013).

Index

A Posteriori (Criteria) 37
Abbott, A. 232, 239
Acknowledgements 5, 74, 225–247, 253, 375
– Funding Acknowledgements 227, 236, 239, 241, 244
Acquaintances 184–187, 215, 218
Activity Systems 42
Actor-network theory (ANT) 81, 251, 255
ACUMEN 361
Algorithm 24, 36, 41, 74, 143, 176, 177, 291, 292, 301, 304, 317, 318, 325, 340, 364
Altmetric.com 349, 360, 370, 375
Altmetrics 2, 7, 8, 74, 106, 114, 180, 195, 200, 337, 338, 340, 342–346, 349–352, 355–376, 378, 380, 382, 384, 386, 388, 390, 392, 394, 396–405
Altmetrics Manifesto 360, 361, 369, 372
Angle-Sum Theory 225, 226, 228, 230, 232, 234, 236–238, 240, 242, 244, 246
Applications Programming Interfaces (API(s)) 342, 375
arXiv.org 357, 363
Assessment 15, 17, 45, 78, 88, 89, 94, 111, 112, 180, 190, 226, 228, 263, 275, 344, 350, 352–354, 356–358, 362, 365, 367–369, 371
– Assessment Metrics 354, 358, 362
– Research Assessment(s) 17, 78, 94, 111, 112, 353, 362, 365, 369
Åström, F. 34, 43, 190, 192
Attention 8, 14, 18, 31, 72–74, 79–81, 87, 89, 100, 137, 142–144, 181, 183, 184, 211, 220, 227, 228, 236, 238, 252, 255, 276, 353, 355, 367, 369, 384, 385, 390, 392, 394, 396–399, 401–404
– Attention Economics (also "Attention Economy") 384, 385, 390, 392, 394, 396–399, 401, 402
– Architecture of Attention 367
Author(s) 1, 2, 4–9, 14–18, 27, 31, 33, 34, 39, 46, 51, 52, 54, 56, 59–64, 66, 73, 76, 77, 85–87, 89, 97–99, 101–104, 107, 110, 111, 114, 119, 121, 127–129, 139–141, 149–152, 158–168, 170, 175–178, 188, 199–210, 212–228, 231, 232, 234–244, 247, 250, 251, 256, 261, 266, 267, 274, 280, 282, 289–291, 293–295, 297, 299, 305, 307, 308, 315, 320–322, 332, 360, 363–366, 368, 372, 376, 381–383, 386–394, 396, 398, 399
Authorship 5, 7, 9, 103, 107, 110, 111, 114, 175–178, 188, 202, 203, 214, 226–228, 236–244, 253, 256

Bacon, F. 24, 57, 366, 368, 371
"Bacon Number" 188
Bar-Ilan, J. 219, 337, 338, 340, 343, 344, 346, 361, 370, 371, 396, 404
Barabási, A.-L. 2, 166, 175, 177, 195, 214, 222, 321, 323, 325, 326, 331, 383, 399
Bawden, D. 1, 2, 4, 180, 182–184, 186, 188, 190, 192–194, 196, 385
Ben-David, J. 59, 68, 250, 256
Bernal, J. D. 305, 322–324, 327
Bias 2, 3, 15, 29, 34, 36–39, 53, 229, 232, 236, 338, 346, 382, 387, 393, 402
– Systematic Bias 38
Bits 112, 183, 284, 288, 293, 294, 297, 298
Björneborn, L. 94, 114, 187, 188, 193, 337–339, 341, 344
Blog(s) 13, 94, 114, 177, 189, 195, 340, 346, 350, 354, 357, 360, 365, 368, 371, 372, 376, 378, 379, 387, 395–398, 401, 403, 404
– Blogger 354, 395, 396
– Scholarly Blogs 360, 365, 368, 371
Bollen, J. 107, 109, 354, 358, 363, 371
Borgman, C. L. 1, 3, 4, 93–96, 98–104, 106, 108–115, 144, 219, 338, 344
Börner, K. 1, 7, 86, 90, 304, 306, 308, 310, 312, 314, 316, 318, 320–322, 324–328, 330, 332–334
Bornmann, L. 1, 3, 7, 8, 89, 90, 299, 343, 344, 347, 348, 350, 352–356, 358, 361, 373, 386, 387, 397, 400
Boundary Objects 248, 256

Bourdieu, P. 5, 226, 227, 234, 237–239, 327, 376, 384, 391, 400
Bowker, G. C. 100, 109, 111
Boyack, K. 33, 36, 43, 52, 70, 86, 90, 324
Bradford, S. C. 5, 20, 127, 128, 144, 145, 147, 166, 177, 190, 193, 195, 200, 331, 333
Bradford's Law 20, 127, 128, 147, 195
Brookes, B. C. 166, 177, 218
Buckland, M. K. 100, 109, 208

Callon, M. 280, 283, 286, 292, 300
Capital 78, 88, 227, 238, 241, 327, 334, 348, 349, 384, 385, 389–392, 394, 396–400, 402–404
– Social Capital 348, 384, 385, 389–392, 394, 396–400, 402–404
– Symbolic Capital 78, 227, 238
Case, D. O. 110, 193
Champernowne, D. G. 142, 144, 190, 191, 193
– Champernowne Constant 190, 191
Characteristic Scores and Scales (CSS) 172, 177
Chen, C. M. 23, 43, 101, 111, 164, 245, 301, 302, 332, 333, 401
Citation(s) 1–9, 13–20, 33, 34, 36, 38–40, 43–46, 49, 51, 54, 55, 60–80, 82–108, 110–114, 119, 127, 128, 139, 148–156, 159, 161–166, 176–178, 180, 187, 193, 194, 199, 201–204, 206–210, 212–228, 236–239, 243, 280, 289–291, 293, 295, 300–303, 306–308, 316–320, 324, 327–330, 337–339, 342–347, 349–352, 354–359, 362–365, 368–375, 378–383, 386–398, 400–405
– Citation Analysis 3, 9, 15–19, 33, 38–40, 43–46, 70, 72, 76–79, 88, 91, 110, 114, 164, 180, 187, 193, 194, 199, 207, 210, 213, 216, 220, 222–224, 302, 324, 328, 338, 339, 345, 352, 357, 358, 362, 363, 370, 373, 374, 380, 381, 400, 401, 403
– Co-citation Analysis 33, 38, 39, 43, 44, 46, 70, 207, 213, 216, 223, 224
– Citation Behavior 14–17, 69, 77, 106, 301, 371, 402
– Citation Context(s) 54, 55, 62, 65–67
– Citation Identity 33, 68, 202, 207, 214, 217, 218
– Citation Index(es) (Indices) 4, 6, 18, 20, 39, 74–79, 83–88, 91, 112, 204, 213, 221, 223, 228, 290, 300, 307, 328, 329, 337, 345, 357, 369, 370, 401
– Citation Relations 6, 70, 85, 112, 238, 280
– Citation Theory 2–5, 19, 49, 70, 72, 73, 77–79, 82–84, 87, 89, 90, 219, 351, 374, 379, 380, 388, 395, 397, 404
– Negational (or Negative) Citation(s) 62, 382, 391
– Perfunctory Citation(s) 382
Citing 5, 6, 14, 16, 18, 39, 54, 62, 63, 66, 73, 75, 76, 84, 85, 87, 90, 94, 97, 102, 104, 107, 110, 138, 149, 150, 204, 209, 210, 212, 213, 215, 219, 221, 222, 289, 290, 294, 295, 297, 300, 342, 344, 351–353, 356, 363, 372, 374, 375, 380–383, 387–390, 395, 397, 398, 400
– Citing Behavior(s) 14, 90, 351, 352, 356, 380
Cladism 40
Classification(s) 7, 37, 40, 44, 135, 143, 145, 146, 172, 184, 193, 228, 230, 231, 235, 256, 261, 263–265, 268, 278, 279, 307, 309–313, 317, 320–322, 324, 326, 329, 350, 363, 369
– Facets 184, 252–254, 269, 279, 320, 376, 380, 388
– Folksonomy (Folksonomies) 263, 264, 274, 278
– Nomenclature(s) 63, 261, 263, 264
– Ontological Politics 83
– Ontology (Ontologies) 81–83, 91, 122, 143, 145–147, 192, 261, 263–269, 273, 276–279, 402
– Tennis Problem 271, 273, 276
Code of Communication 282
Cognitive Norms 57
Cole, S. 13, 52, 62, 63, 68, 165, 167, 169, 173, 174, 177, 327, 384, 400
Collaboration 5, 78, 103, 109, 177, 178, 180, 202, 222, 234, 238, 240, 242, 244, 245, 256, 320, 367, 369, 377, 379, 392, 402
Collective Intelligence 366, 367
Collin, F. 18, 20, 28, 29, 43, 51, 68, 109, 256, 306, 324, 352, 356

416 — Index

Collins, H. 51, 68, 109, 251, 256, 306, 324, 352, 356

Communication 1–9, 14, 17, 18, 22, 30, 38, 43–45, 54, 69, 70, 73, 74, 80, 90, 91, 93–95, 97, 100, 106–110, 112–114, 146, 169, 176, 177, 180, 185, 186, 191, 194, 202, 205, 207, 210–212, 216, 221–228, 230, 233, 239–244, 246, 247, 253, 256, 261, 280–290, 292–294, 296, 298–303, 306, 307, 313, 314, 316, 317, 320, 324, 325, 327, 328, 330, 331, 344, 349, 354, 356, 357, 359, 361, 362, 365, 366, 369, 371–373, 380, 384, 389, 397–399, 402, 404

Communism 249, 380, 381, 388, 391

Community 3–5, 7, 17, 21, 24, 49, 59, 63, 66, 70, 72, 73, 77, 79, 87–89, 91, 95–97, 113, 142, 170, 172, 176, 190, 225, 238, 249, 291, 302, 317, 318, 329, 347, 351, 360, 361, 372–374, 376, 382, 384, 387, 391, 398, 401, 404

– Community-finding 291

– Scientific Community 5, 21, 24, 59, 87, 89, 225, 238, 249, 329, 360, 361, 373, 374, 382, 391, 398

– Paradigm-centered Scientific Communities 24

– User Communities 374

Competition 3, 49, 50, 52, 54, 56, 58, 60, 62–64, 66–70, 100, 241, 244, 254, 328

Computerization 7, 360–366, 368–370, 373

– Computerization Movement 361, 370, 373

Concept(s) 2, 7, 8, 13, 21, 27–29, 32, 34, 42, 43, 45, 53, 57, 67, 69–73, 75, 78, 81, 82, 84, 91, 95, 107, 120, 123, 125, 129, 137, 139, 141, 146, 150, 175, 176, 183, 184, 186–188, 192, 196, 208, 214–216, 226, 233, 234, 240, 243, 248, 254, 255, 261, 263–277, 279, 282, 289, 298, 301, 302, 307, 310, 313, 322, 330, 333, 337, 341, 346, 351–353, 355, 356, 359, 360, 362, 364, 366, 367, 369, 373–376, 380, 382–384, 386, 389, 392, 394, 396–399, 401, 404

– Concept Symbol(s) 70, 215, 216, 355, 359, 380, 383, 389, 392, 394, 396–398, 404

Confidence Interval 38

Consensus 31, 54, 62, 68, 100, 166, 339, 352, 393

Consequences 18, 35, 55, 56, 78, 82, 89, 90, 269, 362, 368

Consilience 54, 56, 67, 71

Context 5–7, 19, 24, 28, 42, 49, 51, 54, 55, 56, 62, 65–70, 73, 74, 77–79, 84–87, 91, 96, 101, 106, 112, 127, 129, 132, 141, 142, 164, 169, 181, 184, 185, 187, 188, 191, 192, 195, 200, 204–206, 209–212, 214, 220, 221, 224, 229, 234, 236, 238, 241, 243, 246–249, 252, 254, 256, 257, 261, 272, 274, 278, 281, 285–288, 298, 305–307, 321, 333, 344, 348, 352–354, 356–359, 365, 368–369, 372, 373, 375–377, 380–382, 386, 387, 389, 395, 397, 398, 402

– Context of Discovery 287

– Context of Justification 287

Cooperation 3, 49, 50, 52, 54, 56, 58, 60, 62–64, 66–70, 326

Correlations 137, 184, 280, 292, 298, 355, 387, 395

Costas, R. 1, 3, 7, 8, 90, 226, 232, 236, 239, 244, 245, 343, 344, 346, 349, 351, 355, 357, 359, 372, 374, 376, 378, 380, 382, 384, 386–390, 392–398, 400, 402, 404, 405

Cozzens, S. E. 62, 65, 68, 280, 300

Credit 5, 59, 61, 63, 65, 68, 93–97, 99, 102–105, 107, 228, 239, 240, 242–245, 252, 253, 351–353, 381, 388, 390

Critical Studies 21

Cronin, B. 1–9, 13–19, 37, 42, 43, 49, 69, 72–78, 80, 81, 83, 90, 94, 102, 103, 105–108, 110–112, 123, 144, 162–165, 175, 177, 180, 188, 191–193, 195, 199, 202, 203, 205, 206, 213, 218–220, 222, 223, 225–227, 231–240, 242–245, 252–254, 256, 263, 275, 277, 280, 289, 290–292, 294, 295, 297, 299, 300, 302, 305, 306, 308, 317, 324, 327, 337, 338, 343–345, 347, 352, 355, 357, 358, 369, 370, 372, 374, 375, 380, 389, 390, 393, 397, 400–403

Cultural-political Agent 6, 41

Culture 4, 18, 26, 42, 43, 50, 92, 109, 110, 163, 181, 222, 228, 230, 234, 240–244, 248, 250, 251, 255, 256, 303, 304, 328, 334, 348, 357, 381, 401, 405
– Epistemic Cultures 42, 43, 110, 248, 256
Cumulative Advantage 63, 70, 165, 166, 170, 174–176, 178, 214, 223, 225, 325, 345, 358, 383, 389, 391, 394, 403

Davenport, E. 103, 107, 111, 219, 242, 256, 375, 385, 401
Day, R. E. 90, 91
Deconstruction 30, 253
Deviant 66, 71, 249, 250, 257, 353
Differentiation 61, 65, 256, 285, 286, 299
Dilemma(s) 255
Dimensions 75, 88, 106, 254, 261, 274, 281, 285, 288, 289, 292–294, 297–299, 302, 323, 354, 355, 366, 368, 401
– Axiological 27
– Evolutionary 27
– Historical 27
Discipline(s) 2, 5, 20, 23, 26, 35, 46, 58, 74, 77, 110, 180–182, 185, 190, 215, 216, 220, 226, 229, 232, 235, 239, 242, 245, 246, 304, 305, 312, 313, 315, 318, 320–322, 340, 348, 355, 363, 364, 366, 369, 376, 384, 387
– Disciplinarity 302
– Disciplinary 2, 18, 69, 71, 72, 110, 188, 195, 223, 227, 232, 239, 241, 244, 247, 305, 317, 343, 344, 346, 356, 357, 400, 402
Discourse 3, 5, 16, 69, 79, 113, 200, 239, 241, 243, 245, 246, 251, 286, 301, 329, 361
Disinterestedness 57, 59, 249, 380, 381, 388, 391
Dispute(s) 24, 60, 68, 142
Distribution(s) 5, 35, 36, 63, 73, 88, 114, 119, 126–130, 132–134, 136, 138–144
– Waring Distribution(s) 165, 166, 170–172, 174, 178
Diversity 1, 8, 95, 99, 133, 366, 367, 372, 403
Document(s) 2, 6, 20, 22, 30, 33, 34, 37, 40–42, 45, 70, 74, 85, 91, 93, 98, 100, 101, 105, 109, 113, 125, 182, 201, 211, 212, 216, 228–232, 235, 238, 261, 263, 264, 266, 267, 269–271, 274, 280, 289–295, 297, 299, 337, 338, 352, 358, 359, 375–379, 383, 386–392, 394–398, 404
– Policy Document(s) 100, 375, 377, 378
– Scholarly Document(s) 376–379, 386, 387, 396, 397
Domain(s) 1, 2, 7, 8, 22–28, 34–36, 39–42, 44, 72, 78, 80, 83, 86, 90, 97, 102–104, 123, 134, 187, 193, 203, 209, 217, 261, 263, 265, 266, 268–271, 276, 277, 279, 281, 284, 294, 306, 308, 310, 312–314, 321, 322, 361, 362, 365, 367–369, 392
Download(s) 107, 289–291, 324, 326, 350, 363, 364, 371, 372, 374, 375, 378, 401, 402
Dunbar, R. 184–186, 191–196
Durkheim, E. 250, 328

Egghe, L. 73, 91, 139–141, 144, 145, 150, 162, 164, 190, 194, 219, 220, 321, 324, 328, 337, 338, 345
Einstein, A. 32, 44, 52, 65, 69, 192, 286, 303
Ekbia, H. 5, 6, 203, 248, 250, 252, 254, 256
Elsevier 15, 68, 70, 194, 324, 328, 333, 347, 363
Embodiment 5, 43, 80, 81, 255, 256
Empiricism 24, 25, 44, 45, 248
– Empirical 2, 5, 21–23, 25, 28, 31, 32, 35, 38, 49, 56, 57, 61, 67, 70, 89, 92, 102, 106, 112, 119, 127, 128, 136, 141, 143, 144, 147, 153, 164, 165, 174–176, 180, 185, 187, 200, 225, 233, 234, 240, 241, 243, 250, 256, 262, 263, 289, 298, 299, 301, 304, 306, 321, 325, 329, 331, 332, 338–340, 342, 343, 345, 355, 358, 362, 366, 368, 375, 389, 399, 403, 404
– Logical empiricism 44, 45, 248
Engagement 7, 8, 18, 40, 255, 338, 377–379, 387, 388, 392, 403
Entropy 284, 285, 288, 298, 300, 301
Error(s) 15, 19, 39, 51, 67, 161, 191, 249, 250, 267, 271, 272, 276, 277, 284, 387, 397
– Circularity Error(s) 267, 271, 272, 276
– Redundancy Error(s) 276
– Skipping Error(s) 272, 276
Ethics 3, 69, 107, 110, 111, 233, 243, 311
– Ethical 3, 17, 35, 69, 83, 94
Ethnography 252

Evaluation(s) 3, 14, 17, 28, 45, 70, 79, 80, 85–88, 90, 91, 110–112, 162–164, 176, 210, 211, 229, 242, 243, 261–263, 265–268, 273–279, 289, 331, 339, 340, 343–350, 357–359, 370, 373–375, 380, 399, 402–405
Evolutionary 2, 3, 27, 46, 49, 57, 61, 63–68, 184, 287, 288, 303, 316–319, 327, 328, 330, 332, 334, 347, 351, 355, 359, 364
– Evolutionary Biology 2, 3, 49, 64
Expectations 53, 61, 67, 179, 211, 274, 281, 284–286, 302, 346, 376, 390
Explanatory Coherence 54, 66

F1000 (also "Faculty of 1000") 344, 346, 350, 379, 387, 393–395, 397, 398, 400, 403, 405
– F1000 Reviews 393, 398
Facebook 14, 350, 352, 354, 360, 378, 386, 401, 404
Falsificationism 21
Female Colleagues 162
Findable 6, 41
Flagship Publications 35
Floridi, L. 182, 183, 189, 194
Folksonomy (Folksonomies) 263, 264, 274, 278
Forcell 97, 100, 109–111, 306
Foundationalism p.42
– Anti-foundationalism 42
Framework 1, 4, 6–8, 27, 28, 42, 43, 50, 52, 60, 78, 79, 87, 89, 111, 114, 140, 150, 163, 168, 171, 175, 191, 199, 202, 226, 227, 229, 235, 248, 265, 267, 277, 278, 322, 324, 339, 341, 344, 346, 347, 357, 358, 366, 367, 369, 373–377, 379, 380, 385, 386, 397, 402
– Framework Concepts 28, 42
Fraud 51, 59, 67, 250
Furner, J. 1, 2, 4, 5, 37, 44, 94, 100, 109, 111, 119, 120, 122, 124, 126, 128, 130, 132, 134, 136, 138, 140, 142, 144, 146, 166, 200, 338, 344

Garfield, E. 15, 18, 19, 23, 44, 85, 91, 94, 109–111, 158, 202, 203, 205, 206, 213, 218, 219, 223, 280, 300, 305, 308, 317, 324, 327, 329, 352, 357, 383, 401

Genre(s) 41–43, 71, 98, 240, 241, 244, 246, 247, 308, 309, 320
Gibbons, M. 306, 317, 321, 325, 329, 332
Giddens, A. 281, 300
Gieryn, T. F. 70, 253, 256, 329
Gilbert, G. N. 13, 19, 52, 61, 69, 329, 374, 382, 401
Gingras, Y. 54, 69, 151, 164, 240, 245, 325, 346, 347, 357, 374, 379, 383, 394, 399, 402
Glänzel, W. 2, 4, 162, 165–179, 200, 219, 220, 331, 374, 383, 401
Goal(s) 15, 27, 51, 57, 80, 81, 97, 105, 119120, 143, 229, 255, 265, 313, 337, 340–342, 384
Goffman, W. 168, 169, 178, 306, 325, 326, 385, 386, 391, 401
Google 41, 111, 165, 201, 220, 340
Griffith, B. C. 23, 32, 33, 44, 202, 203, 205–207
Group 3, 8, 17, 51, 64, 66, 67, 77, 79, 84, 86, 89, 90, 93, 95, 97, 100, 104, 110, 111, 113–115, 137, 145, 146, 149, 152, 168, 169, 175, 181, 182, 184–186, 188, 189, 191–196, 217, 223, 227, 241, 245, 253, 262, 275, 287, 291–293, 295, 310, 312, 314, 318, 332, 343, 349, 352, 357, 358, 360, 362, 365, 366, 370–372, 374–376, 384, 402

h-index 20, 149, 152, 159, 160, 162, 164, 166, 175, 176, 177, 267, 355–357
Habermas, J. 285, 301
Habitus 227
Hagstrom, W. O. 13, 19, 60, 63, 69, 329
Handicap Principle 64, 380
Haustein, S. 1, 3, 7, 8, 107, 112, 114, 267, 274, 278, 343, 345, 346, 351, 355, 357, 362, 372–376, 378, 380, 382, 384, 386–388, 390–392, 394–396, 398, 400–404
Hermeneutic(s) 3, 21–24, 26, 31, 34, 35, 45, 366
– Hermeneutic Circle 3, 22, 35
Hicks, D. 38, 44, 88, 91
Hirsch, J. E. 160, 161, 165, 166, 168, 170, 172, 174–178, 355, 357
Historiographic(al) 18, 44

Hjørland, B. 1–3, 6–8, 20, 22, 24, 26, 28, 30, 32–34, 36, 38, 40, 42, 44–46, 183, 190, 194, 195, 208, 209, 374
Humanities 23, 101, 208, 228, 239, 297, 300, 305, 312, 314, 329, 345, 362, 369, 403
Hyland, K. 16, 50, 69, 219, 227, 232, 235, 240, 246
Hyperlink(s) 338–342

Illusio 227–229, 238, 239, 330
Impact 4, 7, 18, 20, 24, 33, 45, 52, 55, 72, 73, 76, 77, 79, 81, 88, 89, 91, 92, 109, 112, 119, 148, 151, 152, 159, 164, 166, 176, 177, 190, 229, 237, 238, 240, 245, 251, 277, 302, 304, 324, 338, 342, 343, 345–352, 354–360, 362, 365, 368, 370–375, 379, 380, 383, 384, 389, 391, 394, 397, 399–403, 405
– Scholarly Impact 18, 33, 91, 92, 164, 277, 302, 324, 345, 360, 374
– Scientific Impact 77, 89, 240, 338, 345, 347–349, 351, 372, 397, 401
– Societal Impact 7, 348–352, 354–356, 362, 373, 380, 397, 400
ImpactStory 349, 350, 357, 372, 375
Impartial 24–29
Impression Management 384–386, 390–392, 395–399
Incommensurable
 (also "Incommensurability") 27, 83, 298, 349
Independent 2, 28, 35–37, 41, 59, 66, 67, 77, 97, 100, 106, 108, 125, 152, 166, 167, 170, 174, 218, 228, 238, 251, 263, 355
Indicator(s) 3, 4, 8, 17–19, 36, 45, 72, 74, 77, 79–81, 87–92, 112, 139, 145, 148, 149, 151, 152, 154, 162–164, 176, 177, 205, 245, 261, 263, 265–271, 274–278, 288, 300, 302, 304, 324, 328, 343–347, 349, 351, 355, 357–359, 365, 370, 373–376, 379, 380, 383, 397, 400–403
Information 5–9, 17–22, 27, 30–35, 37–46, 49, 61, 65, 68, 70, 80, 84, 90, 91, 93, 96, 98–103, 105, 106, 108–114, 139, 140, 142, 144–147, 149, 153, 164, 165, 177–196, 200, 203, 207, 208, 210–213, 216–218, 220, 222–224, 228, 232–235, 239–246, 256, 261, 262, 264, 267–270, 276–285, 288–290, 294, 295, 297–303, 307, 309, 311, 312, 314, 315, 317, 321, 324, 325, 327–329, 333, 337, 339–346, 350, 352, 356–358, 361–366, 370, 371, 378, 384–388, 390, 391, 394, 396, 399–405
– Bits of Information 183, 288, 293, 294, 297, 298
– Information Service(s) 21, 22, 31, 188, 239, 261, 262, 270, 278
– Information Users 262
– Mutual Information 280, 288
Ingwersen, P. 43, 94, 108, 187, 193, 213, 217–219, 222, 223, 274, 278, 337–339, 341, 344, 345, 372, 399
Input-output Indicators 4, 163
Interpretive 37, 222
Invisible Labor 254
Irvine, J. T. 72, 91
Iterative Process 35

Journal Websites 338, 378
Journal of the American Society for Information Science and Technology (JASIST) 9, 18, 43, 70, 91, 109–111, 113, 144, 145, 149, 153–156, 159, 162–164, 177, 193, 194, 223, 233, 239–244, 279, 290, 297, 300, 325, 344–346, 356, 358, 370, 371, 378, 400, 402

Kaplan, N. 60, 69, 218, 280, 301, 374, 380, 402
Kessler, M. M. 86, 91
Klavans, D. 33, 36, 43, 52, 54, 70, 86, 90, 324
Knorr-Cetina, K. D. 50, 59, 60, 69, 248, 251, 256, 352, 358
Knowledge 2, 4–7, 14, 16, 19–22, 24–29, 31, 33, 37, 40–44, 50, 51, 53, 57, 60–62, 65–69, 71, 73–75, 77–79, 81, 83–87, 95, 99, 103, 108–113, 135, 159, 176, 181, 184–186, 190, 191, 199, 203–205, 208–211, 216, 222, 223, 225–228, 232, 238–241, 243–247, 249–251, 253, 255–257, 261–266, 268–272, 274, 276, 278, 280, 281, 283, 284, 287, 295, 300–307, 310, 312–314, 316–319, 321, 324–332, 343, 345, 348, 351, 352, 354,

358, 361, 366–368, 370, 375, 379–381, 383, 388, 390, 399, 401, 403
– Knowledge Claim(s) 27, 42, 43, 51, 61, 67, 256, 351, 368, 381, 390
– Knowledge Domain(s) 44, 261, 263, 265, 266, 268–270
– Knowledge Organization System(s) (KOS(s)) 6, 7, 184, 204, 261–276, 278, 313, 370
– Recorded Knowledge 22
– Spectator Theory of Knowledge 33
– Subject Knowledge 20, 22, 29, 31
– Tacit Knowledge 24, 103
Kuhn, T. S. 20, 21, 23, 24, 26–28, 30–32, 38, 40–46, 51, 57, 58, 69, 248–250, 256, 305, 320, 321, 325, 330, 347, 358, 359, 373, 402

Laboratory Studies 251
Language 43, 51, 62, 65, 91, 119, 123, 127, 135–137, 140, 142, 144–147, 180, 191, 194, 196, 204, 208, 223, 228, 234–236, 239, 241, 245, 247, 248, 261, 264, 267, 269, 277, 282–285, 300, 308, 320, 371, 385, 398
Larivière, V. 5, 74, 107, 114, 151, 162, 164, 225, 226, 228, 230, 232, 234, 236, 238, 240, 242, 244–246, 308, 324, 325, 343, 345–347, 355, 357, 362, 374, 375, 379, 383, 386, 387, 390, 391, 394, 399, 401–403
Larsen, B. 43, 72, 90, 213, 218, 222, 223
Latour, B. 50–53, 62, 64, 69, 70, 81, 91, 100, 105, 112, 219, 220, 248, 251, 252, 255, 256, 302, 330, 352, 358
Law, J. 91, 300, 301
Layout 291, 315, 377
Leibnizian Ideal 24, 27, 31
Lenoir, T. 89–91
Leydesdorff, L. 1–3, 6, 13, 19, 77, 90–92, 219, 280–290, 292–303, 328, 330, 338, 343–345, 347, 358, 380, 402
Linguistics 2, 5, 72, 119, 124–126, 134, 136, 137, 139, 145, 147, 200, 210, 222, 223, 232–234, 239, 245–247
Link(s) 7, 22, 41, 54–57, 72, 74, 76, 79, 85–87, 90, 98, 99, 102, 105, 106, 113, 114, 139, 144, 163, 186–189, 191, 193, 199, 203, 206, 207, 213, 217, 263, 273, 276, 304, 307, 312, 315–321, 323, 326, 329, 338–342, 344–346, 351, 361, 362, 367, 370, 372, 378, 382, 388, 391–393, 398, 401, 404
– Link Analysis 7, 339–341, 346
– Link Networks 339
Lipetz, B.-A. 107, 112
Logistic Regression 159, 160
Lotka, A. 5, 20, 127–129, 139, 140, 145–147, 150, 166, 190, 194, 200, 306, 310, 325, 328, 330
Luhmann, N. 282, 283, 285, 286, 298–302, 330, 331
Luukkonen, T. 62, 70, 81, 91, 280, 302

MacRoberts, B. R. 15, 19, 38, 39, 45, 78, 91
MacRoberts, M. H. 15, 19, 38, 39, 45, 78, 91, 219
Mapping Studies 35
Material Semiotics 4, 79–81, 83
Matthew Effect 70, 162, 178, 225, 358, 382, 383, 389, 391, 394, 396, 398, 399, 402, 403
Matthew's Principle 165
McCain, K. W. 34, 46, 203, 205, 206, 215, 216, 219, 225, 226, 234, 235, 241, 244
Meadows, A. J. 32, 45, 219, 220
Measurement 23, 58, 73, 77, 146, 274, 284, 298, 303, 330, 345, 348–352, 354–356, 361, 375, 380
Memory 21, 109, 171, 183, 193, 210, 214, 215
Mendeley 99, 342, 345, 349, 350, 354, 360, 365, 375, 376, 378, 387–390, 397, 398, 402–405
– Mendeley Readership 345, 387, 388, 403
Merton, R. K. 2, 4, 13–15, 19, 49, 57, 59, 60, 62, 63, 70, 78, 166, 178, 203, 205, 219, 225–227, 238, 241, 248–250, 257, 305, 321, 325, 328, 331, 338, 345, 351, 353, 358, 380–383, 388, 390, 391, 393, 398, 403, 404
– Mertonian Norms 57, 63, 381, 390, 391, 393, 398
Metaphysics 24, 120, 145, 147, 193

Metrics 1–3, 5–9, 13–24, 26, 28, 30–44, 49, 69–74, 77–79, 86–94, 96, 98, 100, 105–114, 119, 120, 122, 124– 130, 132, 134, 136, 138–140, 142, 144–147, 164, 166–168, 176–180, 187, 188, 190–194, 196, 200, 204, 208–210, 216, 218, 222–224, 232, 233, 238, 240, 242, 244, 246, 248, 252, 262, 263, 265, 266, 276, 277, 279, 280, 291, 293, 300–303, 305, 316–319, 321, 324, 326, 328, 330, 337–347, 349–376, 378–380, 382, 384, 386–388, 390, 392, 394, 396–405
– Altmetric.com 349, 360, 370, 375
– Altmetrics 2, 7, 8, 74, 106, 114, 180, 195, 200, 337, 338, 340, 342–346, 349–352, 355–376, 378, 380, 382, 384, 386, 388, 390, 392, 394, 396–405
– Article-level Metrics 342, 402, 405
– Bibliometric(s) 3, 5, 7, 9, 14–18, 20, 32, 33, 35, 37, 49, 69, 72–74, 77–79, 86, 87, 90–94, 96, 98, 100, 105–113, 119, 120, 122, 124, 126–128, 129, 131, 133, 135, 137–140, 142, 144, 146, 166–168, 176, 180, 188, 190, 193, 200, 208, 210, 216, 223, 232, 238, 240, 244, 262, 263, 277, 280, 291, 293, 302, 305, 316–319, 324, 328, 341, 344–346, 355, 358, 359, 371, 374, 400–404
  – Bibliometric Coupling 33
  – Bibliometric Map 22, 29, 31, 33, 34
  – Evaluative Bibliometrics 9, 15–17, 69, 72–74, 77–79, 86, 87, 90, 91, 111, 144
– Cybermetrics 180, 328, 344, 345, 401, 404
– Influmetrics 193, 240, 244, 375, 401
– Informetrics 1–3, 5, 6, 8, 13, 20–24, 26, 28, 30, 32–44, 70, 91, 92, 94, 106, 140, 144, 145, 164, 176, 178, 179, 191, 192, 194, 204, 218, 222–224, 262, 263, 276, 279, 321, 324, 328, 339, 341, 344–346, 356, 357, 370, 400–402, 404
  – Critical Informetrics 2, 3, 8, 13, 35
– Scientometrics 6, 7, 17, 19–22, 31, 34, 37, 43, 69–71, 77, 78, 89–94, 106, 108, 110, 139, 144, 147, 164, 166, 177, 178, 190, 193, 196, 209, 222, 223, 233, 242, 246, 252, 262, 300–303, 305, 326, 330, 337–339, 341, 343–347, 349, 351, 354–357, 371, 373, 374, 380, 399–405
– Social Media Metrics 362, 375, 387, 398, 400, 402
– Webometrics 7, 20, 22, 94, 106, 108, 114, 187, 193, 200, 262, 337–344, 346, 372, 374, 375, 399
Milgram, S. 186–188, 191, 192, 195
Miller, G. 183, 184, 195
Mirror Metaphor 7, 33
Mitroff, I. I. L. 53, 70
Moed, H. 7, 178, 219, 331, 342, 360–366, 368, 370, 371, 373, 380, 381, 403
Mulkay, M. 57, 58, 62, 70, 329
Multidimensionality 2, 5, 18, 361
Multiple Discovery 65, 68

Narin, F. 73, 91, 203, 206
National Information Standards Organization (NISO) 354, 358, 362, 371, 402
Network 6, 7, 14, 19, 42, 45, 53, 54, 63, 66–68, 70, 81, 85, 92, 97, 109, 111, 113, 114, 149, 163, 166, 175–179, 181, 182, 185, 187, 188, 189, 191–196, 199, 207, 214–216, 222, 223, 251, 255, 269–271, 278, 280–282, 284, 286, 288, 290–292, 294, 296, 298, 300–303, 307, 313, 315–321, 323–329, 331–334, 339, 350, 353, 360, 362, 365, 367, 371, 378, 380, 383–385, 390, 392, 398, 399, 401, 403, 404
– Link Networks 339
– Network Analysis 188, 223, 280, 291, 302, 316, 318, 319, 321, 324, 326, 327, 329, 331, 333, 334
– Network Theory 81, 188, 251, 255, 302, 383
– Socio-cognitive Networks 42, 380
Newman, M. E. J. 2, 63, 70, 127, 144, 146, 175, 178, 195, 214, 215, 222, 317, 325, 331, 380, 383, 403
Nicolaisen, J. 61, 64, 70, 72–74, 77, 79, 91, 152, 164, 190, 195, 280, 302, 380, 381, 403
Nomenclature(s) 63, 261, 263, 264
Norm(s) 3, 13–16, 21, 22, 26, 30, 35, 49, 51, 53, 56–71, 74, 78, 87, 92, 94, 96, 126, 128, 134, 136, 141, 142, 146, 151, 152,

164, 185, 193, 209, 216, 245, 248, 249, 284–286, 288, 291, 292, 299, 301, 306, 309, 347, 351–353, 355–357, 361, 366, 368, 374, 380–382, 388–391, 393, 395, 397, 398, 402, 404
– Ab/normal Science: p.248
– Norm of Originality 381
– Normal Science 248, 347, 351, 355, 356
– Normative Theory 62, 64, 70, 351–353, 380–382, 389, 393, 395, 398, 404
– Norms of Science 70, 381
Noyons, E. C. 86, 92, 164
Numbers 5, 26, 86, 98, 101, 113, 142, 143, 151, 152, 159, 162, 180–186, 188–192, 194, 195, 200, 237, 273, 310, 312, 322, 360
– Numerology 180–182, 184, 186, 188, 190, 192–194

Objectivity 23, 24, 26, 28–30, 38, 45, 69, 113, 255, 330
Obliteration by Incorporation 62, 380, 383, 392
Obsolescence 308, 363, 364
Online Events 376, 378, 379, 384, 386, 387
Open Access 95, 112, 114, 326, 361, 363
Open Science 361, 369, 371
Open Source 367, 369
Ordinary Least Squares (OLS) 159, 160
Organization 2, 6, 7, 18, 36, 40, 44, 60, 88, 97, 99, 100, 103, 184, 185, 194–196, 204, 208, 216, 221, 222, 225, 235, 246, 249, 257, 261–264, 266, 268, 270, 272, 274, 276, 278–280, 282, 284–290, 292, 294, 296, 298–303, 312, 313, 316–319, 323, 325, 326, 328–332, 334, 362, 365, 366, 369–371, 376, 384, 392, 401, 404
– Intellectual Organization 280, 282, 284, 286–290, 292, 294, 296, 298–302
– Self-organization 195, 287, 288, 301, 302, 317, 330, 331
Organized Skepticism 249, 380, 381, 388, 389

Paradigm(s) 23, 24, 27, 28, 30, 31, 35, 40–43, 114, 227, 236, 237, 248, 249, 263, 264
Paratext 13, 18, 234, 240–243, 246, 252, 253
Pareto 126–128, 146, 166, 190, 222, 403

Partnership Ability Index 176
Payback Times 149, 150, 164
Perception 25–27, 52, 80, 146, 210, 212, 226, 252, 274, 275, 278, 310, 331, 398
Perspective(s) 1–3, 6, 20, 22, 30–35, 37, 39–41, 44, 63, 66, 69, 71, 72, 78, 81, 82, 89, 112, 114, 143, 181, 185, 192, 193, 226, 230, 231, 234, 236, 240, 243, 248, 249, 252, 271, 274, 280, 281, 283–285, 287, 292, 298, 302, 306, 307, 317, 318, 322, 325, 330, 332, 337, 338, 340, 344, 357, 363, 370, 376, 381, 390, 392, 394, 396, 398, 400
– Foundational Perspective(s) 20
– Individualistic Perspective(s) 20
– Pragmatic Perspective(s) 20
– Processual Perspective 248
– Translations among Perspectives 280
Persuasion 13, 19, 51, 52, 67, 69, 71, 381, 382, 391, 396, 401, 405
– Persuasion Hypothesis 382
Phenomenology 251, 303
– Phenomenological 255
– Phenomenologists 255
Philosophy 20–28, 30–33, 35, 36, 40, 41, 43–45, 69, 71, 72, 81, 83, 111, 122, 142, 143, 145, 147, 191, 233, 241, 242, 246, 255, 256, 287, 300, 301, 303, 305, 311, 312, 315–319, 323, 324, 327, 330, 332, 333, 358
Picture Theory 33, 142
PLOS 111–114, 324, 346, 372, 375, 401–405
Plum Analytics 375
Polymorphous Mentions 375, 397
Polyrepresentation 267, 274, 276
Popper, K. R. 21, 192, 248, 287, 303, 327, 332
Positions 21, 23, 24, 49, 50, 62, 72, 79, 125, 141, 142, 227, 267, 280, 281, 284, 289, 298, 302, 316–319
Positivism 21, 23–26, 28–30, 32, 35, 45
– Logical Positivism 21, 23–25, 29, 45
Post Hoc Justification 37
Post-Kuhnian 20, 23, 26–28, 30–32, 42
Post-publication Peer Review 393
Power Laws 141, 145, 146, 192, 194, 222, 316, 318, 319, 328, 403
Pragmatism 18, 21, 40

Preferential Attachment 63, 142, 166, 175, 176, 214, 383, 398, 403
Price, Derek J. de Solla (aka de Solla Price, D.) 13, 19, 32, 44, 45, 73, 83, 166, 168, 173, 178, 203, 205–207, 214, 219, 223, 282, 305, 306, 320, 321, 325, 332, 338, 345, 380, 382, 401, 403
Priem, J. 342, 343, 345, 349, 358, 360, 371–374, 397, 403, 404
Principal Unavoidability 37
Productivity 7, 119, 127–129, 132, 133, 140, 146, 166, 169, 170, 174–176, 179, 237, 256, 325, 337, 349, 350, 361
Proximity 6, 37, 50, 202, 203, 222, 253, 254
Publishing 5, 59, 70, 71, 91, 94, 106, 110, 112, 167, 195, 233, 242, 245, 323, 326, 327, 331–333, 344, 361, 362, 366, 368, 371, 372

Quality 3, 6, 18, 40, 63, 72, 73, 81, 87–89, 133, 134, 149, 166, 207, 261–263, 265, 267, 268, 274–276, 278, 279, 304, 327, 332, 343, 354, 356, 358, 359, 370, 388, 390, 393–395

Rational 2, 4, 15, 16, 21, 24, 25, 29, 49, 50, 57, 58, 67, 68, 100, 140–141, 149, 162, 240, 244, 248, 250, 281, 283, 284, 286, 287, 289, 298, 299, 333, 347, 355, 401
– Rationalism 21, 25
– Rationalist 21, 24, 250
Ravetz, J. R. 13, 19
Realism 23, 24, 30, 38, 70, 248, 250, 251, 254, 255
– Naïve realism 30, 251
– Sociological Realism 250
Reception History 33
Redundancy 6, 15, 265, 267, 271, 276, 280, 288, 289, 291, 293, 294, 297–299, 301, 302
Reference(s) 2–4, 8, 9, 13, 14, 18, 31, 43, 51, 52, 54, 56, 60–63, 65, 66, 68, 72–80, 83, 85, 87, 89, 90, 94, 99, 107, 108, 127, 144, 148–156, 158–160, 162–164, 177, 178, 192, 202, 204, 222, 225, 230, 236, 239, 256, 277, 278, 289, 290, 295, 297–300, 307, 308, 322, 323, 344, 348, 353, 356, 362, 370, 379, 382, 391, 399
– Cited References 9, 18, 43, 54, 68, 90, 108, 144, 164, 177, 192, 204, 222, 239, 255, 277, 289, 290, 295, 299, 300, 323, 344, 356, 370, 399
– Referencing 3, 13, 16, 17, 19, 49–52, 54, 56, 58, 60–70, 73, 77, 78, 89, 96, 97, 99, 105, 381, 400, 401
– Reference Manager(s) 345, 360, 365, 377, 378, 387, 389
– Mendeley 99, 342, 345, 349, 350, 354, 360, 365, 375, 376, 378, 387–390, 397, 398, 402–405
– Zotero 99, 115, 360, 365, 378
Relatedness 40, 76, 206
Relational 2, 5, 6, 280, 284, 291, 292, 298, 404
Relativist(ic) 14, 27, 30, 83
Relevance 1, 15, 17, 36, 41, 55, 60, 63, 71, 188, 204–206, 209–214, 216, 217, 220–223, 226, 228, 287, 307, 309, 356, 358
Repositories 95, 98–100, 102, 104, 105, 360, 378, 386
Research 2–4, 7, 8, 15–17, 21–23, 25, 26, 28–38, 42, 43, 45, 49, 52–54, 57, 62, 67–74, 77–80, 84–92, 94–104, 106, 107, 109–114, 137, 139, 143, 145, 147, 159, 162–164, 171, 172, 174, 176–178, 180, 186–188, 193–196, 199, 203, 207, 213, 220, 223, 225, 226, 228–236, 238–246, 249, 253, 262, 263, 267, 271, 275–277, 279, 301, 303–307, 310, 312–319, 321, 323–325, 327, 329, 331, 332, 337–380, 384–387, 391, 393–395, 397–405
– Information Centred Research (ICR) 340, 346
– Mainstream Research 35–37
– Research Assessment(s) 17, 78, 94, 111, 112, 353, 362, 365, 369
– Research Evaluation(s) 70, 80, 88, 90, 162, 176, 242, 345, 346, 348, 350, 357–359, 373, 374, 380, 399, 402–405
– Research Objects 2, 21, 96, 97, 106, 109, 375–378, 386
ResearchGate 350, 360, 378, 379
Reward Triangle 5, 225–227, 236–239, 244

Rip, A. 300, 303, 359
Robinson, L. 180, 182–184, 186, 188, 190, 192–194, 196
Rousseau, R. 1, 4, 15, 19, 73, 91, 148, 150, 152, 154–156, 158–160, 162, 164, 176, 178, 179, 190, 192, 195, 218–220, 280, 300, 302, 321, 324, 328, 337, 338, 340, 345, 354, 358, 375, 383, 404

Scharnhorst, A. 1, 7, 86, 304, 306–308, 310, 312, 314, 316–318, 320, 322, 324–326, 328, 330, 332–334, 383, 399
Scholar(ly) 1–9, 13–18, 20, 26, 30, 32, 33, 35, 38, 40, 41, 43, 45, 60, 61, 70, 72–74, 79–81, 86, 87, 91–110, 112–114, 136, 143, 146, 164, 165, 176, 177, 180, 182, 191, 193, 195, 201, 207, 216, 220, 222, 223, 225–228, 230, 233, 234, 237, 240, 242–246, 252–254, 256, 261, 277, 284, 286, 293, 302, 304–307, 324, 342, 344–346, 350, 354–357, 359–363, 365, 366, 368–380, 385–387, 389, 392–399, 402–405
– Scholarly Agents 376, 386
– Scholarly Communication 1–9, 14, 17, 18, 30, 93–95, 97, 100, 106–110, 112–114, 177, 180, 191, 225–228, 230, 242, 253, 256, 261, 293, 306, 307, 344, 356, 372, 373, 380, 389, 397, 399, 402
– Scholarly Documents 376–379, 386, 387, 396, 397
– Scholarly Impact 18, 33, 91, 92, 164, 277, 302, 324, 345, 360, 374
– Scholarly Traditions 40
Science 2–7, 9, 14, 15, 18–36, 38–46, 49–52, 54, 56–60, 62–64, 66–72, 79–83, 85, 86, 88–92, 95, 97, 100, 108–114, 135, 137, 139, 142, 144–147, 149, 150, 153, 154, 162, 164, 165, 172, 177–184, 186–196, 201–203, 207, 208, 210, 212, 213, 216, 218, 220–228, 230–236, 238–246, 248–257, 261, 262, 264, 268, 277–279, 285, 287–291, 295, 297, 300–308, 310–334, 337, 340, 342, 344–352, 354–359, 361–364, 366, 368–371, 374, 380, 381, 389, 391, 393, 395, 396, 398–405
– Ethos of Science 363, 366, 368, 369, 380, 393
– History of Science 20, 31, 44, 49, 54, 68, 253, 254, 256, 305
– Metascience 20, 30
– Non-scientific Domains 22
– Normal Science 248, 347, 351, 355, 356
– Norms of Science 70, 381
– Objective Science 25
– Reward System of Science 5, 226–228, 238, 381
– Science Citation Index 20, 79, 86, 228, 328, 401
– "Science of Science" 20, 315
– Science Studies 5, 6, 20, 43, 49, 64, 248, 250, 251–255, 287, 317, 330
– Scientific Fact 69, 81, 91, 112, 256, 330, 358, 362, 368
– Scientific Impact 77, 89, 240, 338, 345, 347–349, 351, 372, 397, 401
– Scientific Method(s) 21, 23, 57, 67–69, 366
 – A Priori Scientific Method 21
 – Qualitative Method and Methodology 21, 241, 252
 – Quantitative Method and Methodology 23, 39, 91, 136, 180, 188, 252, 321, 324, 328, 340
– Scientific Opinion 362, 368
– Scientific Paper(s) 45, 54, 67, 89, 91, 325, 349, 352, 373, 387, 390–392, 401
– Scientific Revolution(s) 7, 23, 24, 40, 44, 45, 51, 58, 68, 69, 256, 305, 320, 321, 325, 330, 347, 348, 350, 352, 354, 356, 358, 373, 400, 402
– Sociology of Science 19–21, 28, 29, 31, 70, 228, 238, 241, 245, 249, 256, 287, 305, 317, 321, 325, 329, 331, 345, 352, 358, 380, 403
 – Sociology of Scientific Knowledge 250, 257
– Somatics of Science 6, 203, 252, 254, 255
– Theory of Science 20, 42, 44, 329, 351
Scopus 15, 201, 202, 221, 347, 363, 364, 371
Semantic(s) 7, 79, 91, 110–113, 137, 145, 187, 200, 204, 215, 222, 261, 263–265,

267–273, 275–279, 282, 284, 289, 291, 298, 299, 302, 307, 329
- Semantic Consistency 275
- Semantic Inconsistency 271, 272, 276, 277
- Semantic Relation(s) 261, 263–265, 268–271, 273, 278, 279

Separation 72, 81, 186–188, 194, 196
Shannon-Weaver Model 281
Shapin, S. 52, 59, 70, 219, 220, 250, 255, 256
Similarity Measure(s) 1, 37, 274, 300
Simon, H. A. 58, 105, 114, 142, 147, 173, 179, 232, 286, 293, 303, 333, 385, 404
Small, H. 2, 36, 45, 52, 54, 61, 62, 64, 65, 70, 85, 91, 92, 351, 359, 380, 383, 404
Small World 185–188, 191–196, 344
Social 2, 3, 8, 16, 19–21, 23–31, 34–36, 38, 43–46, 49–51, 54, 57–60, 63, 64, 66–72, 74, 78–84, 88, 91, 92, 102, 114, 127, 145, 162, 166, 176, 177, 179–181, 184, 185, 187–196, 203–205, 208, 215, 216, 218, 220, 223, 226, 228, 232, 233, 236, 239, 242, 243, 245, 248–251, 254, 256, 257, 262, 278, 280, 285, 287, 289, 297, 299–303, 305, 306, 311–319, 321, 323, 324, 326–334, 340, 342, 345, 346, 348–354, 357–365, 369, 370, 372–375, 378–382, 384–387, 389–405
- Social Capital 348, 384, 385, 389–392, 394, 396–400, 402–404
- Social Construction 3, 28–30, 49, 50, 54, 66, 69, 216, 251, 330, 351–354, 358, 380–382, 389, 391, 397, 398
- Social Constructivist Theory 380–382, 389
- Social Context 187, 249
- Social Epistemology 24, 46, 359
- Social Media 2, 8, 185, 189, 190, 352–354, 357, 360, 362, 365, 369, 370, 372, 374, 375, 380, 384, 385, 387, 395, 398–402
- Social Media Platforms 354, 375, 385
- Social Norms 57, 59, 67–69, 78
- Social Science(s) 21, 23, 38, 43, 81–83, 91, 162, 177, 179, 181, 187, 226, 228, 232, 233, 236, 239, 242, 245, 249, 289, 297, 300, 301, 303, 305, 311–314, 316–319, 321, 324, 326, 328–331, 334–346, 362, 363, 364, 369, 400, 403
- Social Structure of Science 249

- Social Theory 8, 70, 300, 329, 351, 372, 379, 384, 386, 390, 392, 397, 400, 403
- Social Tradition 24
- Social Web 114, 342, 365
Soft Data 40
Stock, W. G. 1, 6, 7, 22, 43, 187, 196, 204, 223, 261–264, 266, 268, 270, 272, 274, 276, 278, 279, 370, 391, 401
"Strong Programme" 28, 30, 50, 250
Strong Reciprocity 64, 67–69
Subject 7, 13–15, 20–22, 24, 25–27, 29–31, 34, 36–39, 53, 55, 58, 70, 81, 138, 141, 142, 144, 166, 180, 183, 187, 192, 194, 200, 201, 204, 205, 207, 220, 238, 262, 271, 274, 275, 278, 291, 301, 307–324, 347, 351, 363, 369–371, 381, 383, 393
- Subject Knowledge 20, 22, 29, 31
Subjective Idealism 26
Success(es) 4, 16, 21, 22, 29, 31, 35, 53, 58, 66, 67, 137, 148–156, 158–172, 174–179, 250, 277, 278, 342, 352, 368, 383, 384, 391
- Success-breeds-success 4, 165, 166, 168, 170, 172, 174, 176, 178, 179, 383
- Success Index Family 149
- Success Multiplier 148–154, 156, 158, 160, 162, 163
Sugimoto, C. R. 1–4, 6, 8, 9, 14, 15, 18, 37, 43, 94, 107, 110–112, 114, 163, 164, 180, 193, 240, 243, 263, 277, 299, 302, 306, 323, 324, 343, 345–347, 352, 355, 357, 358, 362, 369–371, 378, 390, 391, 393, 401–403
Swales, J. M. 51, 52, 71
Symmetry 29, 58, 248, 251, 254, 255
Synergy 288, 289, 294, 297, 299, 303

Tague-Sutcliffe, J. 139, 147, 166, 179, 262, 279, 341, 346
Taxonomy 37, 40, 44, 184, 279, 339, 347, 348, 354, 373
- Numerical Taxonomy 37
- Taxonomic Changes 347, 348
Technical Norms 57–60, 62, 66, 67
Thagard, P. 54, 57, 63, 71, 333
Thelwall, M. 1, 7, 8, 94, 105, 107, 112, 114, 159, 164, 219, 337–346, 355, 357, 365, 369,

371, 372, 374, 375, 386–388, 390, 391, 393, 395, 396, 402–404
Theory 1–8, 13, 14, 16–24, 26–36, 38–42, 44, 45, 49–54, 56–59, 62–64, 66–73, 77–79, 81–84, 87, 89–94, 96, 99, 102, 106–110, 119, 120, 122–124, 127, 129, 131, 133–137, 139, 141–147, 169, 175, 176, 178, 183, 188, 189, 191, 194, 195, 205, 208, 209, 212, 219, 221–223, 225, 226, 228–230, 232, 234, 236–238, 240–244, 246, 251, 252, 254, 255, 257, 263, 276, 280, 282–284, 288, 298, 300–304, 310, 311, 315–319, 321, 323–334, 338–341, 343–345, 348, 351–353, 356, 372, 374, 377, 379–386, 388–390, 392–404
– Critical Theory 35, 40, 44
– Theoretical Divergence(s) 37
– Theoretical Framework of Social Media Metrics 374
– Theory-laden 27
Tools 13, 17, 33, 68, 72, 79, 99, 105, 201, 234, 241, 263, 349, 360, 362–367, 369, 370, 374, 378, 382, 385, 398
Trivial 29, 36, 38, 40, 52, 73, 94, 122, 136, 172, 173, 248, 253
Trust 59, 60, 102, 107, 111–113, 203, 209, 234, 239, 240, 242–244, 250, 254, 274, 392
Twitter 14, 114, 189, 341, 342, 345, 346, 350, 354, 360, 365, 370, 375, 377, 378, 385, 386, 390–392, 395, 397, 398, 401, 402, 404
– Hashtag(s) 392, 398
– Tweet(s) 14, 106, 341, 342, 345, 349, 357, 372, 386, 387, 390–392, 398, 401–404

Uncertainty 37, 38, 280, 281, 283, 284, 286, 289, 294, 297–299, 332
Universalism 26, 57, 59, 249, 380–382, 388, 391
Usability 265, 268, 274–278, 393
Usage 73, 109, 135, 138, 187, 262, 355, 358, 362–364, 371, 372, 374, 392, 401, 402
Users 22, 31, 43, 102, 106, 137, 140, 184, 189, 262, 266, 267, 269, 274, 275, 343, 344, 346, 354, 359, 385, 387–392, 396–398, 405

Values 27, 31, 57, 67, 78, 87, 88, 119, 126–129, 131, 133, 134, 144, 151, 153, 155, 156, 158, 159, 162, 168, 171, 172, 175, 192, 211, 227, 238, 241, 244, 288, 302, 306, 354, 380, 388, 395
van Eck, N. J. 86, 89, 92
van Raan, A. F. J. 62, 70, 89, 92, 219, 337–339, 346
Vector Space 281, 289, 291, 292, 299
View from Nowhere 28, 42
Visualization 216, 236, 291, 293, 302, 303, 305, 315, 322, 364

Waltman, L. 74, 86, 89, 90, 92, 343, 346, 386, 393, 394, 405
Wasserman, S. 199, 223, 321, 324, 326, 327, 334
Web of Science (WoS) 6, 15, 154, 160, 162, 165, 201, 202, 221, 228, 231, 232, 236, 241, 245, 289, 290, 295, 297, 347
White, H. D. 46, 71, 114, 223, 405
Wolfram, D. 164, 196, 262, 279, 310, 325
Women 26, 91, 187, 242, 254, 256
Woolgar, S. 69, 91, 112, 256, 257, 303, 330, 358
Wouters, P. 4, 17, 19, 72–74, 76–80, 82–84, 86, 88–90, 92, 94, 113, 221, 222, 280, 303, 340, 343, 344, 346, 349, 357, 359, 374, 380, 386–389, 392, 395, 397, 400, 405
Wray, K. B. 24, 30, 46, 347–349, 355, 359

Ziman, J. 334, 350, 359, 381, 405
Zipf, G. K. 5, 20, 119, 127–129, 134–139, 146, 147, 166, 170–175, 177, 190, 200, 222, 321, 326, 334, 403
Zotero 99, 115, 360, 365, 378
Zuckerman, H. 51, 52, 57, 59, 71, 203, 248–250, 257

www.ingramcontent.com/pod-product-compliance
Lightning Source LLC
Chambersburg PA
CBHW070747230426
43665CB00017B/2277